A Select Collection of Scarce and Valuable Tracts and Other Publications on Paper Currency and Banking

From the Originals of Hume, Wallace, Thornton, Ricardo, Blake, Huskisson, and Others, with a Preface, Notes and Index

J.R. McCulloch

Cambridge University Press

CAMBRIDGE
UNIVERSITY PRESS

University Printing House, Cambridge, CB2 8BS, United Kingdom

Cambridge University Press is part of the University of Cambridge.
It furthers the University's mission by disseminating knowledge in the pursuit of education, learning and research at the highest international levels of excellence.

www.cambridge.org
Information on this title: www.cambridge.org/9781108083744

This edition first published 1857
This digitally printed version 2018

ISBN 978-1-108-08374-4 Paperback

SCARCE AND VALUABLE TRACTS, &c.,

ON

PAPER CURRENCY

AND

BANKING.

*** This volume has been printed by Lord Overstone for distribution among his friends: the duty of editing it was undertaken by J. R. M'Culloch, Esq.

A

SELECT COLLECTION

OF

SCARCE AND VALUABLE TRACTS AND OTHER PUBLICATIONS,

ON

PAPER CURRENCY

AND

BANKING,

FROM THE ORIGINALS OF

HUME, WALLACE, THORNTON, RICARDO, BLAKE, HUSKISSON, AND OTHERS.

WITH A PREFACE, NOTES, AND INDEX.

LONDON:
MDCCCLVII.

[ONE HUNDRED AND FIFTY COPIES PRINTED.]

PREFACE.

THIS collection, of the most valuable of the English tracts and publications on paper currency and banks, may be regarded as supplementary to the volume of tracts on metallic currency, printed for the Political Economy Club. It does not, however, contain any tract having especial reference to paper money, properly so-called, that is, to notes which are legal tender without being convertible at the pleasure of the holder into certain amounts of coin. The value of this variety of paper currency depends on the extent to which it may be issued compared with the demand, or rather with the business it has to perform. Whether those by whom it is issued are in good or bad credit is immaterial. It obtains currency by its issuers having power to make it legal tender; and nothing more is required to sustain its value than that it should be issued in moderate quantities. The value of the assignats issued during the French Revolution was at first nearly equal to that of metallic money; but the quantities of them thrown into circulation being rapidly and enormously increased, their value proportionally declined, till in the end they became all but worthless. And such has invariably been the case wherever inconvertible paper notes have been made legal tender. In Russia, Austria, and other states, which have resorted to this description of paper, its value has always been proportioned to the magnitude of the issues; progressively declining with every addition to its amount, and increasing according as it is diminished. And it is obvious, though we had no experience to which to appeal, that such must be the case. A country has a certain number of payments to make in a given time; and, *cæteris paribus*, it follows, if the coins or notes employed in making these payments be doubled or trebled, that they will only pass at a half or a third part of their former value.

With the exception of the period from 1797 down to 1819, the paper currency of Great Britain has always been convertible at pleasure into an equivalent amount of coin of the standard weight and purity. Our bank-notes are not, strictly speaking, money, but only substitutes for money. Inasmuch, however, as no doubt is entertained of their immediate convertibility into coins, and as they perform some of the principal functions of the latter, and are in many respects more commodious, they are practically held to be money. To use the words of Lord Mansfield "these notes are not, like bills of exchange, mere securities or documents for debts, nor are so esteemed; but are treated as money in the ordinary course and transactions of business, by the general consent of mankind; and on payment of them whenever a receipt is required, the receipts are always given as for money not as for securities or notes."*

The promissory notes issued in the reign of Charles II, by the Goldsmiths of London, who then acted as private bankers, paved the way for those issued by the Bank of England established in 1694. But it is a curious fact that the notes, both of the former and the latter, however convenient and well secured, were objects of great jealousy on their first appearance. The courts of law would not con-

* Chitty on Bills, &c., 8th ed. p. 555.

sider them in the light of inland bills of exchange; and ruled that no action could be maintained on a promissory note, which they held was merely an evidence of debt. So long as this doctrine prevailed the circulation of notes was much obstructed. And the obstruction continued till Parliament, impressed with a sense of the inconveniences thence arising, passed the Act 3 and 4 Anne, c. 92, which conferred on promissory notes the same privileges that had been conferred on bills of exchange, and made them recoverable by action in like manner.

When first established, the Bank of England, owing in part to the circumstances now alluded to, but more to the disordered state of the coin and the novelty of the institution, was involved in considerable difficulties. These, however, were speedily overcome, and for about a century the notes of the Bank, which were immediately convertible into coin, continued to circulate on a par with gold without any interference of any kind on the part of Government. The continuance of this equable system, and the unlimited confidence that was always placed in the ability of the Bank to fulfil her engagements, seem to be the principal reasons why, for a lengthened period, very few tracts or other publications appeared on the subject of paper currency and banking. But the previous scarcity was changed into abundance after the suspension of cash payments in 1797 had awakened the attention of the public to the subject; and still more after the publication of the Bullion Report in 1810. Few if any parliamentary papers ever occasioned so much controversy as the latter. It gave birth to myriads of pamphlets. But of these by far the greater number evinced the zeal rather than the knowledge of their authors. And with the exception of those of Messrs. Ricardo, Blake, and Huskisson, most part of the others have fallen into an oblivion from which they do not deserve to be rescued.

The circumstances now stated suffice to explain why we have reprinted so few tracts published previously to 1797. Others either do not exist, or are not entitled to any special notice. The first tract in this volume, or that on the "Currencies of the Plantations in America," published at Boston, in New England, in 1740, is however of the highest excellence. There was hardly a colony but what had issued large amounts of bills receivable as cash; and as no effectual provision was made for the payment of these bills, while frequent additions were made to their amount, their value continued to decline, and the exchange with England to become more and more unfavourable to the colonies. The history of these proceedings, and their pernicious influence are fully set forth in the tract now referred to. We have not learned the name of the author; but whoever he may be, he has the merit of having very clearly exhibited, the principles that should be kept in view in the issue of paper money, and the abuses which follow from their being neglected.

Following this tract the reader will find extracts from Hume's Essays on Money and the Balance of Trade. They discover all his ingenuity and unrivalled felicity of illustration. But he had no clear idea of the fundamental distinction between paper money and bank-notes payable on demand at the pleasure of the holders. The former may sink far below the value of the sums they profess to represent; and being legal tender, will most likely expel coin from circulation. But no such consequences can follow from the issue of bank-notes, such as were then circulated in all parts of Great Britain. They were fully equivalent to the gold which might be obtained in exchange for them the moment it was required. The latter was not forced abroad; but a portion of it being rendered unnecessary by the employment of notes, which were found to be more commodious, was exported in exchange for commodities, which made a corresponding addition to the wealth and capital of the country. Hume, who survived the publication of the Political Essays for about five and twenty years must have seen, in the extension of banking, and in the rapid progress of all sorts of improvements in Scotland after the peace of Paris in 1763, a practical refutation of his statements in regard to the mischievous influence of bank-notes.

The same confusion of paper money with notes payable on demand which suggested Hume's remarks, pervades the third tract in this volume, the "Essay on Paper Money and Banking," written by Patrick, the fifth Lord Elibank, and published with some other tracts in 1755. Its brevity is its principal recommendation. It is a poor performance, in which the errors of Hume are repeated without any portion of his philosophy, and is chiefly worth notice as showing the crude opinions that were then not unfrequently entertained by well-informed persons with regard to bank-notes. His Lordship supposes that the notes of the Scotch Banks, to which his tract specially refers, by adding to the currency and depreciating its value, had raised the price of labour and all sorts of produce "to the destruction of trade and manufactures." But it is obvious, for the reasons already stated, that their issue could have no such effect; and instead of manufactures being destroyed or injured, they were then beginning to be carried on with an energy and success unknown at any previous period!

The fallacy of the theories in regard to bank-notes, put forth by Hume and Lord Elibank has been clearly shown in the next tract in this volume, an "Essay on Banks and Paper Credit." It is extracted from a volume entitled "Characteristics of the Present State of Great Britain," which appeared in 1758. Though anonymous, it is believed, apparently on good grounds, to be the work of the Rev. Dr. Robert Wallace, one of the ministers of Edinburgh, and well known from his controversy with Hume in regard to the populousness of ancient nations. But though totally wrong in his theory and conclusions upon this latter subject, Wallace entertained more correct opinions than his illustrious antagonist with respect to banks and public credit. The essay we have printed, is both liberal and ingenious; and the other essays in the volume from which it is taken are not unworthy of the reader's attention.

We have given in the Note on the Suspension of Cash Payments at the Bank of England, in 1797, a brief account of the circumstances which led to that measure. The novelty of the position in which the Bank and, with her, the paper currency of the country was then placed, powerfully excited the public attention, and led to much discussion both in and out of Parliament.

Of the tracts that appeared subsequently to this crisis, we have reprinted one on the "Utility of Country Banks," published in 1802. It gives what may be considered as being on the whole a just, though rather too favourable a view of these establishments. Of their importance, indeed, as reservoirs into which the unemployed capital of the surrounding districts may be collected, and from which it may be readily distributed to those by whom it is wanted, it is impossible to speak too highly; while, by affording convenient places of deposit for the smallest savings, and conducting all sorts of pecuniary transactions, they promote a spirit of economy, and enable the business of the country to be transacted with infinitely greater facility and, at the same time, with a much smaller amount of money than would otherwise be necessary.

But these advantages may all be obtained without giving provincial banks the power to issue notes. This, in truth, is a privilege which has nothing whatever to do with the business of banking, and which they are all but certain to abuse. In saying this we do not wholly refer to the heavy losses which the public have often sustained from the discredit brought upon the currency by the mismanagement and failure of banks of issue; for though that cause of loss might be to a considerable extent removed by taking sufficient security for the notes issued, it is impossible, unless their issue be confined to a single source, that their amount in circulation should be uniformily determined, as it ought to be, by the state of the exchange, or by the influx and efflux of bullion. But, though it overlooks the important principle now referred to, the tract on the Utility of Country Banks is a valuable publication. It helped to correct some of the erroneous notions that were previously current in relation to these establishments.

The essay on the "Utility of Country Banks" is followed by the "Enquiry into the Nature and Effects of the Paper Credit of Great Britain," by Henry Thornton, Esq., M.P., published in 1802. This important work contains a much greater amount of useful information with respect to the pecuniary transactions carried on in the country than had previously been communicated to the public. Being an extensive merchant and a director of the Bank of England, Mr. Thornton, was placed in the most favourable position for becoming well acquainted with the various subjects of which he treats. His connexion with the Bank appears, however, to have biassed, though perhaps unconsciously, his judgment. His theoretical principles are, for the most part, sound, and are sometimes laid down with much precision. But when he comes to consider their application he interprets them so that his statements and reasonings have all an evident leaning in favour of the Bank; and are intended to vindicate the suspension of cash payments and her subsequent proceedings. Although, however, we agree with Mr. Thornton in thinking that the suspension was necessary at the time when it was passed, he has not shewn that it should have been continued after the alarms of invasion, in which the drain for gold originated, had subsided; and it is needless to add that he has wholly failed in shewing that there is or can be any real security other than their conversion into coin at the pleasure of the holder, for that limitation of the issue of bank-notes which he admits is indispensable to sustain their value. Mr. Thornton ascribes the fall of the exchange in 1800 and 1801 to payments abroad on account of the war and the heavy importations of corn caused by the scarcity. But these circumstances, though they might, and probably did, affect the *real* exchange, will in no degree account for the excess of the market over the mint price of bullion in those years. That excess, which sometimes exceeded 10 per cent., showed conclusively that the currency was depreciated to that extent. And it is plain, had the Bank been paying her notes in coin, that no such depreciation would have been possible. Their value and that of gold would then have been identical, and there could not have been the smallest discrepancy between the mint and market price of the latter.

But, despite these and other grave errors, the practical character of Mr. Thornton's work, and the many interesting discussions which it embraces, render it a most valuable contribution to our commercial literature.

The suspension of cash payments in 1797, extended to Ireland as well as Great Britain. The directors of the Bank of Ireland did not, however, exercise the privilege of issuing notes with which they were thus intrusted with the same moderation as the directors of the Bank of England. On the contrary, during the same period (from the suspension till February, 1804) in which the issues of the Bank of England had increased in the ratio of 1 to 1·766, the issues of the Bank of Ireland had increased in the ratio of 1 to 4·802. In consequence, the exchange between Dublin and London, which, previously to the suspension, diverged but slightly from par, became from 12 to 16 per cent. against the former. But at the very moment when the exchange between Dublin and London was so unfavourable to the former, the exchange between London and Belfast which, owing to peculiar circumstances, had a gold currency, was about 3 per cent. in favour of the latter! We have explained this case more at large in a Note on the exchange between London and Dublin in 1804. It affords one of the most striking examples to be found of the influence of over-issues of paper in depressing the exchange.

The Treatise of the first Earl of Liverpool on the Coins of the Realm, which appeared in 1805, is one of the most valuable of that class of publications. But its bulk, and the fact of its having been reprinted within these few years, have prevented our giving it a place in these collections. We have, however, inserted in this volume that part of Lord Liverpool's work which refers to the paper currency of the kingdom. And it is eminently deserving of attention from the historical information which it embodies, as well as from its proper appreciation of the mischief which the suspension of cash payments could not fail to produce.

The next, and one of the ablest tracts in this volume, "The High Price of Bullion a Proof of the Depreciation of Bank Notes," appeared in 1810. It was written by Mr. Ricardo, and led the way in the memorable bullion controversy. From 1804 to 1808 inclusive, the market price of gold was nearly uniform at 4*l.* an ounce, being 2*l.* 14*s.* 6*d.* per cent. above the mint of 3*l.* 17*s.* 10½*d* an ounce, and shewing that the currency was depreciated to that extent. But in 1809 and 1810, the issues of the Bank of England and of the country banks were greatly increased; and in consequence the market price of gold rose in March 1809 to 4*l.* 10*s.* an ounce, shewing a depreciation of the currency of no less than 15*l.* 11*s.* 4*d.* per cent. But the real cause of the rise of the market price of gold was then comparatively unknown; and the adverse exchange with which it was accompanied was ascribed to payments on account of the war, the interruption of trade, and so forth. In these circumstances Mr. Ricardo applied himself to the consideration of the subject; and the result of his inquiries appeared in a series of letters in the Morning Chronicle, the first being published on the 6th September, 1809. They made a considerable impression and elicited various answers. This success and the increasing interest of the subject led Ricardo to embody them in a more enlarged and systematic form in the tract now reprinted. It issued from the press some considerable time previously to the appointment of the Bullion Committee, and is believed to have materially assisted in forwarding that important measure.

In this tract Ricardo showed that redundancy and deficiency of currency are only relative terms; and that so long as the currency of a country consists partly of gold and silver coins, and partly of paper immediately convertible into such coins, its value can neither rise above nor fall below the value of the metallic currencies of other countries, by a greater sum than will suffice to defray the expence of importing foreign coin or bullion if the currency be deficient, or of exporting a portion of the existing supply if it be redundant. But when a country issues inconvertible paper notes (as was then the case in England), they cannot be exported to other countries in the event of their becoming redundant at home; and whenever, under such circumstances, the exchange with foreign countries is depressed below par, or the market price of bullion rises above its mint price, more than the cost of sending coin or bullion abroad, it proves that too much paper has been issued, and that its value is depreciated from excess.*

In stripping these important conclusions of the irrelevant matter with which they had previously been encumbered, and making them readily appreciable, Ricardo contributed in no ordinary degree to perfect the theory of money.

Owing to the heavy and continued fall of the exchange, the question in regard to the depreciation of the currency, became of the greatest importance, and was taken up in the House of Commons. It was brought before that assembly by

* Sketch of the Life of Ricardo prefixed to his works.

Mr. Francis Horner, who moved on the 19th February, 1810, that a Select Committee be appointed to "Inquire into the Cause of the High Price of Gold Bullion, and to take into Consideration the State of the Circulating Medium and of the Exchanges between Great Britain and Foreign Parts." The motion was agreed to; and the Committee, which comprised some of the ablest men in the House, after due inquiry, presented their Report on the 8th of June.

The Bullion Report, which is reprinted in this volume, though not wholly exempt from theoretical errors, without any claim to originality, and not very skilfully composed, is nevertheless one of the most valuable papers that has ever proceeded from a Committee of the Legislature. It was principally written by Mr. Horner, who was Chairman of the Committee, portions of it being, however, contributed by Messrs. Thornton and Huskisson; and to this divided paternity may be ascribed that want of sequence in its reasonings, and of uniformity in its style, that are so very observable. Having taken much evidence,* and entered at great length into an examination of the subject, the Committee came to the conclusion that the paper currency was depreciated from excess; and they recommended as the only means by which the evil could be checked, and the value of paper maintained on a par with gold, that cash payments should be resumed within the space of two years.

Such being the character and recommendation of this famous Report, we need not wonder that its publication should have been the signal for a violent and long-continued

* The evidence of the Governor, Deputy-Governor, and such of the Bank Directors as came before the Committee, was anything but creditable to them. It was, in truth, a mere apology for the existing state of things, founded, for the most part, on erroneous assumptions, and false or perverted theories.

controversy. The principles laid down in it were said to be contradicted by the evidence. And besides being strenuously opposed by Government, and by the greater number of bankers, merchants, and practical men, they were assailed by a host of writers. But all the great authorities were on the side of the Bullionists. And in 1819 the triumph of sound principles was completed by the legislature reverting to cash payments at the old standard.

Among the pamphlets to which the state of the currency in 1810 gave birth, a very high place must be assigned to the "Observations on the Principles which regulate the course of Exchange, and on the present depreciated state of the Currency," by William Blake, Esq., F.R.S. We have reprinted this tract, which gives within a moderate compass an extremely clear and satisfactory exposition of an important and at the same time complex and difficult subject. Mr.Blake has enumerated the various circumstances, whether arising out of the state of trade or of the currency, that determine the real, the nominal, and the computed or actual course of exchange. He has farther traced with equal skill and sagacity, the mode in which they respectively operate; and set their separate and combined influence in a very striking light.

The last tract in this volume, "The Question respecting the Depreciation of the Currency Stated and Examined," by William Huskisson, Esq., M.P., appeared in 1810. The author intended it should be at once an explanation and a defence of the doctrines laid down in the Bullion Report. And these objects are most successfully accomplished. The doctrines referred to have nowhere been stated with greater, or, perhaps, equal clearness, or in a way more likely to recommend them to the public.

It would have been useless, even had our space permitted, to have made any additions to the tracts now brought together. They comprise a full exposition of the principles that determine the value of paper currency; with an examination and refutation of the various objections, entitled to any consideration, that have been or may be made to these principles. But they do not inquire, or only briefly and perfunctorily, into the nature of the measures that should be adopted to give a practical and real effect to these principles. This is the grand monetary problem which is now (1857) before the country. Its satisfactory solution must, however, in great measure, depend on the principles established in this volume being properly understood and appreciated.

CONTENTS.

A

DISCOURSE

Concerning the

CURRENCIES

OF THE

BRITISH PLANTATIONS

IN

AMERICA.

Eſpecially with regard to their

PAPER MONEY.

WITH A

POSTSCRIPT thereto.

BOSTON: Printed, MDCCXL.

AND

LONDON: Reprinted, MDCCLI.

CURRENCIES

OF THE

BRITISH PLANTATIONS IN AMERICA, &c.

THE many Schemes at present upon the Anvil in *Boston*, for emitting enormous Quantities of Paper Currencies; are the Occasion of this Discourse. The Writer does not vainly pretend to dictate to Government, or prescribe to Trade; but with a sincere Regard to the Publick Good, has taken some Pains to collect, digest, and set in a proper Light, several Facts and Political Experiences, especially relating to Paper Currencies; which, tho' plain in themselves, are not obvious to every Body. If any expressions should sound harsh, they are not to be understood as a Reflection upon this Province in general: It was always my Opinion, That the Province of the *Massachusetts-Bay* is, by far, the most vigorous and promising Plant (with proper Cultivation) of all the *British* Plantations: In the best of Countries at Times, bad Administrations, and private evil Men of Influence have prevailed. The Author is not a transient Person, who, from Humour, or Caprice, or other malevolent Views, may expose the Province: but is by Inclination induced, and by Interest obliged to study the Good of the Country.

All Commerce naturally is a *Truck-Trade*, exchanging Commodities which we can spare (or their Value) for Goods we are in want of. *Silver itself is a Merchandize*, and being the least variable of all others, is by general Consent made the *Medium of Trade.* If a Country can be supposed to have no Dealings but within itself, the Legislature, or tacit Consent of the People, may appoint or receive any Currency at Pleasure: But a trading Country must have Regard to the universal commercial Medium, which is Silver; or cheat, and trade to a Disadvantage: It is true, that in some Countries of Europe *Billon* (a base Mixture of Metals) is used for small Change, but not as a Medium of Trade.

Every Country or Society have their own peculiar Regulations, which may be called their *Municipal*, or By-Laws in Trade; but the universal trading Part of the World, as one tacit Confederacy, have fallen into some *general Rules*, which, by Custom of Merchants, are become as fundamental: One of these is a *Silver Medium of Trade*, that all Contracts (Specialties excepted) are understood to be payable in this Medium, being always of the same fixed Value, or easily adjusted by the *Par*, and accidental small Differences of Exchange from one Country to another.

There can therefore be no other proper *Medium* of Trade, but Silver, or Bills of Exchange and Notes of Hand, payable in Silver at certain Uso's or Periods, which, by a current Discount, are reducible to Silver ready Money, at any Time. The Debitor Party (I am ashamed to mention it) being the prevailing Party in all our depreciating Paper-money Colonies, do wickedly endeavour to delude the unthinking Multitude, by persuading them, that all Endeavours of the Governor, or Proposals and Schemes of private Societies, to introduce a Silver Medium, or a Credit upon a Silver Bottom, to prevent the honest and industrious Creditor from being defrauded; are Impositions upon the Liberty and Property of the People.

Depreciating of the Value of *nummary Denominations*, to defraud the Creditors of the Publick and of private Persons; by Proclamations of Sovereigns, by Recoinages, and by a late Contrivance of a depreciating Paper-credit Currency; were never practised, but in notoriously bad Administrations.

All over *Europe*, for many Ages preceding the 14th Century, the *nummary* Pound, and the *Ponderal* or Pound Weight of Silver, were the same: But in some following Ages, in bad Administrations, the Values of nummary Denominations were gradually reduced; as in *England* to

4oz. Silver value (upon all Occasions I use the nearest round Numbers) one Third of its original Value; in *Holland* the Pound *Ulams* (6 Guilders) to 2 oz. Silver, being only one Sixth of its original Value. A general Stop has been put to those notorious publick Frauds ever since Trade began to flourish: The Civil Governments becoming more polite, found it their Interest, in Affairs of a *Medium* of Trade, to be advised by the more knowing and experienced Traders: Thus, since the Reign of *Edward* VI. in *England*, the Shilling Denomination hath lost only 2 gr. Silver. We have two or three Instances of late in *Europe*, that have deviated from that *Maxim* of a fixed Value of Silver in Trade: These were in arbitrary Governments, under most arbitrary Administrations. 1. *France by Recoinages* from A. 1689, to the wise Administration of *Cardinal Fleury*, was obliged to defraud the Subject, to maintain unjust Wars and Rapines upon its Neighbours, and lessened the Value of nummary Denominations from a *Mark* of Silver at 27 *Livres* to 80 *Livres*. 2. *The King of Spain*, A. 1688, lowered his Denominations 25 *per Cent.* A heavy Piece of *Eight*, formerly 8 *Ryals* Plate, passed for 10 *Ryals* current. 3. *Sweden*, under the Administration of Baron *Gortz*.

In all Sovereignties in *Europe*, where *Paper-Money* was introduced, great Inconveniencies happened; upon cancelling this Paper Medium all those Inconveniencies did vanish. 1. In *Sweden, Baron Gortz* by imposing *Government Notes* (and *Munt Tokyns*) reduced the People to extreme Misery (this was one of the principal Crimes alledged against him, when he suffered capital Punishment); but these being called in, and the *Coin* settled upon the same Foundation as it was before *Charles* XIIth's Accession, *Sweden* flourished as formerly. 2. The late *Regent of France*, by the Advice of Mr. *Law*, did form a Project *A.* 1720, and by his arbitrary Power, endeavoured to put it in Execution; to defraud State Creditors and others, by banishing of Silver Currency, and by substituting a *Paper Credit:* The Effect was, the greatest Confusion, and almost utter Subversion of their Trade and Business. The *Remedy* was, (Mr. *Law* having sneaked off, became a *Profugus*, and at last died obscurely) after a few Months, the Court of *France* were obliged to ordain, That there should be no other legal Tender but Silver Coin; and Commerce has since flourished in *France* more than ever. At present, under the wise Administration of Cardinal *Fleury*, (who allows of no Paper Currencies, nor Recoinages, which had the same Effect in depreciating nummary Denominations in *France*, that frequent and large Emissions of Paper-Money have in our Colonies) their Trade bids fair to outdo the Maritime Powers, (as *Great Britain* and *Holland* are called) and has a much better Effect in advancing the Wealth and Glory of *France*, than the *romantick* butcherly Schemes of Conquest over their Neighbours, under the Administrations of *Richlieu*, *Mazarine*, and others, in the Reigns of *Lewis* XIII. and XIV. 3. In *Great Britain*, A. 1716, were current four and a half Millions of Pounds Sterling in *Exchequer Notes*, being the largest Quantity current at one Time: Although they bore about half of legal Interest, and not equal to one Third of the concomitant national Silver Currency, they laboured much in Circulation; and the Government, to prevent their being depreciated, was obliged to give considerable *Premiums* to the *Bank* for cancelling some of them, and circulating the Remainder.

It is not easily to be accounted for, how *England*, *France*, and *Holland*, have tacitly allowed their several *American Colonies*, by *Laws* of their several Provinces, by *Chancerings* in their Courts of Judicature, and by *Custom*; to depreciate, from Time to Time, the Value of their original Denominations, to defraud their Principals and Creditors in *Europe*. The *British Plantations* have not only varied from Sterling, but have also very much varied from one another; to the great Confusion of Business, and Damage of the Merchant. This will appear plain, by inserting at one View the State of the Currencies in the several *British* Plantations; whereof some are *per Exchange*, some in *Spanish Silver* Coin, and some in *Paper-Money*, called Colony or Province Bills of Publick Credit.

Originally, and for some Years following, in all the *English American Colonies*, 5*s.* Denomination was equal to an *English* Crown Sterling. After some time, *Pieces of Eight*, being the general Currency of all foreign *American* Colonies, became also their Currency; and they remitted or gave Credit to the Merchants at home (by *home* is meant *Great Britain*) a Piece of Eight (Value 4*s.* 6*d.* Sterl.) for a Crown or 5*s.* Sterl. *This was a Fraud of* 11 *per Cent.* In sundry of our Colonies were enacted Laws against passing of light Pieces of Eight: These Laws not being put in Execution, *heavy and light Pieces of Eight passed promiscuously;* and, as it always happens, a bad Currency drove away the good Currency; heavy Pieces of Eight were shipped off. This current Money growing daily lighter, a Difference was made between heavy Money which became Merchandize, and light Money, in which they paid their Debts, gradually from 10, 15, 20, to 25 *per Cent.* as at present in *Jamaica: This was another and continued Course of cheating their Creditors and Employers at home.* From a Complaint of Merchants and others dealing to the Plantations, Queen *Anne* by Proclamation, and the Parliament of *Great Britain* afterwards by the *Proclamation Act*, ordered, That after *Anno* 1709, *A heavy Piece of Eight and other Pieces in Proportion to their Weight, in all our Colonies, should not pass exceeding* 6*s. Denomination.* This Act continues to be observed in none of our Colonies, excepting in *Barbadoes* and *Bermudas*. *Virginia* Currency was formerly, and continues still, better than what the Act directs.

In *NEWFOUNDLAND*, all large Sums are transacted in *Sterling Bills of Exchange:* Small Dealings are in *English Coin* Sterling Value, and in *Pieces of Eight* at 4*s.* 6*d.* being the Sterling Value.

In *NOVA SCOTIA*, the *Sterling Bills of Exchange*, on the Pay of the Troops, Garrison, and Train, supply them with what they may have occasion for from *New England:* Small Dealings are in *New England publick Bills, and in French Coin* from Cape *Breton;* one *Livre* equal to 4*s.* *New England* Currency. At *Canso* Fish and Oil are purchased by *Bills of Exchange, New England* Money, upon *Boston.*

In the Four Colonies of *New England,* viz. *New Hampshire, Massachusetts Bay, Rhode Island,* and *Connecticut,* their Currency being Paper, is promiscuously the same.

NEW HAMPSHIRE (too diminutive for a separate Province, of small Trade and Credit) their *Publick Bills are so much counterfeited,* they scarce obtain a Currency; hence it is (the Governor's Instruction limiting Sum and Period is also a Bar) that at present, their outstanding Bills of public Credit, some on Funds of Taxes, some on Loan, do not exceed 12,000*l.*, gradually to be cancelled by *December* 1742. Their ordinary Charge of Government is about 1500*l. New England* Currency per Annum.

MASSACHUSETTS-BAY: This being more especially the Scene of our Discourse, we shall be more particular. At the first settling of the *New England* Colonies, their Medium was Sterling Coin at Sterling Value, and Barter; some Part of their Taxes was paid in Provisions and other Produce, called *Stock in the Treasury.* When they got into Trade a heavy Piece of Eight passed at 5*s.* *A.* 1652, *They proceeded to coin Silver Shillings, six Pences, and three Pences, at the Rate of* 6*s. to a heavy Piece of Eight;* Silver continued current at this Rate by sundry subsequent Acts of Assembly till *A.* 1705, by a Resolve of the General Court Silver was to pass at 7*s. per Oz.* *A.* 1706 the Courts of Judicature chancered Silver to 8*s. per Oz.* in satisfying of Debts, being nearly after the Rate of 6*s.* a light Piece of Eight as then current. At this Rate Silver and Province Bills continued upon *Par* until *A.* 1714, the Assembly or Legislature fell into the Error of making, from Time to Time, large superfluous Sums of *Paper Money upon Loans,* and the Emissions for Charges of Government not cancellable for many Years; so that these *Publick Bills have been continually depreciating for these last* 26 *Years, and are now arrived to* 29*s. per Oz. Silver.*

Massachusetts-Bay was the Leader of Paper Currencies in our Colonies. Their first Emission was of 40,000*l.* *A.* 1690

& 1691, to pay off the publick Debts incurr'd by that expensive, unsuccessful Expedition against *Canada;* of this Sum 10,000*l.* was cancelled and burnt in *October A.* 1691: In the following Years no more new Emissions, but some Re-emissions of the Remainder, and that only for the necessary Charges of Government, called in by Rates or Taxes within the Year; the last Re-emission of these Bills was *A.* 1701, of 9,000*l.* Bills all this Period continued at the Rate of 6*s.* a heavy Piece of Eight, and were called *Old Charter Bills. A.* 1702 began new Emissions of Province Bills; but, as it ought to be in all wise Administrations, cancelled by Taxes of the same and next following Year, until *A.* 1704, the Rates for calling them in, were in Part postponed two Years; they began *A.* 1707 to postpone them in Part for three Years; *A.* 1709 for 4 Years; *A.* 1710 for 5 Years; *A.* 1711 for 6 Years; *A.* 1715 for 7 Years; *A.* 1721 for 12 Years; *A.* 1722 for 13 Years: *Thus, unnaturally, instead of providing for Posterity, they proceeded to involve them in Debt.* This long publick Credit and the enormous publick Loans, have depreciated our Province Bills to the small Value they bear at present; the Issues and Cancellings of their Bills being for a long Series of Years, is too tedious to be particularly and minutely inserted.

The Province of the *Massachusetts-Bay,* besides the Emission and Re-emissions of the 40,000*l.* old Charter Bills, have since *A.* 1702 emitted and re-emitted Bills of publick Credit, 1,132,500*l.* upon Funds of *Taxes,* and 310,000*l.* upon *Loans,* being in all near one and a half Million; whereof about 230,000*l.* still outstanding, and if publick Faith be better kept will be gradually cancelled by *A.* 1742. The ordinary Charges of Government may be about 40,000*l. New England* Currency per Ann. *Exchange with Great Britain* 450 *per Cent. Advance,* or five and an half *New England* for one Sterl.

RHODE-ISLAND, their first Emissions were *A.* 1710, towards paying more readily their Quota of Charges on the Expedition against *Port Royal* (now *Annapolis Royal*) in *Nova Scotia,* and have emitted from Time to Time, in all

399,300*l.* whereof only 19,300*l.* upon Funds of *Taxes* for Government Charges, and 360,000*l.* upon *Loans,* whereof there is at present outstanding (all upon Loans) 330,000*l.* circiter; which, if their publick Faith should chance to be kept in Time coming, will not be finished cancelling until *A.* 1759. The Interest of those publick Loans defrays the Charges of Government, and of their Towns.

I shall embrace this Opportunity of exemplifying the Iniquity of Colony publick Bills of Credit by the Instance of *Rhode-Island,* a small Colony containing about 18,000 Souls, under an old Charter very lax and general; they admit of no Instructions from the *King,* Council, or Board of Trade and Plantations; the *King* having no Representative or *Commissioned Governor* in their Legislature. This handful of People have lately made a *very profitable Branch of Trade and Commerce by negociating their own Paper Money in various Shapes:* their Money being Loans of Paper Credit called Bills, from their Government to private Persons upon Land Security; to be repaid not in the same real Value, but in the same depreciating fallacious Denominations.

1. Their first Loan was *A.* 1715 for 10 Years, but have by subsequent Acts postponed and prolonged the Payments, so that the last Payment was *A.* 1738. Thus *A.* 1715 Exchange was at 65 *per Cent.* with *England; A.* 1738 Exchange was at 400*l. per Cent.* Advance; that is, for 100*l.* Sterl. Value received, they pay only after the Rate of 33*l.* Sterl. Suppose further, that the same Person upon the same Land Security, borrows again of the new Emission *A.* 1738, this 33*l.* Sterl. value; and, as formerly, by repeated large Emissions, Exchange becomes as at present in *North-Carolina* 10 for 1 Sterl. by *A.* 1758 the Period of this Loan, *the original* 100*l. Sterling Value will be redeemed with* 16*l. Sterl. Value.* And if this Paper Money Loan Trade, could be supposed to continue, the Land Security would gradually vanish, *the Land redeemed, and the Debt paid with nothing.*

2. They who take up this Loan Money are called *Sharers;* and for the first ten Years pay into the Treasury 5 *per Cent*

per Annum Interest; and for the other ten Years pay 10 *per Cent.* per Annum of the Principal, without Interest. The *Sharers* let out this Money, in their own and neighbouring Colonies at 10 *per Cent.* for the said twenty Years (some let it at a higher Interest) is at the Expiration of the twenty Years 300*l.* for every 100*l.* Loan, Principal and simple Interest; for which only 150*l.* is paid into the Colony Treasury, and 150*l.* is clear Gain: *So that in this Shape for every* 100,000*l. Emission, their People in the space of twenty Years, have after the Rate of* 150,000*l. clear Profits.*

3. In another Shape; upon a new Emission, Interest is made with the *Managers,* to obtain Shares in the Loan: the Sharers immediately sell (or may sell) their *Privilege,* as it is called, for *ready Money Præmium;* at the Emission *A.* 1738 the Præmium was 35 *per Cent:* that is, *the Emission of* 100,000*l. does immediately produce after the Rate of* 35,000*l. ready Money profit.*

4. *Rhode-Island* purchases from their neighbouring large Province of the *Massachusetts-Bay,* all Sorts of British and Foreign Goods with this Paper Manufacture which cost nothing; which enables them to rival us in Trade, (particularly in that valuable Branch of it to the *West-India* Islands) and to which by some unaccountable Infatuation we give a Currency; while at the same Time our Merchants cannot make Returns by any Colony Paper Money, for these Goods; it is true, sometimes they bring us Molasses from our Sugar Islands, but mostly from Foreign Colonies, uncustomed, but naturalized upon Oath in *Rhode-Island.* We have a late good Law against the Currency of such Bills, but not being put in Execution, is of no Effect. *The only Reason that can be assigned for giving the Rhode-Island Bills a Currency,* is that they are received in all Payments by Consent: The same Reason may hold good for passing of any Bills, even the 500,000*l.* lately proposed without Fund or Period; and of counterfeit Bills, as in Fact some Bills of *Connecticut* of small Denominations, tho' known to be Counterfeit, have a Currency.

CONNECTICUT, a Charter Colony of industrious

Husbandmen, having, with much Prudence, emitted only small Quantities of Bills; Silver would have continued with them at 8*s.* per Oz. as it did in *New York* their neighbouring Government westward, if their People had not given a Currency to the publick Bills of their Brethren, in the neighbouring Colonies of *New England. Connecticut* emitted Bills only for the present necessary Charges of Government upon Funds of *Taxes,* until *A.* 1733, having granted a *Charter* for Trade and Commerce to a Society in *New-London,* this Society manufactured some Bills of their own; but their Currency being soon at a stand, the Government were obliged in Justice to the Possessors, to emit 50,000*l.* upon *Loan* to enable those concerned in the Society to pay off their Society Bills in Colony Bills; their Charter was vacated, and a wholesome Law enacted, *That for any single person, or Society of Persons, to emit and pass Bills for Commerce or in imitation of Colony Bills, Penalty should be as in Case of Forgery, or of counterfeiting Colony Bills.* Their first Emission of Colony Bills was in *A.* 1709, and may have emitted in all 155,000*l.* whereof only the above 50,000*l.* upon Loan. There are at present outstanding about 60,000*l.* which will be gradually cancelled by *A.* 1742, if the present good Assistants (Council) continue to be annually elected. They have at Times been guilty of emitting small Sums for the present Supply of Government (by oversight and not with any sinister Design) without annexing a Fund or Period; but have soon after been cancelled by Taxes. Their ordinary Charge of Government does not exceed 3,000*l.* *New England* Currency per Annum.

N.B. This promiscuous Currency in the four Governments of *New England,* that is, one Colony giving a Currency to the enormous Paper Credit Emission of one of the other Colonies, has the same Effect as if that Colony did emit Bills of its own: thus *the King's instructions to the commissioned Governments are evaded,* by the popular Charter Governments, rendering them of no Effect, having as it were no Dependance on the Crown. *A Parliamentary Regulation is the only adequate Remedy.*

NEW-YORK chancered Proclamation Money to 8*s*. per Oz. of Silver, at the same Time and for the same Reasons, as has been said of *Massachusetts-Bay-Government: A.* 1709, towards the Charge of an intended Expedition against *Canada* (upon this same Occasion, began the first Paper Money Emissions of *New Jerseys and Connecticut*) they issued 13,000*l.* publick Bills of Credit bearing interest: *A.* 1710 the Interest was taken off upon pretence, that it occasion'd them to be hoarded up as Bonds, and did frustrate their Currency; and 10,000*l.* more Bills without Interest were issued. All these Bills being small Sums and faithfully paid off and sunk in Taxes, *did not affect Exchange with England.*

A. 1714. By *collusion* of the Governor, Council and Representatives, a large sum of 27,680*l.* in Bills, was issued, to pay off Government Debts, whereof some Part consisted of *their own ill founded Claims;* gradually to be cancelled by *Excise* on Liquors to *A.* 1734: these were issued with the *Royal* Assent.——*A.* 1717 for paying of Government Charges and Debts were issued 16,607*l.* without waiting for the *Royal* Approbation, gradually to be cancelled by a *Duty* upon Wines and Rum for 17 Years and *Excise* continued from *A.* 1734 to *A.* 1739: this Emission was connived at by the *Boards* of Council, Trade and Plantations at home; lest many Persons who had *bona fide* received them for valuable Considerations, might suffer by their being suppressed. Which Indulgence this Government have abused, by never waiting for the Royal Assent in their future Emissions.

In the intermediate Years were some small Emissions for Charges of Government, and regularly cancelled.——*A.* 1734 issued 12,000*l.* in Bills for *Fortifications* to be gradually sunk before *A.* 1746 by *Imposts.*——*A.* 1738 issued 48,300*l.* Bills, whereof 40,000*l.* upon Loan; all to be sunk and paid in by *A.* 1750: this rais'd Exchange to 70 *per Cent.* and Silver to 9*s.* 3*d.* per Oz. *The Lieut. Governor to obtain of the People a Governor's Allowance, consented to humour them in this Emission.*

A. 1739, the Funds being otherways applied, it was found that, *contrary to publick Faith,* 15,000*l.* of the Emissions *A.* 1714 and 1717 were still current, and fifteen Years more upon *Excise* were enacted to cancel them. So that now there is about 70,000*l.* in Bills of *New York* current.

NEW JERSIES, A. 1709 issued 3,000*l.* publick Bills of Credit upon the intended Expedition against *Canada*; and *A.* 1711 upon another intended *Canada* Expedition 5,000*l.* more Bills were emitted, to be cancelled gradually before *A.* 1713; but were by Acts of Assembly *postponed,* and many Bills of both Emissions were current *A.* 1723.

A. 1724 emitted 40,000*l.* in Bills, whereof some small Part was to cancel the old outstanding Bills, and the rest upon Loan, to be paid in gradually in twelve Years. This being *too large an Emission* for a small Colony, their Bills became of less Value than those of *New-York*; but being yearly *in good Faith,* sunk, they became equal, and after some Years 2*s.* in the Pound better than *New-York* Bills. This is a Demonstration, that the Quantity of Paper Money increasing or faithfully decreasing, sinks or raises the Value of it.—*A.* 1733, was issued 20,000*l.* more upon Loan to be gradually paid in sixteen Years: this Emission *fell* their Bills to near Par with *New-York.*——*A.* 1734, the first Loan of *A.* 1724, being near sunk, the Assembly enacted a 40,000*l.* Loan, but was not issued till *A.* 1736, having then obtain'd the *Royal* Approbation, and *passed scarce at Par with New-York*; but upon the *New-York* Emission of 48,300*l.* *A.* 1738, the *Jersey* Bills are 6*d.* in the Pound better than *New-York* Bills, and 1*s.* in the Pound better than those of *Pensylvania.*

The *Jersey* Bills keep their Credit better than those of *Pensylvania* and *New-York* for these two Reasons, 1. *New-York* Bills not being current in *Pensylvania,* and *Pensylvania* Bills not current in *New-York*; but *Jersey* Bills current in both, all Payments between *New-York* and *Pensylvania* are made in *Jersey* Bills. 2. In the *Jerseys* failure of the Loan Payments, at the Days appointed, is confessing Judgment, and thereafter only 30 Days Redemption of Mortgages is allowed.

The 5 *per Cent.* Interest of publick Loans defrays all *Charges of Government.* In the *Jerseys* at present about 60,000*l.* in publick Bills current all upon Loan.

In the two Governments of *PENSYLVANIA* their Currency continued Silver Proclamation Value, until *A.* 1723: The three Upper Counties (strictly called *Pensylvania*) emitted upon Loan 15,000*l.* in Bills, and *A.* 1724 emitted 30,000*l.* more; but *A.* 1726 finding that in strictness of the two preceding Acts 6,100*l.* part of the Capital of 45,000*l.* was sunk, the Encouragers of Paper Money procured an Act for re-emitting what should be annually paid in of the remainder by the Borrowers; and *A.* 1729 emitted 30,000*l.* which have generally been continued out by *re-emitting Acts* from Time to Time. *A.* 1739 they made an Addition of about 11,100*l.* upon Loan on the same Terms: so that at present they have 80,000*l.* all upon Loan. Exchange with *London* 75 *per Cent.* before Emissions of Paper Money, it was only 33 *per Cent.*

The three Lower Counties have also Paper Currency in small Quantities, and upon the same footing.

In MARYLAND, Silver continued at Proclamation Value until *A.* 1734, with a considerable Concomitant *Truck Trade* as a *Medium*, viz. *Tobacco*; they then emitted 90,000*l.* in Bills, which tho' payable to the Possessors in Sterling well secured, the Sum being too large, and the Periods too long, viz. three partial payments of 15 Years Periods each; *Exchange immediately rose from* 33 *to* 100 *and* 150 *per Cent.*

VIRGINIA has the same considerable *Truck Trade Medium*, viz. *Tobacco*; and with regard to Silver Currency, have kept their Integrity better than the other Colonies. It is true, *Lord Culpeper* their Governor, about *A.* 1680, by an arbitrary Proceeding in the quality of the King's Representative, did, by virtue of his own Proclamation, alter the Value of their Silver Coin for his own Profit, to defraud an English Regiment then paid off and disbanded, (this Regiment was sent from *England* to quell an Insurrection or Mutiny in *Virginia* under *Bacon*) but soon finding that it occasioned much Confusion in Business, and did particularly affect his own Perquisites; he reduced it again to the former Standard. Silver a few Years ago was 6*s.* a Crown British, or 6*s.* 3*d.* per Oz. Silver, at present it is 6*s.* 8*d.* per Oz.

of Silver, and 5*l.* per Oz. Gold; *is* 25 *per Cent, worse than Sterling.*

NORTH CAROLINA, an inconsiderable Colony scarce capable of any Fund for Paper Emissions; have notwithstanding 40,000*l.* upon *Loan*, and 12,500*l.* upon Funds of *Taxes.* At present Exchange is settled by their Legislature at 10 *North Carolina* for 1 *Sterling*, but in drawing upon *London* 12 to 14 for 1 *Sterling.*

In *SOUTH CAROLINA*, their first Emission of publick Paper Credit was *A.* 1702, towards the Charges of an Expedition against St. *Augustine.* Their Legislature have been most *notoriously guilty of breach of publick Faith*, in not cancelling their Bills. Besides the Emissions for ordinary Charges of Government, and their Expeditions against the *North Carolina Indians*, *A.* 1711, and against the *Southern Indians*, A. 1715, they have large Sums upon *Loans.* They may have at present outstanding about 250,000*l.* in Province Bills, (whereof above 100,000*l.* without Fund or Period) besides private Notes of substantial Merchants negociated, payable upon Demand in Province Bills; they have also a valuable *Truck*, viz. *Rice.* Their present Exchange with *London*, as settled by their Legislature, to ascertain the Value of Debts contracted, *is* 8 *South Carolina for* 1 *Sterling.*

In the new Colony of *GEORGIA*, their Currency are the Trustees *sola Bills Sterling:* the Funds are the Allowances by Parliament, and private Subscriptions to carry on the Settlement.

PROVIDENCE, including the rest of the *Bahama* Islands, is scarce reckoned a Colony.

In *BERMUDAS*, a Colony of Sea Carriers; their *Currency continues Proclamation* Value.

BARBADOES: Their Currency is Proclamation Value by weight 6*s.* 10*d. farthing* per Oz. Silver. By the Advice of Mr. *W.* from *New England*, they made the Experiment of a Paper Currency, and emitted 16,000*l.* upon the Negro *Tax* Fund, and soon after 80,000*l.* more upon *Loan;* these Bills immediately fell 40 *per Cent.* below Silver, and upon Complaint were directly suppressed by an Order from *England;*

and some of the Possessors who gave them a Currency, have Quantities of them to show, as a Monument of this Folly, and of Paper Money becoming waste Paper.

Here, as in all our Sugar Islands, *Sugar* according to its Quality at the Market Price, serves as a *Truck Medium* to pay Debts. *The Par of Exchange is* 33 *per Cent.* but generally lower and in favour of *Barbadoes.*

The *CARRIBEE LEEWARD ISLANDS* of *Antegoe Newis,* St. *Christophers, Montserrat, and the Virgins,* have depreciated from Silver Proclamation Value, to 8*s.* per Oz. in the same Manner as has been said of *Massachusett's-Bay;* but never proceeded to that Fraud, Paper-Money: light Pieces of Eight are current by Tale. *Exchange* 50 *per Cent. Advance.*

In *JAMAICA,* formerly a heavy Piece of Eight current at 5*s.* but light Money taking Place as a Currency; the heavy Money was shipped off in course of Time, at 10, 15, 20, and 25 *per Cent.* as at present Difference. At this Time a light Piece of Eight passes at 5*s.* a heavy Piece of Eight at 6*s.* 3*d.* and Silver at 7*s.* 2*d.* *per* Oz. *The Par of Exchange with London is about* 36 *per Cent. difference,* but generally higher and in favour of London.

Thus we see, that particularly in our Paper Money Colonies, the Currencies have incredibly depreciated from Sterling, and from one another. Exchange with Great Britain *being at this Time* (Feb. 1739) *in New England* 450 *per Cent. in New York, Jerseys and Pensylvania* 70 *to* 75 *per Cent. in* Maryland, 150 *per Cent. in North Carolina,* 1100 *to* 1300 *per Cent in South Carolina* 700 *per Cent. worse than Sterling.*

To make a Bill or Note bearing no Interest, and not payable till after a dozen or score of Years, a legal ready Money Tender in Payment of Debts, is the highest of *despotick* and arbitrary Government: *France* never made their State Bills a common Tender. Our Paper Money Colonies have carried the Iniquity still further; the popular or *Democratick* Part of the Constitution are generally in Debt, and by their too great Weight or Influence in Elections, have made a depreciating Currency, a Tender for Contracts done many Years before; that is, *they impose upon the Creditor side in private Contracts,* which the most despotick Powers never assumed. An Instance of a still further arbitrary Proceeding in relation to Paper Money, was an Act of Assembly in *New Jerseys, A.* 1723, whereby *Executions for Debt were stayed until Paper Money should be issued.*

The Mystery of the Infatuation of our Colonies running headlong into a depreciating Paper Currency may be this: In many of our Plantations of late Years, by bad Management, and Extravagancies, the Majority of the People are become *Debtors,* hence their elected Representation in the Legislature, have a great Chance to be generally of the Debtors Side: or, in other Words, the *Representatives* being generally Freeholders, and many of them *much in Debt,* by large Emissions their Lands rise in Denomination Value, while their Debts become really less, and the Creditor is defrauded in Part of his Debt. Thus our Colonies have defrauded more in a few Years, than bad Administrations in *Europe* have formerly done in some Centuries. The great Damage done to the generous Merchants at Home, and to the industrious fair Dealers amongst our selves, call aloud for some speedy and effectual Relief from the supreme Legislature, the *Parliament of Great Britain.*

There is an Argument, which tho' not much attended to here, may be of some Weight at Home, viz. *That the Government at Home ought to connive at Paper Money in the Colonies,* because by indulging them in this Error, all the Silver which they acquire from Time to Time, is sent to *Great Britain;* and by the *chimæra* of a fallacious Cash, Extravagancies are encouraged in favour of a great Consumption of British Goods: *This ought to be an Argument with us against that Paper Currency,* which tends to turn the Ballance of Trade so much against us. It is true, That *Great Britain* naturally ought to reap some Profit by its Plantation Improvements: but a good Husbandman improves his Lands not by working them out of Heart (as the Term is) but by manuring them, that they may yield the better Crops: besides, what the British Merchants lose in their Returns, by the Colony Bills depreciating, and by the Bankruptcy of their Factors, and Dealers here; is much more than what *Great Britain* gets, on the abovesaid Accounts.

In the Sequel of this Discourse, I shall 1. Enumerate the Inconveniencies and bad Effects of our large Emissions of Paper Money. 2. Endeavour to remove the Prejudices which some designing Men have infused into the Minds of the Populace, in favour of Bills of Credit. 3. Consider several Projections or Schemes to rectify our Currency and present Circumstances, or to prevent their growing worse.

The Mischiefs arising from a large Paper Currency are,

I. With regard to *the particular and immediate Sufferers thereby.*

1. *The Labourers and Trades-men,* who in all Countries, are the Hands which feed the Belly of the Common Wealth, and therefore *deserve our chief Regard.* How much they have suffered, and continue to suffer is obvious: For Instance, a Carpenter, when Silver was 8*s.* per Oz. his wages were 5*s.* a Day all Cash. The Town House, *A.* 1712, was built at this Rate; whereas at present, *A.* 1739, from the bad Influence of Paper Money, Silver being 29*s.* per Oz. he has only 12*s.* a Day, equal only to 3*s.* 4*d.* of former Times; and even this is further reduced, by obliging him to take one-half in Shop Goods, at 25 per Cent. or more Advance above the Money Price; this Iniquity still grows, by reducing the Goods Part to the least vendable; the Shopkeeper refusing to let them have Provisions, West India Goods, or Goods of *Great Britain,* that are in Demand.

To make the Case more familiar, Suppose a Tradesman laying in his Winter Store, when Wages were at 5*s.* with one Days Labour he purchases 15 Pound of Butter, being 4*d.* per Pound (I use Butter because it rises the most uniformly of all Provisions) at present, his 12*s.* a Day purchases only 7 Pound of Butter, at 20*d.* a Pound. The *Clergy,* or settled Preachers to Congregations in *Boston,* when Silver was at 5*s.* had 3*l.* per Week, at present Silver at 29*s.* per

Oz. they have only 6*l*. to 8*l*. equal to 40*s*. of former Times.

The *Shopkeepers* are become as it were Bankers between the Merchants and Tradesmen, and do impose upon both egregiously. Shop Notes, that great and insufferable Grievance of Tradesmen, were not in Use until much Paper Money took Place: This Pay in Goods which generally are of no necessary Use (Provisions and West India Goods at this Time are removed from That Denomination) encourage Extravagance in Apparel and Furniture much above our Condition.

2. *The Merchants of Great Britain, Adventurers to New England, because of their largest Dealings, have suffered most.* Their Goods are here generally sold at a long Credit, while the Denominations of the Money in which they are to be paid, continues depreciating; so that they are paid in a less Value than was contracted for: thus our Bills have successively depreciated from 8*s*. per Oz. Silver *A*. 1713, to 29*s*. in this Year 1739; that is, if we could suppose the same Person to have constantly followed this Trade (without extraordinary Hits) for that space of Time, *he must have reduced his Estate after the rate of* 8*s*. *only for* 29*s*. For every Shilling in the Pound that Silver rises in Price, or, which is the same, for every Shilling in the Pound that the Denomination of our Paper Money depreciates, the Creditor actually loses 5 per Cent. of his Debt.

There have been from Time to Time *seeking Factors,* who to procure Business from Home have entered into Engagements which could not possibly be complied with: these having little or nothing of their own to lose, soon make desperate Work of it; become Bankrupts, and from a general Insensibility of Discredit, do notwithstanding, keep their Countenance as before.

Many *Factors,* to dazle their Employers for a Time, and in the mean while to procure more Consignments; send home a high Account of Sales, by the Shopkeepers giving a great Advance, in Consideration of a very long Credit, and to be drawn out in Shop Notes. This practice has so much prevailed, that it is now become a fixed, tho' pernicious and ruinous Custom.

As Paper Money pays no Debts abroad, the Factor is obliged to give an extra Quantity of it, to purchase Silver, and other Returns; which can be exported, to satisfy Debts, in this Shape also the Merchant becomes a Sufferer.

3. *Widows, Orphans, Funds for Charity*, at Interest, and all other Creditors; by Bonds, Notes, and Book Debts, acquired by Industry, good Management, and Frugality; are great Sufferers from Time to Time: For instance, from Autumn *A.* 1733, to Autumn *A.* 1734, Silver rose from 22*s.* to 27*s.* per Oz. this was a Loss of 23 per Cent. of the Principal.

II. *The repeated large Emissions of Paper Money are the Cause of the frequent rise of the Price of Silver and Exchange;* that is, of the publick Bills of Currency depreciating in all the Paper Money Colonies; which do as regularly follow the same, as the Tides do the *Phases* or course of the Moon. When no larger Sums are emitted for some Time, than what are cancelled of former Emissions; Silver and Exchange are at a Stand; when less is emitted than cancelled (which seldom happens) Silver and Exchange do fall. This is plain to a kind of Demonstration, from the Instance in the History of our Paper Money Emissions in *New England.*

After Silver had rose *A.* 1706 to 8*s.* per Oz. by light Pieces of Eight superseding the heavy Pieces; it continued at that Rate, while Paper Emissions did not exceed a due Proportion to the current Silver. *A.* 1714 we emitted 50,000*l.* upon Loan, and *A.* 1715 in *Rhode-Island* 40,000*l.* besides Emissions on distant Funds for Charges of Government; in the Autumn *A.* 1715 Silver became 15 per Cent. Advance, above 8*s.* that is about 9*s.* 2*d.* per Oz. *Massachusett's-Bay A.* 1717 emitted 100,000*l.* upon Loan, and a very long Period; Silver rose to 12*s.* per Oz. *A.* 1721 *Massachusetts-Bay* emitted 50,000*l.* and *Rhode-Island* 40,000*l.* upon Loan. Silver *A.* 1722, became 14*s.* per Oz. From that Time a chargeable Indian War, required large Emissions, and Silver rose to 16*s.* per Oz. it continued at this Rate till *A.* 1728, Emissions not being larger than Cancellings. *A.* 1727,

Massachusetts-Bay emitted 60,000*l.* and *A.* 1728 *Rhode-Island* emitted 40,000*l.* upon Loans; Silver became 18*s.* per Oz. *A.* 1731, *Rhode-Island* emitted 60,000*l.* upon Loan. (*N.B.* Besides the several Loans in the course of this History all the Charges of the four Governments were defrayed by Paper Emissions) and Silver became *A.* 1732, 21*s.* per Oz. *A.* 1733, *Massachusetts-Bay* emitted 76,000*l.* upon Funds of Taxes, *Rhode-Island* 104,000*l.* upon Loan and Taxes, *Connecticut* 50,000*l.* upon Loan, and *A.* 1734, Silver became 27*s.* per Ounce. From *A.* 1734 to *A.* 1738, more Bills were cancelled than emitted, Exchange fell from 440 to 400 per Cent. Advance. *A.* 1738 *Rhode Island* emitted 100,000*l.* upon Loan, Silver rose from 27*s.* to 29*s.* per. Oz.

In *New-England*, as in all other trading Countries, from some particular Accidents and Circumstances, there happened at Times, some small Fluctuations in Exchange, without any regard to Emissions of Paper-Money. At all Times, when Returns in Ship-building, Whale Oil, and Fins, Naval Stores, &c. turn out well at Home; Silver and Exchange here suffer a small fall: at other Times when these prove bad Returns, Silver and Exchange rise a small Matter; the most noted Instance, was *A.* 1729, when the usual Returns to *Great Britain* turned to bad Account; the Merchants from Home, directed their Factors here, to make Remittances in Silver or Exchange only, and at any Rate; together with an Agency from this Province, and that of *Connecticut*, fitted out with a Silver Supply; Silver rose very considerably, but after a few Months fell again to the former Price.

The Instance of *Barbadoes* must put this Assertion beyond all Dispute with sober thinking honest Men. *A.* 1702, by the Persuasion of Mr. *W.* from *New-England*, *Barbadoes* emitted 16,000*l.* Bills of publick Credit on a Fund of 3*s.* 9*d.* Negro Tax; at first they passed at a Discount, but no more being emitted, and the Period of cancelling being short, they rose again to near *Par:* This encouraged them to make an enormous Emission of 80,000*l.* Bills on Land Security at 4 *per Cent.* Principal, payable after 5 Years; These Bills immediately fell 40 *per Cent.* below Silver: By an Order from Home, they were soon suppressed, and their Currency became Silver Value as before. That Province has ever since kept their Currency up to Proclamation Value, Ballance of Trade in their Favour, Exchange to *Great Britain* being generally under 33 *per Cent.* the Par.

III. *Large repeated Emissions of publick Bills of Credit, called Paper Money, is no Addition to the Medium of Trade.* No Country can have an indefinite or unlimited Credit; the further a Country endeavours to stretch its Credit beyond a certain Pitch, the more it depreciates. The Credit of a Country may be compared to that of a private Trader; if his Credit is equal to 100,000*l.* Sterl. his Notes of Hand for 100,000*l.* will be as good as Silver; if it be known that he passes Notes of Hand for 200,000*l.* Sterl. their full Credit will be suspected, and eventually be worth no more than his real Credit 100,000*l.* Sterl. if he can be supposed to utter 500,000*l.* Bills or Notes, his 5*l.* Note will be worth 20*s.* Sterling.

In *New England, A.* 1713, there were about *two thirds* Bills to *one third* Silver Current, equally at 8*s. per* Oz. Silver Value; there being an Allowance of 5 *per Cent.* in all publick Payments in favour of Bills only, gave them a Credit beyond their natural Stretch. At that Time the publick Bills of the four Provinces were about 175,000*l.* at 8*s. per* Oz. Silver Value (we use always the nearest round Numbers) is 438,000 Oz. Value, with 219,000 Oz. of Silver Currency, is 657,000 Oz. Silver Value. *A.* 1718, the publick Bills of *New England* were 300,000*l.* (Silver all drove away by the worse Currency of Bills) at 12*s. per* Oz. Silver, is 500,000 Oz. Value in Silver. *A.* 1731, *New England* publick Bills were 470,000*l.* at 20*s. per* Silver, is 470,000 Oz. Silver Value. *A.* 1739, the current Paper Money of *New England* was 630,000*l.* at 29*s. per* Oz. Silver is in Value 434,000 Oz. Silver. Here it is plain, that the more Paper Money we emit our real Value of Currency or *Medium* becomes less, and *what we emit beyond the trading Credit of the Country, does not add to the real Medium, but rather diminishes from* *it, by creating an Opinion against us, of bad Oeconomy and sinking Credit.*

A Country may exceed in any Commodity or *Medium*, excepting in that universally Staple Commodity and *Medium* Silver; and a smaller Quantity of any other Commodity or *Medium* will turn to the same or better Account than a larger. In *Holland*, upon a too large Importation of Spices, they destroy some Part, to keep up the Value of Spices. Not long since in *Virginia*, finding that Tobacco (their Currency as well as Export) by its too large Cultivation began to depreciate; by Act of Assembly they restricted it to 1000*l.* wt. *per Annum per Tythable.* In *Maryland, A.* 1734. & *A.* 1735, for the same Reason they burnt yearly 150*l.* wt. *per Rateable.* If our House of Representatives allow our Paper Money to be cancelled in Course, and be sparing in the Manufacture of more; the Value of the Remainder, would be equal to the Value of the whole now current, or proposed to be added to the Currency.

It is therefore vain and inconsistent to make *Provincial* or Municipal Bills of Credit, for a *Medium* of general Trade: Merchants know how to find their own Tools, or *Medium* of Trade, better than any Civil Administration can prescribe: In Fact, they who call out loudest for this Paper *Medium*, are not our large Traders; but such as would take up Money at any bad Lay, *viz.* the Idle, those in desperate Circumstances, and the Extravagant; who never can have any other Claim to Money but by Fraud; we must except some, who tho' naturally honest are misguided. Publick Bills of Credit in a proper Sense are only to defray the incident Charges of Government which may accrue, before the proper Ways and Means of Taxes can take Place; but so soon as can be, to be cancelled by those Taxes. We know of no Country in *Europe*, where Exchequer Notes, State Bills, or other Bills of publick Credit, have been issued by the Government for a *Medium* of Trade.

IV. *This Infatuation in favour of Paper Money, has had a mutinous bad Effect upon the Civil Government in several of our Colonies.* The Representatives of the People, have frequently refused to provide for the necessary Charges of Government, and other wholesome Laws; because the Governors and Councils, would not (in Breach of their Instructions from the Crown) concur in emitting large Sums of Paper Money to defraud the industrious Creditor and fair Dealer. I shall mention only a few Instances in *S. Carolina*, *A*. 1719, the People deposed the Proprietors Governor on this Account: It is true, the *King* did not much resent this Mutiny; perhaps, that the Proprietors might be weary of their Property and Government; and accordingly seven of the eight Proprietors, for a small Consideration, did *A*. 1729, resign and sell to the Crown: Upon Governor *Johnson's* arrival in *S. Carolina, A*. 1731, there had been no Supply granted in the four preceding Years. The Government of the *Massachusetts Bay*, has from Time to Time been distressed, by our Representatives refusing Supplies for the necessary Charges of Government, and other publick Affairs, neglected on this Account: *Our present Governour's Fortitude and steady Adherence to the King's Instructions, and his having shortened the long Periods of Emissions for Charges of Government* (*I am under no Obligation to flatter*) *are highly laudable. New Hampshire* Representatives for five Years preceding *A*. 1736, granted no Supply. As the *French* Humour of building Forts, to protect their Settlements against an Enemy, is perverted to the enslaving of the Subjects; and as the *Spanish* Humour of Devotion, in building Churches and Convents, is perverted, by their becoming Nurseries of Idleness and other Vices; so the *English Liberty and Property of the Subject*, in many of our Plantations are sometimes abused, to Levelling and Licentiousness; it is true, all Men are naturally equal, but Society requires Subordination.

V. *Long Credit, is not one of the least of the bad Effects of Paper Money*. People run in Debt, endeavour after a long Credit, and refuse paying their Debts when due; because while Bills are continually depreciating, the longer the Debt is outstanding, they pay their Creditors with a less and less Value, than was contracted for. Sir *Alexander Cumings* in his Defence, wrote *A*. 1729. says, That in his Time in *South*

Carolina, Pay after twelve Months, was reckoned as ready Money. Long Credit thus obtained, does in its turn, forward a bad Currency, they go Hand in Hand. A Creditor after being long out of his Money, chuses rather to take the bad Currency and run the Risque of passing it off again (as was the Case of the *Rhode-Island* Emissions, *A.* 1733 and 1738) than of losing his Debt, if another Creditor should take it, and the Debtor afterwards become insolvent.

With ready Money, or short Credit, Business goes on brisk and easy. *Long Credit* occasions the Unthinking of all Conditions and Occupations, to involve themselves. A Merchant over-trades himself, a Shop-keeper buys more Goods, and at a greater Advance than he can afterwards comply with; the Countryman buys and mortgages Lands, to his final Ruin.

VI. *Insensibility of Discredit, does naturally follow long Credit:* All Shame and Modesty is banished even in the Creditor; who, tho' formerly a modest forbearing Man, is now obliged to Dun incessantly, or lose his Debt. Ready Money and short Credit, give a quick Circulation; the quicker the Circulation, the less Quantity of *Medium* is required to carry on the same Trade and Business: Long Credit, and Insensibility of Discredit, have the contrary Effect. There are at present extant of *New England* publick Bills of Credit about 630,000*l.* a much larger Sum than ever was extant at any other Time; yet Money was never so scarce, and Debts worse paid: *People chuse rather to hoard it up*, and wait for better Times, than put it out and not be able to recover it again, but after an unreasonable Length of Time and much Trouble; Money hoarded up, is the same as if not in being, as to Currency. If a Shopkeeper does not clear with his Merchant, till after two or three Years due; he is notwithstanding esteem'd as honest as his Neighbour: Our Courts are full of plain Bonds, and Notes of Hand; Appeals on them are allowed, Executions delay'd, *&c.* This Insensibility of Discredit, breaks all Friendship; it makes a Man cautious of lending his Money to his best Friend, and nearest Relation.

A general Clamour for a depreciating Paper Currency, is

a certain Sign of the Country being generally in bad Circumstances; that is, *in Debt*; because all Creditors, who by their Industry and Frugality, have acquired Rents, Bonds, Notes, and Book Debts, lose by its depreciating; and the Debtors (the Idle and Extravagant Part of the People) come off easy by the Creditors Loss. Seeing they who are desperately in Debt, and want to pay a smaller Value than contracted for, or *they who have nothing to lose, are generally of the Party for Paper money*; this ought to be a strong Prejudice against it, with sober thinking Men.

We have *some prevailing Customs and some Laws in force*, which seem to encourage this *Insensibility of Discredit* in Debtors; 1. *A Maxim amongst Shopkeepers*, That the most ready Way to grow rich, without any Expence of Industry, is, to run boldly in Debt, procure a long Credit; after Time of Payment is elapsed, to bear Dunning with a good Face, and finally to let the Debt take its full Course in the Law, which further requires twelve Months or more, at a small Cost: Notwithstanding this Chain of Iniquity, the Debtor keeps his Countenance, and many Factors continue to trust him with their Employer's Goods, as formerly. 2. *Estates too easily allowed to be represented as Insolvent*; whereby Creditors are defrauded of some Part of their Due. 3. *Appeals upon plain Bonds, Notes of Hand, and Defaults*, to the great Relief of the fraudulent Debtor, and Damage of the honest Creditor. 4. *Sheriffs* impune *Delay of Executions*, while the Creditor is allowed neither Interest nor Damage upon the Debt. 5. *The too general Laws for the Relief of insolvent Debtors*, whereby the Fraudulent, the Idle, and the Extravagant, when sent to Goal, are too soon, and at too easy a Rate, turned loose to follow the same Courses. What I have here said, *cannot be understood in Contempt of our Legislative Authority*; because of that valuable Privilege belonging to our Constitution, viz. of repealing, amending, or explaining what Laws from Experience may be found to require the same.

The Arguments current amongst the Populace in favour of Paper Money are,

I. In most of the Paper Money Colonies one of the

principal Reasons alledged for their first Emissions; was, *to prevent Usurers imposing high Interest upon Borrowers, from the Scarcity of Silver Money.* It is true, that in all Countries the increased Quantity of Silver, falls the Interest or Use of Money; but large Emissions of Paper Money does naturally rise the Interest to make good the sinking Principal: for Instance, in the Autumn, *A.* 1737, Silver was at 26*s.* to 27*s.* per Ounce, but by a large *Rhode-Island* Emission, it became in Autumn 1739, 29*s.* per Oz. this is 7 per Cent. Loss of Principal, therefore the Lender, to save his Principal from sinking, requires 13 per Cent. natural Interest (our legal Interest being 6 per Cent.) for that Year. In Autumn, *A.* 1733, Silver was 22*s.* per Oz. by large Emissions it became 27*s.* in the Autumn, *A.* 1734; is 22 per Cent. loss of Principal; and the Lender to save his Principal; requires 28 per Cent. *natural Interest* for that Year. Thus *the larger the Emissions, natural Interest becomes the higher*; therefore the Advocates for Paper Money (who are generally indigent Men, and Borrowers) ought not to complain, when they hire Money at a dear nominal Rate.

If Bills were to depreciate after a certain Rate, Justice might be done to both contracting Parties, by imposing the Loss which the Principal may sustain in any certain Space of Time (the Period of Payment) upon the Interest of a Bond or Price of Goods: but as Depreciations are uncertain, great Confusions in Dealings happen.

II. *That the Merchants arbitrary Rise upon the Price of Goods, does from Time to Time depreciate the Denominations of our Paper Money,* is imposed upon the unthinking Part of the People, as a certain Truth, by designing Men. It is certain, that in all Countries of *Europe*, where, by Recoinages or Proclamations, the current Specie has been debased, the nominal Price of Goods did naturally rise in Proportion: is it not more natural to say, that formerly in *France* their Recoinings or lessening the Value of their Denominations, did raise the Price of Goods; than to say, that the Rise of the Price of Goods was the Cause of their Recoinages? A continued Rise on Goods in general is from a depreciating

Medium; but Fluctuations in particular Goods, are from the Quantities and Demand; thus *A.* 1739, Provisions, the most Staple of all Commodities, have been cheap, *viz.* Wheat at 10*s.* per Bushel, Silver being 29*s.* per Ounce, whereas *A.* 1738, Wheat was at 18*s.* per Bushel, when Silver was only 27*s.* per Oz.

When a large Emission can be foreseen, the Price of Goods rises; because, being sold upon long Credit, the Effects of the Emission will take Place before the time of Payment: hence it is that, *generally, the Price of Goods advances, before Exchange and Silver do rise*; Exchange and Silver being bought with ready Money, cannot take Place until the Addition is made to the Currency by this new Emission, and then only gradually as the Merchant receives his Pay; thus the large Emissions of *A.* 1733 did not bring Silver to its Height, 27*s*, per Oz. until Autumn, *A.* 1734: Hence proceeds that inculcated Fallacy of the Advance on Goods rising the Price of Silver and Exchange. The same Reason for Lenders of Money, imposing a high Interest, holds in the Rise of the Price of Goods: Custom has given a long Credit, Insensibility of Discredit, makes it still longer, and before the Merchant is paid, the Currency is become much depreciated.

III. *The Sticklers for Paper Credit, requiring long Periods, as well as large Emissions, is a most natural Desire.* Some of *the Massachusetts-Bay* Loan, of *A.* 1717, is still outstanding *A.* 1739: The several *Rhode-Island* Loans do not terminate in less than 20 Years: By this unnatural Contrivance they oblige Posterity to supply the Extravagancies of their Parents and Ancestors, instead of the common and natural Instinct of Parents providing for their Children.

IV. *It is not repeated large Emissions of a base Paper-Currency, but our Imports exceeding our Exports, that occasions Silver to be ship'd off in Ballance; therefore we are not to expect a Silver-Currency, supposing all Bills cancelled.* Before Paper-Money took place in *New England*, Silver abounded in Currency as much, and perhaps more, than in many of our Colonies: Our Exports are always in Demand, *viz.* Ship-building, all Branches of Fishery, Naval-Stores to *Great Britain,* Logwood from the Bay of *Honduras,* Lumber, Stock, and other Provisions to the other Colonies; and (*Bermudians* excepted) our Navigation is the cheapest of all Carriers. Silver began to be generally ship'd off as Paper became the Currency; which gave the Merchant the Liberty of shipping off his Silver as Merchandize, which otherways he must have kept as Cash, seeing no Business can be carried on to Advantage without Cash. In all Countries, if a bad *Medium* is introduced, People take Care to secure the better *Mediums,* and they are no more current.

The Fallacy of Quantities of Paper-Money, has increased our superfluous Imports, much beyond what was in former Times. The *seeking Factors* upon a large Emission, advise the Merchant in *Great Britain,* that Money being now very plenty, a large Quantity of Goods will sell: Accordingly a Glut of Goods is sent to *New England,* more than can be sold for ready Money and short Credit; the Consequence is, a long Credit, with its consequential Multitude of Evils; that is, Returns or Exports in full, are never, or not till after a long Time, ship'd off.

Our Paper-Money being only passable amongst ourselves, is the Reason, why, *they who deal only in buying and selling ashore, get the most Money;* all their Profits are upon ourselves, and run no Risque of precarious Returns; while the generous Merchant loses upon his Exports to a foreign Market. This is a ruinous Case.

As Paper-Money grows scarce, Imports will be less, and be sold cheaper; no Country can want a true real Medium of Trade, while their Exports exceed their Imports; Let us then lessen our Imports by our Frugality, and add to our Exports by our Industry; and we shall have no occasion for this *chimerical ill founded Medium, Paper Money.*

V. *The goodly Appearance, which* Boston *and the Country in general at present, make in fine Houses, Equipage, and Dress, is owing to Paper Money.* All our Plantations, from some Infatuation, are inclinable to run into Prodigality, Profuseness, and Show: these Paper Loans, (from publick or private Schemes) upon long Periods, give the unthinking and unwary, Opportunities of involving themselves, by thus sinking what they have borrowed; by repeated Emissions, they have Opportunities of paying a former Debt, by running further in Debt, till at length they become Insolvents. People do not consider, that all Emissions upon Funds of Taxes, or upon Loans, is running the Country more and more in Debt, and will in Course fall heavy upon every Individual. Never were greater Complaints of want of Money, while at the same Time, never more Extravagance in Equipages and Dress. *Boston, like a private Man of a small Fortune, does not become richer but poorer, by a rich goodly appearance.*

What Part of these Emissions have we laid out in Improvements of Produce, or Manufacture? Not any. It is true, it gave some Men Opportunities of building Vessels, and running into Trade; but their Education and Experience not lying that Way, and having no other Bottom of their own, they soon became *broken Merchants.*

Expending in fine Houses and Apparel what ought to have purchased Exports, is one of the Reasons, why Ballance of Trade is against us.

There is another Fund for all this Finery, and of which we ought not to boast, but be ashamed. By the Means of a depreciating Currency the Merchant at Home, has been paid in less Value, than was contracted for; his Loss was our Gain. Several Factors, from Time to Time, have, by Artifice and Assurance, procured large Commissions from Home, and with Effrontery and Insensibility of Discredit, have become Bankrupts: Thus the Produce of these Effects remained here, and makes good in some Sense, that Position of Dr. *Mandeville's;* Private Vices are Publick Benefits.

VI. *This Country formerly had but a small Trade, now our Trade being much enlarged, we require a large Medium.* This, like all the Arguments commonly used to pervert the People, is very unnatural: because the more a Country grows in good Trade, the more true *Medium* of Trade it acquires, and would have no Occasion to have Recourse to a fallacious *Succedaneum*, or Shift. Notwithstanding the vast Floods of Paper Money lately emitted, and our Trade also more general: we find that, in former Times, the People were more willing and able to pay high Rates, than at present. The first Assembly upon the new Charter, did, in *June A.* 1692, lay a Tax of 30,000*l.* (equal to upwards of 120,000*l.* present Currency) payable within the Year, *viz.* one half before the 25th of *December A.* 1692, and the other half before the first of *May* 1693; towards paying off Charges formerly incurred by the *Canada* Expedition, and Charges of that Year. *A.* 1694 the Tax was 17,589*l.* (equal to upwards of 70,000*l.* present Currency) towards paying off the Government Charges of that and the preceding Year. Whereas, we who reckon ourselves so much increased in Trade at present *A.* 1739 refuse a small Rate of about only 50,000*l.* towards paying Government Charges incurred *A.* 1728, *A.* 1733, and *A.* 1737.

VII. *How can we pay our Taxes and Debts, if the Government do not make large Emissions of Paper Money?* In all Countries, excepting in Paper Money Colonies, the People support the Government: it is absurd to imagine that a Government finds Money for its People, it is the People who, by their Trade and Industry, provide not only for their own Subsistence, but also for the Support of Government, and to find their own *Tools* or *Medium* of Trade. It is true, the Government, that is, the Stewards of the Publick, may (by the Consent of their Principals, the collective Body of the People) raise Money upon the Credit of the real and personal Estates of the People: but this, in propriety of Speech is not making, (or acquiring) of Money, as we term it, but the reverse: A Prodigal who involves his Estate to raise ready Money, is it not ridiculous to say he has made so much Money? whereas, in effect, he has spent so much Money by sinking some Part of his Estate. The unthinking Part of our People do not consider, that *every Emission of Paper Credit, called Money, is laying a heavy Tax upon us,* which in Time will contribute to our Misery: and is really analogous to the Negroes in *Guinea,* who sell their Progeny into Slavery, for the sake of raising some ready Pence.

Our present Rates, are only a calling in Bills formerly Emitted, and therefore are supposed in being, and do not require a new Emission. This Cry is the same as if a private Person borrows of another 100*l.* payable after some Time, and in the mean while, by profuseness and bad Œconomy, becomes incapable of satisfying the Debt when the Term of Payment is come: But says to the Lender, you use me very ill, if you do not lend me 200*l.* to enable me to pay the first 100*l.* and for other Occasions: if the Lender proceeds thus to indulge the Borrower, this bad Husband must at length be reduced to a State of Bankruptcy: *Province Bills are as much a Debt upon the collective Body of the People, as a private Man's Bonds and Notes of Hand, are a Debt upon himself.*

VIII. *The Emission of* 35,000*l. to* 40,000 *per Ann. for the Ordinary Charges of Government, is a small insignificant Addition to our Currency; publick Loans have been found inconvenient; let us then emit large Sums in Province Bills* (*the Charge of making Bills is a Trifle*) *towards publick Edifices, Fortifications, Guarda Costas, Bridges, Castles in the Air, or any Thing, tho' of no use or Consequence: They will draw out larger Sums, and considerably increase our Currency.* They do not consider, that this contracting a large unnecessary Debt, to be redeemed after some Years, by heavy Rates and Taxes, will occasion a Clamour, perhaps a Mutiny, worse than the present groundless Complaints of Oppression. Such unnecessary Impositions are frequently Grounds of Complaint in the People against some Governors: but that the People should thus impose upon themselves, is one of the unnatural Effects of Paper Money.

IX. *Seeing there is like to be no Stop to our Infatuation in receiving the depreciating Bills of* Rhode-Island; *why should they reap all the Profit in our Ruin: Why should not some of our merciful Selves* (as the Authors of the 500,000*l.* Scheme call themselves) partake with them in the Plunder, by taking the Advantage of our present Indispositions and Weakness?

Carry the Imposition further than that of *Rhode-Island;* even beyond what could have entered into the Heart of Man, at any other Time or Place, to conceive: I mean the emitting of 500,000*l.* in Notes, without Fund or Period; a Project to out-do the *Rhode-Islanders* in Fraud, and to make these Bills more Current, because worse than those of *Rhode-Island:* It is almost incredible to what a Pitch of Iniquity some People are arrived, even prophanely to lard their Proposals with Scripture Phrases, *to impose upon the Vulgar waste Paper, instead of a valuable Medium.*

The several Projections or Schemes which occur at present, towards rectifying our Currency, or at least to prevent its growing worse, are,

I. Of a publick Nature.

1. *Is palliative, to prevent its growing worse, by bringing it to a Standard.* By Act of Assembly let *the Governor and Council be impowered, with the Advice of Merchants, to settle once or twice a Year the Price of Exchange to* London, *or of Silver, in Province Bills;* all Bonds, Notes, and Book, Debts, when paid, shall be received in Province Bills, equal in Value to the Exchange or Price of Silver, as it was thus settled at the Time of contracting: For Instance, if I contract for 500*l.* *New England* Bills of Credit, when Exchange is settled at 5 *New England* for 1 Sterling, and when the Contract is to be satisfied, Exchange is settled at 6 for 1; I must pay the true or Sterling Value, which is 600*l.* *New England* Bills: This is strict Equity and natural Justice; it will effectually obviate the fraudulent Practices of those who are constantly clamouring for more Province Bills, and prevent the neighbouring Colonies from imposing their depreciating Bills upon us. Both *Carolinas* have given us a successful Precedent.

2. As private Credit, being under Coercion, is better than publick Faith, which being above the Law, is lawless, *Let the Legislature give a Sanction to some Society, of good substantial Men, who may be willing to emit Bills upon a good Silver Bottom,* continually meliorating at a small Rate, *v. g.* 3 per Cent. per Ann. to prevent their being hoarded up;

and receivable in Taxes, and all publick Payments: Such Bills will soon bring a Discount upon all other Bills. We have at this Time (*Christmas, A.* 1739,) a remarkable Instance of private Credit being good, and publick Faith of no Account: *Merchants Notes* (a private Emission some Years ago upon a Silver Bottom) are sold at 33 *per Cent.* Advance, their true Value above common Currency; at the same Time, *our Province Bills of the New Tenor,* which in *good Faith* are 25 *per Cent.* better than the other Currencies, pass promiscuously with the bad Currencies at *Par.*

3. Let *Massachusetts-Bay* Bills only, be receivable by the Treasurer of the Province, Counties, and Towns; all Bills of the old Tenor, when brought into their Treasury, to issue out no more: *That all publick Bills hereafter to be emitted, be of the Nature of our late Bills of a New Tenor,* with this additional Clause, "And after the last of *December An.* . . . . the Treasurer is hereby directed, without further Advice or Order, to pay to the Bearer—Silver, or—Gold, upon Sight:" The Fund for bringing in this Silver and Gold from abroad, to be Impost upon Goods, Tonnage, and Light-House Money, payable in Silver or Gold only. At the several Emissions let there be an equal Sum taxed on subsequent Years within the Period; and these Taxes, at the same Time, assessed on the several Towns, ordering the Province Treasurer at the stated Times to issue out his Warrants accordingly, without further Order; to prevent Breach of Faith in future Assemblies, refusing to assess the Taxes of the Year, which is the same as postponing. Thus all these Bills will have the *Credit of a Silver Bottom,* tho' in their Nature they will be cancelled in Course by Taxes, before the Period of redeeming them by *Silver* arrive; that is, *there will be none left to make a Demand upon the Treasury;* The Silver lodged, will, after the Period, be ready for any Exigency of Government. In Fact, if Breach of publick Faith do not intervene, *the present Bills of the new Tenor will, by the End of* December *A.* 1742, *bring Silver to* 20*s. per Oz.*—Let all new Emissions be in *Bills of a second new Tenor,* two for three of the first new Tenor, payable in Silver or Gold, after the last of *De-*

cember, A—if not paid in by Taxes as above. Thus *Silver will be brought to* 13*s.* 4*d. per Oz.*—Finally, after some Years, let all future Emissions be in *Bills of a third new Tenor,* 1 for 2 of the second Tenor, payable in Silver or Gold, after the last of *December A.*—, with the forementioned Circumstances ; *Silver will then be* 6*s.* 8*d. per Oz.* It is plain, that 100,000*l.* of this last Money, will be a larger *Medium* of Trade, than 400,000*l.* of the present Currency. *This promises best, and would be a gradual, gentle, and easy Method of making our Currency as valuable as that of Virginia,* which is the most valuable of all our Colony Currencies.

4. *The Parliament of Great Britain* are at this Time, perhaps, taking some more *summary Method* of settling our *Plantation Currencies,* towards redressing the injured Merchants at home: and the fair Dealers in the Colonies : They made some Steps towards it last Sessions of Parliament. It is probable, they may abridge the Plantations of this Privilege, which they have assumed, of making their *publick Bills of Credit, a Tender* at any Rate they please to impose, which is *equal to the King's Prerogative in Coins.* And to prevent private Societies from *bubbling* the People, perhaps, they may extend the Act 6th *Annæ,* to the Plantations, viz. *That no Partnership exceeding Six shall act as Bankers.*

II. *Private Schemes.* It happens unluckily for our Paper-money Advocates, that, at this Time, when the Parliament are about redressing these Grievances, they should *madly* advance many more Schemes (some fraudulent, some foolish, and some good, but impracticable) than ever before, for multiplying of Paper-money : This makes good the old Saying, *Quem Deus vult perdere, prius dementat.*

All *private Banks* for large Sums upon Subscription, have the same bad Consequence which attends publick Loans, viz. *a Snare to the People,* by giving the Unwary, and the Prodigal, Opportunities of borrowing, that is, of involving and ruining themselves. Our *Legislature,* from Experience, are become sensible of this Error, and for many Years have issued no publick Loans.

1. *Land Banks.* The famous Mr. *Law,* noted for his

Knowledge in the Chances of the Games called Hazard, and for these Fallacies called Sharping; in Favour of a Land Bank, being preferable to Silver says, That *Land mortgaged serves for Money, and Culture,* or Produce at the same Time; whereas Silver cannot serve for Money and Plate at the same Time. As he did not understand Trade, he did not consider that *Silver serves for Money and Merchandize* at the same Time, and that Trade is more profitable than Agriculture. A Land Credit or Bank may do in a Country of no Trade; but it is ridiculous to imagine, that it can serve as a *Medium* for foreign Commerce. It cannot be shipt off as Merchandize or Returns, as is the Case of Silver: It cannot be transferred by Bills of Exchange; for so many Ounces of Silver received in *Boston,* I can draw upon my Correspondent for so many Ounces of Silver payable in *London;* but for so many Acres of Land made over to me in *New England,* I cannot draw upon *England* for any number of Acres, Quantity and Quality adjusted.

In a Country where the Denominations of their Currency depreciates, Land being fixed in itself, rises in Denomination Value; whilst what is owing upon the Land, becomes so much less as the Denominations do depreciate: Hence it is, that a Land Bank is so much desired, by those who are in Debt by Mortgage, or who desire to run in Debt by mortgaging their Lands.

2. *A Credit, or Bank of Produce, and Manufacture,* will never answer in a Country where Idleness and Indolence prevails: A late large *Bounty upon Hemp* did not encourage the raising of any considerable Quantity thereof: It would prove a most perplexed labouring Affair, *viz.* inspecting the Quality, settling from Time to Time the Market-price, Deficiencies in case of bad Crops, and other Misfortunes: Notes payable at these *unwieldy Stores,* would be of the same Nature, and attended with the same Inconveniencies, as the so much deservedly exclaimed-against Shop-Notes. In the Infancy of Countries, particularly of this *Province,* some Part of the Taxes were paid in Produce, called *Stock in the Trea-*

sury; but as our foreign Trade did grow, it was found most convenient to discontinue it.

I shall exemplify our present Projections of Banks upon Land, Produce, or Manufacture, by only one Instance. *The Bubble of* 450,000*l. upon Land and Produce,* which fills by Subscriptions at a great Pace; the Subscribers by their Articles, give their *Twelve Directors a Negative in the whole Management;* a Power never before heard of in any Society of Bankers or joint Stocks: It is true, they deserve it; because, by the Face of their Bills, the Directors or *Signers promise to circulate the whole* 450,000*l. upon Sight.* But is it possible that any Man, who gives himself the Trouble of thinking seriously, can imagine, that 12 Men of small Fortunes (who perhaps do not trade for 30,000*l. per Ann.*) should in their Trade immediately circulate 450,000*l.*? Can it be supposed possible to *negotiate Notes of so great a Sum upon so small a Bottom?* In short, this Scheme is so full of Inconsistencies, that it seems to *exceed any of the Bubbles* (which were upwards of 100 in Number) projected in *London,* in that Year of Bubbles *A.* 1720.

3. *A Credit upon a Silver Fund,* well regulated as to Periods and Discounts, would answer if there were no concomitant bad Currency: But as a bad Currency already prevails, and will in all Probability increase, by Two Years Charges of this Government to be emitted at once, by a 100,000*l. Rhode-Island* Emission, which they may throw in upon us at Pleasure; and by a new Emission of 10,000*l.* from *Connecticut,* which they have been endeavouring from Time to Time, by trying to drop a Majority of the present *Assistants* or Council; Silver will then rise in Price, and these Notes on a Silver Bottom becoming more valuable, will be hoarded up, lie dormant, and *answer no Design of a Currency:* It is true, *they will secure to the Possessor his Principal, with a growing Interest;* but as to Currency, they are worse than common Bills, which, being daily let upon Bond, do circulate and promote Business, tho' at the same Time the Owner or Creditor sinks part of his Principal, by its depreciating; and his Interest is ill paid, from a general Insensibility of

Discredit. *Such Bills will never obtain a Currency until they force a Discount upon the bad Currency.*

An Experiment of this Kind has already been made by the *Merchants Notes* so called, without any good Effect: They never became a Currency; they proved a Snare to many of the Subscribers and Borrowers: Silver did rise in Price as much, and perhaps more, than if they had never been emitted. Any Scheme of this Nature, if upon a longer Period, will, on that Account, be the more defective.

If the Scheme for emitting Company Notes or *Bills, to be paid after* 15 *Years, with Silver at* 20*s. per Oz.* can be so contrived, as to bring a growing Discount upon the bad Currency, it will be of the greatest Service to this Province. It seems to bid fair for it (I am no Undertaker nor Promoter thereof, and therefore may be deemed *impartial*); the Undertakers are Men of known Probity, of the best Estates and of the largest Trade in this Place: By their Articles they oblige themselves, under high pecuniary Penalties, to circulate these Bills at a certain annually growing Value, until they arrive at 20*s. per Oz.* and, in Conformity to a late Law of this Province, to refuse all future Emissions of the neighbouring Governments, unless founded upon a Silver Bottom.

It may perhaps be adviseable to suspend the Execution of any Paper-money Schemes, as the Affair of Colony Paper-Credit is, this present Sessions, under the immediate Consideration of the Parliament of Great Britain, *our supreme and absolute Lawgiver; lest the Subscribers (Undertakers) or Possessors of these Bills and Notes should suffer some considerable Damage, by their peremptory Suppression.*

The Projectors of the many various private Banks for Currency, seem to presume too much upon the Indulgence or *Connivance of our Legislature:* Some audaciously question their Power to prevent the People from *bubbling* one another, being (as they call it) an *Act of Liberty and Property to pass and receive Notes of Hand:* Others impudently impeach the Integrity of the Majority of the Legislature, as being, in a private Capacity, Promoters and Encouragers of these

Bubbles. Doubtless our Legislature, as the *natural Guardians* of the People, will compassionately prevent their ruining of themselves, by proper Laws; such as those in *Great Britain*, 6th of *Annæ*, against Bankers, and sundry Acts against Bubbles; or, to go no further for a Precedent, that of our neighbouring Colony *Connecticut*, *A.* 1733, against private Society or Bank Bills. There seems, at least for the present, an absolute Necessity to suppress those which will unavoidable have a riotous Consequence; I mean, the passing upon the Unwary, for a valuable Consideration, *Bills without any true Fund or Bottom:* Such Bills soon stop in Currency, and the poor innocent Possessors, the Tradesmen and Artificers, who, for special Reasons (as they express it) are made their *Dupes*, will be provoked to use the Persons and Effects of the Projectors and Signers of those Bills in a *riotous* Manner. Our Assembly did formerly effectually suppress the pernicious Bubbles of private *Lotteries.* Our Law enacted in *January*, *A.* 1738, may be extended, so as to comprehend private Societies amongst ourselves. *This Act forbids passing or receiving Bills to be issued by the neighbouring Governments, unless redeemable by lawful Money,* (Silver, Proclamation Value) *upon good Security,* (*to appear upon the Face of the Bill*) *within ten Years after their first Emission.*

While this Affair of *Colony Paper-Money* is under Consideration of Parliament for Redress, it will appear as a *daring Presumption* to proceed to large Emissions, especially in those Colonies who have *valuable Charters* to lose. I mention this with a particular Regard to *Connecticut*, who have hitherto behaved well; but at present their Eastern Borders, being tainted by a bad (I had almost said *abandonded*) Neighbourhood, the Colony in general ought to be upon their Guard.

In redressing of this Error, in which many of our Plantations have obstinately persisted for many Years, it is to be hoped the *Parliament of Great Britain* will not use any rigorous sudden Methods; but give us Time, gently and gradually to extricate ourselves; That we may be allowed, upon any sudden extraordinary public Exigences, toemit *Government Notes* to be a Tender only in publick Taxes, and to be called in as soon as may be, by subsequent Taxes: That publick Bills may never be a Tender in Trade and Business. As to the calling in of publick Bills already extant; in those Governments where the Periods are short, (in *New Hampshire, Massachusetts Bay*, and *Connecticut*, they do not extend beyond *A.* 1742,) they may be allowed to run their Course: Where the Periods are long; if upon *Taxes*, as the Governments have the Privilege of Taxing at any Time, they may be required to assess the same at any Time sooner; if upon *Loan*, the Borrowers may be obliged to pay in yearly, for a few Years, a certain Part of the Debt; but, if they insist upon the original long Period, let the Governments give *Premiums* upon all such Bills, as they are brought in: Thus few or none of these Bills will be left with the Borrowers; and at the Expiration of the Periods of the Loans, they must pay in Lawful Money, Proclamation Value; which they will by all Means endeavour to avoid, by paying as is directed.

POSTSCRIPT.

IN the Discourse, I enumerated and endeavoured to answer in so plain, clear and easy a Manner, all the Arguments, and Suggestions, then current amongst the Populace in Favour of Paper-Money; that nothing but the raising a Mist of Obscurity, together with bold Assertions in Place of Argument, could affect it: accordingly there soon followed a Pamphlet called *An Enquiry, &c.* in Favour of Paper Currencies, consisting of a new kind or Set of Arguments in *Abstracto* (as the School's Term is) without any Regard to Matter of fact, but supported with Mobbish Hints, such as, "The Author of the Discourse shakes his Rod over us, by threatning us with Parliamentary Enquiries — His numerous and gross Reflections upon the civil Administration.—— What he says is to distress the Province, *&c.*" This Piece is swelled to a considerable Bulk, by some idle digressions; giving an imperfect Account of the Banks of *Venice* and *Amsterdam*, of Baron Gorts *Munt tokyns* in *Sweden*, of Mr. *Law's* projected Land Bank, and his pernicious unsuccessful Paper Money-Scheme in *France*, together with some Scraps from Mr. *Locke* and others concerning Money, Banks, and the like.

To write satisfactorily to competent Judges, and to enlighten, but not to amuse the Vulgar with empty Words, is my present Design, lest his bare, but bold Affirmations, in favour of Paper-money, might have some Influence in carrying on the Delusion in weak Minds: Weak Minds in all Ages, after being well advis'd, do in Time come to the Truth and Right of Affairs: It is therefore the Duty of good Men, according to their Capacity, candidly, and with Fortitude, to inform those who are not conversant in such Matters, but are blindly led away by evil Men; political Constitutions have at Times been subject to Maladies which require and do admit of a Cure.

Before I proceed to prevent Misrepresentations and Prejudices, I must observe, that by the *Vulgar and Populace,* I always mean the unthinking Part of Mankind, who are not capable of consulting their own Interest; the *Mobility,* who do not reason for themselves, but are tossed about with every Wind of designing ill Men. The Word *Vulgar* is injuriously applied to the honest Tradesmen, Artificers, and common Labourers, who are the Support of the Commonwealth: Amongst them are found great Souls, who at Times, in several Countries have excell'd as Prime Ministers and other Officers of State.

This Postscript, tho' a short, just, and serious Abstract of his Book and Scheme, I am afraid will seem to any Person who has not perus'd his Book, to be a Piece of Banter, or ludicrous Representation, because the Enquiry itself appears to be not properly an accidental temporary Aberration of Mind, called a *Delirium,* but the Produce of a certain native *Anomaly* of Mind called by an *English* cant Expression WRONG-HEAD. The Enquiry being *Anonymous,* allows any Freedom consistent with Truth, without the Imputation of designed Reflections against the Author.

The Author must excuse me if, for the Sake of Propriety of Expression, I class his Positions or Arguments by the Name of *Paradoxes.* He may also allow me, with Regard to his perplexed, diffused, tedious, and trifling Manner of expressing Things, to utter them more concisely and distinctly, but without deviating from his Sense.

I. The principal and fundamental Paradox. *Bills, without any other Fund or Period than common Consent, and no other Standard than a variable Market Price, are the only valuable Bills: all Bills promising Silver at a certain Price and Period, ought to be prohibited.* Because (says he) as they promise nothing, they cannot be negociated by proper *Premiums* and Discounts; and do thus prevent *usurious* Practices, Suits in Law, and other Inconveniencies—If they depreciate, they cannot properly be said to have suffered a Discount, because a Discount signifies something fixed from which the Discount is made. Having no other Fund but common Consent, if this is gradually and at length finally withdrawn (nothing is more precarious than the *incertum Vulgus*) the suffering Possessors can lay the Blame no where but upon their own Folly, in giving Consent: They are remediless in Law, and according to the Nature of the Scheme are fairly dealt with, and ought to take Care not to deal in such perishable Commodities in Time to come.

How is it possible to imagine, that this perishable Consent should be better than *Silver*, an adequate *Depositum*, which abides for ever? Is it not plain that such Bills promising nothing but waste Paper, if left free to their Course in the Market, their Market Price would be accordingly?

By common Consent, he means the *Vox Populi*, because he frequently mentions Government and common Consent, as distinct Things. If common Consent were to take Place, all the Effects in the Province would be equally divided amongst the People, because we are all born equal: After some Time the Idle and Extravagant becoming empty-handed, while the Frugal and Industrious become rich, common Consent would divide again. Our depreciating Paper Currency, by taking from Time to Time Part of the Estates of the Creditors, in favour of the Debtor, has the same Tendency: Is this to encourage Industry? Who would labour in Produce and Manufacture, to be thus stript of his Earnings? Suppose a Company of Men, who have little or nothing to lose, valuing themselves upon their Numbers (which is our Author's common Consent) should proceed in a Scheme of Bills without any other good Foundation; at first they pass them amongst themselves and Friends, and in Course will be made a Tender to others, under Penalty of the Forfeiture of Goods and Merchandize for which they are offered, the *supreme Lex* of the Mob being *Rapine*: That is, the inevitable Consequence will be Riots and Mutiny, without any Regard to the general Rules of Commerce or particular Acts of Government.

II. *All Standards of Currencies are pernicious: Currencies, like Commodities ought to have their free Course in the Market, not to be limited by Funds or Periods, which are Imperfections.* He excludes our Bills of the new Tenor from his Currencies, because they promise something, *viz.* Silver, at a definite Period. He instances, 1st. *Barbados* Bills of *A.* 1702, which, because redeemable at a certain Time, suffered a proper Discount, whereas if there had been no Period there could have been no Discount, or rather, he should have said, no Acceptance or Currency at any Rate. 2d. *Maryland* Bills, immediately upon their Emission suffered a large Discount, because they promised Sterling Value after a long Period: If they had promised nothing, or if any Thing, never to be paid; a Discount would not have been fixed, and they would have proved a good Currency, which they are not, tho' a Tender in Law.

III. *Silver is not the best Measure, nor the best Instrument in Commerce.* All the Trading World at present, and Time out of mind, have used a *Silver Medium.* The Patriarch *Abraham* purchased a Field with Silver, which he calls the Merchant's Currency. 2. *Silver, in a Course of Years, changes its Value more than most Commodities.* In *England*, since King *Edward* the Sixth's Time a Silver Shilling hath lost but two Grains of its Value. Since we begun to manufacture Bills, which have undergone vast Alterations, Silver Currency in the trading World has suffered no Alteration. 3. *The Imperfection of Silver is the true Cause of the Introduction of Banks.* He should have added, and for the same Reason, of Merchants keeping Cash Books; whereas the universal, fixed, and durable Value of Silver, is the Foundation of all Banks. 4. *An Impression upon Paper is better than an Impression upon Silver.* Whereas the first is a most tender Matter, and of no intrinsick Value; the other is a durable intrinsically adequately valuable Metal. 5. *The Fluctuation of Silver as a Commodity, as in* London, *from* 5*s.* 3*d.* *to* 5*s. and* 6*d. per Oz. is the same as our Bills depreciating many Hundreds per Cent.* 6. *Whether we had made Paper Money or not, all Contracts and Debts would have depreciated after the same Rate*; that is, 3 Oz. of Silver contracted would have at present weighed only 1 Oz. Such Paradoxes do admit of no Comment. 7. *One Years small Payment of Impost in Silver did rise Silver from* 27 *to* 31*s. per Oz.* Why did not the preceding and subsequent Years of Silver Impost Money, raise Silver after the same Rate? Why did Silver rather fall than rise in Price from *A.* 1734 to 1738, notwithstanding the large Silver Payments upon Account of calling in the Merchants Notes? 8. *Bills promising Silver at a certain Value and Period, their present Value is much less than the Value of our Province Bills.* He seems as much prejudiced agaiust Matters of Fact, as against a Silver Currency. We all know that last Christmas, Merchants Notes payable after four Years in Silver, were negotiated at 15 per Cent. better than Province Bills.

IV. *Every Country's, every Man's natural Pound is according to his Circumstances.* That is; if I borrow of a Man ten Times richer than myself a certain Sum of Money, and at the Period of Payment, let him have my natural Pound, being only one Tenth of the real original Value which I borrowed, I have in Equity satisfied the Debt. As People's Circumstances differ as much as their Faces, what Confusion would this occasion in Dealings! Do not the Courts of Judicature in all Nations make up Judgments against Debtors indifferently, without Distinction of Circumstances. *A Bankrupt,* (he says) by Imprudence, Misfortunes or Viliany without Distinction, *who pays only 5 or* 10*s. in the Pound, pays his Pound, and satisfies his Debt as honestly and laudably as he who pays* 20*s. in the Pound.* A nominal Pound is as good as a real Pound: no Standard of Justice: Or, as he elsewhere (deviating from himself) well observes, we deal as if we had no Yard nor Bushel: This is pleading the Cause of Bankruptcy, and exposes this Country much, by comparing our depreciating Paper Money, to a Bankrupt's Pound: What we do not return, he says, is so much forgiven us by the Merchants at home. But to carry on the Comparison: If a Bankrupt pays his Creditors only one Shilling for a Crown, ought this Bankrupt's one Shilling be made a Tender for a Crown in all Dealings?

V. *Bills are a Commodity, and therefore do naturally rise*

and fall in the Market. If so, ours are a very bad Commodity, because always a falling in the Market Price. A Commodity, in the general Acceptation and Letter of the Word, signifies what is materially useful, as a Necessary or Conveniency of Life; take from Bills the Notion of Currency, they are only waste Paper, as to their Matter; whereas Silver is equally valuable as a Commodity, or as a Currency. 2. *Silver being a universally staple Commodity, and Bills only a local Commodity, makes no Difference.* 3. *Our* (fluctuating or rather continually depreciating) *Paper Bills are a Standard for Silver.* That is, a Ship upon the Coast progressively under Sail, stands still, while the Fields and Trees fluctuate.

VI. *Our Bills are emitted upon the best Plan the World ever did see; all the essential Parts of the Banks of* Venice *and* Amsterdam, *are to be found in our Province Bills of the Old Tenor.* This Hint seems borrowed from a facetious Writer, who finds all the Beauties of the best Greek and Latin Authors, in the History of *Tom Thumb.* The Credit of those Banks, is the universal Consent or Acceptance of the whole trading World, an adequate *Depositum* in Silver, and *Agio* above the current Price of Silver: Our Bills have only a small local Provincial Consent, no *Depositum,* many per Cts. worse than Silver, and continually depreciating or growing worse than themselves from Time to Time. Forgetting himself, in another Place, he says, our bad Circumstances are the Reason, why our Bills are not upon the same good Establishment as the Transfers of the Banks of *Venice* and *Amsterdam*: How then can they be essentially as good? He should have plainly expressed it thus; at present our Circumstances render us incapable of having a solid Bank of Credit.

For the great Benefits accruing to a Country from Paper Money, he unluckily instances *South Carolina,* where its bad Effects have been the most notorious, by occasioning the greatest Confusions, even *Mutiny* itself. The flourishing State of that Province, proceeds from its Soil and Climate, producing a good Staple, the best of *Rice*; and from a neighbouring vast Indian Country, affording large Quantities of *Deer Skins:* Their large Dealings are not transacted in Paper Money, but in Rice, and Bills of Exchange.

VII. *The cancelling of publick Bills, according to publick Faith, is a publick Fraud or iniquitous Administration; it is establishing of Iniquity by a Law, because as they promise no effective Payments, the Postponing of them is Justice and Righteousness.* He hints at what he imagines a Sort of *Magna Charta,* granted *A.* 1712 by our Assembly to the People, whereby they virtually took upon themselves, to supply the Province with Bills to serve as Money, therefore if we do not postpone these Bills, the Legislature are guilty of a Breach of *Magna Charta.* Was there ever a *Heresy* from any Scriptural System, so enthusiastically imagined, and so ill founded?

VIII. *Paper Money borrowed is not running in Debt, Province Bills are only a Debt amongst our selves, and therefore improperly to be called a Debt.* The publick Debts in *England* to the several Companies or Stocks there, are upon all Occasions called heavy Debts, and the Poor the Consumers are very sensible of the Load of the Funds, the grievous Taxes upon Coals, Candles, Soap, Leather, and some other Necessaries of Life: We murmur yearly because of our great Taxes or Rates, occasioned by this Paper Money Debt; every Emission of our Paper Money, is sensibly found to be contracting of Debt, when the Taxes or Mortgages on which they are founded come to be paid. 2. *We grow daily richer by means of this Paper Money, we are three Times richer than we were at the introducing of these Bills.* If this could be supposed true, while we daily pay less and less in the Pound, how should we avoid the Imputation of a fraudulent Bankruptcy; a Country or Town may look well to outward Appearance, and yet be in a Galloping Consumption, as the vulgar Phrase is. In *London* a Merchant or Tradesman making a more than usually splendid Appearance, is frequently a Fore-runner of Bankruptcy.

The Paper Money Advocates represent our 630,000*l.* present Paper Currency, as a clear *Medium* of Trade, and say that it is not too much for *New England*, and is but a Trifle when reduced to a Sterling Value: whereas it is really an Incumbrance or Debt to be paid, and is already without Additions, too heavy upon the good People of this Province, and will oblige them to sink Part of their trading Stock (instead of inlarging their Trade) to pay their large Taxes.

By Experience we find, that our Credit does not allow of so large a Debt, without depreciating; therefore all new Emissions being additional Debts, do sink the Credit of our Bills more and more. Our inordinate Desire of more, may be compared to Thirst in a *Dropsy*, which by endeavouring to satisfy with Drink, increases the Distemper. *Cressit indulgens sibi dirus Hydrops.*

IX. *The Mother Country, Widows, and Orphans, have suffered for want of a sufficiency of Bills.* That the Merchants of *Great Britain* have been the greatest Losers by Discounts in their Returns of some Hundreds per Cent. is acknowledged by all Parties. Widows, Orphans, Societies incorporated or voluntary, who have a considerable Part of their Stock at Interest, have suffered very much. *The College of* Cambridge *in* New England, have sunk above 10,000*l.* *A charitable Scots Society in* Boston (formed in Imitation of the *Scots* charitable Corporation in *London*) have suffered very much; some of their Bonds are lately paid in, at the Rate of 29*s.* per Oz. Silver, which were contracted when Silver was at 7*s.* per Oz.; this is 300 per Cent. loss of Principal: *Ministers of religious Congregations*, are not paid the real and true Value of their Stipends contracted for: In short, *all Creditors* who have dealt in Honesty and Simplicity of Heart, have been thus sharped upon. Our Author with an open Countenance, says, That the *Rhode-Islanders* outwitting of us, by their repeated large Emissions, is doing for their own Interest, what all wise People ought to do.——The Paper Money Solicitors in Answer, say, That the reducing of Contracts to Specialties, *i.e.* to *Silver* by Weight, is not forbid; therefore private Men must blame themselves, Orphans must blame their

Guardians, and Widows their Advisers, for not making their Contracts in Silver Value, and not in those Bills: This is giving up the Cause of a good Currency, and allowing that every prudent Man should have refused the Currency of those fallacious Bills; or that our *Legislature*, the common Guardian of us all, to prevent our being cheated by others, and our cheating of ourselves, ought to have established a Specialty, as has lately been done in the *Carolinas* with good Effect.

Sufficiencies of Bills, properly speaking, are the Sums which the trading Credit of a Paper Money Country can bear; the more that these Sums are exceeded, the more they become a negative Sufficiency (as *Mathematicians* to say of positive Quantities in a continued Progression to certain Limits, after which they become more and more negative) and their Credit depreciates, and the Creditors or Acceptors of such Bills suffer more and more. This negative Sufficiency multiplied, is what our Author proposes for our Relief, and for the introducing of Silver again; but as Bills, by their increasing Quantity, superceded and drove away Silver, Silver can never be again thus introduced, unless, at length, Bills, by their Quantity and bad Bottom, become as Waste-Paper, then Silver must take Place.

X. *The Legislature to make Laws to bring the Balance of Trade in our Favour.* This is as unnatural and impracticable as the Legislature making a *Medium* of Trade; both which can only be effected by Trade itself. Balance of Trade, when against a Country, is answered by exporting the current Cash, equal to what the Exports in Merchandize fell short of the Imports; our Paper Currency is not exportable to pay a foreign Debt, and therefore will answer no Balance of Trade. 2. *Our Bills have depreciated, in Proportion to the Balance of Trade increasing against us.* In *S. Carolina,* where the Balance of Trade is much in their Favour, many of the Inhabitants having large Sums of Money lodged in *England*; their Paper Money notwithstanding is much more depreciated than ours, because of their greater Paper Money Emissions, and Breach of publick Faith.

XI. *Contracts reduced to Writing, but not the Silver contracted for, is the Money or Medium.* He might perhaps have the Hint of this, from the Analogy of many Spendthrifts amongst us, who after being long dunn'd for a Book Debt, if the Creditor accepts of their Notes or Bonds, they become as easy as if they had paid the Money. *Medium* of Trade in its proper Sense, signifies some intermediate adequately valuable Commodity, such as is Silver. Some Colonies of peculiar Produce, allow of a local (*therefore imperfect*) *Medium*; as Sugar, Tobacco, Rice, in some of our Colonies are Tenders.

XII. *Every landed Man, even to the mortgaging of his last Acre, has a Right to make Money.* He should have added, and finally has a Right to the Alms-House. Thus these projected Banks give the Idle and Extravagant Opportunities of borrowing or involving of themselves, that is, these Banks tend to the Ruin of the Province; we allow, that in Prudence a landed Man may sell off some Part, the better to improve the Remainder.

XIII. *The projected Bank or Scheme, commonly called* J—— C—— *and others, is built upon the best and only good Foundation we have: the Subscribers are Men of Judgment, Integrity, and Estates.* Notes of a dubious, some say, desperate Credit, not receivable in Taxes, no legal Tender, bearing no Interest to the Possessor, obligatory only for Goods at a precarious Price, and not actionable till after 20 Years. *Shop Notes,* which our Author (happening accidentally to be in the right) deservedly, tho' inconsistently with himself, so much exclaims against, are much preferable to such Bills, because payable upon Sight, and in Case the Shopkeeper uses the Bearer very ill, are immediately returnable to the Merchant. Such Bills, being ill founded, will soon stop in Circulation, the Possessor, in time, must have a Law-suit with the Signers, who perhaps prove insolvent: But if they may be supposed solvent, the Signers, for their own Redress, must sue a numerous Tribe of (perhaps generally) insolvent Subscribers, *and occasion a Convulsion in the Government.*

To give a Hint, of such Notes satisfying of Contracts payable in Province Bills, is the Height of ———

A *Depositum* of Silver, Land Security, Government Security, are proper collateral or additional Securities; but we know of no Bank without an adequate Depositum of Silver, if they negociate on Transfers; or Silver sufficient to answer all their Cash Notes upon Demand, if they deal in Cash Notes. It is impracticable to circulate Produce and Manufacture, being perishable, unweildly, uncertain, fallacious Matters. The Land Bank projected in *England* in K. *William's* Reign, tho' established by an Act of Parliament, like a Mushroom, soon came to nothing. The only proper Land Banks, are our Country Registers, where Lands are regularly transferred daily.

I shall dismiss this Paper Money Agent, by observing, that his Memory sometimes gives him the slip, and, *inconsistently with himself, he deviates into Truth.* I shall mention a few Instances. Contracts ought to be paid in Silver, at the current Market Price as when made, but not as it now is, if depreciated.—All other Commodities keep Pace with Silver, *is it not the most natural Medium ?*—When People were obliged to receive light Pieces of Eight in Currency, they advanced upon their Goods in their Contracts accordingly: *This equally holds good with respect to a depreciating Currency (our Bills) of any kind.* Upon a large Emission of Bills, Silver and other Returns must remarkably rise. By emitting and calling in of Bills, their Value may be fixed or diminished: *This is our grand Argument against large and frequent Emissions,* viz. *the depreciating of our Currency.*—Thus unwarily he gives a full Answer to his own Book.—Further, I must observe, that in Recommendation of his Land Banks, he says, The Mother Country will sooner make Abatements in our Pay, than take Lands.

I shall conclude with a Recapitulation of some general Remarks, concerning our Paper Money.

1. If Bills, provincial or national, would answer all the Intentions of Money, no Country, in the most chargeable,

unsuccessful Wars, or in the greatest Bankruptcy as to Trade, would be distressed for want of Money. If Bills upon Land Security could answer the Intention of Money, the Emperor would not have given into that late inglorious Peace with the *Turks*, for want of Money to support his Forces. The *Spaniards* might make themselves easy, though their Flota's, Galleons, Flotillas, Assogues, and Register Ships proceed no more. A Manufacture from Copper Plates, Paper, and Ink (a late Invention of the *British* Colonies in *America*) is a more compendious, and infinitely less chargeable Method of Currency and Medium of Trade. A sort of *Philosophers Stone* (a Term used by the *Alchymists*) or Art, by which no Country (a Country always supposes Land) can be without a sufficient Quantity of Money: The *Spanish* Mines in *America*, an industrious Trade, are becoming mere Chimeras and Deceptions; if Land should be exhausted, there remains still a better Fund, *viz.* common Consent, without any other Bottom.

2. The Party for multiplying a depreciating Paper Currency, are, 1. *The Idle and Extravagant*, who want to borrow Money at any bad Lay, tho' finally to their own Ruin. 2. *The fraudulent Debtors*, that they may pay their Creditors in less Value than contracted for, and notwithstanding retain their Credit without being reckoned Bankrupts; a mortgaged Estate can be redeemed by a smaller dismembering, a Shopkeeper pays his Merchant at a great Discount. Some Men of Substance, and industrious, but of a *natural Improbity and Depravity of Mind*, who by Experience have found, that the greater Confusion such Emissions occasion in Business, the greater Latitude is given for cheating: For Instance, in a depreciating Paper Money Country, the only Method (much practised by the Advocates for Paper Money) of growing rich, is by a Series of the greatest Acts of Injustice, *viz.* to owe to others more than is due to themselves, to procure long Credit, when due, to postpone Payments, and bear dunning, and finally, to let the Law, which in this Province is tedious, and not chargeable, take Place. 4. *The Weak and Ignorant*, (here I include a large Number of good honest

Men, but misled) who imagine, or are taught, that the Legislature can give every individual Person of the Government, what Money they may desire, without any other Bottom, but an Act of Assembly; and that the with-holding of it is Step-Father or Step-Mother's Usage.

3. The Party against a depreciating Paper-money Currency, are, 1. *The Industrious and Frugal,* our considerable foreign Traders and rich Men; who, because of their great Substance deposited in the Country, are obliged to have the Interest of the Country most at Heart: Thus in *Great Britain* (to compare great Things with small) the *Peers,* by reason of their great Estates in the Kingdom, are deemed the natural and standing Council of the *King* and Country. The Industrious and Frugal have Reason to withstand the raising of Money upon Taxes by a Paper-Credit, because by the other Party, who are the most numerous, they are loaded with almost the whole Burthen of the Assessments: The Assessors ought to consider, that the easing of the Extravagant in their Taxes, is so much Encouragement allowed them to carry on their Extravagancies: In other Countries, Extravagancies and the Extravagant are much taxed. 2. *The honest Creditors,* who are for fixing the Value of their Contracts and Debts by a Standard: This is called by the Paper-money Party, endeavouring after unlawful Gain: 3. *The fair Dealer,* who desires neither to bubble nor be bubbled. 4. *The considerate* thinking Man, who, from Experience, finds that all Emissions are contracting of Debts.

4. All Mankind exclaim against clipping of Coin, because it is a Fraud to tender Denominations of a lessened Value; making of a depreciating Paper Money Currency, a Tender in Law, has the same Effect. It is allowed by every Body, that the most glorious Action of K. *William's* Reign, was the calling in of the clip'd Money, and ascertaining the Value of it by a *mill'd Recoinage:* The Progress our late Assemblies are making towards sinking of our precarious Bills of the Old Tenor, and reforming them into new Tenor Bills of a fixed Value, will have the same good Effect. A depreciating Paper Money, has a vastly worse Effect than

clipping of Silver Coin, which never reached further than a Fraud of 25 or 30 *per Cent.* but the other has reached in *New England* to 450 *per Cent.* in *S. Carolina* to 700 *per Cent.* in *N. Carolina* to 900 *per Cent.* As the effectual Cure of the clip'd Coin in most Nations in *Europe*, was reducing it to mill'd Money; or to Weight as in *Bardadoes*: So our Provincial Bills may be brought to a Sterling Price, by fixing Exchange from Time to Time, as in the *Carolina's*.

5. *The Paper Money Men (some anomalous excepted) generally allow, that Silver is a better Medium than Paper; but as it is impossible (so they express it) for Silver ever to be made Current with us, they are for continuing and increasing the Paper Money Currency.* Let us not despair, it is not impossible to give Silver again it's Currency; let us tread our Foot Steps back, and we shall naturally return to where we came from: That is, as the increasing Quantity of Paper Money drove away Silver, a gradual lessening of the same, will make Room for this better Currency; 1. As Bills grow scarce, the Merchants will be obliged to convert some Part of that Commodity Silver into Cash, as in other trading Countries; no Man can trade to Advantage without Cash. 2. The Scarcity of our Province Bills will effectually bring a Discount upon the Bills of the neighbouring Colonies, because *Præmiums* will be given in other Bills, for Bills of our own Province to pay Taxes; and no more Bills being emitted from Time to Time than sufficient for the present Charge of Government, our Bills may be brought to Proclamation, or Sterling Value. 3. Bills growing scarce, our extravagant Way of Living, that is, our Imposts will lessen for some Time; we find at present the Homespun is more in Wear by the Country People, and Spinning is more practised, than at any Time since the Beginning of this Century. If this Scarcity of Currency oblige us to go further into Shop Notes for small Dealings, and into Barter for larger Transactions, it will be only for a Season, (in *Sweden*, from Baron *Gortz's Munt tokyns*, they went into Barter, and from thence back again unto their intrinsically good Currency) until the Inconveniencies thereof become still more sensible, and then the

very good Husbands will retain Silver for Cash, whereby they can deal to better Advantage; and seek out for other Returns, to supply its Place as a Commodity. Bills are in their own Nature, only proper to be returned by Taxes into the Treasury, from which they issued; and perhaps in small Quantities may pass as Inland Notes, but are not fit for a *Medium* of foreign Trade.

FINIS.

BANKS

AND

PAPER-MONEY;

FROM

ESSAYS,

MORAL, POLITICAL, &c.,

BY

DAVID HUME, Esq.

PUBLISHED IN

1752.

* * * THIS has made me entertain a doubt concerning the benefit of *banks* and *paper-credit*, which are so generally esteemed advantageous to every nation. That provisions and labour should become dear by the encrease of trade and money, is, in many respects, an inconvenience; but an inconvenience that is unavoidable, and the effect of that public wealth and prosperity which are the end of all our wishes. It is compensated by the advantages, which we reap from the possession of these precious metals, and the weight, which they give the nation in all foreign wars and negociations. But there appears no reason for encreasing that inconvenience by a counterfeit money, which foreigners will not accept of in any payment, and which any great disorder in the state will reduce to nothing. There are, it is true, many people in every rich state who having large sums of money, would prefer paper with good security; as being of more easy transport and more safe custody. If the public provide not a bank, private bankers will take advantage of this circumstance; as the goldsmiths formerly did in LONDON, or as the bankers do at present in DUBLIN: And therefore it is better, it may be thought, that a public company should enjoy the benefit of that paper-credit, which always will have place in every opulent kingdom. But to endeavour artificially to encrease such a credit, can never be the interest of any trading nation; but must lay them under disadvantages, by encreasing money beyond its natural proportion to labour and commodities, and thereby heightening their price to the merchant and manufacturer. And in this view, it must be allowed, that no bank could be more advantageous, than such a one as locked up all the money it received,* and never augmented the circulating coin, as is

* This is the case with the bank of AMSTERDAM.

usual, by returning part of its treasure into commerce. A public bank, by this expedient, might cut off much of the dealings of private bankers and money-jobbers; and though the state bore the charge of salaries to the directors and tellers of this bank (for, according to the preceding supposition, it would have no profit from its dealings), the national advantage, resulting from the low price of labour and the destruction of paper-credit, would be a sufficient compensation. Not to mention, that so large a sum, lying ready at command, would be a convenience in times of great public danger and distress; and what part of it was used might be replaced at leisure, when peace and tranquillity was restored to the nation.

* * * * *

I scarcely know any method of sinking money below its level, but those institutions of banks, funds, and paper-credit, which are so much practised in this kingdom. These render paper equivalent to money, circulate it throughout the whole state, make it supply the place of gold and silver, raise proportionably the price of labour and commodities, and by that means either banish a great part of those precious metals, or prevent their farther encrease. What can be more short-sighted than our reasonings on this head? We fancy, because an individual would be much richer, were his stock of money doubled, that the same good effect would follow were the money of every one encreased; not considering, that this would raise as much the price of every commodity, and reduce every man in time to the same condition as before. It is only in our public negociations and transactions with foreigners, that a greater stock of money is advantageous; and as our paper is there absolutely insignificant, we feel, by its means, all the ill effects arising from a great abundance of money, without reaping any of the advantages.*

* We observed in Essay III. that money, when encreasing, gives encouragement to industry, during the interval between the encrease of money and rise of the prices. A good effect of this nature may

Suppose that there are 12 millions of paper, which circulate in the kingdom as money (for we are not to imagine that all our enormous funds are employed in that shape), and suppose the real cash of the kingdom to be 18 millions: Here is a state which is found by experience to be able to hold a stock of 30 millions. I say, if it be able to hold it, it must of necessity have acquired it in gold and silver, had we not obstructed the entrance of these metals by this new invention of paper. *Whence would it have acquired that sum?* From all tho kingdoms of the world. *But why?* Because, if you remove these 12 millions, money in this state is below its level, compared with our neighbours; and we must immediately draw from all of them, till we be full and saturate, so to speak, and can hold no more. By our present politics we are as careful to stuff the nation with this fine commodity of bank-bills and chequer-notes, as if we were afraid of being overburthened with the precious metals.

It is not to be doubted, but the great plenty of bullion in FRANCE is, in a great measure, owing to the want of paper-credit. The FRENCH have no banks: Merchants bills do not there circulate as with us: Usury or lending on interest is not directly permitted; so that many have large sums in their coffers: Great quantities of plate are used in private houses; and all the churches are full of it. By this means, provisions and labour still remain cheaper among them, than in nations that are not half so rich in gold and silver. The advantages of this situation, in point of trade as well as in great public emergencies, are too evident to be disputed.

The same fashion a few years ago prevailed in GENOA, which still has place in ENGLAND and HOLLAND, of using services of CHINA-ware instead of plate; but the senate, foreseeing the consequence, prohibited the use of that brittle

---

follow too from paper-credit; but it is dangerous to precipitate matters, at the risk of losing all by the failing of that credit, as must happen upon any violent shock in public affairs.

commodity beyond a certain extent; while the use of silver-plate was left unlimited. And I suppose, in their late distresses, they felt the good effect of this ordinance. Our tax on plate is, perhaps, in this view, somewhat impolitic.

Before the introduction of paper money into our colonies, they had gold and silver sufficient for their circulation. Since the introduction of that commodity, the least inconveniency that has followed is the total banishment of the precious metals. And after the abolition of paper, can it be doubted but money will return, while these colonies possess manufactures and commodities, the only thing valuable in commerce, and for whose sake alone all men desire money?

What pity LYCURGUS did not think of paper-credit, when he wanted to banish gold and silver from SPARTA! It would have served his purpose better than the lumps of iron he made use of as money; and would also have prevented more effectually all commerce with strangers, as being of so much less real and intrinsic value.

It must, however, be confessed, that, as all these questions of trade and money are extremely complicated, there are certain lights in which this subject may be placed, so as to represent the advantages of paper-credit and banks to be superior to their disadvantages. That they banish specie and bullion from a state is undoubtedly true; and whoever looks no farther than this circumstance does well to condemn them; but specie and bullion are not of so great consequence as not to admit of a compensation, and even an overbalance from the encrease of industry and of credit, which may be promoted by the right use of paper-money. It is well known of what advantage it is to a merchant to be able to discount his bills upon occasion; and every thing that facilitates this species of traffic is favourable to the general commerce of a state. But private bankers are enabled to give such credit by the credit they receive from the depositing of money in their shops; and the bank of ENGLAND in the same manner, from the liberty it has to issue its notes in all payments. There was an invention of this kind, which was fallen upon some years ago by the banks of EDINBURGH; and which, as it is one of the most ingenious ideas that has been executed in commerce, has also been thought advantageous to SCOTLAND. It is there called a BANK-CREDIT; and is of this nature. A man goes to the bank and finds surety to the amount, we shall suppose, of a thousand pounds. This money, or any part of it, he has the liberty of drawing out whenever he pleases, and he pays only the ordinary interest for it, while it is in his hands. He may, when he pleases, repay any sum so small as twenty pounds, and the interest is discounted from the very day of the repayment. The advantages, resulting from this contrivance, are manifold. As a man may find surety nearly to the amount of his substance, and his bank-credit is equivalent to ready money, a merchant does hereby in a manner coin his houses, his household furniture, the goods in his warehouse, the foreign debts due to him, his ships at sea; and can, upon occasion, employ them in all payments, as if they were the current money of the country. If a man borrow a thousand pounds from a private hand, besides that it is not always to be found when required, he pays interest for it whether he be using it or not; His bank-credit costs him nothing except during the very moment in which it is of service to him: and this circumstance is of equal advantage as if he had borrowed money at a much lower interest. Merchants, likewise, from this invention, acquire a great facility in supporting each other's credit, which is a considerable security against bankruptcies. A man, when his own bank-credit is exhausted, goes to any of his neighbours who is not in the same condition; and he gets the money, which he replaces at his convenience.

After this practice had taken place during some years at EDINBURGH, several companies of merchants at GLASGOW carried the matter farther. They associated themselves into different banks, and issued notes so low as ten shillings, which they used in all payments for goods, manufactures, tradesmen's labour of all kinds; and these notes, from the established credit of the companies, passed as money in all payments throughout the country. By this means, a stock of five thousand pounds was able to perform the same operations as if it were six or seven; and merchants were thereby enabled to trade to a greater extent, and to require less profit in all their transactions. But whatever other advantages result from these inventions, it must still be allowed that, besides giving too great facility to credit, which is dangerous, they banish the precious metals; and nothing can be a more evident proof of it, than a comparison of the past and present condition of SCOTLAND in that particular. It was found, upon the recoinage made after the union, that there was near a million of specie in that country: But notwithstanding the great encrease of riches, commerce, and manufactures of all kinds, it is thought, that, even where there is no extraordinary drain made by ENGLAND, the current specie will not now amount to a third of that sum.

FINIS.

E S S A Y

On PAPER-MONEY and BANKING;

FROM ESSAYS ON THE

PUBLIC DEBT, FRUGALITY, &c.

Publiſhed in

M. DCC. LV.

PAPER-MONEY, BANKING, &c.

IT is with the greatest concern I have heard, for some years past, the daily complaints made by all ranks of people in this part of the country, in common with the rest of the kingdom, upon the scarcity of gold and silver money; the decay of trade and manufactures; the slow progress of husbandry; and lastly, (what one would scarcely believe could be a concomitant evil with those just mentioned) the increase of luxury, and expence of living. And it is with no less astonishment, that I have so long observed the supine sloth and careless indifference of my countrymen about the causes or cure of this complicated mischief, which threatens poverty and ruin to themselves and their posterity for some generations. It might have been expected, at least, that some one of public spirit, endowed with sufficient abilities, would have drawn his pen in such a national cause, and, in that belief, I had no inclination to undertake a task, for which I found myself very unequal; but when I reflected that the greatest events have been brought to pass, and taken their rise from the smallest beginnings,—that the *Roman* empire was saved by the cackling of a goose,—I was not without hopes that my own weak endeavours might be successful, in some measure, to awaken my countrymen to a sense of their present misery, and perhaps be assistant to them in finding a remedy: if what I now write can have that effect, I shall be well pleased.

Frugality and industry are the two great sources of riches; and when we consider that a desire of gain and an application to the means by which it is to be attained are inseparable from the common principle of self-preservation, one would think there would be little occasion to recommend the practice of these virtues to mankind; but if we reflect, that among such a number as that of mankind, all pursuing the same end, of providing for themselves, and, as it were, running to one common goal, the more active, cunning and vigilant will soon over-reach those of less abilities, it must follow, that the views and interests of individuals thus interfering, will beget a sort of universal war among mankind, and in proportion, as one set of men prevail in their pursuits, the opposite interests must be sunk and discouraged; thus industry and frugality may be swallowed up by rapine and violence.

Now, I take this to be the case with agriculture, trade and manufactures in this country: every one is sensible of the slow progress of the first, and of the stagnation and decay of the other two; and, I imagine, it is no less obvious, that this effect cannot have been produced by any cause flowing from the nature of the things themselves; for industry sets no bounds to itself, and 'tis but a foolish pretence to say that trade can be overstocked, so long as the numbers of mankind and their wants are in proportion, the cause therefore must be extraneous; our industry must be borne down and oppressed by the superior industry, weight or interest of those whose pursuits after gain are inconsistent with the good of trade and manufactures.

The arts by which industry may be oppressed, are as various as those whereby it is promoted; every quality in nature hath its contrary; but we need not search very deep to find out the cause of our present misery, one presents itself, which will solve the whole phænomena and symptoms of it, and that is, the currency of PAPER-MONEY or BANK-NOTES, which by increasing the quantity, has sunk the intrinsic value of our money, and introduced all the real inconveniencies of plenty of money, without the smallest advantage to any individual but the bankers themselves.

I may venture to affirm that there is, at least, twice the value of bank-notes as there is of real money circulating in *Scotland*, (if I had said six times the value, perhaps I had spoke within bounds) and these notes have equal currency with the money itself, which they represent; so that

4

here is the whole cash of the kingdom tripled by a fiction, without any addition to our riches: let us attend to its operation, and the inconvenience will be obvious.

It is a maxim, that the price of labour and commodities is always regulated by the quantity of money circulating in a state; increase or diminish the money, and prices must rise or fall in a certain proportion: the consequence to agriculture, trade and manufactures, is apparent; when money is augmented, the farmer and handy-craftsman must pay higher wages to his servants, and must raise the price of his grain or commodity, to indemnify himself. The merchant buying these at a high price, must sell accordingly, if he can, but will soon find himself undersold at foreign markets, where the same goods manufactured or produced in other states, which have less money, can be sold, perhaps, a half or a third cheaper, and to more profit; this obliges the merchant to give over his trade, or be ruined; and the industry of the merchant being thus stopt, the stagnation must operate backwards from one trade to another, till it affects agriculture, where it begun.

These inconveniencies, when arising from a plenty of real money, are fully compensated by the riches which occasioned them, and the above stagnation of trade will last no longer than other states continue to undersell us, which cannot be very long; for the trade of any state will be an inlet to riches, and money will flow in upon it till that state be likewise full, and its entrance be stopt by the same repletion: from that state it will go to another, and so on, till it becomes on a perfect level and equality throughout the whole.

But what must be the miserable situation of trade and manufactures, in a state, where the policy and interested motives of individuals have so contrived it, that the entrance of money, which would be the necessary consequence of its trade, is debarred by a kind of stratagem or illusion, *viz.* by creating an imaginary money of paper, which the substance, credit or interest of the projectors makes to supply the place of real money?

5

Now, such is our own situation, an immense value of bank-notes hath been poured in upon us, and increaseth daily. Every body takes them for money, without the smallest scruple, and believes himself as rich when possessed of them, as if he had the value in gold and silver; with this imagination, the price of labour and every commodity, and consequently the expence of living is raised, industry, arts, and trade overwhelmed and discouraged, and every other inconveniency felt, that can be produced by the plenty of real gold and silver. Under such a pressure, it must add greatly to our mortification, when we consider that all the real specie, which these notes falsely represent, would have actually entered into the country, by the means of trade, before prices could have been raised, or trade sunk to such a degree as they are at present; and when that inconveniency happened, we should, at least have had the consolation to think that we had got our fill before we removed from the feast, and might then have said:

———*Edisti satis atque bibisti*
tempus abire tibi est————

whereas all we gain by our present œconomy, is to look fat and fair while we consume away with a dropsy. But this public calamity, however destructive of the general good of the society, hath been contrived and brought upon us, as I have said, by the policy and interested motives of individuals, whose fortunes are thus built upon the ruins of their fellow-subjects; the certainty of which may be easily demonstrated; for it is apparent, that the value of all the immense quantity of notes circulating in the kingdom, must have been paid to these bankers, when they were first issued, either in money, labour, or commodities; and if we shall suppose the quantity of those circulating notes to be double to the real circulating specie, it follows that two-thirds of the substance and trade of the nation have got into the hands of the bankers; for as the whole money in a state represents, and is the value of the whole stock of labour and commodities which it produces, so two-thirds of the one must be equal to two-thirds of the other.

And altho' these bankers by the creation of so much money, have raised the price of labour and commodities to such an excessive height, as must be the destruction of trade and manufactures, yet they are the only individuals in the state who do not suffer by it; for by continually increasing their imaginary money, they balance the increase of the price, and so are no poorer by buying dearer than they were before.

One may be apt to wonder how these pernicious practices of bankers should remain so long unchecked in a well regulated society; and it must be confessed, that such an imposture could never have been palmed upon us, but under favour, and by the assistance of a spirit of blindness and delusion, which has thrown, as it were, a mist before our eyes, to lead us astray: no man, with his eyes open, would tamely behold another picking his pocket; and is it to be supposed, that a thinking people would give away two-third parts of their stock for a bit of paper which a foreigner would not take for a farthing, and which any commotion in the state may reduce to as little value at home?

But here it may be asked, Is there then no national advantage arising from this institution of banks and paper-credit, in a state? Is there no plausible plea, at least founded either on reason or experience, for a practice so universal? For answer, I beg leave to refer to the following verses of Mr. *Pope:*

Blest paper credit! last and best supply!
That lends corruption lighter wings to fly!
Gold, imp'd by thee, can compass hardest things,
Can pocket states, can fetch or carry Kings;
A single leaf shall waft an Army o'er,
Or ship off senates to some distant shore;
A leaf, like Sybil's, scatter to and fro
Our fates and fortunes as the winds shall blow;
Pregnant with thousands flits the scrap unseen,
And silent sells a King, or buys a Queen.

But after all, it must be confessed that banks, if under due regulations, might be of use to facilitate commerce in a state; such for instance, as a bank, constituted on the model of that of *Amsterdam,* (where all the money that comes into it is lockt up, and never again sees the light, no payments being there made again in money, but by way of transfers of stock), or such a bank, where no more notes should be issued than exactly corresponded to the money given in; in which case, the notes would be much more convenient than the money itself, as being of more easy transport, and safe custody; and the bankers would become a very usefel and harmless part of the society, as being a sort of public servants for keeping and telling out our money: but as for our present scheme, which leaveth an unlimited dictatorial power to bankers to send abroad notes to what value they please, tho' perhaps twenty times as much as the value of all the money in the kingdom, and impose the same upon us for gold and silver, I make no hesitation to pronounce it absolutely pernicious, and destructive of all trade, industry, and manufactures. I cannot represent this our mismanagement, or the advantage of a contrary scheme, in better words than those of the ingenious Mr. *Hume,* in his Political Essays, from which I have borrowed some of the foregoing arguments: after taking notice that the practices of bankers will introduce paper-credit into every opulent kingdom, he adds: "But to endeavour artificially to increase such a "credit, can never be the interest of any trading nation; "but must lay them under disadvantages, by increasing money "beyond its natural proportion to labour and commodities, "and thereby heightening their price to the merchant and "manufacturer. And in this view it must be allowed, that "no bank could be more advantageous than such a one as "lockt up all the money it received, and never augmented the "circulating coin, as is usual, by returning part of its trea-"sure into commerce. A public bank, by this expedient, "might cut off much of the dealings of private bankers and "money jobbers; and tho' the state bore the charge of "salaries to the directors and tellers of this bank, (for "according to the preceding supposition, it would have no "profit from its dealings) the national advantage, resulting "from the low price of labour and destruction of paper-

"credit, would be a sufficient compensation. Not to men-"tion, that so large a sum, lying ready at command, would "be a great convenience in times of public danger and "distress; and what part of it was used might be replaced "at leisure, when peace and tranquillity were restored to the "nation."

As I would be loath to ominate bad things, I shall not take upon me to foretel the evil consequences of this implicit faith, this unlimited trust, this lethargic carelessness of my countrymen, with regard to paper-credit;—I need only say, that it is a maxim, that security is always dangerous, and often the fore-runner of destruction.

But I hope that the evil consequences to trade, industry and arts, which have been already produced and so heavily felt, by the means of this paper-money, will be sufficient to awaken the spirit of every one who wishes well to the country, and to make him stand up in self-defence, to oppose this torrent which threatens to swallow up our trade and industry, to close up the sluices by which it has entered, and endeavour to force it back to the fountains from whence it proceeded.

I am sensible how difficult a matter it will be to remedy this evil of so long standing, which like an inveterate malady hath become part of our constitution, and is not to be conquered by sudden or violent applications. It is not to be supposed, that the bankers, who are possessed of such a share of the riches, trade, and consequently the power of the nation, will submit to be spoiled of all by those who are weaker than themselves: a very considerable part of our merchants are furnished with credit by those bankers, to near the full extent of their trade, and so have become obliged, thro necessity, to circulate their notes, or lose the credit which supports their trade; the reformation therefore cannot be expected to begin from them, though it is they who must give it the finishing stroke: it must therefore proceed from those who are not immediately dependent on the bankers, that is, the landed gentlemen, farmers, and manufacturers, who have the command of all the labour and native commo-

9

dities in the kingdom. There is no law that obligeth us to take bank-notes for money; and if these three classes would make a vigorous resolution not to circulate any such, or receive them in payment for their grain, labour, or manufactures, unless at an advanced price, we should very soon see these notes shrink into a narrow compass, and, with the same pace as they retire, we shall see trade, industry and arts advance, and assume new life and vigour; for by this vast diminution of our circulating money, the prices of labour and every thing must soon fall in a certain proportion; the farmer will soon get servants at reasonable wages, which will be a spur to his industry, and enable him to cultivate his ground, produce more grain, and to pay a higher rent to his landlord; the cheapness of all the necessaries of life will enable the landlord to sell his grain, and every artizan his commodity, at a lower price, without diminution of his profit; the merchant buying all these at a lower price, can afford to carry them to foreign markets, where he is sure of a ready sale and profitable returns. This will encourage him to enlarge his trade, arts and industry will flourish, and money will flow in upon us, till its entrance is checked again by its plenty and high prices.

All these good effects, which I have mentioned, will be the necessary consequence of the diminution of the quantity of our circulating money. Add to this, the pleasure and satisfaction which it must be to every one's mind, when he reflects that the money he acquires by his industry or good fortune is his own, and will afford him the necessaries or pleasures of life, at home or abroad, independent of any commotions or credit of bankers: this consideration alone, I say, ought to banish paper-money for ever.

FINIS.

ESSAY

Of BANKS and of PAPER CREDIT;

FROM

CHARACTERISTICS of the

PRESENT STATE OF

GREAT BRITAIN,

Publiſhed in

M.DCC.LVIII.

BANKS and PAPER CREDIT.

IN order to form a true judgment of the political state of Great Britain, it is necessary to consider the nature of Paper-credit, and whether Banks are useful or dangerous to a nation.

One would think, the advantages of Banks must have been so manifest from *experience*, that, long before this time, no doubt could have been entertained of their usefulness. But, instead of any universal agreement in their favour, such violent prejudices have been contracted against them, that not only the vulgar, who have never considered the subject, but some very inquisitive and ingenious gentlemen, have fallen into considerable mistakes in this matter, and look on Banks as detrimental to trade and industry.

However, as *experience* hath convinced the *trading part* of the world of the advantages of Banking; it will not be difficult to shew, *from the nature of the thing*, in what manner Banks become useful in commerce.

In a nation that is chiefly addicted to agriculture and to pasturage, where the people, satisfying themselves with a simple life, and wanting only a few conveniencies, deal but little in trade and in manufactures; money will not be very necessary. Much of their commerce may be carried on by barter. But, where there is a great variety of manufactures and commodities, where all sorts of arts are encouraged, and where elegance is studied; much money will not only be *profitable*, but be *absolutely necessary* for the exigencies of the state.

However, there *may be* too much money in a nation. And there is certainly too much, if it renders the great body of the people idle, and enables them to purchase what they want, from foreigners, without any labour or industry of their own. This was the case with Spain, two or three hundred years ago, and did great harm to that country.

But it will scarce be possible to procure so much money by trade alone.

Industry and labour are far better than money, and will soon be able to procure it in exchange for commodities. Yet industry stands sometimes in need to be *quickened;* and money is very serviceable for this purpose.

Let us suppose, that there is a certain quantity of money and of commodities in any country. The quantity of money may be said to represent the commodities, and to determine the prices of them. The prices of *particular* commodities may vary in different circumstances; but, if the *sums* of the money and of the commodities continue much *the same,* the prices, *on the whole,* cannot much alter. In such a case, if no more money comes into the country, unless the dispositions of the people are remarkably changed by some extraordinary accident or revolution, it will be very difficult to carry on a great deal of more work on a sudden, or speedily to increase the sum of the commodities.

But, if a great sum of money should be brought into the nation at once, and be distributed any way whatever, provided the labouring and industrious part of the nation do not get such sums as will keep them idle; though some part of it would undoubtedly be hoarded up, and would thereby be rendered useless, yet the greatest part of it would be employed, and become useful. The great people would immediately lay out part of it in adding to their houses, to their furniture, to their equipages, and to their tables. The merchants and manufacturers would employ more hands, and carry on a greater trade. The farmers would improve their lands. The graziers would breed a greater and a better stock of cattle. Every one would be enabled to spend a little more, and to carry on his business better. By these means there would be every where more labour. Of course, the commodities, or *real* riches, which are quite *different* from *money,* would be greatly increased.

Again: If the stock of money should be increased by this industry; or, if *another sum* of money should be introduced by other means, and be distributed as before; this would again increase the stock of commodities. And so on continually, or to a certain limit.

Now, Banks, settled by public authority under right regulations, continually increase the current species, by issuing notes, which circulate as money. By giving credit, they furnish men of substance with the means of giving greater employment to the industrious, and enable merchants to carry on a more extensive trade. The more notes the Banks can circulate in this way, the more will industry and trade be promoted. Nor can their be any limit, while the borrowers from these banks can give good security, and the managers take care to issue no more notes, than, by experience, they have learned, they can answer, according to the ordinary course of demand. Whatever sums landed men, merchants, or others, borrow, provided they can give good security, and borrow on reasonable prospects; this is so far from being a loss, that it increases industry and consumption. A great quantity of Bank-notes only shews, that great sums have been borrowed by one part of the nation from another, upon good security, for carrying on trade, and for other reasonable purposes: Which is so far from being either a sign, or the cause, of poverty, that it is both the sign, and a mean, of greater riches.

It is of no consequence, in this argument, that there may be more paper-money than silver and gold, and that the proportion betwixt them may not be ascertained; provided the former regulations are duly observed.

It is of no consequence that foreign nations will not take our *Bank-notes.* They will take our *goods,* which are produced by the circulation of these notes among ourselves.

It is of no consequence, though the value of the Bank-notes should happen to extend to a vast sum, provided the Banks, which are to answer these notes, have an equal value in coin, bullion, lands, goods, and good debts, to which there is convenient access.

It is of no consequence, though landed men mortgage part of their estates for Bank-notes, and may be said to coin their lands, and to bring them into the market. On the contrary, the more the lands of any country are *locked up*, the country must be less improved. And the more easily lands can be transferred and exchanged in commerce; industry, trade, and manufactures will be more speedily and successfully promoted.

Banks are not only *profitable*, but may be said, in many cases, to be *necessary*. When a spirit of industry is any way excited in a nation, if, by this industry, both the commodities, and the number of the people, shall be increased, before they have much commerce with foreign nations to fetch them money; in *such* a *condition*, either there *must be* a currency of Paper-credit, or the industrious part of the people will be continually obliged to use barter, which will expose them to many inconveniencies.

In fact, we see that nations have prospered by setting up Banks. This is true of Holland, of Genoa, and of other places; and it will be found to be true both of England and of Scotland.

By making the interest of money fall, Banks must promote industry and trade.

Public Banks are preferable to private Bankers.

It may be observed, that Banks have greatest credit under free governments, or such as have a mixture of the aristocratical or democratical form; a strong presumption in their favour. Absolute monarchies seem hardly capable of such a wise institution. Under arbitrary governments the credit of Banks cannot be firm. Absolute princes would be disposed to lay them under contribution, and would have too ready access to their treasures. It is easy to see, how the ingenious author of the Querist would answer the 303d query, which he hath proposed*, "Whether it be possible "for a national Bank to subsist and maintain its credit

* Fifth edition, printed 1750.

No man hath explained the general nature of Banking, hath shown the advantages of Banks, and hath answered the objections against them, more concisely, and with greater force of argument, than this ingenious author; whose Querist deserves well to be perused by every lover of his country, and of mankind.

"under a French government?" Perhaps, it might flourish for a *little time*, under a *very wise* and *just* prince: but it must sink under one of another character, who would be tempted to lay hold on its treasures, as our King Charles II. shut up his exchequer, and seized the money which belonged to his creditors.

In this manner we may better account for the want of Banks and of Paper-credit in France, than by the supposition of a superior policy in that country, in order to acquire and retain greater quantities of silver and gold. Thus, the French policy in not instituting Banks, in not admitting such a circulation of merchants bills as in England, and in not *directly* permitting lending on interest, which Mr. Hume imagines to be a mighty advantage to the French*, appears to be quite the reverse, and is truly a disadvantage, arising from the pernicious nature of an absolute monarchy.

However, Banks, like all other political institutions, are attended with inconveniencies. The four following are much insisted on.

First; That too great a run may be made upon Banks, and they may not be able to answer their notes; by which many innocent persons may suffer, and a great deal of confusion may be raised in the country. But in answer: Though this indeed *is possible*, there is *little danger of its happening*; if the Bank is not originally on a bad footing, and the mismanagements are not very great. Banks have continued long in Europe, without such disorders; and may be so well constituted and managed, as to prevent them in times to come.

Secondly; It is said, that Banks cannot be depended on during civil wars, or when a foreign enemy is in the heart of the country. But *what* can be preserved in *such* a case? Shall we make no wise establishments in time of peace, because we cannot secure them in time of war? 'Tis true, if we cannot defend ourselves against the French King, or the Pretender, our Banks will be of little use to us. But, in such circumstances, we must lay our account with greater

* In his Political Discourse of the Balance of Trade.

losses than the loss of our Paper-credit. We should lose our more substantial riches. We should lose our religion and liberty. In short, we should be able to secure nothing but the soil of our island; and that too we should be obliged to cultivate, not for ourselves, but for others.

Besides these objections, which may be reckoned inconsiderable, there are two of greater importance. The one, That Paper-money prevents the acquisition of greater quantities of silver and gold. The other, That it heightens the price of labour, and therefore hurts our foreign trade. But neither of these objections rests on a solid foundation.

" Suppose, (says an ingenious writer*) there are twelve " millions of paper, that circulate in a kingdom as money; " and suppose, that the real cash is eighteen millions. Here " is a state, which is found by experience able to hold a " stock of thirty millions : I say, if it be able to hold it, it " must of necessity have acquired it in gold and silver, had " it not obstructed the entrance of these metals by this new " invention of Paper. *Whence would it have acquired that* " *sum?* From all the kingdoms of this world. *But why?* " Because, if you remove these twelve millions of paper, " money in this state is below its level compared with its " neighbours, and it must immediately draw from all of " them, till it be full and saturate, so to speak, and can hold " no more." This is the argument brought to prove that paper-money prevents the entrance of silver and gold. But it is too subtile to be convincing.

If at any period, the coin in any kingdom is eighteen millions, this nation may carry on a considerable trade, and in time may acquire twelve millions more in silver and gold, without Paper-credit. But if, at the time at which they have only eighteen millions in coin, the nation should fall into the use of Paper-credit, and should circulate a sum of twelve millions in paper-money, in order to quicken industry, and to enable the people to carry on a more extensive trade; it is evident, they may carry on a greater trade with the *thirty* millions of *paper and coin*, than with the *eighteen*

* Mr. Hume in his Political Discourse of the Balance of Trade.

millions of *coin alone.* And, as they don't take paper in payment from foreign nations, if they are gainers by trade, they must receive the balance in silver and gold. Consequently, the national stock must be sooner increased in the one case than the other. If we shall suppose, further, that we could remove the twelve millions of paper-money, without any shock or confusion, by allowing less credit; we would only put a stop to so much industry, and would disable the people from carrying on so extensive a trade. This is not the way of bringing in either silver or gold. How is it possible, therefore, that the want of so much credit can add to the treasure of the nation in any way whatever?

The other objection is more plausible, and is stated in this manner by Mr. Hume*: "That, by increasing the current "species of a country, we increase the price of labour and "provisions; consequently, enable poorer nations, where "labour and provisions are cheaper, to work cheaper, and "undersell us at foreign markets: That this is even a "necessary consequence of a great trade, in whatever way "it is upheld, and is inseparably connected with great plenty "of silver and gold. On which account, trade must neces-"sarily circulate; and the poorer nations must gradually "carry it off from the richer. However, there is some "comfort (it is said) in losing our trade by plenty and "fulness; but it is extremely foolish to lose it by an "imaginary wealth, and artificially to increase the natural "disadvantages of plenty."

This is the most plausible objection, that ever has been made against Paper-credit. But, when fully examined, it will appear to be ill founded.

Credit of *some kind or other* is *necessary* wherever there is much trade. In nations, where there is great simplicity of manners and little trade, there is little necessity either of borrowing, or of buying, upon credit. But as commerce is enlarged, credit must be enlarged in proportion. There can be little trade, where every one buys for ready money.

---

* In his Political Discourse of Money.

If therefore we would encrease our trade, we must submit to the disadvantages or rather natural consequences, arising from credit; since credit is *absolutely necessary* to an extensive commerce.

In whatever manner this credit is given, it may be said to come in the place of money, to answer for it, or to supply the want of it. It may be reckoned money, and is truly a kind of money.

Credit can never be given without end. None will give credit but to men either of substance, or of integrity, prudence, and activity. Here then are *natural* checks and limits, beyond which credit will not be extended.

Regard being had to these *natural* limits, credit must always be useful to a nation, while it supports and encreases industry and useful labour.

Besides the credit given by private dealers one to another, and the advantages arising from such credit, equal or greater advantages may be gained by a more regular and publick credit, given by Banks under proper regulations, and established by proper authority.

The credit of these Banks, as well as credit of all other sorts, may be said to create a new species of money; which, like all other kinds of money, must contribute to raise the prices of labour, of provisions, and of all other commodities. But this is necessary in commerce, promotes industry, and is, upon the whole, a manifest advantage.

It may be granted therefore to Mr. Hume, that Bank-notes contribute to encrease the price of labour, and, perhaps, of all sorts of commodities. But this is not a valid argument against banking; since it is only by increasing *industry* and *consumption*, that Bank-notes encrease these prices. Mr. Hume, confesses, that even a greater quantity of silver and gold doth not encrease prices immediately; that a certain interval is required, before it produces this effect; that it must first quicken the diligence of every individual, before it encreases the price of labour*. In no other way can

* In his Political Discourse of Money.

Bank-notes encrease the prices of labour or of goods: Notes must, therefore, be beneficial. Nor does any other disadvantage arise from them which doth not arise equally from money. It is true, they have no *intrinsic* value; in which respect money is preferable to them. But they are equally useful in all kinds of domestic commerce. They produce as much industry, as is produced by the same quantity of money, and serve for money in every case, except in transacting with foreigners.

But might not we have the same industry *without* the notes? It is absolutely impossible. As no man can trade to so great an extent without credit, as with it; so paper, taken in payments, must go farther than money alone. When a spirit of industry is once raised, it may require a larger circulation of specie to support it, than the gold or silver in the country can supply. In this case there is an absolute necessity for Paper-credit. When there are many industrious merchants or manufacturers, who could usefully employ greater sums than they possess, or can have on credit from private hands, they can never carry their trade to the utmost length, if there is not a *Bank* for furnishing them with *this necessary* credit. It may therefore be allowed, that Bank-notes raise the prices of labour and goods; but this is not so properly the effect of the notes, as of that industry which they raise and assist, and which, with all its disadvantages, is confessed to be beneficial to a nation.

Whether in any one year half a million is brought into a commercial country by trade, or issued out by Banks, in notes, upon good security, it will serve for the same purposes. Part of it will be laid out in producing more of the same kinds of commodities which the country produced before; another part in making these kinds better; another in raising new manufactures at home; another in procuring more foreign goods. The farmer will raise more and better grain; the grazier breed more and better cattle; the manufacturer make more and better cloth; the artisan make better work, and in a greater quantity; and the merchant will extend his foreign trade. Thus, the notes will propagate and support greater industry; which will do greater service, by encreasing the substance of a nation, than it can do harm, by raising the prices of labour and of provisions.

Besides; it is not upon the quantity of current specie *alone*, that prices depend; they rather depend on the proportion between the number of buyers, and that of sellers. If there are more buyers than sellers, the prices rise, and rise in proportion to the greater number of buyers. When the demand is lessened, or the sellers exceed the buyers, the prices fall: if the demand is much lessened, they fall greatly. Again, this proportion between buyers and sellers depends on a thousand accidents, that make one sort of goods more necessary, fashionable, or saleable, than another. Thus, when money abounds most, the prices of *some* things fall very low; and when it is very scarce, the prices of *other* things are high. The most necessary things, such as corn and cattle, will depend least upon fashion. Yet these depend upon it in *some* measure. At some times, and in some nations, greater quantities of those necessary commodities are consumed than in others. But corn, and other things that are most necessary, depend oftener upon worse and better crops and seasons, and upon the proportion between the crops of different countries.

Besides the quantity of money, the manners of the people have a great influence in altering the methods of living, and determining the prices of labour and of commodities. These manners are changeable, and are found very different after long intervals of time. It is commonly said, that a crown, two or three hundred years ago, served the same purpose which a pound does at present*. This is true; but not always, perhaps, in the sense in which it is commonly understood. In some cases, no doubt, one could have purchased, for one crown, as much, as he can now purchase for four. In other cases he could not. But considering the different methods of living, there is a sense, in which it is

* Mr. Hume's Political Discourse of Money.

always true. In those days, in which a quarter of a pound was equivalent to a whole pound at present, men needed less than they do now. They wanted only corn, beef, and beer, coarse cloaths and coarse furniture. A little money purchased them. Men of the same rank in our days want finer cloaths, finer furniture; and, besides corn, beef and beer of a better kind, they must have spiceries, fruits, and wines, and stand in need of more money to procure them. Thus, the methods of living and men's opinions are constantly changing; and a variety of circumstances, besides the quantity of current specie, contributes to make labour and provisions dearer at one time than at another.

Mr. Hume* seems to be no less mistaken in the limits, which he assigns to trade, than in his opinion of Banking. According to his maxims, trade gives check to itself; and there is a limit, beyond which it *cannot* be encreased. Poorer nations, that is, nations with less money or foreign commerce, can work cheaper than those that are richer; and must, therefore, carry away their trade. On this head, much has been said of the dearness of labour and of provisions in England, of their cheapness in France; that the French can work cheaper by a third. It is foretold that the French must gradually carry away the whole foreign trade of England; since they can undersell the English in foreign markets.

As to this particular fact, that the French work cheaper than the English, I shall not examine it. It cannot, however, be true in all cases. An Englishman must, no doubt, be better fed, and earns higher wages by the day; but he will work many things *by the piece*, as cheap, or cheaper than a Frenchman. He works harder, and can do more work in the same time. Further, there are places in Britain and Ireland, where provisions are as cheap as in France. But, be this as it will, and though it should be granted, that, in several cases, poorer nations will work cheaper, and be able to undersell those that are richer;

* In his Political Discourse of Money.

and more commercial nations, will, in general, be able to make many things, which poorer nations either cannot make at all, or cannot make so well, Hence they may maintain a greater foreign trade, notwithstanding a greater quantity of money. Trade is, indeed, limited, because the earth and every thing in it are limited. One nation can never extend its trade *in infinitum*, or over all the earth. But a richer nation, by a proper management, may always maintain its superiority in trade over a poorer. Nay a greater quantity of money or credit, instead of being a loss, will often be an advantage for this end. It is not evident either from reason or from experience, that there must be an equilibrium in trade, as in fluids. One may easily account, from other principles, for the circulation of trade, and for its shifting its seat from one nation to another.

But, in truth, neither the riches, nor the happiness of a nation depends so much on foreign trade, as many merchants are apt to imagine. Though such gentlemen are better furnished, than others, with the knowledge of *particular* facts, they are often misled by prejudices, are too confined in their views, and too much consider their own particular traffic. After all that they have asserted concerning the necessity of foreign trade, it may justly be maintained, that such a nation as Britain, with a large territory, may be great and flourishing, may be more powerful than ever it has been hitherto, by industry and domestic commerce, without an extensive foreign trade.

A nation, where the people are not bred to war, but are chiefly employed in agriculture, manufactures, and other arts of peace; if they lye on a continent, where their neighbours have great standing armies, they also must have a standing army, or a very good militia, to defend them from foreign invasions. If they possess an island, such as Britain, and have not a great standing army, or a good militia, they must have as much foreign or domestic trade, as will enable them to support a good navy for their security. Foreign trade is likewise an advantage in other respects. It opens an easy communication with all parts of the globe. It gives us the means of enlarging our knowledge of nature and of mankind, and of acquiring a share of the riches of every nation. If it be managed with wisdom, it may be a more speedy mean of acquiring wealth than domestic commerce alone. If there are no mines in a country, without foreign trade it cannot have either silver or gold. But such an island as Britain, can never be said to depend chiefly on its foreign trade for its greatness and riches. A nation, whose territory is so small, that its native produce is not sufficient to feed and cloath its inhabitants, cannot subsist without a foreign trade. The British are in different circumstances. Their island is more than sufficient to feed and to cloath its inhabitants, though they were much more numerous than they are. No doubt they will be the better for some foreign delicacies and ornaments. They will stand in need of some foreign materials for improving their domestic commerce. But these can be procured without an *extensive* foreign trade. If the people be generally industrious in improving their lands, and in making the best use of the produce of their own island, they may both become very numerous, and enjoy the necessaries and comforts of life in great plenty, with little foreign trade. This is made out by the author of the Querist beyond the possibility of a reply. This is confessed by Mr. Hume*; who acknowledges, that, when industry and manufactures are once introduced into a nation, they may lose most of their foreign trade, and continue, notwithstanding, a great and powerful people. Nay, this gentleman scruples not to affirm, that the disadvantages to the foreign trade of England, arising from the high price of labour, are not to be put in competition with the happiness of so many millions of the commons of England, with whose superior riches, above those of any other people, the high price of labour is so closely connected.

Such a maxim is suitable to a humane disposition. Agreeably to such a benevolent sentiment, we ought to

* In his Political Discourse of Commerce.

extend our notions of trade, and consider not only how much money it gains to a nation, but how far it is conducive to the happiness of the people. That government and policy is best, where most people are most happy and easy. Neither government nor trade ought to be managed with the *sole* view of procuring vast riches to a *few*, at the expence of *grinding* the faces of the poor, and of rendering the labouring people, who are the great body of a nation, miserable. The systems of too many, both merchants and landed gentlemen, tend to no other purpose. While such gentlemen swim in luxury, and *have more than heart could wish*, they grudge a small pittance to the lower classes of mankind. We ought to propose more *equitable* and more *merciful* schemes. By considering things in this light, we may see, how much the policy of England is preferable to that of France.

It is not proposed to compare the taxes of England with those of France, or to determine, which of them are highest or imposed with the greatest judgment. When the expences of the French armies and government are so great, when such vast sums are actually levied, when both the people and their parliaments make such loud complaints of their taxes being so burdensome, it is scarce to be conceived, that the difference in the price of labour and of provisions in France and in England should arise from the difference of taxes. So far as it is real, it arises from another source. The English gentry in general are richer than the gentry in France, excepting those of very high rank. The middling people in England are richer than those of the same rank in France. The commons in France are much poorer, and live more poorly, than the commons in England. Riches are more universally diffused in England, than in France. Wherever this is to be found, *cæteris paribus*, prices must be higher. Hence, the difference in the prices of labour and of provisions in France and in England is chiefly owing to the poverty of the commons in France, and to the riches of the commons in England: a truth, which ought to be acknowledged for the honour of English policy. Accordingly, Mr. Hume* confesses, that the great advantage of England above any nation at present in the world, or that appears in the records of any story, consists in the riches of its artizans and common people: which, in his esteem, is most suitable to human nature, augments the power of the State, makes the burden of taxes feel light on every shoulder, and ought to endear to Englishmen that free Government under which they live. Thus, were we obliged to make a choice, compassion, as well as good policy, might engage us to prefer a scheme, by which the *bulk* of a people will be easy, to another, that bears hard upon the *multitude*. But, in truth, England may have abundance of foreign trade, notwithstanding the higher price of labour. An extensive foreign trade is the natural consequence of a great domestic commerce; since it is scarce possible, that an industrious nation, consisting of ten millions of people, should not work up many commodities, which they do not want at home, and should not exchange them for the commodities of foreign nations.

* In his Political Discourse of Commerce.

FINIS.

NOTE

On the SUSPENSION of CASH PAYMENTS, AT THE BANK OF ENGLAND, IN 1797.

SUSPENSION OF CASH PAYMENTS.

WITH the exception of a run for gold occasioned by the advance of the Highlanders to Derby in 1745, there was no considerable run on the Bank of England till 1792. But owing to the previous over-issue of country bank paper, a fall of the exchange, and a revulsion, accompanied by a good deal of mercantile distress, took place in the latter part of that year, and the early part of 1793. This crisis proved fatal to numerous country banks. And the vacuum caused by the withdrawing of their notes from circulation having restored the currency to its proper value, the exportation of bullion ceased, and the exchange rose to par, or became favourable.

The next, and by far the most important crisis in the history of the paper currency of Great Britain took place in 1797. Owing partly to events connected with the war in which we were then engaged, to loans to the Emperor of Germany, to bills drawn on the treasury by the British agents abroad, and partly and chiefly, perhaps, to the large advances made by the Bank of England to Government, the exchange became unfavourable in 1795, and in that and the following year large quantities of specie were demanded from the Bank. No doubt, however, the ultimate crisis was wholly owing to political causes. Alarms with respect to invasion, and reports of descents, said to have been made on the coast, became exceedingly prevalent in the latter part of 1796, and the beginning of 1797. This produced a strong desire among many individuals, but chiefly among the small farmers and retail dealers, to convert as much as possible of their property into cash. Heavy runs were in consequence made upon most country banks; and the bankruptcy of some of these establishments at Newcastle and other parts of the country gave additional force to the previous panic. Demands for supplies of cash poured in upon the Bank of England from all parts of the country; and the stock of coin and bullion in her coffers, which amounted to £7,940,000 in March, 1795, was reduced on Saturday, the 25th of February, 1797, to £1,272,000, with every prospect of a violent run taking place on the following Monday. In this emergency, a meeting of the Privy Council was held, when it was resolved to *suspend payments in cash at the Bank* until the sense of Parliament could be taken on the matter; and an Order in Council to that effect was issued on Sunday, the 26th of February, 1797.

Much difference of opinion has been entertained with respect to the policy of this measure. But the circumstances were so peculiar, and, at the same time, so urgent, that it appears to have been altogether indispensable. The run was not one that could be checked by ordinary measures. Not having originated in commercial causes, in an excess of paper, or in any doubts with regard to the solidity of the Bank, but in the fears and apprehensions caused by alarms of invasion, it was clear, that so long as these continued, no paper convertible into gold would continue in circulation. And as the Bank was without the means of immediately converting her capital into cash, it is difficult to see how her downfall, and that of the country banks, who all depend on her for supplies of bullion, could have been averted otherwise than by the interference of Government. The crisis was confessedly fraught with the greatest hazard, and required to be promptly dealt with. Had the Bank been forced to stop payment, every sort of credit and confidence would have been paralyzed; and it is impossible to estimate what might have been the effect of the sudden stoppage of the circulation of bank paper that would have been experienced. Under any circumstances such an event would most likely be attended with disastrous results; and had it occurred during war, and in a period of great danger and difficulty, it might have led either to a public bankruptcy, or to some serious convulsion.

Hence it would seem that this was a crisis in which Government were not justified only, but bound to interpose. The really objectionable part of their conduct consisted in their continuing the suspension after the alarms of invasion which had occasioned the panic had completely subsided; when the confidence of the public in the stability of the Bank stood higher than ever; and there was no longer any thing to fear from a return to cash payments. Various motives have been assigned for this conduct; but ill-founded apprehensions as to a recurrence of the run, and the facilities which the restriction gave the Bank of making large advances to Government, without subjecting herself to a drain for bullion, through a fall of the exchange, were most probably the chief causes of its being continued. Much opposition was made to the measure in Parliament, but without effect. After repeated discussions the suspension was ultimately prolonged for an indefinite period, or until six months after the signature of a definitive treaty of peace.

Though not declared by law to be legal tender, the notes of the Bank of England became such in effect from the period of the suspension. Immediately upon its taking place, a meeting was held of the principal merchants, bankers, and traders of the metropolis, when they agreed to subscribe resolutions expressive of their readiness to accept Bank of England notes in payment of all debts and obligations due to them, and pledging themselves to use all their influence to make them be accepted by others. A Committee of the House of Commons was at the same time appointed to inquire into the affairs of the Bank, and it soon after reported, that exclusive of the debt due by the public to the Bank of £11,684,800, she had a surplus fund of £3,825,890, after providing for every claim that could be made upon her. No doubt, therefore, could be entertained in regard to the more than perfect solvency of the Bank. And this circumstance, coupled with the ready acceptance of her notes as cash by the merchants and bankers, and in all payments to the Exchequer, secured their currency; while the moderation with which they were issued hindered their value from being depreciated from excess, so that they continued for a considerable period nearly on a par with gold.

Owing in great measure to the fortunate circumstance of no such crisis having previously occurred in this country, the reader will not be surprised to learn that many very absurd theories were broached in regard to the circumstances which were to determine the value of notes, now that the Bank was no longer obliged to pay them on demand. But it was immediately seen, at least by all the more intelligent inquirers, such as Sir Francis Baring, Mr. Thornton, and Lord King, that a limitation of their quantity was indispensable to prevent their sinking below their previous level. And shortly after the suspension, and while the discussions with respect to it were going forward in the House of Commons, Sir F. Baring published a tract, in which he recommended that during its continuance, the issue of bank notes should be limited, and that they should be made legal tender.* The avowed object of this proposal was to take from the Bank Directors the ability to abuse the privilege conferred on them by the suspension. But it was contended, as is usual on such occasions, that there was no reasonable ground for anticipating any abuse; and the power to regulate the value of the currency was committed without any kind of check, to the discretion of the Directors.

And it is but just to state that for awhile these gentlemen exercised the unparalleled powers with which they were invested with exemplary moderation. It was not, indeed, till 1800 that the value of notes began to fall as compared with the standard. But for some years their depreciation was inconsiderable. And it will be afterwards seen that until 1809 and 1810 the fall in their value had not become so great as to attract and fix the public attention.

* Observations on the Establishment of the Bank of England, and on the Paper Circulation of the country, by Sir Francis Baring, Bart., 2nd edit. p. 72, &c.

THE

UTILITY

OF

COUNTRY BANKS

CONSIDERED, &c.

LONDON:

PRINTED FOR J. HATCHARD, PICCADILLY.

MDCCCII.

UTILITY OF COUNTRY BANKS.

THE Bank of England, which is allowed to be the Bank of greatest circulation in Europe, was incorporated pursuant to Act of Parliament, by a Charter under the Great Seal, dated 27th of July, 1694. It advanced at that time 1,200,000*l.* for an annuity of 100,000*l.* being 96,000*l.* a year interest, at eight per cent. and 4,000*l.* a year for the expence of management. During the recoinage of the silver in 1696, the Bank discontinued the payment of its notes, which brought them into such discredit that they were at twenty per cent. discount. Tallies had been at forty, fifty, and sixty per cent. discount. For the support of public credit, the Bank was allowed in 1697, to enlarge its capital stock by ingrafting on it 1,001,171*l.* 10*s.* Its whole capital stock therefore amounted at this time to 2,201,171*l.* 10*s.* In 1708, in pursuance of the 7th Anne, c. vii. the Bank paid into the Exchequer the sum of 400,000*l.* making in all the sum of 1,600,000*l.* which it had advanced upon its original annuity of 96,000*l.* interest, and 4,000*l.* for expence of management. In pursuance of the same Act, the Bank cancelled Exchequer Bills to the amount of 1,775,029*l.* 17*s.* 10½*d.* at six per cent. interest, and was at the same time allowed to take in subscriptions for doubling its capital. In 1708 therefore the capital of the Bank amounted to 4,402,343*l.* and it had advanced to Government the sum of 3,375,027*l.* 17*s.* 10½*d.* In 1709, by a call of fifteen per cent. there was paid in and made stock 656,204*l.* 1*s.* 9*d.* and in 1710, by another of ten per cent. 501,448*l.* 12*s.* 11*d.* In consequence of those two calls, then the capital of the Bank amounted to 5,559,995*l.* 14*s.* 8*d.** In pursuance of the 3d Geo. I. c. 8.

* Postlethwayt's Hist. of the Revenue, p. 301.

the Bank delivered up to be cancelled two millions of Exchequer Bills. At this time, therefore, it had advanced to Government 5,375,027*l.* 17*s.* 10*d.* The Bank purchased of the South Sea Company, in pursuance of the 8th Geo. I. stock to the amount of 4,000,000*l.* and in 1722 its capital stock was increased by 3,400,000*l.* in consequence of the subscriptions which it had taken in to enable it to make this purchase. The Bank then had advanced to the public at this time 9,375,027*l.* 17*s.* 10½*d.* and its capital stock amounted only to 8,959,995*l.* 14*s.* 8*d.* It was now that the Bank began to have an undivided capital over and above its divided one, and it has continued to have an undivided one of the same kind ever since. The Bank in 1746 had, upon different occasions, advanced to the public 11,686,800*l.* and its divided capital had been raised by different calls and subscriptions to 10,780,000*l.* In pursuance of the 4th Geo. III. c. 25. the Bank paid to government for the renewal of its charter 110,000*l.* without interest or re-payment. This sum therefore did not increase either of the two other sums. The Bank dividends have varied according to the rate of interest received for money advanced to the public, and other circumstances, from eight to three per cent. The Bank dividends for some years have been at five and a half per cent. The Bank of England not only acts as an ordinary Bank, but it must be viewed as a great engine of state. It advances to government the annual amount of the land and malt tax, it circulates exchequer bills, receives and pays the greater part of the annuities which are due to the creditors of the public, and in various other ways aids the operations of government.

On several occasions the Bank has supported the credit of the principal houses in England, Hamburgh, and Holland. It likewise discounts merchants' bills. The operations of this Bank during the war are too well known to require any detail in this place. By a late act of parliament it has been provisionally empowered to pay all demands upon it in its own paper.

The invention of Bank credit, as it is called in Scotland,

has tended much to the prosperity of that country. It is the practice in Edinburgh and Glasgow for the merchants to open an account at a Bank, by getting some one to join as their surety in a security to the amount they require —suppose five thousand pounds. This money, or any part of it, he has the liberty of drawing out whenever he pleases, and he pays only the ordinary interest for it, while it is in his hands. He may when he pleases repay any sum, so small as twenty pounds, and the interest ceases on the day of repayment. The advantages of this contrivance, says Mr. Hume, are manifold—"as a man may find surety nearly to the amount of his substance, and his Bank credit is equivalent to ready money, a merchant does hereby in a manner coin his houses, his household furniture, the goods in his warehouse, the foreign debts due to him, his ships at sea, and can upon occasion employ them in all payments, as if they were the current money of the country. If a man borrows five thousand pounds from a private hand, besides that it is not always to be found when required, he pays interest for it whether he be using it or not; his Bank credit costs him nothing except during the very moment in which it is of service to him. And this circumstance is of equal advantage as if he had borrowed money at much lower interest. Merchants likewise, from this invention, acquire a great facility in supporting each other's credit, which is a considerable security against bankruptcies. A man, when his own Bank credit is exhausted, goes to any of his neighbours who is not in the same condition, and he gets the money, which he replaces at his convenience."*

The practice of the Country Banks in Yorkshire, and I believe in most parts of England, is very much like the Bank Credit in Scotland. The Bankers advance sums on the joint note of any two traders, or persons of credit. The usual period of the bill is one or two months, and many Banks will discount bills of this kind at two months date, for one month's interest, which is in fact to lend money at two and a half per cent. interest.

* Essay V. of the Balance of Trade, p. 96.

"A paper money consisting in bank notes, issued by people of undoubted credit, payable upon demand without any condition, and in fact always readily paid as soon as presented, is in every respect equal in value to gold and silver money, since gold and silver money can always be had for it. Whatever is bought or sold for such paper, must necessarily be bought or sold as cheap as it could have been for gold and silver."* A paper money consisting of bills of exchange, or promissory notes, payable at a future day, might have a different operation, as such paper would bear a discount, and not be convertible into ready money without a loss to the holder; such paper, therefore, would not have the same consequences on the circulating medium as cash.

It was some years ago the custom in Scotland for some of the banking companies to insert into their bank notes what they called an optional clause, by which they promised payment to the bearer, either as soon as the note should be presented, or in the option of the directors, six months after such presentment, together with the legal interest for the said six months. It will readily be supposed, that such a practice degraded the currency of these banking companies, and sunk it below the value of gold and silver.

During the continuance of this abuse, in 1762, 1763, and 1764, while the exchange between London and Carlisle was at par, that between London and Dumfries would sometimes be four per cent. against Dumfries, though this town is only thirty miles from Carlisle. But at Carlisle, bills were paid in gold and silver, and at Dumfries in Scotch Bank notes—the uncertainty of getting gold and silver coin for those bank notes had degraded them four per cent.

These optional clauses were very wisely abolished by that act of parliament which suppressed ten and five shilling bank notes, by which means the exchange between Scotland and England was restored to the fair rate which the course of trade and remittances happen to make it. These optional clauses found their way into Yorkshire, and we smile to read

---

* Smith's Wealth of Nations, vol. i. p. 490.

as a clause in a bank bill for sixpence, that the bearer must bring change for a guinea, as the condition of receiving the cash. Notwithstanding the prohibition by act of parliament, I am told that notes for half a guinea are at present circulated at Sheffield, and some of the large towns in the West Riding of Yorkshire. The paper currencies of North America consisted of a government paper, not payable to the bearer on demand, but the payment of which could not be demanded till several years after it was issued; and the colony governments, though they paid no interest to the holders of this paper, declared it to be a legal tender of payment for the full value for which it was issued. Such an act of injustice, such want of security in the property of a state, as might have been foreseen, depreciated the currency to an astonishing degree. It appeared from the course of exchange with Great Britain, that one hundred pounds sterling was considered as equivalent to one hundred and thirty pounds, and in others even to eleven hundred pounds currency—this difference arising from the different quantities of paper circulated in different colonies, and the period and probability of its final discharge and redemption. In the course of the French Revolution we have seen great changes in their paper currency. In the year 1792 I received at Paris one hundred and sixty pounds in assignats, for one hundred pounds sterling, and though the price of most things was regulated by the worth of the louis-d'or in assignats, yet many things bore only the paper-price. Amongst these, posting was to the traveller a material article. Assignats were at that time received in payment as cash at all the posts; and in a journey from Calais through Paris to Geneva I saved many pounds, by providing myself with assignats, instead of gold or silver coin. Books were sold for paper currency, and I availed myself of this circumstance by the purchase of several editions of French authors, with which I had an opportunity of obliging my friends in England. In considering the effects of a paper currency, it must be remembered, that whilst the trade and commerce of any place continue the same, the whole paper money of every kind, which can easily find circulation in it, can never exceed the value of the gold and silver, of which it supplies the place. To increase the circulation, it will be necessary to increase the trade—hence the beneficial effects of those Banks in all countries, which enable the trader and merchant to extend their concerns.

It is very evident that the system of banking multiplies prodigiously the specie of the country; when from the confidence placed in the character and responsibility of any particular firm, its promissory notes have the same currency as gold and silver money. The stock added to the capital of the community is precisely to the extent of its issues, over and above the sum necessary to be kept in its coffers, for the purpose of answering the demands of those who prefer, or have occasion for coin, instead of its paper.

It would not be very easy to calculate the precise sum necessary for this purpose, but it is very readily seen that a small comparative sum may, on most occasions, be sufficient. By the introduction of paper, therefore, a very large sum can be spared. Let us suppose that the whole circulating money of Yorkshire amounts to two millions sterling, which sum is found to be sufficient for circulating the whole annual produce of land and labour. Let us take the issues of all the bankers in that county at two millions in promissory notes payable in cash, on demand; to answer which sum, suppose that they have in their coffers four hundred thousand pounds. There would then be sixteen hundred thousand pounds in gold and silver, and two millions of their bank notes, or thirty-six hundred thousand pounds of paper and money together. The goods to be bought and sold remaining precisely the same, two millions of money will be sufficient for buying and selling them; the overplus, or sixteen hundred thousand pounds thus created, being over and above what is wanted in that part of the country, will be at hand for the profitable purposes of trade and commerce.

As the paper cannot go abroad, where the money seeks for a profit in foreign trade, gold and silver, or bills of exchange will be employed. If the money thus added to the trading capital on the credit of the Yorkshire Bankers be employed in purchasing goods in a foreign country, to supply the consumption of another, or in what is called the carrying trade, whatever profit they make will be an addition to the neat revenue of their own country. It is in fact a new fund, raised for the purpose of carrying on a new trade, the gold and silver being converted into a fund for this new trade, by the contrivance of transacting the business of the country by means of paper currency.

If the money be employed in purchasing foreign goods for home consumption, it may either procure a return of foreign wines, foreign silks, &c. or it may purchase an additional stock of materials, tools, and provisions, which may serve to maintain and employ an additional number of industrious people, who re-produce with a profit, the value of their annual consumption. The latter is the most usual way in which the gold and silver is employed, that is thus forced abroad by the operations of banking, in purchasing foreign goods for home consumption. "When paper," says a great writer, "is substituted in the room of gold and silver money, the quantity of the materials, tools, and maintenance, which the whole circulating capital can supply, may be increased by the whole value of gold and silver which used to be employed in purchasing them. The whole value of the great wheel of circulation and distribution, is added to the goods which are circulated and distributed by means of it. The operation in some measure resembles that of the undertaker of some great work, who in consequence of some improvement in mechanics, takes down his old machinery, and adds the difference between its price and that of the new to his circulating capital, to the fund from which he furnishes materials and wages to his workmen."*

When the gold and silver necessary for circulation, is reduced by the substitution of paper to perhaps a fifth part of the former quantity, if the value of only the greater part of the other four-fifths be added to the funds appropriated

* Smith on the Wealth of Nations, vol. i. p. 441.

for the maintenance of industry, a very considerable addition will be made to the quantity of that industry, and consequently to the value of the annual produce of land and labour. How desirable then for every country to have these advantages? What a source of wealth and happiness are we now contemplating? To those whose prejudices will call these facts visionary theories, I will produce historical truth in support of my argument. The doctrine was first verified in Scotland, where the business of the country has for forty years been carried on by means of the paper currency of different banks; and what country, let me ask, has flourished so much in so short a time? In Scotland the whole face of the country has been changed; beautiful cities, elegant towns, comfortable villages, fertile fields, increased population, thriving manufactories, extensive commerce, and a happy people have arisen. We need not heighten the colouring of this picture by the recollection of rags and beggary of former times. It is asserted, and the fact is pretty well established, that the trade of Glasgow doubled in about fifteen years after the first erection of the banks there, and that the trade of Scotland has more than quadrupled since the first erection of the two public banks at Edinburgh.

The Bank of Scotland was established by act of parliament in 1695; the other, called the Royal Bank, by royal charter, in 1727. Whoever has been in Scotland knows that, notwithstanding the appearances which denote real wealth, no coin but that of copper is common; gold and silver are scarcely visible; it is even difficult sometimes to get silver in change of a twenty shillings Bank Note. Purchases and payments of all kinds are commonly made in paper.

The whole paper money which can find a ready circulation in any country, never can exceed the value of the gold and silver of which it supplies the place, or which, commerce being the same, would circulate there, if there was no paper money. Should the circulating paper at any time exceed that sum, it must immediately be returned to the banks that issued it, to be exchanged for gold and silver, since the excess could neither be sent abroad, nor employed in the circulation of the country. To those who imagine that the Country Banks are mere paper mills which can issue an indefinite number of sheets, these observations may afford some consolation. Nothing is more demonstrable than that a superfluous issue of paper would cause a run upon the bank which issued it. On their own account therefore Country Bankers are obliged to be careful in balancing the amount of their issues. Let us suppose that all the paper of a particular bank which can be easily employed in the circulation of the country, amounts to exactly eighty thousand pounds, and to answer this demand, this bank has at all times twenty thousand pounds of gold and silver in its coffers, let this bank attempt to circulate eighty-eight thousand pounds, the surplus of eight thousand pounds above what the circulation can easily employ, would return upon it almost as fast as they were issued. To answer its occasional demands, this bank must in that case keep an additional sum in readiness, equal to the surplus issue; instead of twenty, it must keep twenty eight thousand pounds at hand, which as it would increase the expence, and diminish the profits of the firm, no judicious bankers would ever continue to do. It follows then that the safety of the public is connected with the real interest of the bankers; and it may be worth while to observe, that the multiplication of banking companies, so far from being an evil, is itself a good, as it increases the security of the public, by obliging all of them to be very circumspect in their conduct, and not extend their issues beyond a due proportion to their cash, to prevent those heavy and malicious runs, which are often occasioned by rival competitors; the consequences of a failure of any one company become less injurious to the public, and a free competition will induce the bankers to be liberal in their transactions with their customers.

It being true that the Country Banks can only issue as much paper currency as will supply the place of the coin, which would otherwise be required for the same purposes of circulation, it follows that to render a bank profitable, the money thus obtained on the credit of the firm, must be employed; if it were all to lie dead in the coffers of the banking shop, it might as well lie in the coffins of the churchyard; it would be as effectually withdrawn from the circulating-mass. What is employed in circulation alone yields a profit; hence it follows, that the smaller quantity of coin with which a banking-house can carry on its business, the greater good it does to the community. Suppose the issue of a house to be precisely fifty thousand pounds, if to answer that issue fifty thousand pounds in coin were always ready in a chest to answer the demand of every holder of the notes, it is evident that no profit could arise from such issue; nothing would be gained by the bank; nothing would be added to the public stock. Suppose again, that to answer the issue of fifty thousand pounds, five or ten thousand pounds in specie should be kept ready in an unproductive state, then forty or five and forty thousand pounds would in this way be added to the capital stock of the nation, and as effectually added by the circulation of this country paper, as by the importation of an equal quantity of gold and silver from the mines of Peru. In this point of view then every Country Bank must be considered as a mine to the kingdom and the bankers as the workers of this mine for the public good. As they can only make a profit by employing their capital in some way or other, and in whatever way money is employed, it is of use to some part of the community, so it follows that the greater their profits, the greater good results to the public. We never need be afraid of too great a circulation, for the market will not admit of a surplus; the only danger is, that the profits of the bank should fail; and as the best concerted projects will sometimes miscarry, so it may happen that the large speculations into which bankers, as well as merchants sometimes enter, may prove unsuccessful. Even in such a case, if the partners of the firm had assets, no holder of a bill would in the end be a loser, since the law secures their claim, wherever there is a property. That failures of this kind may have sometimes been attended with calamitous circumstances cannot be denied; but whilst the law protects, as it now does, the claims of the holders of Country Bank Notes, and whilst gentlemen of great property and well known integrity engage in these concerns, there is no very great danger from the generality of Country Banks. Security is the primary object of the bankers; and their interest and that of the public is so intimately connected, that it will very rarely happen that they will be tempted to engage in visionary projects, when their sure, safe, and real profits are so large.

The country is much indebted to gentlemen of large landed property for emerging from the indolence of their forefathers, and entering into the commercial concerns of a Bank. They have given a degree of respectability to these undertakings, at the same time that they have added to the confidence and security of the people; yet notwithstanding the certainty of the intrinsic value of the notes issuing from a Bank of this kind, it is surprising to see what a panic has sometimes suddenly seized a whole country, arising from the prejudices of the people, or sometimes from the jealousies, or illiberal arts of rival competitors.

About the commencement of the War, it may be remembered that a great alarm was excited, and if it had not been for the stand made at that time by many bankers of large landed property, the country might have lost all the benefits which it has since derived from these institutions. A Bank in Yorkshire had at that time a run upon it, which created as much clamour, confusion, and bustle, as the invasion of a foreign enemy could have done. A sudden panic having seized the holders of the bills of this Bank, all the carriages, carts, horses, and even asses, were put in a state of requisition; and though every holder of a guinea bill knew that one of the partners had a landed estate of above twenty thousand pounds in the neighbourhood of the Bank, they clamorously demanded cash for his promissory notes; and the security of twenty thousand pounds a year, with the collateral security of the other respectable partners of this firm, was not deemed sufficient, in the minds of these poor, terrified, ignorant persons. Clamours of this kind are much to be deprecated; and the promoters of them should be severely punished.

It is the duty of every man who has the welfare of his country at heart, to place a rational confidence in the respectability of character. Whilst our provincial Banks maintain the confidence of the public, and by an unsullied integrity and by a liberal accommodation to the mercantile part of the community, promote the industrious endeavours of an enterprising people, it will be impossible for the empire of Great Britain to be outrivalled in her commerce. By extending the trading capitals of the merchants, the wealth of the country is put into a progressive state of improvement, and from the largeness of the capitals employed in trade, we must command a great superiority over other nations.

Whatever tends to increase the mass of industry and quantity of labour, must have a material operation on the state of society. The industrious poor, when they can have work, will never be burdensome to their parishes; hence amongst the good effects may be reckoned the tendency of these establishments to diminish the poor rates. And here I cannot help expressing the hope that some regulation or modification of the system of poor laws may soon be effected. By removing the difficulties of gaining a settlement, many hardships to the poor, and very expensive litigations and oppressions might be prevented to parishes. Certificates should be abolished, and every honest, industrious man, married or single, should be at liberty to settle wherever he could gain a livelihood; by which means the scarcity of hands in one parish, would be relieved by the superabundance in another. The law of settlements as it now stands, is a public grievance, which the wisdom of parliament would do well to take into its serious consideration. The great increase of population, and the encouragement necessary to be given to industrious artists and labourers, most especially on the conclusion of a war, imperiously call on the legislature for its immediate attention to this subject.

The populousness of ancient nations is a theme which has

occupied the attention of many philosophic writers, and notwithstanding the investigation which it has received, it appears to be involved in much obscurity. Mr. Hume, unable to account for the amazing population of some parts of Greece, as described by some authors, boldly ventures to assert, that there is often a mistake in the arithmetical figures of the ancients; and in one instance he tells us, that we should read only forty thousand, instead of four hundred thousand. Athenæus says, that by the enumeration of Demetrius Phalereus, there were in Athens 21,000 citizens, 10,000 strangers, and 400,000 slaves. This number is much insisted on by those who are advocates for the extreme populousness of the ancients, but the arguments of Mr. Hume carry with them great probability. There can be no doubt, however, that the free states of Greece were extremely populous. Egypt and Rome were likewise well peopled. Pliny* tells us, that Seleucia, the seat of the Greek empire in the East, contained 600,000 people; and Carthage is said by Strabo† to have contained 700,000. The cities of Pekin, Paris, and Constantinople, are supposed to contain about the same number at present.

A circle of two hundred miles radius drawn from Dover or Calais would comprehend London, Paris, the Netherlands, the United Provinces, and some of the best cultivated parts of France and England. Perhaps we might safely affirm with Mr. Hume, that no spot of ground can be found in antiquity, of equal extent, which contained near so many great and populous cities, and was so stocked with riches and inhabitants. To balance in both periods the states which possessed most art, knowledge, civility, and the best police, seems the truest method of comparison, and in this point of view it will appear, that the moderns have the superiority.

Were it possible for the prolific virtue of man to act in its full extent, the number of the human species would perhaps be doubled in every generation. Poverty and necessity impose restraints, which in some countries are so great as to

---

* Lib. vi. cap. 28. † Lib. xvii.

prevent an increase. Such countries require a supply from others, where a happier state of things prevail. Poverty, it must be admitted, does not prevent generation, neither does it altogether exclude marriage. In Ireland, and in the Highlands of Scotland, the lower orders of people marry at a very early age, and the women bring forth many children; but it has been remarked, that in the Highlands of Scotland in particular, it is not uncommon for a mother who has borne twenty children, not to have two alive. In Ireland likewise the children of the cottars look very sickly, and though from the readiness with which they are supplied with milk and potatoes, proper food of infants, many live over the period of childhood, yet when nature requires a more substantial food, and more expensive clothing, those who are not so fortunate as to be otherwise provided for either by entering into the service of their richer neighbours, or the service of the state, generally fall victims to maladies of some kind or other. Poverty being thus unfavourable to the rearing of children, it follows that whatever tends to ameliorate the comforts and situation of the poor, must be politically viewed as one great cause of the populousness of a country; and in this point of view, I consider the institutions we are viewing, as of great national importance. All animals multiply naturally in proportion to their means of subsistence, and no species can ever multiply beyond it. In civilized society the scantiness of subsistence among the lower ranks of the people sets a limit to the multiplication of the human species, by destroying a great part of the children produced by their fruitful marriages. When labour is to be had and is liberally rewarded, the lower orders are enabled to provide better for their children. A greater number is consequently reared, and added to the national stock of population. It necessarily does this too as nearly as possible in the proportion which the demand for labour requires. In this point of view we may consider the institutions which tend to set it in motion, the manufactures of a country, as inventions for the multiplication of the human species, and the propagation of intellectual beings; they are the creative powers of thought, happiness, and moral existence. Without such fostering establishments, life would decay, and society wither at its root. With such aid the demand for man increases, and the reward of labour necessarily encourages the marriages and multiplication of labourers, so that a continual increasing demand is supplied by a continually increasing population. An increase of wealth produces the liberal reward of labour, which is the cause of increasing population. To complain of it, is to lament over the necessary cause and effect of the greatest public prosperity.

The present flourishing state of America affords a strong proof of this doctrine. From the address of the president Mr. Jefferson to the representatives, just published, it appears that from the census taken of the population for a period of ten years, the whole population of that extensive country will be doubled in about twenty-two years. Throughout the greater part of Europe the number of inhabitants is not supposed to double in less than five hundred years.

Agriculture, manufactures, and foreign commerce, are the three great sources of riches to a nation, and on all of these we see the action of the establishments we are considering. According to the natural course of things the lands are first cultivated; but as we do not live in a state of nature, we must not look for natural orders alone in the present state of society. Accordingly we find that the cultivation of lands in many commercial countries has not kept pace with the extension of its commerce; but there is a species of re-action which has an effect on the agriculture of a country, and it is very observable in many parts of Great Britain, where we find the inhabitants of a sea-port, or large trading town grown rich by trade, begin to turn their attention to the improvement of the country adjacent to such towns. Every one who has travelled through the different counties of England and Scotland, must have noticed these improvements. Agriculture may, therefore, in these cases, be said to owe its improvement to the increase of manufactures, or foreign commerce. In other instances, manufactures have been the offspring of agriculture. The manufactures of Leeds, Halifax, Sheffield, Birmingham, &c. are of this kind. The cheapness of living in those places, appears to have induced the manufacturers to settle in those parts of the country. The workmen found that in those places, by their industry, they could procure more of the necessaries and conveniencies of life, than in other places. By working up the materials of manufacture which the land produces, and exchanging their finished work for more materials and provisions, or what is the same thing, for the price of them, they give a new value to the surplus part of the rude produce, and furnish the cultivators of the land with something in exchange. Thus the farmer and manufacturer are mutually encouraged by each other's industry, and enabled to increase this surplus produce by a further improvement in the cultivation of the land. And as the fertility of the land gave rise to the manufacture, so the extension of the manufacture re-acts upon the soil, and increases the produce of the farm. When manufactures have arrived at a considerable degree of perfection, the price of a great quantity of rude produce is frequently contained in a small bulk. A piece of cloth, for instance, which weighs one hundred pounds, when it reaches the Cloth Hall at Leeds, contains not only the price of one hundred pounds of wool, but of many quarters of corn, pounds of meat, and pots of beer, the maintenance of the different working people, and of the persons immediately employing them.

The produce of agriculture then, in the form of corn, cattle, and malt liquor, is in this manner in the shape of complete manufacture; a finished bale of cloth, virtually exported, and may be sent to any corner of the world. In the history of modern times, the manufactures which have sprung from foreign commerce, have generally been sooner extended and improved, than those which were the offspring of agriculture. The English manufacture of fine cloths made of Spanish wool, was famous for above a century before any of those which now flourish in the above-mentioned places were fit for a foreign market. The improvement and extension of these arose from the extension and improvement of agriculture, the last and greatest effect of foreign commerce, and of the manufactures immediately produced by it. The commerce and manufactures of large towns, instead of being the effect, have been the cause of the improvement and cultivation of the country. To this sort of re-action of the prosperity of the towns on the face of the country, we may attribute the great improvements which have lately been made, and are now making, in the neighbourhood of Hull, Liverpool, Gainsborough, and other trading towns. They are peculiarly remarkable in the vicinity of the latter, which is a small inland town on the banks of the navigable river Trent, inhabited by very wealthy, respectable, and industrious merchants, who, as well as the carrying trade to London and the coast, carry on a very considerable trade to the Baltic and other places, from which even during the war they have derived great wealth, which has lately been employed in improving the agriculture of the adjacent country. Sandy heaths and marshy bogs have been converted into fertile fields, and several extensive inclosures have been undertaken, to the great advantage of the country, and profit of individuals, which improvements have been greatly promoted by the Banks of that thriving town. To purchase land has been, till lately, every where in Europe, a most unprofitable employment of a small capital.

It has been remarked that the improvements in the agriculture of Great Britain have by no means kept pace with the advances of commerce and manufactures, but the rapid progress of a few years, shows the attention which has been paid to this source of wealth.

It is probable that the greatest part of the country was in a state of cultivation before the reign of Elizabeth; but the improvements in every part of agriculture, and the science of farming are of modern date and rapid growth. The plentifulness of ready money, it cannot be doubted, has greatly contributed to this desirable object. No country in which the right of primogeniture takes place, which pays tithes, and where, though contrary to the spirit of the law, perpetuities are admitted in some cases, can give more advantage to agriculture than England does. The attention lately given by several patriotic noblemen and gentlemen, has produced advantages not to be appreciated; but they are only secondary causes which serve to put into motion the cash manufactories of the respective counties.

The state of agriculture in, France previous to the Revolution, was certainly inferior to that of England. We are told by Guicciardin, that before the invasion of Charles VIII. Italy was cultivated in the most barren and mountainous parts of the country, as well as in the fertile plains. Nothing, in my opinion, can shew the real wealth of a commercial nation so much, or prove it so clearly, as improvements in agriculture. It is the real demonstration of wealth, realized by trade and commerce; for the profits of agriculture in general are so small, when compared with the profits arising from trade and commerce, that when we observe the re-action before mentioned, we may be assured that the increase of wealth has given rise to these improvements.

No part of the wealth obtained by merchandize, can properly be said to belong to any particular country, till it has spread itself over the face of that country in buildings, or the durable improvement of lands. The great wealth said to have been possessed by some of the Hans Towns, and of which we read in the obscure histories of the thirteenth and fourteenth centuries, has totally disappeared, and it is not thoroughly ascertained where some of them were situated, or to what towns in Europe the Latin names given to some of them belong. Lombardy and Tuscany are still reckoned among the most populous and best cultivated countries in Europe, though the troubles of Italy in the end of the fifteenth and beginning of the sixteenth centuries, greatly diminished their commerce and manufactures. The great trade of Antwerp, Ghent, and Bruges, was driven from Flanders by the civil wars, and the bad policy of the

Spanish government which succeeded; yet Flanders is at this time one of the richest, most populous, and best cultivated parts of Europe. From the observations which I was able to make in passing through the Pays-Bas, Holland, Lombardy, Tuscany, and various parts of Italy, the Austrian Nethelands appeared to me the most fertile and best cultivated, but Holland the most populous.

The revolutions and wars of governments not unfrequently exhaust or annihilate the springs of riches which flow from trade and commerce; but the wealth derived from the more solid improvements of agriculture, will resist the convulsive shocks of barbarous hostility, as we learn from the history of the fall of the Roman empire in the western provinces of Europe.

It is truly grateful to the feelings of every patriotic breast, to observe the progress which of late years has been made in the agriculture, manufactures, and commerce of Great Britain; and, in tracing the effects, we are gradually led to an examination of the causes; amongst which the establishment of Country Banks holds a primary place. To those who think we mistake an effect for the cause, and would willingly attribute the rise of the Banks to the previous increase of money derived from the flourishing state of the manufactures and commerce, we would produce Scotland as the instance of the cause preceding the effect. In that country, no sooner had the banking system began to operate, than its effects were observable. The Bankers, by advancing money to their customers, enabled them to increase their trading capitals, by which means more hands were employed, the mass of industry increased, and the natural consequences of this order of things, were observable in the opulence which followed. This will serve to shew that we have not mistaken an effect for a cause. The operations of banking are creative of wealth; for wherever a Bank can flourish, it will convert the product of industry into money.

It may not be amiss to pursue this enquiry, by making some observations on the nature and effects of war on the productive capital of a nation; and by duly considering the real sources of wealth, we shall probably be able to explain some phenomena which have surprised the reasoners on finance.

The increasing prosperity of the nation, during a long and expensive war, its gradual and progressive advances in opulence, have been causes of surprise to those most versed in political disquisitions. If we shall be able to shew that the establishments now under our consideration have in any degree tended to this prosperity, we shall enhance their value in a political point of view. We shall considerably increase the magnitude of their operations, by making them engines of war, as well as peace. Whatever contributes to give strength to an empire groaning under the afflictions of war, deserves the attention of every wise statesman. We shall begin by stating, that it must be admitted as a fact, that Great Britain is not, in the present refined state of commerce, compelled, as in former times, to accumulate large quantities of gold and silver, to enable her to carry on foreign wars, and to maintain fleets and armies. It is not with gold and silver that fleets and armies are maintained, but with consumable goods. "The nation which from the annual produce of its domestic industry, from the annual revenue arising out of its lands, and labour, and consumable stock, has wherewithal to purchase those consumable goods in distant countries, can maintain foreign wars there"*

The last French war prior to that which is now on the eve of being terminated, cost Great Britain upwards of ninety millions sterling, including not only the seventy-five millions of new debt that was then contracted, but the additional two shillings in the pound land tax, and what was annually borrowed of the sinking fund. More than two-thirds of this expence were laid out in distant countries; in Germany, Portugal, America, the ports of the Mediterranean, and in the East and West Indies. The kings of England had not, as in former times, an accumulated treasure; the enormous expence then of that war, and the same

* Smith's Wealth of Nations, vol. ii. p. 157.

observation equally applies to the present or late war, could not have been defrayed by the exportation of gold or silver, but by that of British commodities of some kind or other. That a great, an enormous quantity of gold and silver were exported at different periods of the war is beyond a doubt, and that the Country Banks considerably aided these operations of government cannot likewise be doubted. We may truly assert, that without the intervention of paper currency, all the real gold and silver of the nation would not have paid the expences of one year of the war; and though the parliament had enacted sooner than it did the payment of all demands at the Bank of England in their own paper, yet even that could not have supplied the currency of the country; for it is a fact very well known, that the people at large have not the same confidence in the Bank of England, that they have even in some of the Country Banks. And it may be safely affirmed that the gold and silver of the country can be more readily collected by the circulation of Country Bank Notes, than those of the Bank of England: each Bank being indeed a depôt of the cash which would otherwise necessarily be employed in the circulation of its adjacent circuit. In viewing these depôts of coin then as so many public funds ready to be called into action for the advantage of the community, we first see the activity of country banks in collecting the specie. We next find their utility in increasing the quantity of those commodities, which during a war serve as the great medium of payment to a commercial country. When government, or those who act under them, contract with a merchant for a remittance to a foreign country, he consequently endeavours to pay his foreign correspondent upon whom he has drawn a bill, by sending abroad commodities of some kind or other, rather than gold and silver. Even if the products of the empire were not in demand in that country, he would endeavour to send them to some other country, in which he could purchase a bill upon that country. When gold and silver are sent abroad to purchase foreign commodities the profits of the merchant arise, not from the purchase, but from the sale of the returns; but when these are sent abroad merely to pay a debt, he gets no returns, and consequently no profits.

The national currency of a country receives its direction and movement from the commodities circulated in the neighbourhood of each particular country; the money of the mercantile republic from those circulated between the different countries with which it communicates. Both are employed in facilitating exchanges, the one between the different individuals of the same, the other between those of different nations. Part of this money of the great mecantile republic probably was employed in carrying on the late war, and we may suppose that during a war large sums necessarily circulate around the seat of war, and are employed in purchasing there, and in the neighbouring countries, the pay and provisions of the different armies. But it is a fact, that whatever part of this money of the mercantile republic may have been annually employed in this manner by government, it must have been annually purchased either with British commodities, or with something else that had been purchased with them. In whatever way we consider it then, commodities, the annual produce of the land and labour of the country, are the ultimate resources by which we have been enabled to carry on the late expensive war.

The finer manufactures, which contain a great value in a small bulk, and can therefore be exported to a great distance at little expence, are the commodities most proper, and most usually employed to purchase the pay and provisions of troops on foreign service. It is by means of our manufactures then that we have been enabled to carry on the war, they being the resource; and the banking system the source of our whole prosperity. The ability of Great Britain to carry on war is as durable as her home trade, foreign commerce, and paper credit; but destroy all, or any one of these, and her fleets and armies perish. Without these three resources there would be no fleets to make conquests, no armies to command victories. When we look into the history of our own country, and compare the present with the past, the retrospect is truly gratifying; dreadful as war is, a consolation will arise to the people, who feel that when involved in its horrors, they have the power of defence.

Formerly the monarchs of England, when they had exhausted their treasure, could not continue the expences of war without violent and often oppressive exactions on their subjects; and though we must acknowledge that the evils of war have been, and always must be felt by individuals, yet the resources of Great Britain have been so great, by the surplus produce of her manufactories, that notwithstanding the unparalleled expence, the prosperity of the nation has increased under the pressure of the late war. In former times, when we had nothing with which to purchase the pay and provisions of our armies employed in foreign countries, but the rude produce of the kingdom, or the still ruder coarse manufacture, money was necessarily used and as necessarily exported to the impoverishment of the nation. A sovereign in such a state, and under such circumstances, could seldom draw considerable aid from his people.

Foreign trade carries out that surplus part of the produce of land and labour for which there is no demand at home, and brings back that for which there is a demand. It gives value to superfluities and opens an extensive market for the surplus of home consumption; it gives encouragement to the productive powers of the real revenue and wealth of society. The country which is employed in sending out the greatest quantity of superfluities, is generally the greatest gainer by foreign trade. All nations, however, may be more or less enriched by it.

As grand political machines, moving the great levers of the empire, and raising the ponderous powers of war, National Banks may be contemplated as national bulwarks, towers of strength, and edifices of defence.

What the Bank of England is to government and merchants of the metropolis, Country Banks are to traders and gentlemen of landed property in the country. They assist them in their necessities, and aid them in their enterprises. By discounting the bills of the former, they render money plentiful, where it otherwise would never appear. At no period have their good effects been more manifest than during a war, which having drained the nation of its cash, must have ended in the ruin of its trade, had it not happily met with support from gentlemen of respectability and property forming themselves into Banking Companies, to the great advantage of the community. At a time when money was not to be borrowed on mortgage, many men of the greatest landed property could not have raised money for their occasions but by means of the Country Banks, which I am informed has been very extensively given throughout the country. At the time when government opened its subscriptions for the war, and levied the triple assessment, money was not to be had on mortgages, and such persons as had not ready money, whatever might be the amount of their real property, were extremely distressed and perplexed how to raise it. A nobleman of my acquaintance who paid above a thousand pounds to government on that occasion, borrowed the money at a Country Bank, and from that bank alone he was supplied with twenty thousand pounds, which enabled him to make considerable alterations and improvements on his estate, by which means he employed a great number of persons who would otherwise have been out of employment, and probably a burden to their parishes. When we consider the many instances of this kind, on a larger and smaller scale throughout the country, we shall learn to appreciate the value of Country Banks, which have served to sustain the poor, support the rich, and adorn the nation. Many of the greatest undertakings of the kingdom could not have been carried on at all during the war without this aid. I am told that many of the canals intersecting the interior of the kingdom, and opening a communication from the most inland counties to the farthest extent of navigated seas, could never have been effected, but from the facility with which money was obtained from the bankers where the undertaking was carried on. Many, if not all large manufacturers, have received continual or occasional accommodations of the same kind. Building, though considerably checked during the war, has in many parts of the country proceeded with vigour, and houses, streets, and towns, have been raised as substantially on paper currency, as brick or stone cemented by gold or silver, could have built them. Agriculture, and all the spirit of farming, never was pursued with such ardour in its various branches as at this present time, and though we must view the large profits as the spur, yet we must consider the Country Banks as the means by which these large farming concerns have been carried on. And here one cannot but lament the prejudice of those who attempt to deny the utility of these Banks, and who attribute to them bad consequences, without admitting the good.

The high price of provisions, it has been said, and more especially that of corn,* is owing to the facility with which a set of monopolists are supplied with cash by Country Banks. That there should be monopolies or combinations amongst individuals which have the effect of raising the price of the necessaries of life, is much to be lamented, and I am ready to admit that restrictive laws would be desirable, if they could exist without injury to the freedom of trade. But admitting this opinion in its full force, and allowing that the Country Banks advance money on what they think proper security, to monopolists and speculating cornfactors, by which

---

* The Athenians, to prevent corn from rising above its ordinary price, prohibited every citizen, under pain of death, from buying above a certain quantity. Five drachmas, (three shillings and nine-pence English) the medimnus was reckoned the ordinary price.—The medimnus was about four of our bushels, (Goguet, de l'Origine des Lois, &c. t. iii. p. 260.) The quantity which each citizen might purchase, was according to the text of Lysias *πεντηκοντα φορμῶν*, which may be rendered fifty baskets—it is a measure, the exact value of which is not known.—The punishment of death was likewise denounced against the inspectors of corn, if they neglected to prevent a monopoly—a practice at all times forbidden to individuals, but in some places employed by the government to increase its revenues. Lys. in Darden, p. 392. Aristot. de Rep. lib. i. cap. 11.

The Athenians brought yearly from Pontus 400,000 medimni of corn, as appeared from entries in the books at the custom-house, and which, as Mr. Hume observes, was the greatest part of their importation of corn: but Mr. Hume was mistaken in supposing the medimnus only equal to our bushel. Mr. Goguet has shewn it to be equal to a quantity, which in English or Winchester measure, is about four bushels.

means the price in some instances may be raised beyond its level: yet in this trade, injurious as it appears, as well as in every branch of commerce, it is for the advantage of the community that there should be many competitors, for it is by competition alone that the market can be fairly regulated and brought to its due level. If therefore the Country Banks aid many to purchase, as whatever is purchased must be brought to market to fetch a profit, for no profit can arise from constantly hoarding a perishable substance like corn, so the greater the number of dealers, the greater is the probability of the price being lowered. It is highly improbable, therefore, that the Country Banks, by aiding many persons to speculate in corn, are the means of enhancing its price, for it is clear that a general aid to speculators must have a contrary tendency, and effectually do away monopoly. The fact seems to be, that in some places two or three monied men, who act from their own weight in the scale of prices, independent of any bank, for such men are in themselves banks, and whether they pay in Bank of England, or Country Bank Notes, or guineas, is exactly the same thing, perhaps do combine to keep up the price. We have seen this observation verified in the case of hops, where one wealthy individual, solely from the operation of his own weight in the scale, could regulate and raise the price of what we now deem a necessary of life. But it did not appear that the individual alluded to received any aid in his operations from Country Banks.

That the high price of corn might, in some measure, arise from combinations of this kind amongst wealthy persons in some markets, I am ready to admit, and that such persons may keep an account with a Country Banker, and pay in his notes; but such an occurrence is no proof of the bad effects to be attributed to the Country Banks; it must be attributed solely to the operation of wealth on the free trade of a free country. Men with large capitals will naturally endeavour to command the price of the articles in which they trade, and those who trade in corn will be as anxious to sell at a great price as any other traders.

If the Country Banks had acted as has been asserted, they must have had an effect very different from what those gentlemen who made the assertion seem to have imagined. If they had really advanced large sums of money to many persons to purchase corn, the greater the number of persons so employing their capital, the lower must necessarily have been the price — competition produces cheapness. It is evident, therefore, that the high price of provisions is totally independent of any system of banking known in this country.

For all the purposes of agriculture the establishment of Country Banks has its utility. Most of the enclosures of land have been promoted and carried into effect by their means. Even during the war the progress of this improvement has been rapid beyond example. Except in the vicinity of the metropolis, we everywhere find the face of the country enriched, by the cultivation of its heaths, its moors, and waste land.

These improvements could not have taken place in many parts of the country without the assistance of the Country Bankers, who, on various species of security, advanced the money necessary for such very considerable undertakings. By these means many hundred thousand acres of land have become productive; many thousand quarters of wheat and other grain added to the national stock; many thousand families of labourers, artificers, husbandmen, and others supported. These reflections are truly gratifying to every lover of his country, and friend of humanity.

In a tour which I made in the course of the Summer, I had an opportunity of observing the improvements which have taken place, within a very few years, in one of the most barren, desolate, parts of England, I mean the Wolds of Yorkshire, whose bleak mountains, which hardly furnished a blade of grass to a few famished sheep, are now waving with fields of corn. The crops of oats and barley were, this last harvest, immense; and where the fields had been sown with seeds, a most luxuriant crop of grasses appeared. Improvements like these are objects of national importance; and it is my opinion, that they never could have been effected without the aid derived from Country Banks. The Bank of England would not have advanced to individuals the sums necessary, and as they were vested for such enterprises, and on mortgages from common individuals, the money could not have been procured.

In many instances the Country Bankers set the example of improvement. One of the large tracts of the wolds, of of which I have been speaking, has been enclosed, cultivated, and ornamented with several excellent farm-houses by a banker of Hull, to whom the country is greatly indebted. The support given to the manufacturers in the country has been very extensive.

I know a very large manufactory which would have failed early in the war, but for the support it received from a Country Bank. There are, doubtless, many instances of the kind. The foreign trade, and every branch of commerce, has been greatly promoted by these establishments.

Having pointed out the utility of Country Banks, as applied to the improvements which have taken place in the nation by an increase of its trade, commerce, manufactures and agriculture, let us take a view of the advantages which arise to government by the operations of these Banks. As a source of revenue, let us first notice the sums annually paid to government by the bankers themselves, for stamps on which their notes are issued. This will amount to a considerable sum; to which add the consumption of bill stamps, and we shall be astonished at the sum paid to government by means of this circulation. We must likewise take into account the quantity of paper, all of which pays a duty. And lastly, let us attend to the sums paid for postage of letters arising solely from these transactions. Considered then as an object of revenue, the Country Banks are of considerable importance to government. By the aid given to the manufacturer his capital becomes enlarged; he employs and supports a greater number of individuals than he otherwise would have been able to do; these individuals add to the riches and wealth of the nation by their industry: marriage is encouraged; whole families are called into existence; population is increased, and poverty banished from parishes, which otherwise would have been oppressed with an indigent, unemployed poor. This employment of the poor, and encouragement of industry, by facilitating the comforts of marriage, may be considered amongst the happiest effects of an increase of riches to any nation. An increased population, with an increased means of support, forms the strength and is the sure sign of a tendency to improvement in any state — increased population causes an increased consumption of those articles which give rise to and support the various trades, arts, and manufactures of a country. An increased consumption augments the revenues by an increased addition to the duties and taxes paid in a great variety of ways to government, in the form of excise, house-tax, window-tax, &c.

In this point of view, then, these establishments demand the fostering care of government. It is indeed to the security of our admirable Constitution that these institutions owe their rise—the protection given by law to the property of the subject, encourages the commercial spirit of an enterprising people. From what has been said, it will appear that we can have nothing to fear, generally speaking, from an excess of paper currency payable on demand in gold or silver coin, for the nature of its circulation is such as to limit its extent: neither have we any thing to fear from the multiplication of the banks, since they operate as checks on each other, and like all other competitions in trade, are for the benefit of the public. If it be objected that gold, the sight of which so gratifies the human eye, is now seldom to be seen, let it be remembered that it is invisibly performing its magic effects on the commerce of the nation. We may be assured that every guinea, though unseen, is actively employed for the good of the community; its paper representative is not intended to supply its place, that it may sleep in idleness; on the contrary, it goes forth to seek new adventures; the chrysal of the day is not bred up in idleness; he seldom sleeps long in the iron chests of bankers.

The intention and object of all bankers, it must be obvious, is to use the coin which they get in exchange for their paper; and let it be remembered, that it is scarcely possible for them to employ it to the disadvantage of the country. They may, though they seldom do, employ it unskilfully, but even in that case, the employment may have its utility. When we recollect that it is the real interest of the bankers to employ with great caution the coin which they borrow of the public, and when we consider the property which they have at stake, the most timid reasoner, can see but little danger to the holders of country bank-notes in general. It is seldom that persons without real *bonâ fide* property can engage in banking concerns; and if we examine the firms of the banks throughout the country, we shall find that they consist very generally of gentlemen of well known, and often of very large property; and as the bankrupt laws are very wisely framed, and very uprightly administered, we have very little to fear from fraudulent failures, which can hardly ever happen in banking partnerships. If, therefore, from any sudden run upon any of these banks, they should not be able, as might accidentally happen to the most respectable of them, to pay in gold or silver on such occasion, no person who really believed in the validity of the assets of the firm, would have any real cause of alarm, for though he might experience an inconvenience, he could not ultimately be a loser by such an occurrence. The credit, it is true, of such a house, would receive a shock, but it is with pleasure, that every honest man, has seen the recovery of some firms from blows of this kind, malignantly aimed by illiberal competitors. To comprehend fully the utility of any establishment it must be examined in various points of view. I have endeavoured to treat my subject in this manner, and if I am not mistaken, the arguments in favour of the banking system are drawn from facts fully admitted, and established by the best writers and most accurate political enquirers.

It might be curious to ascertain the precise sum now added to the mass of the circulating medium of the country by the present establishments, but I must own that I am not sufficiently acquainted with practical concerns of this kind to offer any thing like an arithmetical calculation on this subject; but it seems probable, that some millions of money are thus added to the productive capital of the nation; and it is a satisfaction to think, that the mines from which these riches spring, must be as durable as the constitution of the country, and this coinage, if I may so term it, be as plentiful as the wants of industry require it. It is a source whence wealth flows precisely as it is wanted; whilst Great Britain increases in industry, she may safely increase her paper currency, and multiply her banks. The period is very far distant that will obstruct the operations of banking; our merchants have great scope for their enterprises, and our manufacturers for their produce. The rapid increase of population will give rise to new towns or villages; the rapid improvements in agriculture will give employment to new labourers; and under the administration of a wise and enlightened government, the empire of Great Britain may flourish for ages yet to come in a progressive state of improvement. Ireland will afford an ample field for the employment of the largest capitals: and when the good effects of the Union shall manifest themselves to the people of that hitherto distracted country, they will soon begin to emerge from the wretched state in which they have so long been sunk; and by the pursuits of industry raise themselves from the miseries of poverty, to the enjoyment of wealth, comfort, and happiness. Now that the Union has so happily united the interests of the two nations, and done away that spirit of jealousy which so long obstructed the springs of commerce, we may hope soon to see the same improvements take place in Ireland, which have followed the union of Scotland with England. Everything that science, humanity, and virtue can accomplish, will be effected by the noble Lord who now governs that country.

It is well worth the Irish politician's attention, to consider how far the example of Scotland might safely be followed, and the trade of Ireland increased by the establishment of a greater number of banks. Whatever may be the sum added to the capital stock of the country, when it is viewed as the circulating capital, we shall be astonished at its effects —"The circulation of money is money, and so much that it cannot be computed by any calculation.

"We every day see bankers, living not only in affluence, but magnificence, building palaces, and purchasing estates, by the sole profits of capitals, very inconsiderable; *continually* circulated; and some, by circulating the wealth of others, without any capital at all. A few thousand pounds diffused through the various occupations and professions of a small town, will maintain all the families, of which it is composed, better than the same sum would support one family, if it remained unemployed in the hands of a single person. The butcher and the baker feed the taylor and the draper, who clothe them in return; the farmer employs the carpenter, the bricklayer, and the labourer, and they assist him by consuming part of his crop; the parson maintains a wife and six children, and the attorney builds a house and buys land, and they are all paid in their turns by the perpetual rotation of the same money. If, then, the circulating a small sum, within such narrow limits can do all this, what will not the circulation of so many millions be able to effect in the hands of a great and powerful nation, when employed in improving commerce, agriculture, and manufactures."*

From the observations which I have already made, it will appear that the Country Banks may be considered as political machines of great power in a commercial state. Their operation is extensive, and not local or limited to the spot on which they are erected. The circulation of the paper, it is true, may, and generally is, very limited to a county, or often to a few parishes; but their efforts may extend to the utmost boundaries of commerce. Nations in every region of the globe may be acted upon by these power-

---

* Soame Jenyn's Essays, vol. ii. p. 284.

ful engines; for as they promote and facilitate trade, their operations become as extensive as the trade they produce; and when we consider the effects of an extended commerce, we may trace the twenty shilling note of a Glasgow bank, from its embarkation in the Clyde, in its form of manufacture, through the West or East Indies, till it returns, in the suite of a Nabob, who fixes it in a palace which he builds in the neighbourhood of his native city, on his return from Asia, whither he himself was probably first sent by the operation of paper currency.

As trade produces reciprocal advantages, so the good effects, so evidently manifested in our own country, may be in a considerable degree promoted in very distant parts of the world. The industry of Indostan may be increased; the inhabitants of Calcutta multiplied; the woods of America cleared, the marshes drained, and its agriculture improved; the produce and population of Africa and the West Indies may all be affected by the establishment of a new bank in any part of Great Britain; which, by increasing the trading capital of a great commercial nation, may produce political consequences in every quarter of the world.

I shall conclude this work with a few brief observations on the balance of trade, the course of exchange, and the causes of the export of gold or bullion from the country.

The commercial exports and imports of any state, readily become proportionate to each other:—they seldom continue for any length of time greatly favourable or unfavourable to any particular country.

The balance must be paid in bullion, or it must remain a debt. The unwillingness of the richer state to lend, and the disinclination of the poorer to borrow to an unlimited extent, promote the equalization of the commercial exports and imports. A great inequality, however, will not fail to arise occasionally from various causes.—War, scarcity, and, above all, a bad or good harvest will produce very manifest effects. In consequence of the late bad harvests, the large imports of corn have cost the nation many millions of ready money;

which served alike to drain the country of gold, and to turn the course of exchange considerably against Great Britain.

In speaking of the commercial exports and imports, we here mean those articles for which an equivalent is given. Many of our commodities which are exported, and some which are imported, furnish no return. The numerous stores which were shipped during the war, for the support of the navy and army in foreign parts—loans and subsidies to our Allies—dividends transmitted to the foreign proprietors of British Stock—the capital sent annually from this kingdom to the West Indies, to be employed in the cultivation of lands are of this kind: whilst, on the other hand, a very considerable capital is brought into this country from the East Indies, both by the India Company and by individuals.

Exports and imports of this kind tend, like a bad harvest to render the balance of trade unfavourable, and by creating a debt to foreign countries, promote the exportation of bullion.

The commercial exports and imports seldom continue long disproportionate: they have a tendency to equalization from two causes: first, the limitation of the debt which foreigners will suffer British merchants to contract; and secondly, from the quantity of English bullion which is exportable.

Gold itself being an article of intrinsic value as well as the medium of payments, is exported and imported by merchants accordingly as the export or import is likely to yield a profit.

It is contrary to law to export gold coin, or gold which has been melted down from coin, but it is generally believed that when the profit on exportation is very great, the law is evaded, and large quantities of English gold find their way into foreign countries. Whilst our paper currency maintains its credit we have no great reason to lament this occurrence, for it should be remembered that gold is an unproductive part of our capital; by the exportation of it, the country saves the interest of the sum exported, and the exchange with foreign countries, is improved by discharging the debt due on account of an unfavourable balance of trade—it is said likewise to prevent the depreciation of our own paper currency as compared with the current money payments of other countries.*

* Thornton on Paper Currency, p. 134.

FINIS.

AN

ENQUIRY

INTO

THE NATURE AND EFFECTS

OF

THE PAPER CREDIT

OF

GREAT BRITAIN.

BY

HENRY THORNTON, ESQ.
M. P.

LONDON:

PRINTED FOR J. HATCHARD, AND MESSRS. F. AND C. RIVINGTON.

1802.

INTRODUCTION.

THE first intention of the Writer of the following pages was merely to expose some popular errors which related chiefly to the suspension of the cash payments of the Bank of England, and to the influence of our paper currency on the price of provisions. But in pursuing his purpose, many questions occurred which it seemed important to discuss, partly on account of their having some bearing on the topics under consideration, and partly because they appeared to be of general importance, and had either been left unexplained, or had been inaccurately stated by those English writers who have treated of paper credit. This work has, therefore, assumed, in some degree, the character of a general treatise.

The first Chapter contains a few preliminary observations on commercial credit. The object of the two following Chapters is distinctly to describe the several kinds of paper credit: to lay down some general principles respecting it; and, in particular, to point out the important consequences which result from the different degrees of rapidity in the circulation of different kinds of circulating medium, and also in the circulation of the same medium at different periods of time.

The nature of the institution of the Bank of England is then explained; the necessity of maintaining the accustomed, or nearly the accustomed, quantity of its notes, however great may be the fluctuations of its cash, is insisted on: and the suspension of its cash payments is shewn to have resulted neither from a deficiency in its resources, nor from a too great extension of its loans to government, nor from rashness or improvidence in its directors, but from circumstances which they had little power of controuling: this event being one to which a national establishment, like the Bank of England, is, in some situations of the country, unavoidably subject.

The manner in which an unfavourable balance of trade

affects the course of exchange, and in which an unfavourable exchange creates an excess of the market price above the mint price of gold, and a profit on the exportation of our coin, are the subjects of a succeeding Chapter.

The circumstances, also, which have led to the multiplication of our country banks, and the several advantages and disadvantages of those institutions, are fully stated.

The earlier parts of the work having tended to shew the evil of a too great and sudden diminution of our circulating medium, some of the latter Chapters are employed in pointing out the consequences of a too great augmentation of it. The limitation of the amount of the notes of the Bank of England is shewn to be the means of restricting the quantity of the circulating paper of the kingdom, of preventing a rise in the price of commodities in Great Britain, and of thus extending our exports and restraining our imports, and rendering the exchange more favourable. Some objections to the limitation of the Bank of England paper are likewise stated and answered.

The last Chapter treats of the influence of paper credit on the price of all the articles of life: a subject, the difficulties of which are in some degree removed by the antecedent discussions.

In the course of this enquiry, several passages in the work of Dr. A. Smith on the Wealth of Nations are animadverted on, as are also some observations made by Mr. Hume in his Essays on Money and on the Balance of Trade, and by Sir James Steuart in his book on Political Œconomy, as well as some remarks in the writings of Locke and Montesquieu.

The mode in which the subjects of coin, of paper credit, of the balance of trade, and of exchanges (subjects intimately connected with each other), have been treated by those writers, was suggested by the circumstances of more early times: and we ought not to be surprised, if, in treatises necessarily in some degree theoretical, or written for the purpose of establishing a particular truth, certain incidental observations should not be just, nor even if some main principles should have been laid down in terms not sufficiently guarded.

A person who presumes to differ from the authorities which have been mentioned, and who proposes to correct the public opinion on the important subject of our paper credit, ought, undoubtedly, to be very cautious lest he should propagate new errors while he is endeavouring to remove the old. A sense of the duty of mature consideration has caused some delay in the publication of the following work. That its leading doctrines are just, the writer feels a confident persuasion. That it may have imperfections, and some, perhaps, which greater care on his part might have corrected, he cannot doubt. But he trusts, that a man who is much occupied in the practical business of life, will be excused by the public, if he should present to them a treatise less elaborate, and, in many respects, more incomplete, than those on which he has found it necessary to remark. Future enquirers may possibly pursue, with advantage, some particular topics on which he has felt a certain degree of distrust.

It may not be irrelevant or improper to observe, that the present work has been written by a person whose situation in life has supplied information on several of the topics under discussion, and that much use has been made of those means of correcting the errors of former writers which recent events have afforded.

CONTENTS.

CHAP. VI.

AN ENQUIRY

INTO THE

NATURE AND EFFECTS

OF THE

PAPER CREDIT OF GREAT BRITAIN.

CHAP. I.

Of commercial Credit.—Of Paper Credit, as arising out of it. —Of commercial Capital.

COMMERCIAL credit may be defined to be that confidence which subsists among commercial men in respect to their mercantile affairs. This confidence operates in several ways. It disposes them to lend money to each other, to bring themselves under various pecuniary engagements by the acceptance and indorsement of bills, and also to sell and deliver goods in consideration of an equivalent promised to be given at a subsequent period. Even in that early and rude state of society, in which neither bills nor money are as yet known, it may be assumed, that if there be commerce, a certain degree of commercial credit will also subsist. In the interchange, for example, of commodities between the farmer and the manufacturer, the manufacturer, probably, will sometimes deliver goods to the farmer on the credit of the growing crop, in confidence that the farmer will come into possession of the fruits of his labour, and will be either compelled by the law of the land, or induced by a sense of justice, to fulfil his part of the contract when the harvest shall be over. In a variety of other cases it must happen, even in the infancy of society, that one man will deliver property to his neighbour without receiving, on the spot, the equivalent which is agreed to be given in return. It will occasionally be the interest of the one party thus to wait the other's convenience: for he that reposes the confidence will receive in the price an adequate compensation for the disadvantages incurred by the risk and the delay. In a society in which law and the sense of moral duty are weak, and property is consequently insecure, there will, of course, be little confidence or credit, and there will also be little commerce.

This commercial credit is the foundation of *paper credit;* paper serving to express that confidence which is in the mind, and to reduce to writing those engagements to pay, which might otherwise be merely verbal. It will hereafter be explained in what manner, and to how very great a degree, paper credit also spares the use of the expensive article of gold; and how the multiplication of paper securities serves to enlarge, confirm, and diffuse that confidence among traders, which, in some measure, existed independently of paper, and would, to a certain degree, remain, though paper should be abolished.

If there may be a convenience in giving credit in the infancy of society, when the interchange of commodities is small, there may be, at least, the same convenience when goods begin to be multiplied, when wealth is more variously distributed, and society is advanced.

The day on which it suits the British merchant to purchase and send away a large quantity of goods, may not be that on which he finds it convenient to pay for them. If it is made necessary for him to give ready money in return, he must always have in his hands a very large stock of money; and for the expence of keeping this fund (an expence consisting chiefly in the loss of interest) he must be repaid in the price of the commodities in which he deals. He avoids this charge, and also obtains time for preparing and adjusting his pecuniary concerns, by buying on credit; that is to say, by paying for his goods not by money, but by the delivery of a note in which he promises the money on a future day He is thus set more at liberty in his speculations; his judgment as to the propriety of buying or not buying, or of selling, or not selling, and also as to the time of doing either, may be more freely exercised.

The general principle, according to which the length of the customary credit in different trades has adjusted itself, seems clearly to have been that of mutual advantage and convenience. For example, if we suppose the merchant importers of any particular article for home consumption to be generally rich, and the retailers of it to be poor—that is, to have a capital insufficient to enable them to keep the assortment and stock of goods necessary in their retail commerce—the credit customarily given by the importers, and taken by the retail traders, will naturally be long. In other words, it will be the custom of the importers to lend part of their capital to the retail dealers, in consideration of an advantage in the price proportionate to the benefit conferred by the loan. Sometimes two or more customs prevail, as to the period of credit, in the same trade; and to each custom there are individual exceptions. The deviations from the rule obviously arise out of that principle of mutual advantage and convenience on which the rule itself has been founded.

The option of buying and of selling on longer or shorter credit, as it multiplies the number of persons able to buy and to sell, promotes free competition, and thus contributes to lower the price of articles. A variety of degrees in the length of credit which is afforded, tends more especially to give to some of the poorer traders a greater power of purchasing, and cherishes that particular sort of competition most adapted to lower prices, namely, the competition of dealers likely to be contented with a very moderate rate of gain. Opulent merchants sometimes complain of the intrusion of dealers who possess a small capital and take long credit, for this very reason, that such dealers reduce the profits of trade.

But the custom of taking and giving long credit has its inconveniences as well as its advantages. It encreases the amount of the bad debts incurred in the course of commercial transactions. The apprehension of loss, is, therefore, continually operating on the mind of the lender as a restraint on the custom of giving credit, while the compensation he receives for the use of the capital which he supplies, acts as an encouragement to the practice. The subsisting state of credit may, in general, be considered as resulting out of a comparison made both by lenders and borrowers of the advantages and disadvantages which each discover that they derive from giving and taking credit.

Mercantile confidence, however, is not always dealt out in that proportion in which there is reasonable ground for it. At some periods it has risen to a most unwarrantable height, and has given occasion to the most extravagant and hurtful speculations. Of these the cases of the Ayr bank, and of the South Sea scheme, are instances. Evils of this kind, however, have a tendency to correct themselves. In a country possessed of commercial knowledge and experience, confidence, in most instances, will not be misplaced.

Some persons are of opinion, that, when the custom of buying on credit is pushed very far, and a great quantity of individual dealings is in consequence carried on by persons having comparatively little property, the national commerce is to be considered as unsupported by a proper capital; and that a nation, under such circumstances, whatever may be its ostensible riches, exhibits the delusive appearance of wealth.

It must, however, be remembered, that the practice of buying on credit, in the internal commerce of the country, supposes the habit of selling on credit also to subsist; and to prevail, on the whole, in an exactly equal degree. In respect to the foreign trade of a country, the practice of dealing on credit indicates poverty or riches, in proportion as the credit generally taken is longer or shorter than the credit given. The custom which tradesmen have of selling to the consumers on credit, is also an indication of wealth in the commercial world; the traders must possess a surplus of wealth, either their own or borrowed, which bears an exact proportion to the amount of debts due to them by the consumers. Thus that practice of trading on credit which prevails among us, so far as it subsists between trader and trader, is an indication neither of wealth nor of poverty in the mercantile body; so far as it respects our transactions with foreign countries, is an indication of extraordinary wealth belonging to the merchants of Great Britain; and so far as it respects the trade between the retailer and the consumer, implies a deficiency of wealth in the consumers, and a proportionate surplus of it among commercial men. The existing customs imply, that, on the whole, there is among our traders a great abundance of wealth.

It may conduce to the prevention of error, in the subsequent discussions, to define, in this place, what is meant by commercial capital. This consists, first, in the goods (part of them in the course of manufacture) which are in the hands of our manufacturers and dealers, and are in their way to consumption. The amount of these is necessarily larger or smaller in proportion as the general expenditure is more or less considerable, and in proportion, also, as commodities pass more or less quickly into the hands of the consumer. It further consists in the ships, buildings, machinery, and other dead stock maintained for the purpose of carrying on our manufactures and commerce, under which head may be included the gold found necessary for the purposes of commerce, but at all times forming a very small item in this great account. It comprehends also the debts due to our traders for goods sold and delivered by them on credit; debts finally to be discharged by articles of value given in return.

Commercial capital, let it then be understood, consists not in paper, and is not augmented by the multiplication of this medium of payment. In one sense, indeed, it may be encreased by paper. I mean, that the nominal value of the existing goods may be enlarged through a reduction which is caused by paper in the value of that standard by which all property is estimated. The paper itself forms no part of the estimate.

This mode of computing the amount of the national

capital engaged in commerce, is substantially the same with that in which each commercial man estimates the value of his own property. Paper constitutes, it is true, an article on the credit side of the books of some men; but it forms an exactly equal item on the debit side of the books of others. It constitutes, therefore, on the whole, neither a debit nor a credit. The banker who issues twenty thousand pounds in notes, and lends in consequence twenty thousand pounds to the merchants on the security of bills accepted by them, states himself in his books to be debtor to the various holders of his notes to the extent of the sum in question; and states himself to be the creditor of the accepters of the bills in his possession to the same amount. His valuation, therefore, of his own property, is the same as if neither the bills nor the bank notes had any existence. Again; the merchants, in making their estimate of property, deduct the bills payable by themselves which are in the drawer of the banker, and add to their estimate the notes of the banker which are in their own drawer; so that the valuation, likewise, of the capital of the merchants is the same as if the paper had no existence. The use of paper does not, therefore, introduce any principle of delusion into that estimate of property which is made by individuals. The case of gold, on the other hand, differs from that of paper inasmuch as the possessor of gold takes credit for that for which no man debits himself. The several commercial capitals of traders, as estimated in their books, would, unquestionably, be found, if deducted from their other property and added together, to correspond, in amount, with a general estimate of the commercial stock of the country, calculated under the several heads already stated.

It is true, that men, in estimating their share in the public funds of the country, add to their estimate a debt due to them which no *individual* deducts from his valuation. On this head, it may be observed, that the nation is the debtor. But the commercial capital, which has been described, exists independently of capital in the public funds. The man in trade has property in trade. If he has property in the stocks, he has the property in trade in addition to it. In speaking, therefore, of the commercial capital, whether of the nation or of an individual, the idea that any part of it is composed either of the paper credit or of the stocks of the country, is to be totally excluded.

CHAP. II.

Of Trade by Barter.—Of Money.—Of Bills of Exchange and Notes.—Of Bills and Notes, considered as discountable Articles.—Of fictitious Bills, or Bills of Accommodation.

SOCIETY, in its rudest state, carries on its trade by the means only of barter. When most advanced, it still conducts its commerce on the same principle; for gold and silver coin, bankers' notes, and bills of exchange, may be considered merely as instruments employed for the purpose of facilitating the barter. The object is to exchange such a quantity of one sort of goods for such a quantity of another, as may be deemed, under all circumstances, a suitable equivalent*.

Barter being soon felt to be inconvenient, the precious metals are resorted to as a measure of value, they being, at once portable, steady in their price, and capable of subdi-

* By the term suitable equivalent, is not intended that equivalent which an impartial umpire, determining according to the strict rule of equity, might dictate. The equivalent obtained by men dealing in the way of barter is not exactly of this sort; for that power which the proprietors of a scarce and necessary commodity have over the consumers of it, will always lead them to demand a much higher price than the production of it may have cost.

In Africa, for example, where the mode of barter prevails, the price of rice is at some times equal to about two pounds, and at others to about sixteen pounds per ton. It cannot be supposed that the variations in the crops of different seasons can bear any proportion to this variation of prices. Monopoly also is an evil which is incident to trade as trade. It is, indeed, more particularly apt to exist in the infancy of commerce.

visions. The state fixes a stamp upon them, in order thus to certify the quantity and fineness of each piece.

The precious metals, when uncoined (or in the state of bullion), are themselves commodities; but when converted into money they are to be considered merely as a measure of the value of other articles. They may, indeed, be converted back into commodities; and it is one recommendation of their use as coin, that they are capable of this conversion.

We shall now advert to some of the simplest forms in which it may be supposed that paper credit will first exist.

To speak first of bills of exchange.

It is obvious, that, however portable gold may be in comparison of any other article which might be made a measure of value, to carry it in quantities to a great distance must prove incommodious. Let it be supposed, that there are in London ten manufacturers who sell their article to ten shopkeepers in York, by whom it is retailed; and that there are in York ten manufacturers of another commodity, who sell it to ten shopkeepers in London. There would be no occasion for the ten shopkeepers in London to send yearly to York, guineas for the payment of the York manufactures, and for the ten York shopkeepers to send yearly as many guineas to London. It would only be necessary for the York manufacturers to receive from each of the shopkeepers, at their own door, the money in question (for we may assume a sufficient quantity to be usually circulating in the place): giving in return letters which should acknowledge the receipt of it; and which should also direct the money, lying ready in the hands of their debtors in London, to be paid to the London shopkeepers, so as to cancel the debt in London in the same manner as that at York. The expence and the risk of all transmission of money would thus be saved; and the traders in question would of course be, on the whole, enabled to sell their article at a price proportionably lower than that which they would otherwise require. Letters ordering the transfer of the debt, are termed, in the language of the present day, bills of exchange. They are bills by which the debt of one person is exchanged for the debt of another: and the debt, perhaps, which is due in one place for the debt due in another.

To speak next of *Promissory Notes.*

When goods are delivered in consideration of an equivalent in money to be received at a subsequent period, it becomes desirable that, for the sake of precisely recording the day on which payment is to be made, and the exact amount of the sum, a note, expressing each of these particulars, should be given The term "value received" is introduced into the note, as also into every bill of exchange; that expression being deemed necessary in law to make the bill or the note binding.

Bills of exchange and notes have been hitherto considered as created only for those simple purposes for which they seem originally to have been drawn, and which are professed by the form always used in drawing them. Both these sorts of paper must now be spoken of as possessing an additional character, namely, that of being *Discountable Articles,* or articles which there is an opportunity of converting, at any time, into money; such a discount or deduction from the amount of the bill or note as is equal to the interest upon it, during the period for which it has to run, being paid as the price of the conversion. The bills of exchange, which were described as drawn from York on London, and as serving to transfer debts, would equally answer that purpose at whatever date they might be payable. It is customary, however, to make almost all bills payable at a period somewhat distant. Country bankers, for instance, and shopkeepers, who often act in this respect as bankers, indemnify themselves for the trouble and expence attending the drawing of bills, not by a commission, but by a protraction of the time at which the bills are to become payable. Thus is created a paper credit, which shall remain in existence for perhaps one or more months, and may serve, during any part of that time, as a discountable article.

Promissory notes were before represented as drawn on the occasion of the sale of goods, and made payable at a distant period. In returning to the more careful consideration of them, we shall discover the existence of the same disposition to multiply paper credit.

When a merchant in this country sells his goods on credit, it is, perhaps, not very important to him that he should receive from the buyer a promissory note (or an accepted bill, which is the same thing), if the only object of taking the note or bill is the ascertainment of the exact amount of the debt, and of the period of payment. It is true that the law gives superior facility to the recovery of debts for which promissory notes have been given. Nevertheless, if the sum be small, and the party in credit, all these advantages, in the present high state of confidence, would, in many cases, be thought scarcely to compensate even the trifling expence of the note stamp. The debt will be a book debt, if no note be taken; and, as such, may be sufficiently secure.

Notes, even for goods sold and delivered, are therefore to be considered as given chiefly for the sake of a convenience of another kind, which the seller finds in having them. The note, like the bill of exchange just spoken of, is a discountable article. It may be turned, if circumstances require, into money; or into bank notes, which answer the same purpose. It is not, perhaps, fully intended to turn the note or bill into money; they are taken rather as a provision against a contingency. The holder is rendered secure against the effect of disappointments in the receipt of cash. It is in this manner that his credit is fortified, and that he is enabled to fulfil with punctuality his pecuniary engagements; for there is a certain sort and quantity of bills and notes, on the turning of which into money, at the common rate of discount, the holder, if he be a man of credit, may almost as confidently rely as on the changing of a bank note into guineas, or of a guinea into silver.

The interest which traders have in being always possessed of a number of notes and bills, has naturally led to a great multiplication of them; and not only to the multiplication of notes given for goods sold, or of regular bills of exchange, but to the creation of numerous other notes and bills. Of these, some are termed notes and bills of accommodation: and the term fictitious is often applied to them. It may be useful to describe them particularly.

It was before shewn, that the principal motive for fabricating what must here be called the real note, that is, the note drawn in consequence of a real sale of goods, is the wish to have the means of turning it into money. The seller, therefore, who desires to have a note for goods sold, may be considered as taking occasion to ingraft on the transaction of the sale, the convenient condition of receiving from the buyer a discountable note of the same amount with the value of the goods. A fictitious note, or note of accommodation, is a note drawn for the same purpose of being discounted; though it is not also sanctioned by the circumstance of having been drawn in consequence of an actual sale of goods. Notes of accommodation are, indeed, of various kinds. The following description of one may suffice.

A, being in want of 100*l*., requests B to accept a note or bill drawn at two months, which B, therefore, on the face of it, is bound to pay; it is understood, however, that A will take care either to discharge the bill himself, or to furnish B with the means of paying it. A obtains ready money for the bill on the joint credit of the two parties. A fulfils his promise of paying it when due, and thus concludes the transaction. This service rendered by B to A is, however, not unlikely to be requited at a more or less distant period by a similar acceptance of a bill on A, drawn and discounted for B's convenience.

Let us now compare such a bill with a real bill. Let us consider in what points they differ, or seem to differ; and in what they agree.

They agree, inasmuch as each is a discountable article; each has also been created for the purpose of being discounted: and each is, perhaps, discounted in fact. Each therefore, serves equally to supply means of speculation to the merchant. So far, moreover, as bills and notes constitute what is called the circulating medium, or paper currency, of the country (a topic which shall not be here anticipated), and prevent the use of guineas, the fictitious and the real bill are upon an equality; and if the price of commodities be raised in proportion to the quantity of paper currency, the one contributes to that rise exactly in the same manner as the other.

Before we come to the points in which they differ, let us advert to one point in which they are commonly supposed to be unlike; but in which they cannot be said always or necessarily to differ.

"Real notes," it is sometimes said, "represent actual "property. There are actual goods in existence, which are "the counterpart to every real note. Notes which are not "drawn, in consequence of a sale of goods, are a species of "false wealth, by which a nation is deceived. These supply "only an imaginary capital; the others indicate one that is "real."

In answer to this statement it may be observed, first, that the notes given in consequence of a real sale of goods cannot be considered as, on that account, *certainly* representing any actual property. Suppose that A sells one hundred pounds worth of goods to B at six months credit, and takes a bill at six months for it; and that B, within a month after, sells the same goods, at a like credit, to C, taking a like bill; and again, that C, after another month, sells them to D, taking a like bill, and so on. There may then, at the end of six months, be six bills of 100*l.* each existing at the same time; and every one of these may possibly have been discounted. Of all these bills, then, one only represents any actual property.

In the next place it is obvious, that the number of those bills which are given in consequence of sales of goods, and which, nevertheless, do not represent property, is liable to be encreased through the extension of the length of credit given on the sale of goods. If, for instance, we had supposed the credit given to be a credit of twelve months instead of six, 1,200*l.* instead of 600*l.* would have been the amount of the bills drawn on the occasion of the sale of goods; and

1,100*l.* would have been the amount of that part of these which would represent no property.

In order to justify the supposition that a real bill (as it is called) represents actual property, there ought to be some power in the bill-holder to prevent the property which the bill represents, from being turned to other purposes than that of paying the bill in question. No such power exists; neither the man who holds the real bill, nor the man who discounts it, has any property in the specific goods for which it was given: he as much trusts to the general ability to pay of the giver of the bill, as the holder of any fictitious bill does. The fictitious bill may, in many cases, be a bill given by a person having a large and known capital, a part of which the fictitious bill may be said, in that case, to represent. The supposition that real bills represent property, and that fictitious bills do not, seems, therefore, to be one by which more than justice is done to one of these species of bills, and something less than justice to the other.

We come next to some points in which they differ.

First, the fictitious note, or note of accommodation, is liable to the objection that it professes to be what it is not. This objection, however, lies only against those fictitious bills which are passed as real. In many cases, it is sufficiently obvious what they are. Secondly, the fictitious bill is, in general, less likely to be punctually paid than the real one. There is a general presumption, that the dealer in fictitious bills is a man who is a more adventurous speculator than he who carefully abstains from them. It follows, thirdly, that fictitious bills, besides being less safe, are less subject to limitation as to their quantity. The extent of a man's actual sales form some limit to the amount of his real notes; and, as it is highly desirable in commerce that credit should be dealt out to all persons in some sort of regular and due proportion, the measure of a man's actual sales, certified by the appearance of his bills drawn in virtue of those sales, is some rule in the case, though a very imperfect one in many respects.

A fictitious bill, or bill of accommodation, is evidently,

in substance, the same as any common promissory note; and even better, in this respect,—that there is but one security to the promissory note, whereas, in the case of the bill of accommodation, there are two. So much jealousy subsists lest traders should push their means of raising money too far, that paper, the same in its general nature with that which is given, being the only paper which can be given, by men out of business, is deemed somewhat discreditable when coming from a merchant. And because such paper, when in the merchant's hand, necessarily imitates the paper which passes on the occasion of a sale of goods, the epithet fictitious has been cast upon it; an epithet which has seemed to countenance the confused and mistaken notion, that there is something altogether false and delusive in the nature of a certain part both of the paper and of the apparent wealth of the country.

Bills of exchange are drawn upon London to a great amount, from all parts, not only of Great Britain, but of the world; and the grounds on which they have been drawn in a great degree elude observation. A large proportion of them, no doubt partakes of the nature of bills of accommodation. They have, however, in general, that shape communicated to them, whatever it may be, which is thought likely to render them discountable; and it is not difficult, as the preceding observations will have shewn, to make use of some real, and, at the same time, of many seeming, transactions of commerce as a ground for drawing, and as a means of multiplying such bills.

The practice of creating a paper credit, by drawing and re-drawing, has been particularly described by Dr. Adam Smith; and is stated by him to have a tendency which is very ruinous to the party resorting to it. This practice, however, is often carried on at much less expence to those engaged in it than Dr. Smith imagines. A, for instance, of London, draws a bill at two months on B, of Amsterdam, and receives immediate money for the bill. B enables himself to pay the bill by drawing, when it is nearly due, a bill at two months on A for the same sum, which bill he sells or discounts; and

A again finds the means of payment by again drawing a bill, at two months, on B. The transaction is, in substance, obviously the same as if A and B had borrowed, on their joint security, the sum in question for six months. The ground on which transactions of this sort have been stated by Dr. Adam Smith to be ruinous is, that of the heavy expence of a commission on every bill drawn, which is paid by him who raises money in this manner. If, for instance, one-half per cent. is the commission, and the bills are drawn at two months, and a discount of five per cent. per annum is paid, the money is raised at an interest of eight per cent. Such transactions, however, are often carried on alternately for the benefit of each of the two parties; that is to say, at one time the transaction is on the account of A, who pays a commission to B; at another it is on the account of B, who pays a commission to A. Thus each party, on the whole, gains about as much as he pays in the shape of such commissions; and the discount in turning the bill into money, which is the same as that on any other bill, may, therefore, be considered as the whole expence incurred. Money may be raised in this manner at an interest of only five per cent. In the case recently proposed, the drawing and re-drawing were imagined to be only between A, of London, and B, of Amsterdam. This practice, however, is often carried on between three or more parties drawing from three or more places. In such case, the draft is drawn on the place on which the existing course of exchange shews that it will best answer to draw it. An operation of this sort may obviously be carried on partly for the purpose of raising money, and partly for that of profiting by a small turn in the exchange. Transactions which are the converse to this, are, on the other hand, entered into by those who happen to possess ready money. They remit, if the exchange seems to favour their remittance, and draw in consequence of having remitted. To determine what bills are fictitious, or bills of accommodation, and what are real, is often a point of difficulty. Even the drawers and remitters themselves frequently either do not know, or do not take the trouble to reflect, whether the bills ought

23

more properly to be considered as of the one class or of the other; and the private discounter, or banker, to whom they are offered, still more frequently finds the credit of the bills to be the only rule which it is possible to follow in judging whether he ought to discount them.

CHAP. III.

Of circulating Paper—of Bank Notes—of Bills considered as circulating Paper—different Degrees of Rapidity in the Circulation of different Sorts of circulating Medium and of the same Sort of circulating Medium at different Times—Error of Dr. A. Smith—Difference in the Quantities wanted for effecting the Payments of a Country in Consequence of this Difference of Rapidity—Proof of this taken from Events of 1793*—Fallacy involved in the Supposition that Paper Credit might be abolished.*

WE proceed next to speak of circulating paper, and first of *Notes payable to Bearer on Demand,* whether issued by a public bank or by a private banker.

When confidence rises to a certain height in a country, it occurs to some persons, that profit may be obtained by issuing notes, which purport to be exchangeable for money; and which, through the known facility of thus exchanging them, may circulate in its stead; a part only of the money, of which the notes supply the place, being kept in store as a provision for the current payments. On the remainder interest is gained, and this interest constitutes the profit of the issuer. Some powerful and well accredited company will probably be the first issuers of paper of this sort, the numerous proprietors of the company exerting their influence, for the sake of the dividends which they expect, in giving currency to the new paper credit. The establishment of a great public bank has a tendency to promote the institution of private banks. The public bank, obliged to provide itself largely with money for its own payments, becomes a reservoir of gold to which private banks may resort with little difficulty, expence, or delay, for the supply of their several necessities.

Dr. A. Smith, in his chapter on Paper Credit, considers the national stock of money in the same light with those machines and instruments of trade which require a certain expence, first, to erect, and afterwards to support them. And he proceeds to observe, that the substitution of paper, in the room of gold and silver coin, serves to replace a very expensive instrument of commerce with one much less costly, and sometimes equally convenient. "Thus," he says, "a "banker, by issuing 100,000*l.* in notes, keeping 20,000*l.* in "hand for his current payments, causes 20,000*l.* in gold and "silver to perform all the functions which 100,000*l.* would "otherwise have performed; in consequence of which, "80,000*l.* of gold and silver can be spared, which will not "fail to be exchanged for foreign goods, and become a new "fund for a new trade, producing profit to the country."*

Dr. Smith, although he discusses at some length the subject of Paper Circulation, does not at all advert to the tendency of bills of exchange to spare the use of bank paper, or to their faculty of supplying its place in many cases.

In the former Chapter it was shewn that bills, though

* Dr. Smith, in conformation of this, remarks how greatly Scotland had been enriched in the twent -five or thirty years preceding the time at which he wrote, by the erection of new banks in almost every considerable town, and even in some country villages, the effects having been, as he affirms, precisely those which he had described. The trade of Glasgow he states to have been doubled in about fifteen years after the erection of its first bank, and the trade of Scotland to be thought to have been more than quadrupled since the first erection of its two first public banking companies. This effect, indeed, he conceives to be too great to be accounted for by that cause alone; though he deems it indisputable, that the banks have essentially contributed to the augmentation of the trade and industry of Scotland. The gold and silver of Scotland, circulating before the union, is estimated by him at full a million; the quantity since the union at less than half a million; and the paper circulating in Scotland since the union at about one million and a half.

professedly drawn for the purpose of exchanging a debt due to one person for a debt due to another, are, in fact, created rather for the sake of serving as a discountable article, and of forming a provision against contingencies; and that, by being at any time convertible into cash (that is, into either money or bank notes) they render that supply of cash which is necessary to be kept in store much less considerable.

But they not only spare the use of ready money; they also occupy its place in many cases. Let us imagine a farmer in the country to discharge a debt of 10*l.* to his neighbouring grocer, by giving to him a bill for that sum, drawn on his cornfactor in London for grain sold in the metropolis; and the grocer to transmit the bill, he having previously indorsed it, to a neighbouring sugar-baker, in discharge of a like debt; and the sugar-baker to send it, when again indorsed, to a West India merchant in an outport, and the West India merchant to deliver it to his country banker, who also indorses it, and sends it into further circulation. The bill in this case will have effected five payments exactly as if it were a 10*l.* note payable to bearer on demand. It will, however, have circulated in consequence chiefly of the confidence placed by each receiver of it in the last indorser, his own correspondent in trade; whereas, the circulation of a bank note is owing rather to the circumstance of the name of the issuer being so well known as to give to it an universal credit. A multitude of bills pass between trader and trader in the country in the manner which has been described; and they evidently form, in the strictest sense, a part of the circulating medium of the kingdom.*

Bills, however, and especially those which are drawn for

* Mr. Boyd, in his publication addressed to Mr. Pitt on the Subject of the Bank of England Issues, propagates the same error into which many others have fallen, of considering bills as no part of the circulating medium of the country. He says, "by the words means of circulation," "circulating medium," and "currency," (which are used as "synonymous terms in this Letter) I understand always ready money, "whether consisting of bank notes or specie, in contradiction to *bills of* "*exchange*, navy bills, exchequer bills, or any negotiable paper which "form no part of the circulating medium, as I have always understood

large sums, may be considered as in general circulating more slowly than either gold or bank notes, and for a reason which it is material to explain. Bank notes, though they yield an interest to the issuer, afford none to the man who detains them in his possession; they are to him as unproductive as guineas. The possessor of a bank note, therefore, makes haste to part with it. The possessor of a bill of exchange possesses, on the contrary, that which is always growing more valuable. The bill, when it is first drawn, is worth something less than a bank note, on account of its not being due until a distant day; and the first receiver of it may be supposed to obtain a compensation for the inferiority of its value in the price of the article with which the bill is purchased. When he parts with it, he may be considered as granting to the next receiver a like compensation, which is proportionate to the time which the Bill has still to run. Each holder of a bill has, therefore, an interest in detaining it.

Bills, it is true, generally pass among traders in the country without there being any calculation or regular allowance of discount; the reason of which circumstance is, that there is a generally understood period of time for which those bills may have to run, which, according to the custom of traders, are accepted as current payment. If any bill given in payment has a longer time than usual to run, he who receives it is considered as so far favouring the person from whom he takes it; and the favoured person has to compensate for this advantage, not, perhaps, by a recompence of the same kind accurately calculated, but in the general adjustment of the pecuniary affairs of the two parties.

This quality in bills of exchange (and it might be added of interest notes, &c.) of occupying the place of bank paper,

---

"that term. The latter is the circulator; the former are merely objects "of circulation."....See note to the first page of Mr. Boyd's Letter to Mr. Pitt.

It will be seen, in the progress of this work, that it was necessary to clear away much confusion which has arisen from the want of a sufficiently full acquaintance with the several kinds of paper credit; and in particular, to remove, by a considerable detail, the prevailing errors respecting the nature of bills, before it could be possible to reason properly upon the effects of paper credit.

and of also throwing the interest accruing during their detention into the pocket of the *holder,* contributes greatly to the use of them. The whole trading world may be considered as having an interest in encouraging them. To possess some article which, so long as it is detained, shall produce a regular interest, which shall be subject to no fluctuations in price, which, by the custom of commerce, shall pass in certain cases as a payment, and shall likewise be convertible into ready money by the sacrifice of a small discount, is the true policy of the merchant. Goods will not serve this purpose, because they do not grow more valuable by detention; nor stocks, because, though they yield an interest, they fluctuate much in value; and, also, because the expence of brokerage is incurred in selling them, not to mention the inconveniences arising from the circumstance of their being transferable only in the books of the Bank of England. Stocks, however, by being at all times a saleable and ready money article, are, to a certain degree, held by persons in London on the same principle as bills, and serve, therefore, in some measure, like bills, if we consider these as a discountable article, to spare the use of bank notes. Exchequer bills will not fully answer the purpose, because there is a commission on the sale of these, as on the sale of stocks; and because, not to speak of some other inferior objections to them, they fluctuate, in some small degree, in price.

Bills, since they circulate chiefly among the trading world, come little under the observation of the public. The amount of bills in existence may yet, perhaps, be at all times greater than the amount of all the bank notes of every kind, and of all the circulating guineas.*

The amount of what is called the circulating medium of a country has been supposed by some to bear a regular proportion to the quantity of trade and of payments. It has,

* Liverpool and Manchester effect the whole of their larger mercantile payments not by country bank notes, of which none are issued by the banks of those places, but by bills at one or two months date, drawn on London. The bills annually drawn by the banks of each of those towns amount to many millions. The banks obtain a small commission on these bills.

however, been shewn, that such part of the circulating medium as yields an interest to the holder will effect much fewer payments, in proportion to its amount, than the part which yields to the holder no interest. A number of country bank notes, amounting to 100*l.*, may, for instance, effect on an average one payment in three days; while a bill of 100*l.* may, through the disposition of each holder to detain it, effect only one payment in nine days.

There is a passage in the work of Dr. Adam Smith which serves to inculcate the error of which I have been speaking; a passage on which it may be useful to comment with some particularity.

He says, "The whole paper money of *every kind* which "can *easily* circulate in any country, never can exceed the "value of the gold and silver of which it supplies the place, "or which (the commerce being supposed the same) would "circulate there, if there was no paper money."

Does Dr. Smith mean to include, in his idea of "the "*whole* paper money of *every kind* which can easily circulate," all the bills of exchange of a country, or does he not? And does he also include interest notes, exchequer bills, and India bonds, and those other articles which very much resemble bills of exchange? In an earlier part of his chapter, he has this observation—"There are different sorts of paper money; "but the circulating notes of banks and bankers are the "species which is best known, and which seems best adapted for this purpose." We are led to judge by this passage, and also by the term "paper money of *every kind*" in the passage before quoted, that it was his purpose to include bills of exchange; on the other hand, if *all* the bills of exchange of a country are to be added to the bank notes which circulate, it becomes then so manifest, that the whole of the paper must be more than equal to the amount of the money which would circulate if there were no paper, that we feel surprised that the erroneousness of the position did not strike Dr. Smith himself. He introduces, indeed, the qualifying word "easily;" he speaks of "the whole paper money of every "kind which can *easily* circulate." But this term, as I ap-

29

prehend, is meant only to refer to an easy, in contradistinction to a forced, paper circulation; for it is on the subject of a forced circulation that a great part of his observations turn. He seems, on the other hand, to have paid no regard to the distinction on which I have dwelt, of a more slow and a more rapid circulation; a thing which is quite different from an easy and a difficult circulation. He appears, in short, not at all to have reflected how false his maxim is rendered (if laid down in the terms which he has used) both by the different degrees of rapidity of circulation which generally belong to the two different classes of paper of which I have spoken, and also by the different degrees of rapidity which may likewise belong to the circulation of the same kinds of paper, and even of the same guineas, at different times.

The error of Dr. Smith, then, is this:—he represents the whole paper, which can easily circulate when there are no guineas, to be the same in quantity with the guineas which would circulate if there were no paper; whereas, it is the quantity not of "the thing which circulates," that is, of the thing which is *capable of* circulation, but of the actual circulation which should rather be spoken of as the same in both cases. The quantity of circulating paper, that is, of paper capable of circulation, may be great, and yet the quantity of actual circulation may be small, or *vice versa.* The same note may either effect ten payments in one day, or one payment in ten days; and one note, therefore, will effect the same payments in the one case, which it would require a hundred notes to effect in the other.

I have spoken of the different degrees of rapidity in the circulation of *different kinds* of paper, and of the consequent difference of the quantity of each which is wanted in order to effect the same payments. I shall speak next of the different degrees of rapidity in the circulation of the *same* medium at *different times:* and, first, of bank notes.

The causes which lead to a variation in the rapidity of the circulation of bank notes may be several. In general, it may be observed, that a high state of confidence serves to quicken their circulation; and this happens upon a principle which shall be fully explained. It must be premised, that by the phrase a more or less quick circulation of notes, will be meant a more or less quick circulation of the whole of them on an average. Whatever encreases that reserve, for instance, of Bank of England notes which remains in the drawer of the London banker as his provision against contingencies, contributes to what will here be termed the less quick circulation of the whole. Now a high state of confidence contributes to make men provide less amply against contingencies. At such a time, they trust, that if the demand upon them for a payment, which is now doubtful and contingent, should actually be made, they shall be able to provide for it at the moment; and they are loth to be at the expence of selling an article, or of getting a bill discounted, in order to make the provision much before the period at which it shall be wanted. When, on the contrary, a season of distrust arises, prudence suggests, that the loss of interest arising from a detention of notes for a few additional days should not be regarded.

It is well known that guineas are hoarded, in times of alarm, on this principle. Notes, it is true, are not hoarded to the same extent; partly because notes are not supposed equally likely, in the event of any general confusion, to find their value, and partly because the class of persons who are the holders of notes is less subject to weak and extravagant alarms. In difficult times, however, the disposition to hoard, or rather to be largely provided with Bank of England notes, will, perhaps, prevail in no inconsiderable degree.

This remark has been applied to Bank of England notes, because these are always in high credit; and it ought, perhaps, to be chiefly confined to these. They constitute the coin in which the great mercantile payments in London, which are payments on account of the whole country, are effected. If, therefore, a difficulty in converting bills of exchange into notes is apprehended, the effect both on bankers, merchants, and tradesmen, is somewhat the same as the effect of an apprehension entertained by the lower class of a difficulty in converting Bank of England notes or bankers' notes into guineas. The apprehension of the approaching difficulty makes men eager to do that to-day, which otherwise they would do to-morrow.

The truth of this observation, as applied to Bank of England notes, as well as the importance of attending to it, may be made manifest by adverting to the events of the year 1793, when, through the failure of many country banks, much general distrust took place. The alarm, the first material one of the kind which had for a long time happened, was extremely great. It does not appear that the Bank of England notes, at that time in circulation, were fewer than usual. It is certain, however, that the existing number became, at the period of apprehension, insufficient for giving punctuality to the payments of the metropolis; and it is not to be doubted, that the insufficiency must have arisen, in some measure, from that slowness in the circulation of notes, naturally attending an alarm, which has been just described. Every one fearing lest he should not have his notes ready when the day of payment should come, would endeavour to provide himself with them somewhat beforehand. A few merchants, from a natural though hurtful timidity, would keep in their own hands some of those notes, which, in other times, they would have lodged with their bankers; and the effect would be, to cause the same quantity of bank paper to transact fewer payments, or, in other words, to lessen the rapidity of the circulation of notes on the whole, and thus to encrease the number of notes wanted. Probably, also, some Bank of England paper would be used as a substitute for country bank notes suppressed.

The success of the remedy which the parliament administered, denotes what was the nature of the evil. A loan of exchequer bills was directed to be made to as many mercantile persons, giving proper security, as should apply. It is a fact, worthy of serious attention, that the failures abated greatly, and mercantile credit began to be restored, not at the period when the exchequer bills were actually delivered, but at a time antecedent to that æra. It also deserves notice, that though the failures had originated in an extraordinary demand for guineas, it was not any supply of gold which effected the cure. That fear of not being able to obtain guineas, which arose in the country, led, in its consequences, to an extraordinary demand for bank notes in London; and the want of bank notes in London became, after a time, the chief evil. The very expectation of a supply of exchequer bills, that is, of a supply of an article which almost any trader might obtain, and which it was known that he might then sell, and thus turn into bank notes, and after turning into bank notes might also convert into guineas, created an idea of general solvency. This expectation cured, in the first instance, the distress of London, and it then lessened the demand for guineas in the country, through that punctuality in effecting the London payments which it produced, and the universal confidence which it thus inspired. The sum permitted by parliament to be advanced in exchequer bills was five millions, of which not one half was taken. Of the sum taken, no part was lost. On the contrary, the small compensation, or extra interest, which was paid to government for lending its credit (for it was mere credit, and not either money or bank notes that the government advanced), amounted to something more than was necessary to defray the charges, and a small balance of profit accrued to the public. For this seasonable interference, a measure at first not well understood and opposed at the time, chiefly on the ground of constitutional jealousy, the mercantile as well as the manufacturing interests of the country were certainly much indebted to the parliament, and to the government.

That a state of distrust causes a slowness in the circulation of *guineas*, and that at such a time a greater quantity of money will be wanted in order to effect only the same money payments, is a position which scarcely needs to be proved. Some observations, however, on this subject may not be useless. When a season of extraordinary alarm arises, and the money of the country in some measure disappears, the guineas, it is commonly said, are hoarded. In a certain degree this assertion may be literally true. But the scarcity of gold probably results chiefly from the circumstance of a considerable variety of persons, country bankers, shopkeepers, and others, augmenting, some in a smaller and some in a more ample measure, that supply which it had been customary to keep by them. The stock thus enlarged is not a fund which its possessor purposes, in no case, to diminish, but a fund which, if he has occasion to lessen it, he endeavours, as he has opportunity, to replace. It is thus that a more slow circulation of guineas is occasioned; and the slower the circulation, the greater the quantity wanted, in order to effect the same number of money payments.

Thus, then, it appears, that the sentiment which Dr. Smith leads his readers to entertain, namely, that there is in every country a certain fixed quantity of paper, supplying the place of gold, which is all that "can easily circulate" (or circulate without being *forced* into circulation), and which is all (for such, likewise, seems to be the intended inference) that should ever be allowed to be sent into circulation, is, in a variety of respects, incorrect. The existence of various hoards of gold in the coffers of bankers, and of the Bank of England, while there are no corresponding hoards of paper, would of itself forbid any thing like accurate comparison between them. Many additional, though smaller, circumstances might be mentioned as contributing to prevent the quantity of notes which will circulate from being the same as the quantity of gold which would circulate if there were no notes; such as their superior convenience in a variety of respects, the facility of sending them by post, the faculty which they have of being either used as guineas, or of supplying the place of bills of exchange, and furnishing a remittance to distant places.

There is a further objection to the same remark of Dr. Smith. It would lead an uninformed person to conceive, that the trade of a country, and of this country in particular, circumstanced as it now is, might be carried on altogether by guineas, if bank notes of all kinds were by any means annihilated. It may already have occurred, that if bank paper were abolished, a substitute for it would be likely to be found, to a certain degree, in bills of exchange; and that these, on account of their slower circulation, must, in that case, be much larger in amount than the notes of which they would take the place. But further; if bills and bank notes were extinguished, other substitutes than gold would unquestionably be found. Recourse would be had to devices of various kinds by which men would save themselves the trouble of counting, weighing, and transporting guineas, in all the larger operations of commerce, so that the amount of guineas brought into use would not at all correspond with the amount of the bills and notes suppressed. Banks would be instituted, not of the description which now exist, but of that kind and number which should serve best to spare both the trouble of gold, and the expence incurred by the loss of interest upon the quantity of it in possession. Merely by the transfer of the debts of one merchant to another, in the books of the banker, a large portion of what are termed cash payments is effected at this time without the use of any bank paper,* and a much larger sum would be thus transferred, if guineas were the only circulating

* The following custom, now prevailing among the bankers within the city of London, may serve to illustrate this observation, and also to shew the strength of the disposition which exists in those who are not the issuers of bank notes to spare the use both of paper and guineas. It is the practice of each of these bankers to send a clerk, at an agreed hour in the afternoon, to a room provided for their use. Each clerk there exchanges the drafts on other bankers received at his own house, for the drafts on his own house received at the houses of other bankers. The balances of the several bankers are transferred in the same room, from one to another, in a manner which it is unnecessary to explain in detail, and the several balances are finally wound up by each clerk into one balance. The difference between the whole sum which each banker has to pay to all other city bankers, and the whole sum which he has to receive of all other city bankers, is, therefore, all that is discharged in bank notes or money; a difference much less in its amount than the *several* differences would be equal to. This device, which serves to spare the use of bank notes, may suggest the practicability of a great variety of contrivances for sparing the use of gold, to which men having confidence in each other would naturally resort, if we could suppose bank paper to be abolished.

medium of the country. Credit would still exist; credit in books, credit depending on the testimony of witnesses, or on the mere verbal promise of parties. It might not be paper credit; but still it might be such credit as would spare, more or less, the use of guineas. It might be credit of a worse kind, less accurately dealt out in proportion to the desert of different persons, and therefore, in some instances, at least, still more extended; it might be credit less contributing to punctuality of payments, and to the due fulfilment of engagements; less conducive to the interests of trade, and to the cheapening of articles; and it would, perhaps, also be credit quite as liable to interruption on the occasion of any sudden alarm or material change in the commercial prospects and circumstances of the country.

CHAP. IV.

Observation of Dr. Smith respecting the Bank of England—Of the Nature of that Institution—Reasons for never greatly diminishing its Notes—Its Liability to be exhausted of Guineas—The Suspension of its Cash Payments not owing to too great Issue of Paper—Nor to too great Loans—Propriety of parliamentary Interference.

DR. ADAM SMITH, after laying down the principle which has been lately animadverted on "that the quantity of "paper which can easily circulate in a country never can "exceed the gold and silver which would circulate if there "were no paper," proceeds to observe, that the Bank of England, "by issuing too great a quantity of paper, of "which the excess was continually returning, in order to be "exchanged for gold and silver, was, for many years toge-"ther, obliged to coin gold to the extent of between eight "hundred thousand pounds and a million a year. For this "great coinage the bank was frequently obliged to purchase "gold bullion at 4*l.* an ounce, which it soon after issued in "coin at 3*l.* 17*s.* 10½*d.* an ounce, losing two and a half and "three per cent. on the coinage." Dr. Smith probably could not be acquainted with the secret of the actual quantity of those bank notes, of the number of which he complains; he must, therefore, have taken it for granted, that they were what he terms excessive, on the ground of the price of gold being high, and the coinage great. He does not proceed, in any respect, to guard or to limit the observation in question; an observation which, when thus unqualified, may lead the reader to suppose, that whenever the bank finds itself subjected to any great demand for gold in consequence of a high price of bullion, the cause of this evil is an excess of circulating paper, and the remedy a reduction of bank notes. There is also danger, lest it should be conceived, that if the remedy should appear to fail, it can fail only because the reduction is not sufficiently great.

The point of which we are speaking is of great importance, and will be the subject of much future discussion. One object of the present and succeeding Chapter will be to shew, that, however just may be the principle of Dr. Smith when properly limited and explained, the reduction of the quantity of Bank of England paper is by no means a measure which ought to be resorted to on the occasion of every demand upon the bank for guineas arising from the high price of bullion, and that such reduction may even aggravate that sort of rise which is caused by an alarm in the country.

It will be proper, first, to describe the nature of the institution of the Bank of England, and the relation in which it stands to the public; in this detail, the event of the late stoppage of its cash payments will be particularly noticed.

Bills are drawn on London from every quarter of the kingdom, and remittances are sent to the metropolis to provide for them, while London draws no bills, or next to none, upon the country. London is, in this respect, to the whole island, in some degree, what the centre of a city is to the suburbs. The traders may dwell in the suburbs, and lodge many goods there, and they may carry on at home a variety of smaller payments, while their chief cash account is with the banker, who fixes his residence among the other bankers, in the heart of the city. London also is become, especially of late, the trading metropolis of Europe, and, indeed, of the whole world; the foreign drafts, on account of merchants living in our out-ports and other trading towns, and carrying on business there, being made, with scarcely any exceptions, payable in London. The metropolis, moreover, through the extent of its own commerce, and the greatness of its wealth and population, has immense receipts and payments on its own account; and the circumstance of its being the seat of government, and the place where the public dividends are paid, serves to encrease its pecuniary transactions. The practice, indeed, of transferring the payments of the country to London being once begun, was likely to extend itself. For, in proportion as the amount and number of payments and receipts is augmented in any one particular place, the business of paying and receiving is more easily and cheaply transacted, the necessary guineas becoming fewer in proportion to the sums to be received and paid; and the bank notes wanted, though encreasing on the whole, becoming fewer in proportion also. On the punctuality with which the accustomed payments of London are effected, depends, therefore, most essentially the whole commercial credit of Great Britain. The larger London payments are effected exclusively through the paper of the Bank of England; for the superiority of its credit is such, that, by common agreement among the bankers, whose practice, in this respect, almost invariably guides that of other persons, no note of a private house will pass in payment as a paper circulation in London.

The bank has a capital of near twelve millions, to which it has added near four millions of undivided profits or savings: all this capital and savings must be lost before the creditors can sustain any loss.

The Bank of England is quite independent of the executive government. It has an interest, undoubtedly (of the same kind with that of many private individuals), in the maintenance of our financial as well as commercial credit. It is also in the habit of lending out a large portion of its ample funds on government securities of various kinds, a comparatively small part only, though a sum not small in itself, being lent to the merchants in the way of discount. The ground on which the bank lends so much to government is clearly that of mutual convenience, as well as long habit. It is the only lender in the country on a large scale; the government is the only borrower on a scale equally extended; and the two parties, like two wholesale traders in a town, the one the only great buyer, and the other the only great seller of the same article, naturally deal much with each other, and have comparatively small transactions with those who carry on only a more contracted business. The bank, moreover, in time of peace, is much benefited by lending to Government. It naturally, therefore, continues those loans, during war, which it had been used to grant at all antecedent periods. It occasionally furnishes a considerable sum to the East India company. If, indeed, it lent more to the merchants during war, and less to the government, the difference would not be so great as might, perhaps, at first view be supposed. If, for instance, it furnished a smaller sum on the security of exchequer bills, that article might then be supposed to fall in price, or, in other words, to yield a higher and more tempting interest; and the bankers, in that case, would buy more exchequer bills, and would grant less aid to the merchants; they would, at least, in some degree, take up whichever trade the Bank of England should relinquish. The preference given by the bank to the government securities, is, therefore, no symptom of a want of independence in its directors; they are subject, in a much greater degree, to their own proprietors than to any administration. The strong manner in which the directors of the bank* at the

* See the correspondence of the bank on this subject, in the Appendix to the Report of the House of Commons respecting the order of council for authorising the suspension of the cash payments of the bank.

time antecedent to the suspension of their cash payments, insisted on having four millions and a half paid up to them by the government—a payment which, though demanded at a very inconvenient time, was accordingly made—may be mentioned as one sufficiently striking mark of the independence of that company. There is, however, another much more important circumstance to be noticed, which is conclusive on this subject. The government of Great Britain is under little or no *temptation* either to dictate to the Bank of England, or to lean upon it in any way which is inconvenient or dangerous to the bank itself. The minister has been able to raise annually, without the smallest difficulty, by means of our funding system, the sum of no less than between twenty and thirty millions. The government, therefore, is always able to lessen, by a loan from the public, if it should be deemed necessary, the amount of its debt running with the bank. To suppose that bank notes are issued to excess, with a view to furnish means of lending money to the minister, is, in a high degree, unreasonable. The utmost sum which he could hope to gain in the way of loan from the bank, by means of an extraordinary issue of bank notes, could hardly be more than four or five millions; and it is not easy to believe, that a government which can raise at once twenty or thirty millions, will be likely, for the sake of only four or five millions (for the loan of which it must pay nearly the same interest as for a loan from the public), to derange the system, distress the credit, or endanger the safety of the Bank of England.* This banking company differs in this most important point from every one of those national banks, which issue paper, on the continent. I understand that the banks of Petersburgh, Copenhagen, Stockholm, Vienna, Madrid, and Lisbon, each of which issues circulating notes, which pass as current payment, are

* The same remark has been made in a short pamphlet lately published by Sir Francis Baring.

all in the most direct and strict sense government banks.* It is also well known, that the governments residing in these several places have not those easy means of raising money, by a loan from the people, which the minister of Great Britain so remarkably possesses. Those governments, therefore, have, in times even of moderate difficulty, no other resource than that of extending the issue of the paper of their own banks; which extension of issue naturally produces a nearly correspondent depreciation of the value of the notes, and a fall in the exchange with other countries, if computed at the paper price. The notes, moreover, being once thus depreciated, the government, even supposing its embarrassments to cease, is seldom disposed to bring them back to their former limits, to do which implies some sacrifice on their part at the time of effecting the reduction; but it contents itself, perhaps, with either a little lessening, or with not further adding to, the evil. The expectation of the people on the continent, therefore, generally is, that the paper, which is falling in value, will, in better times, only cease to fall, or, if it rises, will experience only an immaterial rise, and this expectation serves of course to accelerate its fall. Hence it has happened, that in all the places of Europe, of which mention has been made, there exists a great and established, and, generally, an increasing discount or agio between the current coin and the paper money of the kingdom. Nor, indeed, is this all; several of the governments of Europe have not only extended their paper in the manner which has been described, but have, besides this, depreciated, from time to time, their very coin; and thus there has been a two-fold cause for a rise in the nominal

* The bank of Amsterdam did not issue circulating notes, but was a mere bank for deposits, the whole of which it was supposed by some to keep always in specie. It was discovered, however, when the French possessed themselves of Holland, that it had been used privately to lend a certain part of them to the city of Amsterdam, and a part to the old Dutch government. These loans ought certainly rather to have been furnished in that open manner in which those of our bank are made. Neither of the two debts, as I understand, have yet been discharged. The bank of Amsterdam had no capital of its own.

price of their commodities when exchanged with the current paper. There is, therefore, a fundamental difference between the nature of the paper of the Bank of England, and that of all the national or government banks on the continent. No one supposes that the English guinea contains less and less gold than heretofore, through frauds practised by government in the coinage; and as little is it to be suspected that the Bank of England paper is about to be depreciated by an excessive issue either ordered or needed by the government. There is, moreover, at present, this further ground for assuming that the issue of Bank of England notes is not likely to be excessive,—that it has lately become a practice to make the number of them public. Their quantity, as it now appears, has never, in any short time, varied very greatly; has seldom, in late years, been below ten or eleven millions, even when no one pound and two pound notes were issued; and has at no moment exceeded the sum of about fifteen millions and a half, including two millions and a half of one pound and two pound notes. It is not impossible that the discredit into which the paper of the government banks of the continent of Europe has fallen, into which also the paper of the American banks sunk at the time of the American war, through the same extension of its issues by the then American government; and also that the total annihilation of the paper issued by the successive French revolutionary governments, may have, in some degree, contributed, though most unjustly, to that fall in the exchange which Great Britain has experienced. Foreigners not adverting to that independence of the Bank of England, the grounds of which have been stated, and misled possibly by the abundant misrepresentations which have taken place in this country, may have thought that it was the government which, by its loans, involved the bank in difficulties (a point which shall be discussed presently), and that the bank is merely an instrument in the hands of the government; an instrument which may be turned, as the government banks on the continent have been, to the purpose of issuing notes to an extravagant extent. If such should, in any degree, be their sentiment, it would be just in them to infer from thence, that the Bank of England notes are not unlikely to fall in their value in the same manner as the notes of the continental banks. An unwillingness to leave in this country whatever sums they may have a right to draw from us (sums probably small in the whole) may have been the consequence of this fear, and a great unwillingness to trust with us even a small quantity of property, may happen to cause, under certain circumstances, a considerable fall in the exchange.

It may be mentioned as an additional ground of confidence in the Bank of England, and as a circumstance of importance in many respects, that the numerous proprietors who chuse the directors, and have the power of controlling them (a power of which they have prudently forborne to make any frequent use), are men whose general stake in the country far exceeds that particular one which they have in the stock of the company. They are men, therefore, who feel themselves to be most deeply interested not merely in the increase of the dividends or in the maintenance of the credit of the Bank of England, but in the support of commercial as well as of public credit in general. There is, indeed, both among them and among the whole commercial world, who make so large a portion of this country, a remarkable determination to sustain credit, and especially the credit of the bank; and this general agreement to support the bank is one of the pillars of its strength, and one pledge of its safety. The proprietors of it themselves are not likely to approve of any dangerous extension even of their own paper; both they and the directors know the importance of confining the bank paper, generally speaking, within its accustomed limits, and must necessarily be supposed to prefer its credit, and the paper credit of the nation, to the comparatively trifling consideration of a small increase in their own dividends; an increase which would prove delusory, if it should arise from that extravagant issue of bank notes which would have the effect of depreciating all the circulating medium of the country, since it would thus raise upon the proprietors of bank stock, as well as on others, the price of all the articles of life.* While the proprietors and directors of the bank have thus an interest, on the one hand, in limiting the quantity of paper issued, they are also naturally anxious, on the other, in common with the whole commercial world, to give the utmost possible credit to it: and although an opinion should prevail, even to some extent among persons out of business, that the appearance of gold is the only test of wealth, and that the absence of it, however temporary, implies great danger to the country, the mercantile interest, and in particular the bank proprietors, the bankers, and the traders of London, by whose transactions the value of the London paper is upheld, may be considered as combined in the support of a juster sentiment. The bank itself is known to have experienced, at former times (as appears from the evidence of the directors given to parliament), very great fluctuations in its cash; and, in one period of returning peace and prosperity, a reduction of it below that which took place at the time of the late suspension of its cash payments: the amount of gold in the bank, at any one particular æra, is, perhaps, therefore, on the ground of this experience, not now considered by the commercial world as having all that importance which was given to it when the bank affairs were involved in greater mystery. It is perfectly well understood among all commercial men, that gold coin is not an article in which all payments (though it is so promised) are at any time intended really to be made; that no fund ever was or can be provided by the bank which shall be sufficient for such a purpose; and that gold coin is to be viewed chiefly as a standard by which all bills and paper money should have their value regulated as exactly as possible; and that the main, and, indeed, the only, point is

* If the bank notes were increased even five millions, the additional profit which would accrue to the proprietors would not be more than two per cent. A proprietor qualified to vote in the bank court (that is, having 500*l*. stock) would, therefore, gain by this extravagant issue, supposing it to be maintained for a year, the sum of 10*l*. A large proportion of the bank proprietors do not hold more than 1000*l*. stock. The gain of each of these would not be more than 20*l*.; a sum perfectly insignificant, compared with the interest which they have in the maintenance of the general commercial credit of the country.

to take all reasonable care that money shall in fact serve as that standard.

This is the great maxim to be laid down on the subject of paper credit. Let it, then, be next considered what is necessary, in order sufficiently to secure that, whatever the circulating paper may be, gold shall be the standard to which the value of that paper shall conform itself. It is no doubt important, that there should be usually in the country a certain degree of interchange of gold for paper, for this is one of the means which will serve to fix the value of the latter. Whether the interchange wanted to produce this effect must be more or less large and frequent, depends much on the habits and dispositions of the country, and, in particular, on the degree of knowledge of the nature of paper credit generally prevailing, and on the degree of confidence in it.

In order to secure that this interchange shall at all times take place, it is important that, generally speaking, a considerable fund of gold should be kept in the country, and there is in this kingdom no other depository for it but the Bank of England. This fund should be a provision not only against the common and more trifling fluctuations in the demand for coin, but also against the two following contingencies. First, it should serve to counteract the effects of an unfavourable balance of trade, for this infallibly will sometimes occur, and it is what one or more bad harvests cannot fail to cause. It is also desirable, secondly, that the reserve of gold should be sufficient to meet any extraordinary demand at home, though a demand in this quarter, if it should arise from great and sudden fright, may undoubtedly be so unreasonable and indefinite as to defy all calculation. If, moreover, alarm should ever happen at a period in which the stock of gold should have been reduced by the other great cause of its reduction, namely, that of a call having been recently made for gold to discharge an unfavourable balance of trade, the powers of any bank, however ample its general provision should have been, may easily be supposed to prove insufficient for this double purpose.

To revert, then, to the Bank of England. A short time before the suspension of its cash payments, the gold in its coffers had been reduced materially through an unfavourable balance of trade. The exchange with Europe had, however, so far improved for some time preceding the suspension, as to have caused gold to begin again to flow into the country. When it was thus only beginning to return, the fear of an invasion took place, and it led to the sudden failure of some country banks in the north of England Other parts felt the influence of the alarm, those in Scotland, in a great measure, excepted, where, through long use, the confidence of the people, even in paper money of a guinea value, is so great (a circumstance to which the peçuliar respectability of the Scotch banks has contributed), that the distress for gold was little felt in that part of the island. A great demand on the Bank of England for guineas was thus created, a demand which every one who can possess himself of a bank note is entitled to make by the very terms in which the note is expressed. In London, it is observable that much distress was beginning to arise, which was in its nature somewhat different from that in the country. In London, confidence in the Bank of England being high, and its notes maintaining their accustomed credit, its guineas were little called for with a view to the mere object of London payments. The guineas applied for by persons in London, was, generally speaking, on the account of people in the country. The distress arising in London, like that which took place in 1793, was a distress for notes of the Bank of England. So great was the demand for notes, that the interest of money, for a few days before the suspension of the payments of the bank, may be estimated (by calculating the price of exchequer bills, the best test that can be referred to, as well as by comparing the money price of stocks with their time price) to have been about sixteen or seventeen per cent. per ann. The bank, on this occasion, pursued, though only in a small degree, the path which a reader of Dr. Smith would consider him to prescribe, as in all cases the proper and effectual means of detaining or bringing back guineas. They lessened the number of their notes, which, having been for some years before near eleven millions, and having been reduced, for some time, to between nine and ten millions, were at this particular moment brought down to between eight and nine millions.

It has been shewn already, that, in order to effect the vast and accustomed payments daily made in London, payments which are most of them promised beforehand, a circulating sum in bank notes, nearly equal to whatever may have been its customary amount is necessary. But a much more clear idea of this subject will be gained by entering into some detail.

There are in London between sixty and seventy bankers, and it is almost entirely through them that the larger payments of London are effected. It may be estimated (though the conjecture is necessarily a loose one) that the sums paid daily by the bankers of London may not be less than four or five millions. The notes in their hands form, probably, a very large proportion of the whole circulating notes in the metropolis. It is certain, at least, that only a very small proportion of Bank of England notes circulate far from London, and that it is to the metropolis itself that all the larger ones are confined. The amount of the bank notes in the hands of each banker, of course, fluctuates considerably; but the amount in the hands of all probably varies very little; and this amount cannot be much diminished consistently with their ideas of what is necessary to the punctuality of their payments, and to the complete security of their houses. Thus there is little room for reduction as to the whole of that larger part of the notes of the Bank of England which is in the hands of the London bankers: the notes which may chance to circulate among other persons, especially among persons carrying on any commerce, if we suppose the usual punctuality of payments to be maintained, and the ordinary system of effecting them to proceed, can admit also of little diminution. A deficiency of notes in London is a very different thing from a deficiency either of country bank notes or of coin in the country. A large proportion of the London payments are payments of bills accepted by considerable houses, and a failure in the punctuality of any one such payment is deemed an act of insolvency in the party. The London payments are, moreover, carried on by a comparatively small quantity of notes; and they, perhaps, cannot easily be effected, with due regularity, by a much smaller number, so complete has been the system of economy in the use of them which time and experience have introduced among the bankers. There is, moreover, no substitute for them. They have an exclusive, though limited, circulation. They serve, at the same time, both to sustain and regulate the whole paper credit of the country. It is plain, from the circumstances which have just been stated, that any very great and sudden diminution of Bank of England notes would be attended with the most serious effects both on the metropolis and on the whole kingdom. A reduction of them which may seem moderate to men who have not reflected on this subject—a diminution, for instance, of one-third or two-fifths, might, perhaps, be sufficient to produce a very general insolvency in London, of which the effect would be the suspension of confidence, the derangement of commerce, and the stagnation of manufactures throughout the country. Gold, in such case, would unquestionably be hoarded through the great consternation which would be excited; and it would, probably, not again appear until confidence should be restored by the *previous* introduction of some additional or some new paper circulation.

The case which has been put, is, however, merely hypothetical; for there is too strong and evident an interest in every quarter to maintain, in some way or other, the regular course of London payments, to make it probable that this scene of confusion should occur; or, even if it should arise, that it should continue. Whether there might chance to be much or little gold in the country, steps would be taken to induce the bank to issue its usual quantity of paper, or measures would be resorted to for providing, by some other means, a substitute for it. The credit, however, of even the best substitute, would be far inferior to that of the old and known Bank of England notes; for the new paper would be guaranteed by a capital probably far less ample than that of the Bank of England: it would also be just as impossible for the issuers of it to procure, at the time in question, a supply of guineas to be given in payment of it, as it would for the Bank of England to provide a supply of guineas for payment of their notes. The new paper, then, though it should be the same in its general nature, would be inferior to that of the bank. It would yield, indeed, a profit to the issuers, a profit which the bank would lose the opportunity of gaining; and the desire of this profit might co-operate in producing a disposition in new bodies of men to proceed to the creation of it. If we suppose it to be created, and to form one part of the current circulating medium of the metropolis; and if we suppose, also, as we necessarily must, a reduced quantity of Bank of England notes to continue current at the same time, the new paper would then be easily exchangeable for the Bank of England paper; and every holder of the new paper would, therefore, be able, by first exchanging it for the bank paper, to draw gold out of the bank. The directors of the bank, therefore, by proceeding to such a reduction of their notes, as should create a necessity for the bankers and merchants to create a new paper among themselves, would only increase the general paper circulation in London. They have now, by their exclusive power of furnishing a circulating medium to the metropolis, the means of, in some degree, limiting and regulating its quantity; a power of which they would be totally divested, if, by exercising it too severely, they should once cause other paper to become current in the same manner as their own. Projects for the introduction of a new circulating medium into the metropolis have, at different times, been formed; all such schemes, however, must necessarily fail, as long as there continues to be an unwillingness among the bankers to unite in giving currency to the new paper. This unwillingness would, of course, diminish in proportion as the pressure should become general and severe.

The idea which some persons have entertained of its being at all times a paramount duty of the Bank of England to diminish its notes, in some sort of regular proportion to that diminution which it experiences in its gold, is, then, an idea which is merely theoretic. It must be admitted, however, to be very natural.

It has been supposed by some, that the pressure on the mercantile world which a great diminution of notes must cause, would, especially if it were a severe one, induce the merchants to send for gold from abroad, in order to supply their own want of money. The supposition, when thus put, is stated in much too vague a manner to be susceptible of that close examination which I wish to give to it. There can be no doubt that we shall find it altogether false, when pushed to the extent of assuming that the extreme *severity* of the pressure is to be the remedy. Let us consider this point in as practical a way as possible.

It was supposed that the difficulty of obtaining bank notes would cause *the* merchants to send abroad for gold, in order to effect their payments. But *what* merchants? Certainly not those merchants whose goods are unfit for a foreign market, and are in no demand there. They must first exchange these unsuitable goods for goods which are suitable, that is, they must sell them; and if they sell them, they must sell them, in the first instance, for money, or what passes as money, and answers, in their view, all the same purposes. Thus they get possession of the very thing, to supply their want of which they are supposed to send abroad. The trader acts, in this respect, like any one who is not a trader. If distressed for the means of effecting what is called cash payment, he no more turns his thoughts to a foreign country for a supply of gold, than the farmer or landed gentleman who is equally pressed. He considers only what part of his property he can turn into bank notes. These he sees to be at hand; of the gold which is in foreign countries he knows nothing.

It will be allowed, then, that it is not on our traders in general that the pressure will so operate as to induce them to send for gold from the continent. It will, perhaps, however, be said to operate on our foreign merchants: but we must now distinguish, also, between one foreign merchant and another. The export trade to foreign countries is, generally speaking, one trade: the trade of importing from foreign countries is a second; the trade of sending out and bringing home bullion, in order to pay or receive the difference between the exports and imports, may be considered as a third. This third trade is carried on upon the same principles with any other branch of commerce, that is, it is entered into just so far as it is lucrative to the speculator in bullion, and no farther. The point, therefore, to be enquired into is clearly this,—whether the pressure arising from a scarcity of bank notes tends to render the importation of bullion a more profitable speculation.

In solving this question, there is not, perhaps, all the difficulty which might be supposed; for it is obvious that, generally speaking, it will answer to import gold into a country just in proportion as the goods sent out of it, in the way of trade (that is the goods which must be paid for), are greater in value than the goods which are, in the way of trade, brought into it. We may, therefore, now dismiss also the case of the mere dealer in bullion from our consideration. We have only to examine in what way the pressure arising from the suppression of bank notes will affect the quantity of goods which are in the way of trade either exported or imported.

That a certain degree of pressure will urge the British merchants in general who buy of the manufacturers, as well as the manufacturers themselves, to sell their goods in order to raise money; that it will thus have some influence in lowering prices at home; and that the low prices at home may tempt merchants to export their articles in the hope of a better price abroad, is by no means an unreasonable supposition. But, then, it is to be observed on the other hand, first, that this more than ordinary eagerness of all our traders to sell, which seems so desirable, is necessarily coupled with a general reluctance to buy, which is exactly proportionate to it: it must be obvious, that, when the general body of merchants, being urged by the pecuniary difficulties of the time, are selling their goods in order to raise money, they will naturally also delay making the accustomed purchases of the manufacturer. They require of him, at least, that he shall give them a more than usually extended credit; but the manufacturer, experiencing the same difficulty with the merchants, is quite unable to give this credit. The *sales* of the manufacturer are, therefore, suspended; but though these are stopped, his daily and weekly payments continue, provided his manufacture proceeds. In other words, his money is going out while no money is coming in; and this happens at an æra when the general state of credit is such, that he is not only not able to borrow, in order to supply his extraordinary need, but when he is also pressed for a prompter payment than before of all the raw materials of his manufacture. Thus the manufacturer, on account of the unusual scarcity of money, may even, though the selling price of his article should be profitable, be absolutely compelled by necessity to slacken, if not suspend, his operations. To inflict such a pressure on the mercantile world as necessarily causes an intermission of manufacturing labour, is obviously not the way to increase that exportable produce, by the excess of which, above the imported articles, gold is to be brought into the country.

But, secondly, that very diminution in the *price* of manufactures which is supposed to cause them to be exported, may also, if carried very far, produce a suspension of the labour of those who fabricate them. The masters naturally turn off their hands when they find their article selling exceedingly ill. It is true, that if we could suppose the diminution of bank paper to produce permanently a diminution in the value of all articles whatsoever, and a diminution, as it would then be fair that it should do, in the rate of wages also, the encouragement to future manufactures would be the same, though there would be a loss on the stock in hand. The tendency, however, of a very great and sudden reduction of the accustomed number of bank notes, is to create an *unusual* and *temporary* distress, and a fall of price arising from that distress. But a fall arising from temporary distress, will be attended probably with no correspondent fall in the rate of wages; for the fall of price, and the distress, will be understood to be temporary, and the rate of wages, we know, is not so variable as the price of goods. There is reason, therefore, to fear that the unnatural and extraordinary low price* arising from the sort of distress of which we now speak, would occasion much discouragement of the fabrication of manufactures.

Thirdly, a great diminution of notes prevents much of that industry of the country which had been exerted from being so productive as it would otherwise be. When a time either of multiplied failures, or even of much disappointment in the expected means of effecting payments arises, plans of commerce and manufacture, as well as of general improvement of every kind, which had been entered upon,

* It may, perhaps, be supposed, that a diminution of the quantity of Bank of England notes, if permanent, would produce that permanent diminution of the price of articles which is so much desired, and the observation made above may be thought to give some countenance to this supposition. Such permanent reduction in the price of commodities could not, however, as I apprehend, be by any such means effected. The general and permanent value of bank notes must be the same as the general and permanent value of that gold for which they are exchangeable, and the value of gold in England is regulated by the general and permanent value of it all over the world; and, therefore, although it is admitted that a great and sudden reduction of bank notes may produce a great local and temporary fall in the price of articles (a fall, that is to say, even in their gold price, for we are here supposing gold and paper to be interchanged), the gold price must, in a short time, find its level with the gold price over the rest of the world. The continuance of the great limitation of the number of bank notes would, therefore, lead either, as has already been observed, to the creation of some new London paper, or possibly to some new modes of economy in the use of the existing notes; the effect of which economy on prices would be the same, in all respects, as that of the restoration of the usual quantity of bank notes. What seems most probable, is, that the continuance of any great limitation of the number of bank notes would lead to the transfer of the present cash payments of London to some other place or places in which the means of effecting payments should not be obstructed through the too limited exercise of that exclusive power of furnishing a paper circulation with which the Bank of England has, by its charter, been invested. This subject of the influence of paper credit on prices will be more fully entered into in a future chapter.

are changed or suspended, and part of the labour which had been bestowed proves, therefore, to have been thrown away. If, for instance, expensive machinery had been erected, under an expectation of regular employment for it, a pressing want of the means of effecting payments may cause that machinery to stand idle. The goods which ought to form part of the assortment of the factor or the shopkeeper, and to be occuying their premises, are loading the warehouse of the manufacturer,* and, perhaps, are suffering damage by too long detention. On the other hand, some sales are forced; and thus the goods prepared for one market, and best suited to it, are sold at another. There cease, at such a time, to be that regularity and exactness in proportioning and adapting the supply to the consumption, and that dispatch in bringing every article from the hands

* When an interruption of the usual credit arises, it naturally happens that the individuals having the least property, and the fewest resources, are the most pressed; and it is sometimes assumed by the public, rather too readily, that those who suffer are justly punished for the too great extent of their speculations. It is true, undoubtedly, that those who prove to be the first to fail, have probably been men of too eager and adventurous a spirit. Let the spirit of adventure among traders, however, have been either more or less, the interruption of the usual credit cannot fail to cause distress; and that distress will fall upon those who have merely been *comparatively*, the more adventurous part of the trading world. It is often also assumed by the public (and without the least foundation) that the want not of gold merely, but of *bonâ fide* mercantile capital in the country is betrayed by a failure of paper credit. The error of this supposition is not only plain, from the general principles laid down in the first chapter of this work, but it is also distinctly proved by the circumstance stated above, that while the premises of the factor and of the shopkeeper are becoming empty of goods, the warehouse of the manufacturer is growing proportionably full. The time soon comes, indeed, when that suspension of labour (which, it should be remembered, is the *consequence* of the suspension of credit) causes the general stock of goods (or the mercantile capital of the country) to be diminished. The evil, therefore, consists not in the want of *bonâ fide* capital, but in the want of such a quantity of the circulating medium as shall be sufficient, at the time, to furnish the means of transferring the goods of the manufacturer from his own warehouse to that of the factor and the shopkeeper. The quantity wanted to be employed in the circulation, and especially the quantity of gold, becomes more, as was observed in the third chapter, when confidence is less, because the rapidity of the circulation is less. The substitution of gold for paper, and of better paper for that which is worse, and some temporary increase of the gold and good paper actually circulating, are obviously the remedy.

of the fabricator into actual use, which are some of the great means of rendering industry productive, and of adding to the general substance of a country. Every great and sudden check given to paper credit not only operates as a check to industry, but leads also to much of this misapplication of it. Some diminution of the general property of the country must follow from this cause; and, of course, a deduction also from that part of it which forms the stock for exportation. It can hardly be necessary to repeat, that on the quantity of exported stock depends the quantity of gold imported from foreign countries.

It will be supposed, perhaps, that the limitation of bank notes, by lessening the means of payment of the importing merchant, may induce him to suspend his imports; and that, since it is the excess of exports above the imports which causes gold to enter the country, the limitation of paper may, with a view to the diminution of imports, be very desirable. There is, probably, some justice in this supposition. It should, however, be observed on this subject, that Great-Britain, at that period of an unfavourable balance which we are now supposing, may be considered as importing chiefly either, first, corn, of which no one would wish to check the import by a limitation of paper; or secondly, that class of articles which are brought from one country in order to be transported to another; articles which come chiefly from very distant parts, and of which the payment cannot be declined, it having been promised long before hand; articles, also, which soon serve to swell the exports in a somewhat greater degree than they had increased the imports; or, thirdly, that rude produce of other countries which forms the raw materials of our own manufacture, and serves, after a short time to supply exportable articles to a very increased amount.

The limitation of credit at home will chiefly be of use by urging the exporting merchant to press the sale of the goods which he has abroad, and to direct them to be sold, if he can, at a short credit; and also by its urging, in like manner, the importing merchant to delay buying abroad, as long as he can, and to buy at a long credit. In other words, it may be of use in leading English merchants, in their dealings with foreigners, to anticipate their receipts, and to delay their payments; on the other hand, it is carefully to be remembered, that an anticipation of receipts, and a delay of payments, are only a temporary benefit; while a suspension of manufactures operates, as far as it goes, as so much permanent and entire loss to the country. It is, moreover, to be borne in mind, that a very severe pressure is *sure* to produce a suspension of manufactures, while it is not sure to cause British merchants to obtain an extension of credit from foreigners. Any *very extraordinary* suppression of bank notes must produce distrust abroad through the failures at home, to which it is known abroad to give rise. It, therefore, indisposes foreign merchants to lend money to England, and it induces those foreigners, who have debts due to them from Englishmen, to urge the payment of those debts. England, during the prevalence of any great distrust, is obliged to send abroad manufactures, not for the payment of goods imported, or for the purchase of gold, but for the extinction of debt.

Although, therefore, it may possibly admit of a doubt whether some moderate restriction of the paper of the bank may not be expedient with a view to mend for the time an unfavourable balance, it seems sufficiently clear that any very sudden and violent reduction of bank notes must tend, by the convulsion to which it will lead, to prevent gold from coming into the country rather than to invite it, and thus to increase the danger of the bank itself. The observation which was before made may, therefore be repeated, *that it is not the severity of the pressure which is to be the remedy.* It is, indeed, in every respect plain that it must be important to maintain, and to maintain carefully, the credit of the country, at that time in particular, when its guineas are few, and are also leaving it; that is the time when our own funds are necessarily low, when the most regular industry should by every means be promoted, and when there is the most need of the aid both of our domestic and foreign credit; and it belongs to the Bank of England, in particular, to guard and to superintend the interests of the country in this respect. The very policy of the bank differs, in this particular, from that of the individual country banker, whose own share of the evil resulting to the country, from the sudden suppression of his own notes, is small; who may trust, moreover, that there will be a substitution either of guineas or of other paper in the place of his own paper which is suppressed; and who, it may be remarked, supplies himself with the means of discharging his own notes by obtaining guineas from the Bank of England.

But the Bank of England, has no bank to which it can resort for a supply of guineas proportioned to its wants in the same manner in which it is resorted to by the country banks; nor have the bankers and traders in London, to whom at present is transferred the business of effecting the great cash payments of the whole country, the same resource in case Bank of England notes are suppressed which traders in the country have, supposing country bank notes to be withdrawn. The country payments being not strictly promised before hand, may, many of them, bear to be postponed. Bills of exchange on London may also form some substitute for country bank notes, and may pass as such in the manner which was some time ago described; but if Bank of England notes are suppressed, and are suppressed, as we have been supposing them to be, in consequence of guineas being scarce, there then remain no means whatever of effecting the London payments. There can be no doubt that the extinction or very great diminution of bank notes would be a far greater evil, in the present circumstances of the metropolis, than the disappearing of guineas. If guineas disappear, notes may be substituted in their place; and through that general confidence which may be inspired by the agreement of bankers and other leading persons to take them, they will not fail, provided the issues are moderate, and the balance of trade is not very unfavourable to the country, to maintain exactly the gold price. The punctuality thus introduced into all the larger operations of commerce, will facilitate contrivances for effecting the smaller payments.

Differences of opinion, undoubtedly, may exist as to the exact degree in which the notes of the Bank of England ought, under any given circumstances, to be diminished. It may be hoped, however, that at least one point has now been fully and completely established, namely, that there may be an error on the side of too much diminishing bank notes, as well as on the side of too much increasing them. There is an excessive limitation of them, as every one must admit, which will produce failures: failures must cause consternation, and consternation must lead to a run upon the bank for guineas. There must, in short, then, be some point at which the bank must stop in respect to the reduction of its notes, however progressive may be the drain upon it for guineas.

But if its notes are not lessened, or if even they are lessened, but are not entirely extinguished, it is then in the power of any one who can possess himself of a bank note to possess himself also of guineas, and as long as the bank pays in guineas; and it will be found to follow, moreover, that the bank is thus rendered liable to be totally exhausted of guineas. I mean, that it is liable to be totally exhausted of them, however great their number may have been, if it determines to *maintain* even the *smallest* number of notes. By maintaining, that is to say, five millions, or two millions, or even one million, of notes, the bank cannot avoid being exhausted (supposing the alarm to rise high enough to do it) of even five millions, or ten millions, or, if it had them, of twenty or fifty millions of guineas. It will depend, in such case, on the degree of alarm, and not on the maintenance of the greater or of the less quantity of notes, whether the guineas shall be more or less rapidly called for from the bank; or, in other words, the bank may be as much exhausted of guineas if it maintains five millions of notes as if it maintains ten millions, provided the alarm is only the same in the one case as in the other. If, therefore, the maintenance of the five millions of notes is sure to produce more alarm than the maintenance of ten, then the maintenance of the larger quantity of notes will serve to diminish the demand for guineas, and the maintenance of the smaller number to increase it.

The following is the manner in which that operation, which is finally to exhaust all the guineas of the bank, may be supposed to proceed. A, for instance, the holder of a note of 1000*l.* (and it is what any man may obtain by selling goods) carries it to the bank and demands 1000*l.* in gold. The bank gives the gold; which gold, let it be remarked, either goes abroad to pay for an unfavourable balance of trade, or, as we are now rather supposing, fills a void in the circulation of the country, occasioned by the withdrawing of country bank notes in consequence of alarm, or serves as an addition to the fund of country banks, or forms a hoard in the hands of individuals. The 1000*l.* in gold, thus furnished by the bank, does not supply, in any degree, the place of the 1000*l.* note for which it was given; for the 1000*l.* note had been employed in London in making the larger payments. It is hardly ever, in almost any degree, as a substitute for Bank of England notes, that the gold taken from the bank is wanted. The bank, therefore, having paid away this 1000*l.* in gold, and having received for it their own note for 1000*l.* must now re-issue this note, if they are resolved to *maintain the amount of their paper circulation.* How, then, is the bank to issue it? The only means which the bank on its part, is able to take for the extension of its paper circulation, is to enlarge its loans. It must, therefore, re-issue the 1000*l.* note, in the shape of a loan, to some person who offers a bill to discount. It receives, therefore, a bill of 1000*l.* and gives a note of 1000*l.* in return for it. For the same note, thus re-issued, we may suppose 1000*l.* in money to be again demanded, and to be again paid. The paper circulation of the bank is now again diminished 1000*l.* and, therefore, there arises a necessity for issuing the same 1000*l.* note, or some other note or notes to like amount a third time, in order to maintain the amount of notes in circulation. The like transaction, or rather a number of such transactions, may be supposed to be repeated either five, or fifty, or a hundred, or a thousand times. Even if we should suppose the bank to bring down its paper circulation to one hundred thousand pounds, and to *maintain it at that sum*, it is obvious that this same operation might be so reiterated, from day to day, as to extract at length from the bank even the greatest imaginable number of guineas. Thus, then, the bank is rendered liable to be exhausted of its guineas, by its determination to maintain the number of its notes, whether that number be greater or smaller; and here, also, let it be remarked by the way (a point on which more shall be said presently), that the bank, in consequence of its determination to maintain a given number of notes, is placed under an absolute necessity of increasing its loans to the very same extent to which it is deprived of its guineas. The bank, let it be remembered, was stated to lend an additional 1000*l.* on the occasion of each reiterated demand upon it for 1000*l.* in guineas. It thus clearly appears that the Bank of England is placed, by the very nature of its institution, in a situation in which it may not be possible to avoid a temporary failure in the regularity of its cash payments.

An idea has, indeed, prevailed, than which nothing can be more natural, that because an individual merchant is presumed to be blameable if he is not able to make good his payments, therefore, also, a national bank, in case of failure, may be presumed to be censurable in like manner; and, on account of the greater importance of its transactions, to be censurable even in a still higher degree. But the total disparity in the circumstances of the two cases should be taken into consideration. Private houses may, in general, be fairly presumed to be in fault if they fail in the punctuality of their cash payments, supposing the bank of England to pay in money, because, if they have made on their part a tolerably prudent provision, they may be in general considered as having in the bank a sure resource. Take away from them that resource, and they will then be not only as liable as the Bank of England to the like accident, but they will be much more so, their means of supplying themselves with guineas becoming then exceedingly precarious. It may be apprehended, also, that, if instead one national bank two or more should be instituted, each having a small capital; each would then exercise a separate judgment; each would trust in some measure to the chance of getting a supply of guineas from the other, and each would allow itself to pursue its own particular interest, instead of taking upon itself the superintendence of general credit, and seeking its own safety through the medium of the safety of the public; unless, indeed, we should suppose such a good understanding to subsist between them as to make them act as if they were one body, and resemble, in many respects, one single institution.

The accident of a failure in the means of making the cash payments of a country, though it is one against which there can be no security which is complete, seems, therefore, to be best provided against by the establishment of one principal bank. It, however, becomes the public not to judge the bank, which is thus rendered its servant, and is completely subjected to its interests, by the same rules by which it judges of smaller banking and commercial establishments, but to advert to the peculiarity of its case.

If there has been any fault in the conduct of the Bank of England, the fault, as I conceive, has rather been, as has just been stated, on the side of too much restricting its notes in the late seasons of alarm, than on that of too much enlarging them. In doing this, it has happened to act (though but in part) according to what seems likely to have been the advice of Dr. A. Smith in the case. It has also taken that course which is the natural one for smaller banks, and which might, perhaps, have been the proper one for the Bank of England itself, in the infancy of its establishment, when the country was less dependent upon it for the means of effecting its payments. It has, probably, pursued a principle which had been acted upon, by its own directors, in all former times. It has also followed what was, at the very period in question, the common opinion of the public on the subject. It has, moreover, only diminished those notes, perhaps, in too great a degree, which there might possibly be found to be some argument for restraining with a more gentle hand. I venture, however, with deference, to express a suspicion that the bank may have, in some measure, aggravated, perhaps, rather than lessened, the demand upon itself for guineas through the suppression of too many notes at the time preceding the suspension of its cash payments; and I will hazard an opinion, that it might also, with propriety, have somewhat extended the temporary issue of its paper, in the year 1793, when that alarm, arising from the failure of country banks, which has been already spoken of, took place. It is clear, at least, that it did not, in the more recent instance, succeed by the diminution of its notes in curing the evil which it thus aimed to remedy.

A suspicion prevailed, at the time of which we have been chiefly speaking, that the loans afforded by the bank to the government had caused the distress of the bank. But the government, it should be remembered, has no supply of guineas with which it can discharge any debt. It is circumstanced in this respect, like any other debtor of the bank. It must, if forced to pay its debt, pay it in bank notes, an article which the bank cannot refuse to take. And the government must collect these notes wherever they are to be obtained; that is, from the bankers and traders, and other persons in possession of them, to whom it must, in return, give new stock or exchequer bills, which it may, at all times, easily create; though, at a period of mercantile distress, this would be done at a somewhat unfavourable price. We learn, from the evidence given to parliament, that the government was urged by the bank to pay up four and a half millions of existing debt a short time before the period in question, and that it complied with the demand; that is, the government collected some of the bank notes which were in circulation, and paid them into the bank; and then a part, but only a part, of the notes so paid in were re-issued to the merchants. If the whole of the notes paid into the bank by the government had been immediately re-issued in loans to private traders, *then the sum of notes in circulation* would have been the same. The government is only one large borrower from the bank; the merchants are a number of similar, though smaller, borrowers. Whether, therefore, the bank lent more to individuals and less to government, or less to government and more to individuals, the effect as to the number of notes allowed to be in circulation, must have been equal. The Exchequer, after receiving notes from the bank, almost as quickly pays them away, and thus sends them into the common circulation as the merchant does; and it is the total quantity of circulating notes, and not the manner in which they come into circulation, that is the material point.

It may be thought, indeed, that commerce would be encouraged, and commercial credit, as well as general paper credit, would be supported in a much greater degree by the bank sending their notes into circulation, through the medium of a loan to the merchants, than through that of a loan to government. But the difference would not, as I apprehend, be so great as many commercial men themselves at that time imagined. Those merchants who obtained an increase of the accustomed advances from the bank, would, some of them, probably invest, in the new exchequer bills which were created, a part of that very sum with which the bank favoured them. The merchants in higher credit, of course, would have the preference at the bank; and they were certainly under a very strong temptation to borrow of the bank at five per cent. interest for the sake of investing the sum so borrowed in exchequer bills, yielding five and a half or six, or, for a time, even seven or eight per cent. or more. As far as this was the case, it is obvious that the bank, instead of lending to the government, would only lend to those who lent to the government, the government paying an additional interest, and the merchants receiving it. Where this did not take place, that might happen which would be exactly equivalent. The bankers finding that the merchants were, many of them, allowed to become larger borrowers at the bank than before, would think it less necessary to lend to them, and would, therefore, add to the sum which they themselves kept in exchequer bills, the great profit on that article tempting them, at the same time, to do this. The bank, on this supposition, would lend to the merchants, who would forbear to borrow of the banker (which is the same thing for the present purpose as lending to the banker), who would lend to the government. But let us put a third case. Let us imagine it to be a gentleman in the country who invested the property in the new exchequer bills. That property would probably, since we must suppose it easily applicable to such investment, have been lying in some private hand at interest. Let us imagine it to consist of 100*l.* which had been in the hands of a country banker: the country banker, in this case, would draw upon his London banker; the country banker's account with the London banker would then be worse by 100*l.*: and the London banker having 100*l.* less deposits, would be able to lend 100*l.* less to the London merchants. In other words, the Bank of England, in this case, instead of lending to the government, would lend to the London merchant, who would forbear to borrow of the London banker, who would lend to, or, perhaps, forbear to borrow of the country banker, who would forbear to borrow of the country gentleman, who would lend to the government; which also seems to be much the same as if the Bank of England themselves lent to the government. This detailed case has been put partly for the sake of observing upon it, that the necessity which would be created for the transfer of this 100*l.* through so many hands, would produce a want of some degree of *additional* circulating medium in order to effect these several payments. It would, however, be chiefly by the means of a bill on London that the transaction just now supposed would be conducted; but the bill must finally be paid by a Bank of England note.—Let us imagine a fourth case. Let us suppose a sum to be invested in the new exchequer bills by a person obtaining money for the purpose of the investment, not by calling in a sum lying at interest, as was last assumed, but by selling goods, land, or any other article. We must, then, necessarily suppose a buyer of those goods, of that land, or of that other article to be created by such sale. We shall find, also, that it is necessary to suppose either that buyer to become a borrower, or to become the seller to one who would become a borrower; or, at least, we must come to a borrower at last. We are supposing one man to *sell* goods for 100*l.* and not to *restore* this 100*l.* *to* trade, but to *lend* it out. We must, then, necessarily suppose some other man to borrow 100*l.* and by thus borrowing to add that 100*l.* capital to trade which the other had taken from it; for since the trade goods in the country remain the same, the capital invested in trade must be the same also. The body of lenders, therefore, whoever they might be, who lent the four and a half millions to government, necessarily created a body of borrowers to exactly the same amount in what may be called the general money market of the country. Thus a pressure was, on the whole, created, which was just equal to that which was relieved; a pressure, in the first instance, falling in some degree (though by no means entirely, or even principally) in a different quarter than before; a pressure, however, very soon extending itself to the same persons; for there is a competition among the several classes both of borrowers and of lenders in the money market, which, notwithstanding some inequality occasioned by the usury laws, causes the increased distress brought upon any one class of the accustomed borrowers very soon to distribute itself among all. The bank, it is true, would, by lending the four and a half millions in bills at two months, possess more means of at any time diminishing its loans, and of thus lessening also its notes, than if the same sum had been invested in exchequer bills, since the latter are at a longer date; and it was natural for the bank to call in its loan to government for this reason. If, however, the calling in of the loan to government was only to furnish the means of limiting the notes, then that question returns which has already been discussed, namely, whether the diminution of the notes was not carried possibly somewhat farther than was desirable, even for the sake of the bank itself. During the existence of this loan to government, that reduction of notes, which has been supposed to have been too great, may have been, perhaps, to a certain degree obstructed, though by no means necessarily precluded; since an opportunity of diminishing the discounts to the merchants, and of thus lessening the notes, at all times existed. On the whole, there appears to be no reason to infer, from the circumstance of the demand for the four and a half millions having been made upon government, that the government was either the more remote or the more immediate cause of the suspension of the cash payments of the bank, except, undoubtedly, so far as the war in general, or the particular circumstance of a remittance of a subsidy to the Emperor a short time before the event in question, might be considered as affecting the balance of trade, and thus contributing to draw gold out of the country.

It is, on public grounds, so important to shew that the more than usual largeness of the bank loans to government (for it can hardly fail to be true that they were more than commonly extended) was not the cause of the suspension of the cash payments of the bank, that I shall dwell for some time longer on this subject. This was continually charged as the cause, and it was not unnatural to suppose it to be so. The paper circulation of the bank, however, it has been observed, was at this time not increased. It was, on the contrary, much reduced. It was by no means higher than was necessary for securing the regularity of the payments of the metropolis. Now, if it be allowed that there was this necessity for maintaining the existing quantity of notes, it then was not the notes which must be considered as issued for the purpose of making the loans, but the loans must be considerd as made in consequence of the issue of notes. When the notes of the bank are increased, the loans must be increased also; when the notes are maintained, the loans must be maintained in as great proportion; when the notes are decreased, the loans can be decreased *only in that proportion.* There can, then, be no matter of blame on account of the magnitude of the loans, unless there be matter of blame on account of the magnitude of the notes. But the notes I have stated to have been probably rather too few than too many. If the reader has agreed with me in this, he must then agree with me that the loans were too scanty rather than too large. In other words, then, the bank, at the time of the failure of its cash payments, had lent too little rather than too much. If the bank would have somewhat diminished its danger by issuing more notes, the granting of more loans would have also diminished its danger. Thus the very converse to the common opinion on this subject seems to be the truth.

There is, however, another point of importance here to be remarked. The loans which the bank had made on the whole, that is, the loans to government and to individuals taken together, at the time of the suspension of its cash payments, were not only maintained in that proportion in which the notes were maintained, but they were increased beyond that proportion. This increase beyond that proportion was also a matter of necessity.

The loans of the bank do not simply keep pace with the notes. The loans necessarily increase or diminish through another cause; they diminish as gold flows in to the bank, and increase as gold goes out, supposing, as we generally may, the article of deposits to remain the same; that is, they necessarily increase and diminish in a ratio directly contrary to that which a theorist would prescribe, and which the public naturally would suppose.

To those who are but slightly acquainted with these subjects, this truth will probably be made much clearer by a statement of the whole disposable effects of the Bank of England, and of the manner in which those effects are employed. The statement is important, because it will serve to prove, beyond the possibility of contradiction, that the extraordinary largeness of the loans of the bank, at the critical period in question, ought to be considered not as a consequence of any disposition in the bank to be great and adventurous lenders at a time when their guineas grew low, but as arising out of the necessity under which they were placed. I mean that they could not avoid lending to the whole extent to which they did, provided even that small number of notes which they kept in circulation was maintained.

The effects of the bank on the 25th February 1797, I

mean those effects which were their own, as well as those placed in their hands belonging to other persons, may, in conformity to the account rendered by themselves to parliament, be stated, in round numbers, to have been as follows.

(It may be premised, that they had a capital of their own of about 11,626,000*l.* which shall be excluded from our present consideration, it being lent to government at three per cent. per annum interest).

1. They had a sum of undivided profits which formed an additional and disposeable capital of nearly - -	L.3,800,000
2. They had of deposits lodged with them by customers of various classes about - - - - - -	5,100,000
These deposits include, as may be presumed, the dividends belonging to many proprietors of stock, which may be viewed in the same light with the cash kept by an individual in the hands of his banker.	
3. They had what may be considered as disposeable effects, or deposits placed in their hands in return for bank notes issued* - - - - - - -	8,600,000
Thus the bank had, at that time, disposeable effects amounting in all to - - - - - -	L.17,500,000

* The reader, perhaps, may not understand upon what principle it is that the amount of the notes of the Bank of England is classed among the deposits. The amount of them was placed on this side of the account in the statement given to parliament by the bank, and very properly, or rather very necessarily. It is not, however, the notes which themselves form deposits. They are given *in return for* deposits; and they are, therefore, the measure of those deposits. It is in substance the same thing whether a person deposits 100*l.* in money with the bank, taking no note, but obtaining a right to draw a draft on a banking account which is opened in his name, or whether he deposits the same 100*l.* and receives for it a bank note. The possession of the right to draw obtained in the one case, is exactly equivalent to the possession of the note obtained in the other. The notes, it is true, are commonly issued not in consideration of money received, but of bills discounted; but the deposits, it may also be observed, are generally formed by the same means of bills discounted. The manner of transacting the discounting business at the bank is this:—the discounter opens a banking account with the bank, and usually keeps a small balance upon it; when he sends bills to be discounted, those bills, if the bank consents to discount them, are placed to the credit of his banking account; and when he draws for them, or for any part of them, the bearer of his draft receives the amount of it in bank notes. The numerous balances, therefore (in general small ones), which the discounters keep with the bank, are included, no doubt, in the bank account, under the head of deposits, and form a part of the second item in the statement above. The sum which I have considered as deposited in the bank, by those who take

It will much illustrate what is about to be added, if the following observations respecting these three several heads of disposeable effects are here made.

First, let it be remarked, that the first sum of 3,800,000*l.* does not fluctuate; it only increases gradually, and in a small degree.

Secondly. The second sum of 5,100,000*l.* fluctuates probably but little; and as far as it does so, it fluctuates not at the pleasure of the bank, but at the will of its customers.

Thirdly. The third, then, is the only one of the three component parts of the disposeable effects of the bank which it is in the power of the bank to increase or diminish at its own option. The bank exercised their power of diminishing this article, at the time in question, so far as to bring it down to about 8,600,000*l.* To reduce it thus far was, as has been repeatedly stated, to reduce it, perhaps, somewhat too much; but let us assume only, that the reduction was sufficient, or nearly sufficient. The bank, then, it must be admitted, had 17,500,000*l.* of disposeable effects, and it was not to be ascribed to them as a matter of blame that these effects then stood at about the sum at which they did.

Having, then, these effects, and being under a necessity of disposing of them in some way or other, let us state next how they did in fact employ them.

In proceeding to make this statement, it will be necessary, with a view to the object for which it is made, to name some specific sum (it matters not whether more or less than the real one) for the amount of that part of the effects of the bank which was, on the 25th February, 1797, invested in bullion. In the account rendered to parliament, the value of the bullion and of the bills discounted, &c. are put together, and are stated at nearly seven millions. Let it be supposed that the bullion was either one, two, or three millions; and that the bills discounted, &c. were, therefore,

---

away the notes, they opening no account, is not termed deposits in the bank statement. I have, however, thought it necessary so to term it, in order to make the subject the more clear to the reader.

either four, five, or six millions. The mode of disposing of the 17,500,000*l.* will then be as follows.

The bank invested in government securities, that is, in exchequer bills, in loans to government made on the security of the land and malt tax which was coming in, and in treasury bills of exchange growing due, about - - - - - -	L.10,500,000
They invested, as shall for the present be assumed in conformity to the estimate which it was before proposed to make, "in bills discounted to the merchants," in what is termed in their account, "money lent," and in some other (probably small) "articles," - - -	4,000,000
And they had property invested in bullion, as shall for the present be assumed, amounting to - - -	3,000,000
Making together, as the investment necessarily must, the same sum exactly which the disposeable effects were before stated to amount to, namely - - -	L.17,500,000

This same account of the investment may be given more briefly and conveniently for our present purpose, in the following manner, viz. the total sum lent both to government and to individuals, or, in other words, the total loans were - - - - L.14,500,000

The total of the bullion was - - - - -	3,000,000
Making together - - - - - -	L.17,500,000

It will now be obvious to the reader, that if the bullion, instead of three millions, is supposed to have been only two millions, then the total of the loans must be supposed to be increased one million; and that if the bullion, instead of three millions, is supposed to be only one million, then the loans must be supposed to be increased two millions.

In other words, the account of the investment may either be stated as has been just done, or it may be stated as follows:

Total loans - - - - -	L 15,500,000
Bullion - - - - -	2,000,000
Making together, as before, - - -	17,500,000
Or total loans - - - - -	16,500,000
Bullion - - - - -	1,000,000
Making together, as before, - - -	L.17,500,000

It thus appears, that the loans necessarily must increase in proportion as the gold decreases, provided the disposeable effects remain the same.

It follows, on the principle which has just been explained, that if we suppose, as we necessarily must, the bullion to have been, twelve months before the time of the suspension of the cash payments of the bank, much higher than at the period of the suspension, the loans would, during the course of those twelve months, necessarily increase. Let us (for the sake of illustration) suppose the gold to have been a year before the suspension eight millions, and to have fallen on the 26th February, 1797, to the sum of two millions. In that case, if we were to suppose the disposeable effects of the bank to have been at both periods the same, there must necessarily have been, in the course of the year, an increase of the bank loans of no less than six millions. But the effects of the bank were not quite the same at the two periods. They probably were higher by about two millions at the former period; for the notes were higher by nearly that sum. The notes, then, fell in the year two millions, but the bullion fell six. The loans, therefore, would be decreased two millions through the decrease of notes; but would be increased six millions through the decrease of bullion; that is, they would *necessarily* be increased, in the course of the year, four millions. I have dwelt thus particularly on this circumstance, because the whole of the suspicion, that the magnitude of the bank loans were the cause of the failure of its cash, seems to me to rest upon it. The largeness of those loans was not the *cause* of the guineas going from them, as has been ordinarily supposed; it was the *effect*. Nothing could be more natural than for the public to call that the cause, in this instance, which was the effect, and that the effect which was the cause. In the case of private persons it is often very justly said, that a man fails in his payments because he has lent so largely; and it would seem very strange to reply that this was not the case, for that the man in question had found it necessary to lend largely, because his cash failed him; and that the failure of the cash was the cause, and the lending merely an effect. That, however, which could not be affirmed of an individual, is true in the case of the bank, and the circumstances which give occasion for this peculiarity in our reasonings respecting that institution, are these two; first, the difficulty in obtaining a supply of guineas which the bank experiences, a difficulty totally unknown to individuals who draw their guineas from the bank itself; and, secondly, the singular necessity under which the bank is placed of maintaining at all times its notes.

It was thought by some, that the interference on the part of the government and parliament was improper, inasmuch as the bank ought not to have been prevented from continuing to pay in cash as long as it had any remaining ability to do so. Every bank note, it was urged, is a contract to pay money entered into between the bank and the possessor of it, in consequence of what has been deemed a valuable consideration; and no authority of parliament ought, except in a case of the last necessity, to interpose itself to prevent the fulfilment of such a contract. To this it seems to be a fair answer to say, that the question is not whether any one holder of a note shall have his claim to receive money for it interfered with, but that it is a question respecting *all* the holders of notes, *as well as all other persons having a right to demand any cash payments in any quarter whatever.* Now, there are few or no creditors who are not also debtors; and a very large proportion of debtors owe as much to others, as others owe to them. Bankers and traders are greater debtors than other men; but they are also greater creditors. The bank itself is a great creditor, its credits, indeed, being far greater than its debts, and it is intitled to receive a part of its debts almost immediately. The case, then, is this: a comparatively very small portion of the persons having a right to demand cash, are led, by sudden alarm, to urge their claim for guineas to such an extent as to invest even a large portion of their capital in that article of which a quantity has been provided which is sufficient only for the purpose of the ordinary kind of payments. All the cash in the world would not satisfy claims of this sort, if all men, having a right to urge them, were disposed equally to do so. The very persons who press for these payments do not reflect, that they themselves, perhaps, have creditors who might, with equal justice, exact the immediate money payment of a still larger debt against them. The law authorizing the suspension of the cash payments of the bank, seems, therefore, to have only given effect to what must have been the general wish of the nation in the new and extraordinary circumstances in which it found itself. If every bill and engagement is a contract to pay money, the two parties to the contract may be understood as agreeing, for the sake of a common and almost universal interest, to relax as to the literal interpretation of it, and as consenting that "money should "mean money's worth," and not the very pieces of metal: and the parliament may be considered as interposing in order to execute this common wish of the public.

By authorising the suspension of the cash payments of the bank, while a certain quantity of guineas still remained in its coffers, the parliament, moreover, much diminished the shock which this extraordinary event might naturally be expected to occasion; and also provided the means of furnishing the guineas actually necessary after that æra for some smaller current payments, as well as the means of securing the credit of bank notes, thus rendering them a more valuable medium of exchange for goods, and a fairer substitute for guineas than they might otherwise have been. The parliament, then, were led by the practical view which they took of the subject, to disregard theory, as well as some popular prejudice, for the sake of more effectually guarding the public safety, and promoting real justice.

The danger chiefly to be apprehended in London, was, that the common class of people, not receiving their pay in the usual article of coin, and not knowing at the first that one and two pound notes would purchase every thing in the same manner as gold, might be excited to some tumultuous proceedings. It was also feared that, through the discredit cast on small notes by the common people, this new paper might fall, at the first issue of it, to a discount. It was important, therefore, to continue for a time to pay the labouring people in money; and to circulate the new one and two pound notes, in the first instance, by the medium of the higher classes. Of the sum remaining in the bank, a small part was issued to each of the bankers, after the suspension took place, for the convenience of common workmen. It was obviously desirable, that a farther sum should be reserved in the bank as a provision for any subsequent and important uses.

Immediately after this event, the bank extended the quantity of its notes nearly to the amount of the sum usually in circulation: and not only was credit revived, but in no long time guineas became remarkably abundant. The bank, as is commonly supposed, was replenished with them. And there is this infallible proof, that gold flowed into the country; that the course of exchange became much in favour of it.

CHAP. V.

Of the Balance of Trade—Of the Course of Exchange—Tendency of an unfavourable Exchange to take away Gold—Of the Probability of the Return of Gold—Of the Manner in which it may be supposed that exported Gold is employed on the Continent—Reasons for having renewed the Law for suspending the Cash Payments of the Bank of England.

THE law which authorised the suspension of the cash payments of the bank having been re-enacted; the high price of provisions having given occasion to much speculation on the subject of paper credit; the course of exchange having again turned greatly against the country; and gold having to a material degree disappeared, its place being occupied by small paper notes; it is not surprising that suspicions of the necessity of an alteration in the system of our paper credit should have become prevalent. Some consideration shall here be given to that unfavourable state of the exchange between this country and Europe, which operated during the last two years of the war, in again drawing away our guineas.

It may be laid down as a general truth, that the commercial exports and imports of a state (that is to say, the exported and imported commodities, for which one country receives an equivalent from another) naturally proportion themselves in some degree to each other; and that the balance of trade, therefore (by which is meant the difference between these commercial exports and imports), cannot continue for a very long time to be either highly favourable or highly unfavourable to a country. For that balance must be paid in bullion, or else must constitute a debt. To suppose a very great balance to be paid, year after year, in bullion, is to assume such a diminution of bullion in one country, and such an accumulation of it in another, as are not easy to be imagined: it may even be questioned whether the commercial prosperity of a state does not tend, on the whole, to reduce, rather than augment, the quantity of gold in use, through that extension of paper credit to which it leads. To suppose large and successive balances to be formed into a debt, is to assume an accumulation of debt, which is almost equally incredible. A prosperous nation commonly employs its growing wealth, not so much in augmenting the debts due to it from abroad, as in the enlargement of its capital at home; I mean, in the cultivation of its lands, in the encrease of its buildings, the extension of its machinery, the multiplication of its docks and its canals, and in a variety of other improvements, which become the sure sources of an encreasing income. The state may be progressive in these respects, even in years in which the balance of trade is unfavourable. There is a customary length of credit in foreign parts which the British exporter, however overflowing his capital may be, is not very willing to enlarge. And events fail not occasionally to arise, which remind him of the danger of committing too great a portion of his property into the hands of those who are not subject to the same laws with himself; and whose country may suddenly be involved, at any moment, in a war with Great Britain.

The equalization of the commercial exports and imports is promoted not only by the unwillingness of the richer state to lend to an unlimited extent, but also by a disinclination to borrow in the poorer. There is in the mass of

75

the people, of all countries, a disposition to adapt their individual expenditure to their income. Importations conducted with a view to the consumption of the country into which the articles are imported (and such, perhaps, are the chief importations of a poor country), are limited by the ability of the individuals of that country to pay for them out of their income. Importations, with a view to subsequent exportation, are in like manner limited by the ability to pay which subsists among the individuals of the several countries to which the imported goods are afterwards exported. The income of individuals is the general limit in all cases. If, therefore, through any unfortunate circumstance, if through war, scarcity, or any other extensive calamity, the value of the annual income of the inhabitants of a country is diminished, either new economy on the one hand, or new exertions of individual industry on the other, fail not, after a certain time, in some measure, to restore the balance. And this equality between private expenditures and private incomes tends ultimately to produce equality between the commercial exports and imports.

But though the value of the commercial exports and imports of a country will have this general tendency to proportion themselves to each other, there will not fail occasionally to arise a very great inequality between them. A good or a bad harvest, in particular, will have a considerable influence in producing this temporary difference. The extra quantity of corn and other articles imported into Great Britain in this and the last year, with a view to supply the deficiency of our own crops, must have amounted in value to so many millions, that it may justly excite surprise that we should have been able, during an expensive war, to provide the means of cancelling our foreign debt so far even as we have done; especially when the peculiar interruptions to our commerce are also considered. In this country, however, as in all others, the two principles of economy and exertion are always operating in proportion to the occasion for them. But the economy and exertion follow rather than accompany the evil which they have to cure. If the harvest fails, and imports are necessary, in order to supply the deficiency, payment for those imports is almost immediately required: but the means of payment are to be supplied more gradually through the limitation of private expenditure, or the encrease of individual industry. Hence a temporary pressure arises at the time of any very unfavourable balance. To understand how to provide against this pressure, and how to encounter it, is a great part of the wisdom of a commercial state.

By the commercial exports and imports which have been spoken of, those articles have been intended for which an equivalent is given; not those which form a remittance, for which nothing is obtained in exchange. Many of our exported and some of our imported commodities are of that class which furnish no return.

For example, numerous stores were shipped, during the war, for the support of our navy and army in foreign parts. Remittances were made, in the way of loan and subsidy, to our allies. Some dividends may be supposed to have been transmitted to the foreign proprietors of British stock. Much property is also sent out of the kingdom, which constitutes a capital employed in the cultivation of lands in the West Indies. On the other hand, capital is transmitted *to* Great Britain from the East Indies, both by the India Company and by individuals.

Although exports and imports of this class form no part of the commercial exports and imports which have been spoken of, they affect the quantity of those commercial exports and imports, and they contribute, exactly like the circumstance of a bad harvest, to render the balance of trade unfavourable;* they tend, that is to say, in the same

* This point may be illustrated in the following manner:—

Let us suppose a subsidy, for example, of two millions to be remitted to the Emperor of Germany, through the medium of bills to that amount, directed to be drawn by Vienna on London. By these bills, Great Britain is laid under a necessity of exporting two millions, either of goods or of bullion, or of both, for which no foreign commodities will be given in return. These two millions of exports diminish our fund of exportable goods: and they also satisfy a part of the foreign demand for British articles. They tend, in both these respects, to reduce the manner, to bring Great Britain into debt to foreign countries, and to promote the exportation of our bullion. Our mercantile exports and imports, nevertheless, by whatever means they may be rendered disproportionate, necessarily become, in the long run, tolerably equal; for it is evident that there is a limit, both to the debt which foreigners will permit British merchants to incur, and also to the quantity of British bullion which is exportable.

Gold has been spoken of in this Chapter as that article by which a balance of trade is discharged, and not as itself constituting a commodity. Gold, however, when exported and imported, may be considered in the same light with all other commodities; for it is an article of intrinsic value: its price, like that of other commodities, rises and falls according to the proportion between the supply and the demand; it naturally seeks, like them, that country in which it is the dearest; and it is, in point of fact, like them, exported by our merchants accordingly as the export or import is likely to yield a profit. Some description of the circumstances which cause the export of gold to become a profitable speculation to the merchant may serve to illustrate this subject.

When a bill is drawn by one country on another—by Hamburgh, for instance, on London—it is sold (or dis-

---

quantity of goods which can be exported by us in the way of ordinary commerce, and to turn the balance of trade against us. Capital transferred to our colonies, dividends transmitted to foreigners, and articles shipped for the use of our fleets and armies, contribute in the same manner as foreign subsidies to render the balance of trade unfavourable. It may be added, that articles consumed at home, in the support of similar fleets and armies, as well as all other expenditure in Great Britain, must have the same general tendency.

It may be worthy of remark, that since an additional internal expenditure, in the same manner as the remittance of a subsidy to foreign parts, contributes to an unfavourable balance of trade, and therefore, also, to the exportation of our gold, it follows, that, if the remittance of a small subsidy tends to produce at home a large saving; if, for instance, it spares the expense of maintaining a great naval and military force for the defence of our own island, through the continental diversion to which it leads, the subsidy may conduce to render our balance of trade more favourable; and may, on the whole, prevent rather than promote the exportation of our coin—A circumstance which, in considering the policy of furnishing an aid to foreign allies, is not always taken into contemplation.

counted) in the place in which it is drawn, to some person in the same place; and the buyer or discounter gives for the bill that article, whatever it may be, which forms the current payment of the spot. This article may consist either of gold or silver coin, or of bank paper, or, which is much the same thing as bank paper, of a credit in the books of some public bank.

Let us now suppose that the exporter of corn from Hamburgh to London draws a bill for 100*l.* on London, and offers it for sale on the Hamburgh Exchange at the season when great exportations of corn to London are taking place. The persons in Hamburgh having occasion to buy bills are fewer, in such a case, than those who want to sell them; and the price of the bill, like that of any other article, fluctuates according to the proportion subsisting between the supply and the demand. The disproportion, then, between the number of those persons at Hamburgh who want to sell London bills for Hamburgh coin, and the number of those who want to sell Hamburgh coin for London bills, causes the price of London bills to fall, and of Hamburgh coin to rise. Thus gold is said to rise at Hamburgh; and the exchange between London and Hamburgh becomes unfavourable to London. This fluctuation in the exchange will, in the first instance, be small. It will be limited to that trifling sum which it costs to transport bullion from the one place to the other, so long as there is bullion to be transported. But let us now suppose the number of Hamburgh bills on London, drawn for the payment of the goods imported into the latter place, to be so numerous, that the exportation of all the bullion which is purchasable in Great Britain, has not sufficed for their payment. Gold coin, in this case, will be exported, being first melted down for the purpose. Coin, indeed, is not allowed to be exported from Great Britain, nor gold which has been melted down from coin; an oath being required of every exporter of gold, that the gold which he exports does not consist of guineas which have been melted. There are, however, many ways of escaping the law which imposes this oath. The law is dishonestly evaded either by the clandestine exportation of guineas, no oath at all being taken; or by taking a false oath; or by contriving that the person taking the oath shall be, in some degree, ignorant of the melting which has been practised. The operation of the law is avoided without this dishonesty, through the exportation of gold which had been turned, or had been about to be turned, to the purposes of gilded and golden ornaments, the place of this gold being supplied by gold melted down from coin. The state of the British law unquestionably serves to discourage and limit, though not effectually to hinder, that exportation of guineas which is encouraged by an unfavourable balance of trade; and, perhaps, scarcely lessens it, when the profit on exportation becomes very great. The law tends, indeed, to produce a greater interchange of gold for paper at home. But it encreases whatever evil arises from an unfavourable state of the exchange with foreign countries.

Let it now be considered how this high price of gold in London must operate in respect to the Bank of England. Great demands for guineas will be made on the bank; and, in general, probably by persons not intending to melt or export guineas themselves, but wishing only to supply that want which all have begun to experience in consequence of the large illicit exportations carried on by a few unknown persons. It is assumed, for the present, that the bank is paying in guineas. What, then, is the course which the bank will naturally pursue? Finding the guineas in their coffers to lessen every day, they must naturally be supposed to be desirous of replacing them by all effectual and not extravagantly expensive means. They will be disposed, to a certain degree, to buy gold, though at a losing price, and to coin it into new guineas; but they will have to do this at the very moment when many are privately melting what is coined. The one party will be melting and selling, while the other is buying and coining. And each of these two contending businesses will now be carried on not on account of an actual exportation of each melted guinea to Hamburgh, but the operation (or, at least, a great part of it) will be confined to London; the coiners and the melters living on the same spot, and giving constant employment to each other.

The bank, if we suppose it, as we now do, to carry on this sort of contest with the melters, is obviously waging a very unequal war; and even though it should not be tired early, it will be likely to be tired sooner than its adversaries.

The dilemma in which the bank is thus placed, is evidently one which implies no deficiency in its wealth, in its credit, or in the strength of its resources. The public, during all this time, may have the highest confidence in it. The notes of the bank may be of the same number as usual, possibly somewhat lower in number; its capital and savings may be immensely great, and perfectly well known; its stock may be selling at much above par; its clear annual profits may be considerable. Its gold, nevertheless, through the operation of that one cause which has just been named, may be growing less and less. And it is not at all impossible, if an alarm at home should draw away the gold at the same time, that, however ample its general fund may have been, it may be reduced to its last guinea; and may actually be brought under the necessity of making a temporary suspension of its payments.

An important subject of enquiry here suggests itself. Dr. Smith, as was remarked in the beginning of the former chapter, in some degree leads his reader to assume the Bank of England to be in fault (that is, to have issued too many notes) whenever an excess of the market price above the mint price of gold takes place, an excess which produces, as shall immediately be shewn, that difficulty in replenishing the coffers of the bank which has been recently described. If the observation of Dr. Smith be, without exception or qualification true, then the quantity of paper issued by the Bank of England has undoubtedly been excessive throughout the last two years; for the excess of the market price above the mint price of gold has been, during that time, considerable. Then, also, it is the bank which has placed in its own way that obstacle to the purchase of gold which has been spoken of. Any enquiry tending to indicate the causes which place the bank under this singular difficulty, seems to be important.

I shall here endeavour clearly to explain what is meant by the high and the low price of gold; and also by that difference between the mint price and the market price, which has such material consequences.

Gold must be considered as dear, in proportion as goods for which it is exchangeable are cheap; and as cheap, in proportion as goods are dear. Any circumstance, therefore, which serves to make goods generally dear must serve to make gold generally cheap, and *vice versa;* and any circumstance which serves to make goods dear at any particular time or place, must serve to make gold cheap at that time or place, and *vice versa.*

The reason of the difference between the mint price and the market price of gold, does not easily occur. If the bank, from time to time, buys gold at a high price, that is, if it gives for gold a large quantity of goods (or something convertible into a large quantity, which is the same thing); it is natural, on the first view, to suppose that the high price given by the bank, which is the principal and almost the only English purchaser, must form the current English price; and that this high current price of gold in England will prove the means both of bringing it hither, and of detaining it here; causing goods, which are cheap, to go abroad; and gold, which is dear, to come hither, and also to remain in the country. Undoubtedly gold would remain in England, when tempted hither by the high price given for it by the bank, if it were not for the following circumstance. Gold is bought by the bank, in order to be converted into coin; and, when turned into coin, it forms a part of the circulating medium of the country, paper constituting another part. If, then, this paper is by any means rendered cheap, and if the paper so rendered cheap is currently interchanged for one sort of gold, namely, for gold which has been coined, then the coined gold will partake in the cheapness of the paper; that is, it will buy, when in the shape of coin, a smaller quantity of goods than it will purchase when in the form of bullion. In other words, an ounce of gold coming from the mint in the shape of guineas, and making 3*l.* 17*s.* 10½*d.* (for that is the sum into which an ounce always is coined at the mint), will be worth less than the same ounce of gold was worth before it went to the mint, and less than it would again be worth if converted back into bullion. There arises, therefore, a temptation to convert back into bullion, and then to export; or, which is the same thing, to export, and then convert back into bullion; or, which is also the same thing, to convert back into bullion, and then sell to the bank, at the price which would be obtained by exportation, that gold which the bank had turned from bullion into coin. In proportion as the difficulty of collecting, melting, and sending abroad the gold coin is augmented (and it encreases as the quantity of coin diminishes), the difference between the mint and market price of bullion will become more considerable, supposing the demand for gold in foreign countries to continue. Thus it is through the interchangeableness of gold coin with paper, that gold coin is made cheap in England; or, in other words, that goods, in comparison with gold coin, are made dear. The goods which are dear remain, therefore, in England; and the gold coin, which is cheap (for the bank is indisposed to buy it, on account of the loss sustained on each coinage,) goes abroad.

There is, undoubtedly, much ground for the supposition of Dr. Smith, that a diminution of the quantity of paper has a tendency to cure this evil. It tends to render the paper more valuable, and, therefore, to make that gold coin more valuable for which the paper is interchangeable, and thus to destroy that excess of the market price above the mint price of gold, which forms the obstacle to the introduction of a supply of gold into the coffers of the bank. There seems, nevertheless, to be much of inaccuracy and error in the doctrine of Dr. Smith on this subject. He begins by representing the quantity of paper which may properly circulate, as to be measured by that of the gold which would circulate if there were no paper. The reader is, therefore, led to believe, that a difference between the mint price and the market price of gold arises from an issue of a greater quantity. Dr. Smith also too much countenances an idea, that the excess consists of paper *forced* into circulation; for he terms the proper quantity that paper which will "easily circulate." He, moreover, induces his reader to suppose, that the excessive issue is an issue to a more than usual amount. At the time of a very unfavourable balance of trade (an event which Dr. Smith leaves totally out of his consideration), it is very possible, as I apprehend, that the excess of paper, if such it is to be called, is merely an excess above that very low and reduced quantity to which it is necessary that it should be brought down, in order to prevent the existence of an excess of the market price above the mint price of gold. I conceive, therefore, that this excess, if it arises on the occasion of an unfavourable balance of trade, and at a time when there has been no extraordinary emission of notes, may fairly be considered as an excess created by that unfavourable balance, though it is one which a reduction of notes tends to cure.

The fair statement of the case seems to be this. At the time of a very unfavourable balance (produced, for example, through a failure of the harvest), a country has occasion for large supplies of corn from abroad: but either it has not the means of supplying at the instant a sufficient quantity of goods in return, or, which is much the more probable case, and the case which I suppose more applicable to England, the goods which the country having the unfavourable balance is able to furnish as means of cancelling its debt, are not in such demand abroad as to afford the prospect of a tempting or even of a tolerable price; and this want of a demand may happen possibly through some political circumstance which has produced, in a particular quarter, the temporary interruption of an established branch of commerce. The country, therefore, which has the favourable balance, being, to a certain degree, eager for payment, but not in immediate want of all that supply of goods which would be necessary to pay the balance, prefers gold as part, at least, of the payment; for gold can always be turned to a more beneficial use than a very great overplus of any other commodity. In order, then, to induce the country having the favourable balance to take all its payment in goods, and no part of it in gold, it would be requisite not only to prevent goods from being very dear, but even to render them excessively cheap. It would be necessary, therefore, that the bank should not only not encrease its paper, but that it should, perhaps, very greatly diminish it, if it would endeavour to prevent gold from going out in part of payment of the unfavourable balance. And if the bank do this, then there will arise those other questions, which Dr. Smith leaves totally out of his consideration; namely, whether the bank, in the attempt to produce this very low price, may not, in a country circumstanced as Great Britain is, so exceedingly distress trade and discourage manufactures as to impair, in the manner already specified, those sources of our returning wealth to which we must chiefly trust for the restoration of our balance of trade, and for bringing back the tide of gold into Great Britain. It is also necessary to notice in this place, that the favourable effect which a limitation of bank paper produces on the exchange is certainly not instantaneous, and may, probably, only be experienced after some considerable interval of time; it may, therefore, in many cases, be expected that the exchange will rectify itself before the reduction of bank paper can have any operation. It is also to be recollected (a point, indeed, which Dr. Smith himself states), that gold is retained or drawn away, not by the limitation or the encrease of the Bank of England paper alone, but by that of their paper, conjointly with that of the other paper of the country. The bank paper serves, it is true, to regulate, in a great degree, that other paper; but not with exactness. The bank, by proceeding to that reduction of its own paper which is necessary to bring gold into the country, may possibly annihilate, before it is aware, a part or even almost the whole of the circulating country bank notes, and much other paper also; and it may, in that case, have to supply gold sufficient to fill the whole void, perhaps more than the whole void, which it has created; for it may be called upon to furnish large additional sums which may forthwith be hoarded in consequence of the alarm thus occasioned. Hence, even though it should encrease the supply of gold from abroad; it may augment, in a far greater degree, the demand for it at home. For this reason, it may be the true policy and duty of the bank to permit, for a time, and to a certain extent, the continuance of that unfavourable exchange, which causes gold to leave the country, and to be drawn out of its own coffers: and it must, in that case, necessarily encrease its loans to the same extent to which its gold is diminished. The bank, however, ought generally to be provided with a fund of gold so ample, as to enable it to pursue this line of conduct, with safety to itself, through the period of an unfavourable balance; a period, the duration of which may, to a certain degree, be estimated, though disappointment in a second harvest may cause much error in the calculation.

The more particular examination of this subject of an unfavourable exchange, brings us, therefore, to the same conclusion to which we were led in the former Chapter; namely, that the bank ought to avoid too contracted an issue of bank notes. The absence of gold, though itself an evil, may prevent other evils of greater moment; and may thus conduce, under certain circumstances, to the good of the country. Our gold has lately furnished the prompt payment for a part of that corn, which has been necessary for our consumption. The common manufacturer, if he understood his own interest, would approve rather than complain of the temporary substitution of paper for gold, which has been thus occasioned: for the export of gold has served to ease him in the first instance: his labour, indeed, must hereafter purchase back again the gold which has been exported, but he will have to buy it back by exertions less severe than would otherwise have been needful. The price of the goods which he manufactures, and, consequently, the price also of his own labour, is rendered somewhat higher by not glutting the foreign market with a quantity of articles altogether disproportionate to the demand. It should farther be remembered, that gold is an unproductive part of our capital: that the interest upon the sum exported is so much saved to the country: and that the export of gold serves, as far as it goes, to improve the exchange, by discharging the debt due on account of an unfavourable balance of trade; and to prevent the depreciation of our own paper currency, as compared with the current money payments of other countries.

It may probably be thought that the exported gold will not return. This subject may deserve a careful enquiry. It should be observed, in the first place, that, in order to produce an improvement in the exchange, we have only to suppose the present degree of the *pressure for payment* of goods imported to abate. It may happen, for instance, that in consequence of Hamburgh having become richer through the favourable harvest enjoyed in the surrounding countries, and through the high price obtained for its exported corn, while Britain has become poorer; the antecedent custom of Hamburgh merchants being in debt to London merchants may change, and a contrary custom may become prevalent. If this new debt of London to Hamburgh should be permitted to exist in the same manner as the Hamburgh debt may be supposed to have existed before, the exchange will not be affected by it. The debt which affects the exchange is only that sort of debt, the payment of which is more or less eagerly demanded. A country, therefore, seems likely soon to arrive at a limit in this respect. It has only to diminish not the debt itself, but the pressure of the demand for payment, and the exchange begins to mend. Let the two countries become equally satisfied to allow the debt to continue as it is, and the exchange finds its level. Again; let the country in debt prove itself to be somewhat more desirous to pay its debt, a debt of course running at interest, than the creditor country is to receive payment; and the exchange will be even in favour of the debtor country.

It may naturally be enquired what becomes of the gold which has been supposed to go from this country to Hamburgh; and how it comes to pass that it is there demanded in such large quantities. When Britain has already spared out of its circulation, and out of the coffers of its principal bank, many millions, perhaps, of gold; whence happens it that Europe, having only the same trade as before, uses all that is sent, and continues to call, by means of the exchange, for a still encreasing supply?

I understand that, at the period of every very favourable exchange to Hamburgh, most of the gold poured in thither is melted down into the several sorts of coin which are current on the continent; and that it then becomes an article of remittance to various places. It is, of course, remitted to those parts in which the balance of trade with Hamburgh is unfavourable to that city. Still, however, the difficulty of accounting for the new and *general* demand for gold seems to remain. The following considerations may afford some solution of it. When the trade of the world, or of many separate and considerable places, is more than usually fluctuating, as in times of political uncertainty or convulsion it can hardly fail to be, a larger quantity of gold is wanted than when confidence is high, and when the several exports and imports of different countries more nearly balance each other. Gold, during any extraordinary irregularity in trade between independent states, is the most commodious of all articles of remittance. It is a species of return which Hamburgh, for instance, can send to every place from which its spirit of speculation may have called for articles of commerce. It is, indeed, only the balance of the accounts which is paid in money; but, at different times, there may be balances of different sizes to be thus discharged. Whatever event, therefore, so disturbs the course of trade over the continent as to cause an encrease in the balances of the trade of independent countries, seems likely to cause an augmentation of the general demand for gold. But the general demand for gold is also affected by the degree of confidence at the same time subsisting. It has been already shewn, that the quantity of gold requisite for the circulation of any single country may be very different at different periods, and that the difference is proportioned to the degree of confidence between man and man existing at the several seasons. The quantity of gold wanted for the general trade of the world may also fluctuate, in some degree, from the same cause. It is, however, likely also to vary from a variation in the confidence subsisting between independent countries. For the sake of illustration, let us suppose that Hamburgh owes to some town in Prussia, one hundred miles distant, 100,000*l.* sterling, in consequence of an unfavourable balance of trade occasioned by corn purchased there, and exported by Hamburgh merchants to London; a balance which, if the creditors in the Prussian town were willing to wait six months, would probably by that time be repaid, and even more than repaid, through the importation into the same town of West India articles which Hamburgh would have received within that period from Great Britain. If confidence is high, the merchants of this town will be content, for the sake, perhaps, of an addition of one per cent. to the stipulated interest, to permit the debt to remain unextinguished for the six months; and in this case the course of exchange between the Prussian town and Hamburgh will alter to the extent of one per cent. But if, through the want of confidence subsisting between the Prussian town and Hamburgh, an addition not of one, but of two per cent. to the current interest should be considered to be the adequate compensation for the risk incurred, the exchange will fluctuate two per cent.; and a variation of two per cent. in the exchange will produce, let it be supposed, to the Hamburgh debtors a greater loss than would be incurred by the expence of transporting 100,000*l.* in gold to the Prussian town in question. Gold is, therefore, in that case, transported. On the two circumstances, taken together, of the largeness of the balance between the independent places, and the degree of confidence subsisting between them, appears to depend the quantity of bullion required. It seems, therefore, by no means difficult to account for the manner in which large quantities of gold exported from this country may be employed on the continent in seasons of general distrust, even though we should not suppose any great portion to be hoarded.

Bullion to a very large amount was retained in the Spanish settlements, during the latter period of the war, through the fear of capture; and perhaps, therefore, we might trace in part the want of gold, of which we have complained, to those successful exertions in watching the ports of the enemy which have been made by the British navy.

The immediate cause, however, of the exportation of our coin has been an unfavourable exchange, produced partly by our heavy expenditure, though chiefly by the superadded circumstance of two successively bad harvests. When the recurrence of a favourable balance of trade is long delayed, the fluctuation of the exchange may be expected to be not an immaterial one. The exchange is, in some degree, sustained for a time, which is thought likely to be short, through the readiness of foreigners to speculate in it; but protracted speculations of this sort do not equally answer, unless the fluctuation in the exchange is very considerable. If, for example, a foreigner remits money to London, at a period when the exchange has become unfavourable to England to the extent of three per cent., places it at interest in the hands of a British merchant, and draws for it in six months afterwards, the exchange having by that time returned to its usual level, he gains two and a half per cent. for a half year's interest on his money, and also three per cent. by the course of exchange, which is five and a half per cent. in half a year, or eleven per cent. per annum. But if the same foreigner remits money to England when the exchange has, in like manner, varied three per cent., and draws for it not in six months but in two years, the exchange having returned to its usual level only at the end of that long period, the foreigner then gains ten per cent. interest on his money, and three per cent. by the exchange, or thirteen per cent. in two years: that is to say, he gains in this case six and a half per cent. per annum, but in the other eleven per cent. per annum. If a variation of three per cent. is supposed necessary to induce foreigners to speculate for a period which is expected to end in six months, a variation of no less than twelve per cent. would be necessary to induce them to speculate for a period which is expected to end in two years. The improvement of our exchange with Europe having been delayed through a second bad harvest, it is not surprising that the expectation of its recovery within a short time should have been weakened in the mind of foreigners. Indeed, many circumstances, some of which have been already touched upon,* concurred, towards the conclusion of the war, in rendering our exchange unfavourable.

Some gold, it may be presumed, was retained in the bank coffers, which, if the cash payments of that company had not been suspended, would have found its way to foreign countries, and have contributed to remedy the existing evil.

We depended chiefly, as will be shewn hereafter, on the proper limitation of the quantity of our circulating paper, though partly, also, on the degree of expectation which was kept up abroad of the future improvement of our exchange; an expectation which might be rendered greater or less by a variety of circumstances. Great Britain has had this great advantage over those countries which are in the habit either of depreciating their coin or of allowing a discount on their paper, that they, in anticipating the return of a more favourable state of their trade, look forward only to a time when

---

* A mistaken idea of the bank payments having been suspended through the improper largeness of its loans to government, and of its resembling the continental banks which have issued excessive quantities of paper for the service of their several governments, was before stated to be not unlikely to have prevailed abroad, too much countenance having been given in this country to such a sentiment. Foreigners, if such was their opinion, would conceive that our exchange was a permanently declining one, and that it would, therefore, answer better to them to draw than to remit, and to draw immediately than to delay drawing. The idea that foreign property might be seized in England as an act of retaliation for the British property seized in the north of Europe, may also have had some influence. The expectation of seizures on each side would prejudice the exchange of whichever country was in debt, and the country in debt happened to be Great Britain.

their uncertain and unstable rate of exchange may be meliorated in a degree not easy to be calculated; whereas we have anticipated a period when an intrinsically valuable and specific standard would be restored, when our banks would be obliged to pay fully in guineas containing the same weight of gold as before, and when our exchange, therefore, might be expected completely to return to its former level.

Undoubtedly, circumstances of so great and extraordinary a nature may arise as to prevent the return of gold at an early or assignable period. It may, however, be safely affirmed, that when the main sources of a country's wealth are unimpaired; when its population, its industry, its manufacturing and trading capital, its general commerce, its credit, its colonial possessions, its political strength and independence, its laws and constitution remain; and when, moreover, its paper is confined within its accustomed bounds; the absence of its gold, more especially if it be the obvious consequence of one or more unfavourable seasons, is an evil which is likely neither to be durable, nor in any respect very important.

Under such circumstances, to alter materially the old and accustomed system of paper credit, and, in particular, to restrain in any very extraordinary degree the issues of paper of more responsible banks, is to deprive a country of those means of recovering itself which it naturally possesses. This seems to be the fair inference from the observations which have been stated in the present and preceding Chapters. The return of gold is to be promoted not so much by any legislative measure directed to that immediate object, as by cherishing the general industry, and attending to the higher and more leading interests of the community.

It may be proper here to add, that the experience of past times, both of war and peace, leads us to suppose, that the exchange between Great Britain and foreign countries is not likely to remain for any long period unfavourable to Great Britain. Experience has likewise proved, that the return of gold has not been precluded by the law which authorized the continuance of the suspension of the cash payments of the bank; for, while that law was in force, there occurred one season during which gold flowed with a remarkably strong tide into the country.

It seems scarcely necessary now to dwell on the reasons which evince that the repeal of the law in question, in the last period of the war, would have been inexpedient. It would have been to repeal it at a time not a little resembling that in which the parliament first thought proper to enact it: for it would have been to repeal it when gold had been recently drawn out of the country by an unfavourable exchange; and when we were subjected, as before, to alarms of invasion. To have opened the bank would have been, moreover, to have subjected it not only to a demand for gold on these two accounts but also to such extra calls as might have arisen from the anxiety of the country banks to provide for the event of the first opening more amply than might have been permanently necessary. The renewal, therefore, of the law for suspending the cash payments of the bank stood on the ground of the particular circumstances of the times, and not on any principle which necessarily implied the permanence or even the long continuance of the suspension.

Chap. VI.

Error of imagining that Gold can be provided at the Time of actual Distress—Reasons for not admitting the Presumption that the Directors of the Bank must have been to blame for not making beforehand a more adequate Provision.

The impracticability of encreasing the fund of gold in the Bank of England, when an alarm at home has already taken place, or even during the period of a very unfavourable balance of trade, has been manifested in the preceding pages.

There is a peculiar inconsistency in the supposition that

a country ought, at such a season, to take its measures for encreasing the quantity of its gold. The argument for such an attempt would run thus—" The stock of gold has been in " past time too low, as appears by the experience of the pre- " sent period; for it is not now sufficient to supply what " is necessary for our own circulation, and to enable us also " to pay our unfavourable balance. We ought, therefore, " to take due care that, in time to come, there shall be a " larger provision of gold in the country." So far, undoubtedly, there may be some general justice in the reasoning. But if the further inference is added, that we must, therefore, *now* begin to make the provision, this is to propose to take measures to provide against a want, which is future and contingent, at a time when that very want which we would prevent is actually pressing upon us. With as fair an appearance of justice it might have been argued in respect to the stock of corn in hand in the country—" The stock of " corn has been, as now appears, for some time too low; for " it is, at the present season, insufficient for the due supply " of the country. We ought, therefore, to take care that, " in time to come, there shall be a better provision for such " contingencies as the present." So far, undoubtedly, there might be justice in the observation. But to proceed in our reasoning as to corn, in the same manner as is sometimes done in respect to guineas, would be to add—" Therefore, " now, while the scarcity is pressing upon us, let us begin " to make this provision; let us instantly stock our granaries " with a surplus quantity of corn; let us divert the little " grain which we possess from those most necessary uses to " which it is now destined. Let us encrease our present diffi- " culty, in order that the country may be put, for the future, " out of the reach of the danger which it is experiencing at " the present hour." The two cases are not, indeed, precisely parallel; but there seems to be sufficient resemblance to justify the elucidation.

There is, however, another ground on which the directors of the bank may possibly be thought censurable—that of having failed to supply themselves with a sufficient quantity of gold at an antecedent period. Let us, therefore, enquire whether the public has sufficient reasons for entertaining this suspicion.

Let it be premised, that, since the directors of the Bank of England can have no particular temptation to improvidence; and since our national bank is, from its very nature, liable to that accident which has lately, for the first time, befallen it, a liability which, for obvious reasons, it may have been the custom too studiously to conceal, there is not all that previous presumption of blame which might be supposed. There can be no doubt that the credit of the Bank of England has been, at all periods, most anxiously consulted by its directors; and that present profit has uniformly been only the second consideration.

There are, however, certain limits which, even when gold is most easily purchased, the bank naturally prescribes to itself in respect to its stock of that article. The amount of the disposable effects of the bank, on the 26th of February, 1797, was stated under three heads in a former place; and it was then observed, that the only part of them which the bank itself could enlarge was the deposits lodged in return for bank notes issued. But even the bank notes cannot safely be encreased in a degree which is very considerable. Indeed, experience has proved, that there may be some sort of limit to the demand for them; for the applications for loans have often amounted, during peace, to less than the bank has been disposed to afford on the credit of good bills at the existing rate of discount.

Let us, then, proceed to illustrate our subject by supposing the disposable effects of the bank to have usually stood, for some years antecedent to the suspension of its cash payments, at the sum of about nineteen millions; that is to say, let us allow them to have been about a million and a half more than they amounted to at that period.

It must not be imagined that these nineteen millions could, at any time, be with propriety invested in gold. For the Bank of England, like every other mercantile establishment, carries on its business on such principles as will produce a profit. And the very lowest profit which can serve as a sufficient inducement to pursue the trade of banking, must be somewhat higher than the mere current interest of money. Let us reckon this *necessary profit* of the bank to be six per cent. The bank makes no more than three per cent. interest on the capital subscribed by its members, which is permanently lent to government. It must, then, so manage its disposable effects as to gain an annual sum equal to an additional three per cent. upon its own capital, that is, about 350,000*l.* This it must do by lending out at interest a part of the nineteen millions; and it must lend out, at interest, a still farther part of it, both in order to defray the annual charges of its establishment, and in order also to furnish the means of paying those occasional sums to government which are required as the price of the renewal of its charter. It will be found, perhaps, that not less than ten or twelve of the nineteen millions must be always at interest in order to provide for these objects; and, consequently, that eight or nine millions will have formed the highest average sum which the bank can have kept in gold, consistently with the acquisition of merely the necessary profit on its capital. But neither is it fair to suppose, that these eight or nine millions ought to have been the general or average sum kept in gold. The cash of the bank fluctuates very greatly; and in order to secure the keeping of cash and bullion to the average amount of eight or nine millions, it will occasionally have been necessary to keep twelve or fourteen millions, or possibly even more. This sum would be most unreasonably large; for during the time when twelve or fourteen millions are invested in gold, the bank, instead of gaining six per cent. on its capital, will not gain above three or four; and, moreover, it cannot exactly know how long this extraordinary quantity of gold may continue in its coffers. It certainly can never count beforehand on those great reductions of cash which may serve, by increasing the sum at interest, to compensate for what is lost by a large detention of bullion: for the reduction of cash happens not through any measures taken by the bank, but in consequence of events difficult to be foreseen, and, as has been already shewn, by no means easy to be controlled. The bank, therefore, without impeachment of the character of its directors, may be reasonably presumed to have been at least somewhat indisposed to make investments in bullion, which, while they lasted, should reduce its income very far below the necessary annual profit.

Thus the bank, in endeavouring to secure what has been termed the necessary annual profit, would naturally be led to make, on the whole, something more than that profit; and, indeed, a variety of circumstances have lately occurred which have had a tendency to encrease its gains to a degree which must have been unexpected by the bank itself. Let us, then, suppose that the profits which the bank, considering all circumstances, may fairly and properly have derived from its business for some years past, may have been not six per cent. (which was spoken of as the lowest sum necessary for carrying on the trade of banking), but seven or eight per cent. Now seven or eight per cent. or a little more, seems likely to be that profit which the bank has, in point of fact, been gaining. The dividends which it has paid to the proprietors have been, for some time, seven per cent.; and it has also added 3,800,000*l.* to its capital. This addition has been accruing, no doubt, during a long course of years. If we assume that it has accumulated at the rate of about 116,000*l.* per annum, the bank will have gained annually one per cent. on its capital, besides the seven per cent. which has been divided; if at 232,000*l.** per annum, the bank will have gained annually two per cent. on its capital, besides the seven per cent. which has been divided.

The bank, then, let it be supposed, has been gaining eight or nine per cent. when seven or eight per cent. is as much as it is reasonable that it should have acquired. I

* This is to suppose that the savings of the bank have been between sixteen and seventeen years in accumulating, a period certainly much too short; but the accumulation must have been more rapid during the last years.

have entered into this detail, which, in various parts, may be somewhat erroneous, merely for the sake of shewing that any proposed enquiry whether the quantity of gold kept by the bank may or may not have been too small, must necessarily be much narrower than many persons may imagine. According to the supposition just made, it can relate only to the propriety of a past annual gain of about one per cent. or at most of two per cent. on the bank capital. A gain of one per cent. would have been about 116,000*l.* per annum; and consequently the bank, by taking this gain, have, on an average, kept a stock of gold which has been smaller than it would otherwise have possessed by about 2,300,000*l.* Whether this sum of 2,300,000*l.*, or whether any sum somewhat greater than this, or somewhat short of it, ought or ought not, in time past, to have been invested in gold in addition to the sum which was invested, is a point on which all that it seems safe to affirm with confidence, is, that no person, unacquainted with the affairs of the bank can be capable of pronouncing any clear judgment. There must have existed many arguments, and some standing even on the ground of safety and credit, against maintaining the additional fund which has been mentioned.

If the whole profits of the bank had been lately restricted to seven per cent., they would have been limited to that sum which the bank proprietors had been for some time in the habit of receiving. They would have been confined to a sum which would not easily have admitted of accumulations. By obtaining a higher profit the directors have secured to the proprietors the continuation of the same regular dividend, and have thus prevented that uncertainty which would have encouraged gambling in bank stock.

They have also made, in the course of years, an important addition to their capital; an addition which has caused it to maintain nearly an uniform proportion to the growing extent of the transactions of the bank, and to the advancing commerce of the country; an addition also, by the help of which they have lately lent to government three millions without interest, for a short term of years, as the price of the renewal of their charter. They have thus strengthened that security which the creditors of the bank possess, so far as additional capital can strengthen it; and they will be able hereafter, if it shall seem necessary, to invest in gold, in addition to what they could otherwise have invested, a much larger sum than they could with any propriety have so invested in time past.

It must farther be borne in mind, that the necessity under which the bank has been placed of providing gold which is to fill the void occasioned by the disappearing of country bank notes, has been, in part, a new necessity, country bank notes not having circulated, at remoter periods, in so great a degree as they have lately; and that the additional sum of two or even of three or four millions would have been no security against the effects of a general alarm in the country. The fluctuation in the balance of trade with foreign countries, which we experience, is also become, in consequence of the greater extent of our population and commerce, larger than heretofore. The scale of all things having encreased, the scale of this balance may have encreased also to a degree unexpected by the bank. A war, moreover, unprecedented as that in which we have lately been engaged was not to be anticipated; and the case of a succession of two bad harvests, and of an importation of corn, amounting in two years to the value of fifteen or twenty millions, is felt by all to have been an extraordinary event. We need not wonder, then, if events unforeseen by others, were not foreseen by the Bank of England; nor if for unforeseen events an adequate provision was not at hand.

On the whole, it may be suggested to those who cast blame on the bank for its improvidence in time past, that they should consider well the several points which have here been briefly pointed out; and that if, afterwards, they continue to think the bank censurable, they should ask themselves, before they become the censurers, whether they are sure that, in taking upon themselves the office, they exercise that candour with which they would expect to be judged if they had been themselves, during the late difficult and trying period, directors of that institution.

It has already been observed, that, in that crisis during which the conduct of the directors has been more particularly known, they proceeded, perhaps, with too great fear and caution rather than with too little. There seems, therefore, to be a presumption, that a character, if not for caution, at least for tolerable prudence, must have generally been their due. To say the least, there appears to be no ground for charging them with having acted in antecedent times on a directly opposite principle.

CHAP. VII.

Of Country Banks—their Advantages and Disadvantages.

THE country banks in Great Britain appear to have amounted, in the year 1797, to three hundred and fifty-three. By a numeration taken in 1799, they appear to have been three hundred and sixty-six. By a third numeration taken in 1800, they were three hundred and eighty-six.* It seems, therefore, that no material addition to their number has arisen in these three years.

A great increase of country banks took place during the time which intervened between the American and the present war, and chiefly in the latter part of it; a period during which the trade, the agriculture, and the population of the country must have advanced very considerably. The circumstance of so many of our country banks having originated at such a time, affords a presumption that they are consequences and tokens of the prosperity, rather than

* This statement of the number of country banks is taken from three printed accounts of them, the first of which may not have been very accurate, but may be presumed to state them at too low rather than too high a number. The two later enumerations were made in a more careful manner.

indications of the declining state of the country. No banks have arisen in France during the period of its troubles, though several attempts to erect them have been made. It was with difficulty that any banks supported themselves in America during the war; but after the establishment of peace, banks were instituted in most of the American states. They seem naturally to belong to all commercial countries; but are more particularly likely to be multiplied in a state like ours, in which the mercantile transactions are extended, the population is great, and the expenditure of individuals considerable; and where also a principal bank exists, which, through the necessity imposed on it by its situation, undertakes the task of providing a constant reservoir of gold accessible to every smaller banking establishment. The creation of the large bank operates as a premium on the institution of the smaller.

A description of the origin of one of our smaller country banks may elucidate the subject before us. In every town, and in many villages, there existed, antecedently to the creation of what were afterwards termed banks, some trader, manufacturer, or shopkeeper, who acted, in many respects, as a banker to the neighbourhood. The shopkeeper, for example, being in the habit of drawing bills on London, and of remitting bills thither, for the purposes of his own trade, and receiving also much money at his shop, would occasionally give gold to his customers, taking in return their bills on the metropolis, which were mixed with his other bills, and sent to his London correspondent.

Persons who were not customers being also found to want either money for bills, or bills for money, the shopkeeper was led to charge something for his trouble on accommodating them: and the trade of taking and drawing bills being thus rendered profitable, it became an object to encrease it. For the sake of drawing custom to his house, the shopkeeper, having as yet possibly little or no view to the issuing of bank notes, printed "The Bank" over his door, and engraved these words on the checks on which he drew his bills.

It may be assumed, also, to have been not uncommon, before country banks were established, for the principal shopkeeper in a town to take at interest some of the money of his neighbours, on the condition, however, that he should not be required to pay it back without some notice. The money thus deposited with him, or borrowed by him (it is difficult to say which term is the more proper), might either be thrown into his trade, or employed in discounting bills soon to become due; but the latter would evidently be the more safe and prudent way of investing it.

All these parts of the banking business arose out of the situation and circumstances of the country; and existed in many places before the name of banker was assumed.

The practice of issuing country bank notes, that is to say, notes payable to the bearer on demand, may, undoubtedly, be considered as a separate branch of business. These notes, however, have been shown to be not so very different in their nature from other paper as is commonly imagined.

For the sake of more particularly proving this point, let us advert to the nature of interest notes, a species of paper which some country banks have issued to a great extent. Even the shopkeeper, it was lately observed, would take sums at interest. For each of these sums, especially if he became a banker, he would give out his note, in which would be expressed the sum lent or deposited, the rate of interest upon it, and the time which was to intervene before payment could be demanded. This note would be transferable to any third person. There would, however, be some impediments to its circulation. The interest must be calculated as often as it should change hands. Some of the persons to whom it was offered might not be disposed to accept it as a payment, especially if it had a long time to run. Although these notes might circulate, they would circulate heavily. In order to promote their circulation, and thus encrease the whole number of issuable notes, the banker would be inclined to lessen the time within which they should be payable; and he would find that, in proportion as he adopted this practice, a lower rate of interest on the notes would suffice to induce persons to take them. Notes carrying no interest would circulate, if due within a short time, better than notes bearing interest which should be due at a very distant period. But the only notes which would circulate freely would be those which should be payable, or at least paid, without any notice. Some banks wishing, on the one hand, to encourage the circulation of their paper, and, on the other, to avoid the inconvenience of a strict obligation to pay without notice have issued notes payable after a certain time, and yet have been in the regular practice of giving money for them whenever payment was demanded, and have taken no discount for the accommodation.

Thus, then, the shorter the notice is, the greater is the currency of the note; and in proportion, therefore, as the circumstances of a country render it more safe for the banks to shorten their notice, in the same proportion it may be expected that notes to the bearer on demand will be issued, and gold displaced.

Some speculative persons have imagined, that the practice pursued by bankers of emitting notes payable on demand is founded on an altogether vicious and unwarrantable principle, inasmuch as such paper is issued with a view to a profit which is to be obtained only by lending out part of the sum necessary for the payment. A number of promises, it is said, are thus made, which the banker has evidently placed it out of his power to perform, supposing the fulfilment of them all to be required at the same time, an event by no means impossible. This objection implies, that the banker ought not, after receiving the deposits left with him by his customers, to lend out part of the sum necessary for the payment of those deposits; for he is as much bound to discharge demands for deposits without notice, as to pay without notice all his notes. The Bank of England, the London banker, the country banker, the merchant, and also the individual of every class, proceed, in respect to all their promises to pay money, not on any principle of moral certainty, but on that of reasonable and sufficient probability. The objection to bank notes, *as such,* if pushed to that extent to which, if it is at all just, it might be carried, would apply to all verbal promises to pay money, and, indeed, to almost all promises whatever; for there is scarcely any class of these for the performance of which a *perfectly sure* provision is always made at the time of giving the promise. The objection implies, therefore, that men ought to be prohibited from acting in their commercial concerns according to that rule of sufficient probability by which all the other affairs of human life are conducted.*

It is completely understood by the holders of notes, as well as by the customers of banks, that instant payment is provided for only a part of that sum which may, by possibility, be demanded; and the banker, therefore, seems fully justified if he makes such provision as the general and known usage of others in the same profession (for he is supposed, by those who trust him, to follow this usage), and a prudent regard to all the circumstances of his own case teach him to consider as sufficient.

The practice of issuing notes payable to bearer on demand became very common a few years antecedent to the present war, when various circumstances united to encourage this part of the country banker's employment. Confidence was then high, the number of traders in the country had been greatly multiplied, the income and expenditure of individuals were much encreased, and every branch, therefore, of the banking business had naturally enlarged itself. Some addition had been made to the number of London bankers; and a few of these took forward and active measures to encourage the formation even of very small banks

* In some of the democratic pamphlets of the present day, bank notes of every kind are spoken of not merely as liable to be carried to excess, or to be issued by irresponsible persons, or as producing particular evils, but as radically and incurably vicious; they are considered in the light of a complete fraud upon the public, which is practised by the rich, and connived at by the government; and the very issue of them has been stigmatised as equivalent to the crime of forgery. The resemblance of bank notes to other paper, and the resemblance of a promise on paper to any other promise, have been here touched upon with a view of exposing the absurdity of those doctrines.

in the country, with a view to the benefit expected from a connection with them. In many of our great towns, a fair opening was afforded for the erection of additional banks. These new establishments having taken place, various country traders, who had before made use of their own correspondents in London, fell into the practice of transacting their business with the metropolis through the medium of the country banker with whom they kept their cash. The country banker drew largely on a London banker on the account of the country traders, and the London banker was willing to execute the extensive country business which he thus acquired, in consideration of a much lower commission than had before been paid by the several country traders to their separate correspondents in London, who had been, for the most part, London merchants. The reduction of the rate of commission arose from two causes: first, from the new security which was afforded to the transactions between the town and the country, by the interposition of the credit of rich and responsible country banks; and, secondly, from the transfer to one house of that labour of keeping accounts, writing letters, and receiving and paying bills, which had, before, been divided among many. The risk and trouble being diminished, a proportionate abatement in the rate of commission could be afforded.

The multiplication even of country banks, purposing to deal chiefly in bills, would tend, in many ways, to produce an encreased issue of notes on demand. Some deposit of gold would be kept by banks of every class, with the view of satisfying the demands of their customers; and the stock, maintained for this purpose, would form a part of the necessary provision for the payment of notes payable on demand, and it would, therefore, become an encouragement to the issue of them. The multiplication of deposits of gold through the country would, moreover, furnish, in many cases, more prompt means of obtaining gold on any sudden emergency; since one country bank might often procure a supply from a neighbouring one, especially if a good understanding on this subject should subsist between them. The establishment of mail coaches afforded, at the same time, a more cheap and ready method than before of bringing gold from London, as well as of transmitting thither any superfluity of it which might arise in the country. In proportion to the facility of obtaining gold, the unproductive stock of it kept in hand might be reduced; or, if the same stock should be maintained, the issue of notes payable on demand would be less hazardous. Indeed, a few old and respectable country banks had long been in the habit of emitting much paper of this sort, and had seldom experienced any inconvenience from doing it. The new ones, therefore, many of which were not at all inferior in property to the old, were led into the practice partly by example.

The circumstance which chiefly operated in procuring currency to the new circulating paper, was that participation of the benefit resulting from it which was enjoyed by the customers of the country banker; for he lent among them the capital which was acquired by the issue of his paper, and they became his instruments in sending it into circulation, by accepting it as a ready-money payment in return for bills discounted. In consideration of their obligations to the banker, and of the interest which they had in his stability, they were also forward, on most occasions, in the support of his credit. Such appear to have been the chief circumstances which led to that great encrease of our country banks, and to that substitution of paper in the place of gold, which have been, for some years past, so much the subject of complaint.

In order to assist the reader in judging whether a preponderance of good or of evil results from our numerous country banks, an endeavour shall now be made to enumerate the principal benefits as well as inconveniences of them.

That country banks have, in a variety of respects, been highly advantageous, can scarcely admit of a doubt. They have afforded an accommodation to many descriptions of persons; but more especially to those who are engaged in commerce. They may be regarded as an effect of that division of labour which naturally takes place in every opulent country. The receipts and the payments of money are now no longer conducted at home, even by the middling trader, but are become a separate branch of business in the hands of bankers. It was to be expected that they to whom this employment has been transferred would find means of abridging labour, and of sparing the use of coin, the most expensive circulating medium. By their skill in attaining these objects, they transact an important portion of the business of the trader at an expence far inferior to that which he must incur were he to conduct it by his own clerks; and they derive a profit to themselves, which, no less than the saving to the customer, may be regarded as clear gain to the kingdom.

Country banks are also useful by furnishing to many persons the means of laying out at interest, and in a safe manner, such money as they may have to spare. Those banks, in particular, which give interest notes for very small sums, afford to the middling and to the lower class of people an encouragement to begin to lay up property, and thus to make provision for the time of sickness or old age. Country banks also furnish a very convenient method of distributing to one class of men the superfluity of another. All who have money to spare know where they can place it, without expence or loss of time, not only in security, but often with pecuniary advantage: and all commercial persons of credit understand in what quarter they can obtain such sums, in the way of loan, as their circumstances will fairly warrant them in borrowing. While country banks thus render a benefit of the first magnitude to fair and prudent commerce, they are important barriers against rash speculation, though not unfrequently they are loudly accused of favouring it. However some few banks may have subjected themselves to this charge, banks in general, and particularly those which have been long established, take care to lend the sums which have been deposited in their hands, not to the imprudent speculator, or to the spendthrift, by whom they are in danger of suffering loss, but to those who, being known to possess some wealth and to manage their concerns with prudence, give proof that they are likely to repay the loan. Borrowers of this class are not apt to enter into very large and perilous undertakings; for they are unwilling to risk the loss of their own capital. Bankers, especially men of eminence, feel a special motive to circumspection, in addition to that which operates with other lenders. The banker always lends under an impression that, if he places in any one a boundless or immoderate confidence, the imprudence will necessarily be known, in case the borrower should fail, as the affairs of every bankrupt are laid open to the body of creditors; and that his rashness is, therefore, liable to become the subject of conversation among his customers. Indiscretion of this kind, even if the particular instance be of no prominent magnitude, may thus prove an occasion of injuring the character and credit of the banking house, and of lessening the general profits of the business.

The banker also enjoys, from the nature of his situation, very superior means of distinguishing the careful trader from him who is improvident. The bill transactions of the neighbourhood pass under his view; the knowledge, thus obtained, aids his judgment; and confidence may, therefore, be measured out by him more nearly than by another person, in the proportion in which ground for it exists. Through the creation of banks, the appreciation of the credit of numberless persons engaged in commerce has become a science; and to the height to which this science is now carried in Great Britain we are in no small degree indebted for the flourishing state of our internal commerce, for the general reputation of our merchants abroad, and for the preference which in that respect they enjoy over the traders of all other nations. It is certainly the interest, and, I believe, it is also the general practice, of banks to limit not only the loan which any one trader shall obtain from themselves, but the total amount also, as far as they are able, of the sum which the same person shall borrow in different places; at the same time, reciprocally to communicate intelligence for their mutual assistance; and, above all, to discourage bills of accommodation. While the transactions of the surrounding traders are thus subject to the view of the country banks, those of the country banks themselves come under the eye of their respective correspondents, the London bankers; and, in some measure, likewise, of the Bank of England. The Bank of England restricts, according to its discretion, the credit given to the London banker. Thus a system of checks is established, which, though certainly very imperfect, answers many important purposes, and, in particular, opposes many impediments to wild speculation.

Country banks, also, as well as the Bank of England, have been highly beneficial, by adding, through the issue of their paper, to the productive capital of the country*. By this accession our manufactures, unquestionably, have been very much extended, our foreign trade has enlarged itself, and the landed interest of the country has had a share of the benefit. The common charge which is brought against country banks, of having raised up a fictitious capital in the country, admits of the following answer. They have substituted, it is true, much paper in the place of gold: but the gold which has gone abroad has brought back, as Dr. Smith observes, valuable commodities in return. The guinea spared from circulation has contributed to bring

* Dr. Smith remarks, that it is not by augmenting the capital of the country, but by rendering a greater part of that capital active and productive than would otherwise be so, that the most judicious operations of banking can encrease the industry of the country. "Dead stock," he observes, "is converted into active and productive stock." Whether the introduction of the use of paper is spoken of as turning dead and unproductive stock into stock which is active and productive, or as *adding* to the stock of the country, is much the same thing. The less the stock of gold is, the greater will be the stock of other kinds; and if a less stock of gold will, through the aid of paper, equally well perform the work of a larger stock, it may be fairly said that the use of paper furnishes even *additional* stock to the country. Thus, for example, the use of a new sort of machinery which costs less in the erection than that which was employed before, and which just as effectually does the work required, since it enables the owner to have always more goods in the course of manufacture, while he has exactly the same means of manufacturing them, might not improperly be described as adding to the stock of the country.

home the timber which has been used in building, the iron or the steel which has been instrumental to the purposes of machinery, and the cotton and the wool which the hand of the manufacturer has worked up. The paper has thus given to the country a *bonâ fide* capital which has been exactly equal to the gold which it has caused to go abroad; and this additional capital has contributed, just like any other part of the national stock, to give life to industry.

It has lately been objected to paper credit, that, by supplying the farmers with large loans, it has enabled them to keep back their corn from the market, and enhance the price. It is true, that farmers, both in the last and many preceding years, may have obtained larger loans than they would have procured if no country bank notes had existed. The capital so furnished to the farmers may possibly have induced some of them, at certain times, to keep in hand a larger quantity of grain than they would otherwise have found it convenient to hold. We know, however, that the general stock of grain in the autumn of 1800 was particularly low. Since, therefore, but a small part of the capital of the farmers, whether borrowed or their own, was then vested in grain, the principal share would probably be laid out on their land, and would encrease its produce; for, unquestionably, the value of a crop obtained from a farm depends chiefly on the sum employed in cultivation and improvement. Country bank notes have thus added to the general supply of grain; and, by doing so, have contributed to prevent a rise in its price: they have, probably, in this manner, afforded much more than a compensation for any temporary advance in price to which they may have given occasion by enabling farmers to keep a larger quantity in hand. The very possession of a large quantity in hand is to be considered as, in general, a benefit rather than a disadvantage; for it is our chief security against scarcity, and, consequently, also against dearness. To the want of a larger surplus stock at the end of the years 1799 and 1800 is to be ascribed, in a great degree, the subsequent high price of provisions. The tendency, therefore, of country bank paper to encrease generally the stock of grain in the hands of the farmer is to be ranked among the advantages of country banks. The tendency to encrease it at the particular time of actual scarcity, is to be classed among the evils which they produce; and it is an inconsiderable evil, which is inseparable from a great and extensive good. To those who are disposed to magnify this occasional evil, it may be further observed, that the farmer is enabled to enlarge his stock by the encrease of his own as well as of the general wealth, much more, no doubt, than by the share which he obtains of that particular part of the new capital of the kingdom which is created through the substitution of country bank notes for gold; only a portion, therefore, of the mischief complained of is to be referred to country bank notes. It is principally to be ascribed to the growing riches and prosperity both of the farmers and other inhabitants of the country.

It is no small additional recommendation of the use of our paper, that the public draws a large yearly revenue from the tax imposed on bills and notes. If paper credit did not exist, a sum equal to that which is thus raised must be supplied by taxes either burthening the industry, or paid out of the property of the people. The public has, since the late additional tax, become a very considerable sharer in the profits of the country bankers' business.

Since, therefore, a paper medium has served the purposes which have been described, and has been, generally speaking, quite as convenient an instrument in settling accounts as the gold which it has displaced, the presumption in favour of its utility seems to be very great; and, if it could be added, that no other effects than those which have as yet been stated have arisen or are likely to arise from it, the advantage of it would be beyond dispute. To reproach it with being a merely fictitious thing, because it possesses not the intrinsic value of gold, is to quarrel with it on account of that quality which is the very ground of its merit. Its merit consists in the circumstance of its costing almost nothing. By means of a very cheap article the country has been, for some years, transacting its money concerns, in which a very expensive material had previously been employed. If this were the whole question, the substitution of paper for gold would be as much to be approved as the introduction of any other efficacious and very cheap instrument in the place of a dear one. It would stand on the same footing with the substitution, for example, of cast iron for wrought iron or steel; of water-carriage for land carriage; of a steam-engine for the labour of men and horses; and might claim a high rank among that multitude of ingenious and economical contrivances to be found among us, by the aid of which we have attained to the present unrivalled state of our manufactures and commerce.

Some very solid objections, however, may be urged against the system of banking in the country.

The first which I shall mention, is, the tendency of country banks to produce, occasionally, that general failure of paper credit, and with it that derangement and suspension of commerce, as well as intermission of manufacturing labour, which have been already spoken of.

Country bank notes, and especially the smaller ones, circulate, in a great measure, among people out of trade, and pass occasionally into the hands of persons of the lower class; a great proportion, therefore, of the holders of them, have few means of judging of the comparative credit of the several issuers, and are commonly almost as ready to take the paper of any one house calling itself a bank, as that of another. A certain degree of currency being thus given to inferior paper, even the man who doubts the ultimate solvency of the issuer is disposed to take it; for the time during which he intends to detain it is very short, and his responsibility will cease almost as soon as he shall have parted with it.* Moreover, the amount of each note is so

* I apprehend that, supposing a country bank to fail, the holder of one of its notes, who should have parted with it in sufficient time to afford to the next holder an opportunity of applying for the discharge of it before the day of failure, could not be called upon for the payment of the value of it. The responsibility, therefore, of him who has been the holder of a country bank note commonly ceases in about one

small, that the risk seems, also, on that account, insignificant. The notes of the greater and of the smaller country banks, thus obtaining, in ordinary times, a nearly similar currency, they naturally fall at a season of alarm into almost equal discredit. If any one bank fails, a general run upon the neighbouring ones is apt to take place, which, if not checked in the beginning by pouring into the circulation a large quantity of gold, leads to very extensive mischief. Many country bankers, during a period of danger, prescribe to themselves a principle of more than ordinary reserve in the issue of their notes, because they consider these as the more vulnerable part of their credit. They know, that if the character of their house should be brought into question, through the fears or even the caprice of any of those strangers into whose hands their circulating paper passes, some distrust may be excited among their customers, the effect of which may be a sudden demand for the payment of large deposits. The amount, therefore, of the country bank notes circulating in the kingdom is liable to great fluctuation. The country banker, in case of an alarm, turns a part of the government securities, bills of exchange, or other property which he has in London, into Bank of England notes, and those notes into money; and thus discharges many of his own circulating notes, as well as enlarges the fund of gold in his coffers. The Bank of England has, therefore, to supply these occasional wants of the country banker; and, in order to be fully prepared to do this, it has, ordinarily, to keep a quantity of gold equal to that of the notes liable to be extinguished, as well as a quantity which shall satisfy the other extraordinary demands which may be made at the same season of consternation either by banking houses, or by individuals. Thus the country banker by no means bears his own burthen, while the Bank of England sustains a burthen which is not its

or two days after it has been parted with. That of the holder of a bill continues till after the bill is due, namely, for a period, perhaps, of one or two months.

own, and which we may naturally suppose that it does not very cheerfully endure.*

The national bank, indeed, may fairly be called upon, in consideration of the benefits enjoyed through its monopoly, to submit to a considerable expence in supplying gold for the country; but there must be some bounds to the claims which can equitably be made upon it: and, in estimating the benefit arising to the kingdom from the use of country bank notes, we have either to deduct the loss which the Bank of England incurs by maintaining an additional supply of gold sufficient to answer the demands which they occasion, or else we have to take into consideration the risk which the bank incurs by only keeping a fund of gold which is somewhat inadequate. The country banks may, perhaps, cause the bank in some measure to encrease its general fund of gold, though not to hold so much of this unproductive article as to afford a security equal to that which the bank would enjoy if no country bank notes existed.

It is obvious, that the additional capital given to the kingdom through the use of country bank notes must not be measured by the amount of those notes, but that a deduction must be made of the sum kept in gold in the coffers of the issuers, as their provision for the occasional payments to which their bank paper subjects them. The other deduction, which has been spoken of, is of the same nature. It is a second deduction, which must be made on account of a similar, and, perhaps, no less considerable provision for the payment of country bank notes, which is rendered necessary to be kept in the coffers of the Bank of

* At the time of the distress of 1793, some great and opulent country banks applied to the Bank of England for aid, in the shape of discount, which was refused on account of their not offering approved London securities: some immediate and important failures were the consequence. The Bank of England was indisposed to extend its aid to houses in the country. The event, however, shewed that the relief of the country was necessary to the solvency of the metropolis. A sense of the unfairness of the burthen cast on the bank by the large and sudden demands of the banking establishments in the country, probably contributed to produce an unwillingness to grant them relief.

England. In other words, the capital given to the country, through the use of country bank notes, is only equal (and it was so stated in speaking of that subject) to the amount of the gold which they cause to be exported.

I shall endeavour here to explain more particularly than has yet been done, some of those circumstances which cause a great diminution of country bank notes to bring distress on London, and to end in a general failure of commercial credit.

In a former chapter it was observed, that when that alarm among the common people, which produces an unwillingness to take country bank paper, and an eagerness for gold has risen to a considerable height, some distrust is apt to be excited among the higher class of traders; and that any great want of confidence in this quarter produces an encreased demand for that article, which is, among London bankers and merchants, in much the same credit as gold; I mean Bank of England notes, and which forms, at all times, the only circulating medium of the metropolis in all the larger transactions of its commerce. This more than usual demand for Bank of England notes the bank is at such a time particularly unwilling to satisfy, for reasons which I shall endeavour fully to detail. The reader will have been prepared to enter into them by the observations on the subject of the bank, introduced towards the close of the chapter which treated of that institution.

First, the bank may be supposed to be unwilling to satisfy that somewhat *encreased* demand for its notes which a season of consternation is apt to produce, because it is not unlikely to partake, in some degree, in the general alarm, especially since it must necessarily be supposed to have already suffered, and to be still experiencing a formidable reduction of the quantity of its gold. The natural operation of even this general sort of fear must be to incline it to contract its affairs, and to diminish rather than enlarge its notes.

But it must also be recollected, that the bank has necessarily been led already to encrease its loans in the same degree in which its gold has been reduced, provided it has maintained in circulation the accustomed quantity of notes. This point was explained in the chapter on the subject of the bank. The directors, therefore, must seem to themselves to act with extraordinary liberality towards those who apply to them for discounts, if they only go so far as to maintain the usual, or nearly the usual, quantity of notes. The liberality in lending which they must exercise, if, when the gold is low, they even augment their paper, must be very extended indeed.

In order to render this subject more clear, let us suppose that an extra demand on the Bank of England for three millions of gold has been made through the extinction of the paper of country banks, and through the slower circulation and hoarding of gold which have attended the general alarm. Let us assume, also, that the bank, during the time of its supplying this gold, has thought proper to reduce its notes one million. It will, in that case, have necessarily increased its loans two millions. Let us further assume, as we not very unreasonably may, that the two millions of additional loans have been afforded, not to the government, who owe a large and standing sum to the bank (suppose eight or ten millions besides the bank capital), but exclusively to the merchants; and let the total amount of loans antecedently afforded to the merchants be reckoned at four millions. The bank, in this case, will have raised its discounts to the merchants from four millions to six; that is, it will have encreased them one half, even though it has diminished its notes one million. This extension of the accustomed accommodation to the mercantile world must appear to call for the thanks of that body, rather than to leave any room for complaint; and yet it is plain from reasoning, and, I believe, it might be also proved from experience, that it will not ease the pressure. The difficulties in London, notwithstanding the additional loan of *two* millions to the merchants, will be somewhat encreased; for a sum in gold, amounting to *three* millions, has been drawn from the bank by the London agents of the country bankers and traders, and has been sent by those agents into the country. London, therefore, has furnished for the country circulation three millions of gold; and it has done this by getting discounted at the bank two additional millions of bills, for which it has received two of the millions of gold, and by sparing one million of its circulating notes as a means of obtaining the other million. This reduction of the usual quantity of notes is borne by the metropolis with peculiar difficulty at a time of general alarm. However liberally, therefore, the bankers and merchants may acknowledge themselves to have been already relieved by the bank, they will repeat, and will even urge more than ever, their application for discounts.

It may be observed, with a view to the further elucidation of this part of our subject, that both the bank, and they who borrow of it, are naturally led to fix their attention rather on the amount of the loans furnished than on that of the notes in circulation. The bank is used to allow to each borrower a sum bearing some proportion to his supposed credit; but seldom or never exceeding a certain amount. It is true, the various borrowers do not always in an equal degree avail themselves of their power of raising money at the bank; and, therefore, a material enlargement of the sum total of the bank loans may take place at a moment of difficulty, through the encreased use which some of the richer merchants then make of their credit, as well as through the creation of a few new borrowers at the bank. The directors also, in particular cases, may suffer their rule to be relaxed. The circumstance, however, of the general principle on which the bank ordinarily, and, indeed, naturally proceeds, being that of a limitation of the amount of each of its loans to individuals, must tend, as I conceive, to place something like a general limit to the total sum lent. It must conduce to prevent the fluctuation in the bank loans from keeping pace with the variation in the necessities of the public, and must contribute to produce a reduction of notes at that season of extraordinary distrust, when the state of the metropolis, as was more fully remarked in a former part of this Work, calls rather for their encrease.

That the borrowers at the bank are likely to pay no attention to the subject of the total quantity of notes in circulation is easily shewn. They have, indeed, no means of knowing their amount. They can only judge of the liberality of the bank by the extent of its loans; and of this they form an imperfect estimate by the sum which they or their connexions have been able to obtain. Scarcely any one reflects, that there may be a large encrease of the general loans of the bank, as well as possibly an extension of each loan to individuals, while there is a diminution of the number of bank notes; and that the amount of the notes, not that of the loans, is the object on which the eye should be fixed, in order to judge of the facility of effecting the payments of the metropolis.

It was remarked, in a former chapter, that the bank, at the time antecedent to the suspension of its cash payments, having diminished the sum lent by it to government, and enlarged, though not in an equal degree, that furnished to the merchants, the pressure on the merchants was not relieved, as was expected, by the encreased loan afforded them, but even grew more severe. It was also shewn, that this could not fail to be the case, since the bank notes necessary for effecting the current payments of the metropolis were then diminished, and since the additional loans afforded to the merchants only in part compensated for the new pressure which was created in the general money market of the kingdom, by the circumstance of the government being obliged to become a great borrower in that market. Whenever the bank materially lessens its paper, a similar pressure is likely to be felt. Neither the transfer of the bank loans from the government to the merchants, nor even a large encrease of its loans, when that encrease is not carried so far as is necessary to the maintenance of the accustomed, or nearly the accustomed, quantity of bank paper, can prevent, as I apprehend, distress in the metropolis; and this distress soon communicates itself to all parts of the kingdom. The short explanation of the subject is this. Many country bank notes having disappeared, a quantity of gold is called for, which is so much new capital suddenly needed in the country. The only place in which any supply of gold exists is the Bank of England. Moreover, the only quarter from whence the loan of the new capital, under all the circumstances of the case, can come, is also the Bank of England: for the gold in the bank is the only dead or sleeping stock in the kingdom which is convertible into the new active capital which is wanted. The bank, therefore, must *lend*, the gold which it furnishes; it must lend, that is to say, to some individuals a sum equal to the gold which other individuals have taken from it: otherwise it does not relieve the country.

If it should be asked, Why does not the bank in such case demand something intrinsically valuable, instead of contenting itself with mere paper in return?—the answer is, first, that if the bank were to receive goods in exchange for its gold, or, in other words, were to purchase goods, it would have afterwards to sell them; and it would then become a trading company, which it is forbid to be by its charter; it is allowed to traffic only in bullion. The answer is, secondly, that if it were to take goods as a mere security, and to detain them as such, it would then prevent their passing into consumption with the desirable expedition. By proceeding on either of these plans, it would also involve itself in a degree of trouble which would not be very consistent with the management of the business of a banking Company.* It may be answered, thirdly, that the bills which the bank discounts, are, generally speaking, so safe, that the security either of goods, or stocks, or land, none of which are received in pledge by the directors, may be considered as nearly superfluous. A very small proportion of the five per cent. discount, gained upon the bills turned into ready money at the

* Of the parliamentary loan of exchequer bills in 1793, which was directed to be granted on the security either of sufficient bondsmen, or of a deposit of goods, only a small proportion was taken on the latter principle, on account of the great obstruction to the sale of goods, which was thought to arise from warehousing them on the account of the commissioners appointed by parliament. It has been already remarked, that no part of the sum lent was lost.

bank, has compensated, as I believe, for the whole of the loss upon them, even in the years of the greatest commercial failures which have yet been known.

The observations which have now been made sufficiently shew what is the nature of that evil of which we are speaking. It is an evil which ought to be charged not to any fault in the mercantile body, but to the defects of the banking system. It is a privation which the merchants occasionally experience of a considerable part of that circulating medium which custom has rendered essential to the punctual fulfilment of their engagements. In good times, the country banks furnish this necessary article, which they are enabled to do through the confidence of the people in general; but when an alarm arises, the country banks cease to give it out, the people refusing what they had before received; and the Bank of England, the only body by whose interposition the distress can be relieved, is somewhat unwilling to exercise all the necessary liberality, for the reasons which have been so fully mentioned. The merchants are some of the chief sufferers, and they are generally, also, loaded with no inconsiderable share of censure; but the public, the country banks, and the Bank of England, may properly divide the blame.

The mischief produced by a general failure of paper credit is very considerable. How much such a failure interrupts trade and manufacturing industry, and, therefore, ultimately also tends to carry gold out of the country, has been already stated at large. It also causes a great, though merely temporary, fall in the market price of many sorts of property; and thus inflicts a partial and very heavy loss on some traders, and throws extraordinary gain into the hands of others; into the hands, I mean, of those who happen to have superior powers of purchasing at the moment of difficulty. By giving to all banking, as well as mercantile, transactions the appearance of perilous undertakings, it deters men of large property, and of a cautious temper, from following the profession of bankers and merchants. It creates no small uneasiness of mind, even among traders who surmount the difficulties of the moment. Above all, it reduces many respectable, prudent, and, ultimately, very solvent persons to the mortifying necessity of stopping payment; thus obliging them to share in that discredit, in which, it is much to be desired, that traders of an opposite character only should be involved. If, indeed, we suppose, as we necessarily must, that, on account of the multitude of failures which happen at the same time, the discredit of them is much diminished, then another evil is produced, which, in a commercial country, is very great. Acts of insolvency, leaving less stigma on the character, become not so much dreaded as might be wished. The case of some, who bring difficulties on themselves, being almost unavoidably confounded with that of persons whose affairs have been involved through the entanglement of paper credit, to stop payment is considered too much as a misfortune or accident, and too little as a fault; and thus a principal incentive to punctuality in mercantile payments is weakened, and an important check to adventurous speculation is in some measure lost.

The observations which have been made, will, however, shew that the tendency of country bank paper to produce a general failure of paper credit, is an evil which may be expected to diminish; for, first, if the Bank of England, in future seasons of alarm, should be disposed to extend its discounts in a greater degree than heretofore, then the threatened calamity may be averted through the generosity of that institution.* If, secondly, the country bankers should be taught (as, in some degree, unquestionably they must), by the difficulties which they have experienced, to provide

* It is by no means intended to imply, that it would become the Bank of England to relieve every distress which the rashness of country banks may bring upon them: the bank, by doing this, might encourage their improvidence. There seems to be a medium at which a public bank should aim in granting aid to inferior establishments, and which it must often find very difficult to be observed. The relief should neither be so prompt and liberal as to exempt those who misconduct their business from all the natural consequences of their fault, nor so scanty and slow as deeply to involve the general interests. These interests, nevertheless, are sure to be pleaded by every distressed person whose affairs are large, however indifferent or even ruinous may be their state.

themselves with a larger quantity of that sort of property which is quickly convertible into Bank of England notes, and, therefore, also, into gold, then the country bankers will have in their own hands a greater power of checking the progress of an alarm. Still, indeed, their resource will be the gold which is in the bank. The encreased promptitude, however, with which the greater convertibility of their funds will enable them to possess themselves of a part of the bank treasure, will render a smaller supply of it sufficient; and this smaller supply may be expected to be furnished, without difficulty, either by means of such a trifling addition to the bank loans as the bank will not refuse, or by sparing the necessary sum from the paper circulation of the metropolis, which, if commercial confidence is not impaired, will always admit of some slight and temporary reduction. The Bank of England will itself profit by the circumstance of its gold becoming more accessible to the country banks; for the untoward event of a general failure of paper credit will thus be rendered less probable, and, therefore, a smaller stock of gold will be an equally sufficient provision for the extraordinary demands at home to which the bank will be subject. Or if, thirdly, those among whom country bank notes circulate should learn to be less variable as to the confidence placed by them in country paper, or even to appreciate more justly the several degrees of credit due to the notes of different houses, then the evil which was before supposed to be obviated by the liberality of the Bank of England, or by the prudence of the country banker, will abate through the growth of confidence and the diffusion of commercial knowledge among the public. It seems likely that by each of these means, though especially in the second mode which was mentioned, the tendency of country bank notes to produce an occasional failure of commercial credit will be diminished. In time past, the mischief has been suffered to grow till it appeared too formidable to be encountered; and this has happened partly in consequence of our wanting that knowledge and experience which we now possess.

Another evil attending the present banking system in the country is the following.

The multiplication of country banks issuing small notes to bearer on demand, by occasioning a great and permanent diminution in our circulating coin, serves to encrease the danger, lest the standard by which the value of our paper is intended to be at all times regulated should occasionally not be maintained.

The evils of a great depreciation of paper currency are considerable. In proportion as the article which forms the current payment for goods drops in value, the current price of goods rises. If the labourer receives only the same nominal wages as before the depreciation took place, he is underpaid. Antecedent pecuniary contracts, though nominally and perhaps, legally fulfilled, are not performed with due equity. It is true that the general stock of wealth in the country may remain nearly the same; and it is possible that the circulating paper may be restored to its full value when the period of the particular difficulty shall have passed by. Some degree, however, of unfairness and inequality will, in the mean time, have been produced, and much pressure may have been felt by the lower classes of people, whose wages are seldom raised until some time after the occasion for a rise has begun to exist.

In those countries in which the government is the chief banker or issuer of notes, a temptation arises, on the occasion of every public pressure, either to lessen the quantity of precious metal contained in the chief current coin, as one of the means of detaining it in the country, or to allow paper to pass at a considerable and professed discount, which is another mode of preventing the coin from being exported. These are evils from which we consider ourselves as happily secured by the established principles of good faith which prevail in Great Britain. Those principles, however, should, perhaps, lead us even to place ourselves at a distance from that temptation to depreciate coin, or to permit a discount on paper, to which so many other countries have yielded. The possession, in ordinary times, of a very considerable quantity of gold, either in the bank or in general circulation, or both, seems necessary for our complete security in this respect. The substitution of country bank notes for gold tends to lessen that security. The evil of them is not that they create any false and merely ideal riches, or that they do any constant prejudice to the country. They enable the trader to vest a capital in merchandize, which, without them, he would not possess, and thereby add to the annual income of the nation. In their immediate effect, therefore, they are beneficial; but they leave us more exposed to an occasional evil, against which it is prudent to guard, provided we can accomplish that purpose without too great a sacrifice of present advantages. It seems, on this account, as well as on some others, very undesirable to render permanent the temporary law passed some years since, and subsequently renewed, for the purpose of permitting the issue of English notes under five pounds. When it shall have expired, the power of re-enacting it, which we shall possess, will be a valuable resource. If, moreover, any measure can be devised, which, by encreasing the public confidence in good paper, will lessen the danger of a general failure of paper credit, and of a run upon the bank for gold, and which, also, by obstructing the issue of five and ten pound notes by smaller and less respectable banks, will somewhat extend the use of coin, on the whole, it will have a twofold argument to recommend it*.

The reader will observe, that even our circulating gold coin has here been considered in the light of a provision against an unfavourable balance of trade with foreign countries, and, therefore, as exportable. Part of our coin will, in fact, always be exported when the balance is very unfavourable,

* Various objections, however, occur against almost every parliamentary measure for the regulation of country banks. Dr. Smith is of opinion, that a law prohibiting the issue of small notes is alone a sufficient remedy for the evils attending these institutions, and that the danger arising from banks is lessened by the multiplication of them. It is the object of this Work not so much to canvass any question respecting the particular means of regulating paper credit, as to lay down some general principles concerning it.

and the exportation, under such circumstances, is beneficial to the country. We are apt to think that it is the interchange of the usual gold coin for paper at home which alone maintains the value of our paper; and we are partly, on this account, much more anxious to detain our gold at home, than we are to discharge by means of it an unfavourable balance of trade, and thereby to improve our exchange with foreign countries. I apprehend, however, that an unfavourable course of exchange, which the export of our gold would cure, will, in many cases, tend much more to depreciate our paper, and to produce a rise in the nominal price of articles, than the want of the usual interchange of gold for paper at home. Our coin itself, as has been already remarked, when paper is depreciated, passes not for what the gold in it is worth, but at the paper price; though this is not generally observed to be the case. It is the maintenance of our general exchanges, or, in other words, it is the agreement of the mint price with the bullion price of gold which seems to be the true proof that the circulating paper is not depreciated.

Chap. VIII.

Of the Tendency of a too great Issue of Bank Paper to produce an Excess of the Market Price above the Mint Price of Gold —Of the means by which it creates this Excess, namely, by its Operation on the Price of Goods and on the Course of Exchange — Errors of Dr. A. Smith on the Subject of excessive Paper—Of the Manner in which the Limitation of the Quantity of the Bank of England Paper serves to limit the Quantity and sustain the Value of all the Paper of the Kingdom.

A THIRD objection commonly made to country banks, is, the influence which their notes are supposed to have in raising the price of articles.

By the principles which shall be laid down in this Chapter, I propose to prove, that, though a general encrease of paper has this tendency, the objection, when applied to the paper of country banks, is particularly ill founded.

It will be necessary, in the discussion which is now about to take place, to join the consideration of two subjects, that of the influence which an enlarged emission of paper has in lifting up the price of commodities, and that of its influence, also, in producing an excess of the market price above the mint price of gold, and in thus exposing the bank to failure, and the country to considerable inconvenience. It is through the medium of the enhanced price of commodities that I conceive the ill effect on the mint price of gold to be brought about.

The discussion of these topics will best be introduced by a statement of the principle which regulates the value of all the articles of life.

The price of commodities in the market is formed by means of a certain struggle which takes place between the buyers and the sellers. It is commonly said, that the price of a thing is regulated by the proportion between the supply and the demand. This is, undoubtedly, true; and for the following reason. If the supply of an article or the demand for it is great, it is also known to be great; and if small, it is understood to be small. When, therefore, the supply, for example, is known to be less than the demand, the sellers judge that the buyers are in some degree at their mercy, and they insist on as favourable a price as their power over the buyers is likely to enable them to obtain. The price paid is not at all governed by the equity of the case, but entirely by the degree of command which the one party has over the other. When the demand is less than the supply, the buyers, in their turn, in some degree, command the market, giving not that sum which is calculated to indemnify the seller against loss, but so much only as they think that the seller will accept rather than not sell his article. The question of price is, therefore, in all cases, a question of power, and of power only. It is obvious, that a rise in the price of a scarce commodity will be more or less considerable in proportion as the article is felt to be one of more or less strict necessity.

The principle which has been laid down as governing the price of goods, must be considered as also regulating that of the paper for which they are sold; for it may as properly be said, on the occasion of a sale of goods, that paper is sold for goods, as that goods are sold for paper: thus the sale of a single commodity, as it is called, is a twofold transaction, though not commonly understood to be so: I mean, that the price at which the exchange (or sale) takes place depends on two facts; on the proportion between the supply of the particular commodity and the demand for it, which is one question; and on the proportion, also, between the state of the general supply of the circulating medium and that of the demand for it, which is another.

Paper, moreover (of which I shall here speak as if it were the only circulating medium, it being the only one used in the larger payments), is, to some persons, somewhat in the same manner as bread is to all, an article of necessity. It is necessary to traders, partly because they have come under engagements to make payments which are only to be effected by means of their own previous receipts: and partly because they hold goods which must, within no long time, be sold for money, that is to say, for paper, since a continually growing loss accrues from the detention of them. Paper, therefore, must be bought by the trader: and if there is a difficulty in obtaining it, the buyer of it is brought under the power of the seller, and, in that case, more goods must be given for it.

Let us, now, trace carefully the steps by which an encrease of paper serves to lift up the price of articles. Let us suppose, for example, an encreased number of Bank of England notes to be issued. In such case the traders in the metropolis discover that there is a more than usual facility of obtaining notes at the bank by giving bills for them, and that they may, therefore, rely on finding easy means of performing any pecuniary engagements into which they may enter. Every trader is encouraged, by the knowledge of this facility of borrowing, a little to enlarge his speculations; he is rendered, by the plenty of money, somewhat more ready to buy, and rather less eager to sell; he either trusts that there will be a particular profit on the article which is the object of his speculation, or else he judges, that, by extending his general purchases, he shall at least have his share of the ordinary profit of commercial business, a profit which he considers to be proportioned to the quantity of it. The opinion of an encreased facility of effecting payments causes other traders to become greater buyers for the same reason, and at the same time. Thus an inclination to buy is created in all quarters, and an indisposition to sell. Now, since the cost of articles depends on the issue of that general conflict between the buyers and sellers, which was spoken of, it follows, that any circumstance which serves to communicate a greater degree of eagerness to the mind of the one party than to that of the other, will have an influence on price. It is not necessary to suppose either a monopoly, or a combination, or the least unfairness, to exist, or even large and improper speculations. The encrease in the eagerness of each buyer may be trifling. The zeal to buy, being generally diffused, may, nevertheless, have a sensible operation on price.

That, on the other hand, a reduction of the quantity of paper causes a fall in the price of goods, is scarcely necessary to be proved. It may be useful, however, in some degree, to illustrate this point by facts. I understand, that at the time of the great failure of paper credit in 1795, the price of corn fell, in a few places, no less than twenty or thirty per cent. The fall arose from the necessity of selling corn under which some farmers were placed, in order to carry on their payments. Much of the circulating medium being withdrawn, the demand for it was in those places far greater than the supply; and the few persons, therefore, who were in possession of cash, or of what would pass as cash, having command of the market, obliged the farmers to sell at a price thus greatly reduced. It was a new and sudden scarcity of cash, not any new plenty of corn, which caused the price of corn to drop.

It has been already observed, that some few days antecedently to the suspension of the cash payments of the bank, exchequer bills, as well as stocks, when sold for ready money, that is to say, for bank notes, fell in price. Not many days afterwards, although no material event had occurred except that of the stoppage of the bank, they rose. This fall and rise in the price of government securities evidently did not result from any corresponding fluctuation in the national confidence in them; for the fall took place when the national credit would naturally be the highest, namely, when the bank was as yet paying in cash, and the approaching stoppage was not known; and the rise happened when the national credit would be the lowest, namely, within a few days after that discouraging event. The reason of each of the fluctuations unquestionably was the fluctuation in the quantity of the Bank of England notes, which, as it has since appeared, were, during the day or two which preceded the suspension, about a million less than they were either a short time before or a short time afterwards. The notes being fewer during those few days, the price of them was, at the same time, higher. It was, in fact, therefore, the price of notes which rose, rather than that of stocks which fell, on the days immediately preceding the suspension; and it was the price of notes which a few days afterwards fell, rather than that of stocks which rose.*

* In the event of any great public alarm, such, for instance, as that which might be occasioned by the landing in this country of any considerable body of enemies, it is likely that the price of Bank of England notes, compared with that of stocks, or other articles for which there is a ready money market, would in like manner rise, even though the quantity of paper should continue the same: this would happen in consequence of that encreased demand for bank notes, to which it has been repeatedly observed that a state of consternation always gives occasion. Many bankers, at such a time, would feel a doubt whether they might not be drawn upon more largely than usual by some of their more timid customers; and whether, also, they might not be subjected to more than common difficulty in selling government securities, an article which, in ordinary times, they are used to turn into cash on the shortest notice, and which, while a prompt sale of them is to be

I shall, for the present, consider the doctrine which has been laid down, as being sufficiently established, namely, that paper fluctuates in price on the same principles as any other article, its value rising as its quantity sinks, and *vice versâ*; or, in other words, that an augmentation of it has a general tendency to raise, and a diminished issue to lower, the nominal cost of commodities, although, partly for reasons which have been already touched upon, and partly for some which shall be hereafter given, an exact correspondence between the quantity of paper and the price of commodities can by no means be expected always to subsist.

The reader possibly may think that, in treating of this subject, I have been mistaking the effect for the cause, an encreased issue of paper being, in his estimation, merely a consequence which follows a rise in the price of goods, and not the circumstance which produces it. That an enlarged emission of paper may often fairly be considered as only, or chiefly, an effect of high prices, is not meant to be denied. It is, however, intended to insist, that, unquestionably, in some cases at least, the greater quantity of paper is, more properly speaking, the cause. A fuller explanation of this apparently difficult and disputable position will be given in the further progress of this Work.

I proceed, in the next place, to show in what manner a

---

depended on, they prefer to bank notes, because an interest is gained by holding the one, and not by detaining the other.

During the short crisis of an invasion, the advantage of accruing interest would be little regarded, and each banker, therefore, would make an effort to exchange his exchequer bills, or perhaps, his stocks, for Bank of England notes, an effort which must prove generally ineffectual, supposing the quantity issued to be the same; but which, however, would have the effect of bringing down the comparative price of the article so eagerly offered in exchange for notes. Thus the price of government securities would appear to fall, when, in part at least, it would rather be the price of bank notes, which should be said to rise. Some encrease of the bank issues seems very justifiable at such a time; such an encrease, I mean, as should be sufficient only to prevent what may be termed an unnatural rise in the value of bank notes. This issue would be the means of preventing a misconception among the public respecting the degree of distrust in government securities entertained by the dealers in them, a circumstance which might be of some political importance in a moment of general consternation.

general rise in the cost of commodities, whether proceeding from an extravagant issue of paper, or from any other circumstance, contributes to produce an excess of the market price above the mint price of gold.

It is obvious, that, in proportion as goods are rendered dear in Great Britain, the foreigner becomes unwilling to buy them, the commodities of other countries which come into competition with our's obtaining a preference in the foreign market; and, therefore, that in consequence of a diminution of orders from abroad, our exports will be diminished; unless we assume, as we shall find it necessary to do, that some compensation in the exchange is given to the foreigner for the disadvantage attending the purchase of our articles. But not only will our exports lessen in the case supposed; our imports also will encrease; for the high British price of goods will tempt foreign commodities to come in nearly in the same degree in which it will discourage British articles from going out. I mean only, that these two effects (that of a diminished export, and that of an encreased import) will follow, provided that we suppose, what is not supposable, namely, that, at the time when the price of goods is greatly raised in Great Britain, the course of exchange suffers no alteration. For the following reason, I have said that this is not supposable. Under the circumstances which have been described of a diminished export, and an encreased import, the balance of trade must unavoidably turn against us; the consequence of which must be, that the drawers of bills on Great Britain in foreign countries will become more in number than the persons having occasion to remit bills. This disparity between the number of individuals wanting to draw, and of those wanting to remit, as was remarked in a former Chapter, must produce a fall in the price at which the overabundant bills on England sell in the foreign market. The fall in the selling price abroad of bills payable here, will operate as an advantage to the foreign buyer of our commodities in the computation of the exchangeable value of that circulating medium of his own country with which he discharges the debt in Britain contracted by his purchase. It will thus obviate the dearness of our articles: it will serve as a compensation to the foreigner for the loss which he would otherwise sustain by buying in our market. The fall of our exchange will, therefore, promote exportation and encourage importation. It will, in a great degree, prevent the high price of goods in Great Britain from producing that unfavourable balance of trade, which, for the sake of illustrating the subject, was supposed to exist.

The compensation thus made to the foreigner for the high British price of all articles is necessary as an inducement to him to take them, somewhat in the same manner as a drawback or bounty on exportation is the necessary inducement to take those particular goods which have been rendered too dear for the foreign market by taxes laid on them in this country. In each case the British consumer pays the high price, and the foreigner is spared, because otherwise he will not accept our commodities.

The fall in our exchange was just now defined to be an advantage gained in the computation of the exchangeable value of that foreign circulating medium with which the foreigner discharges his debt in Great Britain, a debt paid in the circulating medium of this country. It implies, therefore, a high valuation of his circulating medium, and a low valuation of our's; a low valuation, that is to say, both of our paper and of the coin which is interchanged with it.

Now, when coin is thus rendered cheap, it by no means follows that bullion is rendered cheap also. Coin is rendered cheap through its constituting a part of our circulating medium; but bullion does not constitute a part of it. Bullion is a commodity, and nothing but a commodity; and it rises and falls in value on the same principle as all other commodities. It becomes, like them, dear in proportion as the circulating medium for which it is exchanged is rendered cheap, and cheap in proportion as the circulating medium is rendered dear.

In the case, therefore, which has now been supposed,

we are to consider coin as sinking below its proper and intrinsic worth, while bullion maintains its natural and accustomed price. Hence there arises that temptation, which was formerly noticed, either to convert back into bullion and then to export; or, which is the same thing to export and then convert back into bullion; or which is also the same thing, to convert back into bullion, and then sell to the bank, at the price which would be gained by exportation, that gold which the bank has purchased, and has converted from bullion into coin.

In this manner an encrease of paper, supposing it to be such as to raise the price of commodities in Britain above the price at which, unless there is some allowance afforded in the course of exchange, they will be received in foreign countries, contributes to produce an excess of the market price above the mint price of gold, and to prevent, therefore, the introduction of a proper supply of it into the Bank of England, as well as to draw out of its coffers, that coin which the directors of the bank would wish to keep in them.

Dr. Smith appears to me to have treated the important subject of the tendency of an excessive paper circulation to send gold out of a country, and thus to embarrass its banking establishments, in a manner which is particularly defective and unsatisfactory. It is true, that he blames the Bank of England for having contributed to bring on itself, during several successive years, a great expence in buying gold through a too great circulation of its paper; and that he also charges the Scotch banks with having had, through their excessive issues, a share in producing this evil. Thus, therefore, he seems to give to his reader some intimation of the tendency of an excessive issue of paper to create an excess of the market price above the mint price of gold.*

It appears, however, in some degree, from the passage in question, though much more clearly from other parts of his

* Enquiry into the Nature and Causes of the Wealth of Nations, vol. i. page 451, 4th edit. 8vo.

work, that he considers every permanent excess, whether of the market price above the mint price, or of the mint price above the market price of gold, as entirely referable to "something in the state of the coin."*

In one place he remarks, that a high price of bullion arises from the difference between the weight of our more light and that of our more heavy guineas; the value of the gold in the heavier guineas, as he represents the case, determining the general current value of both the lighter and the heavier pieces of coin; and the superior quantity of gold in the heavier guineas constituting, therefore, so much profit on the melting of those heavier pieces: a supposition manifestly erroneous, and contradicted by experience; for it implies that the excess of the market price above the mint price of gold both never is and never can be greater than the excess of the weight of the heavier above the lighter guineas; and, also, that the price of bullion cannot fluctuate while the state of our coinage remains in all respects the same. We havé lately experienced fluctuations in our exchange, and correspondent variations in the market price, compared with the mint price of gold, amounting to no less than eight or ten per cent., the state of our coinage continuing, in all respects, the same.

Dr. Smith recommends a seignorage, as tending to raise the value both of the lighter and heavier coin; and thus, also, to diminish, if not destroy, the excess of the market price above the mint price of gold.†

---

* Wealth of Nations, vol. i. page 69, 4th edit. 8vo.

† "Were the private people who carry their gold and silver to the "mint to pay themselves for the coinage, it would add to the value of "those metals in the same manner as the fashion does to that of plate. "Coined gold and silver would be more valuable than uncoined. The "seignorage, if it was not exorbitant, would add to the bullion the "whole value of the duty, because the government having every where "the exclusive privilege of coining, no coin can come to market cheaper "than they think proper to afford it.

"A seignorage will, in many cases, take away altogether, and will in "all cases diminish, the profit of melting down the new coin. This "profit always arises from the difference between the quantity of "bullion which the common currency ought to contain, and that which "it actually does contain. If this difference is less than the seignorage,

It is remarkable, that this Writer does not, in any degree, advert either to that more immediate cause (a fall of our exchanges), from which I have, in this as well as in a former Chapter, described the excess in question, as in all cases, arising; or to that more remote one on which I have lately dwelt, namely, a too high price of goods, which produces a fall of our exchanges.

"there will be loss instead of profit. If it is equal to the seignorage, "there will neither be profit nor loss. If it is greater than the seignor-"age, there will, indeed, be some profit; but less than if there were no "seignorage."—Wealth of Nations, vol. ii. Book iv. Chap vi. pages 333, 334, and 335.

These observations, on the subject of a seignorage, seem erroneous in the following respects. Plate, when bought, is purchased in order not to be sold again, but to be retained by the possessor; and the price paid by the original buyer, may, therefore, be not unfairly considered, as it is by Dr. Smith, to be the current price of the article. Gold, on the contrary, is no sooner bought and coined, than it is sent into circulation; it is sold, that is to say (or exchanged for commodities), again and again. What we mean, therefore, by the current price of gold coin, is that price at which it passes, not in the original bargain for bullion between the seller of it, and the bank, but in the general course of this subsequent circulation. Guineas, moreover, not only circulate at home, but are liable to be sent abroad in the event of any unfavourable balance of trade. They are worth, in that case, just as much as the foreign country will give for them; and the foreign country, in estimating their value, since it means to melt them, does not at all take into its calculation the expence of the coinage of the piece of metal. It acts like a buyer not of new but of old plate, who destines it to the melting pot, and, therefore, refuses to allow any thing for "the fashion."

This foreign price of our coin principally determines the current value of the price of coin in England. It appears to me to do this in the following manner.

When the price which our coin will fetch in foreign countries is such as to tempt it out of the kingdom, the directors of the bank naturally diminish, in some degree, the quantity of their paper, through an anxiety for the safety of their establishment. By diminishing their paper they raise its value; and in raising its value, they raise also the value in England of the current coin which is exchanged for it. Thus the value of our gold coin conforms itself to the value of the current paper, and the current paper is rendered by the bank directors of that value which it is necessary that it should bear in order to prevent large exportations; a value sometimes rising a little above, and sometimes falling a little below, the price which our coin bears abroad; a price, in the formation of which no regard is had to the fashion.

A seignorage, nevertheless, might add to the current value of the coin of the kingdom for the following reason. It might incline the directors of the bank to improve the value of their paper by a stricter limitation of it, for the sake of more effectually exempting themselves

Dr. Smith does not, in any of his observations on this subject, proceed sufficiently, as I conceive, on the practical principle of shewing how it is through the medium of prices (of the prices of goods in general, and of bullion in particular, compared with the price of the current circulating medium), that the operations of importing and exporting gold are brought about. He considers our coin as going abroad simply in consequence of our circulation at home being over full. Payment in coin, according to his doctrine is demanded of every bank for as much of its paper as is excessive, because the excessive paper can neither be sent abroad nor turned to any use at home; whereas, when it is changed into coin, the coin may be transmitted to a foreign part, and may there be advantageously employed.*

The reader will perceive, that, according to the principle which I have endeavoured to establish, coin does not merely leave the country because, the circulation being full, no use can be found at home for additional circulating medium; but that every encrease of paper has been represented as enhancing the price of goods, which advanced price of goods affords employment to a larger quantity of circulating medium, so that the circulation can never be said to be over full. This advanced price of goods is the same thing as a reduced price of coin; the coin, therefore, in consequence of its reduced price, is carried out of the country for the sake of obtaining for it a better market. The heavier pieces, undoubtedly,

---

from an occasional burthen, which is now borne for them by the government. The point *below* which they would wish to prevent their paper from falling would still be the same as it is now, namely, the selling price of our coin when melted and carried to foreign countries: the care, however, which they would take to prevent its falling below that price would, perhaps, be greater, and would be such as to raise its average price, if, in the event of each depression, they should be subject not only as they are now, to loss in the purchase of gold, but to a further loss in coining it. There seems no reason, however, to suppose, that the degree of fluctuation which is now apt to subsist between the market price and mint price of gold could, by any efforts of the bank, be materially lessened. It results from the fluctuations in the exchange; and those fluctuations, in general, proceed from variations in the markets of Europe, which affect the balance of trade, and cannot, by any management of bank paper, be exactly counteracted.

* Wealth of Nations, vol. i. page 450.

will be preferred, if there is a facility of obtaining and transporting them; but the lighter guineas will also be exported, when the state of the exchange shall be sufficiently low to afford a profit on such a transaction. One of the consequences of Dr. Smith's mode of treating the subject, is, that the reader is led into the error of thinking, that when, through an excessive issue of paper, gold has been made to flow away from us, the expence of restoring it consists merely in the charge of collecting it and transporting it from the place to which it is gone. It follows, on the contrary, from the principles which I have laid down, that, in order to bring back gold, the expence not only of importing it may be to be incurred, but that also of purchasing it at a loss, and at a loss which may be either more or less considerable: a circumstance of great importance in the question. If this loss should ever become extremely great, the difficulties of restoring the value of our paper might not easily be surmounted, and a current discount or difference between the coin and paper of the country would scarcely be avoidable.

Dr. Smith, indeed, represents the expence of bringing back gold as considerable; but he seems to impute the greatness of it to the circumstance of its recurring again and again: and he describes it as continuing to recur in the case of each individual bank, whether in town or country, which persists in the false policy of issuing more paper than is sufficient to fill the circulation of the neighbouring district. I shall here take occasion to notice some great inaccuracies in one part of his reasoning upon this point.

He says—"A banking company which issues more paper "than can be employed in the circulation of the country, "and of which the excess is continually returning upon them "for payment, ought to encrease the quantity of gold and "silver which they keep at all times in their coffers, not only "in proportion to this excess, but to a much greater propor- "tion. Suppose, for instance, all the paper of a particular "bank, which the circulation of the country can easily "absorb, amounts to forty thousand pounds, and the bank "keeps usually ten thousand pounds in gold and silver for its "occasional demands. If this bank should attempt to cir- "culate forty-four thousand pounds, the excess of four "thousand pounds will return as fast as it is issued. Four- "teen thousand pounds must then be kept instead of ten "thousand pounds, and the bank will gain nothing by the "excessive circulation. On the contrary, it will lose the "whole expence of continually collecting four thousand "pounds in gold and silver, which will be continually going "out of its coffers as fast as they are brought in."

He then adds—"Had every particular bank always "understood and attended to its own interest, the circulation "would never have been overstocked with paper money."

There is, no doubt, some sort of ground for saying that an excess of paper will come back upon the banks which issue it, and that, in coming back, it will involve the issuing banks in expence. Much exception, however, might be taken against Dr. Smith's mode of estimating the expence which the quantity which would come back would bring upon the issuing banks. But the objection which I shall, in the first place, urge against the remark of Dr. Smith, is, that, even granting it to be just, it can be just only in a case which can scarcely ever occur among the country banks of this kingdom. I mean, that it can apply solely to the case of a single bank of which the paper circulates exclusively through a surrounding district: it obviously cannot hold in the case of many banks, the paper of all of which circulates in the same district.

In order to explain this clearly, let us make the following supposition. Let us imagine the circulation of country bank paper which a certain district will bear to be one hundred thousand pounds, and ten banks to be in that district, each usually circulating and able to keep in circulation ten thousand pounds. Let us also suppose an excessive issue of four thousand pounds, and let us allow the effect of this on the ten banks to be that which Dr. Smith describes, a point which might certainly be disputed, namely, that a necessity will arise for *always* keeping (for this is what Dr. Smith's language implies) an additional stock of gold amounting to exactly four thousand pounds, and also that a reiterated expence will be incurred (Dr. Smith does not say how frequently reiterated) in collecting and transporting these four thousand pounds of gold. Still it must be observed, that we may suppose the issue of the four thousand pounds excessive paper to be made by some one only of the ten banks, while the charge incurred by such issue may be divided among them all. It may, therefore, on Dr. Smith's own principles, answer to one of several banks emitting paper which circulates in the same place, to issue the paper which is considered by him as excessive; and the practice of doing so may be owing to the country banker's too well knowing his own interest, and not, as Dr. Smith supposes, to his too ill understanding it.

But the case which I have supposed has been put merely by way of illustration. When many banks issue notes circulating over the same district, it is impossible to say whose paper constitutes the excess. Whatever temptation to excess exists, must be a general one. It is, however, counteracted not only by the charge of transporting gold on which alone Dr. Smith dwells, but likewise by all the other charges, as well as by all the risks to which country bank notes subject the issuers; not to mention the difficulty of finding a channel through which a quantity of paper much larger than common can be sent by the country bank into circulation.

Dr. Smith supposes, in the passage which has just been quoted, that, when there is an excessive circulation of country bank paper, the excess returns upon the banks to be exchanged for gold and silver. The fact is, that it returns to be exchanged not for gold and silver only, but either for gold and silver, or for bills on London. A bill on London is an order to receive in London, after a certain interval, either gold or Bank of England notes. This order imposes on the country banker the task of providing a fund in London sufficient to answer his draft: it serves, however, to spare that expence of transporting gold, as well as to lessen that necessity of maintaining a stock of guineas, which Dr.

Smith assumes to be the consequence of every excessive emission of notes, and to be the certain means, if bankers do but understand their interest, of limiting their issue.

The remark which has just been made derives particular importance from the circumstances of the period through which we have passed. For, if the usual means of preventing an excess of country bank notes were nothing else than the liability of the issuers to be called upon for a money payment of them, it might fairly be assumed, that, at a time when the money payment of them has been suspended, we must necessarily have been exposed to the greatest inundation of country paper, and to a proportionate depreciation of it. The unbounded issue of country bank notes has been restrained by the obligation under which country bankers have considered themselves to be of granting bills on London; that is to say, orders to receive in London Bank of England paper in exchange for their notes, if required to do so: and it is certain that they would be required to do so whenever the quantity of their notes should be much greater in proportion to the occasion for them, than the quantity of the notes of the Bank of England in proportion to the occasion for those notes.

For the sake of explaining this, let it be admitted, for a moment, that a country bank has issued a very extraordinary quantity of notes. We must assume these to be employed by the holders of them in making purchases in the place in which alone the country bank paper passes, namely, in the surrounding district. The effect of such purchases, according to the principles established in this Chapter, must be a great local rise in the price of articles. But to suppose a great and merely local rise, is to suppose that which can never happen or which, at least, cannot long continue to exist; for every purchaser will discover that he can buy commodities elsewhere at a cheaper rate; and he will not fail to procure them in the quarter in which they are cheap, and to transport them to the spot in which they are dear, for the sake of the profit on the transaction. In order that he may be enabled to do this, he will demand to have the notes which pass current in the place in which we have supposed goods to have been rendered dear by the extraordinary emission of paper, converted into the circulating medium of the place in which goods are cheap: he will, therefore, require to have his country bank note turned into a Bank of England note, or into a bill on London, which is nearly the same thing, provided Bank of England notes are fewer in proportion to the occasion for them than the country bank notes; that is to say, provided Bank of England notes have less lifted up the price of goods in London than country bank notes have lifted up the price of goods in the country.

This point may be still more fully illustrated in the following manner. Let us imagine a mercantile house to consist of two branches, the one placed in the metropolis, the other in the country, and each branch to be accustomed to make certain payments in the spot in which it is situated, each, however, to be in the habit of borrowing as largely as it is able, the one of a neighbouring country bank, the other of the Bank of England, and of applying these loans to the joint use of the trading concern. Let us next suppose an extraordinary facility of borrowing at the country bank to arise, while the opportunities of obtaining loans at the Bank of England remain the same.* In such case the mercantile house, provided its London payments continue to bear the same proportion as before to its country payments, which will hardly fail to be the case, will exchange some part of its encreased loans in the country, consisting in country bank notes, for bills on London, or, in other words, for Bank of England notes. It will thus adjust, with the greatest nicety, the quantity of London and of country paper to the

* The case here put is assumed to exist only by way of argument. The point intended to be shewn, is, that the case cannot happen; or, at least, that such cannot be the case, at the same time, of all the country banks in the kingdom. A single individual, it is true, may find his means of borrowing at a particular country bank to encrease in the manner which is here supposed; for he may obtain a preference over other borrowers. A single bank, also, may find its means of lending to encrease; for its notes may usurp the place of those of other banks. There can, however, be no material enlargement on the whole of the paper of the country, while the facility of borrowing in London remains the same.

amount of the pecuniary demands upon it in each quarter; and, in doing so, it will contribute to prevent the supply of notes in either place from becoming greater in proportion to the demand than in the other. What has been supposed of one house, may be supposed of many similar ones; and not only of houses of the particular description which has been spoken of, but also of the several independent establishments in the two distant places which have pecuniary transactions together, and have an interest in accommodating each other. Their general operations, of a pecuniary kind, must be such as always to check a local rise in the price of commodities in either place, while it is as yet so small as to be scarcely perceptible. In this manner, therefore, the exchangeableness of country paper for London paper will never fail very nearly to equalize the value of them both. It is, moreover, important clearly to point out that their value will be equalized, or nearly equalized, not by a tendency in the London paper to partake in a low value which the country paper has acquired in consequence of its not being limited by any voluntary act of the issuers; nor by a tendency in each to approximate in value to the other; but by a tendency in the country paper to take exactly the high value which the London paper bears in consequence of its being restricted by the issuers. That this must be the case is plain, from the remark which has just been made; for it has been shewn, that the country paper, however it may fail to be limited in quantity by any moderation or prudence of the issuers, becomes no less effectually limited through the circumstance of their being compelled by the holders to exchange as much of it as is excessive for the London paper which is limited; which is limited, I mean, in consequence of a principle of limitation which the directors of the Bank of England have prescribed to themselves.

The country paper, let it then be observed, does not add any thing to the quantity of the London paper; for the effectual limitation of the London paper is the great point, which it must be borne in mind, that we have assumed. The country paper, therefore, does not in any degree diminish the price of the London paper; for its price must remain fixed so long as its quantity continues fixed, supposing, as we do in our present argument, that the demand for it is the same. It has been proved, however, that the country paper is rendered, by its exchangeableness with the London paper, almost exactly equal to it in value. It is, then, rendered almost exactly equal in value to a paper of which the value is completely sustained. Thus, therefore, the limitation of the supply of the single article of London paper, of which, however, we are taking for granted that the demand continues the same, is the means both of sustaining the value of London paper, and also of sustaining the value as well as limiting the quantity of the whole paper of the country.

It is, however, necessary here to point out to the reader, that, in the immediately preceding observations, we have assumed certain facts to exist, for the sake of stating clearly a general principle. It will be the object of a succeeding Chapter to shew in what respects the case which has been supposed differs from the actual one.

Chap. IX.

Of the Circumstances which cause the Paper of the Bank of England, as well as all the other Paper of the Country, to fail of having their Value regulated according to any exact *Proportion to the Quantity of Bank of England Notes.*

Several points may be considered as having been assumed, for the sake of describing clearly the principle which was laid down in the close of the former Chapter. They may be stated to have been the following.

First, the notes of the Bank of England were spoken of as forming exclusively the whole circulating medium of the district which surrounds the metropolis, and as having no circulation beyond the boundaries of that district. The object was, then, to evince, that supposing, secondly, the quantity of Bank of England paper to continue the same; and supposing, thirdly, the payments within the district to be the same; and supposing also, fourthly, the general circumstances to be such as to render the same quantity of circulating medium just as sufficient as before to effect the same payments; the Bank of England paper could not fail both to maintain its own value, and also to maintain the value as well to restrict the quantity of the general paper of the country.

In attempting to shew in what respects the case thus put may have differed from the actual one, I shall advert to each of the four points which have just been mentioned.

First, the notes of the Bank of England have a circulation, which is not perfectly exclusive, over any definable district. In the metropolis itself, and in its neighbourhood, they are the only current paper, some coin circulating also. In many distant parts of the country a very small quantity of Bank of England notes circulate, and also much other paper, as well as a certain quantity of coin. This London and country coin, as well as country paper, may happen through various causes to supplant the Bank of England paper, or to be supplanted by it, either in a greater or in a less degree; and every such variation will have an effect which it is necessary to consider. If, for example, a larger quantity than usual of Bank of England notes should circulate in the country; then the quantity of them which remains applicable to the uses of the London district will be smaller, supposing the total amount issued to be the same. In the case, therefore, of more Bank of England notes circulating in the country, and in the case also of some Bank of England notes occupying the place of guineas antecedently current in London, an issue of a larger total quantity of Bank of England paper will be necessary, in order to give the same means as before of effecting London payments, and in order to produce the same limitation as before of the total quantity of circulating paper in the country.

All the one and two pound notes of the Bank of England (a species of paper which has been issued only since the suspension of its cash payments) have clearly formed that sort of addition to the bank paper of which I have been speaking. These have circulated, some in London, and many of them in the country, in the place of guineas, which have disappeared; and the amount of them has lately been two millions. In order, therefore, to produce the same effect on the country paper as before the suspension, the total amount of Bank of England notes lately circulating ought to have exceeded the quantity issued before the suspension by about two millions, supposing all other things the same. There are other causes which occasionally produce variations in that part of the Bank of England paper, which assists in supplying the distant country circulation: and these variations may sometimes be considerable, and may not easily be estimated. They probably, however, have not lately been material. For though, while the practice of paying in gold has been suspended, country banks, on the one hand, may have been encouraged somewhat more than before to push their notes into circulation, and may thus have supplanted some of the paper of the Bank of England usually passing in their neighbourhood; they certainly, on the other hand, have many of them kept lately in their drawer a fund of Bank of England notes, which was not heretofore deemed necessary, for the sake of being able to offer these in payment of their own paper.*

I have to consider, secondly, how far, allowing for that difference of two millions of which mention has been made, the circulating quantity of Bank of England paper has lately corresponded with that of antecedent periods.

The average amount of Bank of England notes in circulation during three years ending in December 1795, appears to have been 11,975,573*l.* The amount in circulation on the 26th of February 1797, the day antecedent to the suspension of the cash payments of the bank, has been already stated to have been about 8,600,000*l.*, this being that very

* Some Bank of England notes have also been recently employed in the place of small bills on London, the use of which has been discouraged by the late additional duty on bills and notes.

low sum to which they were then reduced. By a statement of their amount on the 6th December 1800, laid before the House of Commons, they appear to have been then 15,450,970*l.* This last mentioned sum includes the two millions of one and two pound notes. If these two millions are deducted, the amount on the 6th December 1800 will exceed the average amount in three years antecedent to the suspension of the cash payments of the bank by 1,475,397*l.* It remains, however, to be observed, that the notes of the Bank of England were stated to the House of Commons by the governor of that company, in the spring of 1801, to have been then reduced to a sum less by about a million and a half than their amount on the 6th December 1800. The total quantity, therefore, of the Bank of England notes in circulation in one part of the spring of 1801, if the two millions be deducted, almost exactly agrees with their average amount during the three years ending December 1795.*

---

* This account of the comparative quantities of the Bank of England notes circulating before, and of those circulating after the suspension of the cash payments of the bank, differs greatly from that of Mr. Boyd, who has, in his pamphlet, minutely investigated the same subject. The causes of this disagreement are the following.

He mentions, as I have done, the amount of Bank of England notes to have been, on the 6th December 1800, 15,450,970*l.* He then compares this their highest amount (for such, or nearly such, I consider it to be), first with their lowest amount, namely, with their amount on the 26th February 1797, which was 8,640,250*l.*, and then with their average amount for three years antecedent to the suspension of the cash payments of the bank, viz. 11,975,573*l.*, the same average amount at which I have reckoned them, for I have adopted Mr. Boyd's own statement. He then infers, that, on the first of his principles of comparison, an addition of nearly four-fifths, and, on the second, of three-tenths, had been made to the sum in circulation.

To this representation the answer is, as will appear from the text, first that of the 15,450,970*l.* stated to the House of Commons to be the amount of Bank of England notes in circulation on the 6th December 1800, the sum of about two millions, consisting in one and two pound notes, ought to have been deducted by Mr. Boyd in forming his comparison. These notes evidently filled the place which was before occupied by guineas. They were, for that reason, not added to the 13,450,970*l.* in the return made by the bank to parliament, as they have been in the pamphlet of Mr. Boyd, but were set down as a separate article. Bankers have commonly given out these one and two pound notes as a substitute for guineas; and every individual, whether in London or in the country, who has had a note of this description in his pocket, has obviously kept it in the place of gold.

We have to consider, thirdly, whether the payments of the metropolis may be likely to have been the same in the last year as in some preceding years.

A subject, in the examination of which there may seem to be some difficulty, shall here, in the first place, be discussed. It has been already observed, that the quantity of Bank of England notes is limited by the bank directors who issue them; and that the quantity of country bank paper, though restricted in an equal degree, is limited not by the act of the issuers, but through the circumstance of its exchangeableness for London paper. By saying that the country paper is limited in an equal degree, I always mean not that one uniform proportion is maintained between the quantity of the London paper and that of the country paper, but only that the quantity of the one, in comparison with the demand for that one, is the same, or nearly the same, as

---

It is to be replied, secondly, that the sum of 8,640,250*l.* with which one of the comparisons of Mr. Boyd is made, is that remarkably low sum to which the bank improperly, as I have ventured to suspect, and certainly to the no small distress of the metropolis, had suffered their notes to fall on the day antecedent to the suspension of their cash payments, a sum of the smallness of which Mr. Boyd himself has complained. Their notes on the 18th February, that is, exactly one week

before, were	£.9,137,950
They were two weeks before	9,431,550
Three weeks before	9,667,460
A month before	10,024,740
And five weeks before	10,550,830

Their notes also, immediately after they were at that lowest sum of 8,640,250*l.*, with which Mr. Boyd forms the first of his comparisons, were encreased considerably: they were, on the 4th March, that is, one week after, 10,416,520*l.*, and they were gradually raised still higher.

There can, therefore, be no doubt that the comparison ought to have been made with the number which were in circulation, not at the remarkable æra of the 26th February, 1797, but only during an average of years preceding the suspension.

The fact of the Bank of England notes having been reduced near a million and a half in the spring of 1801, a circumstance which renders the amount of them almost exactly equal at the two periods at which both I and Mr. Boyd have made our comparison, could not be known to Mr. Boyd at the time of writing his pamphlet.

Mr. Boyd founds, on the supposed fact of the vast encrease of Bank of England notes, the opinion which he states in the beginning of his Work, that "to the augmentation of bank paper not convertible into specie, more than to any other cause, is to be ascribed the high price of provisions."

the quantity of the other in proportion to the call for the other.

The reader, in reasoning on this state of the case, may, perhaps, be inclined to infer, and it is a question which seems to deserve consideration, that when the Bank of England paper is more than usually restricted, the pressure in London which in such case takes place (for it is there that the general pressure originates), may be likely to relieve itself either by drawing to London a large part of the Bank of England paper usually circulating in the country, the place which it occupied being supplied by country paper, or by causing many of the payments of London to transfer themselves to the country. If either of these two consequences should result from every pressure in London, then, even though the total amount of Bank of England paper should be diminished, that part of it which circulates in London may possibly continue to be just as sufficient as before to perform the task assigned to it of effecting the London payments; and in that case the country paper also, since it always takes the price of the London paper, will so far encrease itself as to become in the same manner as before commensurate with the country payments. If any considerable effect of this kind should follow from every limitation of the London paper; then the principle which was laid down in the close of the former Chapter in a great measure fails: and the bank has not that power which was ascribed to it of restricting the quantity and regulating the value of the paper of the country.

That a pressure in London is not likely to produce the first of the two effects which have been mentioned, that of drawing to London the Bank of England notes circulating in the country, is a point on which I shall not separately dwell, except so far as to observe, that a pressure in London, if it be very sudden and severe, may be suspected of having a tendency directly contrary to that of bringing Bank of England notes from the country to London; for it is apt, through the alarm which it excites, to produce, as was formerly explained, an extraordinary diminution of country bank notes; a diminution, I mean, which is even greater in proportion to the country payments to be effected than that of the notes of the Bank of England in proportion to the London payments. In such case, a necessity is created for the substitution of other circulating medium in the place of the country paper which has been suppressed. The substitute principally demanded will be gold; but some Bank of England paper is not unlikely to be also employed in filling the void.

In proceeding to enquire whether a pressure in London, arising from the restriction of Bank of England paper, is likely to cause the transfer to the country of many of the payments usually made in London, I shall advert to past experience.

It was mentioned in an early Chapter of this Work, that there seems to have existed, for some time, an encreasing disposition to transfer to London the pecuniary part of even those commercial transactions which belong properly to the country. It here naturally occurs to us to enquire for what reason the restriction of the notes of the Bank of England by the issuers in time past, has not served to remove this disposition, and even to cause the quantity of London payments, compared with those of the country, continually to lessen, rather than to encrease. The Bank of England paper, let it here be observed, operated before the suspension of the cash payments of the bank in restricting the country paper, exactly in the same manner as it has done since that event. It is commonly and very naturally supposed, that it was the exchangeableness of the country paper for guineas which used to sustain its value. This, however, was not the case: its value was sustained by its exchangeableness for Bank of England notes. The country paper bore always and necessarily the same value as the notes of the Bank of England; and not always or necessarily the same value as the gold contained in the coin, for which the country paper was exchangeable. It is true, indeed, that the quantity of gold in our coin had an influence on the value of country paper. It had, however, only an influence which was imperfect and indirect. It served to dictate to the directors of the Bank of England what was that quantity of paper which they might properly emit. For, if at any time the exchanges of the country became so unfavourable as to produce a material excess of the market price above the mint price of gold: the directors of the bank, as appears by the evidence of some of their body given to parliament, were disposed to resort to a reduction of their paper as a means of diminishing or removing the excess, and of thus providing for the security of their establishment. They, moreover, have at all times been accustomed to observe some limit as to the quantity of their notes, for the same prudential reasons.

This interest in the prevention of any great excess of the market price above the mint price of gold was in no degree felt by the country banker; for the loss sustained by every new conversion of bullion into coin was borne not by him, but by the bank of England, out of whose coffers all the guineas called for in every part of the kingdom were supplied. The bank of England, if coin was demanded of it, had to purchase bullion at a losing price. The country banker, if coin was in like manner required of him, had only to possess himself of a Bank of England note, which was exchangeable at the bank for guineas without any discount. If, therefore, the directors of the Bank of England suffered their paper to be worth less than the gold contained in the coin for which their paper was exchangeable, the country paper was worth less also; or, in other words, the degree of expence and difficulty which the country banker incurred in obtaining guineas was to be measured by the degree of expence and difficulty incurred in obtaining Bank of England notes, and not by the degree of expence and difficulty incurred in buying and then coining gold. The necessity which the Bank of England felt of curing any great excess of the market price above the mint price of gold, caused the limitation of Bank of England paper; and then this limitation, in proportion as it took place, produced the limitation of the paper of the country. It was in this manner that an excessive issue of the paper of the kingdom was restrained before the suspension of the cash payments of the Bank of England. If then, the directors of the bank were used before the suspension of their cash payments to limit their issues through a necessity which sometimes urged them, and if thus they limited the paper of the country in the manner which has been described, it follows that, supposing them after that event to have restrained their issues in like manner, though through a somewhat less urgent motive, the general effect must have been the same. There can, therefore, be no more reason to suppose a transfer to have lately taken place of London payments to the country, or of Bank of England notes circulating in the country to London, than there is to suppose the same transfer to have taken place in the time when the bank paid in gold. Both the nature of the pressure, and the principle on which our paper credit stood, were the same at both periods.

It remains for us to enquire, how far the payments of London are likely to have varied through any other cause. It is probable that, under ordinary circumstances, they do not fluctuate in any very considerable degree within a short distance of time. War seems likely, on the whole, to encrease them, both by the additional business in the stocks, and also by the other pecuniary transactions on the account of government (transactions generally carried on entirely in London), to which it gives occasion. It also encreases the payments of London, in common with those of the country, by contributing to a general rise in the price of articles. It is, however, necessary to guard this observation. In respect to the total *quantity* of consumable articles produced and sold in the kingdom, war, perhaps, may be considered as usually making little difference; for, while it gives a spur to some, it operates as a check to other branches of industry; and, while it encreases national consumption, it may possibly diminish, in an almost equal degree, that of individuals. It raises, however, the *price* of commodities, and thus enlarges the general amount of payments, though it more particularly augments those payments which are made in the metropolis. This general augmentation, however, of the price of our articles, unattended by a similar rise in the price of the commodities of other countries, obstructs as has been already shewn, the exportation of our goods; since it renders them less able to stand the competition to which they are subject in foreign markets, unless a compensation for the rise is afforded to the foreigner in the computation of the exchange between the two countries. The reader may, perhaps, be led here to imagine, that the bank ought to prevent this rise[1] according to the principles which it is the object of this Chapter to establish, a sufficiently considerable reduction of its paper being all that is necessary for the purpose. No doubt the fact is, that the tendency of goods to rise is continually restrained by the limitation of the paper of the Bank of England. And I apprehend that it is restrained just as much as it is proper, or, perhaps, practicable, to restrain it, if the paper of the bank is so far confined as to prevent an excess of the market price above the mint price of gold: for, in that case, it is restrained so far as still to afford to our goods the opportunity of sale in a foreign market, without giving to the foreigner that compensation in the exchange which leads to the exportation of the current coin of the country. To suppose the bank paper to be restrained much farther, is to suppose a profit on the importation of bullion; a profit, to which the continuance of the importations of that article must soon put a period. In saying, therefore, that war enhances the price of goods, and thus causes an encrease of payments, we ought here to bear in mind that it ought only to be allowed to lift them up to that point to which they can be raised consistently with the general maintenance of our exchanges; and that, so far as they *permanently* stand above that point, it is the enlarged and too great quantity of notes of the Bank of England which is to be considered as the cause of the high price of goods, rather than the high price of goods which is to be taken to be the cause of the enlarged quantity of notes of the Bank of England*. There is considerable danger, lest

* It was observed in a former place, that this difficult and disputable point would be again adverted to in the progress of the present Work. The fairest mode, as it appears to me, of determining which ought to be deemed the cause and which the effect, is that which has been

in this respect, we should, in some degree, at least, mistake the effect for the cause; and should too much incline to consider an advanced price of commodities to be both the cause of an encreased issue of paper and the justification of it.

War, on the contrary, may be supposed to lessen the amount of general payments, or, at least, to check their growth, so far as it obstructs the accumulation of wealth and the natural progress of commerce. We know, however, that, during the late war, the amount of our exported and imported articles continued greatly to encrease. This happened partly, no doubt, through the general tendency of our trade to enlarge itself, partly through the advantages resulting from some new colonial acquisitions, and partly from the circumstance of the commerce of our competitors having been still more interrupted than our own. Our exports and imports it is true, form no just measure of the total quantity either of our commercial transactions or of our general payments: they afford, however, some presumption of the enlargement of both. If we take into consideration all the points which have been touched upon, there will appear sufficient reason to believe, that, during the late war, a very considerable and progressive augmentation of the payments of the metropolis must have taken place.

It now remains only to consider, fourthly, how far circumstances may have been such as to have rendered the same quantity of Bank of England notes either more or less sufficient for effecting the same quantity of London payments.

---

adopted in the text; namely, to charge too much paper with being the cause when the price of bullion is rendered permanently higher than that of coin, and, when otherwise, to consider it rather as an effect. By the term "permanently," I, however, mean such a degree of permanence as may serve to shew that the fall of our exchanges, and the rise in the price of bullion, are not referable to any extraordinary and passing event, such as that of one or even of two particularly bad harvests; for these may not unfairly be termed temporary circumstances, though their influence may extend over a period of one or two years. In general it may, perhaps, also be assumed, that an excessive issue of paper has not been the leading cause of a fall in the exchange, if it afterwards turns out that the exchange is able to recover itself without any material reduction of the quantity of paper.

Several causes may have contributed to spare the use of notes. First, it is to be remembered, that a small extension of their quantity may be sufficient to effect a comparatively large number of additional payments; for the private bankers in London, who are the chief holders of Bank of England paper, by no means find it necessary to enlarge their stock of it in full proportion to the encreased number of their pecuniary transactions. The talent of œconomizing bank notes is also a continually improving one; and the very circumstance of the suspension of the cash payments of the bank, by serving to strengthen mercantile credit, has favoured the exercise of œconomy in the use of the paper of the Bank of England. When payments were currently made in gold, the country banks were subject to sudden demands for cash through temporary alarms among the holders of their notes. From these they have lately been more exempt, in consequence of no other option having been given to those who demanded payment of country bank paper than that of receiving Bank of England notes in return. Since the suspension of the cash payments of the bank, credit has been less subject to interruption, and the quantity both of country paper and of Bank of England notes has probably been less variable; or, if the fluctuations of the latter have been as considerable as before, they may have more nearly corresponded with the variations in the wants of the public*.

* Immediately after the payment of the quarterly dividends on the public funds, the amount of Bank of England paper in circulation is considerably encreased; but the expectation that the plenty of it will soon cease, disposes bankers and others to hold for a time a superfluous quantity. In consequence of the additions to the public debt made during the war, the occasional enlargements of the quantity of bank paper, arising from this cause, have become much more considerable. A diminution of notes, if known to be temporary, and if also moderate, produces, on the other hand, little pressure: for the expectation of returning abundance serves to maintain confidence, and to dispose the bankers to deem a somewhat reduced stock of bank paper for the time sufficient. The chief occasion of a diminution of the number of bank notes has been, that of the payment of the instalments on the public loans. The government, during the latter years of the war, issued from week to week a species of exchequer bills, which they received back in part of the payments on the loans. By thus lessening the quantity of paper taken out of circulation at the time of each instalment, they gave new

To sum up the observations which have now been made: it thus appears, that since the suspension of the cash payments of the bank, the number of its notes has been the same, or nearly the same, as before that event, if those two millions of one and two pound notes, which have been a mere substitute for gold, are deducted; that the payments, however, of the metropolis have been much encreased; but that, on the other hand, the same number of notes has probably sufficed of late for more than the same number of payments.

It has not been the object of these remarks to found upon them any exact estimate of the effect which the quantity of Bank of England paper lately issued is likely to have had on the cost of commodities, or on the market price of bullion; but rather, on the contrary, to shew that no such estimate can with confidence be formed, on account of the number of circumstances, some of them very difficult to be appreciated which affect the question. I believe the fact to be, that very little correspondence has subsisted between the fluctuation in the amount of Bank of England notes in circulation at different times, and the variations in the general price of articles at the same periods; and this want of a very discernible connexion between the cause and the effect, seems not unlikely to have led some persons too hastily to conclude, that the enlargement and diminution of Bank of England paper have not that influence on the exchanges or on the price of commodities which has been spoken of*.

---

facility to the operation of raising the public money; an operation which, however great, has in itself no other difficulty than that which arises from the too sudden diminution of London paper to which it is apt to lead. It can scarcely be necessary to add, that a great loan may, nevertheless, portend difficulty in other quarters, and that the degree of ease with which the payment of our loans may be accomplished, is, therefore, no true criterion of the state of the public resources.

* It is not long since the Bank of England first adopted the custom of issuing notes for five pounds. These have circulated for some years in the place partly of gold, partly of country bank notes, and partly also, though it is impossible to say in what degree, in the place of ten pound Bank of England notes. There is, therefore, an unknown number of notes for five pounds which has formed that sort of addition to the Bank of England paper, which has no influence in raising the price of articles. This is only one of many circumstances, some operating in one direction, and some in the contrary, which render it difficult to draw a correct

Let it, therefore, be carefully remembered, that I by no means suppose a limitation of London paper to operate simply by causing an equal reduction of country paper, and then such a fall in the price of goods over the kingdom as is exactly commensurate with the general diminution of paper; and, finally, also such a variation in the exchange as is precisely proportionate to the reduction of paper, and to the fall in the price of goods. Counteracting circumstances of various kinds may prevent these proportions from being maintained; and the full effects may not follow their cause until after the lapse of some period of time.

It must, in particular, be borne in mind, that a limitation of Bank of England paper affects prices in a great measure by its operation on the state of commercial confidence; and this influence on the minds of men will be far from uniform. A small limitation of Bank of England paper may give a great shock to confidence, when the state of credit is delicate; and may, therefore, at such a time, much discourage speculation. The very same limitation, under other circumstances of the country, may be almost without effect.

But although there is so great difficulty in estimating the precise influence on the cost of articles, or on the market price of bullion, which each alteration in the quantity of Bank of England notes may produce, there is no reason, on that account, to doubt the general truth of the proposition which was laid down in the close of the former Chapter, namely, that the restriction of the paper of the Bank of England is the mean both of maintaining its own value, and of maintaining the value, as well as of limiting the quantity of all the paper in the country. Although it should be difficult, or even impossible, to determine to what point the limitation must be carried in order to produce a given effect, it may be sufficiently clear that the tendency of the limitation is to secure the benefit in question.

---

inference from those accounts of the quantity of Bank of England notes circulating at a variety of periods, which have been lately laid before parliament.

The perplexities of this subject being such as I have now described, it naturally occurs to us to reason from the effect to the cause, and to infer a too great issue of paper when we perceive that there is an excess of the market price above the mint price of gold. But this inference is one which, for reasons formerly given, should always be very cautiously made; for it is to be borne in mind, that the excess may arise from other causes besides that of a too great emission of paper. Let the manner in which an extravagant issue of notes operates in producing the excess be recollected. It raises, and probably by slow degrees, the cost of British goods. It thus obstructs the export of them, unless a compensation for the high price is afforded to the foreign buyer in the rate of exchange; and the variation in our exchange produces a low valuation of our coin, compared with that of bullion. The state of the exchange, then, is the immediate cause of the evil in question. Now, a suspension of the foreign demand for British manufactures, or an encrease of the British demand for foreign articles, circumstances which may arise when there is no encrease of bank paper, are the much more frequent as well as the more obvious causes of a fall in our exchange, and, therefore, also of a high price of bullion.

We are thus led back to the point which was dwelt upon some time since. Our two defective harvests, and the interruptions experienced in our export trade, very sufficiently account for the late fluctuation of our exchanges. In these respects there has evidently been much in our situation which has been remarkable; while, as has been proved in the present Chapter, there has been nothing which ought to be deemed extraordinary in the quantity of paper issued by the Bank of England.

It must, however, be admitted, that if an excessive issue of Bank of England notes produces, as it has been shewn to do, an unfavourable exchange; a reduction of them below the accustomed number must have a tendency to improve our exchange, by whatever means it may have been made to turn against us. But, after this admission, it may be remarked, that it may be necessary to encounter much evil in effecting the reduction. We have been lately placed between two dangers; between that of a depreciated paper currency on the one hand, and that of an interruption to our paper credit, and a consequent stagnation of our commerce and manufactures, on the other. And, on the whole, we have, perhaps, owed much to that liberal policy of the directors of the Bank of England, which has led them to maintain a quantity of notes in appearance encreased, and in reality not diminished, in spite of some political as well as popular prejudices on this subject; at a time, also, when their conduct was observed with particular jealousy, on account of the suspension of their cash payments, and even when the course of exchange was much against us. Whether the bank may have erred a little on the one side or on the other, is a point which it would be invidious very critically to examine, and difficult to determine with certainty. It seems sufficiently clear, that if, at the period of the late northern confederacy, when our exchanges were the least favourable, the bank had materially diminished its paper, the embarrassment of our manufacturers and merchants, which the state of the continent had begun to render great, would have immediately become far greater; and that manufacturing labour, which was then in some degree interrupted by a suspension of the demand for British goods on the continent, would have been likewise obstructed at the same season (a season of peculiar pressure on the common people, from the circumstance of the scarcity) by a more than ordinary difficulty which our manufacturers would have experienced in effecting their payments. The stock of goods in our warehouses, made ready for subsequent exportation, would, in this case, have been smaller; and we might, therefore, on the whole, have had to look forward to a less early rectification of our exchanges. The difficulties of 1793 might have been added to those of the spring of 1801; and if commercial confidence had failed, political credit might in consequence have been shaken at one of the most critical periods of our history.

From the principles recently laid down, some additional inferences may be deduced.

It was the object of several former Chapters to point out the evil of a too contracted issue of paper. The general tendency of the present, as well as of the preceding one, has been to shew the danger of a too extended emission. Two kinds of error on the subject of the affairs of the Bank of England have been prevalent. Some political persons have assumed it to be a principle, that in proportion as the gold of the bank lessens, its paper, or, as is sometimes said, its loans (for the amount of the one has been confounded with that of the other), ought to be reduced. It has been already shewn, that a maxim of this sort, if strictly followed up, would lead to universal failure. A sentiment has prevailed among other persons, which has bordered on a very different extreme. They have complained of nothing, except the too scanty liberality of the bank, and have seen no danger in almost any extension of its discounts, or profusion in the issue of its paper, provided only the bills discounted (that is, the bills received by the bank in return for its notes) were real bills, and were those also of sufficiently safe and responsible houses.

But it will appear from the principles laid down in this and the preceding Chapter, that there may be a disposition among very rich and punctual men to borrow a sum far exceeding that which it may be prudent in the bank to lend. Every additional loan obtained from the bank, if we suppose its gold to remain the same, implies an encreased issue of paper, but the measure of such issue has been shewn to be regulated by a principle which is not even connected with the question of the opulence of the borrowers at the bank, or of the nature of the bills discounted. The borrowers make a promise (and we will suppose that there is no reason to doubt the fulfilment of it) that the loan shall be repaid with punctuality. But in what manner is the payment to be effected? It will be made either in notes furnished by the Bank of England itself, or else in gold supplied by the same company, which notes and gold the bank must take care to render interchangeable for each other; and this is only to be done by keeping down their quantity, and thus maintaining their value.

Objections have been made by some to the monopoly of the bank. And its indisposition to lend to safe houses, on the security of real bills, to an extent which is deemed sufficient, has probably been the circumstance which has induced some mercantile persons to favour the idea of the establishment of a rival establishment. Competition, it is thought, would lead to greater liberality; and, in a variety of respects, would operate beneficially in this case, as it is known to do in many others.

It has been evinced, however, in the present Chapter, that we derive a material advantage from the power enjoyed by the Bank of England of exclusively furnishing the paper circulation of the metropolis. To this very circumstance the bank stands indebted for its faculty of regulating all the paper of the kingdom. On the bank is devolved the task of providing guineas for the whole country: with the bank is lodged the power of so restricting the general paper, as to render bullion purchasable, except in some extraordinary cases of alarm or difficulty. If these excepted cases should arise, and the cash payments of the bank should be suspended, an event of the possible recurrence of which we must not altogether exclude the idea; then the same circumstance of the monopoly of the bank affords to it the means of still sustaining the value both of its own paper and of that of the whole island. It serves also to impose upon the directors of this powerful company a complete responsibility. If a rival institution to the Bank of England were established, both the power and the responsibility would be divided; and, through the additional temptation to exercise that liberality in lending, which it is the object of competition to promote, the London notes, and also the country bills and notes, would be more liable to become excessive. Our paper credit would, therefore, stand in every respect on a less safe foundation.

Chap. X.

Objections to the Doctrine of the two preceding Chapters answered.—Of the Circumstances which render it necessary that the Bank should impose its own Limit on the quantity of its Paper.—Effect of the Law against Usury.—Proof of the Necessity of restricting the Bank Loans, drawn from the Case of the Transfer of Capital to Foreign Countries.

Since it is not improbable that the reasoning of the preceding Chapters may have failed to produce full conviction in the mind of those who have been in the habit of deeming all limitation of the bank paper by the bank itself to be unnecessary; some few pages may be usefully employed in answering popular objections to the doctrine which has been laid down, and in more fully elucidating the subject.

"The encrease of Bank of England paper," we will suppose it to be still said by an objector "is the effect and "not the cause of an advanced price of commodities. To "enlarge the Bank of England notes merely in proportion "as safe and real bills are offered in return for them, is only "to exchange one species of paper for another, namely, "Bank of England notes for bills, which, though not so "current or so safe as bank notes, are sufficiently worthy of "credit. It is, therefore, simply to afford a guarantee to "the transactions of the merchant, and thus to render that "accommodation to commerce which it belongs to the bank "to give."

"The depreciation of paper," it may be added, "is apt to "arise not so much from an extension of its quantity, as "from a want of sufficient confidence in it. The great "object of the bank should, therefore, be to maintain the "public confidence; to which it contributes by furnishing, "in return for bills confessedly good, a species of paper still "better. The evil of an unfavourable exchange, and of a "consequent high price of gold, arises from an unfavourable "balance of trade, and from that cause only. The true "mode of preventing this evil, or of remedying it, if unfor-"tunately it exists, is to encrease the national industry. "The way to encourage industry is to give full scope to "trade and manufactures by a liberal emission of paper. "The balance of trade will not fail to be rendered favour-"able by that abundance of exportable articles which the "labour thus excited must necessarily create. The course "of exchange will, consequently, be supported; all excess "of the market price above the mint price of gold will be "prevented; and thus the value of our paper will be sus-"tained by the very means of its encrease."

Suppose a reasoner, on the same side, to add, that when the credit of the assignats of France was overthrown, the fall especially at the first, was owing rather to the prevalence of distrust than to the excessive quantity of the article, and that the depreciation of assignats rarely bore a regular proportion to the extension of their amount.*

It may, with equal truth, be affirmed by the objector, that if a reference be made to the prices of corn in the London corn-market at various æras, and also to the account of the quantity of bank notes stated by the bank to have been in circulation at the same or at immediately preceding periods, the price of grain in London will by no means be found to have been high in proportion as the number of Bank of England notes has been great, and low in proportion as it has been small; but that the very contrary has often been remarkably the case.

To these objections it may be answered, that they who

---

* The following extract from Mr. Arthur Young's Tour through France, seems to establish the above-mentioned fact.

"In September, 1790, four hundred millions of assignats were in "circulation; but the discount at Bordeaux never exceeded ten, at "Paris six, per cent. And in May, 1791, after many hundred millions "more were issued, the discount was from seven to ten per cent. Con-"dorcet, with other theorists, expected that the prices of corn, and of "other necessaries of life, would enormously advance; but the contrary "happened to be the event—the price of corn declined. The assignats "amounted, on the dissolution of the first assembly, to eighteen hundred millions."—Vol. i. 4to edition, page 520.

represent an unlimited issue of Bank of England paper as having no tendency to produce the evils of a rise in the price of commodities in Great Britain, of a fall in our exchange, and of an excess of the market price above the mint price of gold, are bound to prove one of the two following propositions; either, first, that, supposing the directors of the bank to make the most enormous addition to their paper; to raise it, let us suppose, to fifty millions, even this augmentation will not lead to the consequences which have been mentioned; or if they do not affirm this strong position, but admit that there is a certain quantity of notes which will not fail to produce the evils in question, then, secondly, in order to prove that the bank need not place any limit to the issue of its own paper, they are bound to shew that the bank paper has a natural tendency sufficiently to limit itself.

Let us separately investigate each of these two points.

When we assume the fact of the bank paper being raised from its present amount of about fifteen millions to to the sum of fifty millions, we are led, in the first place, to enquire in whose hands the additional sum of thirty-five millions would be placed, and what would be the motive for holding it? I admit, or rather it is a point on which I would insist, that the maintenance of the price of the assignats of France by no means rested entirely, nor, for a time, even principally, on their quantity. It depended much on the opinion entertained by Frenchmen respecting the value of the lands declared to be purchasable by means of this particular kind of paper, and respecting the fidelity of the French government to its engagements. Assignats, it is true, bore no interest; but the prospect of an ultimate profit to be reaped by the possessor of them, would operate, for a time, exactly like an accruing interest, in causing many persons to detain them; and, therefore, although they were used as a circulating medium, it is probable that only a part of them was turned to this purpose, and that even that part circulated but slowly. The reader is here desired to recollect a point which was explained in an early part of this work; namely, that the quantity of circulating medium which can be employed without injury to its value, is to be estimated not merely by its proportion to the quantity of trade or of payments, but also by the relative rapidity of its circulation. A species of circulating medium which changes hands once in ten days, will need to be a hundred times as great in quantity as the paper which passes through ten hands in one day. When that sanguine spirit which had at first inspired the holders of assignats subsided, the article would naturally sink in value with considerable rapidity; and in proportion as its price fell, the French government would be under the necessity of extending its issues. It is therefore, not at all surprising that French assignats should, for a time, have borne a price which was proportionate not so much to their quantity as to their credit. Their quantity, however, after a certain period, operated on their credit, and became a very powerful cause of their depreciation.

Bank of England notes are exactly the converse to assignats in the points which have been mentioned; and their value, on that account, will be found to depend not so properly on their credit as on their quantity. It is true, that when, in consequence of alarm, a run is made upon the bank for guineas, the same confidence which is placed in gold is not reposed in Bank of England paper. Even in this case, however, it is only a small part of the community which is eager for gold: the holders of a very large proportion of the bank paper remain exactly as well contented as before to use it as the medium of their payments. And since the hoarders of gold prefer it not to paper only, but to land, to goods, and to almost every species of property, the paper of the bank cannot be affirmed to fall into discredit in consequence of applications for coin made with a view to hoard it, so properly as gold may be said to come into peculiar demand. In a season of alarm, our guineas are preferred by some persons both to our bank notes and to goods, on the same principle on which, in a state of extreme political convulsion, diamonds, because they may be still more easily transported or concealed, would probably be preferred to gold.

By saying, therefore, that the value of bank notes depends not on their credit, but on their quantity, I mean to affirm that their credit, so far as it affects their value, is always good; and that the common fluctuations of their price, in exchange both for goods and bullion, are not, in the smallest degree, to be referred to variations in the degree of confidence placed by Englishmen in the good faith or the solidity of the Bank of England. The magnitude of its capital is perfectly well known, and not the slightest doubt subsists respecting the sufficiency of its effects to answer much more than all its engagements. If the rise and fall in the public confidence in bank notes were the cause of the gradations in their price, the period at which their value would have been the lowest would have been that which followed the suspension of the cash payments of the bank; an event certainly calculated, more than any other which has been experienced, to affect the reputation of that company. But it is a most remarkable fact, and a fact decisive on the present point, that the exchanges of this country improved, or, in other words, that Bank of England paper rose in value when compared with bullion, in the months subsequent to the suspension of its payments in cash.

Bank of England paper, therefore, is not apt to vary in its value in consequence of the fluctuations of the public confidence in it; but essentially differs in this respect from the late assignats of France. It presents to the holder no hope of future profit from the detention of it. Not only does it bear no interest (in this point, indeed, resembling assignats), but it offers no substitute for interest; it holds out no privileges, certain or contingent, real or pretended, tempting the possessor to detain it. There is, on the contrary, a known and continually encreasing loss sustained by keeping it. On this account the quantity held by each person is only that which the amount of payments to be effected by it renders, in his opinion, necessary.

We are at present assuming, for the sake of illustrating

the subject, that thirty-five millions of additional bank paper are retained in the hands of the public. Imagine a London banker to acquire his share of them. The supply of bank notes which he chuses to reserve in his drawer is always estimated by the scale of his payments; or, to speak more correctly, by the probable amount of the fluctuations in his stock of notes, which fluctuations are proportionate, or nearly proportionate, to the scale of his payments. So long, therefore, as his payments remain the same (and they will not materially alter while the price of goods suffers no variation, supposing his transactions to retain their former proportion to those of the whole kingdom), he will be perfectly indisposed to hold fifty thousand pounds in bank notes, in the place of each fifteen thousand pounds which he has been accustomed to deem necessary. He will make haste to part with the whole superfluous quantity; he will offer to lend it to any safe merchants, and even at a reduced rate of interest, in case he shall find that borrowers cannot otherwise be invited.

If we imagine the merchants to become possessed of the new paper, the same difficulty of accounting for the detention of it remains; unless we admit that the principles laid down in the two former Chapters are just, and that the larger quantity of circulating medium will cause goods to rise in value, and will thus find for itself employment.

There seem to be only two modes in which we can conceive the additional paper to be disposed of. It may be imagined either, first, to be used in transferring an encreased quantity of articles, which it must, in that case, be assumed that the new paper itself has tended to create; or, secondly, in transferring the same articles at a higher price.

Let us examine the first of these cases.

An encreased quantity of articles can only arise from additional commodities either brought from abroad or produced at home through the exertion of new industry. An extraordinary issue of paper will bring goods from abroad only so far as it enables the country to export either gold, or additional commodities created at home, as the means of paying for the foreign articles. The export of gold has its limit. It is, moreover, desirable, for reasons which have been fully stated, that this limit should be narrow. Whether a very great emission of notes tends to encrease the quantity of goods produced at home, is the point which remains to be considered.

In examining this question, an error into which it is very natural to fall must be developed. When the Bank of England enlarges its paper, it augments, in the same degree, as we must here suppose, its loans to individuals. These favoured persons immediately conceive, and not without reason, that they have obtained an additional though borrowed capital, by which they can push their own particular manufacture or branch of commerce; and they are apt, also, though not with equal justice, to infer that the new capital thus acquired by themselves is wholly an accession to that of the kingdom; for it does not occur to them that the commerce or manufactures of any other individuals can be at all reduced in consequence of this encrease of their own.

But, first, it is obvious, that the antecedently idle persons to whom we may suppose the new capital to give employ, are limited in number; and that, therefore, if the encreased issue is indefinite, it will set to work labourers, of whom a part will be drawn from other, and, perhaps, no less useful occupations. It may be inferred from this consideration, that there are some bounds to the benefit which is to be derived from an augmentation of paper; and, also, that a liberal, or, at most, a large encrease of it, will have all the advantageous effects of the most extravagant emission.

Let us also consider the mode in which the new paper operates through the medium of these individual borrowers, as unquestionably it does, in giving life to fresh industry. The bank notes convey to them the power of obtaining for their own use, or of destining to such purposes as they please, a certain portion of purchasable commodities. The extraordinary emission of paper causes no immediate difference in the *total* quantity of articles belonging to the kingdom. This is self-evident. But it communicates to the new borrowers at the bank a power of taking to themselves a larger share of the existing goods than they would otherwise have been able to command. If the holders of the new paper thus acquire the power over a larger portion of the existing stock of the kingdom, the possessors of the old paper must have the power over a smaller part. The same paper, therefore, will purchase fewer goods, or, in other words, commodities will rise in their nominal value. The proprietors of the new paper will become greater encouragers of industry than before; the owners of the old paper, being able to command less property, will have less power of employing labour. For industry is excited, strictly speaking, not by paper, but by that stock which the paper affords the means of purchasing. Money of every kind is an order for goods. It is so considered by the labourer when he receives it, and is almost instantly turned into money's worth. It is merely the instrument by which the purchasable stock of the country is distributed with convenience and advantage among the several members of the community.

It may be said, however, and not untruly, that an encreased issue of paper tends to produce a more brisk demand for the existing goods, and a somewhat more prompt consumption of them; that the more prompt consumption supposes a diminution of the ordinary stock, and the application of that part of it, which is consumed, to the purpose of giving life to fresh industry; that the fresh industry thus excited will be the means of gradually creating additional stock, which will serve to replace the stock by which the industry had been supported; and that the new circulating medium will, in this manner, create for itself much new employment.

The supposition which has now been made is admitted to be just. Let the reader, however, take notice, that it assumes the demand both for goods and labour to become more eager than before.—Now the consequence of this encreased eagerness in the demand must, unquestionably, be an enhancement of the price of labour and commodities, which is the very point for which I am contending. Indeed, whatever view we take of the subject, we seem obliged to admit, that, although additional industry will be one effect of an extraordinary emission of paper, a rise in the cost of articles will be another.

Probably no small part of that industry which is excited by new paper is produced through the very means of the enhancement of the cost of commodities. While paper is encreasing, and articles continue rising, mercantile speculations appear more than ordinarily profitable. The trader, for example, who sells his commodity in three months after he purchased it, obtains an extra gain, which is equal to such advance in the general price of things as the new paper has caused during the three months in question:—he confounds this gain with the other profits of his commerce; and is induced, by the apparent success of his undertakings, to pursue them with more than usual spirit. The manufacturer feels the same kind of encouragement to extend his operations; and the enlarged issue of paper supplies both him and the merchant with the means of carrying their plans into effect. As soon, however, as the circulating medium ceases to encrease, the extra profit is at an end; and, if we assume the augmented paper to be brought back to its ordinary quantity, we must suppose industry to languish for a time, through the ill success which will appear to attend mercantile transactions.

Mr. Hume has an observation in his Essay on Money, which, in some degree, confirms the remarks which have been made in the text. Having represented an influx of money as exciting industry (and we may presume an encrease of paper to have exactly the same effect), "At "first," he says, "no alteration is perceived; by degrees "the price rises first of one commodity, then of another, "till the whole, at last, reaches a just proportion with the "new quantity of specie which is in the kingdom. *In my "opinion, it is only in this interval or intermediate situation "between the acquisition of money and rise of prices*"

(Mr. Hume must mean, no doubt, the completion of the rise, and not the commencement of it) "*that the encreasing quan-*" *tity of gold and silver is favourable to industry.*"*

It must be also admitted, that, provided we assume an excessive issue of paper to lift up, as it may for a time, the cost of goods though not the price of labour, some augmentation of stock will be the consequence; for the labourer, according to this supposition, may be forced by his necessity to consume fewer articles, though he may exercise the same industry. But this saving, as well as any additional one which may arise from a similar defalcation of the revenue of the unproductive members of the society, will be attended with a proportionate hardship and injustice. This supposition also implies the acknowledgment of the point for which we are contending, that an encreased issue of paper tends to raise the price of commodities.

It has thus been admitted that paper possesses the faculty of enlarging the quantity of commodities by giving life to some new industry. It has, however, been affirmed,

---

* Mr. Hume, in observing that, when money encreases, "the price " rises first of one commodity, then of another, till the whole, at last, " reaches a just proportion with the new quantity of specie which is " in the kingdom," appears to me not sufficiently to advert to the tendency of money to go abroad as soon as it shall have raised the gold price of articles above their level in other countries, allowing for the charges of transportation ; a subject which will be more fully treated of in the next Chapter. He also describes the operation of an encrease of coin in raising prices as proceeding somewhat more slowly than, perhaps, it would be found to do. An augmentation of Bank of England notes operates, no doubt, in this resp ct, more quickly than an encrease of money ; for the London bankers, who are the great holders of bank paper, are likely to be much less disposed to detain, for example, a double quantity of it, than all the individuals of the kingdom are to detain in their several drawers, or in their pockets, a double quantity of guineas. The banking system, by committing the business of payments to few hands, has made much difference in respect to the time within which an encreased quantity of circulating medium may be supposed to raise the price of articles. It has given to many great holders of Bank of England paper a very strong interest on the side of not keeping a superfluous quantity of it.

That an encrease of the circulating medium tends to afford temporary encouragement to industry, seems also to be proved by the effects of the Mississippi scheme in France ; for it is affirmed by French writers, that the notes of Mr. Law's bank appeared for a time to have a very powerful influence in extending the demand for labour, and in augmenting the visible and *bonâ fide* property of the kingdom.

that the encrease of industry will by no means keep pace with the augmentation of paper. The question now to be considered, is, whether, if we suppose thirty-five millions of new paper to be suddenly issued, the fresh industry which would, consequently, be excited, would create a quantity of goods, the sale of which would give employment to all the new paper. Let it be admitted, for the sake of illustrating this point, that the thirty-five millions of additional bank notes will have the extraordinary power of calling at once into being thirty-five millions of new goods; still it may be remarked, that even all this additional property would by no means find employment for that equal quantity of paper which is here assumed to have given existence to it.

We shall be able to explain this circumstance, as well as to throw some new light on the general subject, by supposing an individual, A, to become, in consequence of an extraordinary issue of paper, a new borrower at the bank to the extent of twenty thousand pounds. The twenty thousand pounds, while it is held in the shape of paper, affording him no interest; he will make haste to part with it, by purchasing goods, stocks, land, or some other article, to the extent of the sum in question. Suppose him to make the purchase from B, in three days after he received the notes. B is now in possession of twenty thousand pounds in new bank paper, created by the extraordinary emission; and is, in like manner, in haste to part with it. Imagine him, also, to pay away the same paper in return for goods at the end of three days. Thus the same notes will in six days have effected two purchases amounting together to forty thousand pounds. If we imagine the like transaction to be repeated again and again; the same notes will in twelve days have effected the purchase of goods amounting to eighty thousand pounds; in about a month to two hundred thousand pounds; and in a year to about two millions. Thirty-five millions of new paper will thus effect in a year the sale of goods to the extent of two or three thousand millions. In order, therefore, to account for the employment of the thirty-five millions, we must assume, if we allow no rise in prices to take place, such a new quantity of goods to be called into existence by the magic influence of the new paper, as to become a subject for purchases, amounting, in a year, to no less than these two or three thousand millions. We must assume the creation not of thirty-five millions of property, but of five, ten, or, perhaps, twenty times that sum; or else we must suppose, what is not supposable, that the newly created capital of thirty-five millions changes hands as frequently as the thirty-five millions of bank notes which created it; that is to say, that the new property undergoes a fresh sale on every third day.

The case which has been put is inaccurate, inasmuch as the payments effected by bank notes are on the account not merely of goods and other articles sold, but likewise of numberless sums borrowed and repaid. It is probable, however, that payments of this latter kind will always bear a nearly uniform proportion to those of the other class. The general inference which was intended to be drawn from the case, will, therefore, be just.

In speaking formerly of the reduction of bank paper, much pains were taken to point out the important difference between that limitation of loans which leads to a diminution of paper, and that which produces no such diminution; and it was then observed, that it was by the quantity of Bank of England paper, and not by the amount of loans, or by the amount of loans so far only as they influence the quantity of paper, that a judgment was to be formed of the pressure on the metropolis, and of the reduction of prices. Many of the remarks then made respecting the limitation of bank paper, apply with nearly equal force to the subject of its encrease.

It has now been fully shewn, first, that Bank of England paper is an article of such a nature, that a very superfluous quantity of it will never be for a long time retained in any quarter; and, secondly, that the vast encrease of it, which, for the sake of more convenient discussion, was assumed to take place, cannot possibly create such a new capital as shall furnish the new paper with employment. There remains, therefore, no other mode of accounting for the uses to which the additional supply of it can be turned, than that of supposing it to be occupied in carrying on the sales of the same, or nearly the same, quantity of articles as before, at an advanced price, the cost of goods being made to bear the same, or nearly the same, proportion to their former cost, which the total quantity of paper at the one period bears to the total quantity at the other.

We are thus brought, though by a different course, to the point at which we arrived in an early part of a former Chapter. An enlarged issue of paper, it was then observed, produces an encreased facility of borrowing, as well as an opinion of encreased facility; and thus adds to the eagerness of purchasers. It communicates an additional power of purchasing, not only to the original borrower at the bank, but successively, also, as has now been shewn, to all the other individuals into whose hands the new bank notes pass in the course of their circulation.

Very strong confirmation of the present doctrine may be furnished by a reference to the case of gold. No one doubts, that, in the event of an augmented supply of this article from the mines, the value of it would fall nearly in proportion to the extension of its quantity; especially if it were used for the sole purpose of a circulating medium, and were also the only kind of circulating medium. The metropolis of Great Britain is so circumstanced, that the issue of an extraordinary quantity of bank paper for the purpose of effecting the payments of London, in a considerable degree resembles the creation of an extraordinary supply of gold for the general uses of the world.

It was stated in the beginning of this Chapter, as one objection to the doctrine which I have been endeavouring to establish, that "to enlarge the quantity of Bank of England "notes merely in proportion as sufficient and real bills are "offered in return for them, is only to exchange one species "of paper for another, namely, Bank of England notes for "bills, which, though not so current or so safe as bank notes, "are sufficiently worthy of credit. That it was, therefore, "simply to afford a guarantee to the transactions of the

" merchant, and thus to render that accommodation to com-" merce which it belongs to the bank to give." This objection will be sufficiently answered by repeating an observation which has been already frequently made, namely, that the effect produced by paper credit on the price of articles depends not merely on the quantity of paper in existence, but also on its currency, or, in other words, on the rapidity of its circulation. It was admitted in the objection, that bills are not current like bank notes, and that it is the greater currency of the latter which causes the exchange to be desired.

It was mentioned, as another argument against the doctrine which has been laid down, that corn has not usually borne any sort of proportion to the quantity of Bank of England paper in circulation at the same time. The answer is, that the directors of the bank have never augmented their notes in such a degree as to be likely to produce any material alteration in the general price of goods; that one or more of those circumstances which were dwelt upon in the preceding Chapter, may have counteracted the tendency of the fluctuations of the quantity of paper to produce correspondent variations in the price of commodities; and, above all, that even a small reduction of the supply of grain can hardly fail to lead to a rise in its value when exchanged for paper, so great as to forbid all comparison between the effects of an alteration of the quantity of the one article and of an alteration of the quantity of the other. Paper has been spoken of as raising the cost of commodities, at the most, only in proportion to its encreased quantity. But in the case of a diminished supply of corn, the price rises according to a very different ratio; and for this obvious reason, that we cannot accustom ourselves to the use of a reduced allowance of grain, in the same manner in which we are able, by degrees, to accommodate ourselves to a smaller quantity of circulating medium.*

* The following extract from the work of Sir W. Davenant, who wrote from 1695 to 1712, may give some idea of the vast effect which a small failure of the supply of corn has on the price of this necessary of life.

Let the principle which was laid down as regulating the cost of all articles be recollected. The question of prices is a question of power, and of power only; and, in the event of the scarcity of any commodity, the buyers are more or less under the power of the sellers, in proportion as the article in question is of more or less urgent necessity.

That the quantity of circulating paper must be limited, in order to the due maintenance of its value, is a principle on which it is of especial consequence to insist, as it has been overlooked by some writers on paper credit. In the work of Sir James Steuart on Political Œconomy, banks are discussed at considerable length; but little intimation is given of the necessity of confining the total quantity of circulating paper, or of the tendency of an excessive emission to render the exchange unfavourable, and thus to cause gold to be drawn away. On the other hand, the duty of not giving out bank paper, except for sufficient value received (a point on which, at the present time, there is less occasion

---

" It is observed, that but one-tenth defect in the harvest may raise " the price three-tenths ; and when we have but half our crop, which " now and then happens, the remainder is spun out by thrift and good " management, and eked out by the use of other grain ; but this will " not do for above one year, and would be a small help in the succession " of two or three unseasonable harvests.

" We take it, that a defect in the harvest may raise the price of corn " in the following proportions :

" A defect of		above the common rate
" 1 tenth	raises the price	3 tenths,
" 2 tenths		8 tenths,
" 3 tenths		1 six-tenths,
" 4 tenths		2 eight-tenths,
" 5 tenths		4 five-tenths.

" So that, when corn rises to treble the common rate, it may be pre- " sumed that we want above one-third of the common produce ; and if " we should want five-tenths, or half the common produce, the price " would rise to near five times the common rate."

This scale is not likely to be very accurate. It is, indeed, by no means clear, whether it proceeds on the supposition of a deficiency of the antecedent crop only ; or of a deficiency of the total stock, that is to say, of the antecedent crop and of the stock remaining over from a former year taken together; which are two very different questions. And many circumstances may render such calculations, however just, by no means equally applicable to every period. The passage, therefore, is quoted merely for the purpose of giving some general ideas on the subject.

to enlarge), is strongly urged by this writer, and the security of bills of exchange is implied by him to be inadequate, that of land alone being fully approved. Bank notes emitted without obtaining value in return, are termed by him paper issued for "value consumed;" and are represented as the great source both of loss and danger to a banking company. His mode of expressing himself on this point is such as to make him appear to lend much countenance to the error which it is the object of the present Chapter to expose; namely, that of imagining that a proper limitation of bank notes may be sufficiently secured by attending merely to the nature of the security for which they are given.

Dr. A. Smith, who is a more late writer, has asserted the necessity of a limitation of paper, in the passage which was quoted in an early part of this work; but he has done this in terms which are inaccurate, and he has given an erroneous and inadequate idea of the evil which may result from a very extended emission.

Mr. Locke has lent some countenance to the error which I am endeavouring to expose, by his way of considering the subject of the balance of trade, which is the same mode in which I supposed, in the beginning of this Chapter, an objector to conceive of it. "The evil of an unfavourable "exchange," I imagined my opponent to say, "and of a "consequent high price of gold, arises from an unfavourable "balance of trade, and from that only. The true way of "preventing this evil, or of remedying it, if it unfortunately "exists, is to encrease the national industry; and the way "to encourage industry, is to give full scope to trade and "manufactures by a liberal emission of paper. The balance "of trade will not fail to be rendered favourable by that "abundance of exportable articles which the labour thus "excited must necessarily be supposed to create."

Mr. Locke's language respecting an unfavourable balance of trade, and its influence in causing gold to be melted down and exported, is as follows.

"Profit," he says, "can be made by melting down our "money, but only in two cases. First, when the current "prices of the same denomination are unequal and of "different weights, some heavier some lighter; for then "the traders in money cull out the heavier, and melt them "down with profit.—The other case wherein our money "comes to be melted down, is a losing trade, or, which is "the same thing in other words, an over great consumption "of foreign commodities. Whenever the over-balance of "foreign trade makes it difficult for our merchants to get "bills of exchange, the exchange presently rises. If the "law makes the exportation of our coin penal, it will be "melted down; if it leaves the exportation of our coin free, "it will be carried out in specie—one way or other, go it "must. But this melting down carries not away one grain "of our treasure out of England.—*The coming and going of* "*that depends wholly upon the balance of trade.*"*

The error which I consider as encouraged and supported by this passage of Mr. Locke (and much similar language is to be found in other writers), is this;—the passage implies, that it is the comparative state of our exports and imports which regulates the exchange, and not at all the state of the exchange which regulates the comparative state of our exports and imports. It leads us to suppose, that an unfavourable balance of trade (that is, the excess of the goods imported above those exported) is exclusively the cause, and that the bad state of the exchange is altogether the effect. The passage inclines us not at all to suspect a circumstance which Mr. Hume admits in a note in his Essay on Money, namely, "that an unfavourable exchange becomes a new encouragement to export."

The point which I wish here to establish may be still more clearly explained in the following manner. It has been shewn in a former Chapter, and, indeed, it is stated by Mr. Locke, that the selling price of bills determines the rate of exchange. When, therefore, for example, persons abroad wishing to sell bills on England are more numerous than those who are disposed to buy them, the price of bills

* Further Considerations concerning raising the Value of Money.

must drop; and it must continue to fall until it becomes so low as to tempt some individuals to become purchasers of them. They who buy the bills on England, are the buyers of so many orders to receive in England either money or bank notes. The money or bank notes thus received, unless left in some English hand (and they will be so left in some few cases only), must be invested in British articles, and exported. The profit afforded by the fall in the selling price of the bills must, therefore, be sufficient to cause the speculation of the buyers of the bills to answer—the speculation I mean of either bringing over British gold, which would not otherwise have been transferred, or of purchasing and exporting British commodities which would not otherwise have been at that time transported. Thus, therefore, an unfavourable exchange may be considered not only as becoming, according to Mr. Hume's expression, "a new encouragement to export," but as affording all that degree of encouragement to export which is necessary to secure as much actual exportation either of gold or of goods, or both, as shall serve to equalize the exports and imports; unless, indeed, the same cause, namely, the unfavourableness of the exchange, should tempt foreigners to remit money to England, and lodge it for a time in our hands, with a view to the profit to be obtained by this species of speculation.

The principle which I would lay down on the subject now under consideration, is, I think, simple and intelligible, and it applies itself to all periods of time, and to every kind of circulating medium which may happen to be in use. I would be understood to say, that in a country in which *coin alone* circulates, if, through any accident the quantity should become greater in proportion to the goods which it has to transfer than it is in other countries, the coin becomes cheap as compared with goods, or, in other words, that goods become dear as compared with coin, and that a profit on the exportation of coin arises. This profit, indeed, soon ceases through the actual exportation of the article which is excessive.

I would say again, that in a country in which *coin and paper* circulate at the same time, if the two taken together should, in like manner, become, in the same sense of the term, excessive, a similar effect will follow. There will, I mean, be a profit on sending away the coin, and a consequent exportation of it.

I would say, thirdly, that in a country in which *paper alone* circulates, if the quantity be in the same sense excessive, supposing the credit of the banks which issued it to be perfect, the paper will fall in value in proportion to the excess, on an exactly similar principle; or, in other words, that goods will rise; and that a necessity will exist for granting, in the shape of exchange, a bounty on the exportation of them equal to that which would have been afforded in the two former suppositions, assuming the quantity of circulating medium to be excessive in an equal degree in all the three cases.

It thus appears, that "the coming and going of gold" does not (as Mr. Locke expresses it, and as was supposed in the objection at the beginning of this Chapter) "depend wholly on the balance of trade." It depends on the quantity of circulating medium issued; or it depends, as I will allow, on the balance of trade, if that balance is admitted to depend on the quantity of circulating medium issued. Mr. Locke, however, is very far from leading his reader to conceive that the balance of trade depends on the quantity of circulating medium issued; for he describes an unfavourable balance as resulting from a "losing trade," and from an "over great consumption of foreign commodities;" terms which seem to imply an unprosperous state of commerce, and a too expensive disposition in the people, and which naturally lead to the conclusion, that the prosperity of the country will effectually secure us against the danger of the exportation of our coin, whatever may be the quantity of our paper.

It has now, I trust, been made sufficiently to appear, that banks, if they pay in gold, or if, while not paying in gold, they maintain the value of their notes, must observe some limit in respect to their emission of them.

If, indeed, we could suppose a country to have no intercourse with any other, we might imagine an unlimited issue of paper to take place without producing any difference in its value when exchanged for gold. In that case it would be necessary to assume the price of goods to rise indefinitely, but the people to be content to use a less and less proportion of gold to paper, and on that account to continue to consider the relative value of gold and paper as the same. This unlimited rise in the price of goods, and equally indefinite fall in the value of gold, are every where precluded by the commercial communications which take place between different parts of the world; gold in exchange for goods, allowing for the expence of transporting them, necessarily bearing that price, or nearly that price, in each country which it bears in all. The variations in the value of bullion, as compared with that of the circulating medium, serve, therefore, to detect and restrain that too great emission of notes to which all countries would otherwise be prone; and those operations of the exchange, which have been described, are the means by which every bank is compelled to make the value of its paper conform itself to the ancient standard.

Let the case of the continental bank notes, already spoken of, be here adverted to. The depreciation of these has been apt to originate, as I conceive, in the state of the exchanges. The unfavourable exchange has produced a difference between the value of bullion, and that both of the current paper of those banks and of the current coin; and, when this difference has become permanent and considerable, a discount on the paper has established itself; in other words, coin has ceased to bear the price of paper, and has taken the price of bullion, and from that time the paper alone has passed at the reduced rate. The difference between the value of the circulating medium of this country and that of bullion has always been sufficiently small to prevent the like discount from arising; and so long as we avoid a discount, persons, in general, do not discover that any depreciation of our paper exists. But even the most insignificant of those depressions in the value of our circulating medium, which are indicated by the exchange, are to be referred to the same immediate cause from which the depreciation of the bank paper on the continent has originated. I do not mean that our smaller and their greater depreciations are alike to be referred to an excess of paper. I would affirm, however, that they have equally resulted from the circumstance *of goods, at the time in question, being too high in value* (possibly, in the one case, through an excess of paper, and, in the other, through a fluctuation in the markets) *to bear to be exported in sufficient quantity to satisfy the debt for which payment has been demanded, unless an advantage in the exchange was granted to the exporting merchant.*

It may be convenient to the reader here to recapitulate the several points which have been lately dwelt upon.

I have shewn, first, that since Bank of England paper affords no profit to the holder, a very superfluous quantity is not likely to be held in any quarter; and that the additional thirty-five millions, which have been spoken of, must, therefore, be supposed to be employed either in transferring an encreased quantity of goods, which, in that case, it must be assumed to have itself created, or in transferring the same goods at a higher price. I have, then, insisted, that since the fresh industry which is excited cannot be supposed to be commensurate with the new paper, it is necessary to assume (conformably to the principles of a former Chapter), that a great rise in the price of commodities will take place. This rise in the cost of articles in Great Britain must produce, as has been also shewn, a diminution of the demand for them abroad, unless a compensation for their high price is given to the foreigner in the rate of exchange: so that the too great emission of paper will be the cause of a disadvantageous balance of trade, and also of an unfavourable exchange; or, in other words, of a low valuation of the circulating medium of Great Britain when compared with that of other countries.

It has, likewise, been observed, that even the smallest of those depressions in the value of our circulating medium, which are indicated by the exchange, arise out of the same circumstance which has produced the greater depreciations of the continental bank paper; goods, it has been said, being rendered too high (in the one instance, probably, by an excess of paper, in the other by a fluctuation in the markets) to bear to be exported in sufficient quantity to satisfy the debts for which payment has been demanded; unless a bounty, in the shape of the exchange, be granted to the exporting merchant.

We come next to the second topic of enquiry, namely, whether those bounds within which Bank of England paper must be confined, in order to guard against a dangerous depreciation of it, are likely to be observed, in consequence of some natural tendency which it has to limit itself, so that it is unnecessary that the bank should restrain it.

In examining this question, I mean also to enquire whether the adoption merely of such rules as may tend, in a general way, to confine the loans of the bank, may be sufficient; or whether, also, any limitation of the specific sums lent may be necessary.

First, it is obvious that the principle of lending, simply in proportion to the property of those who desire to borrow, cannot be a safe one. If mere capital were to give a title to bank loans, the borrowers might become beyond measure numerous; even all proprietors of the public funds might prefer a claim for assistance.

If it should be said that the bank loans ought to be afforded only to traders, and on the security of real bills, that is to say, of bills drawn on the occasion of an actual sale of goods, let it be remembered that real bills, as was observed in an early part of this work, may be multiplied to an extremely great extent; and, moreover, that it is only necessary sufficiently to extend the customary length of credit, in order to effect the greatest imaginable multiplication of them. If the bank directors were to measure their discounts by the amount of real bills offered, it may be apprehended, that bankers and other discounters, who now take this better kind of paper, might become much more considerable holders of mere notes of hand, or of fictitious bills; and that an opportunity might thus be afforded of pouring a vast additional quantity of real bills into the Bank of England.

It may be imagined, that if the directors were to govern their conduct by a regard partly to the capital of the borrowers, partly to the species of bills offered, but partly, also, to the probability of punctual payment, the addition of this third check to the former might suffice. But it is here to be recollected, that the bank itself, if we suppose a progressive enlargement of notes, must be assumed to furnish perpetually encreasing means of effecting payments, and thus to render punctuality in fulfilling even the most extravagant engagements convenient and easy to the merchants.

It only remains to enquire, lastly, whether any principle of moderation and forbearance on the part of the borrowers at the bank may be likely to exempt the directors of that institution from the necessity of imposing their own limit.

It may possibly be thought, that a liberal extension of loans would soon satisfy all demands, and that the true point at which the encrease of the paper of the bank ought to stop, would be discovered by the unwillingness of the merchants to continue borrowing.

In order to ascertain how far the desire of obtaining loans at the bank may be expected at any time to be carried, we must enquire into the subject of the quantum of profit likely to be derived from borrowing there under the existing circumstances. This is to be judged of by considering two points: the amount, first, of interest to be paid on the sum borrowed; and, secondly, of the mercantile or other gain to be obtained by the employment of the borrowed capital. The gain which can be acquired by the means of commerce is commonly the highest which can be had; and it also regulates, in a great measure, the rate in all other cases. We may, therefore, consider this question as turning principally on a comparison of the rate of interest taken at the bank with the current rate of mercantile profit.

The bank is prohibited, by the state of the law, from

demanding, even in time of war, an interest of more than five per cent., which is the same rate at which it discounts in a period of profound peace. It might, undoubtedly, at all seasons, sufficiently limit its paper by means of the price at which it lends, if the legislature did not interpose an obstacle to the constant adoption of this principle of restriction.

Any supposition that it would be safe to permit the bank paper to limit itself, because this would be to take the more *natural* course, is, therefore, altogether erroneous. It implies that there is no occasion to advert to the rate of interest in consideration of which the bank paper is furnished, or to change that rate according to the varying circumstances of the country.

At some seasons an interest, perhaps, of six per cent. per annum, at others, of five, or even of four per cent., may afford that degree of advantage to borrowers, which shall be about sufficient to limit, in the due measure, the demand upon the bank for discounts. Experience, in some measure, proves the justice of this observation; for, in time of peace, the bank has found it easy to confine its paper by demanding five per cent. for interest; whereas, in war, and especially in the progress and towards the conclusion of it, as well as for some time afterwards, the directors have been subject, as I apprehend, to very earnest solicitations for discount, their notes, nevertheless, not being particularly diminished. It is, therefore, unreasonable to presume that there will always be a disposition in the borrowers at the bank to prescribe to themselves exactly those bounds which a regard to the safety of the bank would suggest. The interest of the two parties is not the same in this respect. The borrowers, in consequence of that artificial state of things which is produced by the law against usury, obtain their loans too cheap. That which they obtain too cheap they demand in too great quantity. To trust to their moderation and forbearance under such circumstances, is to commit the safety of the bank to the discretion of those who, though both as merchants and as British subjects they may approve in the general of the proper limitation of bank paper, have, nevertheless, in this respect, an individual interest which is at variance with that of the Bank of England.

The temptation to borrow, in time of war, too largely at the bank, arises, as has been observed, from the high rate of mercantile profit. Capital is then scarce, and the gain accruing from the employment of it is proportionably considerable.

The reader, possibly, may think that an extension of bank loans, by furnishing additional capital, may reduce the profit on the use of it, and may thus lessen the temptation to borrow at five per cent. It has been already remarked in this Chapter, that capital, by which term *bonâ fide* property was intended, cannot be suddenly and materially encreased by any emission of paper. That the rate of mercantile profit depends on the quantity of this *bonâ fide* capital, and not on the amount of the nominal value which an encreased emission of paper may give to it, is a circumstance which it will now be easy to point out.

I admit, that a large extension of bank loans may give a temporary check to the eagerness of the general demand for them. It will cause paper to be for a time over abundant, and the price paid for the use of it, consequently, to fall.

It seems clear, however, on the principles already stated, that when the augmented quantity of paper shall have been for some time stationary, and shall have produced its full effect in raising the price of goods, the temptation to borrow at five per cent. will be exactly the same as before; for the existing paper will then bear only the same proportion to the existing quantity of goods, when sold at the existing prices, which the former paper bore to the former quantity of goods, when sold at the former prices: the power of purchasing will, therefore, be the same; the terms of lending and borrowing must be presumed to be the same; the amount of circulating medium alone will have altered, and it will have simply caused the same goods to pass for a larger quantity of paper. To assume under such circumstances the same rate of mercantile profit to subsist, is only to suppose that the trader will be situated neither more nor less advantageously than before; and that the annual gain which he will obtain by trading with the same quantity of goods, will bear the same proportion as before to their current cost. If this observation be just, there can be no reason to believe that even the most liberal extension of bank loans will have the smallest tendency to produce a permanent diminution of the applications to the bank for discount. It is the progressive augmentation of bank paper, and not the magnitude of its existing amount, which gives the relief. It thus appears, that the moderation and forbearance among borrowers, which were supposed likely to restrain the too great emission of paper, are only to be excited by the means of its perpetual encrease; by the means, that is to say, of the very evil which it was assumed that they would be sufficient to prevent.

The danger of enlarging the loans of the bank in proportion to the extension of the demand for them, may be more particularly shewn by adverting to the case of the sudden transfer to foreign countries of capital which had been antecedently lodged in this. Let us suppose the foreign owners, either of British stocks, or of property left in the hands of English correspondents, to draw during the space of three months to a very large amount; and let us imagine that, in consequence of such an event, the exchange turns against Great Britain to the extent of five per cent.; and moreover that, at the end of the three months, the drafts ceasing, and the mercantile state of the country improving, the exchange returns to its proper level. In this case any Englishman who can send goods abroad on his own account, and draw for them during the three months in question, will gain an extra profit of five per cent., supposing him to buy them in England for the same English money, and to sell them abroad for the same foreign money, for which goods may be bought and sold at the periods preceding, and following the interval of time of which we are speaking. A similar extra profit will be obtainable during the same three months by a variety of other modes of employing capital. It is obvious, for example, that the public funds may be expected to experience a sudden fall through the great sale of foreign property in the stocks, which we have imagined to take place. He, therefore, who shall buy into the funds at the season of depression, and shall sell out at the expiration of the three months, will be likely to derive a benefit from this species of speculation. It is also plain that the quantity of goods in Great Britain will be reduced through the enlarged exportations, as well as through the suspension of imports, to which the state of the exchange will have given occasion. The profit, therefore, on the use of the remaining stock will be generally augmented. The exportation of bullion will afford a gain of the same sum of five per cent., the expence of transporting it being, indeed, deducted. The demand upon the bank for discounts is, therefore, likely to be particularly earnest during the period of which we are speaking; and it is important here to notice, that the ground on which it will be made will not be that which was spoken of in an early part of this work. It will not be the privation of that quantity of circulating medium which is necessary for carrying on the accustomed payments, for these will be very immaterially encreased; the cause of the extraordinary applications to the bank will be the temporary advantage which may be gained, or the loss which may be avoided, by borrowing, during the three months in question, at the rate of five per cent. A pressure, it is true, may be occasioned by the multitude of foreign drafts, and it may resemble that which would arise from a diminution of Bank of England paper. Some of those merchants in whose hands the foreign property had been placed may not be able, with sufficient readiness, to spare from their commerce the sums necessary to answer the bills drawn upon them. Creditors, not being permitted to demand more than five per cent. interest from their debtors, are apt, at particular junctures, to call in their money, for the sake of taking to themselves the extraordinary benefit to be obtained by the use of capital. The disappointments thus brought on persons trading with borrowed wealth are often productive of much evil. The maintenance of the accustomed quantity of Bank of England notes may, therefore, be insufficient to furnish the means of securing the usual regularity of the payments of the metropolis; and a material diminution of paper may be particularly inconvenient. Possibly an augmentation of it may be necessary to the due maintenance of credit. If we suppose, however, a very great encrease of bank notes to take place (and an encrease, probably, equal to the total capital transferred on account of foreigners, will immediately be desired), the result must be a very important fall in the exchange, in addition to the fall of five per cent. already mentioned; and a new and proportionate danger to the Bank of England.

The point which it has been the object here to explain, might have been equally illustrated by imagining either the case of a strong disposition in many British subjects to transfer their own property to foreign countries, in order to lodge it there; or the case of a general eagerness to extend foreign commerce; for we must assume the transfer to foreign parts of an additional British capital to take place on either of these suppositions.

The preceding observations explain the reason of a determination, adopted some time since by the bank directors, to limit the total weekly amount of loans furnished by them to the merchants. The adoption of a regulation for this purpose seems to have been rendered necessary by that impossibility of otherwise sufficiently limiting, at all times, the Bank of England paper, which it has been the design of this Chapter to point out.

The regulation in question I consider as intended to confine within a specific, though in some degree fluctuating, sum, the loans of the bank, for the sake of restricting the paper. The variations in the amount of loans fail of producing exactly correspondent variations in the amount of paper, in proportion as the gold of the bank fluctuates. But the regulation being a weekly one, opportunity is afforded of correcting this attendant imperfection before any material evil can have arisen. The changes which occur in the amount of the loans to government form another ground for taking into weekly consideration the sum which shall, in the succeeding week, be afforded to the merchants.

To limit the total amount of paper issued, and to resort for this purpose, whenever the temptation to borrow is strong, to some effectual principle of restriction; in no case, however, materially to diminish the sum in circulation, but to let it vibrate only within certain limits; to afford a slow and cautious extension of it, as the general trade of the kingdom enlarges itself; to allow of some special, though temporary, encrease in the event of any extraordinary alarm or difficulty, as the best means of preventing a great demand at home for guineas; and to lean to the side of diminution, in the case of gold going abroad, and of the general exchanges continuing long unfavourable; this seems to be the true policy of the directors of an institution circumstanced like that of the Bank of England. To suffer either the solicitations of merchants, or the wishes of government, to determine the measure of the bank issues, is unquestionably to adopt a very false principle of conduct.

CHAP. XI.

Of the Influence of Paper Credit on the Price of Commodities—Observations on some Passages of Montesquieu and Hume—Conclusion.

THIS subject has been in so great a degree anticipated by the discussions which have taken place; that it will scarcely be necessary to do more than to remind the reader of the principles which have been laid down, and to point out the manner in which they bear upon the present question.

It was observed in a former Chapter, that a very considerable advance in the price of the commodities bought and sold in one quarter of this kingdom, while there was no such rise in any other, was not supposable; because the holders of the circulating medium current in the spot in which goods were imagined to have been rendered dear, would exchange it for the circulating medium of the part in which they were assumed to be cheap, and would then buy the commodities of the latter place, and transport them to the former, for the sake of the profit on the transaction.

The exchangeableness of our country paper for our London paper was represented as always in this manner preventing the quantity of paper circulating in one place from being very disproportionate to the quantity circulating in another; and as also precluding any great local rise in the price of commodities within our own island.

We may justly extend our views, and conceive of Europe, and even of the world, as forming one great kingdom, over the whole of which goods pass and repass, as suits the interest of the merchant, nearly in the same manner in which they spread themselves through this single country.

In one particular, indeed, the resemblance between the two cases fails. Country bank paper, as compared with Bank of England notes, cannot be, to a material degree, excessive in any part of England; because, by the custom of our country banks, it is convertible, without any discount, into the London paper. But British paper is not exchangeable for the circulating medium of the continent, unless a discount, or difference, be allowed. Of this fluctuating discount, or difference, the variations in the course of exchange are the measure.

It is true that the continental circulating medium, like our own, varies in value. Both, however, commonly vibrate only within certain limits; and both may be considered as fluctuating exactly so far as their value differs from that of bullion. To say that bullion varies in its price, is to say that there is an alteration in the general exchangeable value of that article, which constitutes the standard of the world.

We are led, by these observations, to divide our subject into two branches of enquiry: first, into the question how far our paper credit may have raised the price of goods in

Great Britain, by causing their current price here (that is to say, their price in British paper, as well as in British coin) to be higher than their bullion price; and, secondly, how far also the bullion price of our commodities here (that is to say, their value in exchange for the article of bullion) may be suspected of having been enhanced by means of the paper credit of Great Britain.

As to the first question; the highest influence which a too extended paper credit can have had in raising the current price of commodities in Great Britain above their bullion price, must be measured by the difference which has subsisted between the market price and mint price of gold; or, which is nearly the same thing, by the fluctuation in the state of our general exchanges. This difference or fluctuation has at no period been more than about ten or twelve per cent. Even this variation, however, has not been fairly referable to a too great issue of paper, but rather to the peculiar circumstances of the country; and, in particular, to our two bad harvests, which sufficiently account for the unfavourable state of our exchanges.

The second question is, how far the bullion price of our commodities may be suspected of having been raised through the influence of the paper credit of Great Britain.

It was formerly stated, that the bullion price of articles may be considered to be their general price: because bullion necessarily bears that value, or nearly that value, in each country, in exchange for goods, which it bears in all, allowance being made for the expence of their transmission, inclusive of export and import duties, ordinary profit of the merchant, freight, insurance, and other customary charges. The expence of the transportation of commodities from the several places of their growth or manufacture, an expence which is great in some cases, and small in others, is the measure of the difference subsisting between the bullion prices of the same articles, at the same time, in different parts of the world. Each addition to this difference implies an extra profit on the transportation either of bullion or of goods; and must be supposed soon to cause the one or the other to be carried over in such quantity as to restore their due relative price. Every rise, therefore, of the bullion price in Great Britain of those commodities which she is accustomed to export, if we suppose the usual exportation to continue, implies an equal, or nearly equal, enhancement of the bullion price of all articles of the same class in every foreign part in which our commodities are sold.

Great Britain so remarkably takes the lead in manufactures and commerce, that she may not unjustly be deemed to have the power, especially in a time of general war, of prescribing to foreign countries the rate at which they shall buy her commodities.

That monopoly of the supply, however, which I am here supposing Great Britain to possess, is, probably, but temporary, and, in every respect, imperfect. In most of her sales abroad she meets with strong competition; for, though other countries may not rival her in the quality of her goods, they can, generally, furnish a substitute, which, if British prices are much lifted up, will gain, by comparative cheapness, the preference. Every great enhancement of the cost of our articles must lessen the foreign demand for them. It must reduce our exported and augment our imported goods. By thus turning the balance of trade against us, and rendering our exchanges unfavourable, it must cause the rise at home to be a rise not in the bullion price of our articles, the subject which we are now considering, but in the paper or current price, the point which was noticed before. If the advance is in the paper or current price, the bank is compelled to restrict its issues; and the reduction of the quantity of bank notes has a tendency to limit the cost not only of those particular commodities which are the subjects of exportation, but of every commodity in the kingdom.

That the bullion price of some British articles has lately been much encreased, and that the bullion price of all, or of almost all, has in some degree risen, are facts which cannot be doubted. But that this enhancement is to be charged to an encrease of paper, is not equally to be admitted; for it is plain that other causes have powerfully operated, namely, a state of war, new taxes, and two bad harvests, which, by raising the price of bread, have in some degree lifted up that of labour, and of all commodities. Our prices may have also been partly augmented by the enhancement of the cost of raw materials brought from other countries.

Although it should be granted, as it must, either that the amount of our paper has been enlarged in proportion to the extension of pecuniary transactions; or that an encreased œconomy in the use of it has rendered an equal quantity sufficient for more payments (and it seems of little moment which of these two suppositions is adopted): still it may be questioned whether the extended issue of paper ought to be deemed the cause of the high prices; or whether the high prices ought not to be deemed the cause, and the encrease of paper the effect.

It was before remarked, that it seems in general more fair to consider the latter to be the case, when the extension of paper is not such as to be the means of reducing its value below that of bullion. To prove the reasonableness of this observation, let us imagine the paper credit of this country to be abolished, and our payments to be conducted by a circulating medium consisting wholly of gold; and let us assume, that we still find ourselves able to procure for our commodities sent abroad a higher bullion price than before. In this case the bullion price of articles at home will also experience a rise; for the high bullion prices abroad will have the effect of enlarging our exported and diminishing our imported goods; of rendering our balance of trade favourable, and of bringing gold into the kingdom; which encrease of gold will have precisely the same effect as an augmentation of paper, namely, that of raising British prices. The bullion will continue to flow in until it shall have brought the bullion price of goods in England to a level with the bullion price of the same articles in foreign parts, allowing for charges of transportation. On the ability, therefore, of Great Britain to maintain a high bullion price for her goods abroad, would depend the bullion price of her commodities at home, in the event of her employing gold as her only circulating medium.

If we suppose paper to constitute the circulating medium of Great Britain, and an encreased bullion price for her commodities abroad to be in like manner obtainable, the case will in the main be similar, though in one particular it will differ. The case will be similar, inasmuch as Great Britain will experience, exactly as if she made use only of gold, an encrease in the price of her commodities at home, as well as an enlargement of the quantity of her circulating medium; such an enlargement, I mean, as is necessary for effecting her more extended payments. The case will differ, inasmuch as, instead of importing the additional circulating medium which is wanted, she will create it. The production, therefore, of a rather less quantity of exportable articles will be necessary on the one supposition than on the other; and the state of the exchange itself will be in some degree affected by this variation in the circumstances of the two cases.

It may, perhaps, be thought, that I have considered the bullion price of goods in Great Britain as exclusively depending on the bullion price of the same kind of commodities abroad; and that I ought to have stated the converse to be also in some measure the fact, namely, the bullion price of articles abroad to depend in part on the bullion prices of Great Britain. I have intended thus to represent the case. My position has been this,—that the bullion price of articles in Great Britain conforms itself to the bullion price abroad; but that, in the formation of this bullion price abroad, the British price has some share of influence: and this influence I have considered to be proportioned to the degree of our monopoly of the supply of the foreign markets.

There is an additional mode of considering the influence of paper credit on the bullion price of articles.

The encreased use of paper in each individual country must contribute to lower the price of bullion, by lessening the general demand for it in the world. On every advance in the cost of commodities, it may be suspected that the means of effecting the encreased payments are supplied not by bringing more gold into use, but rather by the enlargement of that part of the circulating medium which consists in paper. No inconsiderable portion of British gold coin is employed in effecting the fractional parts of payments; and the total amount of these does not encrease in the same proportion in which the sum total of payments is augmented.* Moreover, the art of œconomizing gold is continually advancing. The very vicissitudes of commerce, probably, tend to improve it. A time of distress, such as was felt in 1793, compels many to resort to new expedients, tending to spare the use both of Bank of England notes and of coin. The measures adopted, at first, through necessity, are afterwards persisted in because they are œconomical. To put the case which we have more recently experienced. An unfavourable balance of trade, arising out of the disadvantageous circumstances of the country, causes our guineas to go abroad. Paper is necessary to supply their place. Experience of the loss incurred by hoarding money, and of the practicability of sustaining both private and public credit during the absence of gold, strengthens the general

---

* The bank notes in circulation commonly are notes for five, ten, fifteen, twenty, twenty-five, thirty, forty, fifty, and one hundred pounds and upwards. If we suppose the price of all articles to be doubled, then we may assume every payment of one guinea to be a payment of two guineas, and to employ a double quantity of gold; every payment of two guineas to be a payment of four guineas, and also to employ a double quantity of gold; but every payment of three guineas will be a payment of six, and it may employ a five pound note, the fractional part only being paid in money. This particular payment will, therefore, require less gold. A payment of four guineas will be a payment of eight, and will also require less gold. The payments of more than four guineas, when, in like manner, doubled, will some of them employ a greater and some a less quantity of gold than before. They will employ, taking them together, the same quantity. It is evident from this statement, that an encrease of the quantity of the circulating medium of a country employing paper in its larger payments, and coin only in the smaller, will consist chiefly of paper; a circumstance which may considerably tend to prevent an encreased demand for bullion on the occasion of an augmentation of prices, and which may, therefore greatly facilitate a rise of the bullion price of articles in the world.

confidence in a paper currency, and encourages a permanently encreased use of it. If we could suppose as large a substitution of paper in the place of coin to take place in other countries as we have lately experienced in our own; the diminution of the demand for bullion might be such as very materially to affect its general value, and to enhance the money price of articles over the world.

There is, however, a limit to this evil. The annual supply of the precious metals is obtained from mines, of which some afford to the proprietors a higher and others a lower revenue, and some probably no revenue at all. If we suppose the encreased use of paper to lower, in any degree, the value of the precious metals; we must assume those mines which have not yielded any rent, to be no longer worked; and the supply of gold and silver to be, in consequence, somewhat reduced. If we imagine the reduction of the price of the precious metals to be progressive, we must conceive a period to arrive when all mines will be unable to defray the charge of extracting the ore, except those which now yield the very highest rent. At this point the fall will necessarily stop. In other words, gold and silver must continue to bear that price, or nearly that price, at which they are now exchangeable for commodities, a deduction being made of the total present rent derived from the richest mines; a deduction which, if Dr. A. Smith's observations on this subject are just, cannot be very considerable.

Mr. de Montesquieu has represented, in the following manner, the principle which regulates the price of the precious metals. He "compares the mass of gold and silver in "the whole world with the quantity of merchandize therein "contained," and "every commodity with a certain portion "of the entire mass of gold and silver:" and then observes, that, "Since the property of mankind is not all at once in "trade, and as the metals or money also are not all in trade "at the same time; the price is fixed in the compound "ratio of the total of things with the total of signs, and that "of the total of things in trade with the total of signs in "trade also." This theory, though not altogether to be rejected, is laid down in a manner which is very loose and fallacious*.

Not to mention the misconception of the subject which may arise from the silence of Mr. de Montesquieu respecting the state of the mines, it may be observed, first, that he alludes, in a manner so imperfect as to be scarcely intelligible, to those effects of the different degrees of rapidity in the circulation both of money and of goods, which it has been one object of this work to explain. It is on the degree of the rapidity of the circulation of each, combined with the consideration of quantity, and not on the quantity alone, that the value of the circulating medium of any country depends.

Mr. de Montesquieu also leaves out of his consideration the custom of transacting payments by means of entries in books, and of other expedients. In proportion as contrivances of this sort prevail; and they must abound more and more as commercial knowledge advances in the world; the demand for bullion will be diminished.

He also does not advert to that reserve of gold and silver in the coffers of the banks of various countries which merely forms a provision against contingencies. The amount of this reserve will depend on the opinion which the banks entertain respecting the extent of the sum likely to be suddenly drawn from them, in consequence either of fluctuations in the national balances of trade, or of temporary interruptions of credit among individuals. In proportion, therefore, as the variations in the national balances of trade, as well as in the state of commercial confidence, are greater or smaller, the fund of gold which is kept out of circulation will be more or less considerable. On the amount of this fund depends, in no inconsiderable degree, the price of bullion in the world.

Mr. de Montesquieu likewise omits to take into his account that now immense and perpetually encreasing influence in sparing the precious metals which arises from the use of paper credit. The false impression which he gives of this

* It is controverted at great length in the work of Sir James Steuart on Political Œconomy.

subject may chiefly be referred to his not having contemplated the effects of the introduction of the banking system.

Mr. Hume has spoken strongly of the influence of paper credit in sparing the use of the precious metals, and in proportionably lowering their value, and raising that of labour and of commodities. He inveighs against bank paper on this account, as well as on some others; but, in so doing, he appears to assume, that paper credit causes a merely local rise in the price of articles; a rise, I mean, which extends itself only over the whole of the single independent country in which the paper is issued. The bank is considered by him as most advantageous to a state, which locks up all the gold received in return for its notes [he admits that it will have no profit on its dealings], and thus causes the total quantity of circulating medium to remain the same. The price of labour, he says, will, in this manner, be kept down. The Bank of Amsterdam is approved by him, on account of its being an establishment of this nature*. In thus representing the subject he appears to forget, that, when the total circulating medium of a country, whether consisting of gold, or of paper, or of both, is rendered excessive; when it has thus lifted up the gold price of articles above the point at which they stand in adjacent countries, the gold is obliged, by the operation of the exchange, to transport itself to those other parts; and that paper credit, therefore, enhances the prices not of that single spot in which it passes, but of the adjoining places, and of the world. The state which issues paper only in such quantity as to maintain its general exchanges, may be considered as substituting paper in the place of gold, and as gaining additional stock in return for whatever coin it may cause to be exported. It derives, therefore, from its own issue, the whole advantage of this augmentation of capital. It participates with other countries in that inconvenience of a generally encreased price of commodities which its paper has contributed to produce.

That the popular opinion which was lately entertained

---

* Hume's Essay on Money.

of the great influence of paper credit in raising the price not only of commodities in general, but of provisions in particular, had no just foundation, is a position which admits of easy proof.

First, that opinion has proceeded on the assumption of the fact of a vast encrease of the total circulating medium of the kingdom, within the last two or three years, the period during which the high prices have subsisted. But I have shewn both that the amount of the notes of the Bank of England has lately not been such as to imply a material augmentation of the circulating medium of the metropolis, and, also, that the quantity of circulating medium in the country necessarily conforms itself to that of London, for which it is exchangeable. It has obviously been the use of country bank notes, and especially of the smaller ones, in the place of gold, not in addition to it, which has been the chief occasion of the prevailing suspicion; for the common complaint has been not only that paper has been multiplied, but, also, that guineas have been hardly to be seen; and it has not been considered, that by this double invective some sort of acknowledgment is made that the one article is only that substitute for the other, by which none of the supposed effect on the price of commodities can be produced.

It is sometimes said, that the additional loans which the paper of the country banks has enabled them to furnish, have encouraged mercantile speculation; and that we may ascribe to the spirit thus excited much of the late rise in the price of articles in general, and of corn in particular.

There is an error in the public sentiment on this subject, which it is important to correct.

It has been already shewn, that it is by the amount not of the loans of the Bank of England, but of its paper; or if of its loans, of these merely as indicating the quantity of its paper, that we are to estimate the influence on the cost of commodities. The same remark may be applied to the subject of the loans and paper of country banks. For the sake of more fully illustrating this point, let us examine into the several ways in which a country banker may be supposed to extend his loans, without augmenting the quantity of circulating medium in the kingdom.

He may be enabled to do this, first, through the enlargement of the deposits lodged with him. In this case some of his customers may be considered as leaving with him, or as lending to him a sum which is lent by him to other customers. This is the same thing as if some individuals were to lend to others, without the intervention of the banker. Loans of this nature will be admitted not to have the supposed influence on prices.

A country banker may also encrease his loans, without augmenting the quantity of the circulating medium of the country, in the following manner. He may extend the issue of his own paper, and then that paper may circulate in the place of gold either hoarded or exported. If the gold is hoarded; if a quantity of coin locked up by one man equals the amount of the new paper issued by another; it is plain that there will not be the supposed influence on prices. If the gold is exported, we must consider it in the same light with any other commodity sent abroad. It is true that the paper, according to this supposition, may be said to give existence to an additional exportable article: but so also does every encreased exertion of the national industry, as well as every favourable harvest. An augmentation of prices is no more to be inferred from the creation of a new exportable commodity in the one case than in the others.

The following facts furnish a convincing proof that the late high prices of corn have not been owing to the enlargement of Bank of England paper.

By the account which the bank rendered to Parliament, it appears, that the amount of Bank of England notes was, on the 25th of February, 1795, 13,539,160*l.* In the three months immediately following the 25th of Februay, 1795, the average price of wheat, in the London corn-market, was about 57*s.* per quarter.

By the same bank account, it appears, that the amount of Bank of England notes was, on the 25th of February, 1796, 11,030,116*l.* In the three months immediately following the 25th of February, 1796, the average price of wheat, in the London corn-market, was about 94*s*. per quarter.

Thus wheat bore a comparatively low price when the amount of bank notes in circulation was greater; and a comparatively high price when their amount was smaller. It bore the moderate price of 57*s*. per quarter, at a time when the amount of Bank of England notes was full as considerable (allowing for about two millionsof 1*l*. and 2*l*. notes) as it is known to have been at any period.

Paper credit may be considered as tending, in some respects, to reduce the price of commodities. It was compared, in a former chapter, to a cheap species of machinery which is substituted in the place of a dear one; and it is obvious, that in proportion as any instrument of manufactures or commerce is less expensive, the articles which it contributes to produce may be afforded at a lower rate.

Paper credit, also, promotes general cheapness, by sparing much expence and trouble in weighing, counting, and transporting, money; and by thus facilitating more particularly the larger transactions of the merchant. Mr. Hume appears to suppose, that, when a great encrease of it takes place, the augmentation is artificially produced. But it has been shewn, that mercantile persons naturally resort more and more to the use of paper, in proportion as wealth accumulates, confidence improves, and commerce advances. The consumers of commodities may be considered as having an interest in permitting the merchants to follow their own plans of œconomy, in this respect, in the same manner as in all others.

But whatever may be the amount of that influence on the price of commodities which ought to be ascribed to paper credit, one point is clear, namely, that, during the period in which our paper has extended itself, our trade has prospered, the state of our agriculture has advanced, and both the capital and the income of the country have been augmented.

The chief mischiefs which, according to Mr. Hume, are to be apprehended from any considerable addition to our paper currency, may be stated to be the following: first, the great enhancement of the price of British labour and commodities, an evil with which we ought unquestionably to connect that of the diminution of the sale of our manufactures in foreign markets; secondly, the inconvenience to which we may be exposed in time of war through the want of sufficient means of making remittances in bullion to other countries; and, thirdly, the confusion which the failure of paper credit may produce at home in the event of any great disorder in the nation.

That the first consequence (the great enhancement of the price of British labour and commodities) cannot follow from the enlargement of our paper currency in the degree which Mr. Hume supposes, has been proved from the circumstance of our paper causing guineas to go abroad, and tending, therefore, to raise the prices of the world rather than those of our own single island. That our prices, however high, have not been such as to lessen the vent abroad of our home made articles, and, have, therefore, not been raised above the prices of other countries, is proved by those documents from our custom-house, which state the continually encreasing quantity of manufactures exported by Great Britain.

That the second evil (that of our being reduced to difficulty in making remittances abroad in time of war through the want of bullion) is one which there is less reason to dread than Mr. Hume has imagined, may likewise be inferred from recent experience. We have been able to maintain the credit of our funds, and to carry on all our financial operations, during the whole of the late expensive and protracted contest, although in the commencement of it our stock of circulating gold was probably less than in many former periods; and although, also, in the last years of the struggle, a period in which we lent considerable sums to Ireland, and had to purchase immense quantities of foreign grain, we were in a great measure deprived of current coin, and the cash payments of the Bank of England remained suspended.

Mr. Hume himself has remarked, "That want of money can never injure any state *within itself*; for that men and commodities are the real strength of any community." He might have added, that Want of money can never injure any state *in its transactions with foreign countries*, provided it sufficiently abounds with commodities which are in demand abroad, and which it can afford to sell at a bullion price lower than that for which foreign articles of a similar kind can be afforded. The power of manufacturing at a cheap rate is far more valuable than any stock of bullion. Even the greatest quantity of gold which can be supposed at any time to possess, bears but a small proportion to our extraordinary expenditure in time of war, and affords a security which is extremely slender in comparison of that which we derive from the commercial capital, the manufacturing skill, and the other resources of the country.

That the third evil (the confusion which the failure of paper credit may produce in the event of any disorder at home) is less a subject for apprehension than Mr. Hume and other British writers have conceived, is a point which a great part of the preceding work will have contributed to establish.

During the late scenes of trouble and consternation on the continent, the possession of a stock of the precious metals probably added little to the security of any nation. When the French armies approached, or when an insurrection was projected, a stock of gold and silver possessed by a government bank might contribute to invite attack; or if the fund should at such a juncture be expended in the public service, it would not long continue to perform the office of a circulating medium. It might even disappear after effecting a single payment.

Our own island has been preserved, through the favour of Providence, from those violent convulsions which have been felt on the continent. We have, however, been exposed to many smaller evils, and, in particular, to the interruption of our mercantile credit. It was probable that the enemy, knowing how much our political strength depended on our commercial prosperity, and our commercial prosperity on the due maintenance of mercantile confidence among us, would direct his endeavours to the very object of exciting alarms over the kingdom, with the view of thus disturbing the course of our trade and manufactures. It therefore became us to protect ourselves by the best means in our power against this species of injury; and the continuance of the law for suspending the cash payments of the Bank of England has been one of the steps which parliament has deemed necessary.

There can be no doubt that, in the situation in which we have thus found ourselves placed, we have been greatly benefited by the circumstance of our having been previously accustomed to the free use of a paper credit. In a commercial country, subjected to that moderate degree of occasional alarm and danger which we have experienced, gold is by no means that kind of circulating medium which is the most desirable. It is apt to circulate with very different degrees of rapidity, and also to be suddenly withdrawn, in consequence of its being an article intrinsically valuable, and capable of being easily concealed. If, during the war, it had been our only medium of payment, we might sometimes have been almost totally deprived of the means of carrying on our pecuniary transactions; and much confusion in the affairs of our merchants, great interruption of manufacturing labour and very serious evils to the state, might have been the consequences.

Paper credit has, on this account, been highly important to us. Our former familiarity with it prepared us for the more extended use of it. And our experience of its power of supplying the want of gold in times of difficulty and peril, is a circumstance which, though it ought not to encourage a general disuse of coin, may justly add to the future confidence of the nation.

FINIS.

NOTE

ON THE

STATE OF THE EXCHANGE

BETWEEN

LONDON AND DUBLIN

FROM 1797 TO 1804.

EXCHANGE.

THE suspension of cash payments in 1797 extended to Ireland as well as Great Britain; and the first decided proof of the depreciation of the paper currency from over-issue was supplied by the former.

The nominal value of the Irish shilling having been raised in 1689 from 12*d.* to 13*d.** 108*l.* 6*s.* 8*d.*, Irish money became equal to only 100*l.* British money; and the exchange between Great Britain and Ireland was said to be at par when it was nominally 8⅓ per cent. against the latter. In the *eight* years preceding 1797, when the paper currency of both countries was convertible into gold, the exchange between London and Dublin fluctuated from 7½ to 9 per cent., that is, from ⅚ per cent. in favour of Dublin to ⅔ per cent. against it. In September 1797 it was at 6 per cent., or 2⅓ per cent. in favour of Dublin. The amount of Bank of Ireland notes in circulation in January 1797 was only 621,917*l.*; whereas in January 1801 they had increased to 2,258,816*l.*, and the exchange was then at 12 per cent., or 3⅔ per cent. against Dublin. In January 1804 the Bank of Ireland notes in circulation amounted to 2,986,999*l.*, and the exchange was then quoted at 16¼ per cent., that is at very near 8 per cent. against Dublin!

The fact of the exchange between London and Dublin having fluctuated but little from par during the eight years previously to the restriction, shows that the circulating medium of Great Britain and Ireland had been adjusted so

* By a proclamation of James II. The arrangement was continued by the revolutionary government, and was confirmed by proclamation, 29th September 1737. But in 1825 the currencies of Great Britain and Ireland were assimilated.

3

as to be nearly of the same value in the two countries. But, in these circumstances, it was evidently impracticable, supposing the value of British currency to remain nearly stationary, that the amount of Irish bank paper could be a good deal more than quadrupled in the short space of seven years, without rendering the currency of Ireland redundant, and sinking its value below that of England. Had the Bank of England increased her notes in something like the same ratio as the Bank of Ireland, then, as the currency of both countries would have been equally depreciated, the exchange between London and Dublin would have continued at par, or near it. While, however, the notes of the Bank of Ireland were increased from 621,917*l.* to 2,986,999*l*, or in the pro-tion of 1 to 4·802, those of the Bank of England were only increased from 9,674,780*l.* (their amount on 28th February 1797), to 17,077,830*l.* (their amount on the 29th February, 1804) or in the proportion of 1 to 1·766. But for this addition to the issues of the Bank of England, the exchange, it is plain, would have been still more unfavourable to Dublin.

It should be observed that a portion of the increased issue in both countries consisted of 1*l.* and 2*l.* notes, that were issued, for the first time, in 1797, in the view of supplying the place of the guineas that had been withdrawn from circulation. Of these the Bank of England had about 1,800,000*l.* in circulation in 1798, and 4,711,150*l.* on the 25th of January, 1804. We have not seen any account of the notes of the Bank of Ireland for less than 5*l.* in circulation at the above periods. But the Committee of the House of Commons, in their Report on the Circulating Paper, &c. of Ireland, state, that "if the whole paper of the Bank of Ireland in circulation in January last (1804) be divided into five parts, one will appear necessary as having existed prior to the restriction; two are to be set down as occupying the place of gold withdrawn; and no sufficient reasons have been given for the issue of the other two parts, or for the bank not having diminished its paper when the exchange rose, in the same manner that they must have done in case the Restriction act had not been in force."

4

In the debates on the Bullion Report, it was contended that the increase of Bank of Ireland paper could not have been the cause of the unfavourable exchange upon Dublin, seeing that it had again become favourable notwithstanding the issues of the Bank of Ireland had been still further increased. But to give this reasoning the least weight, it should have been shown that the currency of Great Britain retained its value in the interim, or that it had not been depreciated to the same extent as that of Ireland. For it is obvious that the depreciation of Irish bank paper might go on subsequently to 1804, and yet, if English bank paper were depreciated still more rapidly, the exchange would become more favourable to Dublin. This is merely supposing the circumstances which took place in the first six years of the restriction to be reversed in the second six. Let us briefly inquire how the fact stands.

We have seen, that in January 1804, when the exchange was nominally 16¼ per cent. against Dublin, the issues of the Bank of England amounted to 17,077,830*l.*, and those of the Bank of Ireland to 2,986,999*l.* And by referring to the accounts of the issues of the latter, it is seen that from 1805 to 1808, they were rather diminished; and that, in 1810, they amounted to only 3,251,750*l.*, being an increase of not more than 264, 751*l.* in the space of six years, or at the rate of 1 477 per cent. per annum; but in the same period (from 1804 to 1810) the issues of the Bank of England were increased from 17,077,830*l.* to 22,541,523*l.*, or at the rate of 5·333 per cent. per annum. And this is not all: For Mr. Wakefield tell us that there were *fifty* registered bankers in Ireland in 1804, and only *thirty-three* in 1810, of which fourteen were new houses, thirty-one of the old establishments having disappeared, and, "I believe," he adds "for the most part failed." And as the reduction of the issues of these banks may be fairly presumed to have been at least proportional to the reduction in their number, this diminution of country paper could not fail greatly to raise its value, and to countervail a corre-

* "Account of Ireland," vol ii. p. 171.

sponding increase, if such there had been, in the issues of the national bank. Now, the reverse of all this took place in England. In 1800 there were 386 country banks in this country; and in 1810, this number, instead of being diminished as in Ireland, had increased to 721, having at least three times the number of notes in circulation in the latter as in the former period!

It appears, therefore, that in the period between 1797 and 1804, when the amount of paper in circulation in Ireland was increased, and its value depressed more rapidly than in England, the exchange between London and Dublin became proportionally unfavourable to the latter; and that in the six years subsequent to 1804, when the paper currency of England was increased more rapidly than that of Ireland, its relative value was diminished, and the exchange became less unfavourable to Dublin.

This is sufficiently conclusive. But there is still better evidence to show that the unfavourable exchange of Dublin upon London, in 1802, 1803, 1804, etc., was entirely owing to the comparative redundancy or depreciation of Irish bank paper. The linen manufacturers and weavers, with the majority of the other inhabitants of a few counties in Ulster, being at the period of the Restriction, strongly disaffected towards government, very generally refused to receive bank-notes in payment either of commodities or wages. The landlords having also stipulated for the payment of their rents in specie, a gold currency was maintained in the north long after it had been banished from the south of Ireland. If, therefore, the depression of the exchange between London and Dublin had been occasioned, as many contended, by an unfavourable balance of trade between Ireland and Great Britain, or by remittances from the former on account of absentees, it would have been equally depressed between London and the commercial towns in the northern counties. But so far was this from being the case, that in December 1803, when the exchange of Dublin on London was about 16 per cent., that of Belfast on London was about 5 per cent.; or, in other words, at the very time that the exchange between Dublin, which had a paper currency, and London, was near 8 per cent. against Ireland, the exchange between Belfast, which had a gold currency, and London, was about 3 per cent. in its favour. And this is not all: For, while there was a difference of 11 per cent. in the rate of exchange between Dublin and London, and Belfast and London, the inland exchange between Dublin and Belfast was about 10 per cent. in favour of the latter; that is, bills drawn in Dublin, and payable in the gold currency of Belfast, brought a premium of ten per cent., while bills drawn in Belfast, and payable in the paper currency of Dublin sold at 10 per cent. discount !*

* Farther information on this subject may be obtained from the Report referred to above, of the Committee of the House of Commons in 1804, on the state of the circulating paper in Ireland, its specie, etc.; from Mr. Foster's very able essay on the Principle of Commercial Exchanges; and from the pamphlets of Sir Henry Parnell, Lord King, Huskisson, etc.

FINIS.

REMARKS

ON

PAPER CURRENCY;

FROM

A TREATISE

ON THE

COINS OF THE REALM,

BY THE

EARL OF LIVERPOOL,

PUBLISHED IN

1805.

PAPER CURRENCY.

* * * I SHOULD stop here, but there is a subject of so great importance, and so nearly connected with the Coins of Your Majesty's realm, that I should not discharge my duty if I left it wholly unnoticed; I mean what is now called paper currency; which is carried to so great an extent that it is become highly inconvenient to Your Majesty's subjects, and may prove in its consequences, if no remedy is applied, dangerous to the credit of the kingdom. It is certain, that the smaller Notes of the Bank of England, and those issued by country Bankers, have supplanted the Gold Coins, usurped their functions, and driven a great part of them out of circulation; in some parts of Great Britain, and especially in the southern parts of Ireland, small notes have been issued to supply the place of Silver Coins, of which there is certainly a great deficiency.

I will first observe, that if this practice is suffered to continue, as at present, without any limitation, there can be neither use nor advantage in converting Bullion or either of the precious metals into Coins, except so far as it may serve for the convenience of Your Majesty's subjects in their most private concerns; that is, no greater quantity than many of the writers, who have of late speculated on this subject, will allow to continue in currency: the Bullion, of which these Coins are made, had better be exported in its natural state, like any other unmanufactured commodity, for the use of which the trade of the country has no occasion. The Coins of Your Majesty, when carried into foreign countries, will only be valued as Bullion; and the precious metals, whether exported in Coins or in Bullion, will equally serve the purpose of a commercial capital; and it is useless and absurd to impose upon the public the expence of making Coins, merely for the purpose of sending them out of the kingdom.

It has been a common artifice, practised by those who have written on Paper currency, to confound Paper credit with Paper currency, and even the higher sorts of Paper currency with the inferior sorts, such as immediately interfere with the use of the Coins of the realm. Paper credit is not only highly convenient and beneficial, but is even absolutely necessary in carrying on the trade of a great commercial kingdom. Paper currency is a very undefined term, as used by speculative writers.* To find arguments in its support, at least to the extent to which it is at present carried, they have been obliged to connect it with Paper credit; so that the principles on which the use of Paper credit is truly founded, may be brought in support of a great emission of Paper currency: I do not mean to say, that even the higher orders of Paper currency may not be very convenient in carrying on many branches of the trade of a country so wealthy as Great Britain: the sort of Paper currency to which I principally object, is that which interferes with the use of the Coins of the realm, more especially in the payment of labourers and artificers, of the sailor and soldier, and in the smaller branches of the retail trade of the kingdom.

Many words are not necessary to point out the evils to which Your Majesty's subjects are exposed by the practice which now prevails of issuing the lower sort of Paper currency by country Bankers; the complaints on this head are universal. The Notes of these country Bankers have credit only within a certain extent or district; if a traveller passes from one district to another, he must provide himsel. with the Notes of other Bankers which have credit within the district on which he is entering; and an inconvenience to which travellers have hitherto been subject, in passing from one small independent state on the continent to another, is experienced by those who travel through Your

* Paper currency, strictly speaking, consists only of bills, or notes payable or convertible into cash on demand by the person who issued the same, at the will of the holder. See Report of the Secret Committee of the House of Lords in 1797, p. 249.

Majesty's dominions, in passing from one district to another; so that the circulating medium of the different parts of Your Majesty's dominions is various; an evil which I believe never existed before in one great United Kingdom.

But I have not hitherto described the principal evils resulting from this Paper currency. It was natural to suppose that the precious metals, being no longer wanted in the same degree for the purpose of being converted into Coins, the price of them would fall in the British market: on the contrary, for a considerable time, Bullion, both of Gold and Silver, has not been generally sold, but at a price above the rate at which each of them is valued at Your Majesty's Mint. It would not be proper for me at present to assign the probable cause of this apparent contradiction: in such a state of things, whatever may be the cause, no Bullion, either of Gold or Silver, will be brought to Your Majesty's Mint to be coined; for it cannot be coined without a loss to the person who brings it; and if it were converted into Coins, the moment they were issued they would be thrown into the melting pot, and reconverted into Bullion, because it would be of more value in the shape of Bullion, than in that of Coins. Till some remedy is applied to this evil no new system of Coinage can be aodpted with any reasonable hope of success.

When the situation of the Bank of England was under the consideration of the two Houses of Parliament, in the year 1797, it was my opinion, and that of many others, that the extent to which Paper currency had then been carried was the first and principal, though not the sole cause of the many difficulties to which that corporate Body was then, and had of late years, from time to time, been exposed, in supplying the Cash occasionally necessary for the commerce of the kingdom; for the Bank of England being at the head of all circulation, and the great repository of unemployed Cash, it necessarily happens, that whenever a sudden increased supply of Coins becomes indispensable, in consequence of private failures or general discredit, by which Notes of the before-mentioned description are driven out of circulation, the Bank of England can alone furnish the Coins which are required to make up this deficiency; and this corporate body is thereby rendered responsible, not only for the value of its own Notes which it may issue, but in a certain degree, for such as may be issued by every private Banker in the kingdom, let the substance, credit, or discretion of such a Banker be what it may: and if the price of both the precious metals in Bullion should then be above that at which they are rated at the Mint, the Bank of England have it not in their power to supply this deficiency, but at a great loss to its proprietors; and even if they were to submit to this loss, and issue new Coins in consequence, it would only be, as has been already observed, in order that they might be thrown into the melting pot and converted into Bullion; so that till some remedy is applied to this evil, the Bank of England cannot, I think, return to the first principles of its institution, under which it has so long and so greatly flourished, and reassume without any restriction its payments in Cash.

The state of the Paper currency of this country, in its manner and extent taken together, is, I believe, without example in the history of mankind. The trade or profession of banking has been exercised in all countries and in all ages; it existed in the Republics of Greece,* and in ancient Rome: there were in all these States men who received money as a deposit, repaid it upon the drafts of those who had entrusted them with it, and derived their profits from having this money in their custody; but it does not appear that they ever issued Notes, such as are now called Paper currency.

In the middle ages, the traffic in money was exercised solely by the Jews; for Christian men, as they were then called, from a mistaken principle of religion, would not engage in it: but the Jews, who interpreted the law of Moses

* For what relates to the Grecian republics see the Voyage du Jeune Anacharsis, ch. 55, and the Grecian authors referred to therein. For what relates to the Roman Republic, see the words Præscribere and Præscriptio, in Gesner's Thesaurus, and the passages of Cicero and other authors referred to by him.

in a different sense from the Christians, thought that they might lawfully carry it on with strangers, and to them every man was a stranger who was not a Jew. The wealth of these Jews, and the extortions and cruelties to which they were exposed on this account, contrary to the principles of humanity and justice, are well known to every one.

When commerce was first revived in the republics of Italy, Banking Companies and private Bankers appeared in numbers, and carried on the trade in money, and particularly in bills of exchange, to a very great extent. The origin and history of the Banks of Venice* and Genoa† need not be here inserted; the wealth‡ of these banks was very great, and many of the principal families in Italy derive their origin and their ample fortunes from persons who once exercised the trade of banking. I cannot, however, discover from history, that either the Jews beforementioned, or the Banking Companies established in Italy, or any of the private Bankers, ever issued what is now called Paper currency: it is certain, at least, that they did not issue it in so great a degree as to drive the Coins out of the country; for it is asserted by historians of undoubted credit,|| that Italy at that time had drawn to itself almost the whole of the Gold of Europe.

After the example of what had been thus practised in Italy, Banking Companies were gradually established in many of the principal cities of Europe, particularly at Hamburgh, Nuremberg, and Amsterdam: many of these Corporate Banks issued Paper currency for the payment of foreign, and sometimes inland, bills of exchange; but this privilege was always exercised under certain regulations and restrictions, sanctioned by the governments of these places,

* Called Banco del Giro.

† Called Banco de Sa° Giorgio.

‡ The wealth of the Bank of St. George at Genoa in process of time became so great, that Machiavel says, there was reason to apprehend that it would become possessed of all the territories of that little state. See *Historia Florentina*, lib. 8.

|| See Histoire de la Ligue de Cambray, liv. v. Bodin, Réponse à Maletroit, p. 49, and Histoire de Louis XI., p. 708.

for the security of the individuals who trusted them, and for the preservation of public credit. It is singular, that it was found necessary to require, that the Notes of these Banks should be accepted and employed exclusively in certain payments: but the privilege thus given never included any payments for which a single piece of Coin, or, as I believe, any small number of them, was sufficient, so as to interfere with the retail trade of the country. The reasons for establishing this Paper currency have been fully explained in a former part of this Letter; and I have never heard that private Bankers issued Paper currency in any European country to the extent in which it is now practised in the British dominions: if it has prevailed anywhere to excess, it has been in the United Provinces of America.

The practice of issuing Paper currency within Your Majesty's dominions first began in Scotland:* it was natural that this device should originate in a country where there was a great want of Coins and capital: the evils it produced were felt so early as the year 1765, when a wise law was passed by the Legislature,[a] to restrain and regulate it within that part of the united kingdom. This law did not extend to England, for the evil at that time had not been felt here: Your Majesty's English subjects, however, soon followed the example of their northern brethren; and in the year 1775 the mischiefs arising from the issue of small Paper Notes were so severely felt, that a law was passed for regulating and restraining it;[b] but it was afterwards found that this law did not remedy the evil, and a second law, still more restrictive, was passed in 1777.[c] These measures were recommended to the Legislature by many of the most eminent of your Majesty's subjects and servants, to whose consultations I, though unworthy, was admitted: I remember, too, that the restrictions then imposed on this practice

---

* See some account of Mr. Law, and of the famous project presented by him to the Parliament of Scotland before the Union, and afterwards to the Regent of France, in Smith's Wealth of Nations, vol. i. p. 478, and the Histoire du Système.

[a] 5th Geo. III. ch. 49.

[b] 15th Geo. III. ch. 51.

[c] 17th Geo. III. ch. 30.

were considered by many as not sufficient.—It was necessary, however, for a temporary purpose to enact a short suspension of these laws, in consequence of the difficulties to which public credit was exposed in the year 1797. At the same time the Bank of England was discharged by the Legislature from the obligation of paying in Cash: but, contrary to expectation, these suspensions have been continued to the present day; and from that period the Bank of England have issued Notes for smaller sums, and to a greater extent than they ever did before; and the number of private Bankers spread over every part of the country during that interval has been more than doubled.*

It is true that there have been a few memorable instances, I believe but three, in which, under the authority of government, Paper currency has been issued to an extravagant extent in a neighbouring country. The first was while France was governed by a Regency, in the beginning of the last century; the two others are of a later date: and each of these experiments has proved, in its results, dishonourable to the Government, and disastrous to the people. During the emission of this Paper currency, the Coins of that country were in a very great degree driven out of circulation; but they re-appeared in considerable quantities as soon as this Paper currency was discredited and annihilated. It ought always to be kept in remembrance, that this Paper currency was issued to so great an excess, either by Corporate Bodies, under the authority and protection of Government, or directly by the Government itself, and not on the sole credit and responsibility of unauthorized individuals.

It is certain, that the principles on which speculative writers would justify the emission of Paper currency in Your Majesty's dominions, would leave it almost without

* It is stated in the summary of the Report of the Secret Committee of the House of Lords in 1797, that the number of Country Bankers, which had in 1792 amounted to 280, had in 1797 been reduced to 230. It appears by the list of Country Bankers now published that they amount to 517.

limitation. The ablest writer on this subject, Dr. Adam Smith, appears, however, sensible that there must be some limitation. That adopted by him is, "that the whole Paper "currency of every kind, which can easily circulate in any "country,[a] never can exceed the value of the Gold and "Silver of which it supplies the place; or which (the "commerce being supposed the same,) would circulate "there, if there was no Paper Money." From this passage it may be inferred, that even in this writer's opinion Paper currency may be issued to so great an extent as to take the place of all the Gold and Silver Coins necessary for carrying on the commerce of the kingdom, though it cannot *easily* be carried to a greater. But later writers pay no attention to the moderation with which this master of political economy has supported his system: and as they are not satisfied with the opinion thus given, we may presume they mean, that Paper currency may be made to represent, according to the system of the well known Mr. Law, even immovable property; that is, a portion at least of the lands and buildings of the kingdom, and as such sent into circulation. It seems to have been discovered of late years in this country, that, by a new sort of alchemy, Coins of Gold and Silver, and almost every other sort of property, may be converted into Paper; and that the precious metals had better be exported, to serve as capital to foreign countries, where no such discovery has yet been made. But this new sort of fictitious capital, thus introduced within the kingdom, has contributed more than any other circumstance to what is called *over-trading;* that is, rash and inconsiderate speculations, and what is almost a necessary consequence, unworthy artifices to support the credit of adventurers already ruined, as well as other evils, which tend to corrupt the morals of the trading part of the community, and to shake the credit on which not only Paper currency, but the internal commerce of the kingdom is founded. In every commercial system capital is certainly a necessary ingredient; but the pros-

[a] Vol. i., p. 448.

perity of the British commerce depends not singly on capital; it depends still more on the good faith, honour, and punctuality of British merchants, for which they are so justly celebrated.

Impressed as I am with the idea, that no system of Coinage can be adopted with the prospect of permanent advantage till some regulations have been made for remedying the evils resulting from the present state of Paper currency, I have thought it right thus to lay before Your Majesty some account of the excess to which it has of late been carried within your kingdoms. I am unwilling to enter into farther discussion on a question so important, and so much agitated, because it is not a fit subject for a Letter to Your Majesty; nor will I treat of the remedies which ought to be applied, because these cannot be administered by the authority of Your Majesty, as in the case of Coins; but they require the authority of the Two Houses of Parliament, in conjunction with that of Your Majesty. Certain I am, that in a kingdom like Great Britain, the most commercial, and for its extent the richest perhaps that ever existed in the world, every branch of circulating medium, of whatever it may consist, should be founded on solid, wise, and honest principles; and Coins in particular, which are the only true measure of property and instrument of commerce, and by which every other circulating medium must be regulated, should be made and kept as perfect as the nature of the subject will admit. * * *

THE HIGH PRICE OF BULLION A PROOF OF THE DEPRECIATION OF BANK NOTES.

BY DAVID RICARDO.

THE FOURTH EDITION, CORRECTED.

LONDON:
PRINTED FOR JOHN MURRAY, 32, FLEET STREET.

1811.

HIGH PRICE OF BULLION

A PROOF OF

THE DEPRECIATION OF BANK NOTES.

THE precious metals employed for circulating the commodities of the world previously to the establishment of banks, have been supposed by the most approved writers on political economy to have been divided into certain proportions among the different civilized nations of the earth, according to the state of their commerce and wealth, and therefore according to the number and frequency of the payments which they had to perform. While so divided they preserved every where the same value, and as each country had an equal necessity for the quantity actually in use, there could be no temptation offered to either for their importation or exportation.

Gold and silver, like other commodities, have an intrinsic value, which is not arbitrary, but is dependent on their scarcity, the quantity of labour bestowed in procuring them, and the value of the capital employed in the mines which produce them.

"The quality of utility, beauty, and scarcity," says Dr. Smith, "are the original foundation of the high price of "those metals, or of the great quantity of other goods for "which they can every where be exchanged. This value "was antecedent to, and independent of their being employed "as coin, and was the quality which fitted them for that "employment."

If the quantity of gold and silver in the world employed as money were exceedingly small, or abundantly great, it would not in the least affect the proportions in which they would be divided among the different nations—the variation in their quantity would have produced no other effect than to make the commodities for which they were exchanged comparatively dear or cheap. The smaller quantity of money would perform the functions of a circulating medium, as well as the larger. Ten millions would be as effectual for that purpose as one hundred millions. Dr. Smith observes, "that "the most abundant mines of the precious metals would add "little to the wealth of the world. A produce of which "the value is principally derived from its scarcity is neces-"sarily degraded by its abundance."

If in the progress towards wealth, one nation advanced more rapidly than the others, that nation would require and obtain a greater proportion of the money of the world. Its commerce, its commodities, and its payments, would increase, and the general currency of the world would be divided according to the new proportions. All countries therefore would contribute their share to this effectual demand.

In the same manner if any nation wasted part of its wealth, or lost part of its trade, it could not retain the same quantity of circulating medium which it before possessed. A part would be exported, and divided among the other nations till the usual proportions were re-established.

While the relative situation of countries continued unaltered they might have abundant commerce with each other, but their exports and imports would on the whole be equal. England might possibly import more goods from, than she would export to, France, but she would in consequence export more to some other country, and France would import more from that country; so that the exports and imports of all countries would balance each other; bills of exchange would make the necessary payments, but no money would pass, because it would have the same value in all countries.

If a mine of gold were discovered in either of these countries, the currency of that country would be lowered in value in consequence of the increased quantity of the precious metals brought into circulation, and would therefore no longer be of the same value as that of other countries. Gold and silver, whether in coin or in bullion, obeying the law which regulates all other commodities, would immediately become articles of exportation; they would leave the country where they were cheap, for those countries where they were dear, and would continue to do so, as long as the mine should prove productive, and till the proportion existing between capital and money in each country before the discovery of the mine, were again established, and gold and silver restored every where to one value. In return for the gold exported, commodities would be imported; and though what is usually termed the balance of trade would be against the country exporting money or bullion, it would be evident that she was carrying on a most advantageous trade, exporting that which was no way useful to her, for commodities which might be employed in the extension of her manufactures, and the increase of her wealth.

If instead of a mine being discovered in any country, a bank were established, such as the Bank of England, with the power of issuing its notes for a circulating medium; after a large amount had been issued either by way of loan to merchants, or by advances to government, thereby adding considerably to the sum of the currency, the same effect would follow as in the case of the mine. The circulating medium would be lowered in value, and goods would experience a proportionate rise. The equilibrium between that and other nations would only be restored by the exportation of part of the coin.

The establishment of the bank and the consequent issue of its notes therefore, as well as the discovery of the mine, operate as an inducement to the exportation either of bullion or of coin, and are beneficial only in as far as that object may be accomplished. The bank substitutes a currency of no value for one most costly, and enables us to turn the precious metals (which, though a very necessary part of our capital, yield no revenue,) into a capital which will yield one. Dr. A. Smith compares the advantages attending the establishment of a bank to those which would be obtained by converting our highways into pastures and cornfields, and procuring a road through the air. The highways, like the coin, are highly useful, but neither yield any revenue. Some people might be alarmed at the specie leaving the country, and might consider that as a disadvantageous trade which required us to part with it; indeed the law so considers it by its enactments against the exportation of specie; but a very little reflection will convince us that it is our choice, and not our necessity, that sends it abroad; and that it is highly beneficial to us to exchange that commodity which is superfluous, for others which may be made productive.

The exportation of the specie may at all times be safely left to the discretion of individuals; it will not be exported more than any other commodity, unless its exportation should be advantageous to the country. If it be advantageous to export it, no laws can effectually prevent its exportation. Happily in this case as well as in most others in commerce where there is free competition, the interests of the individual and that of the community are never at variance.

Were it possible to carry the law against melting or exporting of coin into strict execution, at the same time that the exportation of gold bullion was freely allowed, no advantage could accrue from it, but great injury must arise to those who might have to pay, possibly, two ounces or more of coined gold for one of uncoined gold. This would be a real depreciation of our currency, raising the prices of all other commodities in the same proportion as it increased that of gold bullion. The owner of money would in this case suffer an injury equal to what a proprietor of corn would suffer, were a law to be passed prohibiting him from selling his corn for more than half its market value. The law against the exportation of the coin has this tendency, but is so easily evaded, that gold in bullion has always been nearly of the same value as gold in coin.

Thus then it appears that the currency of one country

can never for any length of time be much more valuable, as far as equal quantities of the precious metals are concerned, than that of another; that excess of currency is but a relative term; that if the circulation of England were ten millions, that of France five millions, that of Holland four millions, &c. &c. whilst they kept their proportions, though the currency of each country were doubled or trebled, neither country would be conscious of an excess of currency. The prices of commodities would every where rise, on account of the increase of currency, but there would be no exportation of money from either. But if these proportions be destroyed by England alone doubling her currency, while that of France, Holland, &c. &c. continued as before, we should then be conscious of an excess in our currency, and for the same reason the other countries would feel a deficiency in theirs, and part of our excess would be exported till the proportions of ten, five, four, &c. were again established.

If in France an ounce of gold were more valuable than in England, and would therefore in France purchase more of any commodity common to both countries, gold would immediately quit England for such purpose, and we should send gold in preference to any thing else, because it would be the cheapest exchangeable commodity in the English market; for if gold be dearer in France than in England, goods must be cheaper; we should not therefore send them from the dear to the cheap market, but, on the contrary, they would come from the cheap to the dear market, and would be exchanged for our gold.

The Bank might continue to issue their notes, and the specie be exported with advantage to the country, while their notes were payable in specie on demand, because they could never issue more notes than the value of the coin which would have circulated had there been no bank.*

If they attempted to exceed this amount, the excess would

* They might, strictly speaking, rather exceed that quantity, because as the Bank would add to the currency of the world, England would retain its share of the increase.

be immediately returned to them for specie; because our currency, being thereby diminished in value, could be advantageously exported, and could not be retained in our circulation. These are the means, as I have already explained, by which our currency endeavours to equalize itself with the currencies of other countries. As soon as this equality was attained, all advantage arising from exportation would cease; but if the Bank assuming, that because a given quantity of circulating medium had been necessary last year, therefore the same quantity must be necessary this, or for any other reason, continued to re-issue the returned notes, the stimulus which a redundant currency first gave to the exportation of the coin would be again renewed with similar effects; gold would be again demanded, the exchange would become unfavourable, and gold bullion would rise, in a small degree, above its mint price, because it is legal to export bullion, but illegal to export the coin, and the difference would be about equal to the fair compensation of the risk.

In this manner if the Bank persisted in returning their notes into circulation, every guinea might be drawn out of their coffers.

If to supply the deficiency of their stock of gold they were to purchase gold bullion at the advanced price, and have it coined into guineas, this would not remedy the evil, guineas would be still demanded, but instead of being exported would be melted and sold to the Bank as bullion at the advanced price. " The operations of the Bank," observed Dr. Smith, alluding to an analogous case, " were upon this " account somewhat like the web of Penelope, the work that " was done in the day was undone in the night." The same sentiment is expressed by Mr. Thornton:—" Finding the " guineas in their coffers to lessen every day, they must " naturally be supposed to be desirous of replacing them by " all effectual and not extravagantly expensive means. They " will be disposed, to a certain degree, to buy gold, though " at a losing price, and to coin it into new guineas; but they " will have to do this at the very moment when many are " privately melting what is coined. The one party will be

" melting and selling while the other is buying and coining. " And each of these two contending businesses will now be " carried on, not on account of an actual exportation of each " melted guinea to Hamburgh, but the operation or at least " a great part of it, will be confined to London; the coiners " and the melters living on the same spot, and giving con- " stant employment to each other.

" The Bank," continues Mr. Thornton, " if we suppose " it, as we now do, to carry on this sort of contest with the " melters, is obviously waging a very unequal war; and even " though it should not be tired early, it will be likely to be " tired sooner than its adversaries."

The Bank would be obliged therefore ultimately to adopt the only remedy in their power to put a stop to the demand for guineas. They would withdraw part of their notes from circulation, till they should have increased the value of the remainder to that of gold bullion, and consequently to the value of the currencies of other countries. All advantage from the exportation of gold bullion would then cease, and there would be no temptation to exchange bank-notes for guineas.

In this view of the subject, then, it appears, that the temptation to export money in exchange for goods, or what is termed an unfavourable balance of trade, never arises but from a redundant currency. But Mr. Thornton, who has considered this subject very much at large, supposes that a very unfavourable balance of trade may be occasioned to this country by a bad harvest, and the consequent importation of corn; and that there may be at the same time an unwillingness in the country, to which we are indebted, to receive our goods in payment; the balance due to the foreign country must therefore be paid out of that part of our currency, consisting of coin, and that hence arises the demand for gold bullion and its increased price. He considers the Bank as affording considerable accommodation to the merchants, by supplying with their notes the void occasioned by the exportation of the specie.

As it is acknowledged by Mr. Thornton, in many parts of

his work, that the price of gold bullion is rated in gold coin; and as it is also acknowledged by him, that the law against melting gold coin into bullion and exporting it is easily evaded, it follows, that no demand for gold bullion, arising from this or any other cause, can raise the money price of that commodity. The error of this reasoning proceeds from not distinguishing between an increase in the value of gold, and an increase in its money price.

If there were a great demand for corn its money price would advance; because, in comparing corn with money, we in fact compare it with another commodity; and for the same reason, when there is a great demand for gold its corn price will increase; but in neither case will a bushel of corn be worth more than a bushel of corn, or an ounce of gold more than an ounce of gold. An ounce of gold bullion could not, whatever the demand might be, whilst its price was rated in gold coin, be of more value than an ounce of coined gold, or 3*l.* 17*s.* 10½*d.*

If this argument should not be considered as conclusive, I should urge, that a *void* in the currency, as here supposed, can only be occasioned by the annihilation or limitation of paper currency, and then it would speedily be filled by importations of bullion, which its increased value, in consequence of the diminution of circulating medium, would infallibly attract to the advantageous market. However great the scarcity of corn might be, the exportation of money would be limited by its increasing scarcity. Money is in such general demand, and in the present state of civilization is so essential to commercial transactions, that it can never be exported to excess; even in a war such as the present, when our enemy endeavours to interdict all commerce with us, the value which the currency would bear, from its increasing scarcity, would prevent the exportation of it from being carried so far as to occasion a void in the circulation.

Mr. Thornton has not explained to us, why any unwillingness should exist in the foreign country to receive our goods in exchange for their corn? and it would be necessary for him to show, that if such an unwillingness were to exist, we should agree to indulge it so far as to consent to part with our coin.

If we consent to give coin in exchange for goods, it must be from choice, not necessity. We should not import more goods than we export, unless we had a redundancy of currency, which it therefore suits us to make a part of our exports. The exportation of the coin is caused by its cheapness, and is not the effect, but the cause of an unfavourable balance: we should not export it, if we did not send it to a better market, or if we had any commodity which we could export more profitably. It is a salutary remedy for a redundant currency; and as I have already endeavoured to prove, that redundancy or excess is only a relative term, it follows, that the demand for it abroad arises only from the comparative deficiency of the currency of the importing country, which there causes its superior value.

It resolves itself entirely into a question of interest. If the sellers of the corn to England, to the amount I will suppose of a million, could import goods which cost a million in England, but would produce, when sold abroad, more than if the million had been sent in money, goods would be preferred; if otherwise, money would be demanded.

It is only after a comparison of the value in their markets and in our own, of gold and other commodities, and because gold is cheaper in the London market than in theirs, that foreigners prefer gold in exchange for their corn. If we diminish the quantity of currency, we give an additional value to it: this will induce them to alter their election, and prefer the commodities. If I owed a debt in Hamburgh of 100*l.* I should endeavour to find out the cheapest mode of paying it. If I send money, the expence attending its transportation being I will suppose 5*l.* to discharge my debt will cost me 105*l.* If I purchase cloth here, which, with the expences attending its exportation, will cost me 106*l.* and which will in Hamburgh sell for 100*l.* it is evidently more to my advantage to send the money. If the purchase and expences of sending hardware to pay my debt, will take 107*l.* I should prefer sending cloth to hardware, but I would send neither in preference to money, because money would be the cheapest exportable commodity in the London market. The same reasons would operate with the exporter of the corn, if the transaction were on his own account. But if the Bank, "fearful for the safety of their establishment," and knowing that the requisite number of guineas would be withdrawn from their coffers at the mint price, should think it necessary to diminish the amount of their notes in circulation, the proportion between the value of the money, of the cloth, and of the hardware, would no longer be as 105, 106, and 107; but the money would become the most valuable of the three, and therefore would be less advantageously employed in discharging the foreign debts.

If, which is a much stronger case, we agreed to pay a subsidy to a foreign power, money would not be exported whilst there were any goods which could more cheaply discharge the payment. The interest of individuals would render the exportation of the money unnecessary*.

Thus then specie will be sent abroad to discharge a debt only when it is superabundant; only when it is the cheapest exportable commodity. If the Bank were at such a time paying their notes in specie, gold would be demanded for that purpose. It would be obtained there at its mint price, whereas its price as bullion would be something above its value as coin, because bullion could, and coin could not, be legally exported.

It is evident, then, that a depreciation of the circulating medium is the necessary consequence of its redundance; and that in the common state of the national currency this

* This is strongly corroborated, by the statement of Mr. Rose, in the House of Commons, that our exports exceeded our imports by (I believe) sixteen millions. In return for those exports no bullion could have been imported, because it is well known, that the price of bullion having been during the whole year higher abroad than in this country, a large quantity of our gold coin has been exported. To the value of the balance of exports, therefore, must be added the value of the bullion exported. A part of the amount may be due to us from foreign nations, but the remainder must be precisely equal to our foreign expenditure, consisting of subsidies to our allies, and the maintenance of our fleets and armies on foreign stations.

depreciation is counteracted by the exportation of the precious metals*.

Such, then, appear to me to be the laws that regulate the distribution of the precious metals throughout the world, and which cause and limit their circulation from one country to another, by regulating their value in each. But before I proceed to examine on these principles the main object of my enquiry, it is necessary that I should shew what is the standard measure of value in this country, and of which, therefore, our paper currency ought to be the representative, because it can only be by a comparison to this standard that its regularity or its depreciation may be estimated.

No permanent† measure of value can be said to exist in

---

* It has been observed, in a work of great and deserved repute, the Edinburgh Review,[a] that an increase in the paper currency will only occasion a rise in the *paper* or *currency* price of commodities, but will not cause an increase in their bullion price.

This would be true at a time when the currency consisted wholly of paper not convertible into specie, but not while specie formed any part of the circulation. In the latter case the effect of an increased issue of paper would be to throw out of circulation an equal amount of specie ; but this could not be done without adding to the quantity of bullion in the market, and thereby lowering its value, or in other words, *increasing the bullion price of commodities.* It is only in consequence of this fall in the value of the metallic currency, and of bullion, that the temptation to export them arises : and the penalties on melting the coin is the sole cause of a small difference between the value of the coin and of bullion, or a small excess of the market above the mint price. But exporting of bullion is synonymous with an unfavourable balance of trade. From whatever cause an exportation of bullion, in exchange for commodities, may proceed, it is called (I think very incorrectly) an unfavourable balance of trade.

When the circulation consists wholly of paper, any increase in its quantity will raise the *money* price of bullion without lowering its *value*, in the same manner, and in the same proportion, as it will raise the prices of other commodities, and for the same reason will lower the foreign exchanges ; but this will only be a *nominal*, not a *real* fall, and will not occasion the exportation of bullion, because the real value of bullion will not be diminished, as there will be no increase to the quantity in the market.

† Strictly speaking, there can be no permanent measure of value. A measure of value should itself be invariable ; but this is not the case with either gold or silver, they being subject to fluctuations as well as other commodities. Experience has indeed taught us, that though the variations in the *value* of gold or silver may be considerable, on a com-

---

[a] Vol. I. p. 183.

any nation while the circulating medium consists of two metals, because they are constantly subject to vary in value with respect to each other. However exact the conductors of the mint may be, in proportioning the relative value of gold to silver in the coins, at the time when they fix the ratio, they cannot prevent one of these metals from rising, while the other remains stationary, or falls in value. Whenever this happens, one of the coins will be melted to be sold for the other. Mr. Locke, Lord Liverpool, and many other writers, have ably considered this subject, and have all agreed, that the only remedy for the evils in the currency proceeding from this source, is the making one of the metals only the standard measure of value. Mr. Locke considered silver as the most proper metal for this purpose, and proposed that gold coins should be left to find their own value, and pass for a greater or lesser number of shillings, as the market price of gold might vary with respect to silver.

Lord Liverpool, on the contrary, maintained that gold was not only the most proper metal for a general measure of value in this country, but that, by the common consent of the people, it had become so, was so considered by foreigners, and that it was best suited to the increased commerce and wealth of England.

He, therefore, proposed, that gold coin only should be a legal tender for sums exceeding one guinea, and silver coins for sums not exceeding that amount. As the law now stands, gold coin is a legal tender for all sums; but it was enacted in the year 1774, " That no tender in payment of money " made in the silver coin of this realm, of any sum ex- " ceeding the sum of twenty-five pounds at any one time, " shall be reputed in law, or allowed to be legal tender within " Great Britain or Ireland, for more than according to its " value by weight, after the rate of 5*s.* 2*d.* for each ounce

---

parison of distant periods, yet for short spaces of time their value is tolerably fixed. It is this property, among other excellences, which fits them better than any other commodity for the uses of money. Either gold or silver may therefore, in the point of view in which we are considering them, be called a measure of value.

"of silver." The same regulation was revived in 1798, and is now in force.

For many reasons given by Lord Liverpool, it appears proved beyond dispute, that gold coin has been for near a century the principal measure of value, but this is, I think, to be attributed to the inaccurate determination of the mint proportions. Gold has been valued too high; no silver, therefore, can remain in circulation which is of its standard weight.

If a new regulation were to take place, and silver to be valued too high, or (which is the same thing,) if the market proportions between the prices of gold and silver were to become greater than those of the mint, gold would then disappear, and silver become the standard currency.

This may require further explanation. The relative value of gold and silver in the coins is as $15\frac{9}{124}$ to 1. An ounce of gold which is coined into 3*l.* 17*s.* 10½*d.* of gold coin, is worth, according to the mint regulation, $15\frac{9}{124}$ ounces of silver, because that weight of silver is also coined into 3*l.* 17*s.* 10½*d.* of silver coin. Whilst the relative value of gold to silver is in the market under 15 to 1, which it has been for a great number of years till lately, gold coin would necessarily be the standard measure of value, because neither the Bank, nor any individual, would send $15\frac{9}{124}$ ounces of silver to the Mint to be coined into 3*l.* 17*s.* 10½*d* when they could sell that quantity of silver in the market for more than 3*l.* 17*s.* 10½*d.* in gold coin, and this they could do by the supposition, that less than 15 ounces of silver would purchase an ounce of gold.

But if the relative value of gold to silver be more than the mint proportion of $15\frac{9}{124}$ to 1, no gold would then be sent to the mint to be coined, because as either of the metals are a legal tender to any amount, the possessor of an ounce of gold would not send it to the mint to be coined into 3*l.* 17*s.* 10½*d.* of gold coin, whilst he could sell it, which he could do in such case, for more than 3*l.* 17*s.* 10½*d.* of silver coin. Not only would not gold be carried to the Mint to be coined, but the illicit trader would melt the gold coin, and sell it as bullion for more than its nominal value in the silver coin. Thus then gold would disappear from circulation, and silver coin become the standard measure of value. As gold has lately experienced a considerable rise compared with silver, (an ounce of standard gold, which, on an average of many years, was of equal value to $14\frac{3}{4}$ ounces of standard silver, being now in the market of the same value as $15\frac{1}{2}$ ounces.) this would be the case now were the Bank Restriction-bill repealed, and the coinage of silver freely allowed at the Mint, in the same manner as that of gold; but in an Act of Parliament of 39 Geo. III. is the following clause:—

> "Whereas inconvenience may arise from any coinage of silver until "such regulations may be formed as shall appear necessary; and "whereas from the present low price of silver bullion, owing to temporary circumstances, a small quantity of silver bullion has been brought "to the mint to be coined, and there is reason to suppose that a still "further quantity may be brought; and it is therefore necessary to "suspend the coining of silver for the present; be it therefore enacted, "That from and after the passing of this act, no silver bullion shall be "coined at the mint, nor shall any silver coin that may have been coined "there be delivered, any law to the contrary notwithstanding."

This law is now in force.

It would appear, therefore, to have been the intention of the legislature to establish gold as the standard of currency in this country. Whilst this law is in force, silver coin must be confined to small payments only, the quantity in circulation being barely sufficient for that purpose. It might be for the interest of a debtor to pay his large debts in silver coin if he could get silver bullion coined into money; but being prevented by the above law from doing so, he is necessarily obliged to discharge his debt with gold coin, which he could obtain at the mint with gold bullion to any amount. Whilst this law is in force, gold must always continue to be the standard of currency.

Were the market value of an ounce of gold to become equal to thirty ounces of silver, gold would nevertheless be the measure of value, whilst this prohibition continued in force. It would be of no avail, that the possessor of 30 ounces of silver should know that he once could have discharged a debt of 3*l.* 17*s.* $10\frac{1}{2}$*d.* by procuring $15\frac{9}{124}$ ounces of silver to be coined at the mint, as he would in this case have no other means of discharging his debt but by selling his 30 oz. of silver at the market value, that is to say, for one ounce of gold, or 3*l.* 17*s.* 10½*d.* of gold coin.

The public has sustained, at different times, very serious loss from the depreciation of the circulating medium, arising from the unlawful practice of clipping the coins.

In proportion as they become debased, so the prices of every commodity for which they are exchangeable rise in nominal value, not excepting gold and silver bullion: accordingly we find, that before the re-coinage in the reign of King William the Third, the silver currency had become so degraded, that an ounce of silver, which ought to be contained in sixty-two pence, sold for seventy-seven pence; and a guinea, which was valued at the mint at twenty shillings, passed in all contracts for thirty shillings. This evil was then remedied by the recoinage. Similar effects followed from the debasement of the gold currency, which were again corrected in 1774 by the same means.

Our gold coins have, since 1774, continued nearly at their standard purity; but our silver currency has again become debased. By an assay at the mint in 1798, it appears that our shillings were found to be twenty-four per cent., and our sixpences thirty-eight per cent. under their mint value; and I am informed, that by a late experiment they were found considerably more deficient. They do not, therefore contain as much pure silver as they did in the reign of King William. This debasement, however, did not operate previously to 1798, as on the former occasion. At that time both gold and silver bullion rose in proportion to the debasement of the silver coin. All foreign exchanges were against us full twenty per cent., and many of them still more. But although the debasement of the silver coin had continued for many years, it had neither, previously to 1798, raised the price of gold nor silver, nor had it produced any effect on the exchanges. This is a convincing proof, that gold coin was, during that period, considered as the standard measure of value. Any debasement of the gold coin would then have produced the same effects on the prices of gold and silver bullion, and on the foreign exchanges, which were formerly caused by the debasement of the silver coins.*

While the currency of different countries consists of the precious metals, or of a paper money which is at all times exchangeable for them; and while the metallic currency is not debased by wearing, or clipping, a comparison of the weight, and degree of fineness of their coins, will enable us to ascertain their par of exchange. Thus the par of exchange between Holland and England is stated to be about eleven florins, because the pure silver contained in eleven florins is equal to the pure silver contained in twenty standard shillings.

This par is not, nor can it be, absolutely fixed; because gold coin being the standard of commerce in England, and silver coin in Holland, a pound sterling, or $\frac{20}{21}$ of a guinea, may at different times be more or less valuable than twenty standard shillings, and therefore more or less valuable than its equivalent of eleven florins. Estimating the par either by silver or by gold will be sufficiently exact for our purpose.

If I owe a debt in Holland; by knowing the par of exchange, I also know the quantity of our money which will be necessary to discharge it.

If my debt amount to 1100 florins, and gold have not varied in value, 100*l.* in our pure gold coin will purchase as much Dutch currency as is necessary to pay my debt. By exporting the 100*l.* therefore in coin, or (which is the same thing) paying a bullion merchant the 100*l.* in coin, and allowing him the expences attending its transportation, such as freight, insurance, and his profit, he will sell me a bill which will discharge my debt; at the same time he will export the bullion, to enable his correspondent to pay the bill when it shall become due.

* When the gold coin was debased, previously to the re-coinage in 1774, gold and silver bullion rose above their mint prices, and fell immediately on the gold coin attaining its present perfection. The exchanges were, owing to the same causes, from being unfavourable rendered favourable.

These expences then are the utmost limits of an unfavourable exchange. However great my debt may be, though it equalled the largest subsidy ever given by this country to an ally; while I could pay the bullion-merchant in coin of standard value, he would be glad to export it, and to sell me bills. But if I pay him for his bill in a debased, coin or in a depreciated paper-money, he will not be willing to sell me his bill at this rate; because, if the coin be debased, it does not contain the quantity of pure gold or silver which ought to be contained in 100*l.*, and he must therefore export an additional number of such debased pieces of money to enable him to pay my debt of 100*l.* or its equivalent, 1100 florins. If I pay him in paper-money; as he cannot send it abroad, he will consider whether it will purchase as much gold or silver bullion as is contained in the coin for which it is a substitute; if it will do this, paper will be as acceptable to him as coin: but if it will not, he will expect a further premium for his bill, equal to the depreciation of the paper.

While the circulating medium consists, therefore, of coin undebased, or of paper-money immediately exchangeable for undebased coin, the exchange can never be more above, or more below, par, than the expences attending the transportation of the precious metals. But when it consists of a depreciated paper money, it necessarily will fall according to the degree of the depreciation.

The exchange will, therefore, be a tolerably accurate criterion by which we may judge of the debasement of the currency, proceeding either from a clipped coinage, or a depreciated paper-money.

It is observed by Sir James Steuart, " That if the foot " measure was altered at once over all England, by adding " to it, or taking from it, any proportional part of its standard " length, the alteration would be best discovered, by com- " paring the new foot with that of Paris, or of any other " country, which had suffered no alteration.

" Just so, if the pound sterling, which is the English unit, " shall be found any how changed; and if the variation it

" has met with be difficult to ascertain, because of a com-
" plication of circumstances; the best way to discover it will
" be to compare the former and the present value of it, with
" the money of other nations which has suffered no varia-
" tion. This the exchange will perform with the greatest
" exactness."

The Edinburgh reviewers, in speaking of Lord King's pamphlet, observe, that "it does not follow because our " imports always consist partly of bullion, that the balance " of trade is therefore permanently in our favour. Bullion," they say, "is a commodity, for which, as for every other, " there is a varying demand; and which, exactly like any " other, may enter the catalogue either of imports or exports; " and this exportation or importation of bullion will not " affect the course of exchange in a different way from the " exportation or importation of any other commodities."

No person ever exports or imports bullion without first considering the rate of exchange. It is by the rate of exchange that he discovers the relative value of bullion in the two countries between which it is estimated. It is therefore consulted by the bullion-merchant in the same manner as the price-current is by other merchants, before they determine on the exportation or importation of other commodities. If eleven florins in Holland contain an equal quantity of pure silver as twenty standard shillings, silver bullion, equal in weight to twenty standard shillings, can never be exported from London to Amsterdam whilst the exchange is at par, or unfavourable to Holland. Some expence and risk must attend its exportation, and the very term *par* expresses that a quantity of silver bullion, equal to that weight and purity, is to be obtained in Holland by the purchase of a bill of exchange, free of all expence. Who would send bullion to Holland at an expence of three or four per cent. when, by the purchase of a bill at par, he in fact obtains an order for the delivery to his correspondent in Holland of the same weight of bullion which he was about to export?

It would be as reasonable to contend, that when the price

of corn is higher in England than on the Continent, corn would be sent, notwithstanding all the charges on its exportation, to be sold in the cheaper market.

Having already noticed the disorders to which a metallic currency is exposed, I will proceed to consider those which, though not caused by the debased state of either the gold or silver coins, are nevertheless more serious in their ultimate consequences.

Our circulating medium is almost wholly composed of paper, and it behoves us to guard against the depreciation of the paper currency, with at least as much vigilance as against that of the coins.

This we have neglected to do.

Parliament, by restricting the Bank from paying in specie, have enabled the conductors of that concern to increase or decrease at pleasure the quantity and amount of their notes; and the previously existing checks against an over-issue having been thereby removed, those conductors have acquired the power of increasing or decreasing the value of the paper currency.

In tracing the present evils to their source, and proving their existence by an appeal to the two unerring tests I have before mentioned, namely, the rate of exchange and the price of bullion, I shall avail myself of the account given by Mr. Thornton of the conduct of the Bank before the restriction, to shew how clearly they acted on the principle which he has expressly acknowledged, viz. that the value of their notes is dependent on their amount, and that they ascertained the variation in their value by the tests I have just referred to.

Mr. Thornton tells us, " That if at any time the exchanges " of the country become so unfavourable as to produce a " material excess of the market above the mint price of " gold, the directors of the Bank, as appears by the evidence " of some of their body, given to parliament, were disposed " to resort to a reduction of their paper, as a means of diminishing or removing the excess, and of *thus providing for* " *the security of their establishment.* They moreover have at "all times," he says, "been accustomed to observe some "limit as to the quantity of their notes, for the same pru-"dential reasons." And in another place: "When the price "which our coin will fetch in foreign countries is such as to "tempt it out of the kingdom, the directors of the Bank "naturally diminish, in some degree, the quantity of their "paper *through an anxiety for the safety of their establishment.* "By diminishing their paper, they raise its value; and in "raising its value, they raise also the value in England of "the current coin which is exchanged for it. Thus the value "of our gold coin conforms itself to the value of the current "paper, and the current paper is rendered by the Bank-"directors, of that value which it is necessary that it should "bear in order to prevent large exportations;—a value "sometimes rising a little above, and sometimes falling a "little below, the price which our coin bears abroad."

The necessity which the Bank felt itself under to guard the safety of its establishment, therefore, always prevented, before the restriction from paying in specie, a too lavish issue of paper money.

Thus we find that, for a period of twenty-three years previously to the suspension of cash payments in 1797, the average price of gold bullion was 3*l.* 17*s.* 7¾*d.* per oz. about 2¼*d.* under the mint price; and for sixteen years previously to 1774, it never was much above 4*l.* per oz. It should be remembered that during these sixteen years our gold coin was debased by wearing, and it is therefore probable that 4*l.* of such debased money did not weigh as much as the ounce of gold for which it was exchanged.

Dr. A. Smith considers every permanent excess of the market above the mint price of gold, as referrible to the state of the coins. While the coin was of its standard weight and purity, the market price of gold bullion, he thought, could not greatly exceed the mint price.

Mr. Thornton contends that this cannot be the only cause. "We have," he says, "lately experienced fluctuations in "our exchanges, and correspondent variations in the market, "compared with the mint price of gold, amounting to no

" less than eight or ten per cent.; the state of our coinage " continuing in all respects the same." Mr. Thornton should have reflected that at the time he wrote, specie could not be demanded at the Bank in exchange for notes; that this was a cause for the depreciation of the currency which Dr. Smith could never have anticipated. If Mr. Thornton had proved that there had been a fluctuation of ten per cent. in the price of gold, while the Bank paid their notes in specie, and the coin was undebased, he would then have convicted Dr. Smith of " having treated this important subject in a defective and " unsatisfactory manner."*

But as all checks against the over issues of the Bank are now removed by the act of parliament, which restricts them from paying their notes in specie, they are no longer bound by "*fears for the safety of their establishment*," to limit the quantity of their notes to that sum which shall keep them of the same value as the coin which they represent. Accord-

* An excess in the market above the mint price of gold or silver bullion, may, whilst the coins of both metals are legal tender, and there is no prohibition against the coinage of either metal, be caused by a variation in the relative value of those metals; but an excess of the market above the mint price proceeding from this cause will be at once perceived by its affecting only the price of one of the metals. Thus gold would be at or below, while silver was above, its mint price, or silver at or below its mint price, whilst gold was above.

In the latter end of 1795, when the bank had considerably more notes in circulation than either the preceding or the subsequent year, when their embarrasssments had already commmenced, when they appear to have resigned all prudence in the management of their concerns, and to have constituted Mr. Pitt sole director, the price of gold bullion did for a short time rise to 4*l.* 3*s.* or 4*l.* 4*s.* per oz.; but the directors were not without their fears for the consequences. In a remonstrance sent to them by Mr. Pitt, dated October 1795, after stating, " that the demand for gold not appearing likely soon to cease," and " that it had excited great apprehension in the court of directors," they observe, " The present price of gold being 4*l.* 3*s.* to 4*l.* 4*s.*† per ounce, " and our guineas being to be purchased at 3*l.* 17*s.* 10½*d.*, clearly demon- " strates the grounds of our fears; *it being only necessary to state those " facts to the Chancellor of the Exchequer.*" It is remarkable that no price of gold above the mint price is quoted during the whole year in Wetenhall's list. In December it is there marked 3*l.* 17*s.* 6*d.*

† It is difficult to determine on what authority the directors made this assertion, as by a return lately made to parliament it appears that during the year 1795 they did not purchase gold bullion at a price higher than 3*l.* 17*s.* 6*d.*

ingly we find that gold bullion has risen from 3*l.* 17*s.* 7¾*d.* the average price previously to 1797, to 4*l.* 10*s.* and has been lately as high as 4*l.* 13*s.* per oz.

We may therefore fairly conclude that this difference in the relative value, or, in other words, that this depreciation in the actual value of bank-notes has been caused by the too abundant quantity which the Bank has sent into circulation. The same cause which has produced a difference of from fifteen to twenty per cent. in bank-notes when compared with gold bullion, may increase it to fifty per cent. There can be no limit to the depreciation which may arise from a constantly increasing quantity of paper. The stimulus which a redundant currency gives to the exportation of the coin has acquired new force, but cannot, as formerly, relieve itself. We have paper money only in circulation, which is necessarily confined to ourselves. Every increase in its quantity degrades it below the value of gold and silver bullion, below the value of the currencies of other countries.

The effect is the same as that which would have been produced from clipping our coins.

If one-fifth were taken off from every guinea, the market price of gold bullion would rise one-fifth above the mint price. Forty-four guineas and a half (the number of guineas weighing a pound, and therefore called the mint price), would no longer weigh a pound, therefore a fifth more than that quantity, or about 56*l.* would be the price of a pound of gold, and the difference between the market and the mint price, between 56*l.* and 46*l.* 14*s.* 6*d.* would measure the depreciation.

If such debased coin were to continue to be called by the name of guineas, and if the value of gold bullion and all other commodities were rated in the debased coin, a guinea fresh from the mint would be said to be worth 1*l.* 5*s.* and that sum would be given for it by the illicit trader; but it would not be the value of the new guinea which had increased, but that of the debased guineas which had fallen. This would immediately be evident, if a proclamation were issued, prohibiting the debased guineas from being current but by weight at the mint price of 3*l.* 17*s.* 10½*d.*; this would be constituting the new and heavy guineas, the standard measure of value, in lieu of the clipped and debased guineas. The latter would then pass at their true value, and be called 17 or 18 shillings-pieces. So if a proclamation to the same effect were now enforced, bank-notes would not be less current, but would pass only for the value of the gold bullion which they would purchase. A guinea would then no longer be said to be worth 1*l.* 5*s.* but a pound note would be current only for 16 or 17 shillings. At present gold coin is only a commodity, and bank-notes are the standard measure of value, but in that case gold coin would be that measure, and bank-notes would be the marketable commodity.

" It is," says Mr. Thornton, " the maintenance of our " general exchanges, or, in other words, it is the agreement " of the mint price with the bullion price of gold, which " seems to be the true proof that the circulating paper is not " depreciated."

When the motive for exporting gold occurs, while the Bank do not pay in specie, and gold cannot therefore be obtained at its mint price, the small quantity that can be procured will be collected for exportation, and bank-notes will be sold at a discount for gold in proportion to their excess. In saying however that gold is at a high price, we are mistaken; it is not gold, it is paper which has changed its value. Compare an ounce of gold, or 3*l.* 17*s.* 10½*d.* to commodities, it bears the same proportion to them which it has before done; and if it do not, it is referrible to increased taxation, or to some of those causes which are so constantly operating on its value. But if we compare the substitute of an ounce of gold 3*l.* 17*s.* 10½*d.* in bank-notes with commodities, we shall then discover the depreciation of the bank-notes. In every market of the world I am obliged to part with 4*l.* 10*s.* in bank-notes to purchase the same quantity of commodities which I can obtain for the gold that is in 3*l.* 17*s.* 10½*d.* of coin.

It is often asserted, that a guinea is worth at Hamburgh 26 or 28 shillings; but we should be very much deceived if we should therefore conclude that a guinea could be sold at Hamburgh for as much silver as is contained in 26 or 28 shillings. Before the alteration in the relative value of gold and silver, a guinea would not sell at Hamburgh for as much silver coin as is contained in 21 standard shillings; it will at the present market price sell for a sum of silver currency, which, if imported and carried to our mint to be coined, will produce in our standard silver coin 21*s.* 5*d.**

It is nevertheless true, that the same quantity of silver will, at Hamburgh, purchase a bill payable in London, in bank notes, for 26 or 28 shillings. Can there be a more satisfactory proof of the depreciation of our circulating medium?

It is said, that, if the Restriction-bill were not in force, every guinea would leave the country.†

This is, no doubt, true; but if the Bank were to diminish the quantity of their notes until they had increased their value fifteen per cent., the restriction might be safely removed, as there would then be no temptation to export specie. However long it may be deferred, however great may be the discount on their notes, the Bank can never resume their payments in specie, until they first reduce the amount of their notes in circulation to these limits.

The law is allowed by all writers on political economy to be a useless barrier against the exportation of guineas: it is so easily evaded, that it is doubted whether it has had the effect of keeping a single guinea more in England than there would have been without such law. Mr. Locke, Sir J. Steuart, Dr. A. Smith, Lord Liverpool, and Mr. Thornton, all agree on this subject. The latter gentleman observes, "That the state of the British law unquestionably serves "to discourage and limit, though not effectually to hinder, "that exportation of guineas which is encouraged by an

* The relative value of gold and silver is on the Continent nearly the same as in London.

† It must be meant that every guinea in the Bank would leave the country; the temptation of fifteen per cent. is amply sufficient to send those out which can be collected from the circulation.

" unfavourable balance of trade, and perhaps scarcely lessens " it when the profit on exportation becomes very great." Yet after every guinea that can in the present state of things be procured by the illicit trader has been melted and exported, he will hesitate before he openly buys guineas with bank-notes at a premium, because, though considerable profit may attend such speculation, he will thereby render himself an object of suspicion. He may be watched, and prevented from effecting his object. As the penalties of the law are severe and the temptation to informers great, secrecy is essential to his operations. When guineas can be procured by merely sending a bank-note for them to the Bank, the law will be easily evaded; but when it is necessary to collect them openly and from a widely diffused circulation, consisting almost wholly of paper, the advantage attending it must be very considerable before any one will encounter the risk of being detected.

When we reflect that above sixty millions sterling have been coined into guineas during his present Majesty's reign, we may form some idea of the extent to which the exportation of gold must have been carried.—But repeal the law against the exportation of guineas, permit them to be openly sent out of the country, and what can prevent an ounce of standard gold in guineas from selling at as good a price for bank-notes, as an ounce of Portuguese gold coin, or standard gold in bars, when it is known to be equal to them in fineness? And if an ounce of standard gold in guineas would sell in the market, as standard bars do now, at 4*l.* 10*s.* per oz., or as they have lately done at 4*l.* 13*s.* per oz., what shopkeeper would sell his goods at the same price either for gold or bank-notes indifferently? If the price of a coat were 3*l.* 17*s.* 10½*d.* or an ounce of gold, and if at the same time an ounce of gold would sell for 4*l.* 13*s.*, is it conceivable that it would be a matter of indifference to the tailor whether he were paid in gold or in bank-notes?

It is only because a guinea will not purchase more than a pound-note and a shilling, that many hesitate to allow that bank-notes are at a discount. The Edinburgh Review supports the same opinion; but if my reasoning be correct, I have shewn such objections to be groundless.

Mr. Thornton has told us that an unfavourable trade will account for an unfavourable exchange; but we have already seen that an unfavourable trade, if such be an accurate term, is limited in its effects on the exchange. That limit is probably four or five per cent. This will not account for a depreciation of fifteen or twenty per cent. Moreover Mr. Thornton has told us, and I entirely agree with him, "That it may be laid down as a general truth, that the com-"mercial exports and imports of a state naturally proportion "themselves in some degree to each other, and that the "balance of trade therefore cannot continue for a very long "time to be either highly favourable or highly unfavourable "to a country." Now the low exchange so far from being temporary, existed before Mr. Thornton wrote in 1802, and and has since been progressively increasing, and is now from fifteen to twenty per cent. against us. Mr. Thornton must therefore, according to his own principles, attribute it to some more permanent cause than an unfavourable balance of trade, and will, I doubt not, whatever his opinion may formerly have been, now agree that it is to be accounted for only by the depreciation of the circulating medium.

It can, I think, no longer be disputed that bank-notes are at a discount. While the price of gold bullion is 4*l*. 10*s*. per oz., or in other words, while any man will consent to give that which professes to be an obligation to pay nearly an ounce, and a sixth of an ounce of gold, for an ounce, it cannot be contended that 4*l*. 10*s*. in notes and 4*l*. 10*s*. in gold coin are of the same value.

An ounce of gold is coined into 3*l*. 17*s*. 10½*d*.; by possessing that sum therefore I have an ounce of gold, and would not give 4*l*. 10*s*. in gold coin, or notes which I could immediately exchange for 4*l*. 10*s*., for an ounce of gold.

It is contrary to common sense to suppose that such could be the market value, unless the price were estimated in a depreciated medium.

If the price of gold were estimated in *silver* indeed, the

price might rise to 4*l.*, 5*l.*, or 10*l.* an ounce, and it would, of itself, be no proof of the depreciation of paper currency, but of an alteration in the relative value of gold and silver. I have, however, I think proved, that silver is not the standard measure of value, and therefore not the medium in which the value of gold is estimated. But if it were, as an ounce of gold is only worth in the market 15½oz. of silver, and as 15½ ounces of silver is precisely equal in weight, and is therefore coined into 80 shillings, an ounce of gold ought not to sell for more than 4*l.*

Those then who maintain that silver is the measure of value cannot prove that any demand for gold which may have taken place, from whatever cause it may have proceeded, can have raised its price above 4*l.* per oz. All above that price must, on their own principles, be called a depreciation in the value of bank-notes. It therefore follows, that if bank-notes be the representative of silver coin, then an ounce of gold, selling as it now does for 4*l.* 10*s.* sells for an amount of notes which represent 17½ ounces of silver, whereas in the bullion market it can only be exchanged for 15½ ounces. Fifteen ounces and a half of silver bullion are therefore of equal value with an engagement of the Bank to pay to *bearer* seventeen ounces and a half.

The market price of silver is at the present time 5*s.* 9½*d.* per oz. estimated in bank-notes, the mint price being only 5*s.* 2*d.*, consequently the standard silver in 100*l.* is worth more than 112*l.* in bank-notes.

But bank notes, it may be said, are the representatives of our debased silver coin, and not of our standard silver. This is not true, because the law which I have already quoted declares silver to be a legal tender, for sums only not exceeding 25*l.* except by weight. If the Bank insisted on paying the holder of a bank-note of 1000*l.* in silver coin, they would be bound either to give him standard silver of full weight, or debased silver of an equal value, with the exception of 25*l.* which they might pay him in debased coin. But the 1000*l.* so consisting of 975*l.* pure money, and 25*l.* debased, is worth more than 1112*l.* at the present market value of silver bullion.

It is said that the amount of bank-notes has not increased in a greater proportion than the augmentation of our trade required, and therefore cannot be excessive. This assertion would be difficult to prove, and if true, no argument but what is delusive could be founded on it. In the first place, the daily improvements which we are making in the art of economizing the use of circulating medium, by improved methods of banking, would render the same amount of notes excessive now, which were necessary for the same state of commerce at a former period. Secondly, there is a constant competition between the Bank of England and the country-banks to establish their notes, to the exclusion of those of their rivals, in every district where the country banks are established.

As the latter have more than doubled in number within very few years, is it not probable that their activity may have been crowned with success, in displacing with their own notes many of those of the Bank of England?

If this have happened, the same amount of Bank of England notes would now be excessive; which, with a less extended commerce, was before barely sufficient to keep our currency on a level with that of other countries. No just conclusion can therefore be drawn from the actual amount of bank notes in circulation, though the fact, if examined, would, I have no doubt, be found to be, that the increase in the amount of bank-notes, and the high price of gold, have usually accompanied each other.

It is doubted, whether two or three millions of Bank-notes (the sum which the Bank is supposed to have added to the circulation, over and above the amount which it will easily bear,) could have had such effects as are ascribed to them; but it should be recollected, that the Bank regulate the amount of the circulation of all the country banks, and it is probable that if the Bank increase their issues three millions, they enable the country banks to add more than three millions to the general circulation of England.

The money of a particular country is divided amongst its different provinces by the same rules as the money of the world is divided amongst the different nations of which it is composed. Each district will retain in its circulation such a proportionate share of the currency of the country, as its trade, and consequently its payments, may require, compared to the trade of the whole; and no increase can take place in the circulating medium of one district, without being generally diffused, or calling forth a proportionable quantity in every other district. It is this which keeps a country bank note always of the same value as a Bank of England note. If in London where Bank of England notes only are current, one million be added to the amount in circulation, the currency will become cheaper there than elsewhere, or goods will become dearer. Goods will, therefore, be sent from the country to the London market, to be sold at the high prices, or which is much more probable, the country banks will take advantage of the relative deficiency in the country currency, and increase the amount of their notes in the same proportion as the Bank of England had done; prices would then be generally, and not partially affected.

In the same manner, if Bank of England notes be diminished one million, the comparative value of the currency of London will be increased, and the prices of goods diminished. A Bank of England note will then be more valuable than a country-bank note, because it will be wanted to purchase goods in the cheap market; and as the country banks are obliged to give Bank of England notes for their own when demanded, they would be called upon for them till the quantity of country paper should be reduced to the same proportion which it before bore to the London paper, producing a corresponding fall in the prices of all goods for which it was exchangeable.

The country banks could never increase the amount of their notes, unless to fill up a relative deficiency in the country currency, caused by the increased issues of the Bank of England.* If they attempted it, the same check

* They might, on some occasions, displace Bank of England notes, but that consideration does not affect the question which we are now discussing.

which compelled the Bank of Eg land to withdraw part of their notes from circulation when they used to pay them on demand in specie, would oblige the country-banks to adopt the same course. Their notes would, on account of the increased quantity, be rendered of less value than the Bank of England notes, in the same manner as Bank of England notes were rendered of less value than the guineas which they represented. They would therefore be exchanged for Bank of England notes until they were of the same value.

The Bank of England is the great regulator of the country paper. When they increase or decrease the amount of their notes, the country banks do the same; and in no case can country banks add to the general circulation, unless the Bank of England shall have previously increased the amount of their notes.

It is contended, that the rate of interest, and not the price of gold or silver bullion, is the criterion by which we may always judge of the abundance of paper-money; that if it were too abundant, interest would fall, and if not sufficiently so, interest would rise. It can, I think, be made manifest, that the rate of interest is not regulated by the abundance or scarcity of money, but by the abundance or scarcity of that part of capital, not consisting of money.

"Money," observes Dr. A. Smith, "the great wheel of "circulation, the great instrument of commerce, like all "other instruments of trade, though it makes a part, and a "very valuable part of the capital, makes no part of the "revenue of the society to which it belongs; and though the "metal pieces of which it is composed, in the course of their "annual circulation, distribute, to every man the revenue "which properly belongs to him, they make themselves no "part of that revenue.

"When we compute the quantity of industry which the "circulating capital of any society can employ, we must "always have regard to those parts of it only which consist "in provisions, materials, and finished work: the other, "which consists in money, and which serves only to circulate "those three, must always be deducted. In order to put

" industry into motion, three things are requisite:—materials " to work upon, tools to work with, and the wages or " recompense for the sake of which the work is done. Money " is neither a material to work upon, nor a tool to work with; " and though the wages of the workman are commonly paid " to him in money, his real revenue, like that of all other " men, consists not in money, but in money's worth; not in " the metal pieces, but what can be got for them."

And in other parts of his work, it is maintained, that the discovery of the mines in America, which so greatly increased the quantity of money, did not lessen the interest for the use of it: the rate of interest being regulated by the profits on the employment of capital, and not by the number or quality of the pieces of metal which are used to circulate its produce.

Mr. Hume has supported the same opinion. The value of the circulating medium of every country bears some proportion to the value of the commodities which it circulates. In some countries this proportion is much greater than in others, and varies, on some occasions, in the same country. It depends upon the rapidity of circulation, upon the degree of confidence and credit existing between traders, and above all, on the judicious operations of banking. In England so many means of economizing the use of circulating medium have been adopted, that its value, compared with the value of the commodities which it circulates, is probably (during a period of confidence*) reduced to as small a proportion as is practicable. What that proportion may be has been variously estimated.

No increase or decrease of its quantity, whether consisting of gold, silver, or paper money, can increase or decrease its value above or below this proportion. If the mines cease to supply the annual consumption of the precious metals, money will become more valuable, and a smaller quantity will be employed as a circulating medium. The diminution in the quantity will be proportioned to the increase of its value.

* In the following observations, I wish to be understood as supposing always the same degree of confidence and credit to exist.

In like manner, if new mines be discovered, the value of the precious metals will be reduced, and an increased quantity used in the circulation; so that in either case, the relative value of money, to the commodities which it circulates, will continue as before.

If, whilst the Bank paid their notes on demand in specie, they were to increase their quantity, they would produce little permanent effect on the value of the currency, because nearly an equal quantity of the coin would be withdrawn from circulation and exported.

If the Bank were restricted from paying their notes in specie, and all the coin had been exported, any excess of their notes would depreciate the value of the circulating medium in proportion to the excess. If twenty millions had been the circulation of England before the restriction, and four millions were added to it, the twenty-four millions would be of no more value than the twenty were before, provided commodities had remained the same, and there had been no corresponding exportation of coins; and if the Bank were successively to increase it to fifty, or a hundred millions, the increased quantity would be all absorbed in the circulation of England, but would be, in all cases, depreciated to the value of the twenty millions.

I do not dispute, that if the Bank were to bring a large additional sum of notes into the market, and offer them on loan, but that they would for a time affect the rate of interest. The same effects would follow from the discovery of a hidden treasure of gold or silver coin. If the amount were large, the Bank, or the owner of the treasure, might not be able to lend the notes or the money at four, nor perhaps, above three per cent.; but having done so, neither the notes, nor the money, would be retained unemployed by the borrowers; they would be sent into every market, and would every where raise the prices of commodities, till they were absorbed in the general circulation. It is only during the interval of the issues of the Bank, and their effect on prices, that we should be sensible of an abundance of money; interest would, during that interval, be under its natural level; but as soon as the additional sum of notes or of money became absorbed in the general circulation, the rate of interest would be as high, and new loans would be demanded with as much eagerness as before the additional issues.

The circulation can never be over-full. If it be one of gold and silver, any increase in its quantity will be spread over the world. If it be one of paper, it will diffuse itself only in the country where it is issued. Its effects on prices will then be only local and nominal, as a compensation by means of the exchange will be made to foreign purchasers.

To suppose that any increased issues of the Bank can have the effect of permanently lowering the rate of interest, and satisfying the demands of all borrowers, so that there will be none to apply for new loans, or that a productive gold or silver mine can have such an effect, is to attribute a power to the circulating medium which it can never possess. Banks would, if this were possible, become powerful engines indeed. By creating paper money, and lending it at three or two per cent. under the present market rate of interest, the Bank would reduce the profits on trade in the same proportion; and if they were sufficiently patriotic to lend their notes at an interest no higher than necessary to pay the expenses of their establishment, profits would be still further reduced; no nation, but by similar means, could enter into competition with us, we should engross the trade of the world. To what absurdities would not such a theory lead us! Profits can only be lowered by a competition of capitals not consisting of circulating medium. As the increase of bank notes does not add to this species of capital, as it neither increases our exportable commodities, our machinery, or our raw materials, it cannot add to our profits nor lower interest.*

* I have already allowed that the Bank, as far as they enable us to turn our corn into "materials, provisions, &c." have produced a national benefit, as they have thereby increased the quantity of productive capital; but I am here speaking of an excess of their notes, of that quantity which adds to our circulation without effecting any corresponding exportation of coin, and which, therefore, degrades the notes, below the value of the bullion contained in the coin which they represent.

When any one borrows money for the purpose of entering into trade, he borrows it as a medium by which he can possess himself of "materials, provisions, &c." to carry on that trade; and it can be of little consequence to him, provided he obtain the quantity of materials, &c. necessary, whether he be obliged to borrow a thousand, or ten thousand pieces of money. If he borrow ten thousand, the produce of his manufacture will be ten times the nominal value of what it would have been, had one thousand been sufficient for the same purpose. The capital actually employed in the country is necessarily limited to the amount of the "materials, provisions, &c." and might be made equally productive, though not with equal facility, if trade were carried on wholly by barter. The successive possessors of the circulating medium have the command over this capital: but however abundant may be the quantity of money, or of bank-notes; though it may increase the nominal prices of commodities; though it may distribute the productive capital in different proportions; though the Bank, by increasing the quantity of their notes, may enable A to carry on part of the business formerly engrossed by B and C, nothing will be added to the real revenue and wealth of the country. B and C may be injured, and A and the Bank may be gainers, but they will gain exactly what B and C lose. There will be a violent and an unjust transfer of property, but no benefit whatever will be gained by the community.

For these reasons I am of opinion that the funds are not indebted for their high price to the depreciation of our currency. Their price must be regulated by the general rate of interest given for money. If before the depreciation I gave thirty years' purchase for land, and twenty-five for an annuity in the stocks, I can after the depreciation give a larger sum for the purchase of land, without giving more years' purchase, because the produce of the land will sell for a greater nominal value in consequence of the depreciation; but as the annuity in the funds is paid in the depreciated medium, there can be no reason why I should give a greater nominal value for it after than before the depreciation.

If guineas were degraded by clipping to half their present

value, every commodity as well as land would rise to double its present nominal value; but as the interest of the stocks would be paid in the degraded guineas, they would, on that account, experience no rise.

The remedy which I propose for all the evils in our currency, is that the Bank should gradually decrease the amount of their notes in circulation until they shall have rendered the remainder of equal value with the coins which they represent, or, in other words, till the prices of gold and silver bullion shall be brought down to their mint price. I am well aware that the total failure of paper credit would be attended with the most disastrous consequences to the trade and commerce of the country, and even its sudden limitation would occasion so much ruin and distress, that it would be highly inexpedient to have recourse to it as the means of restoring our currency to its just and equitable value.

If the Bank were possessed of more guineas than they had notes in circulation, they could not, without great injury to the country, pay their notes in specie, while the price of gold bullion continued greatly above the mint price, and the foreign exchanges unfavourable to us. The excess of our currency would be exchanged for guineas at the Bank and exported, and would be suddenly withdrawn from circulation. Before therefore they can safely pay in specie, the excess of notes must be gradually withdrawn from circulation. If gradually done, little inconvenience would be felt; so that the principle were fairly admitted, it would be for future consideration whether the object should be accomplished in one year or in five. I am fully persuaded that we shall never restore our currency to its equitable state, but by this preliminary step, or by the total overthrow of our paper credit.

If the Bank directors had kept the amount of their notes within reasonable bounds; *if they had acted up to the principle which they have avowed to have been that which regulated their issues when they were obliged to pay their notes in specie, namely, to limit their notes to that amount which should prevent the excess of the market above the mint price of gold, we should not have been now exposed to all the evils of a depreciated and perpetually varying currency.*

Though the Bank derive considerable advantage from the present system, though the price of their capital stock has nearly doubled since 1797, and their dividends have proportionally increased, I am ready to admit with Mr. Thornton, that the directors, as monied men, sustain losses in common with others by a depreciation of the currency, much more serious to them than any advantages which they may reap from it as proprietors of Bank stock. I do therefore acquit them of being influenced by interested motives, but their mistakes, if they are such, are in their effects quite as pernicious to the community.

The extraordinary powers with which they are entrusted, enable them to regulate at their pleasure the price at which those who are possessed of a particular kind of property, called money, shall dispose of it. The Bank directors have imposed upon these holders of money all the evils of a maximum. To-day it is their pleasure that 4*l.* 10*s.* shall pass for 3*l.* 17*s.* 10½*d.*, to-morrow they may degrade 4*l.* 15*s.* to the same value, and in another year 10*l.* may not be worth more. By what an insecure tenure is property consisting of money or annuities paid in money held? What security has the public creditor that the interest on the public debt, which is now paid in a medium depreciated fifteen per cent., may not hereafter be paid in one degraded fifty per cent.? The injury to private creditors is not less serious. A debt contracted in 1797 may now be paid with eighty-five per cent. of its amount, and who shall say that the depreciation will go no further?

The following observations of Dr. Smith on this subject are so important, that I cannot but recommend them to the serious attention of all thinking men.

" The raising the denomination of the coin has been the " most usual expedient by which a real public bankruptcy " has been disguised under the appearance of a pretended " payment. If a sixpence, for example, should either by " act of parliament or royal proclamation be raised to the

" denomination of a shilling, and twenty sixpences to that of " a pound sterling, the person who under the old denomina- " tion had borrowed twenty shillings, or near four ounces of " silver, would, under the new, pay with twenty sixpences, or " with something less than two ounces. A national debt of " about a hundred and twenty millions, nearly the capital of " the funded debt of Great Britain, might in this manner be " paid with about sixty-four millions of our present money. " It would indeed be a pretended payment only, and the " creditors of the public would be defrauded of ten shillings " in the pound of what was due to them. The calamity " too would extend much further than to the creditors of the " public, and those of every private person would suffer a " proportionable loss; and this without any advantage, but " in most cases with a great additional loss, to the creditors " of the public. If the creditors of the public indeed were " generally much in debt to other people, they might in some " measure compensate their loss by paying their creditors " in the same coin in which the public had paid them. But " in most countries the creditors of the public are the greater " part of them wealthy people, who stand more in the rela- " tion of creditors than in that of debtors towards the rest of " their fellow-citizens. A pretended payment of this kind, " therefore, instead of alleviating, aggravates in most cases " the loss of the creditors of the public; and without any " advantage to the public, extends the calamity to a great " number of other innocent people. It occasions a general " and most pernicious subversion of the fortunes of private " people; enriching in most cases the idle and profuse debtor " at the expence of the industrious and frugal creditor, and " transporting a great part of the national capital from the " hands which are likely to increase and improve it, to those " which are likely to dissipate and destroy it. When it " becomes necessary for a state to declare itself bankrupt, in " the same manner as when it becomes necessary for an indi- " vidual to do so, a fair, open, and avowed bankruptcy is " always the measure which is both least dishonourable to " the debtor, and least hurtful to the creditor. The honour "of a state is surely very poorly provided for, when in order "to cover the disgrace of a real bankruptcy, it has recourse "to a juggling trick of this kind, so easily seen through, and "at the same time so extremely pernicious."

These observations of Dr. Smith on a debased money are equally applicable to a depreciated paper currency. He has enumerated but a few of the disastrous consequences which attend the debasement of the circulating medium, but he has sufficiently warned us against trying such dangerous experiments. It will be a circumstance ever to be lamented, if this great country, having before its eyes the consequences of a forced paper circulation in America and France, should persevere in a system pregnant with so much disaster. Let us hope that she will be more wise. It is said indeed that the cases are dissimilar: that the Bank of England is independent of government. If this were true, the evils of a superabundant circulation would not be less felt; but it may be questioned whether a Bank lending many millions more to government than its capital and savings can be called independent of that government.

When the order of council for suspending the cash payments became necessary in 1797, the run upon the Bank was, in my opinion, caused by political alarm alone, and not by a superabundant, or a deficient quantity (as some have supposed) of their notes in circulation.*

This is a danger to which the Bank, from the nature of its institution, is at all times liable. No prudence on the part of the directors could perhaps have averted it: but if their loans to government had been more limited; if the same amount of notes had been issued to the public through the medium of discounts; they would have been able, in all probability, to have continued their payments till the alarm had subsided. At any rate, as the debtors to the Bank would have been obliged to discharge their debts in the space of sixty days, that being the longest period for which any bill discounted by the Bank has to run, the directors would in

* At that period the price of gold kept steadily under its mint price.

that time, if necessary, have been enabled to redeem every note in circulation. It was then owing to the too intimate connection between the Bank and government that the restriction became necessary; it is to that cause too that we owe its continuance.

To prevent the evil consequences which may attend the perseverance in this system, we must keep our eyes steadily fixed on the repeal of the Restriction-bill.

The only legitimate security which the public can possess against the indiscretion of the Bank is to oblige them to pay their notes on demand in specie; and this can only be effected by diminishing the amount of bank-notes in circulation till the nominal price of gold be lowered to the mint price.

Here I will conclude; happy if my feeble efforts should awaken the public attention to a due consideration of the state of our circulating medium. I am well aware that I have not added to the stock of information with which the public has been enlightened by many able writers on the same important subject. I have had no such ambition. My aim has been to introduce a calm and dispassionate enquiry into a question of great importance to the state, and the neglect of which may be attended with consequences which every friend of his country would deplore.

FINIS.

REPORT,

FROM

The Select Committee

OF THE

HOUSE OF COMMONS,

ON THE

HIGH PRICE

OF

GOLD BULLION.

Ordered to be printed, 8 June 1810.

THE following are the Names of the Members who formed the Bullion Committee:

F. HORNER, Esq., Chairman.
Rt. Hon. S. PERCEVAL, Chancellor of the Exchequer.
Rt. Hon. G. TIERNEY.
Earl TEMPLE.
Hon. T. BRAND.
H. PARNELL, Esq.
D. M. MAGENS, Esq.
G. JOHNSTONE, Esq.
D. GIDDY, Esq. (in the room of the Rt. Hon. G. ROSE, who declined.)
W. DICKINSON, Esq.
H. THORNTON, Esq.
Rt. Hon. R. B. SHERIDAN.
A. BARING, Esq.
W. MANNING, Esq.
R. SHARP, Esq.
P. GRENFELL, Esq.
J. L. FORSTER, Esq.
T. THOMPSON, Esq.
J. IRVING, Esq.
W. HUSKISSON, Esq.
Hon. J. ABERCROMBIE.

THE SELECT COMMITTEE appointed to enquire into the Cause of the High Price of GOLD BULLION, and to take into consideration the State of the CIRCULATING MEDIUM, and of the EXCHANGES between Great Britain and Foreign Parts;—and to report the same, with their Observations thereupon, from time to time, to The House;—HAVE, pursuant to the Orders of The House, examined the matters to them referred; and have agreed to the following REPORT:

YOUR Committee proceeded, in the first instance, to ascertain what the price of Gold Bullion had been, as well as the rates of the Foreign Exchanges, for some time past; particularly during the last year.

Your Committee have found that the price of Gold Bullion, which, by the regulations of His Majesty's Mint, is 3*l.* 17*s.* 10½*d.* per ounce of standard fineness, was, during the years 1806, 1807 and 1808, as high as 4*l.* in the market. Towards the end of 1808 it began to advance very rapidly, and continued very high during the whole year 1809; the market price of standard Gold in bars fluctuating from 4*l.* 9*s.* to 4*l.* 12*s.* per oz. The market price at 4*l.* 10*s.* is about 15½ per cent. above the Mint price.

Your Committee have found, that during the three first months of the present year, the price of standard Gold in bars remained nearly at the same price as during last year; viz. from 4*l.* 10*s.* to 4*l.* 12*s.* per oz. In the course of the months of March and April, the price of standard Gold is quoted but once in Wettenhall's tables; viz. on the 6th of April last, at 4*l.* 6*s.* which is rather more than 10 per cent. above the Mint price. The last quotations of the price of Gold, which have been given in those tables, are upon the 18th and 22d of May, when Portugal Gold in coin is quoted at 4*l.* 11*s.* per oz.: Portugal Gold coin is about the same fineness as our standard. It is stated in the same tables, that in the month of March last, the price of new Doubloons rose from 4*l.* 7*s.* to 4*l.* 9*s.* per oz. Spanish Gold is from 4½ to 4¾ grains better than standard, making about 4*s.* per oz. difference in value.

It appears by the Evidence, that the price of foreign Gold coin is generally higher than that of bar Gold, on account of the former finding a more ready vent in foreign markets. The difference between Spanish and Portugal Gold in coin and Gold in bars, has of late been about 2*s.* per ounce. Your Committee have also to state, that there is said to be at present a difference of between 3*s.* and 4*s.* per ounce between the price of bar Gold which may be sworn off for exportation as being foreign Gold, and the price of such bar Gold as the Dealer will not venture to swear off; while the former was about 4*l.* 10*s.* in the market, the latter is said to have been about 4*l.* 6*s.* On account of these extrinsic differences, occasioned either by the expense of coinage, or by the obstructions of law, the price of standard Gold in bars, such as may be exported, is that which it is most material to keep generally in view through the present enquiry.

It appeared to Your Committee, that it might be of use, in judging of the cause of this high price of Gold Bullion, to be informed also of the prices of Silver during the same period. The price of standard Silver in His Majesty's Mint is 5*s.* 2*d.* per ounce; at this standard price, the value of a Spanish Dollar is 4*s.* 4*d.* or, which comes to the same thing, Spanish Dollars are, at that standard price, worth 4*s.* 11½*d.* per ounce. It is stated in Wettenhall's tables, that throughout the year 1809, the price of new Dollars fluctuated from 5*s.* 5*d.* to 5*s.* 7*d.* per ounce, or from 10 to 13 per cent. above the Mint price of standard Silver. In the course of the last month, new Dollars have been quoted as high as 5*s.* 8*d.* per ounce, or more than 15 per cent. above the Mint price.

Your Committee have likewise found, that towards the end of the year 1808, the Exchanges with the Continent became very unfavourable to this Country, and continued still more unfavourable through the whole of 1809, and the three first months of the present year.

Hamburgh, Amsterdam, and Paris, are the principal places with which the Exchanges are established at present. During the last six months of 1809, and the three first months of the present year, the Exchanges on Hamburgh and Amsterdam were depressed as low as from 16 to 20 per cent. below par; and that on Paris still lower. The Exchanges with Portugal have corresponded with the others; but they are complicated by some circumstances which shall be explained separately.

Your Committee find, that in the course of the month of March last, that is, from the 2d of March to the 3d April, the Exchanges with the three places above mentioned received a gradual improvement. The Exchange with Hamburgh rose gradually from 29. 4. to 31.; that with Amsterdam from 31. 8. to 33. 5.; that with Paris from 19. 16. to 21. 11. Since the 3d of April last to the present time, they have remained nearly stationary at those rates, the Exchange with Hamburgh, as stated in the tables printed for the use of the Merchants, appearing as much against this Country as 9*l.* per cent. below par; that with Amsterdam appearing to be more than 7*l.* per cent. below par; and that with Paris more than 14*l.* per cent. below par.

So extraordinary a rise in the market price of Gold in this Country, coupled with so remarkable a depression of our Exchanges with the Continent, very early, in the judgment of Your Committee, pointed to something in the state of our own domestic currency as the cause of both appearances. But before they adopted that conclusion, which seemed agreeable to all former reasonings and experience, they thought it proper to enquire more particularly into the circumstances connected with each of those two facts; and to hear, from persons of commercial practice and detail, what explanations they had to offer of so unusual a state of things.

With this view, Your Committee called before them several Merchants of extensive dealings and intelligence, and desired to have their opinions, with respect to the cause of the high price of Gold and the low rates of Exchange.

I.

It will be found by the Evidence, that the high price of Gold is ascribed, by most of the Witnesses, entirely to an alleged scarcity of that article, arising out of an unusual demand for it upon the Continent of Europe. This unusual demand for Gold upon the Continent is described by some of them as being chiefly for the use of the French Armies, though increased also by that state of alarm, and failure of confidence, which leads to the practice of hoarding.

Your Committee are of opinion, that, in the sound and natural state of the British currency, the foundation of which is gold, no increased demand for Gold from other parts of the world, however great, or from whatever causes arising, can have the effect of producing here, for a considerable period of time, a material rise in the market price of Gold. But before they proceed to explain the grounds of that general opinion, they wish to state some other reasons which alone would have led them to doubt whether, in point of fact, such a demand for Gold, as is alleged, has operated in the manner supposed.

If there were an unusual demand for Gold upon the Continent, such as could influence its market price in this country, it would of course influence also, and indeed in the first instance, its price in the Continental markets; and it was to be expected that those who ascribed the high price here to a great demand abroad, would have been prepared to state that there was a corresponding high price abroad. Your Committee did not find that they grounded their inference upon any such information; and so far as Your Committee have been enabled to ascertain, it does not appear that during the period when the price of Gold Bullion was rising here, as valued in our paper, there was any corresponding rise in the price of Gold Bullion in the market of the Continent, as valued in their respective currencies, *Mr. Whitmore*, indeed, the late Governor of the Bank, stated, that in his opinion it was the high price abroad which had carried our Gold coin out of this Country; but he did not offer to Your Committee any proof of this high price. *Mr. Greffulhe,* a Continental Merchant, who appeared to be remarkably well informed in the details of trade, being asked by the Committee, If he could state whether any change had taken place in the price of Gold in any of the foreign markets within the last year? answered, "No very material change that I am aware of." Upon a subsequent day, having had time to refer to the actual prices, he again stated to the Committee, "I beg leave to observe, that there has been "no alteration of late in the Mint price of Gold in foreign "places, nor have the market prices experienced an advance "at all relative to the rise that has taken place in England; "one of the papers I have delivered shews the foreign "prices reduced into sterling money at the present low rates "of Exchange, and the excess above our market price may "be considered as about equal to the charges of conveyance." The paper he refers to, and the statement made by Mr. Greffulhe throws great light upon this part of the subject; as it shews, that the actual prices of Gold in the foreign markets are just so much lower than its market price here, as the difference of Exchange amounts to. Mr. Greffulhe's paper is confirmed by another, which has been laid before Your Committee. *Mr. Abraham Goldsmid* has also stated to Your Committee, that, during that part of last year when the market price of Gold here rose so high, its price at Hamburgh did not fluctuate more than from 3 to 4 per cent.

Here Your Committee must observe, that both at Hamburgh and Amsterdam, where the measure of value is not Gold as in this Country, but Silver, an unusual demand for Gold would affect its money price, that is, its price in Silver; and that as it does not appear that there has been any considerable rise in the price of Gold, as valued in Silver, at those places in the last year, the inference is, that there was not any considerable increase in the demand for Gold. That permanent rise in the market price of Gold above its Mint price, which appears by Mr. Greffulhe's paper to have taken place for several years both at Hamburgh and Amsterdam, may in some degree be ascribed, as Your Committee conceive, to an alteration which has taken place in the relative value of the two precious metals all over the world; concerning which, much curious and satisfactory Evidence will be found in the documents laid before Your Committee by Mr. Allen. From the same cause, a fall in the relative price of Silver appears to have taken place in this Country for some time before the increase of our paper currency began to operate. Silver having fallen in its relative value to Gold throughout the world, Gold has appeared to rise in price in those markets where Silver is the fixed measure, and Silver has appeared to fall in those where Gold is the fixed measure.

With respect to the alleged demand for Gold upon the Continent for the supply of the French Armies, Your Committee must further observe, that, if the wants of the military chest have been latterly much increased, the general supply of Europe with Gold has been augmented by all that quantity which this great commercial Country has spared in consequence of the substitution of another medium of circulation. And Your Committee cannot omit remarking, that though the circumstances which might occasion such an increased demand may recently have existed in greater force than at former periods, yet in the former wars and convulsions of the Continent, they must have existed in such a degree as to produce some effect. *Sir Francis Baring* has very justly referred to the seven years war and to the American war, and remarks, that no want of Bullion was then felt in this Country. And upon referring for a course of years to the tables which are published for the use of the Merchants, such as Lloyd's Lists and Wettenhall's Course of Exchange, Your Committee have found that from the middle of the year 1773, when the reformation of the Gold coin took place, till about the middle of the year 1799, two years after the suspension of the cash payments of the Bank, the market price of standard Gold in bars remained steadily uniform at the price of 3*l.* 17*s.* 6*d.* [being, with the small allowance for loss by detention at the Mint, equal to the

8

Mint price of 3*l.* 17*s.* 10½*d.*] with the exception of one year, from May 1783 to May 1784, when it was occasionally 3*l.* 18*s.* During the same period it is to be noticed, the price of Portugal Gold coin was occasionally as high as 4*l.* 2*s.*; and Your Committee also observe, that it was stated to the Lords' Committee in 1797 by Mr. Abraham Newland, that the Bank had been frequently obliged to buy Gold higher than the Mint price, and upon one particular occasion gave as much for a small quantity, which their agent procured from Portugal, as 4*l.* 8*s.* But Your Committee find, that the price of standard Gold in bars was never for any length of time materially above the Mint price, during the whole period of 24 years which elapsed from the reformation of the Gold coin to the suspension of the cash payments of the Bank. The two most remarkable periods prior to the present, when the market price of Gold in this country has exceeded our Mint price, were in the reign of King William, when the Silver coin was very much worn below its standard, and in the early part of His present Majesty's reign, when the Gold coin was very much worn below its standard. In both those periods, the excess of the market price of Gold above its Mint price was found to be owing to the bad state of the currency; and in both instances, the reformation of the currency effectually lowered the market price of Gold to the level of the Mint price. During the whole of the years 1796 and 1797, in which there was such a scarcity of Gold, occasioned by the great demands of the country Bankers in order to increase their deposits, the market price of Gold never rose above the Mint price.

Your Committee have still further to remark upon this point, that the Evidence laid before them has led them to entertain much doubt of the alleged fact, that a scarcity of Gold Bullion has been recently experienced in this country. That Guineas have disappeared from the circulation, there can be no question; but that does not prove a scarcity of Bullion, any more than the high price proves that scarcity. If Gold is rendered dear by any other cause than scarcity, those who cannot purchase it without paying the high price, will be very apt to conclude that it is scarce. A very extensive home dealer who was examined, and who spoke very much of the scarcity of Gold, acknowledged, that he found no difficulty in getting any quantity he wanted, if he was willing to pay the price for it. And it appears to Your Committee, that, though in the course of the last year there have been large exportations of Gold to the Continent, there have been also very considerable importations of it into this Country from South America, chiefly through the West Indies. The changes which have affected Spain and Portugal, combined with our maritime and commercial advantages, would seem to have rendered this country a channel through which the produce of the mines of New Spain and the Brazils passes to the rest of the world. In such a situation, the imports of Bullion and Coin give us the opportunity of first supplying ourselves; and must render this the last of the great markets in which a scarcity of that article will be felt. This is remarkably illustrated by the fact, that Portugal Gold coin is now sent regularly from this Country to the Cotton Settlements in the Brazils, Pernambuco, and Maranham, while Dollars are remitted in considerable quantities to this country from Rio Janiero.

It is important also to observe, that the rise in the market price of Silver in this country, which has nearly corresponded to that of the market price of Gold, cannot in any degree be ascribed to a scarcity of Silver. The importations of Silver have of late years been unusually large, while the usual drain for India and China has been stopped.

For all these reasons, Your Committee would be inclined to think, that those who ascribe the high price of Gold to an unusual demand for that article, and a consequent scarcity, assume facts as certain of which there is no evidence. But even if these assumptions were proved,—to ascribe the high price of Gold in this Country to its scarcity, seems to your Committee to involve a misconception, which they think it important to explain.

In this Country, Gold is itself the measure of all exchangeable value, the scale to which all money prices are referred. It is so, not only by the usage and commercial habits of the country, but likewise by operation of law, ever since the Act of the 14th of His present Majesty [finally rendered perpetual by an Act of the 39th year of the reign] disallowed a legal tender in Silver coin beyond the sum of 25*l.* Gold being thus our measure of prices, a commodity is said to be dear or cheap according as more or less Gold is given in exchange for a given quantity of that commodity; but a given quantity of Gold itself will never be exchanged for a greater or a less quantity of Gold of the same standard fineness. At particular times it may be convenient, in exchange for Gold in a particular coin, to give more than an equal quantity of other Gold; but this difference can never exceed a certain small limit: and thus it has happened that the Bank, while liable to pay its notes in specie, has under particular emergencies been put to the necessity of purchasing Gold at a loss, in order to keep up or to repair its stock. But, generally speaking, the price of Gold, being itself measured and expressed in Gold, cannot be raised or lowered by an increased or diminished demand for it. An ounce of Gold will exchange for neither more nor less than an ounce of Gold of the same fineness, except so far as an allowance is to be made, if the one ounce is coined or otherwise manufactured and the other is not, for the expence of that coinage or manufacture. An ounce of standard Gold Bullion will not fetch more in our market than 3*l.* 17*s.* 10½*d.*, unless 3*l.* 17*s.* 10½*d.* in our actual currency is equivalent to less than an ounce of Gold. An increase or diminution in the demand for Gold, or, what comes to the same thing, a diminution or increase in the general supply of Gold, will, no doubt, have a material effect upon the money prices of all other articles. An increased demand for Gold, and a consequent scarcity of that article, will make it more valuable in proportion to all other articles; the same quantity of Gold will purchase a greater quantity of any other article than it did before: in other words, the real price of Gold, or the quantity of commodities given in exchange for it, will rise, and the money prices of all commodities will fall; the money price of Gold itself will remain unaltered, but the prices of all other commodities will fall. That this is not the present state of things is abundantly manifest; the prices of all commodities have risen and Gold appears to have risen in its price only in common with them. If this common effect is to be ascribed to one and the same cause, that cause can only be found in the state of the currency of this Country.

Your Committee think it proper to state still more specifically, what appear to them to be the principles which govern the relative prices of Gold in Bullion and Gold in Coin, as well as of Paper circulating in its place and exchangeable for it. They cannot introduce this subject more properly, than by adverting to those simple principles and regulations, on which a coinage issuing from the King's Mint is founded.

The object is, to secure to the people a standard of a determinate value, by affixing a stamp, under the Royal authority, to pieces of Gold, which are thus certified to be of a given weight and fineness. Gold in Bullion is the standard to which the Legislature has intended that the coin should be conformed, and with which it should be identified as much as possible. And if that intention of the Legislature were completely fulfilled, the coined Gold would bear precisely the same price in exchange for all other commodities, as it would have borne had it continued in the shape of Bullion; but it is subject to some small fluctuations.

First, there is some expense incurred in converting Bullion into coin. Those who send Bullion to be coined, and it is allowed to any one to send it, though they are charged with no seignorage, incur a loss of interest by the detention of their Gold in the Mint. This loss may hitherto have amounted to about 1*l.* per cent., but it is to be presumed that the improvements of the system of the new Mint will cause the detention and consequent loss to be much smaller. This 1*l.* per cent. has formed the limit, or nearly the limit, to the possible rise of the value of coin above that of Bullion; for to suppose that coin could, through any cause, advance much above this limit, would be to assume that there was a high profit on a transaction, in which there is no risk, and every one has an opportunity of engaging.

The two following circumstances conjoined, account for the depression of the Coin below the price of Bullion, and will shew what must have been the limit to its extent before 1797, the period of the suspension of the Cash payments of the Bank of England. First, the Coin, after it had become current, was gradually diminished in weight by use, and therefore if melted would produce a less quantity of Bullion. The average diminution of weight of the present current Gold Coin below that of the same Coin when fresh from the Mint, appears by the Evidence to be nearly 1*l.* per cent. This evil, in more ancient times, was occasionally very great. It was particularly felt in an early period of His present Majesty's reign, and led to the reformation of the Gold Coin in 1773. But it is now carefully guarded against, not only by the legal punishment of every wilful deterioration of the Gold Coin, but also by the regulation of the Statute, that Guineas, of which the full weight when fresh from the Mint is 5 dwts. 9 $\frac{39}{89}$ grains, shall not be a legal tender if worn below 5 dwts. 8 grs.; the depreciation thus allowed being at the utmost 1·11 per cent. A still more material cause of depression is the difficulty under which the holders of Coin have been placed when they wished to convert it into Bullion. The Law of this Country forbids any other Gold Coin than that which has become light to be put into the melting pot, and, with a very questionable policy, prohibits the exportation of our Gold Coin, and of any Gold, unless an oath is taken that it has not been produced from the Coin of this realm. It appears by the Evidence, that the difference between the value of Gold Bullion which may be sworn off for exportation, and that of the Gold produced or supposed to be produced from our own Coin, which by Law is convertible only to domestic purposes, amounts at present to between 3*s.* and 4*s.* per ounce.

The two circumstances which have now been mentioned have unquestionably constituted, in the judgment of Your Committee, the whole cause of that depression of the value of the Gold Coin of this Country in exchange for commodities, below the value of Bullion in exchange for commodities, which has occasionally arisen or could arise at those times when the Bank paid in specie, and Gold was consequently obtainable in the quantity that was desired; and the limit fixed, by those two circumstances conjoined, to this excess of the market price of Gold above the Mint price, was therefore a limit of about 5½ per cent. The chief part of this depression is to be ascribed to that ancient but doubtful policy of this Country, which, by attempting to confine the Coin within the Kingdom, has served, in the same manner as permanent restrictions on the export of other articles, to place it under a disadvantage, and to give to it a less value in the market than the same article would have if subject to no such prohibition.

The truth of these observations on the causes and limits of the ordinary difference between the market and Mint price of Gold, may be illustrated by a reference to the mode, explained in the Evidence, of securing a fixed standard of value for the great commercial payments of Hamburgh. The payments in the ordinary transactions of life are made in a currency composed of the coins of the several surrounding States; but Silver is the standard there resorted to in the great commercial payments, as Gold is in England. No difference analogous to that which occurs in this Country, between the Mint and market price of Gold, can ever arise at Hamburgh with regard to Silver, because provision is made that none of the three causes above specified, [the expense of coinage, the depreciation by wear, or the obstruction to exportation] shall have any operation. The large payments of Hamburgh are effected in Bank money, which consists of actual Silver of a given fineness, lodged in the Hamburgh Bank by the merchants of the place, who thereupon have a proportionate credit in the Bank books, which they transfer according to their occasions. The Silver being assayed and weighed with scarcely any loss of time, the first-mentioned cause of fluctuation in the relative value of the current medium compared with Bullion is avoided. Certain masses of it being then certified (without any stamp being affixed on the metal) to be of a given quantity and fineness, the value is transferred from individual to individual by the medium merely of the Bank books, and thus the wearing of the Coin being prevented, one cause of depreciation is removed. A free right is also given to withdraw, melt, and export it; and thus the other and principal source of the occasional fall of the value of the current medium of payment, below that of the Bullion which it is intended to represent, is also effectually precluded.

In this manner, at Hamburgh, Silver is not only the measure of all exchangeable value, but it is rendered an invariable measure, except in so far as the relative value of Silver itself varies with the varying supply of that precious metal from the mines. In the same manner the usage, and at last the law, which made Gold Coin the usual and at last the only legal tender in large payments here, rendered that metal our measure of value: and from the period of the reformation of the Gold Coin down to the suspension of the Bank payments in specie in 1797, Gold Coin was not a very variable measure of value; being subject only to that variation in the relative value of Gold Bullion which depends upon its supply from the mines, together with that limited variation which, as above described, might take place between the market and the Mint price of Gold Coin.

The highest amount of the depression of the Coin which can take place when the Bank pays in Gold, has just been stated to be about 5½ per cent.; and accordingly it will be found, that in all the periods preceding 1797, the difference between what is called the Mint price and market price of Gold never exceeded that limit.

Since the suspension of Cash payments in 1797, however, it is certain, that, even if Gold is still our measure of value and standard of prices, it has been exposed to a new cause of variation, from the possible excess of that paper

15

which is not convertible into Gold at will; and the limit of this new variation is as indefinite as the excess to which that paper may be issued. It may indeed be doubted, whether, since the new system of Bank of England payments has been fully established, Gold has in truth continued to be our measure of value; and whether we have any other standard of prices than that circulating medium, issued primarily by the Bank of England and in a secondary manner by the country Banks, the variations of which in relative value may be as indefinite as the possible excess of that circulating medium. But whether our present measure of value, and standard of prices, be this paper currency thus variable in its relative value, or continues still to be Gold, but Gold rendered more variable than it was before in consequence of being interchangeable for a paper currency which is not at will convertible into Gold, it is, in either case, most desirable for the public that our circulating medium should again be conformed, as speedily as circumstances will permit, to its real and legal standard, Gold Bullion.

If the Gold Coin of the Country were at any time to become very much worn and lessened in weight, or if it should suffer a debasement of its standard, it is evident that there would be a proportionable rise of the market price of Gold Bullion above its Mint price: for the Mint price is the sum in coin, which is equivalent in intrinsic value to a given quantity, an ounce for example, of the metal in Bullion; and if the intrinsic value of that sum of Coin be lessened, it is equivalent to a less quantity of Bullion than before. The same rise of the market price of Gold above its Mint price will take place, if the local currency of this particular Country, being no longer convertible into Gold, should at any time be issued to excess. That excess cannot be exported to other countries, and, not being convertible into specie, it is not necessarily returned upon those who issued it; it remains in the channel of circulation, and is gradually absorbed by increasing the prices of all commodities. An increase in the quantity of the local currency of a particular country, will raise prices in that country exactly in the same manner as an increase in the general supply of precious metals raises prices all over the world. By means of the increase of quantity, the value of a given portion of that circulating medium, in exchange for other commodities, is lowered; in other words, the money prices of all other commodities are raised, and that of Bullion with the rest. In this manner, an excess of the local currency of a particular country will occasion a rise of the market price of Gold above its Mint price. It is no less evident, that, in the event of the prices of commodities being raised in one country by an augmentation of its circulating medium, while no similar augmentation in the circulating medium of a neighbouring country has led to a similar rise of prices, the currencies of those two countries will no longer continue to bear the same relative value to each other as before. The intrinsic value of a given portion of the one currency being lessened, while that of the other remains unaltered, the Exchange will be computed between those two countries to the disadvantage of the former.

In this manner a general rise of all prices, a rise in the market price of Gold, and a fall of the Foreign Exchanges, will be the effect of an excessive quantity of circulating medium in a country which has adopted a currency not exportable to other countries, or not convertible at will into a Coin which is exportable.

II.

Your Committee are thus led to the next head of their inquiry; the present state of the Exchanges between this Country and the Continent. And here, as under the former head, Your Committee will first state the opinions which they have received from practical men, respecting the causes of the present state of the Exchange.

Mr. Greffulhe, a general merchant, trading chiefly to the Continent, ascribed the fall of Exchange between London and Hamburgh, near 18 per cent. below par, in the year 1809, "altogether to the commercial situation of this Country

" with the Continent; to the circumstance of the imports, and " payments of Subsidies, &c. having very much exceeded " the exports." He stated, however, that he formed his judgment of the balance of trade in a great measure from the state of the Exchange itself, though it was corroborated by what fell under his observation. He insisted particularly on the large imports from the Baltic, and the wines and brandies brought from France, in return for which no merchandize had been exported from this Country. He observed on the other hand, that the export of Colonial produce to the Continent had increased in the last year compared with former years; and that during the last year there was an excess, to a considerable amount, of the exports of colonial produce and British manufactures to Holland above the imports from thence, but not nearly equal, he thought, to the excess of imports from other parts of the world, judging from the state of the Exchange as well as from what fell generally under his observation. He afterwards explained, that it was not strictly the balance of trade, but the balance of payments, being unfavourable to this Country, which he assigned as the principal cause of the rate of Exchange; observing also, that the balance of payments for the year may be against us, while the general exports exceed the imports. He gave it as his opinion, that the cause of the present state of Exchange was entirely commercial, with the addition of the foreign expenditure of Government; and that an excess of imports above exports would account for the rates of Exchange continuing so high as 16 per cent. against this country, for a permanent period of time.

It will be found in the Evidence, that several other Witnesses agree in substance with *Mr. Greffulhe*, in this explanation of the unfavourable state of the Exchange; particularly *Mr. Chambers* and *Mr. Coningham.*

Sir Francis Baring stated to the Committee, that he considered the two great circumstances which affect the Exchange in its present unfavourable state, to be the restrictions upon trade with the Continent, and the increased circulation of this Country in paper as productive of the scarcity of Bullion. And he instanced, as examples of a contrary state of things, the seven years war, and the American war, in which there were the same remittances to make to the Continent for naval and military expenditure, yet no want of Bullion was ever felt.

The Committee likewise examined a very eminent Continental Merchant, whose evidence will be found to contain a variety of valuable information. That Gentleman states, that the Exchange cannot fall in any country in Europe at the present time, if computed in coin of a definitive value, or in something convertible into such coin, lower than the extent of the charge of transporting it, together with an adequate profit in proportion to the risk attending such transmission. He conceives that such fall of our Exchange as has exceeded that extent in the last 15 months, must certainly be referred to the circumstance of our paper currency not being convertible into specie; and that if that paper had been so convertible, and Guineas had been in general circulation, an unfavourable balance of trade could hardly have caused so great a fall in the Exchange as to the extent of 5 or 6 per cent. He explains his opinion upon the subject more specifically in the following Answers, which are extracted from different parts of his Evidence.

"To what causes do you ascribe the present unfavourable course of Exchange?—The first great depreciation took place when the French got possession of the North of Germany, and passed severe penal decrees against a communication with this Country; at the same time that a sequestration was laid upon all English goods and property, whilst the payments for English account were still to be made, and the reimbursements to be taken on this Country; many more bills were in consequence to be sold than could be taken by persons requiring to make payments in England. The communication by letters being also very difficult and uncertain, middle men were not to be found, as in usual times, to purchase and send such bills to England for returns; whilst no suit at law could be instituted in the

Courts of Justice there against any person who chose to resist payment of a returned bill, or to dispute the charges of re-exchange. Whilst those causes depressed the Exchange, payments due to England only came round at distant periods; the Exchange once lowered by those circumstances, and Bullion being withheld in England to make up those occasional differences, the operations between this Country and the Continent have continued at a low rate, as it is only matter of opinion what rate a pound sterling is there to be valued at, not being able to obtain what it is meant to represent."

"The Exchange against England fluctuating from 15 to 20 per cent. how much of that loss may be ascribed to the effect of the measures taken by the enemy in the North of Germany, and the interruption of intercourse which has been the result, and how much to the effect of the Bank of England paper not being convertible into cash, to which you have ascribed a part of that depreciation?—I ascribe the whole of the depreciation to have taken place originally in consequence of the measures of the enemy; and its not having recovered, to the circumstance of the paper of England not being exchangeable for cash."

"Since the conduct of the enemy which you have described, what other causes have continued to operate on the Continent to lower the course of Exchange?—Very considerable shipments from the Baltic, which were drawn for and the bills negotiated immediately on the shipments taking place, without consulting the interest of the Proprietors in this country much, by deferring such a negotiation till a demand should take place for such bills: The continued difficulty and uncertainty in carrying on the correspondence between this Country and the Continent: The curtailed number of houses to be found on the Continent willing to undertake such operations, either by accepting bills for English account drawn from the various parts where shipments take place, or by accepting bills drawn from this Country, either against property shipped, or on a speculative idea that the Exchange either ought or is likely to rise: The length of time that is required before goods can be converted into cash, from the circuitous routes they are obliged to take: The very large sums of money paid to foreign Ship Owners, which in some instances, such as on the article of Hemp, has amounted to nearly its prime cost in Russia: The want of middle men who as formerly used to employ great capitals in Exchange operations, who, from the increased difficulties and dangers to which such operations are now subject, are at present rarely to be met with, to make combined exchange operations, which tend to anticipate probable ultimate results."

The preceding Answers, and the rest of this Gentleman's Evidence, all involve this principle, expressed more or less distinctly, that Bullion is the true regulator both of the value of a local currency and of the rate of Foreign Exchanges; and that the free convertibility of paper currency into the precious metals, and the free exportation of those metals, place a limit to the fall of Exchange, and not only check the Exchanges from falling below that limit, but recover them by restoring the balance.

Your Committee need not particularly point out in what respects these opinions, received from persons of practical detail, are vague and unsatisfactory, and in what respects they are contradictory of one another; considerable assistance however may bè derived from the information which the evidence of these persons affords, in explaining the true causes of the present state of the Exchanges.

Your Committee conceive that there is no point of trade, considered politically, which is better settled, than the subject of Foreign Exchanges. The PAR of Exchange between two Countries is that sum of the currency of either of the two, which, in point of intrinsic value, is precisely equal to a given sum of the currency of the other; that is, contains precisely an equal weight of Gold or Silver of the same fineness. If 25 livres of France contained precisely an equal quantity of pure Silver with twenty shillings sterling, 25 would be said to be the Par of Exchange between London and Paris. If one country uses Gold for its principal measure of value, and another uses Silver, the par between those countries cannot be estimated for any particular period, without taking into account the relative value of Gold and Silver at that particular period; and as the relative value of the two precious metals is subject to fluctuation, the Par of Exchange between two such countries is not strictly a fixed point, but fluctuates within certain limits. An illustration of this will be found in the Evidence, in the calculation of the Par between London and Hamburgh, which is estimated to be 34/3½ Flemish shillings for a pound sterling. That *rate* of exchange, which is produced at any particular period by a balance of trade or payments between the two countries, and by a consequent disproportion between the supply and the demand of bills drawn by the one upon the other, is a departure on one side or the other from the real and fixed Par. But this real Par will be altered if any change takes place in the currency of one of the two countries, whether that change consists in the wear or debasement of a metallic currency below its standard, or in the discredit of a forced paper currency, or in the excess of a paper currency not convertible into specie; a fall having taken place in the intrinsic value of a given portion of one currency, that portion will no longer be equal to the same portion, as before, of the other currency. But though the real Par of the currencies is thus altered, the dealers, having little or no occasion to refer to the par, continue to reckon their course of Exchanges from the former denomination of the par; and in this state of things a distinction is necessary to be made between the *real* and *computed* course of Exchange. The computed course of Exchange, as expressed in the tables used by the Merchants, will then include, not only the real difference of exchange arising from the state of trade, but likewise the difference between the original par and the new par. Those two sums may happen to be added together in the calculation, or they may happen to be set against each other. If the country whose currency has been depreciated in comparison with the other, has the balance of trade also against it, the computed rate of exchange will appear to be still more unfavourable than the real difference of exchange will be found to be; and so if that same country has the balance of trade in its favour, the computed rate of exchange will appear to be much less favourable than the real difference of exchange will be found to be. Before the new coinage of our silver in King William's time, the Exchange between England and Holland, computed in the usual manner according to the standard of their respective mints, was 25 per cent. against England; but the value of the current coin of England was more than 25 per cent. below the standard value; so that if that of Holland was at its full standard, the real exchange was in fact in favour of England. It may happen in the same manner, that the two parts of the calculation may be both opposite and equal, the real exchange in favour of the country by trade being equal to the nominal exchange against it by the state of its currency: in that case, the computed exchange will be at par, while the real exchange is in fact in favour of that country. Again, the currencies of both the countries which trade together may have undergone an alteration, and that either in an equal degree, or unequally: in such a case, the question of the real state of the exchange between them becomes a little more complicated, but it is to be resolved exactly upon the same principle. Without going out of the bounds of the present inquiry, this may be well illustrated by the present state of the Exchange of London with Portugal, as quoted in the tables for the 18th of May last. The exchange of London on Lisbon appears to be 67½; 67½*d.* sterling for a mill ree is the old established par of exchange between the two countries: and 67½ accordingly is still said to be the par. But by the evidence of *Mr. Lyne,* it appears, that, in Portugal, all payments are now by law made one-half in hard money, and one-half in Government paper; and that this paper is depreciated at a discount of 27 per cent. Upon all payments made in Portugal, therefore, there is a discount or loss of 13½ per cent.; and the exchange at 67½, though nominally at par, is in truth 13½ per cent. against this Country. If the exchange were really at par, it would be quoted at $56\frac{65}{100}$, or apparently $13\frac{1}{2}$ per cent. in favour of London, as compared with the old par which was fixed before the depreciation of the Portuguese medium of payments. Whether this $13\frac{1}{2}$ per cent. which stands against this Country by the present Exchange on Lisbon, is a real difference of Exchange, occasioned by the course of trade and by the remittances to Portugal on account of Government, or a nominal and apparent Exchange occasioned by something in the state of our own currency, or is partly real and partly nominal, may perhaps be determined by what Your Committee have yet to state.

It appears to Your Committee to have been long settled and understood as a principle, that the difference of Exchange resulting from the state of trade and payments between two countries is limited by the expence of conveying and insuring the precious metals from one country to the other; at least, that it cannot for any considerable length of time exceed that limit. The real difference of Exchange, resulting from the state of trade and payments, never can fall lower than the amount of such expence of carriage, including the Insurance. The truth of this position is so plain, and it is so uniformly agreed to by all the practical authorities, both commercial and political, that Your Committee will assume it as indisputable.

It occurred however to Your Committee, that the amount of that charge and premium of insurance might be increased above what it has been in ordinary periods even of war, by the peculiar circumstances which at present obstruct the commercial intercourse between this Country and the Continent of Europe; and that as such an increase would place so much lower than usual the limit to which our Exchanges might fall, an explanation might thereby be furnished of their present unusual fall. Your Committee accordingly directed their enquiries to this point.

It was stated to Your Committee, by the Merchant who has been already mentioned as being intimately acquainted with the trade between this Country and the Continent, that the present expence of transporting Gold from London to Hamburgh, independent of the premium of Insurance, is from 1½ to 2 per cent.; that the risk is very variable from day to day, so that there is no fixed premium, but he conceived the average risk, for the fifteen months preceding the time when he spoke, to have been about 4 per cent.: making the whole cost of sending Gold from London to Hamburgh for those fifteen months, at such average of the risk, from 5½ to 6 per cent.—*Mr. Abraham Goldsmid* stated, that in the last five or six months of the year 1809, the expence of sending Gold to Holland varied exceedingly from 4 to 7 per cent. for all charges, covering the risk as well as the costs of transportation. By the Evidence which was taken before the Committees upon the Bank affairs in 1797, it appears that the cost of sending specie from London to Hamburgh in that time of war, including all charges as well as an average insurance, was estimated at a little more than 3½ per cent. It is clear, therefore, that in consequence of the peculiar circumstances of the present state of the war, and the increased difficulties of intercourse with the Continent, the cost of transporting the precious metals thither from this Country has not only been rendered more fluctuating than it used to be, but, upon the whole, is very considerably increased. It would appear, however, that upon an average of the risk for that period when it seems to have been highest, the last half of the last year, the cost and insurance of transporting Gold to Hamburgh or to Holland did not exceed 7 per cent. It was of course greater at particular times, when the risk was above that average. It is evident also that the risk, and consequently the whole cost of transporting it to an inland market, to Paris for example, would, upon an average, be higher than that of carrying it to Amsterdam or Hamburgh. It follows, that the limit to which the Exchanges, as resulting from the state of trade, might fall and continue unfavourable for a considerable length of time, has, during the period in question, been a good deal lower than in former times of war; but it appears also, that the expence of remitting specie has not been increased so much, and that the limit, by which the depression of the Exchanges is bounded, has not been lowered so much, as to afford an adequate explanation of a fall of the Exchanges so great as from 16 to 20 per cent. below par. The increased cost of such remittance would explain, at those moments when the risk was greatest, a fall of something more than 7 per cent. in the Exchange with Hamburgh or Holland, and a fall still greater perhaps in the Exchange with Paris; but the rest of the fall, which has actually taken place, remains to be explained in some other manner.

Your Committee are disposed to think, from the result of the whole evidence, contradictory as it is, that the circumstances of the trade of this Country, in the course of the last year, were such as to occasion a real fall of our Exchanges with the Continent to a certain extent, and perhaps at one period almost as low as the limit fixed by the expence of remitting Gold from hence to the respective markets. And Your Committee are inclined to this opinion, both by what is stated regarding the excess of imports from the Continent above the exports, though that is the part of the subject which is left most in doubt; and also by what is stated respecting the mode in which the payments in our trade have been latterly effected, an advance being paid upon the imports from the Continent of Europe, and a long credit being given upon the exports to other parts of the world.

Your Committee, observing how entirely the present depression of our Exchange with Europe is referred by many persons to a great excess of our imports above our exports, have called for an account of the actual value of those for the last five years; and Mr. Irving, the Inspector-General of Customs, has accordingly furnished the most accurate Estimate of both that he has been enabled to form. He has also endeavoured to forward the object of the Committee, by calculating how much should be deducted from the value of goods imported, on account of articles in return for which nothing is exported. These deductions consist of the produce of Fisheries, and of imports from the East and West Indies, which are of the nature of rents, profits, and capital remitted to Proprietors in this Country. The balance of trade in favour of this Country, upon the face of the Account thus made up, was

In 1805 about - -	£. 6,616,000.
1806 - -	£. 10,437,000.
1807 - -	£. 5,866,000.
1808 - -	£. 12,481,000.
1809 - -	£. 14,834,000.

So far therefore, as any inference is to be drawn from the balance thus exhibited, the Exchanges during the present year, in which many payments to this Country on account of the very advantageous balances of the two former years may be expected to take place, ought to be peculiarly favourable.

Your Committee, however, place little confidence in deductions made even from the improved document which the industry and intelligence of the Inspector-General has enabled him to furnish. It is defective, as Mr. Irving has himself stated, inasmuch as it supplies no account of the sum drawn by Foreigners (which is at the present period peculiarly large) on account of freight due to them for the employment of their shipping, nor, on the other hand, of the sum receivable from them (and forming an addition to the value of our exported articles) on account of freight arising from the employment of British shipping. It leaves out of consideration all interest on capital in England possessed by Foreigners, and on capital abroad belonging to Inhabitants of Great Britain, as well as the pecuniary transactions between the Governments of England and Ireland. It takes no cognizance of contraband trade, and of exported and imported Bullion, of which no account is rendered at the Custom-house. It likewise omits a most important article, the variations of which, if correctly stated, would probably be found to correspond in a great degree with the fluctuations of the apparently favourable balance;

namely, the bills drawn on Government for our naval, military, and other expences in Foreign parts. Your Committee had hoped to receive an account of these from the table of the House; but there has been some difficulty and consequent delay in executing a material part of the Order made for them. It appears from "an Account, as far as it could be made out, of sums paid for Expences Abroad in 1793, 4, 5, and 6," inserted in the Appendix of the Lords' Report on the occasion of the Bank Restriction Bill, that the sums so paid were,

In 1793 - - -	£. 2,785,252.
4 - -	£. 8,335,591.
5 - - -	£. 11,040,236.
6 - -	£. 10,649,916.

The following is an account of the official value of our Imports and Exports with the Continent of Europe alone, in each of the last five years:

	IMPORTS.	EXPORTS.	Balance in favour of Great Britain, reckoned in Official Value.
	£.	£.	£.
1805	10,008,649	15,465,430	5,456,781
1806	8,197,256	13,216,386	5,019,130
1807	7,973,510	12,689,590	4,716,080
1808	4,210,671	11,280,490	7,069,819
1809	9,551,857	23,722,615	14,170,758

The balances with Europe alone in favour of Great Britain, as exhibited in this imperfect statement, are not far from corresponding with the general and more accurate balances before given. The favourable balance of 1809 with Europe alone, if computed according to the actual value, would be much more considerable than the value of the same year, in the former general statement.

A favourable balance of trade on the face of the Account

of Exports and Imports, presented annually to Parliament, is a very probable consequence of large drafts on Government for foreign expenditure; an augmentation of exports, and a diminution of imports, being promoted and even enforced by the means of such drafts. For if the supply of bills drawn abroad, either by the Agents of Government, or by individuals, is disproportionate to the demand, the price of them in foreign money falls, until it is so low as to invite purchasers; and the purchasers, who are generally Foreigners, not wishing to transfer their property permanently to England, have a reference to the terms on which the bills on England will purchase those British commodities which are in demand, either in their own country, or in intermediate places, with which the account may be adjusted. Thus, the price of the bills being regulated in some degree by that of British commodities, and continuing to fall till it becomes so low as to be likely to afford a profit on the purchase and exportation of these commodities, an actual exportation nearly proportionate to the amount of the bills drawn can scarcely fail to take place. It follows, that there cannot be, for any long period, either a highly favourable or unfavourable balance of trade; for the balance no sooner affects the price of bills, than the price of bills, by its reaction on the state of trade, promotes an equalization of commercial exports and imports. Your Committee have here considered Cash and Bullion as forming a part of the general mass of exported or imported articles, and as transferred according to the state both of the supply and the demand; forming, however, under certain circumstances, and especially in the case of great fluctuations in the general commerce, a peculiarly commodious remittance.

Your Committee have enlarged on the documents supplied by Mr. Irving, for the sake of throwing further light on the general question of the balance of trade and the Exchanges, and of dissipating some very prevalent errors which have a great practical influence on the subject now under consideration.

That the real Exchange against this Country with the

Continent cannot at any time have materially exceeded the limit fixed by the cost at that time of transporting specie, Your Committee are convinced upon the principles which have been already stated. That in point of fact, those Exchanges have not exceeded that limit, seems to receive a very satisfactory illustration from one part of the evidence of Mr. Greffulhe, who, of all the Merchants examined, seemed most wedded to the opinion, that the state of the balance of payments alone was sufficient to account for any depression of the Exchanges, however great. From what the Committee have already stated with respect to the par of Exchange, it is manifest that the Exchange between two countries is *at its real par*, when a given quantity of Gold or Silver in the one country is convertible at the market price into such an amount of the currency of that country, as will purchase a bill of Exchange on the other country for such an amount of the currency of that other country, as will there be convertible at the market price into an *equal* quantity of Gold or Silver of the same fineness. In the same manner the real Exchange is *in favour* of a country having money transactions with another, when a given quantity of Gold or Silver in the former is convertible for such an amount in the currency of that latter country, as will there be convertible into a *greater* quantity of Gold or Silver of the same fineness.

Upon these principles, Your Committee desired Mr. Greffulhe to make certain calculations, which appear in his Answers to the following Questions; viz.

"Supposing you had a pound weight troy of Gold of the English standard at Paris, and that you wished by means of that to procure a Bill of Exchange upon London, what would be the amount of the Bill of Exchange which you would procure in the present circumstances?—I find that a pound of Gold of the British standard at the present market price of 105 francs, and the exchange at 20 livres, would purchase a Bill of Exchange of 59*l.* 8*s.*

"At the present market price of Gold in London, how much standard Gold can you purchase for 59*l.* 8*s.*?—At the price of 4*l.* 12*s.* I find it will purchase 13 ounces of Gold, within a very small fraction.

"Then what is the difference per cent. in the quantity of Standard Gold which is equivalent to 59*l.* 8*s.* of our currency as at Paris and in London?—About 8½ per cent.

"Suppose you have a pound weight troy of our standard Gold at Hamburgh, and that you wished to part with it for a Bill of Exchange upon London, what would be the amount of the Bill of Exchange, which, in the present circumstances, you would procure?—At the Hamburgh price of 101, and the Exchange at 29, the amount of the Bill purchased on London would be 58*l.* 4*s.*

"What quantity of our standard Gold, at the present price of 4*l.* 12*s.* do you purchase for 58*l.* 4*s*?—About 12 ounces and 3 dwts.

"Then what is the difference per cent. between the quantity of standard Gold at Hamburgh and in London, which is equivalent to 58*l.* 4*s.* sterling?—About 5½ per cent.

"Suppose you had a pound weight troy of our standard Gold at Amsterdam, and wished to part with it for a Bill of Exchange upon London, what would be the amount sterling of the Bill of Exchange which you would procure?—At the Amsterdam price of 14½, Exchange 31. 6. and Bank agio 1 per cent. the amount of the Bill on London would be 58*l.* 18*s.*

"At the present price of 4*l.* 12*s.* what quantity of our standard Gold do you purchase in London for 58*l.* 18*s.* sterling?—12 oz. 16 dwts.

"How much is that per cent.?—7 per cent."

Similar calculations, but made upon different assumed data, will be found in the evidence of Mr. Abraham Goldsmid. From these answers of Mr. Greffulhe, it appears, that when the computed Exchange with Hamburgh was 29, that is, from 16 to 17 per cent. below par, the real difference of Exchange, resulting from the state of trade and balance of payments was no more than 5½ per cent. against this Country; that when the computed Exchange with Amsterdam was 31. 6. that is about 15 per cent. below par, the real Exchange was no more than 7 per cent. against this Country; that, when the computed Exchange with Paris was 20, that is 20 per cent. below par, the real Exchange was no more than 8½ per cent. against this Country. After making these allowances, therefore, for the effect of the balance of trade and payments upon our Exchanges with those places, there will still remain a fall of 11 per cent. in the Exchange with Hamburgh, of above 8 per cent. in the Exchange with Holland, and of 11½ per cent. in the Exchange with Paris, to be explained in some other manner.

If the same mode of calculation be applied to the more recent statements of the Exchange with the Continent, it will perhaps appear, that though the computed Exchange is at present against this Country, the real Exchange is in its favour.

From the foregoing reasonings relative to the state of the Exchanges, if they are considered apart, Your Committee find it difficult to resist an inference, that a portion at least of the great fall which the Exchanges lately suffered must have resulted not from the state of trade, but from a change in the relative value of our domestic currency. But when this deduction is joined with that which Your Committee have stated, respecting the change in the market price of Gold, that inference appears to be demonstrated.

III.

In consequence of the opinion which Your Committee entertain, that, in the present artificial condition of the circulating medium of this Country, it is most important to watch the Foreign Exchanges and the market price of Gold, Your Committee were desirous to learn, whether the Directors of the Bank of England held the same opinion, and derived from it a practical rule for the control of their circulation; and particularly whether, in the course of the last year, the great depression of the Exchanges, and the great rise in the price of Gold, had suggested to the Directors any suspicion of the currency of the Country being excessive.

Mr. WHITMORE, the late Governor of the Bank, stated to the Committee, that in regulating the general amount of the loans and discounts, he did "not advert to the circum-"stance of the Exchanges; it appearing upon a reference to "the amount of our notes in circulation, and the course of "Exchange, that they frequently have no connexion." He afterwards said, "My opinion is, I do not know whether it "is that of the Bank, that the amount of our paper circula-"tion has no reference at all to the state of the Exchange." And on a subsequent day, Mr. Whitmore stated, that "the "present unfavourable state of Exchange has no influence "upon the amount of their issues, the Bank having acted "precisely in the same way as they did before." He was likewise asked, whether, in regulating the amount of their circulation, the Bank ever adverted to the difference between the market and Mint price of Gold? and having desired to have time to consider that question, Mr. Whitmore, on a subsequent day; answered it in the following terms, which suggested these further questions:

"In taking into consideration the amount of your notes "out in circulation, and in limiting the extent of your dis-"counts to Merchants, do you advert to the difference, when "such exists, between the market and the Mint price of Gold? "We do advert to that, inasmuch as we do not discount at "any time for those persons who we know, or have good "reason to suppose, export the Gold.

"Do you not advert to it any further than by refusing "discounts to such persons?—We do advert to it, inasmuch "as whenever any Director thinks it bears upon the ques-"tion of our discounts, he presses to bring forward the "discussion.

"The market price of gold having, in the course of the "last year, risen as high as 4*l.* 10*s.* or 4*l.* 12*s.* has that cir-"cumstance been taken into consideration by you, so as to "have had any effect in diminishing or enlarging the amount "of the outstanding demands?—It has not been taken into "consideration by me in that view."

Mr. PEARSE, now Governor of the Bank, agreed with

Mr. Whitmore in this account of the practice of the Bank, and expressed his full concurrence in the same opinion.

Mr. PEARSE.—"In considering this subject, with reference to the manner in which Bank notes are issued, "resulting from the applications made for discounts to supply "the necessary want of Bank notes, by which their issue in "amount is so controlled that it can never amount to an "excess, I cannot see how the amount of Bank notes issued "can operate upon the price of Bullion, or the state of the "Exchanges, and therefore I am individually of opinion that "the price of Bullion, or the state of the Exchanges, can "never be a reason for lessening the amount of Bank notes "to be issued, always understanding the control which I "have already described.

"Is the Governor of the Bank of the same opinion which "has now been expressed by the Deputy Governor?

Mr. WHITMORE.—"I am so much of the same opinion, "that I never think it necessary to advert to the price of "Gold, or the state of the Exchange, on the days on which "we make our advances.

"Do you advert to these two circumstances with a view "to regulate the general amount of your advances?—I do not "advert to it with a view to our general advances, conceiving "it not to bear upon the question."

And Mr. HARMAN, another Bank Director, expressed his opinion in these terms;—"I must very materially alter "my opinions, before I can suppose that the Exchanges "will be influenced by any modifications of our paper "currency."

These Gentlemen, as well as several of the Merchants who appeared before the Committee, placed much reliance upon an argument which they drew from the want of correspondence in point of time, observable between the amount of Bank of England Notes and the state of the Hamburgh Exchange during several years; and Mr. Pearse presented a Paper on this subject, which is inserted in the Appendix. Your Committee would feel no distrust in the general principles which they have stated, if the discordance had been greater; considering the variety of circumstances which have a temporary effect on exchange, and the uncertainty both of the time and the degree in which it may be influenced by any given quantity of paper. It may be added, that the numerical amount of Notes (supposing 1*l.* and 2*l.* Notes to be excluded from the statement) did not materially vary during the period of the comparison; and that in the last year, when the general Exchanges with Europe have become much more unfavourable, the notes of the Bank of England, as well as those of the country Banks, have been very considerably increased. Your Committee however, on the whole, are not of opinion that a material depression of the Exchanges has been manifestly to be traced in its amount and degree to an augmentation of notes corresponding in point of time. They conceive, that the more minute and ordinary fluctuations of Exchange are generally referable to the course of our commerce; that political events, operating upon the state of trade, may often have contributed as well to the rise as to the fall of the Exchange; and in particular, that the first remarkable depression of it in the beginning of 1809, is to be ascribed, as has been stated in the evidence already quoted, to commercial events arising out of the occupation of the North of Germany by the troops of the French emperor. The evil has been, that the Exchange, when fallen, has not had the full means of recovery under the subsisting system. And if those occasional depressions, which arise from commercial causes, are not after a time successively corrected by the remedy which used to apply itself before the suspension of the cash payments of the Bank, the consequences may ultimately be exactly similar to those which a sudden and extravagant issue of paper would produce. The restoration of the Exchange used to be effected by the clandestine transmission of Guineas, which improved it for the moment, by serving as a remittance; and unquestionably also in part, probably much more extensively, by the reduction of the total quantity of the remaining circulating medium, to which reduction the Bank were led to contribute by the caution which every drain of Gold naturally excited.

Under the present system, the former of these remedies must be expected more and more to fail, the Guineas in circulation being even now apparently so few as to form no important remittance; and the reduction of paper seems therefore the chief, if not the sole corrective, to be resorted to. It is only after the Bank shall have for some time assumed its cash payments, that both can again operate, as they did on all former occasions prior to the restriction.

The Committee cannot refrain from expressing it to be their opinion, after a very deliberate consideration of this part of the subject, that it is a great practical error to suppose that the Exchanges with Foreign Countries, and the price of Bullion, are not liable to be affected by the amount of a paper currency, which is issued without the condition of payment in specie at the will of the holder. That the Exchanges will be lowered, and the price of Bullion raised, by an issue of such paper to excess, is not only established as a principle by the most eminent authorities upon Commerce and Finance; but its practical truth has been illustrated by the history of almost every State in modern times which has used a paper currency; and in all those countries, this principle has finally been resorted to by their Statesmen as the best criterion to judge by, whether such currency was or was not excessive.

In the instances which are most familiar in the history of Foreign Countries, the excess of paper has been usually accompanied by another circumstance, which has no place in our situation at present, a want of confidence in the sufficiency of those funds upon which the paper had been issued. Where these two circumstances, excess and want of confidence, are conjoined, they will co-operate and produce their effect much more rapidly than when it is the result of the excess only of a paper of perfectly good credit; and in both cases, an effect of the same sort will be produced upon the Foreign Exchanges, and upon the price of Bullion. The most remarkable examples of the former kind are to be found in the history of the paper currencies of the British Colonies in North America, in the early part of the last century, and in that of the assignats of the French Republic: to which the Committee have been enabled to add another, scarcely less remarkable, from the money speculations of the Austrian Government in the last campaign, which will be found in the Appendix. The present state of the currency of Portugal affords, also, an instance of the same kind.

Examples of the other sort, in which the depreciation was produced by excess alone, may be gathered from the experience of the United Kingdom at different times.

In Scotland, about the end of the seven years' war, Banking was carried to a very great excess; and by a practice of inserting in their promissory notes an optional clause of paying at sight, or in 6 months after sight with interest, the convertibility of such notes into specie at the will of the holder was in effect suspended. These notes accordingly became depreciated in comparison with specie; and while this abuse lasted, the exchange between London and Dumfries, for example, was sometimes four per cent. against Dumfries, while the exchange between London and Carlisle, which is not thirty miles distant from Dumfries, was at par. The Edinburgh Banks, when any of their paper was brought in to be exchanged for bills on London, were accustomed to extend or contract the date of the bills they gave, according to the state of the Exchange; diminishing in this manner the value of those bills, nearly in the same degree in which the excessive issue had caused their paper to be depreciated. This excess of paper was at last removed by granting bills on London at a fixed date; for the payment of which bills, or, in other words, for the payment of which excess of paper, it was necessary in the first instance to provide, by placing large pecuniary funds in the hands of their London correspondents. In aid of such precautionary measures on the part of the Edinburgh Banks, an act of parliament prohibited the optional clauses, and suppressed ten and five shilling notes. The Exchange between England and Scotland was speedily restored to its natural rate; and bills on London at a fixed date having ever since been given in Exchange for the circulating notes of Scotland, all material excess of

Scottish paper above Bank of England has been prevented, and the Exchange has been stationary. (Wealth of Nations, vol. i. p. 492.—Report of Committee upon Irish Exchange, 1804. Mr. Mansfield's Evidence.)

The experience of the Bank of England itself, within a very short period after its first establishment, furnishes a very instructive illustration of all the foregoing principles and reasonings. In this instance, the effects of a depreciation of the coin, by wear and clipping, were coupled with the effect of an excessive issue of paper. The Directors of the Bank of England did not at once attain a very accurate knowledge of all the principles by which such an institution must be conducted. They lent money not only by discount, but upon real securities, mortgages, and even pledges of commodities not perishable; at the same time the Bank contributed most materially to the service of Government for the support of the Army upon the Continent. By the liberality of those loans to private individuals, as well as by the large advances to Government, the quantity of the notes of the Bank became excessive, their relative value was depreciated, and they fell to a discount of 17 per cent. At this time there appears to have been no failure of the public confidence in the funds of the Bank; for its Stock sold for 110 per cent. though only 60 per cent. upon the subscriptions had been paid in. By the conjoint effect of this depreciation of the paper of the Bank from excess, and of the depreciation of the Silver coin from wear and clipping, the price of Gold Bullion was so much raised, that Guineas were as high as 30*s.*; all that had remained of good Silver gradually disappeared from the circulation; and the Exchange with Holland, which had been before a little affected by the remittances for the Army, sunk as low as 25 per cent. under par, when the Bank notes were at a discount of 17 per cent. Several expedients were tried, both by Parliament and by the Bank, to force a better Silver coin into circulation, and to reduce the price of Guineas, but without effect. At length the true remedies were resorted to: first, by a new coinage of Silver, which restored that part of the currency to its standard value, though the scarcity of money occasioned by calling in the old coin brought the Bank into streights, and even for a time affected its credit; secondly, by taking out of the circulation the excess of Bank Notes. This last operation appears to have been effected very judiciously. Parliament consented to enlarge the Capital Stock of the Bank, but annexed a condition, directing that a certain proportion of the new subscriptions should be made good in Bank Notes. In proportion to the amount of Notes sunk in this manner, the value of those which remained in circulation began presently to rise; in a short time the notes were at par, and the Foreign Exchanges nearly so. These details are all very fully mentioned in authentic tracts published at the time, and the case appears to Your Committee to afford much instruction upon the subject of their present Enquiry.—(See a short Account of the Bank, by Mr. Godfrey, one of the original Directors; and A short History of the last Parliament, 1699, by Dr. Drake; both in Lord Somers' Collection of Tracts.)

Your Committee must next refer to the confirmation and sanction which all their reasonings receive from the labours of the Committee of this House, which was appointed in a former Parliament to examine into the causes of the great depreciation of the Irish Exchange with England in 1804. Most of the mercantile persons who gave evidence before that Committee, including two Directors of the Bank of Ireland, were unwilling to admit that the fall of the Exchange was in any degree to be ascribed to an excess of the paper currency arising out of the restriction of 1797; the whole fall in that case, as in the present, was referred to an unfavourable balance of trade or of payments; and it was also then affirmed, that "Notes issued only in proportion to the demand, in exchange for good and convertible securities payable at specific periods, could not tend to any excess in the circulation, or to any depreciation." This doctrine, though more or less qualified by some of the Witnesses, pervades most of the evidence given before that Committee, with the remarkable exception of Mr. Mansfield, whose knowledge of the effects of that over issue of Scotch paper, which has just been mentioned, led him to deliver a more just opinion on the subject. Many of the Witnesses before the Committee, however unwilling to acknowledge the real nature of the evil, made important concessions, which necessarily involved them in inconsistency. They could not, as practical men, controvert the truth of the general position, that "the fluctuations of Exchange between two countries are generally limited by the price at which any given quantity of Bullion can be purchased in the circulating medium of the debtor country, and converted into the circulating medium of the creditor country, together with the insurances and charges of transporting it from the one to the other." It was at the same time admitted, that the expense of transporting Gold from England to Ireland, including insurance, was then under one per cent.; that before the restriction, the fluctuations had never long and much exceeded this limit; and moreover, that the exchange with Belfast, where Guineas freely circulated at the time of the investigation by that Committee, was then 1¼ in favour of Ireland, while the Exchange with Dublin, where only paper was in use, was 10*l.* per cent. against that country. It also appeared from such imperfect documents as it was practicable to furnish, that the balance of trade was then favourable to Ireland. Still, however, it was contended, that there was no depreciation of Irish paper, that there was a scarcity and consequent high price of Gold, and that the diminution of Irish paper would not rectify the Exchange. "The depreciation of Bank paper in Ireland (it was said by one of the Witnesses, a Director of the Bank of Ireland) is entirely a relative term with respect to the man who buys and sells in Dublin by that common medium; to him it is not depreciated at all; but to the purchaser of a Bill on London, to him in that relation, and under that circumstance, there is a depreciation of ten per cent." By thus avoiding all comparison with a view to the point in issue, between the value of their own paper and that of either the then circulating medium of this Country or of Gold Bullion, or even of Gold coin then passing at a premium in other parts of Ireland, they appear to have retained a confident opinion, that no depreciation of Irish paper had taken place.

It is further observable, that the value of a considerable quantity of Dollars put into circulation by the Bank of Ireland at this period, was raised to 5*s.* a Dollar, for the professed purpose of rendering the new Silver coin conformable to the existing state of the Exchange; a circumstance on which the Committee animadverted in their Report, and which serves to shew that the Irish paper currency could not stand a comparison with the standard price of Silver, any more than with that of Gold Bullion, with Gold in coin, or with the then paper currency of this kingdom.

A fact was mentioned to that Committee on the evidence of Mr. Colville, a Director of the Bank of Ireland, which though it carried no conviction to his mind of the tendency of a limitation of paper to lower Exchanges, seems very decisive on this point. He stated, that in 1753 and 1754, the Dublin Exchange being remarkably unfavourable, and the notes of the Dublin Bank being suddenly withdrawn, the Exchange became singularly favourable. The mercantile distress produced on that occasion was great, through the suddenness of the operation; for it was effected, not by the gradual and prudential measures of the several Banks, but through the violent pressure which their unguarded issues had brought upon them. The general result, however, is not the less observable.

With a view to the further elucidation of the subject of the Irish Exchanges, which so lately attracted the attention of Parliament, it may be proper to remark, that Ireland has no dealings in Exchange with foreign countries, except through London; and that the payments from Ireland to the Continent are consequently converted into English currency, and then into the currency of the countries to which Ireland is indebted. In the Spring of 1804, the Exchange of England with the Continent was above par, and the Exchange of Ireland was in such a state that

118*l.* 10*s.* of the notes of the Bank of Ireland would purchase only 100*l.* of those of the Bank of England. Therefore, if the notes of the Bank of Ireland were not depreciated, and it was so maintained, it followed that the notes of the Bank of England were at more than 10 per cent. premium above the standard coin of the two countries.

The principles laid down by the Committee of 1804 had probably some weight with the Directors of the Bank of Ireland; for between the period of their Report (June 1804) and January 1806, the circulation of the notes of the Bank of Ireland was gradually (though with small occasional fluctuations) reduced from about three millions to 2,410,000*l.*, being a diminution of nearly 1-5th; at the same time, all the currency which had been issued under the name of Silver Tokens was by law suppressed. The paper currency, both of the Bank of England, and of the English Country Banks, seems during the same period to have gradually increased. The combination of these two causes is likely to have had a material effect in restoring to par the Irish Exchange with England.

The Bank of Ireland has again gradually enlarged its issues to about 3,100,000*l.* being somewhat higher than they stood in 1804, an increase probably not disproportionate to that which has occurred in England within the same period. Perhaps, however, it ought not to be assumed, that the diminution of issues of the Bank of Ireland between 1804 and 1806, would produce a corresponding reduction in the issues of private Banks in Ireland, exactly in the same manner in which a diminution of Bank of England paper produces that effect on the Country Banks in Great Britain; because the Bank of Ireland does not possess the same exclusive power of supplying any part of that country with a paper currency, which the Bank of England enjoys in respect to the metropolis of the Empire. The Bank of England, by restricting the quantity of this necessary article in that important quarter, can more effectually secure the improvement of its value; and every such improvement must necessarily lead, by a corresponding diminution in amount, to a similar augmentation of the value of Country Bank paper exchangeable for it. That the same diminution of the circulation of private Banks took place in Ireland is more than probable, for the private Banks in Ireland are accustomed to give Bank of Ireland paper for their own circulating notes when required to do so, and therefore could not but feel the effect of any new limitation of that paper for which their own was exchangeable.

It is due, however, in justice to the present Directors of the Bank of England, to remind the House, that the suspension of their cash payments, though it appears in some degree to have originated in a mistaken view taken by the Bank of the peculiar difficulties of that time, was not a measure sought for by the Bank, but imposed upon it by the Legislature for what were held to be urgent reasons of State policy and public expediency. And it ought not to be urged as matter of charge against the Directors, if in this novel situation in which their commercial Company was placed by the law, and intrusted with the regulation and control of the whole circulating medium of the Country, they were not fully aware of the principles by which so delicate a trust should be executed, but continued to conduct their business of discounts and advances according to their former routine.

It is important, at the same time, to observe, that under the former system, when the Bank was bound to answer its Notes in specie upon demand, the state of the Foreign Exchanges and the price of Gold did most materially influence its conduct in the issue of those Notes, though it was not the practice of the Directors systematically to watch either the one or the other. So long as Gold was demandable for their paper, they were speedily apprized of a depression of the Exchange, and a rise in the price of Gold, by a run upon them for that article. If at any time they incautiously exceeded the proper limit of their advances and issues, the paper was quickly brought back to them, by those who were tempted to profit by the market price of Gold or by the rate of Exchange. In this manner the evil soon cured itself. The Directors of the Bank having their apprehensions excited by the reduction of their stock of Gold, and being able to replace their loss only by reiterated purchases of Bullion at a very losing price, naturally contracted their issues of paper, and thus gave to the remaining paper, as well as to the Coin for which it was interchangeable, an increased value, while the clandestine exportation either of the coin, or the Gold produced from it, combined in improving the state of the Exchange, and in producing a corresponding diminution of the difference between the market price and Mint price of Gold, or of paper convertible into Gold.

Your Committee do not mean to represent that the manner, in which this effect resulted from the conduct which they have described, was distinctly perceived by the Bank Directors. The fact of limiting their paper as often as they experienced any great drain of Gold, is, however, unquestionable. Mr. Bosanquet stated, in his evidence before the Secret Committee of the House of Lords, in the year 1797, That in 1783, when the Bank experienced a drain of Cash which alarmed them, the Directors took a bold step, and refused to make the advances on the loan of that year. This, he said, answered the purpose of making a temporary suspension in the amount of the drain of their Specie. And all the three Directors who have been examined before Your Committee, represent some restriction of the Bank issues as having usually taken place at those periods antecedent to the suspension of the cash payments of the Bank, when they experienced any material run. A very urgent demand for Guineas, though arising not from the high price of Gold and the state of the Exchange, but from a fear of Invasion, occurred in 1793, and also in 1797, and in each of these periods the Bank restrained their discounts, and consequently also the amount of their Notes, very much below the demand of the merchants. Your Committee question the policy of thus limiting the accommodation in a period of alarm, unaccompanied with an unfavourable Exchange and high price of Bullion; but they consider the conduct of the Bank at the two last-mentioned periods, as affording illustration of their general disposition, antecedently to 1797, to contract their loans and their paper, when they found their Gold to be taken from them.

It was a necessary consequence of the suspension of cash payments, to exempt the Bank from that drain of Gold, which, in former times, was sure to result from an unfavourable Exchange and a high price of Bullion. And the Directors, released from all fears of such a drain, and no longer feeling any inconvenience from such a state of things, have not been prompted to restore the Exchanges and the price of Gold to their proper level by a reduction of their advances and issues. The Directors, in former times, did not perhaps perceive and acknowledge the principle more distinctly than those of the present day, but they felt the inconvenience, and obeyed its impulse; which practically established a check and limitation to the issue of paper. In the present times, the inconvenience is not felt; and the check, accordingly, is no longer in force. But Your Committee beg leave to report it to the House as their most clear opinion, that so long as the suspension of Cash Payments is permitted to subsist, the price of Gold Bullion and the general Course of Exchange with Foreign Countries, taken for any considerable period of time, form the best general criterion from which any inference can be drawn, as to the sufficiency or excess of paper currency in circulation; and that the Bank of England cannot safely regulate the amount of its issues, without having reference to the criterion presented by these two circumstances. And upon a review of all the facts and reasonings which have already been stated, Your Committee are further of opinion, that, although the commercial state of this Country, and the political state of the Continent, may have had some influence on the high price of Gold Bullion and the unfavourable Course of Exchange with Foreign Countries, this price, and this depreciation, are also to be ascribed to the want of a permanent check, and a sufficient limitation of the paper currency in this Country.

In connexion with the general subject of this part of their Report, the policy of the Bank of England respecting the amount of their circulation, Your Committee have now to call the attention of the House to another topic, which was brought under their notice in the course of their Enquiry, and which in their judgment demands the most serious consideration. The Bank Directors, as well as some of the Merchants who have been examined, shewed a great anxiety to state to Your Committee a doctrine, of the truth of which they professed themselves to be most thoroughly convinced, that there can be no possible excess in the issue of Bank of England paper, so long as the advances in which it is issued are made upon the principles which at present guide the conduct of the Directors, that is, so long as the discount of mercantile Bills is confined to paper of undoubted solidity, arising out of real commercial transactions, and payable at short and fixed periods. That the Discounts should be made only upon Bills growing out of real commercial transactions, and falling due in a fixed and short period, are sound and well-established principles. But that, while the Bank is restrained from paying in specie, there need be no other limit to the issue of their paper than what is fixed by such rules of discount, and that during the suspension of Cash payments the discount of good Bills falling due at short periods cannot lead to any excess in the amount of Bank paper in circulation, appears to Your Committee to be a doctrine wholly erroneous in principle, and pregnant with dangerous consequences in practice.

But before Your Committee proceed to make such observations upon this theory as it appears to them to deserve, they think it right to shew from the Evidence, to what extent it is entertained by some of those individuals who have been at the head of the affairs of the Bank. The opinions held by those individuals are likely to have an important practical influence; and appeared to Your Committee, moreover, the best evidence of what has constituted the actual policy of that establishment in its corporate capacity.

Mr. Whitmore, the late Governor of the Bank, expressly

states, "The Bank never force a Note in circulation, and "there will not remain a Note in circulation more than the "immediate wants of the public require; for no Banker, I "presume, will keep a larger stock of Bank Notes by him "than his immediate payments require, as he can at all times "procure them." The reason here assigned is more particularly explained by *Mr. Whitmore,* when he says, "The "Bank Notes would revert to us if there was a redundancy "in circulation, as no one would pay interest for a Bank "Note that he did not want to make use of." *Mr. Whitmore* further states, "The criterion by which I judge of the exact "proportion to be maintained between the occasions of the "Public, and the issues of the Bank, is by avoiding as much "as possible to discount what does not appear to be legitimate "mercantile paper." And further, when asked, What measure the Court of Directors has to judge by, whether the quantity of Bank Notes out in circulation is at any time excessive? *Mr. Whitmore* states, that their measures of the security [*scarcity?*] or abundance of Bank Notes is certainly by the greater or less application that is made to them for the discount of good paper.

Mr. Pearse, late Deputy Governor, and now Governor of the Bank, stated very distinctly his concurrence in opinion with *Mr. Whitmore* upon this particular point. He referred "to the manner in which Bank Notes are issued, resulting "from the applications made for discounts to supply the "necessary want of Bank Notes, by which their issue in "amount is so controlled that it can never amount to an ex-"cess." He considers "the amount of the Bank Notes in "circulation as being controlled by the occasions of the "public, for internal purposes," and that from the manner "in which the issue of Bank Notes is controlled, the public "will never call for more than is absolutely necessary for their "wants."

Another Director of the Bank, *Mr. Harman,* being asked, if he thought that the sum total of discounts applied for, even though the accommodation afforded should be on the security of good bills to safe persons, might be such as to produce some excess in the quantity of the Bank issues if fully complied with; he answered, "I think if we discount "only for solid persons, and such paper as is for real *bonâ* "*fide* transactions, we cannot materially err." And he afterwards states, that what he should consider as the test of a superabundance would be, "money being more plentiful in "the market."

It is material to observe, that both *Mr. Whitmore* and *Mr. Pearse* state that "the Bank does not comply with the "whole demand upon them for discounts, and that they are "never induced by a view to their own profit, to push their "issues beyond what they deem consistent with the public "interest."

Another very important part of the Evidence of these Gentlemen upon this point, is contained in the following Extract;

"Is it your opinion that the same security would exist "against any excess in the issues of the Bank, if the rate of "the discount were reduced from *5l.* to *4l.* per cent.?" Answer.—"The security of an excess of issue would be, I "conceive, precisely the same." *Mr. Pearse.*—"I concur in "that Answer."

"If it were reduced to *3l.* per cent.?"—*Mr. Whitmore,* "I conceive there would be no difference, if our practice "remained the same as now, of not forcing a note into "circulation." *Mr. Pearse.*—"I concur in that Answer."

Your Committee cannot help again calling the attention of the House to the view which this Evidence presents, of the consequences which have resulted from the peculiar situation in which the Bank of England was placed by the suspension of Cash payments. So long as the paper of the Bank was convertible into specie at the will of the holder, it was enough, both for the safety of the Bank and for the public interest in what regarded its circulating medium, that the Directors attended only to the character and quality of the Bills discounted, as real ones and payable at fixed and short periods. They could not much exceed the proper bounds in respect of the quantity and amount of Bills discounted, so as thereby to produce an excess of their paper in circulation, without quickly finding that the surplus returned upon themselves in demand for specie. The private interest of the Bank to guard themselves against a continued demand of that nature, was a sufficient protection for the public against any such excess of Bank paper, as would occasion a material fall in the relative value of the circulating medium. The restriction of cash payments, as has already been shewn, having rendered the same preventive policy no longer necessary to the Bank, has removed that check upon its issues which was the public security against an excess. When the Bank Directors were no longer exposed to the inconvenience of a drain upon them for Gold, they naturally felt that they had no such inconvenience to guard against by a more restrained system of discounts and advances; and it was very natural for them to pursue as before (but without that sort of guard and limitation which was now become unnecessary to their own security) the same liberal and prudent system of commercial advances from which the prosperity of their own establishment had resulted, as well as in a great degree the commercial prosperity of the whole Country. It was natural for the Bank Directors to believe, that nothing but benefit could accrue to the public at large, while they saw the growth of Bank profits go hand in hand with the accommodations granted to the Merchants. It was hardly to be expected of the Directors of the Bank, that they should be fully aware of the consequences that might result from their pursuing, after the suspension of cash payments, the same system which they had found a safe one before. To watch the operation of so new a law, and to provide against the injury which might result from it to the public interests, was the province, not so much of the Bank as of the Legislature: And, in the opinion of Your Committee, there is room to regret that this House has not taken earlier notice of all the consequences of that law.

By far the most important of those consequences is, that while the convertibility into specie no longer exists as a check to an over issue of paper, the Bank Directors have not perceived that the removal of that check rendered it possible that such an excess might be issued by the discount of perfectly good bills. So far from perceiving this, Your Committee have shewn that they maintain the contrary doctrine with the utmost confidence, however it may be qualified occasionally by some of their expressions. That this doctrine is a very fallacious one, Your Committee cannot entertain a doubt. The fallacy, upon which it is founded, lies in not distinguishing between an advance of capital to Merchants, and an additional supply of currency to the general mass of circulating medium. If the advance of capital only is considered, as made to those who are ready to employ it in judicious and productive undertakings, it is evident there need be no other limit to the total amount of advances than what the means of the lender, and his prudence in the selection of borrowers, may impose. But, in the present situation of the Bank, intrusted as it is with the function of supplying the public with that paper currency which forms the basis of our circulation, and at the same time not subjected to the liability of converting the paper into specie, every advance which it makes of capital to the Merchants in the shape of discount, becomes an addition also to the mass of circulating medium. In the first instance, when the advance is made by notes paid in discount of a bill, it is undoubtedly so much capital, so much power of making purchases, placed in the hands of the Merchant who receives the notes; and if those hands are safe, the operation is so far, and in this its first step, useful and productive to the public. But as soon as the portion of circulating medium, in which the advance was thus made, performs in the hands of him to whom it was advanced this its first operation as capital, as soon as the notes are exchanged by him for some other article which is capital, they fall into the channel of circulation as so much circulating medium, and form an addition to the mass of currency. The necessary effect of every such addition to the mass, is to diminish the relative value of any given portion of that mass in exchange for commodities. If the addition were made by notes conver-

50

tible into specie, this diminution of the relative value of any given portion of the whole mass would speedily bring back upon the Bank, which issued the notes, as much as was excessive. But if by law they are not so convertible, of course this excess will not be brought back, but will remain in the channel of circulation, until paid in again to the Bank itself in discharge of the bills which were originally discounted. During the whole time they remain out, they perform all the functions of circulating medium; and before they come to be paid in discharge of those bills, they have already been followed by a new issue of notes in a similar operation of discounting. Each successive advance repeats the same process. If the whole sum of discounts continues outstanding at a given amount, there will remain permanently out in circulation a corresponding amount of paper; and if the amount of discounts is progressively increasing, the amount of paper, which remains out in circulation over and above what is otherwise wanted for the occasions of the Public, will progressively increase also, and the money prices of commodities will progressively rise. This progress may be as indefinite, as the range of speculation and adventure in a great commercial country.

It is necessary to observe, that the law, which in this Country limits the rate of interest, and of course the rate at which the Bank can legally discount, exposes the Bank to still more extensive demands for commercial discounts. While the rate of commercial profit is very considerably higher than five per cent. as it has lately been in many branches of our Foreign trade, there is in fact no limit to the demands which Merchants of perfectly good capital, and of the most prudent spirit of enterprise, may be tempted to make upon the Bank for accommodation and facilities by discount. Nor can any argument or illustration place in a more striking point of view the extent to which such of the Bank Directors, as were examined before the Committee, seem to have in theory embraced that doctrine upon which Your Committee have made these observations, as well as the practical consequences to which that doctrine may lead in periods of a high spirit of commercial adventure, than the opinion which Mr. Whitmore and Mr. Pearse have delivered; that the same complete security to the public against any excess in the issues of the Bank would exist if the rate of discount were reduced from five to four, or even to three per cent. From the Evidence, however, of the late Governor and Deputy Governor of the Bank, it appears, that though they state the principle broadly, that there can be no excess of their circulation if issued according to their rules of discount, yet they disclaim the idea of acting up to it in its whole extent. Though they stated the applications for the discount of legitimate bills to be their sole criterion of abundance or scarcity, they gave Your Committee to understand, that they do not discount to the full extent of such applications. In other words, the Directors do not act up to the principle which they represent as one perfectly sound and safe, and must be considered, therefore, as possessing no distinct and certain rule to guide their discretion in controlling the amount of their circulation.

The suspension of Cash payments has had the effect of committing into the hands of the Directors of the Bank of England, to be exercised by their sole discretion, the important charge of supplying the Country with that quantity of circulating medium which is exactly proportioned to the wants and occasions of the Public. In the judgment of the Committee, that is a trust, which it is unreasonable to expect that the Directors of the Bank of England should ever be able to discharge. The most detailed knowledge of the actual trade of the Country, combined with profound science in all the principles of Money and circulation, would not enable any man or set of men to adjust, and keep always adjusted, the right proportion of circulating medium in a country to the wants of trade. When the currency consists entirely of the precious metals, or of paper convertible at will into the precious metals, the natural process of commerce, by establishing Exchanges among all the different countries of the world, adjusts, in every particular country, the proportion of circulating medium to its actual occasions, according to that supply of the precious metals which the mines furnish to the general market of the world. The proportion, which is thus adjusted and maintained by the natural operation of commerce, cannot be adjusted by any human wisdom or skill. If the natural system of currency and circulation be abandoned, and a discretionary issue of paper money substituted in its stead, it is vain to think that any rules can be devised for the exact exercise of such a discretion; though some cautions may be pointed out to check and control its consequences, such as are indicated by the effect of an excessive issue upon Exchanges and the price of Gold. The Directors of the Bank of England, in the judgment of Your Committee, have exercised the new and extraordinary discretion reposed in them since 1797, with an integrity and a regard to the public interest, according to their conceptions of it, and indeed a degree of forbearance in turning it less to the profit of the Bank than it would easily have admitted of, that merit the continuance of that confidence which the public has so long and so justly felt in the integrity with which its affairs are directed, as well as in the unshaken stability and ample funds of that great establishment. That their recent policy involves great practical errors, which it is of the utmost public importance to correct, Your Committee are fully convinced; but those errors are less to be imputed to the Bank Directors, than to be stated as the effect of a new system, of which, however it originated, or was rendered necessary as a temporary expedient, it might have been well if Parliament had sooner taken into view all the consequences. When Your Committee consider that this discretionary power, of supplying the Kingdom with circulating medium, has been exercised under an opinion that the paper could not be issued to excess if advanced in discounts to Merchants in good bills payable at stated periods, and likewise under an opinion that neither the price of Bullion nor the course of Exchanges need be adverted to, as affording any indication with respect to the sufficiency or excess of such paper, Your Committee cannot hesitate to say, that these opinions of the Bank must be regarded as in a great measure the operative cause of the continuance of the present state of things.

IV.

Your Committee will now proceed to state, from the information which has been laid before them, what appears to have been the progressive increase, and to be the present amount of the Paper circulation of this Country, consisting primarily of the Notes of the Bank of England not at present convertible into specie; and, in a secondary manner, of the Notes of the Country Bankers which are convertible, at the option of the holder, into Bank of England Paper. After having stated the amount of Bank of England Paper, Your Committee will explain the reasons which induce them to think that the numerical amount of that Paper is not alone to be considered as decisive of the question as to its excess: and before stating the amount of Country Bank Paper, so far as that can be ascertained, Your Committee will explain their reasons for thinking, that the amount of the Country Bank circulation is limited by the amount of that of the Bank of England.

1. It appears from the Accounts laid before the Committees upon the Bank Affairs in 1797, that for several years previous to the year 1796, the average amount of Bank Notes in circulation was between 10,000,000*l.*, and 11,000,000*l.* hardly ever falling below 9,000,000*l.* and not often exceeding to any great amount 11,000,000*l.*

The following Abstract of the several Accounts referred to Your Committee, or ordered by Your Committee from the Bank, will shew the progressive increase of the Notes from the year 1798 to the end of the last year.

Average Amount of Bank of England Notes in circulation in each of the following years:

	Notes of 5*l.* and upwards, including Bank Post Bills.	Notes under 5*l.*	TOTAL.
	£.	£.	£.
1798	11,527,250	1,807,502	13,334,752
1799	12,408,522	1,653,805	14,062,327
1800	13,598,666	2,243,266	15,841,932
1801	13,454,367	2,715,182	16,169,594
1802	13,917,977	3,136,477	17,054,454
1803	12,983,477	3,864,045	16,847,522
1804	12,621,348	4,723,672	17,345,020
1805	12,697,352	4,544,580	17,241,932
1806	12,844,170	4,291,230	17,135,400
1807	13,221,988	4,183,013	17,405,001
1808	13,402,160	4,132,420	17,534,580
1809	14,133,615	4,868,275	19,001,890

Taking from the Accounts the last half of the year 1809, the average will be found higher than for the whole year, and amounts to 19,880,310*l.*

The Accounts in the Appendix give very detailed Returns for the first four months of the present year, down to the 12th May, from which it will be found that the amount was then increasing, particularly in the smaller Notes. The whole amount of Bank Notes in circulation, exclusive of 939,990*l.* of Bank Post Bills, will be found on the average of the two Returns for the 5th and 12th May last, to be 14,136,610*l.* in Notes of 5*l.* and upwards, and 6,173,380*l.* in Notes under 5*l.* making the sum of 20,309,990*l.* and, including the Bank Post Bills, the sum of 21,249,980*l.*

By far the most considerable part of this increase since 1798, it is to be observed, has been in the article of small notes, part of which must be considered as having been introduced to supply the place of the specie which was deficient at the period of the suspension of cash payments. It appears however that the first supply of small notes, which was thrown into circulation after that event, was very small in comparison of their present amount; a large augmentation of them appears to have taken place from the end of the year 1799 to that of the year 1802; and a very rapid increase has also taken place since the month of May in the last year to the present time; the augmentation of these small notes from 1st May 1809 to the 5th of May 1810, being from the sum of 4,509,470*l.* to the sum of 6,161,020*l.*

The notes of the Bank of England are principally issued in advances to Government for the public service, and in advances to the Merchants upon the discount of their bills.

Your Committee have had an Account laid before them, of Advances made by the Bank to Government on Land and Malt, Exchequer Bills, and other securities, in every year since the suspension of cash payments; from which, as compared with the Accounts laid before the Committees of 1797, and which were then carried back for 20 years, it will appear that the yearly advances of the Bank to Government have upon an average, since the suspension, been considerably lower in amount than the average amount of advances prior to that event; and the amount of those advances in the two last years, though greater in amount than those of some years immediately preceding, is less than it was for any of the six years preceding the restriction of cash payments.

With respect to the amount of commercial discounts, Your Committee did not think it proper to require from the Directors of the Bank a disclosure of their absolute amount, being a part of their private transactions as a commercial Company, of which, without urgent reason, it did not seem right to demand a disclosure. The late Governor and Deputy Governor, however, at the desire of Your Committee, furnished a comparative Scale, in progressive numbers, shewing the increase of the amount of their discounts from the year 1790 to 1809, both inclusive. They made a request, with which your Committee have thought it proper to comply, that this document might not be made public; the Committee therefore have not placed it in the Appendix to the present Report, but have returned it to the Bank. Your Committee however have to state in general terms, that the amount of discounts has been progressively increasing since the year 1796; and that their amount in the last year (1809) bears a very high proportion to their largest amount in any year preceding 1797. Upon this particular subject, Your Committee are only anxious to remark, that the largest amount of mercantile discounts by the Bank, if it could be considered by itself, ought never, in their judgment, to be regarded as any other than a great public benefit; and that it is only the excess of paper currency thereby issued, and kept out in circulation, which is to be considered as the evil.

But Your Committee must not omit to state one very important principle, That the mere numerical return of the amount of Bank notes out in circulation, cannot be considered as at all deciding the question, whether such paper is or is not excessive. It is necessary to have recourse to other tests. The same amount of paper may at one time be less than enough, and at another time more. The quantity of currency required will vary in some degree with the extent of trade; and the increase of our trade, which has taken place since the suspension, must have occasioned some increase in the quantity of our currency. But the quantity of currency bears no fixed proportion to the quantity of commodities; and any inferences proceeding upon such a supposition would be entirely erroneous. The effective currency of the Country depends upon the quickness of circulation, and the number of exchanges performed in a given time, as well as upon its numerical amount; and all the circumstances, which have a tendency to quicken or to retard the rate of circulation, render the same amount of currency more or less adequate to the wants of trade. A much smaller amount is required in a high state of public credit, than when alarms make individuals call in their advances, and provide against accidents by hoarding; and in a period of commercial security and private confidence, than when mutual distrust discourages pecuniary arrangements for any distant time. But, above all, the same amount of currency will be more or less adequate, in proportion to the skill which the great money-dealers possess in managing and economising the use of the circulating medium. Your Committee are of opinion, that the improvements which have taken place of late years in this Country, and particularly in the district of London, with regard to the use and economy of money among Bankers, and in the mode of adjusting commercial payments, must have had a much greater effect than has hitherto been ascribed to them, in rendering the same sum adequate to a much greater amount of trade and payments than formerly. Some of those improvements will be found detailed in the Evidence: they consist principally in the increased use of Bankers' drafts in the common payments of London; the contrivance of bringing all such drafts daily to a common receptacle, where they are balanced against each other; the intermediate agency of Bill-brokers; and several other changes in the practice of London Bankers, are to the same effect, of rendering it unnecessary for them to keep so large a deposit of money as formerly. Within the London district, it would certainly appear, that a smaller sum of money is required than formerly to perform the same number of exchanges and amount of payments, if the rate of prices had remained the same. It is material also to observe, that both the policy of the Bank of England itself, and the competition of the Country bank paper, have tended to compress the paper of the Bank of England, more and more, within London and the adjacent district. All these circumstances must have co-operated to render a smaller augmentation of Bank of England paper necessary to supply the demands of our increased trade than might otherwise have been required; and show how impossible it is, from the numerical amount alone of that paper, to pronounce whether it is excessive or not: a more sure criterion must be resorted to, and such a criterion, Your Committee have already shown, is only to be found in the state of the Exchanges, and the price of Gold Bullion.

The particular circumstances of the two years which are so remarkable in the recent history of our circulation, 1793 and 1797, throw great light upon the principle which Your Committee have last stated.

In the year 1793, the distress was occasioned by a failure of confidence in the country circulation, and a consequent pressure upon that of London. The Bank of England did not think it advisable to enlarge their issues to meet this increased demand, and their Notes, previously issued, circulating less freely in consequence of the alarm that prevailed, proved insufficient for the necessary payments. In this crisis, Parliament applied a remedy, very similar, in its effect, to an enlargement of the advances and issues of the Bank; a loan of Exchequer Bills was authorised to be made to as many mercantile persons, giving good security, as should apply for them; and the confidence which this measure diffused, as well as the increased means which it afforded of obtaining Bank Notes through the sale of the Exchequer Bills, speedily relieved the distress both of London and of the country. Without offering an opinion upon the expediency of the particular mode in which this operation was effected, Your Committee think it an important illustration of the principle, that an enlarged accommodation is the true remedy for that occasional failure of confidence in the country districts, to which our system of paper credit is unavoidably exposed.

The circumstances which occurred in the beginning of the year 1797, were very similar to those of 1793;—an alarm of invasion, a run upon the Country Banks for Gold, the failure of some of them, and a run upon the Bank of England, forming a crisis like that of 1793, for which, perhaps, an effectual remedy might have been provided, if the Bank of England had had courage to extend instead of restricting its accommodations and issue of Notes. Some few persons, it appears from the Report of the Secret Committee of the Lords, were of this opinion at the time; and the late Governor and Deputy Governor of the Bank stated to Your Committee that they, and many of the Directors, are now satisfied, from the experience of the year 1797, that the diminution of their Notes in that emergency increased the public distress; an opinion in the correctness of which Your Committee entirely concur.

It appears to Your Committee, that the experience of the Bank of England in the years 1793 and 1797, contrasted with the facts which have been stated in the present Report, suggests a distinction most important to be kept in view, between that demand upon the Bank for Gold for the supply of the domestic channels of circulation, sometimes a very great and sudden one, which is occasioned by a temporary failure of confidence, and that drain upon the Bank for Gold which grows out of an unfavourable state of the Foreign Exchanges. The former, while the Bank maintains its high credit, seems likely to be best relieved by a judicious increase of accommodation to the Country: the latter, so long as the Bank does not pay in specie, ought to suggest to the Directors a question, whether their issues may not be already too abundant.

Your Committee have much satisfaction in thinking, that the Directors are perfectly aware that they may err by a too scanty supply in a period of stagnant credit. And Your Committee are clearly of opinion, that although it ought to be the general policy of the Bank Directors to diminish their paper in the event of the long continuance of a high price of Bullion and a very unfavourable Exchange, yet it is essential to the commercial interests of this Country, and to the general fulfilment of those mercantile engagements which a free issue of paper may have occasioned, that the accustomed degree of accommodation to the Merchants should not be suddenly and materially reduced; and that if any general and serious difficulty or apprehension on this subject should arise, it may, in the judgment of Your Committee, be counteracted without danger, and with advantage to the public, by a liberality in the issue of Bank of England paper proportioned to the urgency of the particular occasion.

Under such circumstances, it belongs to the Bank to take likewise into their own consideration, how far it may be practicable, consistently with a due regard to the immediate interests of the public service, rather to reduce their paper by a gradual reduction of their advances to Government, than by too suddenly abridging the discounts to the Merchants.

2. Before Your Committee proceed to detail what they have collected with respect to the amount of Country Bank paper, they must observe, that so long as the Cash payments of the Bank are suspended, the whole paper of the Country Bankers is a superstructure raised upon the foundation of the paper of the Bank of England. The same check, which the convertibility into specie, under a better system, provides against the excess of any part of the paper circulation, is, during the present system, provided against an excess of Country Bank paper, by its convertibility into Bank of England paper. If an excess of paper be issued in a country district, while the London circulation does not exceed its due proportion, there will be a local rise of prices in that country district, but prices in London will remain as before. Those who have the country paper in their hands will prefer buying in London where things are cheaper, and will therefore return that country paper upon the Banker who issued it, and will demand from him Bank of England Notes or Bills upon London; and thus, the excess of country paper being continually returned upon the issuers for Bank of England paper, the quantity of the latter necessarily and effectually limits the quantity of the former. This is illustrated by the Account which has been already given of the excess, and subsequent limitation, of the paper of the Scotch Banks, about the year 1763. If the Bank of England paper itself should at any time, during the suspension of Cash payments, be issued to excess, a corresponding excess may be issued of Country Bank paper which will not be checked; the foundation being enlarged, the superstructure admits of a proportionate extension. And thus, under such a system, the excess of Bank of England paper will produce

its effect upon prices not merely in the ratio of its own increase, but in a much higher proportion.

It has not been in the power of Your Committee to obtain such information as might enable them to state, with any thing like accuracy, the amount of Country Bank paper in circulation. But they are led to infer from all the Evidence they have been able to procure on this subject, not only that a great number of new Country Banks has been established within these last two years, but also that the amount of issues of those which are of an older standing has in general been very considerably increased: whilst on the other hand, the high state of mercantile and public credit, the proportionate facility of converting at short notice all public and commercial securities into Bank of England paper, joined to the preference generally given within the limits of its own circulation to the paper of a well established Country Bank over that of the Bank of England, have probably not rendered it necessary for them to keep any large permanent deposits of Bank of England Paper in their hands. And it seems reasonable to believe, that the total amount of the unproductive stock of all the Country Banks, consisting of specie and Bank of England paper, is much less at this period, under a circulation vastly increased in extent, than it was before the restriction of 1797. The temptation to establish Country Banks, and issue Promissory Notes, has therefore greatly increased. Some conjecture as to the probable total amount of those issues, or at least as to their recent increase, may be formed, as Your Committee conceive, from the amount of the duties paid for stamps on the re-issuable notes of Country Banks in Great Britain. The total amount of these duties for the year ended on the 10th of October 1808, appears to have been 60,522*l.* 15*s.* 3*d.*, and for the year ended on the 10th of October 1809, 175,129*l.* 17*s.* 7*d.* It must, however, be observed, that on the 10th of October, 1808, these duties experienced an augmentation somewhat exceeding one-third; and that some regulations were made, imposing limitations with respect to the re-issue of all notes not exceeding two

Pounds two Shillings, the effect of which has been to produce a much more than ordinary demand for stamps or notes of this denomination within the year 1809. Owing to this circumstance, it appears impossible to ascertain what may have been the real increase in the circulation of the notes, not exceeding two Pounds two Shillings, within the last year; but with respect to the notes of a higher value, no alteration having been made in the Law as to their re-issue, the following Comparison affords tbe best statement that can be collected from the Documents before the Committee, of the addition made in the year 1809 to the number of those Notes.

Number of Country Bank Notes exceeding 2*l*. 2*s*. each stamped in the years ended the 10th of October 1808, and 10th of October 1809, respectively.

	1808	1809.
	No.	No.
Exceeding 2*l*. 2*s*. and not exceeding 5*l*. 5*s*. -	666,071	922,073
Exceeding 5*l*. 5*s*. and not exceeding 20*l*. -	198,473	380,006
Exceeding 20*l*. and not exceeding 30*l*. -	- - -	2,425
Exceeding 30*l*. and not exceeding 50*l*. -	- - -	674
Exceeding 50*l*. and not exceeding 100*l*. -	- - -	2,611

Assuming that the notes in the two first of these classes were all issued for the lowest denomination to which the duties respectively attach, and such as are most commonly met with in the circulation of country paper, viz. Notes of 5*l*. and 10*l*., (although in the second class there is a considerable number of 20*l*.) and even omitting altogether from the comparison the Notes of the three last classes, the issue of which Your Committee understands is in fact confined to the chartered Banks of Scotland, the result would be, that, exclusive of any increase in the number of notes under 2*l*. 2*s*. the amount of Country Bank paper stamped in the year ended the 10th of October 1809, has exceeded that of the year ended on the 10th of October, 1808, in the sum of

3,095,340*l.* Your Committee can form no positive conjecture as to the amount of Country Bank paper cancelled and withdrawn from circulation in the course of the last year. But considering that it is the interest and practice of the Country Bankers to use the same notes as long as possible; that, as the law now stands, there is no limitation of time to the re-issuing of those not exceeding 2*l.* 2*s.*; and that all above that amount are re-issuable for three years from the date of their first issuing; it appears difficult to suppose that the amount of notes above 2*l.* 2*s.* cancelled in 1809, could be equal to the whole amount stamped in 1808: but even upon that supposition, there would still be an increase for 1809 in the notes of 5*l.* and 10*l.* alone, to the amount above specified of 3,095,340*l.*, to which must be added an increase within the same period of Bank of England Notes to the amount of about 1,500,000*l.*, making in the year 1809, an addition in the whole of between four and five millions to the circulation of Great Britain alone, deducting only the Gold which may have been withdrawn in the course of that year from actual circulation, which cannot have been very considerable, and also making an allowance for some increase in the amount of such country paper, as, though stamped, may not be in actual circulation. This increase in the general paper currency in last year, even after these deductions, would probably be little short of the amount which in almost any one year, since the discovery of America, has been added to the circulating coin of the whole of Europe. Although, as Your Committee has already had occasion to observe, no certain conclusion can be drawn from the numerical amount of paper in circulation, considered abstractedly from all other circumstances, either as to such paper being in excess, or still less as to the proportion of such excess; yet they must remark, that the fact of any very great and rapid increase in that amount, when coupled and attended with all the indications of a depreciated circulation, does afford the strongest confirmatory evidence, that, from the want of some adequate check, the issues of such paper have not been restrained within their proper limits.

Your Committee cannot quit this part of the subject without further observing, that the addition of between four and five millions sterling to the paper circulation of this Country, has doubtless been made at a very small expense to the parties issuing it, only about 100,000*l.* having been paid thereupon in stamps to the Revenue, and probably for the reasons already stated, no corresponding deposits of Gold or Bank of England Notes being deemed by the Country Banks necessary to support their additional issues. These parties therefore, it may be fairly stated, have been enabled under the protection of the law, which virtually secures them against such demands, to create within the last year or fifteen months, at a very trifling expense, and in a manner almost free from all present risk to their respective credits as dealers in paper money, issues of that article to the amount of several millions, operating, in the first instance and in their hands, as capital for their own benefit, and, when used as such by them, falling into and in succession mixing itself with the mass of circulation of which the value in exchange for all other commodities is gradually lowered in proportion as that mass is augmented. If Your Committee could be of opinion that the wisdom of Parliament would not be directed to apply a proper remedy to a state of things so unnatural, and teeming, if not corrected in time, with ultimate consequences so prejudicial to the public welfare, they would not hesitate to declare an opinion, that some mode ought to be devised of enabling the State to participate much more largely in the profits accruing from the present system; but as this is by no means the policy they wish to recommend, they will conclude their observations on this part of the subject, by observing, that in proportion as they most fully agree with Dr. Adam Smith and all the most able writers and Statesmen of this Country, in considering a paper circulation constantly convertible into specie, as one of the greatest practical improvements which can be made in the political and domestic economy of any State; and in viewing the establishment of the Country Banks issuing such paper as a most valuable and essential branch of that improvement in this Kingdom; in the same proportion is Your Committee anxious to revert, as speedily as possible, to the former practice and state of things in this respect: convinced on the one hand, that any thing like a permanent and systematic departure from that practice must ultimately lead to results, which, among other attendant calamities, would be destructive of the system itself; and on the other, that such an event would be the more to be deprecated, as it is only in a Country like this, where good faith, both public and private, is held so high, and where, under the happy union of liberty and law, property and the securities of every description by which it is represented, are equally protected against the encroachments of power and the violence of popular commotion, that the advantages of this system, unaccompanied with any of its dangers, can be permanently enjoyed, and carried to their fullest extent.

Upon a review of all the facts and reasonings which have been submitted to the consideration of Your Committee in the course of their Enquiry, they have formed an Opinion, which they submit to the House:—That there is at present an excess in the paper circulation of this Country, of which the most unequivocal symptom is the very high price of Bullion, and next to that, the low state of the Continental Exchanges; that this excess is to be ascribed to the want of a sufficient check and control in the issues of paper from the Bank of England; and originally, to the suspension of cash payments, which removed the natural and true control. For upon a general view of the subject, Your Committee are of opinion, that no safe, certain, and constantly adequate provision against an excess of paper currency, either occasional or permanent can be found, except in the convertibility of all such paper into specie. Your Committee cannot, therefore, but see reason to regret, that the suspension of cash payments, which, in the most favourable light in which it can be viewed, was only a temporary measure, has been continued so long; and particularly, that by the manner in which the present continuing Act is framed, the character should have been given to it of a permanent war measure.

Your Committee conceive that it would be superfluous to point out in detail, the disadvantages which must result to the Country, from any such general excess of currency as lowers its relative value. The effect of such an augmentation of prices upon all money transactions for time; the unavoidable injury suffered by annuitants, and by creditors of every description, both private and public; the unintended advantage gained by Government and all other debtors; are consequences too obvious to request proof, and too repugnant to justice to be left without remedy. By far the most important portion of this effect appears to Your Committee to be that which is communicated to the wages of common country labour, the rate of which, it is well known, adapts itself more slowly to the changes which happen in the value of money, than the price of any other species of labour or commodity. And it is enough for Your Committee to allude to some classes of the public servants, whose pay, if once raised in consequence of a depreciation of money, cannot so conveniently be reduced again to its former rate, even after money shall have recovered its value. The future progress of these inconveniences and evils, if not checked, must, at no great distance of time, work a practical conviction upon the minds of all those who may still doubt their existence; but even if their progressive increase were less probable than it appears to Your Committee, they cannot help expressing an opinion, that the integrity and honour of Parliament are concerned, not to authorize, longer than is required by imperious necessity, the continuance in this great commercial Country of a system of circulation, in which that natural check or control is absent which maintains the value of money, and, by the permanency of that common standard of value, secures the substantial justice and faith of monied contracts and obligations between man and man.

Your Committee moreover beg leave to advert to the temptation to resort to a depreciation even of the value of the Gold coin by an alteration of the standard, to which Parliament itself might be subjected by a great and long continued excess of paper. This has been the resource of many Governments under such circumstances, and is the obvious and most easy remedy to the evil in question. But it is unnecessary to dwell on the breach of public faith and dereliction of a primary duty of Government, which would manifestly be implied in preferring the reduction of the coin down to the standard of the paper, to the restoration of the paper to the legal standard of the coin.

Your Committee therefore, having very anxiously and deliberately considered this subject, report it to the House, as their Opinion, That the system of the circulating medium of this Country ought to be brought back, with as much speed as is compatible with a wise and necessary caution, to the original principle of Cash payments at the option of the holder of Bank paper.

Your Committee have understood that remedies, or palliatives of a different nature, have been projected; such as, a compulsory limitation of the amount of Bank advances and discounts, during the continuance of the suspension; or, a compulsory limitation, during the same period, of the rate of Bank profits and dividends, by carrying the surplus of profits above that rate to the public account. But, in the judgment of Your Committee, such indirect schemes, for palliating the possible evils resulting from the suspension of cash payments, would prove wholly inadequate for that purpose, because the necessary proportion could never be adjusted, and, if once fixed, might aggravate very much the inconveniencies of a temporary pressure; and even if their efficacy could be made to appear, they would be objectionable as a most hurtful and improper interference with the rights of commercial property.

According to the best judgment Your Committee has been enabled to form, no sufficient remedy for the present, or security for the future, can be pointed out, except the Repeal of the Law which suspends the Cash Payments of the Bank of England.

In effecting so important a change, Your Committee are

of opinion that some difficulties must be encountered, and that there are some contingent dangers to the Bank, against which it ought most carefully and strongly to be guarded. But all those may be effectually provided for, by intrusting to the discretion of the Bank itself the charge of conducting and completing the operation, and by allowing to the Bank so ample a period of time for conducting it, as will be more than sufficient to effect its completion. To the discretion, experience, and integrity of the Directors of the Bank, Your Committee believe that Parliament may safely intrust the charge of effecting that which Parliament may in its wisdom determine upon as necessary to be effected; and that the Directors of that great institution, far from making themselves a party with those who have a temporary interest in spreading alarm, will take a much longer view of the permanent interests of the Bank, as indissolubly blended with those of the Public. The particular mode of gradually effecting the resumption of cash payments ought therefore, in the opinion of Your Committee, to be left in a great measure to the discretion of the Bank, and Parliament ought to do little more than to fix, definitively, the time at which cash payments are to become as before compulsory. The period allowed ought to be ample, in order that the Bank Directors may feel their way, and that, having a constant watch upon the varying circumstances that ought to guide them, and availing themselves only of favourable circumstances, they may tread back their steps slowly, and may preserve both the course of their own affairs as a Company, and that of public and commercial credit, not only safe but unembarrassed.

With this view, Your Committee would suggest, that the Restriction on Cash payments cannot safely be removed at an earlier period than two years from the present time; but Your Committee are of opinion, that early provision ought to be made by Parliament for terminating, by the end of that period, the operation of the several Statutes which have imposed and continued that restriction.

In suggesting this period of two years, Your Committee have not overlooked the circumstance, that, as the law stands at present, the Bank would be compelled to pay in cash at the end of six months after the ratification of a definitive Treaty of Peace; so that if Peace were to be concluded within that period, the recommendation of Your Committee might seem to have the effect of postponing, instead of accelerating, the resumption of payments. But Your Committee are of opinion, that if Peace were immediately to be ratified, in the present state of our circulation it would be most hazardous to compel the Bank to pay cash in six months, and would be found wholly impracticable. Indeed, the restoration of Peace, by opening new fields of commercial enterprise, would multiply instead of abridging the demands upon the Bank for discount, and would render it peculiarly distressing to the commercial world if the Bank were suddenly and materially to restrict their issues. Your Committee are therefore of opinion, that even if Peace should intervene, two years should be given to the Bank for resuming its payments; but that even if the War should be prolonged, Cash payments should be resumed by the end of that period.

Your Committee have not been indifferent to the consideration of the possible occurrence of political circumstances, which may be thought hereafter to furnish an argument in favour of some prolongation of the proposed period of resuming cash payments, or even in favour of a new law for their temporary restriction after the Bank shall have opened. They are, however, far from anticipating a necessity, even in any case, of returning to the present system. But if occasion for a new measure of restriction could be supposed at any time to arise, it can in no degree be grounded, as your Committee think, on any state of the Foreign Exchanges, (which they trust that they have abundantly shown the Bank itself to have the general power of controlling,) but on a political state of things producing, or likely very soon to produce, an alarm at home, leading to so indefinite a demand for cash for domestic uses as it must be impossible for any Banking establishment to provide against. A return to the ordinary system of Banking is, on the very ground of the late extravagant fall of the Exchanges and high price of Gold, peculiarly requisite. That alone can effectually restore general confidence in the value of the circulating medium of the kingdom; and the serious expectation of this event must enforce a preparatory reduction of the quantity of paper, and all other measures which accord with the true principles of Banking The anticipation of the time when the Bank will be constrained to open, may also be expected to contribute to the improvement of the Exchanges; whereas a postponement of this era so indefinite as that of six months after the termination of the War, and especially in the event of an Exchange continuing to fall, (which more and more would generally be perceived to arise from an excess of paper, and a constant depreciation of it) may lead, under an unfavourable state of public affairs, to such a failure of confidence (and especially among foreigners) in the determination of Parliament to enforce a return to the professed standard of the measure of payments, as may serve to precipitate the further fall of the Exchanges, and lead to consequences at once the most discreditable and disastrous.

Although the details of the best mode of returning to cash payments ought to be left to the discretion of the Bank of England, as already stated, certain provisions would be necessary, under the authority of Parliament, both for the convenience of the Bank itself, and for the security of the other Banking establishments in this Country and in Ireland.

Your Committee conceive it may be convenient for the Bank to be permitted to issue Notes under the value of *5l.* for some little time after it had resumed payments in specie.

It will be convenient also for the Chartered Banks of Ireland and Scotland, and all the Country Banks, that they should not be compelled to pay in specie until some time after the resumption of payments in Cash by the Bank of England; but that they should continue for a short period upon their present footing, of being liable to pay their own notes on demand in Bank of England paper.

FINIS.

OBSERVATIONS

ON THE

PRINCIPLES WHICH REGULATE

THE

COURSE OF EXCHANGE;

AND ON THE

PRESENT DEPRECIATED STATE

OF THE

CURRENCY.

By WILLIAM BLAKE, Esq., F.R.S.

LONDON.
1810.

ADVERTISEMENT.

THE first intention in writing the following pages, was to animadvert on some opinions relating to the principles of political economy, which had met with a very general circulation, through the medium of several well-written pamphlets on the depreciation of the currency.

It became irksome, however, and seemed but an invidious task, to select from works that possessed generally a very high degree of merit, a few particular passages, merely to dwell upon their errors; and the author therefore determined to arrange his own thoughts upon the subject, in an order that might admit of his incidentally commenting upon such opinions of other writers, as appeared to be in opposition to his own.

It will perhaps be but too apparent that these remarks upon the principles of exchange have been written and sent to the press, with more haste than is altogether consistent with the respect due to the public; and the author would willingly have delayed the publication till he had an opportunity of revising and correcting the style: but the circumstances of the present moment seem so peculiarly suited to a Treatise of this nature, that he has not been deterred by personal considerations, from communicating his opinions to the public, on a subject which has long occupied his attention.

In the execution of his plan, his endeavour has been, to hold a middle course between such a conciseness as might be incompatible with perspicuity, and that degree of superfluous illustration which might appear to insult the understanding of his readers.

He is not without hopes that he may escape being classed with those "who, while they imagined that they "themselves had made important discoveries, uniformly "found that no discoveries had been made by their prede- "cessors," for the author neither pretends to discoveries him self nor denies that merit to others. If the following observations have any claim upon the public attention, it can arise solely from the attempt to discriminate, more accurately than has hitherto been done, the operation of causes that have been long known, and frequently discussed; but which have not met with so distinct and detailed a consideration as the author deems essential to a due comprehension of the subject.

May, 1810.

OBSERVATIONS,

&c., &c., &c.

INTRODUCTION.

THE principles which regulate the exchange will be investigated in the simplest manner, by an arrangement that may lead the mind gradually from the separate consideration of the individual causes by which it is influenced, to the more complicated results that arise from their combined operation.

The effects of the exchange are first practically felt, when the intercourse between foreign nations has rendered it necessary to make a remittance from one country to another.

The usual mode of making a remittance, either for the discharge of debts previously existing, or for the purpose of investing it in foreign produce, is to purchase and transmit, to the person to whom the remittance is to be made, a foreign bill of exchange.

A foreign bill of exchange is an order addressed to some person residing abroad, directing him to pay a determinate quantity of foreign currency to the person in whose favour it is drawn. The quantity, therefore, to be paid, is fixed by the sum specified in the bill; but the amount of British currency to be given here, for the purchase of the bill, is by no means fixed, but is continually varying, from causes which it is the object of this essay to explain.

When the market price of foreign bills is high, the exchange is said to be unfavourable, because a larger sum will be required for discharging a given amount of foreign payments. When the market price is low, the exchange is said to be favourable, because the discharge of the same amount of foreign payments will be effected by a smaller quantity of British currency. Whatever therefore affects the price of a foreign bill will affect the state of the exchange.

Now the price of bills will depend, in the same manner as that of any other commodity, upon two causes:

First, on their abundance or scarcity in the market, compared with the demand for them; and secondly, on the value of the currency in which they are to be paid, compared with the value of that with which they are bought.

If there be a certain quantity of foreign bills in the market, and at the same time a great demand for making foreign payments or investments, the holders of bills will soon feel the effect of the competition for their purchase, and will refuse to part with them, except an additional price be given as a premium. If, on the contrary, there be an abundant supply of bills in the market, and not much demand for foreign payment or investment, there will be more persons inclined to dispose of bills, than there are persons desirous of purchasing them; and the holders, who wish to convert them into cash, will not be able to sell, except at a discount; so that this variation in the market price might take place, though the value of the currency of the respective countries continued absolutely unchanged.

Supposing, however, the quantity of bills in the market sufficient exactly to supply the demand, and that there are no more persons wishing to sell than there are persons wanting to purchase them, so that any alteration in their price, from this cause, is precluded; yet as the currency of all countries is subject to continual fluctuations in its value, the quantity of British currency to be given for a determinate quantity of foreign currency, at any period of time, will depend upon the comparative value of each. An English guinea may be worth, sometimes, a certain number of guilders, florins, or piastres, and at others a very different number, depending either upon alterations in the value of the guinea, or of the guilder, florin, or piastre. The moment that these alterations take place, the information is communicated from one part of the mercantile community to the other, and the price of foreign bills is regulated accordingly.

The rate of the *computed* exchange, then, will vary from two causes, totally distinct from each other. The first, arising from the abundance or scarcity of bills in the market, is the foundation of what may be called the *real* exchange, which depends upon the payments a country has to make, compared with those it has to receive, and has no reference to the state of the currency.

The second, arising from alterations in the value of the currency, is the foundation of what may be called the *nominal* exchange, which has no reference whatever to the state of debt and credit of the country. And as the effects, which the *real* and *nominal* exchange have upon the general dealings and commerce of the country, are as distinct as their causes, the natural mode of investigating the subject will be to follow the order which this division points out; and after tracing the operation of the *real* and *nominal* exchange independently of each other, to consider their combined effect, in treating upon the *computed* exchange.

OF THE REAL EXCHANGE.

In order that the consideration of the *real* Exchange may be kept perfectly distinct from that of the *nominal*, let it be supposed, during the review of this subject, that the Coin of any two countries that have intercourse with each other is in a perfect state as to purity and weight; and that the proportion which the quantity of currency bears to the commodities to be circulated by it in the respective countries, continues unchanged, so as to exclude any alteration in its value.

In the commercial dealings which take place between any two nations, the surplus produce of the one will be exchanged for the surplus produce of the other. When neither of them imports from the other to a greater amount than it exports to the same country, the debts and credits of each will balance; and there will be no difficulty in making remittances from one to the other, without the actual transfer of Bullion or money: for as the Bills drawn *by* the merchants exporting produce would exactly equal, in amount, the Bills drawn *on* the merchants importing produce, their mutual debts and credits would be easily liquidated by the transfer of Bills of Exchange; and as the supply of Bills would be equal to the demand for them, they would neither bear a premium, nor be at a discount, and the *real* Exchange would be said to be at par.

At any particular period of time, however, it may happen that a nation may have imported to a greater amount than it has exported, and consequently have more payments to make than to receive. If at that time payment were demanded, the balance due from the debtor country could only be liquidated by the transfer of money or Bullion; and the merchant, rather than incur the expense of the freight insurance and commission attending its conveyance, will be induced to give more for a Bill of Exchange, than the sum for which it is drawn. A competition will be thereby created among the purchasers of Bills upon the creditor country, and they will bear a premium in proportion to the demand. In that country, on the contrary, there will be more persons holding, than there are persons wanting Bills, and the excess above the demand can only be converted into Coin or Bullion by sending them to the place upon which they are drawn. But this Bullion or Coin cannot be conveyed to the creditor, without his paying the expense of its transit; and the holder of a Bill in the creditor country, if he be desirous of converting it into money, will be content to receive something less than its amount. There will therefore be in the creditor country a competition to sell, and Bills will be at a discount in proportion to the supply. The premium in one country will correspond with the discount in the other.

Whatever, therefore, affects the proportion between the

payments to be made, and those to be received, will alter the state of the *real* Exchange.

This proportion varies principally from the following circumstances: first, from the effects of favourable or unfavourable seasons creating a difference in the customary supply of the annual produce of the land: secondly, from the alterations which take place in the amount of the foreign expenditure of a country, arising either from the expenses of foreign establishments and expeditions, subsidies to foreign powers, or remittances to absentee proprietors.

The population of the countries that have commercial intercourse with each other, though it may vary considerably in long periods of time, is not subject to any sudden changes from year to year; the wants, therefore, for annual consumption may be considered as nearly constant; but the supply of those wants depending principally on the annual produce of the land, will vary to a very great extent. If in any particular country there should be a failure in a commodity which is also the common growth of the neighbouring countries, the deficiency will be supplied, in a greater or less degree, by an increased importation; and where the failure takes place in an article of the first necessity, as for instance, in corn, which forms the principal part of the food of the people, the importation will be augmented nearly in proportion to the extent of the deficiency. The average amount of annual imports will in these cases be exceeded, and the ordinary proportion of payments between the country and foreign nations proportionably affected; and though the effects of the failure of a corn crop, from its magnitude, and its being an article of the first necessity, are most apparent, an alteration similar in kind, but not in degree, will be induced by a failure in the produce of any commodity to the use of which a country has been long habituated. In an article of mere luxury, the deficiency of its produce, by occasioning an increase of its price, may contract the consumption, and thus cause the value of the quantity exported or imported to be in a certain degree uniform; yet it may be easily conceived that a combination of circumstances would, even in commodities of less necessity than corn, lead to an unusual export or import, and therefore materially affect the state of debt and credit of a country.

The second circumstance, which has been stated as affecting the payments and receipts of a country, is the variation in the amount of its foreign expenditure, under which head may be included, the charge of maintaining its foreign establishments, civil and military, subsidies to foreign powers, and the remittances to absentee proprietors: the last of which it may be sufficient merely to mention, since they must bear so very small a proportion to the sum total of the foreign expenditure of a great nation, that any variations in their amount would scarcely have a perceptible effect upon the general state of its payments and receipts. On the contrary, the subsidies to foreign powers, and the expense of maintaining the civil and military establishments abroad, may vary, in times of war, to an enormous extent.

Now this expenditure may be supplied either by the export of Bullion or Specie; by purchasing foreign Bills in the home market, and sending them to the place where the money is wanted; or by authorising the agents abroad to draw Bills upon the government, and discount them at the place where they are drawn, upon the best terms that the Bill-market will allow.

By the export of Bullion or Specie the expenditure would be at once defrayed, without creating any debt against the country, and therefore without producing any effect upon the *real* Exchange; but there are various reasons why this mode has not been generally adopted. In the first place, the quantity of Bullion or Specie in a country which has no mines of its own, is exceedingly limited, and the total amount that can be spared or procured for exportation will bear a very small proportion to the foreign expenditure arising from protracted warfare. In the next place, there must always be a certain expense of insurance and freight attending its transport; and whenever, therefore, foreign Bills can be procured at a less premium than the amount of that expense, or Bills on the government abroad can be negociated at a less discount, the vehicle of Bills will necessarily be preferred to that of Specie or Bullion.

The foreign expenditure of this country, as appears by the account presented to the Committee of Secrecy by Mr. Long, in 1797, was principally paid by the draft of Bills from the Continent upon England. A debt is thus created against the country equal to the amount of the Bills drawn upon the government, which must exist, in a greater or less degree, till the whole of those bills are liquidated by the remittance of value of some kind or other. Whatever, therefore, be the proportion between the payments to be made, and those to be received, at any period of time, arising from the ordinary commercial dealings; whatever be the quantity of Bills in the home or foreign market, which are, in fact, the evidences of that proportion; the foreign expenditure of government must derange the natural state of the balance, and produce an alteration proportional to its amount.* If the Bills be drawn from abroad, they will increase the quantity of British Bills in the foreign Bill market, and lower their value from their abundance. If the foreign Bills be purchased at home for the purpose of remittance, the competition of government will immediately raise their price, and increase their scarcity. Whether the *real* Exchange, therefore, at the time of the expenditure taking place, be favourable or unfavourable, it will always be the less favourable, or the more unfavourable, in consequence of that expenditure.

We have hitherto been considering the demand for foreign Bills, as originating wholly in the necessity of

---

* See the examination of Mr. Huskisson before the Committee for enquiry into the policy and conduct of the Expedition to the Scheldt; where he states the difficulty of making the remittances to Austria without lowering the Exchange, which was already from 18 to 20 per cent. against this country.

See also Mr. Moore's Narrative of the Campaign in Spain, and the difficulty of negociating Bills there, for the supply of the army in that country.

liquidating balances arising from transactions that had already taken place; but there is another cause of demand, which springs from the desire of entering upon new commercial speculations whenever the relative prices in the home and foreign markets are such, as to afford the prospect of an adequate profit. If the current *real* prices abroad are low, compared with those in the home market, there will be an increased demand for foreign Bills, for the purpose of making foreign investments; and the extent of this demand will be in proportion to the probable amount of the profits to be derived, and the unemployed capital that will admit of being diverted into that channel. As soon as a foreign price-current is received, it is compared with the price-currents at home, and the conduct of the merchant is regulated accordingly. If commodities abroad be relatively cheap, there will be more purchasers than usual of foreign Bills; if they be relatively dear, there will be fewer purchasers than usual; and thus whatever be the *real* Exchange under any given balance of payment to be made, and payment to be received, the arrival of a foreign price-current, or an alteration in the home price-current, will have an instantaneous effect upon the foreign Bill market; and the weekly, and sometimes daily, fluctuations in the course of the *real* Exchange, are attributable principally to the variations in this species of demand.

It must not be inferred, however, that because the prices of commodities cause a fluctuation in the course of the *real* Exchange, that therefore the *real* Exchange causes a fluctuation in the prices of commodities. The prices of commodities in the home market (upon the supposition to which we constantly adhere, that the value of the currencies throughout the mercantile republic remains unaltered) cannot depend upon the number of foreign Bills in the same market, but upon the abundance or scarcity of the commodities themselves, compared with the real demand for them, that is, the wants of consumers; and it is essential that this peculiar feature of the *real* Exchange should not escape the reader's attention, since it forms one of the leading distinctions between the *real*, and the *nominal* Exchange, and is the cause of the great difference of their effects upon the general exports and imports of the country.

It may, then, be stated generally, that, whenever there is a balance of debt against a country, arising, either from an excess of imports over exports, a large foreign expenditure of government, or the remittance of foreign subsidies; whenever, in short, there is a demand for foreign payment, or foreign investment, the price of foreign Bills will rise, and may bear a premium; and the price of Bills drawn on the country from abroad will fall, and be at a corresponding discount; and, on the contrary, when there is a balance of debt due to a country, and a diminution of demand for foreign payment or foreign investment, the price of Bills drawn from abroad will increase, and may bear a premium; and the price of foreign Bills will fall in the home market, and may be at a discount.

What effects the *real* Exchange has upon the general exports and imports of the country, it will now be proper to enquire.

The merchant is regulated in the conduct of his business, by a comparison of the prices which commodities bear in the home, and foreign market; his attention is directed to the prices current, accounts of which are constantly published, and immediately communicated by his correspondents abroad. If he finds that the price of any commodity abroad is so much higher than the price of the same commodity in the home market, that its sale abroad will pay the expenses of freight and insurance, and at the same time leave him an adequate profit for his trouble, he will immediately purchase and export the commodity in question. As soon as the bill of lading has been received by his correspondent to whom the goods are consigned, he will draw his Bill upon him for the amount; and if the *real* Exchange be at par, will have no difficulty in procuring money equal to the value specified in the Bill, by negotiating it in the market at home. But if the *real* Exchange should not be at par, it is evident that his calculation upon the profit he is likely to derive from the export, must include the premium, or discount, which he will receive, or pay, in the disposal of his Bill. If the Exchange is unfavourable, or, in other words, if the payments to be made are greater than those to be received, foreign Bills will bear a premium; and consequently, the additional sum which he will receive on the disposal of his Bill, will enable him to export with profit, though the difference of prices of the commodity at home and abroad were such, as would not allow him to export, with the *real* Exchange at par. The more unfavourable the *real* Exchange, the less might be the difference of prices that would induce him to export; so that an unfavourable state of the real Exchange will operate as a bounty upon exportation, to the amount of the premium, which he will receive upon his foreign Bill.

The same calculation upon the state of the *real* Exchange will be necessary, if the difference of prices at home and abroad should lead him to import. But whatever be the state of the *real* Exchange, it will affect the importing merchant, and the exporting merchant, in a directly opposite manner: for the importing merchant must pay for the goods he imports, either by purchasing a foreign Bill to remit to his correspondent abroad, for which, if the *real* Exchange be unfavourable, he must pay a premium; or, if his correspondent abroad is authorised by the importing merchant to draw a Bill upon him for the payment of the goods consigned, as that Bill cannot be converted into money without a loss, he must draw for such an additional sum above the invoice price of the goods, as will counterbalance the discount to be allowed in negotiating his Bill in the foreign market.—This additional sum, therefore, paid by the importing merchant in the premium of the foreign Bill, or drawn for by the correspondent to make up the loss on the discount, will be so much deducted from his profit. Unless, then, the difference of prices at home and abroad be such as to admit of this deduction, the merchant must cease to import; so that an unfavourable *real* Exchange will operate as a duty upon importation, in proportion to the premium on a foreign Bill, or the corresponding discount on the Bill drawn from abroad; and in the same manner it is easy to see, that a favourable *real* Exchange will operate as a duty upon exportation, and will afford a bounty upon importation.

An unfavourable *real* Exchange will, therefore, have the effect of forcing the exports of a country; because, during its unfavourable state, the merchant can afford to sell at a lower price to the foreign consumer, and this diminution of price will naturally lead to an increased consumption. It will contract imports, because the importing merchant must sell foreign produce at a higher rate to the home consumer, to draw back the duty imposed upon him by the unfavourable state of the *real* Exchange, and consequently the high price will diminish the home consumption.

It is evident that during an unfavourable state of the *real* Exchange, the bounty received by the exporting merchant does not depend upon the nature of the commodity he exports. Whatever kind of goods he sends abroad, it gives him the power of drawing upon the person to whom he consigns them, to the amount of their value; and upon this Bill he receives the premium that the market affords. He will of course select those commodities for exportation, which, besides the premium afforded by his Bill, will give him the greatest profit, by the difference of price abroad and at home. Of all the commodities, which are the objects of request among trading nations, there is none perhaps that is subject to so little variation in its *real* price, as Bullion. The annual quantity produced from the mines is very nearly constant,—its distribution, from the facility with which it is transported, is exceedingly uniform,—and its value, and consequently its real price, throughout Europe at least, must be considered as nearly the same. Unless, then, the bounty afforded by the unfavourable state of the *real* Exchange, were greater than the expenses attending the transit of Bullion, it would be of all others the commodity* least likely

* Mr. Thornton, apparently from not being aware of the mode in which the export of ordinary produce was increased by an unfavourable

to be selected by the exporting merchant: but that same uniformity of value and of price, which would prevent its being exported befőre the premium on a foreign Bill exceeded the expenses of the transit of Bullion, would be the very cause, why, as soon as the premium had reached that point, it would immediately be chosen as one of the most eligible for exportation.

The export and import of Bullion are generally conducted by a class of the community remarkable for their shrewdness, and the small profits upon which they transact their business; and as soon as the premium on a foreign Bill exceeds, by a very small amount, the expenses of the transit of Bullion, the certainty of the profit compensates in some degree for its smallness, and the opportunity, when it occurs, is seldom neglected. The adverse debt will then begin to be paid, by the Bullion merchants exporting to take advantage of the premium; and the competition will be such, that the *real* exchange will be very rapidly brought down, so as no longer to afford a profit upon the export of this article. The exporters of consumable produce will during this period co-operate with the Bullion merchants; and when the latter have ceased to derive a profit, the former will still continue their operations, till the unfavourable Exchange is reduced to par, or, in other words, till the exports have been such, as to counterbalance the adverse debt, and render the quantity of foreign Bills in the market equal to the demand.

From this statement it is obvious, that the natural limit to the amount of the *real* Exchange is the expense of the transit of Bullion; and long before it has arrived at that point, the export of ordinary produce will be forced, and its import restrained; so that the *real* Exchange can scarcely begin to deviate from par, without calling into action a principle that will correct its deviation. It may oscillate a little on the one side, or the other, from its point of rest,

---

real Exchange, seems to imagine that the greater part of the adverse balance must necessarily be paid in Bullion.

but can hardly admit of remaining either permanently favourable, or permanently unfavourable, to a nation, in the ordinary course of its transactions.*

It must not be inferred, however, because the expense of the transit of Bullion is the limit of the *real* Exchange, that it is therefore a fixed limit, and capable of being estimated at a certain per-centage on the price of a foreign Bill: for when the *real* Exchange has caused a transit of Bullion to any considerable degree, it will at length create a difference in the market price of Bullion itself. This article will become scarce in the country from which it is sent, and abundant in that into which it is flowing. Its price will rise in the former, and fall in the latter. The exporter, therefore, will then have to calculate the difference of prices in the home and foreign market; and if in the first instance the profit were but just sufficient to induce him to export, it is clear that after the change has taken place, the exportation of Bullion, under the same rate of Exchange, will cease.

Mr. Boyd, in his evidence before the Secret Committee of the House of Lords, in 1797, respecting the mode of remitting the Imperial loan to Vienna, states, "that he "thought the remittances by Bills of Exchange were not "quite so favorable as those in Bullion; but, if he had "stuck exclusively to Bullion, the price of this article would "have risen so high here, and probably sunk so low at "Hambro', that instead of a good, it would have become "a bad remittance." The limit therefore of the *real* Exchange can only be fixed at a certain rate, upon the supposition that the price of Bullion is the same in the home and the foreign market; for when the *real* price of Bullion abroad is less than it is at home, the transit of

* This observation must be understood to apply to the general balance that subsists between any one nation, and the whole of those with which it has commercial intercourse, it being evident that where a nation trades with more than one country, the *real* Exchange may be constantly favourable with one, provided it be constantly unfavourable with another.

Bullion will not take place, unless the rate of Exchange be sufficiently high, not only to pay the expences of transit, but also to compensate for the loss attending the difference of home and foreign prices. When, on the contrary, the price of Bullion abroad is higher than in the home market, it is equally evident that Bullion will be exported, when the *real* Exchange is less than the expenses of the transit of Bullion.

And thus it is that a very small part of the payment of an unfavourable balance is effected by the transit of Bullion, since its transit can scarcely begin to take place, without rendering it a more unprofitable article of export than ordinary consumable commodities. For the former cannot, generally speaking, be considered as a commodity the consumption of which will be augmented by a diminished price, its use being confined to the wealthy few, who are not likely to encrease the quantity of their plate, or indulge themselves more freely in the purchase of ornamental manufactures, from the temporary variations in the market price of Bullion: but it is not so with ordinary produce. The great mass of mankind will always endeavour to purchase their comforts at the lowest possible rate. If by means of an unfavorable Exchange our merchants can supply the nations of the Continent with British manufactures, cheaper than when the Exchange is at par, our manufactures will be bought and consumed; and in proportion to the degree in which the Exchange is unfavourable, in the same proportion, shall we be enabled to enter more easily into a competition with the manufactures abroad, even in their own market.

A possible case may, nevertheless, be supposed, where the government may, from political causes, be induced to continue a scale of warfare, demanding a larger foreign expenditure than can be supplied by a proportional excess of exports over imports; and, consequently, if the quantity of Bullion in the country were extremely limited, the *real* Exchange might, notwithstanding the usual causes that check and prevent its fluctuations, deviate so much from par, and create so great a drain of Bullion, as to raise its market price above its mint price.

It is certain that the Bullion merchants would in that case, rather than pay the advanced market price, endeavour to collect the current Coin for the purpose of exportation. A pound of gold at the English mint is coined into forty-four guineas and a half, or 46*l.* 14*s.* 6*d.** By exchanging, then, bank-notes at the Bank, for coin, they can always procure a pound of gold for 46*l.* 14*s* 6*d.* in notes; and so long as they have this power of purchasing gold at the mint price, at the Bank, they will not give a higher market price elsewhere. If the paper, therefore, be convertible into Coin at the option of the holder, the Bullion merchants will be constantly pouring in their notes upon the Bank, to be exchanged for Coin, which will be exported† as fast as it can be procured; and thus a drain upon the Bank will be established, to a greater or less extent, in proportion to the amount of foreign payment that must be discharged; before the *real* Exchange is sufficiently elevated to prevent any profit upon the export of Bullion. As long as this drain continues, the Bank will be compelled to purchase Bullion, and to coin, for the purpose of supplying the demand occasioned by the return of its notes; and as the purchase must be made at the then market price, it is evident that in whatever degree that shall exceed the mint price, the Bank must sustain a loss proportional to the difference; and that a continuance of the drain, under such circumstances, might eventually lead to its ruin.

* Throughout this pamphlet, the Author, in speaking of Bullion, has confined his observations to Gold Bullion only: first, because the Gold Coin is now the only one in which a legal payment can be made for debts above 25*l.* in amount; and, secondly, because he has derived considerable assistance from, and had frequent occasion to refer to, Mr. Mushet's valuable Tables of the Exchange between London and Hambro', since the year 1760, in which the price of Gold Bullion only is noted.

† It is true the laws have affixed most severe penalties to the melting or exporting the current Coin of the realm; but these penalties have always been found insufficient for its protection, the Coin having uniformly disappeared, whenever either of the above practices has been attended with an adequate profit.

It was upon this ground that the Directors of the Bank, in the year 1795, remonstrated in so urgent a manner against any further loans to the Emperor; lest the drain, which those loans occasioned, should prove fatal to that establishment. In a letter from the Directors to Mr. Pitt, dated October 8, 1795, after observing upon the continual drain that the loan to the Emperor had occasioned; they proceed to state, "that the present price of gold being from 4*l.* 3*s.* to " 4*l.* 4*s.* per ounce, and our guineas being to be purchased at " 3*l.* 17*s.* 10½*d.*, clearly demonstrates the grounds of our " fears, it being only necessary to state these facts to the " Chancellor of the Exchequer."* Now those very facts ought to have led Mr. Pitt to suspect, that the drain upon the Bank, at that time, arose from some other cause than the loans to the Emperor; for it has been already shewn how impossible it is, that the Bullion merchant should for any length of time continue the export of Bullion, without increasing the quantity abroad, and lowering its price so much, that it would no longer afford a profitable speculation. Mr. Pitt should have recollected, that for the last twenty-one years from 1774, when the reformation in the gold Coin took place, though the *computed* Exchange between Hambro' and London had frequently been so unfavourable to London, as far to exceed the expenses of the transit of Bullion, the quantity required for export had been so easily supplied, either from the spare Bullion, or from the export of the Coin, that the market price of bullion had never exceeded the mint price, except only for about six months, at the time of the peace of Versailles, in the year 1783; and then only by about 3*s.* 2½*d.* in 100*l.*, not much more than $\frac{1}{700}$th part. Now as during a great part of that period, the country was engaged in active warfare, which would cause, from the variations in the amount of the foreign expenditure, occasional demands for large foreign payments, one would have expected, that such an excessive increase of the market price above the mint price, as was asserted by the Bank

* P. 152, Secret Committee of the House of Lords, 1797.

Directors to have taken place, amounting to 7*l.* 4*s.* 5½*d.* per cent., being forty-five times greater than any variation that had occurred in the former war, would have led him to receive their remonstrances with considerable suspicion.

If, in addition to this, he had called to mind that the excess of the market price above the mint price, could be accounted for, and might have taken place, though no loan to the Emperor had been in a course of remittance; that the excess of the market price of Bullion over the mint price had existed to a very great extent, attended with a drain upon the Bank, prior to the year 1774, when the gold currency was degraded below its standard weight; that the drain, under such circumstances, would have equally existed, though there had been no demand for the exportation of Bullion, (as will be fully explained, in the Section upon the Nominal Exchange;) it seems unaccountable that he should so easily have yielded to the representations of the Directors; and it is the more to be lamented, since the impressions he then received, seem to have had considerable influence in producing the fatal measure of permanent restriction on Bank payments, which began in the year 1797, only fourteen months after this period.

But assuming it to be the fact, that the foreign expenditure at that period was greater than on any former occasion, and that the real cause of the drain was that assigned by the Bank Directors, still they had the means of prevention within their own power; for it will be shown, in the next Section, on the *nominal* Exchange, that when the currency of a country consists partly of Paper, and partly of Coin, and that the former bears a large proportion to the latter, the Bank can at all times contract the issue of its notes, and produce a considerable diminution in the total amount of the currency. By this means the *nominal* prices of commodities, and amongst the rest, that of Bullion, will be lowered. As soon, therefore, as a reduction has thus been effected in the price of Bullion below its mint price, the drain upon the Bank will at once be stopped; since it will no longer be the interest of the Bullion merchant to purchase gold at the mint price, by exchanging notes at the Bank, when he can procure it at a cheaper rate in the market. The Bank Directors were so well aware of this mode of counteracting the effects of a drain upon them, that they had recourse to it at the very period of making their remonstrances; and the market price of Bullion, which had been 9*s.* 7*d.* per cent. below its mint price, in the beginning of the year 1795, and which probably might never have been raised, had not the Bank, at this period, extended its paper from 11 to 13½ millions, was, by the subsequent contraction of it to 9½ millions, again reduced before the middle of the year 1796, to 9*s.* 7*d.* below the mint price. Unfortunately, too for the country, this same counteracting principle was resorted to, when the drain took place in the beginning of the year 1797, arising, not from a demand for bullion for the purpose of exportation, nor from an excess in its market price above the mint price, neither of which existed at the time;* but solely from the alarm occasioned by the fears of invasion;—a drain that will always occur under similar circumstances, and which will be aggravated, rather than relieved, by a contraction of paper.

It should be carefully remembered, that the profit from the export of Bullion in consequence of an unfavourable *real* Exchange, does not arise from Bullion selling for a higher price in the foreign than in the home market, nor from any scarcity of Bullion abroad occasioning an extraordinary demand for it; but solely from the demand for foreign bills, for the purpose of making foreign payments, being so great, that the premium upon them exceeds the expenses of the transit of bullion; and, consequently, the transit will take place and afford a profit to the exporter, though the price of bullion be precisely the same abroad as it is at home.

* In January, 1797, the *computed* Exchange between Hambro' and London was 5*l.* 4*s.* per cent. in favour of London, and during the year rose to 13 per cent.; it never being, at any part of the year, less than 3*l.* 2*s.* in favour of London. The market price of Bullion, at the same period, was never above its mint price.

When such a quantity of bullion has been exported as to raise its market price above the mint price, the coin being obtainable at the mint price, will be exported in preference to bullion; not in consequence of any depreciation in the value of the coin, for it will purchase the same quantity of ordinary produce after the rise of the price of bullion as before; nor because it is more valuable abroad than it is here, for it will not purchase more in the foreign than the home market; but it will be exported, for the same reason that the bullion is exported, to take advantage of the premium on foreign bills, and will be sent, though the price of bullion be precisely the same in the continental market as the English mint price.

After what has been stated, it will be sufficiently apparent, upon what a false foundation the old notions respecting the advantages of a favourable balance of trade are built, and how futile all attempts must be to procure and detain bullion, beyond the quantity that is actually wanted for consumption. The transit of bullion from a high or low *real* exchange is an unnatural transit, not arising from the wants of the country into which it flows, but depending solely on the profits which a temporary pressure for foreign payments affords to the bullion merchants on the sale of foreign bills; and as soon as the cause that has produced the temporary influx subsides, (an event that will sooner or later necessarily take place, by the import of such ordinary produce as is wanted for the purposes of consumption, and increased enjoyment of the people,) the superfluous and unused quantity of bullion that has been accumulated, will flow back from the country where its abundance has rendered its real price low, to those nations from which it had been unnaturally sent, and where its scarcity will have rendered its real price high.

Much of the confusion that attends this question would have been avoided, had the dealers in bills of exchange, and the dealers in bullion, (that is, the persons who export or import bullion for the supply of consumers,) been two distinct classes of merchants. It would then have been seen that the profits of the dealer in bills of exchange flowed through very different channels from those of the dealer in bullion. If at any time the course of exchange were such as to afford a profit to the bill merchant by the sale of foreign bills, he would export that bullion which had been imported for the use of the manufacturer, and would continue to export till it no longer afforded a profit. The bullion dealer would then begin to re-import, in consequence of the difference of prices in the home and foreign markets, the bullion that the bill merchant had sent away, in consequence of the high premium on foreign bills. Whatever derangement the bill merchants might occasion in the quantity of bullion that would be otherwise naturally distributed among the different countries according to their wants, would be remedied by the operations of the bullion merchants, who would find their advantage in restoring the equilibrium that the bill merchants had destroyed.

The dealer in bills of exchange would have employment, when there was the least difference between the prices of bullion in the home and foreign market, and the *real* exchange at the greatest deviation from par.

The bullion dealer would be most engaged, when there was the greatest difference in these prices, and the *real* exchange at its least deviation from par.

Had this distinction been attended to by Lord King, he would never have entertained such erroneous opinions respecting the exports of silver from this country to India, nor have considered them as indications of an exchange constantly in favour of England against the Continent; for he would have seen, that the export of bullion is not regulated merely by the speculations of the dealers in bills of exchange, but is effected, like that of any other commodity, when there is such a difference in its real prices at any two places, as will afford a profit on its transit, an occurrence that will frequently take place, even with an exchange at par.

OF THE NOMINAL EXCHANGE.

The market price of a foreign bill has been stated to depend upon two circumstances: first, on the scarcity of bills in the market compared with the demand for them; and secondly, on the value of the coin or currency in which they are to be paid, compared with the value of the coin or currency with which they are bought.

The first of these, as connected with the *real* exchange, formed the subject of the foregoing Section; we shall now proceed to examine the nature and effects of the second, on which depend the alterations of the *nominal* exchange; and as in treating of the *real* exchange we endeavoured to keep the subject as distinct as possible from the question of the *nominal* exchange, by supposing no alteration to take place in the value of the currencies in the respective countries; so in tracing the effects of the *nominal* exchange, we shall suppose the state of the *real* exchange to remain unaltered; or the mutual dealings and intercourse between the nations composing the great mercantile republic to be such, that the price of foreign bills is not affected by any variation in their abundance or scarcity, but that the supply of them is constantly sufficient to answer the *real* demand.

In this case the variations in their price can arise only from changes in the comparative value of the currencies in which they are paid, and those with which they are bought.

It will not be necessary, therefore, to enter into any enquiry respecting those changes which have taken place from the discovery of the American mines, or which have arisen from any cause that would affect all currencies in an equal degree; since the object is not to compare the value of currencies now, with what they were at any former period, but to estimate the local alterations that have taken place in the currency of one country, without a corresponding alteration in that of others.

The currency of every nation is subject to continual fluctuations in its value, principally from three circumstances.

First, An alteration in the quality and standard purity of the metal of which the coin is formed.

Secondly, An alteration in the quantity of the metal contained in coin of the same denomination.

Thirdly, An alteration in the total amount of the currency of a country, without a corresponding alteration in the commodities to be circulated by it.

The first of these is now seldom resorted to in a civilized country, even under the most pressing necessities of the government.

The second has been frequently adopted by princes and sovereign states, who through a mistaken policy have imagined that they derived a benefit from diminishing the quantity of metals contained in their coins. The English pound contained, in the time of Edward the First, a pound of silver. The French livre contained a pound weight of silver, in the time of Charlemagne. The English pound contains, at present, only one-third, and the French one-66th part of their original value ;* but I believe, except in Turkey, there is no instance of this practice being countenanced by any of the modern governments. The metallic currencies, however, of most nations, even where the governments have been desirous of maintaining them in a state of the utmost possible perfection, have been much diminished in value by being worn from use, and clipt or otherwise degraded by the illicit practices of the people. To avoid the confusion that would follow from the constant fluctuations in the value of currencies, merchants have adopted a mode by which they endeavour to estimate the extent of these fluctuations; and for this purpose, have ascertained with tolerable accuracy, in what quantities of coin of the mint standard in different countries, an equal weight of gold or silver of the same standard fineness is contained. Thus

* Smith's Wealth of Nations, vol. i. p. 39.

it has been determined, that a pound sterling of the English mint contains the same weight of silver, of a certain fineness, as 33 schillings 8 grotes,* of tho Hambro' banco-money; and in speaking of the exchange with Hambro', 33. 8. is in the technical language of merchants said to be the par of exchange. In the same manner the par of exchange with France is fixed at 24, because 24 livres of the mint standard of France contain the same weight of silver, of a certain fineness, as the pound sterling of the English mint.

By means of this rule, the merchants of one country would never be at a loss to estimate what quantity of their own money would be equivalent to a specific sum of foreign money, so far as regarded the weight of metal, provided the coins of the respective countries contained the due weight of their respective mints. But in some countries the coins are more, in others less worn, and clipt or otherwise degraded below the mint standard. When these alterations have taken place, it would be necessary either to establish a new par of exchange, to guide merchants in their money transactions, or, as is now the general usage, not to alter the par of exchange, but to mark the fluctuation of the currency, by considering it as so much above or below the established par.

---

* From the evidence before the Secret Committee of the House of Lords, in the year 1797, it appears that there is a difference in the mode of estimating the par of Exchange with Hambro'; the house of Goldsmid considering 33. 8. and Mr. Boyd's 34. 8. as the par of Exchange. The difference seems to have arisen, from the former estimating the par according to the standard of Hambro' banco money; the latter, according to the actual currency of Hambro' which appears to be more than 3 per cent. below the standard of the banco money. Upon this supposition there is less difficulty in reconciling the apparent contradiction that 3 schillings above the par, has the same effect one way, upon the transit of gold, that 4 grotes below par has the other; a fact that was stated by Mr. Goldsmid's partner, but which he was unable satisfactorily to explain.

If the Hambro' currency were so much degraded below the banco money, that 35 schillings 4 grotes currency were worth no more than 33 schillings 8 grotes banco money, there would be a *nominal* Exchange of 1 schilling 8 grotes against Hambro', for every pound sterling; and if the par is estimated at 33. 8. 4 grotes, below that sum, and 3 schillings above it, would be equally distant from the *real* par of 35 schillings 4 grotes.

In King William's time, before the reformation of the silver coin, (silver being then the metal in which the payments of the country were legally made,) the current coin was rather more than 25 per cent. below its standard value. The established par, however, was not altered, but the exchange was said to be 25 per cent. against England.* Before the reformation of our gold coin in 1774, the guinea contained so much less than its standard weight, that it was degraded 2 or 3 per cent. when compared with the French coin at the same period; and the exchange between England and France was then computed to be 2 or 3 per cent. against this country;—upon the reformation of the gold coin, the exchange rose to par. The Turkish government, in the course of the last forty years, has made three great alterations in its coin. Before these frauds were committed, the Turkish piastre contained nearly as much silver as the English half crown; and in exchange, the par was estimated at 8 piastres to the pound sterling. The consequence of these repeated adulterations has been, the reduction of the silver in the piastre to one half, and a fall in the exchange of 100 per cent., bills on London having been bought in Turkey, in 1803, at the rate of 16 piastres for every pound sterling.† Now though it is not absolutely conclusive, that these alterations in the *computed* exchange were entirely owing to the fluctuations in the value of coin, because the *real* exchange at the time might not be constant; yet the correspondence of the difference of exchange, with the acknowledged degradation of the coin, renders it more than probable, that the fall of the *computed* exchange arose from an alteration in the *nominal* exchange only.

It is unnecessary to enter further into the detail of the consequences that arise from the degradation of the coin below its mint standard. As soon as that degradation (which never can remain long concealed) is discovered, the inconveniences that would otherwise attend the commercial

---

* Smith's Wealth of Nations, vol. ii. p. 216.
† Foster on Commercial Exchange, p. 93.

intercourse are obviated by a corresponding alteration in the *computed* exchange; and though during the continuance of the degradation, the *nominal* exchange will remain permanently unfavourable to the country in which it prevails, it will be immediately restored to par, by a reformation of the circulating medium. We will, therefore, in the remaining part of this enquiry into the nature and effects of the *nominal* exchange, suppose, that the currencies are not degraded below their mint standards, and confine our observations to the third cause, which has been stated to affect the value of currencies, viz. the ratio, which the total amount of the currency in one country bears to the commodities to be circulated by it, compared with the ratio that the currencies of other countries bear to the commodities which they are respectively employed to circulate. It is the fluctuation from this cause, which at present principally affects the *nominal* exchange.

Had the currencies of commercial states been confined to the precious metals only, it is scarcely possible that any increase of currency, more than was demanded by the wants of increasing wealth, could have taken place, in countries that had no mines of their own. As the metals of which the coin was composed must have been purchased at their value, no possible motive can be conceived, that would induce the holder of bullion to convert it into coin, unless there was a real demand for it. The circulating medium of modern times no longer consists of the metals only, almost all nations having adopted, on a greater or less scale, the use of paper currency, issued generally, under the sanction of government, by corporate bodies or banks, who are responsible for the payment of it in specie on demand. As the profits of these corporate bodies or banks are in proportion to the quantity of the paper they can permanently keep in circulation, there can be no doubt, that every effort consistent with prudence, will be made to augment that quantity. But it is impossible that such an increase can take place in the quantity of any commodity that is given in exchange for others, whose quantity is not augmented in the same proportion, without affecting their comparative value. If the currency of a country is increased, while the commodities to be circulated by it remain the same, the currency will be diminished in value with respect to the commodities, and it will require a larger proportion of the former to purchase a given quantity of the latter; or, in other words, prices will rise. If we were in the habit of considering money as purchased by commodities, instead of commodities being purchased by money, the diminution in the value of money from its abundance, would be immediately apparent. "Mr. "Thornton admits, in the most explicit manner, that if the "quantity of circulating medium is permanently augmented, "without a corresponding augmentation of internal trade, a "rise will unavoidably take place in the price of exchange-"able articles. Indeed this is a principle upon which all the "writers on Commerce, both practical and speculative, are "agreed: they have thought it so undeniable as to require "no particular illustration, and have rather assumed it as an "obvious truth, than as a proposition that depended on "inference. Upon this idea is founded Mr. Hume's well-"known argument against banks, and it is equally implied in "Dr. Smith's confutation of that objection; it forms the "foundation of those presumptions from which Mr. Boyd "has lately inferred an improper increase of Bank of Eng-"land paper; and it is implicitly admitted, likewise, by Mr. "Thornton, one great object of whose book is to persuade "the public that there has been no such increase."* Without entering, therefore, into an unnecessary argument, I shall, for the present, assume as admitted, that the increase of currency, while the commodities to be circulated remain the same, will be attended with an increase of nominal prices, and a correspondent depreciation in the value of money.

Now it is impossible, when the currency of a country has been thus depreciated, that the same amount of it should purchase the same sum of foreign money as before its depreciation. A foreign bill, or an order for payment of

* Edinb. Review, v. i. p. 178.

a given sum of foreign money abroad, will not be sold, unless for such an increased amount of the depreciated currency, as will counterbalance the diminution of its value. Foreign bills will, therefore, bear a premium, in proportion to the depreciation.

In the same manner a bill on the country where the currency is depreciated will be bought abroad, where money retains its value, for a much less *nominal* sum than the amount for which it is drawn; or, in other words, will be at a discount. Suppose, for instance, that the coins being in the utmost state of perfection in England and France, and the *real* exchange at par, the augmentation of the total amount of the currency in England were such as to raise prices here, to double their former amount, it would require, in that case, twice the sum to purchase the same commodity in England that would be required in France. The same *nominal* sum would, therefore, be only of half the value:—24 livres in France would purchase an order for the payment of 2*l.* sterling in England, and the *nominal* exchange, would be 100 per cent. against England.

An augmentation of currency that affects prices, cannot take place without a corresponding alteration in the *nominal* exchange. Merchants, from the average sale of the produce which they receive and remit, and from the uninterrupted correspondence which they hold with each other, expressly for the communication of the prices current, have not much difficulty in distinguishing those fluctuations which are owing to the partial abundance or scarcity of a few articles, from that general increase of price which denotes a depreciation of currency:—or should they, from want of experience, be tempted to engage in commercial speculations, from a difference of prices not depending upon the *real* demand, but arising merely from an over-issue or contraction of currency, the loss upon their returns would infallibly teach them more caution in future.

After the par of exchange, therefore, has been established, an alteration in the value of currency, whether it arises from a debasement of the coin below its standard, a diminution of weight below the mint regulation, or depreciation of its value from relative over-issue, will alike affect the price of a foreign bill, and be made evident by an unfavourable *nominal* exchange.

It now remains to trace the operation of the *nominal* exchange on the several exports and imports of the country.

When foreign bills bear a premium from an unfavourable *nominal* exchange, it appears advantageous, upon a superficial view of the subject, to export produce, in consequence of the profit arising from the sale of the bill, which the merchant would be authorised to draw upon his correspondent abroad. But a very little consideration will show that there is, in this respect a striking difference between the *real* and the *nominal* exchange.

It is true that the merchant will obtain a premium upon his bill, but it is this premium which alone enables him to export. The same cause that has given rise to this premium, has increased the *nominal* prices of the articles, which he buys, for the purpose of exportation, in the home market; whatever he gains upon the bill, he loses in the purchase of his goods. The merchant, therefore, must calculate what is the difference at home and abroad, in the real prices of commodities, by which I mean the prices at which those commodities would be bought and sold, if no depreciation of currency existed. If those prices are such as to admit of a profit, the merchant will continue to export, whether the *nominal* exchange be favourable or unfavourable; — that circumstance can make no difference whatever in his transactions.

Suppose, for instance, the currencies of Hambro' and London being in their due proportions, and therefore the *nominal* exchange at par, that sugar, which from its abundance in London sold at 50*l.* per hogshead, from its scarcity at Hambro' would sell at 100*l.* The merchant, in this case, would immediately export. Upon the sale of his sugar, he would draw a bill upon his correspondent abroad for 100*l.* which he could at once convert into cash, by selling it in the bill-market at home, deriving from this transaction a profit of 50*l.*, from which he would have to deduct the expenses of freight, insurance, commission, &c. Now suppose no alteration in the scarcity or abundance of sugar in London and Hambro', and that the same transaction were to take place, after the currency in England had been so much increased that the prices were doubled, and consequently, the *nominal* exchange 100 per cent. in favour of Hambro'. The hogshead of sugar would then cost 100*l.* leaving, apparently, no profit whatever to the exporter. He would, however, as before, draw his bill on his correspondent for 100*l.*; and as foreign bills would bear a premium of 100*l.* per cent. he would sell this bill in the English market for 200*l.* and and thus derive a profit from the transaction amounting to 100 depreciated pounds, or 50*l.* estimated in undepreciated currency; deducting, as in the former instance, the expenses of freight, insurance, commission, &c.*

The case would be precisely similar, *mutatis mutandis*, with the importing merchant. The unfavourable *nominal* exchange would appear to occasion a loss amounting to the premium on a foreign bill, which he must give in order to pay his correspondent abroad. But if the difference of *real* prices in the home and foreign markets were such as to admit of a profit upon the importation of produce, the merchant would continue to import, notwithstanding the premium; for that would be repaid to him in the advanced *nominal* price at which the imported produce would be sold in the home market.

Suppose, for instance, the currencies of Hambro' and London being in their due proportions, and therefore the *nominal* exchange at par, that linen which can be bought at Hambro' for 50*l.* will sell here at 100*l.* The importer immediately orders his correspondent abroad to send the linen, for the payment of which he purchases at 50*l.* a foreign bill in the English market, and on the sale of the consignment for 100*l.* he will derive a profit amounting to the

* The reader will observe how much the nominal income, and apparent profits, of the merchant are increased by the depreciation of the currency.

difference between 50*l.* and the expenses attending the import.

Now, suppose the same transaction to take place, without any alteration in the scarcity or abundance of linen at Hambro' and London, but that the currency of England has been so augmented, as to be depreciated to half its value. The *nominal* exchange will then be 100 per cent. against England, and the importer will not be able to purchase a 50*l.* foreign bill for less than 100*l.* But as the prices of commodities here will have risen in the same proportion as the money has been depreciated, he will sell his linen to the English consumer for 200*l.* and will, as before, derive a profit amounting to the difference between 100*l.* depreciated money, or 50*l.* estimated in undepreciated money, and the expenses attending the import.

The same instances might be put in the case of a favourable exchange; and it would be seen in the same manner, that *nominal* prices and the *nominal* exchange being alike dependent upon the depreciation of currency, whatever apparent advantage might be derived from the former, would be counterbalanced by a loss on the latter, and *vice versâ.*

For the very same reasons that the *nominal* exchange produces no alteration in the imports or the exports of ordinary produce, it can have no effect on the export or import of bullion. Nothing can be more evident, than that bullion must be subject to the same variation in its prices from an alteration in the value of currency as any other commodity. If the value of currency is diminished, the prices of all commodities must advance, and that of bullion among the rest.* How then is the profit of the merchant, from the export of bullion, to arise? Is it not evident that upon an unfavourable *nominal* exchange, whatever premium he may gain upon his bill, as much will be lost in the advanced price

* "Bullion is a commodity, and nothing but a commodity, and it "rises and falls on the same principle as all other commodities. It "becomes, like them, dear in proportion as the circulating medium for "which it is exchanged is rendered cheap; and cheap in proportion as "the circulating medium is rendered dear."—(Thornton, Paper Credit.)

which he must pay for the bullion?—Yet all writers upon the subject of political œconomy, that I have met with, seem to be persuaded, that when the rate of exchange has deviated from par beyond the expenses of the transit of bullion, bullion will immediately pass: and the error has arisen, from not sufficiently distinguishing the effects of a *real* and a *nominal* exchange. This false opinion seems to have been strongly impressed upon all the merchants and Bank Directors who were examined before the Secret Committee of the Houses of Lords and Commons in the year 1797; nor does Mr. Pitt himself appear to have been exempt from its influence. Mr. Bosanquet expressly declares his opinion " that the favourable state of the exchange afforded a " prospect of purchasing foreign gold, and setting the " mint at work," (p. 32. Com. H. of Lords, & passim.) Now it is absolutely impossible that an exchange, arising from depreciation of currency, can have any effect upon the export or import of bullion. For supposing the *nominal* exchange at par, and the *real* prices of bullion in London and Hambro' precisely the same, it is clear there could be no motive to export bullion, but that, on the contrary, it would be attended with the certain loss of the expenses of transit. Every thing else, then, remaining the same, let the currency in England be augmented so that the prices of commodities shall rise 4 per cent. and bullion of course among the rest; the depreciation of the currency will immediately be indicated by an unfavourable *nominal* exchange of 4 per cent. Is it possible that the bullion merchant can be deluded with the idea, that he can derive any benefit from a premium of 4 per cent. upon his bill, when he purchases bullion here at an advanced price, and sells it at Hambro' 4 per cent. lower? Does he not lose as much from the difference of prices, occasioned by the depreciation, as he gains by the premium on his bill, occasioned by the same depreciation; and consequently subject himself to all the expenses attending the transit, in the same manner as when the *nominal* exchange is at par?

For the same reason, there would be no advantage

derived from the import of bullion if the *nominal* exchange were favourable. Suppose it were 4 per cent. in favour of this country;—it is evident that money here would be 4 per cent. more valuable than at Hambro'; prices, therefore, would be 4 per cent. lower, and foreign bills in the English market would be at 4 per cent. discount. Under those circumstances, if foreign bills were purchased to be invested in bullion at Hambro', and the bullion were sent here, would it not be sold in the English market at 4 per cent. less than was given for it at Hambro'? thus destroying every advantage derived from the *nominal* exchange, and subjecting the importer to the same loss, as in the former instances. Is it then to be wondered at, that with such opinions as the Bank Directors seem to have entertained, they should be so totally at a loss to reconcile the facts with their false theory respecting the export and import of bullion? During the course of the year 1796, for eleven months previous to the Bank restriction, the exchange had been, with only two exceptions, favourable; and at the end of February, 1797, was so high as considerably to exceed the expenses of the transit of bullion; yet when Mr. Raikes, on the 13th March, was examined before the Secret Committee of the House of Commons,* he acknowledged, that measures had been taken by the Bank to procure a supply of bullion, but without effect, as it could not be imported except at a considerable loss. On the 14th, Mr. Bosanquet stated to the same Committee, that the influx of bullion is occasioned by a favourable exchange; that the exchange had not been unfavourable for many months; and, when asked whether the importation had been such as it ought to have been, considering the state of the exchange, replied,† "I am not able to answer these kind of questions." The fact is, that the *nominal* exchange might for years continue in favour of a country, and not cause a single ounce of bullion to flow into it, or have any effect upon the general state of exports and imports, which would proceed in their

* Secret Committee of the House of Commons, p. 23.
† Secret Committee of the House of Commons, p. 28.

usual course, regulated only by the wants of consumers, and the supply of commodities.*

It is in vain therefore to look for any remedy for a high *nominal* exchange from any alteration in the exports and imports of a country. When it arises from a degraded state of the coin, a new coinage immediately restores it to par;—when it arises from the augmentation or contraction of currency, the restoration of the currency to a due proportion with the commodities to be circulated by it, will be the true and only remedy.

In what manner this restoration of the currency to its level is effected, it will now be proper to enquire.

In all countries the weight of bullion contained in any specific quantity of coin issued at the mint is determined by law. At the English mint, a pound weight of gold is coined into 44½ guineas, which, at 21*s.* the guinea, is equal to 46*l.* 14*s.* 6*d.* or 3*l.* 17*s.* 10½*d.* per ounce. This is said to be the mint price of gold in England, or the quantity of coin which the mint returns for standard gold bullion. An ounce of gold, therefore, so long as it remains in the shape of coin, can never be worth more than 3*l.* 17*s.* 10½*d.* because while it retains that form, it cannot be legally tendered in payment for more than that sum. As soon therefore as an over-issue of currency has raised the prices of all commodities, and that of bullion among the rest, the weight of gold contained in any specific quantity of coin will sell for a higher *nominal* value in bullion, than it will pass for in the form of coin, or, as it is usually expressed, the market price of bullion will exceed the mint price, and there will be a profit attending the conversion of coin into bullion proportionate to the difference of the *nominal* value. Accordingly, the conversion immediately takes place, requiring very little greater excess of the market price above the mint price, than will pay for the fire that is to melt the coin. The

* It is not to be inferred, that because the *nominal* exchange has no effect on the general exports and imports, that therefore the country sustains no injury; the contrary of which will be shewn, in treating of the foreign expenditure of government, and the unequal pressure that the depreciation occasions on the different classes of the community.

operation is so simple, and requires so little apparatus, that it may be performed with the utmost secresy, and no penalties of the law, or vigilance of the officers of the Mint or Bank, have ever been found adequate to its prevention.

To account for this, there is no necessity for supposing a demand for bullion abroad. It is the conversion, that prevents the currency from ever exceeding the due proportion that is wanted for the purposes of circulation: for it can* never exceed that proportion, without augmenting the *nominal* price of bullion, and affording, as long as there is a superfluous quantity, a profit to the melter.

It is true that the same conversion may take place, by exporting the coin to any foreign country, where it will be estimated according to its weight in bullion, and pass for its intrinsic value; and probably this circumstance has led so many writers to assign the capability of the transit of coin, as the reason why currency convertible into coin can never be depreciated by excess. But it is evident that, of the two modes of conversion, that by melting will be preferred, since it will be unattended by any expenses of transit. If the market price of bullion in London were 4 per cent. above its mint price, in consequence of the depreciation of currency, while at Hambro' there was no depreciation whatever, 100 guineas conveyed to the latter place would purchase the same value in commodities that 104 guineas would do in London; but as the expense of sending them would amount to 3 per cent.,† there would be a profit to the exporter of one guinea only; whereas the 100 guineas, melted in London, would immediately sell in the market for 109*l.* 4*s.*, leaving a clear profit of four guineas by the operation. It is absurd, then, to suppose that any man would

---

* The reader will apply the proper limitation to this general assertion, which is not meant to convey the idea that the effect will be instantaneous, or that it may not be counteracted by other causes, but that the over-issue of currency will have this tendency, and that ultimately the *nominal* price of bullion will be raised above its natural price, in proportion to the over-issue.

† The expense as stated by Mr. Eliason, is 3*l.* 12*s.* 11*d.* per cent.—Evidence Secret Committee House of Lords, 1797, p. 96.

expose himself to the penalties of the law, by exporting coin for a profit of 1 per cent., when without subjecting himself to severer penalties, he might, by melting it, secure a profit of 4 per cent.

It is the melting, therefore, in consequence of the high market price at home, and not the export in consequence of a high *nominal* exchange, that will cause the disappearance of the coin. It is true, that after the melting has proceeded for some length of time, (unless indeed the melted coin be purchased for the purpose of being recoined,) there will be a gradual accumulation of bullion beyond what may be wanted for consumption; and this abundance may render the commodity so cheap, that the bullion merchant may find his advantage in exporting it, in consequence of the difference of the *real* prices in the home and foreign markets. But this exportation is the effect of the melting, and not the cause of it. It is not a demand for the exportation of bullion that has caused the melting of the coin; but the coin being melted, to take advantage of the high *nominal* price of bullion, has lowered its real price so much, as to afford a profit upon its exportation. It is by no means necessary, however, that the bullion produced by the melting should be exported, since there may be a greater demand for bullion at home, for the purposes of manufacture, than there is abroad. The melter will always derive his profit by selling the melted coin at the high market price, which the bullion merchant will be equally ready to give, whether he sell to the home manufacturer, or the foreigner—whether, at the time, he be effecting the import or the export of bullion.

A want of attention to this distinction, so essentially necessary towards a just conception of the principle, which regulates the quantity of currency and the increase of prices, has led to some very erroneous opinions respecting what is called the universal level of currency: for it has been maintained by many writers upon political economy, and implied by almost all, that specie leaves the country where it is depreciated in consequence of the inferiority of its value to the currency of other countries;* that if the currencies of other nations were depreciated in an equal proportion, there would be no advantage attending the export; and that upon the supposition of the currency being proportionally increased throughout the world, prices might be universally and indefinitely augmented; whereas the export has no relation whatever to the value of currencies in other countries, but arises entirely from the relative value of gold in the form of coin and in the form of bullion.

The coin of this country, when sent abroad, passes only for its intrinsic value, according to its weight, and it will not be sent abroad from an unfavourable *nominal* exchange, unless its value in the shape of bullion is greater than its value in the form of coin. But the real value of bullion on the Continent is no more affected by the depreciation of the currency there, than it is here. If there be a profit upon the export of coin from this country at a time when the currency is depreciated here, and is not depreciated upon the Continent, there would be the same profit, if the currency of the Continent were depreciated also: for the market price of bullion, at which our exported coin would then be sold abroad, would be so much higher in proportion to the depreciation of the foreign currency. Suppose that the currency at London and Hambro' being in their due proportions, and

* This error pervades Mr. Wheatley's Work on the Theory of Money and Principles of Commerce. He was well aware of the fact, that specie is frequently exported in consequence of an unfavourable exchange; but as he does not admit of any alteration in the exchange, from the abundance or scarcity of foreign bills, (which is the real cause of the *export* of specie, when it does take place,) he attributed the effect, to the difference in the value of currencies; and thence inferred, that the export of coin was the remedy for its depreciation—a principle, that leads at once to the conclusion, that prices might be indefinitely augmented, if the currencies of all nations were proportionally increased. Mr. Ricardo and Mr. Mushet have fallen into the same error, respecting the export of specie, and do not seem to be aware, that the alteration in prices, from over-issue or contraction of currency, has no effect upon the exports and imports of ordinary produce; since they uniformly describe commodities as flowing from the nominally cheap, to the nominally dear market, without adverting to the counteracting effects of the *nominal* exchange.

the *nominal* exchange at par, the *real* price of bullion corresponds in both places with the English mint price. Let the currency at London be depreciated by over-issue 4 per cent.; the market price of bullion at London would then exceed the mint price 4 per cent., and the nominal exchange would be unfavourable to the same amount. Under those circumstances, a merchant exporting 100*l.*'s worth of specie to Hambro' and drawing a bill upon his correspondent, would gain 1 per cent. by the transaction: for the specie, on its arrival at Hambro' where the market price of bullion, according to the hypothesis, corresponds with the English mint price, would sell in the bullion market for 100*l.* The English merchant would therefore draw for 100*l.*; and, foreign bills bearing a premium, would sell his bill in the English bill market for 104*l.*, which, after deducting 3 per cent. for the expenses of transit, would leave him a profit of 1*l.* per cent. Now suppose the currency at Hambro' to be also depreciated to the amount of 4 per cent.; the nominal exchange will then be at par, but the market price of bullion at Hambro' will exceed the English mint price 4 per cent. The 100*l.*'s worth of specie will sell at Hambro' for 104*l.*; the merchant will therefore draw upon his correspondent for 104*l.*, and the exchange being at par, will procure 104*l.* for his bill in the English bill market; and deducting 3 per cent for the expenses of transit, he will obtain a profit of 1*l.* per cent. as before.

It has been already demonstrated that bullion will not be exported under an unfavourable *nominal* exchange, merely in consequence of that exchange; and the reason why specie is exported under the same circumstances, is, that the coin, while it remains here, passes for less than its worth, and that abroad it passes for its real value;—in this country it forms a part of the currency, and partakes of the depreciation,—abroad, it passes as bullion, and is relieved from the depreciation. But it is quite clear that even in the export of specie, there would be no profit whatever, unless its depreciation were greater than the expenses attending its export; and therefore were there no other remedy for a depreciated currency than the export of specie, the *nominal* exchange might for any length of time continue unfavourable, to an extent somewhat less than the expenses of the transit of bullion. But the fact is, that no such continuance of an unfavourable exchange, even to that extent, can take place, so long as the currency is capable of being converted into bullion: for as soon as the depreciation is evinced by an elevation of the market price of bullion above the mint price, that moment the conversion of the superfluous currency commences; and it depends upon the comparative demand for bullion in this country, and the demand, upon the continent, whether the melted specie be exported or not.

It must be admitted, that, as soon as the depreciation has exceeded the expenses of the transit of specie, and thus afforded an option as to the mode of converting it into bullion, the foreign merchant, by buying abroad the bills upon England, which will necessarily be at a discount, and ordering his correspondent to whom he sends the bills, to invest them in English specie, will be enabled to procure bullion at the English mint price. So that as long as he can dispose of the bullion at that price abroad, he will derive a profit equal to the excess of the discount at which he has bought the English bills, above the expenses of the transit of specie. But it having been already shewn, that the profit on melting always exceeds the profit on exporting, by the amount of the expenses attending the export, it can never be believed that a merchant would collect the current coin, and by exporting it, subject himself to the penalties of the law, for the sake of obliging his foreign correspondent, and enabling him to acquire a profit of 1 per cent., when by melting the same coin, he might himself, with less risk, obtain a profit of 4 per cent.

Again, if the *nominal* exchange were rendered favourable, 4 per cent. by a forced contraction of the currency, and the price of bullion were lowered with that of other commodities, so as to be 4 per cent. below the mint price; would any merchant purchase foreign bills at a discount of 4 per cent., and send them to Hambro' to be invested in foreign coin, for the sake of gaining 1 per cent. upon its import, when, by employing the same capital in the purchase of bullion in the home market, and converting it into coin at the mint, he would derive a profit of 4 per cent.?

The only case in which a superior advantage would be obtained from the export of specie, rather than from the conversion of coin into bullion, or from the import of specie rather than the conversion of bullion into coin, would be, when the over-issue or contraction of the currency had created a premium or discount of 4 per cent. on foreign bills, without producing an alteration of 1 per cent. in the market price of bullion. But it has been already shewn, that the nominal price of bullion is raised or lowered in the same manner as that of other commodities, to which it would otherwise no longer bear its natural relative value. Such an occurrence, therefore, if possible, can be but temporary, and does not affect the general argument.

When the currency consists partly of coin, and partly of paper convertible at option into coin, it is for the same reason absolutely impossible that it can continue permanently in a state of depreciation: for should the Bank be so imprudent as to issue notes beyond the demands of increasing wealth, as soon as the augmentation of prices, and a consequent unfavourable *nominal* exchange, denoted the depreciation of the currency, the market price of bullion would exceed its mint price, and all that portion of the circulating medium which could be converted into bullion would begin to disappear. The paper of the Bank would be returned to be exchanged for coin, which would be immediately melted, and sold in the form of bullion, for notes, at the advanced nominal price. These, in their turn, would be sent to the Bank to be in the same manner exchanged for coin, which would be melted and sold as soon as procured.

Now this process might be going forward, and continue to drain the Bank of its gold, without the slightest demand for bullion abroad, or without any demand for foreign payments. It would equally take place, though the country were receiving payments instead of making them—though it were importing bullion instead of exporting it. Should the Bank persist in its over-issue, and still endeavour to throw the same quantity of notes into circulation, the Directors would be compelled to purchase bullion, and coin it into guineas, in order to supply the drain occasioned by the return of their notes; and as Mr. Thornton states, "they will have to do this at the very moment when many "are privately melting what is coined. The one party "might be melting and selling, while the other is buying "and coining; and each of these two contending businesses "will be carried on, not on account of an actual exportation "of each melted guinea to Hambro'; but the operation, or "at least a great part of it, will be confined to London— "the coiners and melters living on the same spot, and giving "constant employment to each other."*

Mr. Winthorp, in the evidence he gave before the Secret Committee of the House of Commons in 1797, (p. 46 and 47,) concluded that because there was a drain upon the Bank, there must necessarily be a drain upon the country; and stated "his belief that the coffers of the Bank generally "shew whether money is coming into or going out of the "country." I should hope it would be unnecessary, after what has been already observed, to offer anything further in refutation of such opinions. The drain upon the Bank will begin under any circumstances, whenever the depreciation of currency from over-issue has raised the market price of bullion above its mint price; and it will continue, till the loss which the Bank must suffer by the purchase of bullion to supply the drain, shall compel the Directors to diminish the number of their notes, so as to bring back the currency to its natural level. The price of bullion will then fall to its mint price, and no longer afford a profit on being melted;

* Mr. Thornton admits that the melting is not always connected with the export of bullion; but as the object of his Book was to shew that the currency was not depreciated, it was impossible for him to give even a plausible explanation of this part of his subject, without attributing the effect to an unfavourable *real* exchange.

the *nominal* exchange will invariably mark the amount of the depreciation during its continuance; and when the depreciation ceases, the *nominal* exchange will rise to par.

The adoption of a paper currency, therefore, can never be injurious to a country, so long as it is convertible at option into specie. The temptation to its over-issue will always be sufficiently checked by the principle that has been just explained; and, independently of the convenience of making the larger payments, it will certainly be advantageous to carry on the circulation of a country by a cheap, rather than a costly, machinery.

It is obvious, that as the nominal prices of commodities will be increased by the over-issue of currency, so, for the same reasons, the contraction of it below the natural wants of circulation, will diminish the *nominal* prices in the same proportion. A smaller quantity of currency will then measure the same value, and the nominal exchange will be favourable to the country where the value of the currency is increased. This is an event that does not often occur: for as the profits of a bank that issues paper-money depend upon the quantity it can circulate, the directors of the establishment will generally take care that the supply shall not be less than the demand. When the market price of bullion, however, has from any cause been elevated above the mint price, the Bank has always the power of giving the currency an artificial value by a diminution of its total amount; and it is evident that by such a diminution, the price of bullion will be lowered in the same proportion as that of any other commodity. Bullion will then be of less value in the market than in the form of coin, and the merchant will carry it to the mint, to obtain the profit attending its conversion into specie. If, under such circumstances, there should be a demand for bullion for the purpose of exportation, this would evidently occasion no drain upon the Bank, while it could be procured at a cheaper rate in the market; and should the demand for exportation continue so long as to raise the price of this commodity, in consequence of its scarcity* the Bank would always have the power by a greater contraction of its currency, to lower its *nominal* price, and thus preserve the superiority of its value in the form of coin over its value in the shape of bullion.

It is thus that the value of the currency is made to correspond with that of the precious metals of which it is composed, or into which it is convertible; and as long as they continue to be the standard by which the value of other commodities is estimated, the circulating medium of the whole mercantile republic will suffer no permanent alterations, but what arise from the variation in the intrinsic value of the precious metals themselves.

It is some proof of the truth of these positions respecting the uniformity of the value of currency, that from the period of the reformation of the gold coin in 1774, to the year 1797, the *computed* exchange between London and Hambro' was generally in favour of the former, arising, probably, from the superiority of our coin; and that it seldom varied, except in 1793, more than 5 per cent. on the one side or the other of par. In that year the *computed* exchange rose to 10 and 11 per cent. in favour of this country owing to the sudden contraction of currency that took place in consequence of the run upon and failure of the country banks, at the breaking out of the French revolutionary war, which had the effect of raising the *nominal* value of the currency here to the degree indicated by the favourable exchange. During the whole of this period the market price of bullion never exceeded its mint price, except in the year 1783, by the very trifling amount that has been already specified; and in the year 1795, when the Bank had extended its paper from less than 11 to upwards of 13 millions and a half.

After this review of the subject, and the strong evidence

* The scarcity here spoken of refers only to the partial scarcity arising in particular countries from the temporary unequal distribution of bullion, and not an actual scarcity arising from a permanent diminution of the usual quantity produced at the mines.

which presents itself that the currency of a kingdom, whether consisting of coin only, or partly of coin and partly of paper, can never be augmented beyond its due proportion, so long as the paper is convertible at pleasure into specie—can any one for a moment doubt of the result, should this salutary check be removed, and at the same time the paper currency be made a legal tender for the payment of debts?*

Without this latter provision, motives of prudence might induce the Bank so to restrain its issues, as not to create an open discount upon its notes, and thus introduce a paper and a money price for commodities: but under the protection now afforded by the Restriction Act, there is no reason why it should not push the issue of this currency to the utmost possible limit, and particularly if there be a confidence in the public, that sooner or later the notes will be convertible into gold. There is no doubt, that with respect to the Bank of England this confidence is strongly felt by the public, and with good reason. Bank of England notes are never issued but for a valuable consideration, being principally advanced either upon Exchequer bills or in discounting the bills of merchants. Unless, therefore, the government is unable to redeem the former, or the merchants should be incapable of paying the latter when they become due, there must always be sufficient funds in the Bank to answer the demands upon it.† The depreciation from over issue is therefore by no means necessarily connected with any want of confidence in the resources of the Bank, but rests upon an entirely different foundation, and might equally take place, whether the currency consisted partly of coin and partly of paper, or was composed entirely of the former: for it is not the paper only, but the whole currency, both the paper and the coin, so long as it remains in the form of coin, that is depreciated by over-issue. But as the latter is

* By the Restriction Act, bank notes are not absolutely a legal tender; but if a tender be made in notes, the debtor cannot be arrested.

† There must in fact be more than sufficient, since the value of the outstanding notes must be less than that of the bills upon which they were issued, by the amount of the interest deducted at the time they were discounted.

convertible into bullion by melting, it will be consigned to the crucible, for the purpose of removing the depreciation that it suffers, while it constitutes a part of the currency.

The advocates for the Bank restriction triumphantly ask, how it is possible that the notes can be depreciated, if 100*l.* in bank notes will purchase as much as 100*l.* in specie: but the question, as applied to the depreciation of the currency, is absurd; for the notes and the coin are alike depreciated,* and therefore exchange, as before, for the same quantity of produce in the market. But their intrinsic value is not the same, because guineas being convertible into bullion, the one may be relieved from its depreciation by a change in its form; whereas the other cannot.† This conversion is constantly going on, and must continue till not a piece of coin is left in circulation, unless its weight be so much reduced below the standard as not to be worth the melting. The disappearance of the coin is the proof of its depreciation.

---

* This opinion is controverted in the Edinbro' Review, No. 25, p. 54, apparently under an idea that, as the price of gold and silver is nearly the same in all the countries of the world, a depreciation of the current specie in this country must necessarily be accompanied by a corresponding depreciation of the currency of all nations upon the face of the earth. But there is a material distinction between the depreciation of the specie, and the depreciation of the gold and silver that forms the specie. The first may be effected by the over-issue of the Bank, but that can have no influence on the *real* value of the bullion, which the specie contains. As an *argumentum ad hominem* against Mr. Thornton, it is indeed conclusive, because he imagines the remedy for a depreciated currency consists in the exportation of coin to other countries, where it is not so depreciated. It would be impossible, therefore, for the specie to continue permanently degraded, upon his principles, unless the value of the currency of every other nation were equally so. But it has been shewn that the remedy for depreciated currency from over-issue depends on its conversion into bullion, and not upon its exportation.

The gold and silver currency may therefore fall in value below the level of the currency of neighbouring states, but this cannot be the case with the gold and silver of which it is composed.

† As long as the bank note for a guinea is convertible into gold bullion, at the option of the holder, its intrinsic value may be said to be the same as a guinea. Take away the convertibility, and the intrinsic value of the note is the value of the ink and paper of which it is composed. No banking operation, nor legislative provision, can ever alter the real value of the gold bullion in a guinea, but the number of nominal pounds to be given for that quantity of gold bullion, may be increased in the proportion that the total number of pounds in the currency is increased beyond what is wanted.

The reason why the ordinary shopkeeper does not make a distinction between the payments made to him in gold, and those which he receives in paper, is, the confidence he feels that at some time or other the notes will be paid in specie, and that he is in the meantime deterred by the penalties of the law from melting the guineas—the only mode by which he can derive a superior profit, from a payment in coin. But the occupation of melting the specie is nevertheless followed by a less scrupulous class of the community, who have not hesitated to give a premium for guineas, whenever an opportunity offered of purchasing them, and of profiting by their conversion, without danger of detection.* But the difference in the intrinsic value of the notes and the guineas is not the less real, because it cannot openly be avowed. If the coin were allowed by law to be melted, if the penalties for this offence were less severe, or if guineas could be collected without exciting the suspicion of the officers of the Bank and the Mint, neither the Restriction Bill, nor the provision that bank notes may be tendered as legal payment, would prevent a paper and a money price for commodities, and consequently an open discount upon bank paper.

The drain upon the Bank, in the year 1797, is allowed by all the Directors to have arisen from the alarm of invasion. The market price of bullion was, at the time, below its mint price; the exchange with the Continent was in favour of London; and therefore all the causes, that are usually assigned, as creating a drain upon the Bank, were operating in a contrary direction. The alarm originated, according to the evidence given by Mr. Burdon, one of the proprietors of the Newcastle bank, before the Secret Committee in 1797, from the orders that had been issued for taking an account of the stock of the farms of Northumberland, for the purpose of regulating the mode in which the

* An instance of this has recently come before the public, in consequence of an information against a person charged with selling guineas for more than they are allowed to pass for by law.

county was to be driven, in case of invasion. The farmers immediately sold their produce at very low prices, and the notes which they received from the purchasers were poured in upon the persons by whom they were issued, to be exchanged for specie; in consequence of which, the banks at Newcastle were obliged to stop payment, and their failure was followed by a similar run upon the country banks throughout the kingdom, many of which were in like manner obliged to stop. The alarm was communicated to the metropolis, and occasioned a drain upon the Bank, which had already been called upon for considerable advances, in consequence of the run upon the country banks. The distress of the mercantile class, from the great extent of the failures, and the general distrust they occasioned, aggravated by a violent, and therefore improvident, contraction of the usual quantity of bank paper, combined to produce that crisis which terminated in the restriction of cash payments at the Bank. It is unnecessary now to enquire how far this restriction at the time was politic or otherwise. It probably was a measure of prudence; but as the evil was temporary, so also ought to have been the remedy. It might have been expected, that the complete relief of the merchants, and the returning confidence of the people, would have been considered as the signal for discontinuing a law, which has given the Bank Directors a power of permanently altering the value of the circulating medium of the country. It has, however, been decided otherwise; and the consequence has been, that as the fears of the Bank Directors have been dispelled, the quantity of currency has been gradually increased, and has produced all those symptoms, which any person acquainted with the theory of money and exchange would easily have anticipated;—an augmentation in the price of commodities, an increase of the market price of bullion over the mint price, and an unfavourable *nominal* exchange.

The effect of the over-issue of bank-notes upon the *computed* exchange may be visible from comparing the amount of the notes in circulation in the years 1795 and 1797, with the *computed* exchange at the some periods. The amount was augmented in February 1795, to 13½ millions,* and the exchange between Hambro' and London, which was then 6 per cent. above par, fell, before September, to 3½ per cent. against England. In February 1797, the paper in circulation was reduced to 8½ millions, and the exchange between Hambro' and London rose to 6*l.* 18*s.* per cent. in favour of England. By the last returns presented to Parliament, it appears that the bank notes now in circulation amount to 21 millions, the market price of gold in November was 15*l.* 8*s.* 2*d.* per cent. above the mint price, and the exchange between Hambro' and London 16*l.* 18*s.* per cent. against England.

Should any one still be sceptical on the subject, a short survey of the mode in which the business of the Bank is conducted will probably remove his doubt. It has been already shewn, that so long as its notes are convertible at option into specie, a bank can never permanently keep in circulation more paper than the wants of the country require. But it is not perhaps, quite so clear, in what manner the over-issues of the bank that is not liable to be called upon for cash payments, will augment the *nominal* prices of all commodities.

The notes of the Bank of England are issued to the merchants who are in want of money, on the security of bills of exchange of not more than 60 days date, which are brought to the Bank for discount.

On the receipt of the bill, the Bank gives to the merchant an equal amount in notes, deducting the interest at the rate of 5 per cent. When the bill is due, the Bank presents it for payment, and receives the amount in full, deriving a profit from the transaction equal to the interest of the notes for the time. The oftener this process can be repeated, and the greater the amount of the notes it lends, the greater will be its profits.—Now it is evident, that if the purchases of the merchants could be effected by their own

* Secret Committee of the House of Lords in 1797, p. 176.

bills, it would be unnecessary for them to apply to the Bank for discounts; this application, then, is of itself a decisive proof that the bills of private merchants will not pass in the market with the same facility as the bills of a national Banking Company. The conversion, therefore, of the bills into notes is an increase of currency, which could not take place without the assistance which a bank affords.

Now the merchant regulates the scale of his transactions by the amount of the capital he can command. The greater the extent of this capital, the larger the profits he will expect to derive from its employment. If he can make a profit of 10 per cent. by his business, he will always be willing to extend it by borrowing capital, for which he is to pay an interest of only 5 per cent. Here then are two parties exactly suited to the supply of each other's wants, and co-operating from mutual interest towards the same object. The profits of the Bank are in proportion to the paper currency it can lend, and the expected profits of the merchant are in proportion to the paper currency he can borrow. Under such circumstances it is idle to talk of the Bank Directors having the power to contract their discounts when they perceive there has been an over-issue, unless a motive can be shewn for the exercise of that power. While the Restriction Act is in force, the only rule of their conduct will be the validity of the bills that are offered for discount, and they are bound by the duty they owe to the Bank Proprietors who appoint them, to profit by the facilities thus imprudently granted by the government, and to employ to the greatest possible advantage the funds of which they have the disposal.

It is equally idle to say that the merchant will not employ all the capital he can command, or that his credit will enable him to borrow.* By the facilities that are now

* See a whimsical pamphlet published by Mr. Smith on the Theory of Money. He asks, would bankers and merchants apply to have good bills discounted at the Bank, if bank notes were depreciated? The answer to which is obvious. The depreciation in no way affects the dealings of the merchants; who buy and sell at the high *nominal*

given to discounts, the merchants can always, either by immediate application to the Bank by means of their bankers, or, if in the country, by the intervention of the country banks, coin their credit into currency, which will operate upon the markets wherever it makes its appearance: for the prices of any given supply of produce will depend upon the number of purchasers, and the extent of the capital they can command. The more easily capital can be procured, the greater will be the competition in the market. Whenever the prospect of a profitable speculation offers, merchants will be eager to embark in it, and the demand, which, under ordinary circumstances, would be regulated by the amount of *real* capital capable of being diverted into that channel, will now be augmented in proportion to the *fictitious* capital, called into existence by the facilities afforded from the Bank discounts; and thus an over-issue of notes will immediately take place, creating an additional number of purchasers, or increasing their powers of purchasing in proportion to the over-issue. If the increased currency be employed in a foreign speculation, it immediately acts upon the foreign bill-market, and creating there a fictitious demand, it affects the *nominal* exchange; if it be employed by the bullion-merchant, it raises the market price of that article; if by the home dealer, it augments the prices of native commodities. No sooner has it left the merchants by whose means it was called into existence, than it passes to the wholesale dealers and master manufacturers, who, in their turn, will raise the prices in their respective markets by a competition which is called into action merely by the over-issue.

If the evil were confined to the increased quantity of currency thus thrown into circulation by the Bank of England, it might not be attended with injurious consequences of such magnitude as are now experienced: but the misfortune is, that the same law which protects the National

prices, and whose profits are nominally increased in the same proportion as money is depreciated.

Bank, and enables it thus to derange the natural state of the circulating medium, confers the same power on all the country banks throughout the kingdom, which are now relieved from the fears and inconvenience to which under ordinary circumstances they would be subject, should they at any time be tempted to issue their notes beyond the amount which the wants of their respective districts might require.

The country banks are, in the same manner as the Bank of England, enabled to supply their respective connexions with funds for speculation. If the excess of their paper should at any time excite doubts of their solvency, and create a run, they may be supplied by their correspondents in London with notes from the great central paper mint; and thus are all the lesser establishments throughout the kingdom absolved from every difficulty. They issue their notes almost without limit, and by these means enable the country dealers to enter into speculations and purchases, which, without their assistance, could never have been effected. Can any one then be surprised that prices should rise, when every addition of currency is attended with profit to the Bank by which it is issued; and that there can never be an additional issue of currency without creating additional purchasers to the same amount?

An objection has been urged against this view of the subject, which deserves to be noticed. It has been stated, that if only such bills are discounted at the Bank, as have been drawn in consequence of *bonâ fide* commercial transactions, no additional currency is thrown into circulation, more than the wants of the mercantile community require; that the bills so discounted are the representatives of the property, by the transfer of which they are created; and thus a distinction has been attempted to be drawn between real and fictitious bills; or, as the latter are more generally termed, bills of accommodation. But it will not require much consideration to perceive that this, as far at least as concerns the over-issue of currency, is a distinction with little, if any, difference. Mr. Thornton has well observed, that "notes given in consequence of a real sale of goods "cannot be considered as on that account certainly repre-"senting any actual property.—Suppose that *A.* sells 100*l.* "worth of goods to *B.* at six months credit, and takes a bill "at six months for it; and that *B.* within a month after, "sells the same goods to *C.* at a like credit, taking a like "bill; that *C.* after another month, sells them to *D.*; and "so on: there may, at the end of six months, be six bills of "100*l.* each, existing at the same time, and every one of "them may possibly have been discounted. Of all these "bills, then, one only represents any actual property. If "the credit given be a credit of twelve months instead of "six, 1200*l.* instead of 600*l.* would have been the amount "of the bills drawn on the occasion of the sale of goods, "and 1100*l.* would have been the amount of those that "represented no property. In order to justify the suppo-"sition that a real bill represents actual property, there "ought to be some power in the bill-holder to prevent "the property which the bill represents from being turned to "other purposes than that of paying the bill in question."*

Now had these bills never been discounted, their circulation would have been confined to those persons only, with whom the parties, whose names appear on the bill, had credit; and their effect upon the general currency of the country would in such case have been exceedingly limited, compared with that which they have in the more negotiable form of the notes of a Banking Company.

"One of the motives of the seller who desires to have "a note for goods sold, is, that he may engraft on the trans-"action of the sale the convenient condition of receiving "from the buyer a discountable note of the same amount "with the value of the goods. A fictitious note, or note of "accommodation, is a note drawn for the same purpose of "being discounted, though it is not sanctioned by the cir-"cumstance of its having originated in an actual sale of "goods."† The Bank of England professes to refuse the discounting of any bills except those drawn for *bonâ fide*

* Thornton on Paper Credit, *ante* p. 156. † Ibid.

mercantile considerations; and so far as their own interests are concerned, it may be a very proper and highly prudent regulation: but to the public, it is of little moment upon what degree of security the Bank may think right to lend its notes; nor can the Directors, with all their vigilance, discriminate between real and fictitious bills. Whether real or fictitious, their conversion into notes will alike augment the currency of the country, which, without the check that has been pointed out in the foregoing pages, may be increased in an unlimited degree. In the case of the real bill, a *bonâ fide* transaction takes place prior to its being converted into currency, in consequence of a credit subsisting between the drawer of the bill and the seller of the goods. In the fictitious bill, for want of that credit between the drawer and the seller, the conversion of the bill into currency takes place in the first instance, and the *bonâ fide* transaction follows.

From what has been stated, the distinction between the *real* and *nominal* exchange will be sufficiently apparent;—they have been found to differ most essentially, both in their causes and effects.

The *real* exchange has been proved to depend upon the proportion between the foreign payments which a country has to make, and the payments it has to receive.

The *nominal* exchange depends upon the comparative value of currencies.

The *real* exchange has an immediate effect upon the exports and imports.

The *nominal* exchange, whether favourable or unfavourable, has no effect whatever upon exports and imports.

An unfavourable *real* exchange, if its rate be sufficiently high, will cause an export of bullion, and may, under peculiar circumstances, lead to a drain upon the Bank.

An unfavourable *nominal* exchange, whatever be its rate, will not necessarily lead to any export of bullion, but will immediately cause a drain upon the Bank, for the conversion of coin into bullion.

When the market price of bullion exceeds the mint price,

in consequence of its export from an unfavourable *real* exchange, the currency is not depreciated, for it bears the same relative value to all other commodities; it is the *real* price of bullion that is raised, from a temporary scarcity.

When there is an excess of the market price of bullion above the mint price, together with an unfavourable *nominal* exchange, the *real* price of bullion is not altered, for it bears the same relative value to all other commodities; it is the currency that is depreciated, from a temporary abundance.

The *real* exchange cannot be permanently favourable or unfavourable, whatever be the state of the currency.

The *nominal* exchange may continue for any length of time favourable or unfavourable, provided the value of the currency continues to be depreciated.

Now the *computed* exchange depends upon the combined operations of the *real* and *nominal* exchange; and unless the distinctions just pointed out are kept constantly in view, it will be impossible to reconcile the contradictory results to which it appears to give rise.

OF THE COMPUTED EXCHANGE.

THE *computed* exchange is determined by the fluctuations of the price which a foreign bill bears in the market, but affords no criterion by which to distinguish whether those fluctuations arise from variations in the state of the *real*, or of the *nominal* exchange. As these are perfectly independent of each other, it is evident that if both are favourable, or both unfavourable, the *computed* exchange will denote their sum; but if the one is favourable, while the other is unfavourable, it will express their difference, and may be at par, though neither the *real* or *nominal* exchange are so, provided the unfavourable state of the one be counteracted by the favourable state of the other. Now let any one for a moment consider, what different phenomena would present themselves under an apparently similar state of the exchange, according to the mode in which that similarity was produced. For the *com-*

puted exchange would be at par, if the *real* and *nominal* exchange were so; that is, if the supply of foreign bills were equal to the demand, and the currencies of other countries of the same value with our own, in which case the exports and imports would proceed in their ordinary course.

It would be at par, though the *real* exchange were unfavourable in any degree, if the *nominal* exchange were favourable in the same degree; that is, if the high price of foreign bills, arising from their scarcity, were counteracted by the superior value of our currency over that of other countries. In this case the unfavourable *real* exchange would induce an increased exportation and diminished importation;—it would occasion a demand for bullion for exportation, without creating any drain upon the Bank; because from the contraction of the currency, the market price of bullion would be below the mint price. Ordinary produce would be cheap, the *real* exchange would be gradually restored to par by the operation of the exports and imports; and the *nominal* exchange would be raised to par by the conversion of bullion into coin.

The *computed* exchange would also be at par, though the *real* exchange were favourable, provided the *nominal* exchange were unfavourable in a similar degree; or, in other words, provided the low price of foreign bills, arising from their abundance, were counterbalanced by the depreciation of our currency compared with that of foreign countries. In this case there would be a diminished export and increased import, arising from the favourable state of the *real* exchange, attended with an influx of bullion; but there would at the same time be a drain upon the Bank, in consequence of the market price of bullion exceeding the mint price, from the over-issue of currency. Ordinary produce would be dear; the operation of the exports and imports would gradually restore the *real* exchange to par; and the *nominal* exchange would return to the same level by the conversion of the superfluous currency into bullion.

Again, the *computed* exchange might be in favour of a country, under very opposite states of the *real* and *nominal* exchange. Thus it would be 2 per cent. in favour of this country, if the *real* exchange were 3 per cent. above, and the *nominal* exchange 1 per cent. below par. It would also be two per cent. in favour of this country, with a favourable *nominal* exchange to the amount of 3 per cent. and an adverse *real* exchange of 1 per cent. In the same manner, an adverse *computed* exchange might be shewn to arise from very opposite states of the *real* and *nominal* exchange;* and it would be easy to point out, under any given circumstances, in what manner the merchant would derive his profit from the produce he was engaged either in exporting or importing. Suppose, for instance, the *computed* exchange between Hambro' and London to be 1 per cent. against this country, and that this arises from a *real* exchange which is favourable to the amount of 4 per cent. and a *nominal* exchange unfavourable to the extent of 5 per cent.; let the *real* price of bullion at Hambro' and London be precisely the same, and consequently the *nominal* prices different by the amount of the *nominal* exchange or 5 per cent. Now, if the expences of freight, insurance, &c. on the transit of bullion from Hambro' are 3 per cent. it is evident that a profit would be derived from the import of that article, notwithstanding the *computed* exchange was 1 per cent. against us. In this case the merchant must give a premium of 1 per cent. for the foreign bill to pay for the bullion;—100*l.* worth of bullion at Hambro' would therefore cost him 101*l.* and the charges

* Mr. Wheatley, who assigns the relative values of currencies as the exclusive cause of the fluctuations in the *computed* exchange, has endeavoured to prove, that the rate of exchange has constantly corresponded with the relative issues of currency. But the tables published by Lord King and Mr. Mushet furnish abundant proof of fluctuations in the exchange, without a corresponding alteration in the currency. Since the year 1797, when the correcting principle of the *nominal* exchange was removed in consequence of the Bank Restriction Act, there is, as might be expected, a general coincidence between the increase of bank notes in circulation and the adverse *computed* exchange; yet even within that period, there have been considerable intervals when the *computed* exchange between Hambro' and London has been in favour of the latter, and that too at the time when the greatest issues of currency recorded in Mr. Mushet's tables took place, viz. in May 1804, and January 1805.

of importation would increase this sum to 104*l*. Upon the subsequent sale, then, for 105*l* of depreciated currency in the home market he would derive from the transaction a profit of 1*l*. This sum is precisely the difference between the *real* exchange and the expences of transit, that part of the *computed* exchange which depends upon the *nominal*, producing no effect, since whatever is lost by its unfavourable state, is counterbalanced by a corresponding inequality of *nominal* prices.

In the same manner it might be shewn, that with a favourable *computed* exchange, bullion might be flowing out of the country; but it would be tedious to multiply instances, which, as the intelligent reader will easily conceive, may be infinitely varied. Those which have been now adduced are sufficient to shew, what contradictory conclusions may be drawn from any given rate of the *computed* exchange, and how impossible it is, from that alone, to determine either the relative value of currencies, or whether, what is usually called the balance of trade, be favourable or unfavourable to a nation.*

The merchant, by knowing the *computed* exchange, and

---

* A singular instance of the confusion arising from a want of attention to these distinctions occurs in the following passage from the fifth Number of the Quarterly Review: "Mr. Thornton having used the "following expression—'If at any time the exchanges of the country "become so unfavourable as to produce a material excess of the market "over the mint price of gold'—Mr. Ricardo comments on this represen- "tation by concisely saying, 'Here the cause is mistaken for the effect.' "Mr. Thornton seems to us indisputably correct; not but that the "unfavourableness of the exchange, and the rise in the bullion price of "gold, alternately act as cause and effect; but the former may, in some "cases, not improperly be said to precede the latter, and it certainly "does so in the case of a bad harvest, of which Mr. Thornton is speak- "ing in this case.' P. 157.—Here it is evident that Mr. Thornton's observation, if confined to the *real* exchange is correct. Mr. Ricardo's comment, if limited to the *nominal* exchange, may also be considered as correct, though it would have been more accurate to have stated, the unfavourableness of the exchange, and the excess of the market over the mint price of gold, both, as effects of the depreciation of the currency; and the Reviewer may be correct, if his observations are intended to apply to the *computed* exchange. The apparent contradictions arise from confounding the *real*, the *nominal*, and the *computed* exchange, under the general, unqualified term, exchange.

the current prices in the home and foreign market, and without any acquaintance with the theory of exchange, or the principles which regulate it, will always have sufficient practical data to guide him in his commercial transactions; but the statesman should beware in making general legislative provisions, that he is not misled by the partial statements of men, whose individual interests are frequently in direct opposition to the general welfare of the country.—This remark is not meant to convey any illiberal insinuations against a most useful and respectable class of the community; but experience sufficiently proves that self-interest gives a bias to the mind, which, without its being conscious of the influence, will mislead and pervert the judgment. Perhaps a more than ordinary degree of caution is requisite, in this commercial country, where there seems to be a prevailing opinion, that the riches of the merchants are evidence of the benefits that the nation derives from its foreign trade; it being forgotten, or unnoticed, that the profits of that class of persons are derived from the pockets of their countrymen; and that the advantages of foreign commerce consist in the stimulus it gives to the increase of the produce of the land and labour of the country; and to the opportunity which it affords, of exchanging the surplus produce thus called into existence for an equivalent, and only an equivalent produce, collected from every climate, and materially contributing to the enjoyments and the comforts of the community.

Of the Effects of the Depreciation of the Currency on the Expenditure of Government, and on the Interests of the different Classes of the Community.

The foreign expenditure of government being principally discharged by the remittance or the draft of bills, must be subject to the premium or discount in proportion to the *computed* exchange. Whatever be the amount of that expenditure, it will always be effected with greater or less advantage, according as the computed exchange is favourable or otherwise. It is of no consequence, so far as the disbursements of the Treasury are concerned, in what way the foreign expenditure is ultimately discharged by the country: for as long as bills are made use of, as the immediate mode of payment by the government, so long must the government, whenever the *computed* exchange is unfavourable, pay the premium for foreign bills, or submit to the discount upon its own; and so long, on the other hand, will it derive the advantage of the discount on foreign, and the premium on its own bills, whenever the state of the *computed* exchange is in favour of the country. It is therefore most essential to the interests of government, that the *computed* exchange should at all times be as favourable as possible. Now this can only be produced by a careful attention to the state of the currency, and its effects upon the *nominal* exchange; for the circumstances that affect the *real* exchange are not, at all times, within its control.

Bad harvests and deficient crops will always create an increased and unusual importation; and in the same degree, a demand for foreign payment. This will eventually, indeed, be discharged by an increased exportation; but, in the mean time, and during the continuance of the pressure, the *real* exchange will become unfavourable, and will continue so till the consequent bounty upon all exported, and the duty upon all imported, commodities, shall restore it to par.

The *nominal* exchange, on the contrary, is completely within the control of government, and can never be either permanently favourable or unfavourable, so long as the legislature exercises a due degree of vigilance over the state of the circulating medium. If the coin, in which the legal payments of the country are made, is not degraded, and the paper is convertible at option into specie, it is impossible that the currency can ever be reduced below the almost uniform value, which the precious metals preserve among the different nations of the earth; because the depreciation of the currency will always be prevented, by the conversion of any superfluous quantity of it into bullion.

Should the legislature be induced by temporary circumstances to interfere with this regulating principle, and restrict the issuers of notes from the obligation of paying in specie, the consequences are easily foreseen, and must soon be felt. There will be no longer any limit to the depreciation of the currency; the *nominal* exchange will continue permanently unfavourable, and will render the *computed* exchange so much the less favourable, or so much the more unfavourable, in proportion to the extent to which the currency may have been augmented beyond its natural amount.

The government, under these circumstances, will be utterly unable to relieve itself from the loss which must be incurred upon the total amount of its foreign expenditure, in whatever mode it is discharged; for the *nominal* exchange has a very different effect on the foreign payments of the state, and those of merchants in the course of their commercial transactions. The exporting merchant gains a premium on his bill equivalent to the *nominal* exchange, and by that advantage is repaid what would be otherwise lost in the high price he must give for his goods here, and the low price at which he must sell them abroad;—he derives no profit, and he suffers no loss. The importing merchant gives a premium for the foreign bill with which he pays for the produce he imports, but is repaid by the high *nominal* price at which he sells the produce at home. He also derives no profit, and sustains no loss.

But the government has no means of repaying itself for the loss occasioned by the *nominal* exchange. The equivalent is received abroad, and consumed there, and the bill for which the premium has been given will purchase precisely the same quantity of produce, whatever may have been paid for it here. Neither would the situation of government be altered, if, under an idea of saving the *nominal* exchange, it were induced to export commodities for the immediate supply of its armies, or its foreign establishments; for independently of the expenses of the transit, it would lose the whole amount of the *nominal* exchange, in the high prices at which the commodities would be bought in the home market. If bullion could be procured, there would be still the same loss; first, in the expenses of the transit; and secondly, in the high market price at which it must be bought here, while abroad it would pass for no more than its intrinsic value.

Without access to the documents and vouchers of government, there is no very accurate mode of estimating the amount of the foreign expenditure; but some approximation to it may be made, by a comparison of the exports and imports. It has been already observed, that the foreign expenditure of a country can only be discharged by the export of commodities to an equal amount; and as the equivalent is received and consumed abroad, it follows, that in every country where there is a foreign expenditure, the exports must exceed the imports to that extent:—the larger the expenditure, the greater will be the excess of exports over imports. From this acknowledged truth, the inference seems very obvious, or at least there is strong presumptive evidence to lead to this conclusion, that if a foreign expenditure cause an excess of exports over imports, an excess of exports over imports will denote a foreign expenditure.—Yet even at this day there are not wanting men in the Cabinet, in the Senate, and among the best-informed classes of society, who still adduce as a proof of the gains, that are made by foreign commerce, this same excess, which indicates expenditure, and not receipt.* Mr. Pitt was continually

* The same inference has been drawn, from the excess of exports, by the present Chancellor of the Exchequer, while these sheets have been passing through the press. See his speech upon opening the budget.

The gradual increase, both of the annual imports, and exports, has been frequently adduced as a decisive proof of the flourishing state of our commerce—a conclusion that may be exceedingly fallacious. The *nominal* value of the exports and imports will in some degree keep pace with the increase in the *nominal* price of commodities, and will swell the apparent amount of merchandize exported and imported, without any material addition to the actual quantity. That the present increase arises principally from this cause, is rendered more than probable, by a comparison of the relative amount of tonnage employed for the transport of that merchandize, in the years 1807 and 1809. The following table is drawn up from the returns made to the House of Commons, January 30th and March 24th, 1810:

vaunting of the resources of the nation, as evinced by this circumstance; and Mr. Rose, in his "Brief Examination," states, with the same view, the annual balance of trade in favour of this country at 14,800,000*l.* Mr. Necker, acting upon similar principles, estimated the annual balance in favour of France at 3,000,000*l.*; and all other countries have in like manner prepared official statements of exports and imports, and boasted of a favourable balance.* Those, who have entered into the spirit of the observations upon the *real* exchange, will think it unnecessary that I should dwell upon these absurd opinions respecting a balance of trade, either favourable or unfavourable to a nation; it being

---

Tonnage of Vessels, British and Foreign, including their repeated Voyages, in the several Ports of Great Britain, from and to all Parts of Europe.

Year ended 5th Jan.	Inwards. Tons.	Outwards. Tons.
1808	944,282	811,255
1810	882,255	814,811

Official Value of the Imports and Exports for three Quarters, ending the 10th of October.

Year.	Imports.	Exports.
1807	19,717,396	22,464,875
1809	29,000,782	39,824,104

As the nature of the commodities is specified in the returns, and does not appear to vary materially, as to the proportions of value and bulk in the respective years, the equality in the amount of tonnage employed is conclusive, that the apparent increase of trade is in a great measure *nominal.*

* "There is no mine, however productive, that could supply the "necessary stores for the balances that are claimed by the different "nations of the world. One country claims a balance of 14,800,000*l.* "and another of 5,000,000*l.* another of 3, and others of 2 and 1, to the "aggregate amount of nearly 40,000,000*l.* annually; and as all assert "their commerce to be favourable, it is obvious that their collective "balances must be paid by a continual influx of bullion from the mines "correspondent with their amount; but the annual produce of the

evident, that, though at any particular moment there may have been more produce sent from a country than has been received in return for it, and that bullion does occasionally pass to liquidate the balance, this happens merely in consequence of a derangement of the usual commercial exchanges, and the bullion must eventually again leave the country into which it flows, unless detained there by the wants of the people, either for the purpose of ornamental manufacture, or an extended currency, in consequence of increased wealth.

All trade, whether foreign or domestic, consists in an exchange of equivalents. Gold and silver will be sent as the equivalent, when gold and silver are wanted for use. The hardware and woollens of England are exchanged for the silks and the wines of France, because these are more desired than the bullion of France. It it were the taste of the people of England to use gold and silver for their ordinary utensils, the bullion of France would be demanded as the equivalent. But they prefer the wines and silks, and rather than forego these luxuries, are content with utensils formed of coarser materials. When the exports exceed the imports, (as they must do, when there is a foreign expenditure,) the equivalents for the excess are received "abroad "in as full and ample a manner, as if the produce which they "purchased were actually imported and entered in the "Custom-house books, and afterwards sent to the seat of war "for consumption. But from the circumstance of its not "being inserted in the Custom-house entries as value received "against the produce exported for its payment, the latter is "deemed to constitute a favourable balance, when it is in "reality exported to liquidate a balance against us."*

Notwithstanding, therefore, the inaccuracy of the Custom-house returns, and the difficulty of ascertaining the actual value of the imports and exports,—notwithstanding that the imports from the East and West Indies are confounded

"mines of the world does not exceed 7,000,000*l*." (Wheatley, on the Theory of Money, p. 139.)

* See Wheatley on the Theory of Money, p. 219.

with the imports arising from trade, when in fact they are merely remittances; the one, of territorial revenue invested in produce; the other, of rents and profits remitted to absentee planters resident in this country;—notwithstanding also, that the contraband trade introduces an immense quantity of commodities, which do not appear in the Custom-house returns; yet as the inaccuracies of one period are probably neither much greater nor less than those of another, if the ratio of the excess of exports to the foreign expenditure in one year, is known, it is fair to conclude, that the excess of any other year will be nearly in the same proportion to the foreign expenditure of that year.

It appears from the accounts presented by Mr. Long to the Secret Committee of the House of Lords, in 1797, that the foreign expenditure in the year 1796, the fourth year of the French revolutionary war, amounted to 10,649,000*l.*; and the excess of exports above the imports, for the same year, taken from the Custom-house books, is 7,331,494*l.*; so that the foreign expenditure is to this excess in the ratio nearly of 10 to 7.* The excess of exports over imports for three-quarters of the year 1809, is 17,359,229*l.* or above 23 millions for the year, as appears by the returns from the Custom-house presented to parliament the 10th of January, 1810; but as these returns are exclusive of the imports from India, the amount of those imports must be deducted, to make the calculations correspond with the returns for 1796, in which those imports are included. The sale of the East India Company's goods, from March 1, 1809, to March 1, 1810, amounted to 8,237,035*l.* the excess of exports over imports for the year 1809, after deducting this sum, would be about 15 millions, which, according to the ratio obtained for the year 1796, would give a foreign expenditure of 21 millions; and considering the enlarged scale of our military operations, together with the establishments in Sicily and

* The excess of exports over imports appears to be actually less than the foreign expenditure, in consequence of the produce remitted from the East and West Indies being entered in the Custom-house returns as imports.

Malta, it will perhaps be thought not much beyond the truth. During the whole of the year 1809, the exchange between London and Hambro' was never less than 7 per cent. in favour of the latter; and, increasing gradually towards the end of the year, it rose in the month of November to 16 per cent. Mr. Huskisson, in his examination before the Committee for inquiring into the policy and conduct of the expedition to the Scheldt, states the difficulties of negotiating bills in Spain, and in the Mediterranean, as much greater than at Hambro'; so that it is not improbable an additional expenditure of some millions has been incurred in consequence of the unfavourable state of the exchange, occasioning a correspondent loss to this country, which might have been entirely avoided, had the currency been sufficiently contracted to reduce the *computed* exchange to par.

Without, however, placing too much reliance upon an estimate, which at best can only be considered as an approximation, it must be evident that whatever may be the loss of government from this cause, it can only be supplied by laying additional burthens on the people. But this is not the only injury sustained in consequence of the depreciation of the currency; the same evil pervades the whole expenditure of government.—Whatever purchases are made must be at an increased cost in proportion to the *nominal* high prices that an excessive currency produces. It will be felt through all the departments of the state, and the enlarged scale of expense must be balanced by an encreased scale of taxation. It is a matter of general notoriety, that money within these few years has been considerably reduced in value. The depreciation has been visibly going forwards since the time of the Bank restriction; and as long as it continues, the interests of the Bank are in direct opposition to those of the government and the public.

If the evils of an excessive currency affected all classes of the community equally, there might be less reason for complaint; but the misfortune is, that one class suffers no injury whatever, while another is subjected to the whole pressure, without the possibility of relief. It is of no consequence to the merchant whether he purchase with guineas the commodities which were formerly bought with shillings. His exports and his imports are in no degree affected; he is, in a great measure, relieved from the fear of pecuniary embarrassment: and in the same degree that the value of money is lowered, his *nominal* profits are increased. Without possessing greater means than before, of commanding the comforts and the luxuries of life, he feels himself relatively raised in the scale of society, as far at least as property has the power of raising him, in proportion to the *nominal* thousands he receives.

The landed proprietor is subject to all the evils of a depreciated circulating medium during the continuance of his current leases. As they expire, an opportunity is afforded him of profiting from the high *nominal* prices of produce, by raising his rents, and thus, to a certain degree, of preserving his relative station in life; but the uncertainty of seasons, and the consequent excessive variations in the prices of agricultural produce, will prevent him from increasing the amount of his income in the same proportion that its value is diminished; and as the depreciation proceeds, he must suffer from its effects, in proportion to the length of time for which his leases are renewed.

But it is upon that class of the community, which receives a *nominal* income, that the depreciation of the currency acts with the greatest severity. The public creditor, the annuitant, the clergyman, the physician, the lawyer, the soldier, and the sailor—all the civil officers of government—all persons receiving salaries only,—in short, all those who have no produce to dispose of, by the high price of which they might have the opportunity of remunerating themselves for the losses which the depreciation induces. They not only bear the increased burthens which the government is compelled to impose in consequence of the depreciation, but the remainder of their income no longer possesses the same power of procuring the necessaries and comforts of life.

Let this view of the injury sustained by the class receiving a *nominal* income be contrasted with the advantages which the Restriction Act has conferred on the Bank proprietors.—Since the year 1797, the proprietors of Bank Stock have received,

In 1799, a bonus of	10 per cent.	Loyalty.
In 1801, - - -	5 per cent.	Navy 5 per cent.
In 1802, - - -	$2\frac{1}{2}$ per cent.	Ditto.
In 1804, - - -	5 per cent.	Cash.
In 1805, - - -	5 per cent.	Ditto.
In 1806, - - -	5 per cent.	Ditto.

In 1807, the dividend was raised from 7 to 10 per cent. which, with the payment of the Property Tax, makes more than 11 per cent. regular interest; and 100*l.* stock has increased from $127\frac{1}{2}$*l.* its price in 1797, to 280*l.* its price in 1809.*. Besides which, there is generally understood to be a very large surplus, which has not yet been divided amongst the proprietors; and, if the vast sums of money that have been expended during this period upon the buildings of the Bank, be considered, some idea may be formed of the immoderate profits that have been acquired by this establishment.

The question therefore is simply this, whether the interests of so large a part of the community are to be sacrificed for the benefit of the proprietors of bank stock, and the different banking partnerships throughout the kingdom; and it is yet to be explained on what grounds the continuance of a system can be justified, which, if it were wise at the time of its adoption, has long ceased to be either equitable or politic. It might be called for by imperious necessity, during the moment of alarm, and may be again resorted to should similar circumstances demand it; but in the mean time, it seems no more than right, that the Bank should be content with the profits that are to be acquired in a pursuit, which has at all times afforded an adequate remuneration to those who have embarked in it, without the assistance of a

* Reflections on the Abundance of Paper, &c., by Sir Philip Francis.

legislative provision, that has deranged, and will continue to derange, so long as it exists, the circulating medium of the country.

Applications are continually making to parliament for an increase of salary to those who are unable to meet the pressure of the times, and to keep up appearances suitable to their stations in life. Instances of this have recently occurred, as well in the case of the inferior clergy, as of the officers of the army and navy. The salaries in all public offices, and public trading companies, are obliged to be raised, to enable the persons who are employed in them to purchase the necessaries of life.* Those who sell as well as buy, have the means of transferring the weight from their own shoulders; but the possessor of a *nominal* income receives the same number of pounds, whatever be their value;—he is a buyer only, and must submit to his fate. The effects of *ordinary* taxation are the depression of the same class, and a tendency, as it proceeds to confound the different ranks of society. It is the more incumbent therefore upon the legislature to be careful, that this depressed class be not overwhelmed by that *extraordinary* taxation, which arises from the necessity of increasing the *nominal* revenue of government, in proportion to the depreciation of its value.

The mode in which these evils are to be remedied, it is unnecessary, after what has been already said, for me to point out. When the cause that has produced the mischief is removed, the evils will subside of themselves. Lord King very justly observes, "Had parliament been called upon to "authorize any of those direct frauds upon the currency, "which have often disgraced arbitrary governments; had it "been recommended to them to raise the denominations of the "current coin, there can be no doubt that such a proposal "would have been rejected with indignation. Yet an abuse

* Mr. Rose, in his pamphlet on the Public Expenditure, in speaking of the increase of the expense of collecting the Excise revenue, observes, "The increase in the Excise is nearly altogether for the augmentation "of the salaries of the officers on the establishment, to enable them to "exist." p. 54.

" of the same nature has been established by law in this " country. The power of reducing the value of the cur- " rency by a silent and gradual depreciation, is more danger- " ous, from the very circumstance of its being less direct, " and less exposed to observation."*

The difficulty that now presents itself is, in what manner to revert to the former system, without injury to the Bank, or to the merchants who have so long been indulged with the accommodation of procuring the discount of their bills;—and this difficulty is the more embarrassing, from the very peculiar and unprecedented combination of circumstances that exist at the present moment.

In consequence of the large army now maintained by this country on the Continent of Europe, and in the Mediterranean, our foreign expenditure is unusually great; and the export trade, which under the ordinary facilities of commercial intercourse, would enable us to defray this expenditure, is subjected to impediments from the control exercised by the enemy over the commerce of the Continent, which it is difficult to overcome. Our merchants are compelled to find secret and circuitous modes of introducing their merchandise into foreign countries, which, even after its introduction, is liable to immediate confiscation.†—This must

---

* Thoughts on the Restriction of Cash Payments at the Bank, p. 121.

† It has been said, that, in the countries more immediately under the control of the French, the merchants refuse to take our produce in exchange, and demand specie or bullion in payment for what we import from them. Should this be the fact, it is a strong proof that the French decrees have produced their effect, and that the risk of confiscation has to a certain extent prevented British merchandize from being introduced into those countries. It will be impossible, under these circumstances, much longer to continue such a commercial intercourse, unless the means be found of procuring a very unusual supply of bullion from the American mines: and it will become a question, whether the South American market can take such a quantity of British produce as will be sufficient to supply the bullion that will be wanted for effecting the usual imports from Holland and France, and that part of the Continent, where the French decrees can be enforced. Independently of this, the accumulation of bullion on the Continent will by degrees render its real price so low, that the quantity to be given in exchange for commodities imported from thence, must be continually augmenting, and of

72

operate as a very powerful check upon the export of the staple produce of the country: and great as the comparative excess of exports appears to be, from the last returns of the Custom-house that have been laid before Parliament, it is probable that the foreign expenditure would have demanded and produced a much greater excess, but for the restrictions that the French decrees have imposed upon our commerce. It is said, too, that the deficiency in the last year's harvest has occasioned an increased and unusual importation of foreign grain: so that the *real* exchange has been acted upon by the combined influence of all the causes that can render it unfavourable,—a large foreign expenditure, demanding an excess of exports which the restrictions on commerce obstruct; and an increased importation, to supply the failure of an article of the first necessity, counteracting the effect of the export trade, and diminishing its excess. If the market price of bullion, therefore, were ever raised above the mint price by an unfavourable *real* exchange, it might be expected under the circumstances now enumerated; and should this be the case, and the Bank be immediately rendered liable to the payment of its notes in specie, there would be no possibility of its withstanding the drain that would immediately commence, without such a sudden contraction of paper as would endanger the stability of the merchants. For the *nominal* and the *real* exchange being both unfavourable in a great degree, the process of melting the coin, and the export of bullion, would be carried on at the same time;—the first, to take advantage of the difference between the market aud the mint price of gold; the second, on account of the excess of the premium upon foreign bills above the expenses of the transit of bullion; and this drain would continue till the issues of bank paper were sufficiently contracted, to lower the market price of bullion below its mint price.

It is not easy to ascertain what degree of contraction might be requisite to produce this effect, for the issues of

course the price of continental produce so much enhanced to the consumer here, as at length to stop the consumption altogether.

the country banks are probably to the full as much above their due proportion, as those of the Bank of England. In the year 1795, before the drain took place which became the subject of such serious complaints to Mr. Pitt, the usual amount of bank notes in circulation was about 11 millions; at the time of the drain, the issue had been increased to 13 millions, and from the 25th of February, 1795, to the 25th of February, 1797, had been violently contracted to 8½ millions. At that time bank notes were in common circulation in all parts of the kingdom, and had not been so completely displaced as they have since been, by the country notes. The paper circulating medium, therefore, required for the capital, and parts immediately adjacent, would probably not exceed 10 millions. The quantity of coin at the same period may be estimated by the proportion between the cash and paper payments at the Bank, as given in evidence by Mr. Abraham Newland, before the Secret Committee of the House of Lords.* He states, that previously to the restriction, if the dividends to the public creditor amounted to 14,000,000*l*., not more than from 1,300,000*l*. to 1,400,000*l*. would be paid in cash. If in so large a payment, where cash in any quantity might be demanded, and where there must have been many fractional sums, one tenth only were paid in specie, it is fair to conclude that not more than one tenth would be given in the other money transactions of the metropolis. He adds, that 100,000*l*. would be sufficient for all the cash payments of the Treasury;—that in the gross produce of the Customs, which then amounted to 3,000,000*l*., the Bank did not receive above 3000*l*. in specie;—in the produce of the Excise, stated at 7,000,000*l*., not more than 60,000*l*.;—and in the instalments of a loan, consisting of much larger sums, not above 1 per cent, upon the whole.† So that taking 1 to 10 as the probable proportion of the specie to the notes, there would be about one million of the former in circulation,

* p. 63.

† See Wheatley on the Theory of Money, p. 142.

making, together with the paper, 11 millions for the total amount of the currency of the metropolis. By the last returns of the House of Commons, the bank notes in circulation on the 12th of January in the present year, exclusive of the Bank post bills, amounted to 20,522,810*l.*; and as the quantity of these notes that circulate in the country is very trifling, it is not improbable that the currency of the capital has been nearly doubled in the course of the last thirteen years. The general opinion is, that the country banks have made a still more extensive use of the privileges which the Restriction Bill has afforded, and have multiplied their paper to an enormous amount. There seems every reason, therefore, to conclude, that the circulating medium would be under-rated at double its amount, in the year 1797; and consequently that if the country does not require a greater quantity of currency now, than it did at that time, the Bank must contract its paper one-half, or to about 11 millions, before commodities could be brought back to their natural prices.*

Those who have attended to the distress in which the merchants were involved at the period to which we have referred, by a reduction of bank paper from 13½ to 8½ millions in two years, may conceive how infinitely more they must suffer by a sudden diminution of it from 21 to 11 millions. But this circumstance, which is a cogent reason against the immediate repeal of the Bank Restriction Bill, is also the strongest proof of the effect which the contraction of currency has upon prices; for whence could the distress of the merchants arise, but from their being compelled to dispose of their stock at reduced prices? They have now been so long habituated to the enhanced rates, that their purchases have been made with reference to this system, and under an expectation of deriving their present high *nominal* profits from its continuance. The number of purchasers in the market, occasioned by the increased issues of paper, will

* The increase of prices, arising from the gradual progress of taxation, will probably require a larger circulating medium than might be wanted in 1797.

be withdrawn, when the paper is again contracted, and consequently the holders of produce that has been bought upon credit, and for which bills are outstanding, must sell in the falling markets, in order to meet their acceptances when they become due. The Bank also, in consequence of the drain, will be compelled to reduce its paper, which it cannot effect, without refusing its usual discounts. The merchant, no longer possessing the means as before, of coining his credit into currency, must either sell, or be unable to make good his payments. In the same proportion as an increase of buyers was created by the over-issue, the contraction will create an increase of sellers; and thus it appears evident, that so sudden a diminution of currency, as would be necessary to protect the Bank, if the restriction were immediately withdrawn, would inevitably occasion great pecuniary distress, and be attended with the most injurious consequences to the credit and commerce of the nation.

But there is no necessity for such violence. The Bank may gradually diminish the amount of its paper, in the same manner in which it has for the last thirteen years been gradually increased. It is true such a proceeding will not be so popular with the merchants, but it will not be attended with any real injury to their interests, whilst it will confer a substantial benefit on the possessor of a *nominal* income, a benefit to which he is upon every principle of justice entitled.

It is only necessary for parliament to determine the amount of the annual diminution of the issues of the Bank, and to enforce the continuance of the measure, till it is found that the market price of bullion is permanently reduced, in a trifling degree, below its mint price. The currency will then be of the same value as if it consisted entirely of the precious metals, and the restriction may be removed without the slightest injury to the Bank, or any real injury to the merchant. This experiment may be made with the utmost safety, both to the Bank and the country; because parliament will at any time have the power of increasing or diminishing the annual contraction, should it be found that, in the first instance, too low or too high a limit had been assigned.*

It will require, however, much caution and some firmness, lest the legislature should be misled by the clamours of those who will first feel the effects of the remedy; for as the Bank will immediately experience a diminution of its profits, and probably be at length compelled to lower the interest to the proprietors; as the issues of the country banker will be restrained within their natural limits; and as the merchant, under the first alarm which the falling prices will excite, and without forming any just conception of its cause, will not fail to exclaim against a system apparently so adverse to his interests; there can be little doubt but that the public, during its progress, will be assailed with the most gloomy predictions of the decline of the general wealth, and the ruin of the commercial prosperity of the nation. But a full and accurate acquaintance with this most important subject, will lead the government and the people to disregard and depise such idle and interested clamours,—to consider these effects not as symptoms of decay, but as evidences of the efficacy of a measure tending to restore the energies of the country. It will teach them the necessity of perseverance, not merely for the purpose of obviating those mischiefs which have hitherto been experienced, but in order to prevent the still greater evils, which must infallibly result from an adherence to the same system. Above all, it will induce them to submit with cheerfulness to those trifling and partial inconveniencies, which may

* The Bank has been indulged so long in the exercise of the extraordinary privileges conferred upon it by the legislature, and has, by its extensive advances, acquired such a control over the finances of individuals, and of government, that it may, perhaps, have become questionable, whether the Directors of that establishment have not, at this moment, the power of dictating their own terms; and whether the legislature may not be under the necessity of receiving, rather than of proposing conditions. Should these conjectures have any foundation in truth, they furnish the most cogent reasons for the immediate extinction of a power, whose existence is incompatible with the independence and the supremacy of government.

occasionally be experienced during the progress of the remedy, while they look forward with confidence to the re-establishment of the ancient scale and order of things, and the consequent increase, not only of the comforts of the great mass of the community, but of the resources, the powers, and the independence of the government.

In the following Tables, the figures indicating the per centage in favour of, and against London, denote pounds and the decimal parts of pounds, which are not carried beyond one decimal place.

A Table of the Rates of Exchange between London and Hambro', and of the Market Price of Gold, from 1760 *to* 1810, *extracted from the Tables of Mr. Mushet:*

		Hamburgh.	Per centage in favour of London.	Per centage against London.	Price of Standard Gold per oz.	Per centage above its Mint Price.	Per centage below its Mint Price.
1760	Jan. 1	36 4	7 .9		3 18 6	0 16 0 2	
	March 4	36 1	7 .1		3 18 9	1 2 5 2	
	May 2	35 6	5 .4		3 19 1	1 11 0 1	
	July 1	32 6		3 .5	3 19 0	1 8 10 2	
	Sept. 2	32 2		4 .5	4 0 1	2 16 8 2	
	Nov. 4	31 8		6	3 19 4	1 17 5 1	
1761	Jan. 2	32		5	3 18 10	1 4 7 1	
	March 3	32 3		4 .3	3 19 8	2 6 0	
	May 1	32 2		4 .5	4 0 0	2 14 6 3	
	July 3	31 11		5 .2	4 0 6	3 7 5	
	Sept. 1	32 5		3 .8	4 0 6	3 7 5	
	Nov. 3	33		2	3 19 4	1 17 5 1	
1762	Jan. 1	32 11		2 .3	3 19 0	1 8 10 2	
	March 2	33 9	0 .2		3 18 9	1 2 5 2	
	May 4	34 3	1 .7		3 19 3	1 15 3 3	
	July 2	34 8	2 .9		3 19 10	2 10 3 2	
	Sept. 3	35	3 .9		3 19 4	1 17 5 1	
	Nov. 2	35 1	4 .2		3 18 10	1 4 7 1	
1763	Jan. 4	34 2	1 .4		4 0 0	2 14 6 3	
	March 1	33 11	0 .7		4 0 6	3 7 5	
	May 3	34 2	1 .4		4 1 3	4 6 8	
	July 1	34 3	1 .7		4 0 6	3 7 5	
	Sept. 2	34 7	2 .7		4 1 6	4 13 1 3	
	Nov. 1	34 11	3 .7		3 18 9	1 2 5 2	
1764	Jan. 3	34 5	2 .2		3 18 3	0 9 7 2	
	March 2	35 2	4 .4		3 18 3	0 9 7 2	
	May 1	34 11	3 .7		3 18 3	0 9 7 2	
	July 3	35 1	4 .2		3 18 3	0 9 7 2	
	Sept. 4	35	3 .9		3 18 0	0 3 2 2	
	Nov. 2	35 1	4 .2		3 18 0	0 3 2 2	

		Hamburgh.	Per centage in favour of London.	Per centage against London.	Price of Standard Gold per oz.	Per centage above its Mint Price.	Per centage below its Mint Price.
1765	Jan. 1	35 1	4 .9		3 18 0	0 3 2 1	
	March 1	34 10	3 .4		3 18 0	0 3 2 2	
	May 3	34 11	3 .7		3 18 0	0 3 2 2	
	July 2	34 9	3 .2		3 18 0	0 3 2 2	
	Sept. 3	34 4	1 .9		3 18 8	1 0 3 3	
	Nov. 1	34 4	1 .9		3 18 2	0 7 5 3	
1766	Jan. 3	34 6	2 .4		3 18 7	0 18 2 1	
	March 4	34 9	3 .2		3 18 8	1 0 3 3	
	May 2	34 11	3 .7		3 19 2	1 13 2	
	July 1	35 1	4 .9		3 19 10	2 10 3 2	
	Sept. 2	35 3	3 .7		3 19 0	1 8 10 2	
	Nov. 4	35 8	5 .9		3 19 0	1 8 10 2	
1767	Jan. 2	35 6	5 .4		3 19 3	1 15 3 3	
	March 3	35 8	5 .9		3 19 4	1 17 5 1	
	May 1	35 10	6 .4		3 19 10	2 10 3 2	
	July 3	35 8	5 .9		3 19 8	2 6 0	
	Sept. 1	35 11	6 .6		3 19 5	1 19 7	
	Nov. 3	35 6	5 .4		3 19 5	1 19 7	
1768	Jan. 1	34 11	2 .7		3 18 8	1 0 3 3	
	March 1	34 4	1 .9		3 18 9	1 2 5 2	
	May 3	34 8	2 .9		3 19 1	1 11 0 1	
	July 1	34 7	2 .7		3 19 6	2 1 8 3	
	Sept. 2	34 5	2 .2		3 19 6	2 1 8 3	
	Nov. 1	33 6		6 .5	3 19 5	1 19 7	
1769	Jan. 3	33 2		1 .5	3 19 7	2 3 10 1	
	March 3	33 4		1	3 19 9	2 8 1 3	
	May 2	33 8			4 0 3	3 1 0	
	July 4	33 6		.5	4 0 8	3 11 8 1	
	Sept 1	33 6		0 .5	4 0 4	3 3 1 2	
	Nov. 3	33 1		1 .8	4 0 6	3 7 5	

		Hamburgh.	Per centage in favour of London.	Per centage against London.	Price of Standard Gold per oz.	Per centage above its Mint Price.	Per centage below its Mint Price.
1770	Jan. 2	33 2		1 .5	4 0 6	3 7 5	
	March 2	33 2		1 .5	4 0 4	3 3 1 2	
	May 1	33 3		1 .3	4 0 4	3 3 1 2	
	July 3	33 4		1	4 0 2	2 18 10 1	
	Sept. 4	33 2		1 .5	4 0 0	2 14 6 3	
	Nov. 2	33 5		0 .8	3 19 6	2 1 8 3	
1771	Jan. 1	33 8			3 18 9	1 2 5 2	
	March 1	33 9	0 ·2		3 18 10	1 4 7 1	
	May 3	33 6		0 .5	3 19 2	1 13 2	
	July 2	33		2	3 19 9	2 8 1 3	
	Sept. 3	32 11		2 .3	4 0 8	3 11 8 1	
	Nov. 1	32 9		2 .8	4 0 7	3 9 6 2	
1772	Jan. 3	32 7		3 .3	4 1 0	4 0 3	
	March 3	32 11		2 .3	4 1 0	4 0 3	
	May 1	32 10		2 .5	4 0 9	3 13 10	
	July 3	33 4		1	4 0 0	2 14 6 3	
	Sept. 1	33 5		1 .3	3 19 0	1 8 10 2	
	Nov. 3	33 8			3 18 0	0 3 2 2	
1773	Jan. 5	34	0 .9		3 18 0	0 3 2 2	
	March 2	35	3 .9		3 18 0	0 3 2 2	
	May 4	34 9	3 .2		3 17 11	0 1 0 3	
	July 2	34 11	3 .7		3 17 9		0 3 2 2
	Sept. 3	34 8	2 .9		3 17 9		0 3 2 2
	Nov. 2	34 9	3 .0		3 17 9		0 3 2 2
1774	Jan. 4	34 9	3 .2		3 17 9		0 3 2 2
	March 1	34 10	3 .4		3 17 9		0 3 2 2
	May 3	34 7	2 .7		3 17 9		0 3 2 2
	July 1	34 9	3 .2		3 17 9		0 3 2 2
	Sept. 2	34 5	2 .2		3 17 7		0 7 5 3
	Nov. 1	34 2	1 .4		3 17 7		0 7 5 3

		Hamburgh.	Per centage in favour of London.	Per centage against London.	Price of Standard Gold per oz.	Per centage above its Mint Price.	Per centage below its Mint Price.
1775	Jan. 3	34 3	1 .7		3 17 7		0 7 5 3
	March 3	34 5	2 .2		3 17 7		0 7 5 3
	May 2	34 4	1 .9		3 17 7		0 7 5 3
	July 4	34 5	2 .2		3 17 7		0 7 5 3
	Sept. 1	34 4	1 .9		3 17 7		0 7 5 3
	Nov. 3	34 2	1 .4		3 17 7		0 7 5 3
1776	Jan. 5	34 1	1 .2		3 17 7		0 7 5 3
	March 1	33 9	0 .2		3 17 7		0 7 5 3
	May 3	33 8			3 17 7		0 7 5 3
	July 2	33 3		1 .3	3 17 7		0 7 5 3
	Sept. 3	33 5		0 .8	3 17 7		0 7 5 3
	Nov. 1	33 1		1 .8	3 17 7		0 7 5 3
1777	Jan. 3	33 2		1 .5	3 17 7		0 7 5 3
	March 4	33 0		2	3 17 7		0 7 5 3
	May 2	32 10		2 .5	3 17 7		0 7 5 3
	July 1	32 7		3 .3	3 17 7		0 7 5 3
	Sept. 2	32 2		4 .5	3 17 7		0 7 5 3
	Nov. 4	32 1		4 .8	3 17 7		0 7 5 3
1778	Jan. 2	32 4		4	3 17 7		0 7 5 3
	March 3	32 9		2 .8	3 17 7		0 7 5 3
	May 1	34 2	1 .4		3 17 7		0 7 5 3
	July 3	34 7	2 .7		3 17 7		0 7 5 3
	Sept. 1	34 5	2 .2		3 17 7		0 7 5 3
	Nov. 3	34 10	3 .4		3 17 7		0 7 5 3
1779	Jan. 1	35 6	5 .4		3 17 7		0 7 5 3
	March 2	35 8	5 .9		3 17 6		0 9 7 2
	May 4	36 2	7 .4		3 17 6		0 9 7 2
	July 2	35 10	6 .4		3 17 6		0 9 7 2
	Sept. 3	33 9	0 .2		3 17 6		0 9 7 2
	Nov. 9	34 4	1 .9		3 17 6		0 9 7 2

		Hamburgh.		Per centage in favour of London.		Per centage against London.		Price of Standard Gold. per oz.			Per centage above its Mint Price.				Per centage below its Mint Price.			
1780	Jan. 4	34	6	2	.4			3	17	6					0	9	7	2
	March 3	35	7	5	.6			3	17	6					0	9	7	2
	May 2	35	2	4	.4			3	17	6					0	9	7	2
	July 4	34	8	2	.9			3	17	6					0	9	7	2
	Sept. 1	34	1	1	.2			3	17	6					0	9	7	2
	Nov. 3	33	10	0	.4			3	17	6					0	9	7	2
1781	Jan. 2	34	1	1	.2			3	17	6					0	9	7	2
	March 2	33	11	0	.7			3	17	6					0	9	7	2
	May 1	33	7			0	.3	3	17	6					0	9	7	2
	July 3	32	1			4	.8	3	17	6					0	9	7	2
	Sept. 4	32	2			4	.5	3	17	6					0	9	7	2
	Nov. 2	31	11			5	.2	3	17	6					0	9	7	2
1782	Jan. 1	31	9			5	.7	3	17	6					0	9	7	2
	March 1	32	10			2	.5	3	17	6					0	9	7	2
	May 3	32	11			2	.3	3	17	6					0	9	7	2
	July 2	32	11			2	.3	3	17	6					0	9	7	2
	Sept. 3	32	6			3	.5	3	17	9					0	3	2	2
	Nov. 1	31	8			6		3	17	9					0	3	2	2
1783	Jan. 3	32	7			3	.2	3	17	9					0	3	2	2
	March 4	32	5			3	.8	3	17	9					0	3	2	2
	May 2	31	9			5	.7	3	18	0	0	3	2	2				
	July 1	31	6			6	.5	3	18	0	0	3	2	2				
	Sept. 2	31	6			6	.5	3	18	0	0	3	2	2				
	Nov. 4	32	9			2	.8	3	18	0	0	3	2	2				
1784	Jan. 2	33	6			0	.5	3	18	0	0	3	2	2				
	March 2	33	9	0	.2			3	18	0	0	3	2	2				
	May 4	34	4	1	.9			3	17	10 2								
	July 2	34	4	1	.9			3	17	10 2								
	Sept. 3	34	7	2	.7			3	17	10 2								
	Nov. 2	34	8	2	.9			3	17	10 2								

		Hamburgh.	Per centage in favour of London.	Per centage against London.	Price of Standard Gold per oz.	Per centage above its Mint Price.	Per centage below its Mint Price.
1785	Jan. 7	35	3 .9		3 17 10 2		
	March 1	35 4	4 .9		3 17 10 2		
	May 3	34 11	3 .7		3 17 10 2		
	July 1	35 6	5 .4		3 17 6		0 9 7 2
	Sept. 2	35 4	4 .9		3 17 6		0 9 7 2
	Nov. 1	35 3	4 .7		3 17 6		0 9 7 2
1786	Jan. 3	34 10	3 .4		3 17 6		0 9 7 2
	March 3	34 11	3 .7		3 17 6		0 9 7 2
	May 2	34 5	2 .2		3 17 6		0 9 7 2
	July 4	34 3	1 .7		3 17 6		0 9 7 2
	Sept. 1	34 3	1 .7		3 17 6		0 9 7 2
	Nov. 3	34 6	2 .4		3 17 6		0 9 7 2
1787	Jan. 2	34 5	2 .2		3 17 6		0 9 7 2
	March 2	34 7	2 .7		3 17 6		0 9 7 2
	May 1	34 7	2 .7		3 17 6		0 9 7 2
	July 3	34 8	2 .9		3 17 6		0 9 7 2
	Sept. 4	35	3 .9		3 17 6		0 9 7 2
	Nov. 2	35 1	4 .2		3 17 6		0 9 7 2
1788	Jan. 1	35 1	4 .2		3 17 6		0 9 7 2
	March 4	35 3	4 .7		3 17 6		0 9 7 2
	May 2	35 4	4 .9		3 17 6		0 9 7 2
	July 1	35 1	4 .2		3 17 6		0 9 7 2
	Sept. 2	35	3 .9		3 17 6		0 9 7 2
	Nov. 4	34 9	3 .2		3 17 6		0 9 7 2
1789	Jan. 6	34 10	3 .4		3 17 6		0 9 7 2
	March 3	35 1	4 .2		3 17 6		0 9 7 2
	May 1	35 6	5 .4		3 17 6		0 9 7 2
	July 3	35 7	5 .6		3 17 6		0 9 7 2
	Sept. 1	35 5	5 .1		3 17 6		0 9 7 2
	Nov. 3	35 1	4 .2		3 17 6		0 9 7 2

		Hamburgh.	Per centage in favour of London.	Per centage against London.	Price of Standard Gold per oz.	Per centage above its Mint Price.	Per centage below its Mint Price.	Amount of Bank of England notes in Circulation.
1790	Jan. 29	35	3 .9		3 17 6		0 9 7 2	10,245,280
	March 1	35 2	4 .4		3 17 6		0 9 7 2	11,160,590
	May 4	35 4	4 .9		3 17 6		0 9 7 2	11,348,700
	July 2	35 7	5 .6		3 17 6		0 9 7 2	11,510,270
	Sept. 3	35 6	5 .4		3 17 6		0 9 7 2	11,601,950
	Nov. 2	35 7	5 .6		3 17 6		0 9 7 2	12,060,620
1791	Jan. 4	35 6	5 .4		3 17 6		0 9 7 2	11,764,680
	March 1	35 10	6 .4		3 17 6		0 9 7 2	11,225,840
	May 3	35 11	6 .6		3 17 6		0 9 7 2	11,239,170
	July 1	35 10	6 .4		3 17 6		0 9 7 2	11,765,280
	Sept. 2	35 6	5 .4		3 17 6		0 9 7 2	11,316,790
	Nov. 1	35 2	4 .4		3 17 6		0 9 7 2	11,157,040
1792	Jan. 3	34 6	2 .4		3 17 6		0 9 7 2	11,963,820
	March 2	34 6	2 .4		3 17 6		0 9 7 2	12,100,650
	May 1	34 3	1 .7		3 17 6		0 9 7 2	10,938,620
	July 3	34 5	2 .2		3 17 6		0 9 7 2	10,967,310
	Sept. 4	34	0 .9		3 17 6		0 9 7 2	11,159,720
	Nov. 2	34 3	1 .7		3 17 6		0 9 7 2	10,366,450
1793	Jan. 1	35 4	4 .9		3 17 6		0 9 7 2	10,343,940
	March 1	36 7	8 .6		3 17 6		0 9 7 2	10,927,970
	May 3	37 6	11 .3		3 17 6		0 9 7 2	
	July 2	37 2	10 .3		3 17 6		0 9 7 2	
	Sept. 3	36	6 .9		3 17 6		0 9 7 2	
	Nov. 1	35 3	4 .7		3 17 6		0 9 7 2	
1794	Jan. 3	35 9	6 .1		3 17 6		0 9 7 2	
	March 4	36 4	7 .9		3 17 6		0 9 7 2	
	May 2	36 7	8 .6		3 17 6		0 9 7 2	
	July 1	35 6	5 .4		3 17 6		0 9 7 2	
	Sept. 2	35	3 .9		3 17 6		0 9 7 2	
	Nov. 4	34 5	2 .2		3 17 6		0 9 7 2	

		Hamburgh.	Per centage in favour of London.	Per centage against London.	Price of Standard Gold per oz.	Per centage above its Mint Price.	Per centage below its Mint Price.	Amount of Bank of England notes in circulation.
1795	Jan. 2	34 6	2 .4		3 17 6		0 9 7 2	12,432,240
	March 3	35 10	6 .4		3 17 6		0 9 7 2	10,912,680
	May 1	34 4	1 .9		3 17 6		0 9 7 2	11,034,790
	July 3	32 10		2 .5	3 17 6		0 9 7 2	11,608,670
	Sept. 1	32 6		3 .5				10,824,150
	Nov. 3	32 10		2 .5				10,770,200
1796	Jan. 1	32 7		3 .3				9,720,440
	March 1	33 2		1 .5				9,645,710
	May 3	33 10	0 ·4					8,640,250
	July 1	33 7		0 .3	3 17 6		0 9 7 2	11,103,880
	Sept. 2	33 7		0 .3	3 17 6		0 9 7 2	10,828,880
	Nov. 1	34 7	2 .7		3 17 6		0 9 7 2	11,641,400
1797	Jan. 3	35 6	5 .4					13,043,480
	March 3	34 9	3 .2					13,234,440
	May 2	36	6 .9		3 17 6		0 9 7 2	12,115,640
	July 4	36 6	8 .4		3 17 6 2		0 9 7 2	12,441,070
	Sept. 1	38	12 .8		3 17 10 2			13,202,460
	Nov. 3	38	12 .8		3 17 10 2			13,720,260
1798	Jan. 2	38 2	13 .3		3 17 10 2			13,759,940
	March 2	37 5	11 .1		3 17 10 2			14,006,960
	May 1	37 8	11 .8		3 17 10 2			
	July 3	37 10	12 .3		3 17 10 2			
	Sept. 4	37 6	11 .3		3 17 10			
	Nov. 2	37 10	12 .3		3 17 9		0 3 2 2	
1799	Jan. 1	37 7	11 .6		3 17 9		0 3 2 2	
	March 1	37 7	11 .6		3 17 9		0 3 2 2	
	May 3	35 6	5 .4		3 17 9		0 3 2 2	
	July 2	36	6 .9		3 17 9		0 3 2 2	
	Sept. 3	33 4		1	3 17 9		0 3 2 2	
	Nov. 1	32 6		3 .5				

		Hamburgh.	Per centage in favour of London.	Per centage against London.	Price of Standard Gold per oz.	Per centage below its Mint Price.	Amount of Bank of England Notes in circulation.
1800	Jan. 3	32		5			15,110,060
	March 4	31 4		7			15,213,520
	May 2	32 5		3 .8			
	July 1	32 6		3 .5	4 5 0	9 2 11 3	15,230,410
	Sept. 2	32 2		4 .5	4 5 0	9 2 11 3	15,450,970
	Nov. 4	31 10		5 .5	4 5 0	9 2 11 3	
1801	Jan. 2	29 8		11 .9	4 6 0	10 8 8	16,365,206
	March 3	31 7		6 .2	4 2 6	5 18 9 1	No account of the Bank notes in circulation appears to have been presented for this year, subsequent to March 25.
	May 1	31 6		6 .5	4 5 0	9 2 11 3	
	July 3	31 6		6 .5			
	Sept. 1	31 7		6 .2			
	Nov. 3	32 6		3 .5			
1802	Jan. 1	32 2		4 .5			
	March 2	32 3		4 .3	4 3 6	7 4 5 2	15,956,016
	May 4	32 8		3			
	July 2	33 3		1 .3			16,747,300
	Sept. 3	33 3		1 .3			16,141,636
	Nov. 2	33 5		0 .8			15,838,410
1803	Jan. 4	34	0 .9				
	March 1	34 5	2 .2				16,101,140
	May 3	34 4	1 .9				16,734,510
	July 1	34 4	1 .9				16,622,510
	Sept. 2	32 10		2 .5			
	Nov. 1	34 4	1 .9				17,931,930
1804	Jan. 3	34 10	3 .4				17,274,493
	March 2	35	3 .9				18,033,383
	May 1	35 9	6 .1				
	July 3	35 8	5 .9		4 0 0	2 14 6 3	17,194,138
	Sept. 4	35 10	6 .4		4 0 0	2 14 6 3	16,881,306
	Nov. 2	35 6	5 .4		4 0 0	2 14 6 3	

		Hamburgh.	Per centage in favour of London.	Per centage against London.	Price of Standard Gold per oz.	Per centage above its Mint Price.	Amount of Bank of England notes in circulation.
1805	Jan. 1	35 6	5 .4		4 0 0	2 14 6 3	18,407,380
	March 1	35 8	5 .9		4 0 0	2 14 6 3	17,367,740
	May 3	35 5	5 .1		4 0 0	2 14 6 3	16,449,020
	July 2	35 8	5 .9		4 0 0	2 14 6 3	16,753,490
	Sept. 3	35 5	5 .1		4 0 0	2 14 6 3	17,293,070
	Nov. 5	32 9		2 .8			17,085,150
1806	Jan. 3	33 3		1 .3			17,281,330
	March 4	34 2	1 .4				17,049,720
	May 2	33 8					16,618,390
	July 1	34 5	2 .2				17,536,400
	Sept. 2	34 4	1 .9				17,748,400
	Nov. 4	33 10	0 .4				16,930,200
1807	Jan. 2	34 8	2 .9				17,573,100
	March 3	34 10	3 .4				17,491,900
	May 1	34 10	3 .4				17,644,670
	July 3	34 3	1 .7				17,466,170
	Sept. 4	34 3	1 .7				17,560,060
	Nov. 6	34 4	1 .9				
1808	Jan. 1	34 4	1 .9				
	March 1	34 6	2 .4				
	May 3	34 9	3 .2				
	July 1	35 8	5 .9				
	Sept. 2	34 8	2 .9				
	Nov. 1	32 9		2 .8			
1809	Jan. 3	31 3		7 .2			No account of Bank notes in circulation was presented subsequent to this date.
	March 3	31		8			
	May 2	30 6		9 .5	4 10 0	15 11 4 3	
	July 4	28 6		15 .4	4 11 0	17 1 7 3	
	Sept. 5	29		13 .9	*4 8 0	19 5 2 3	
	Nov. 3	28		16 .9	†4 5 0	15 8 2	

* The Gold quoted this month is doubloons, they are valued in our Gold coins at 3l. 13s. per oz.

† Doubloons.

THE QUESTION

CONCERNING THE

DEPRECIATION

OF OUR

Currency

STATED AND EXAMINED.

By W. HUSKISSON, Esq. M.P.

" It is the interest of every country that the Standard of its Money, once settled, should be inviolably and immutably kept to perpetuity. For whenever that is altered, upon what pretence soever, the Public will lose by it.

" Men, in their bargains, contract, not for denominations or sounds, but for the intrinsic value."

LOCKE *on Money.*

THIRD EDITION CORRECTED.

LONDON:

1810.

PREFACE

From the circumstance of my having been a member of the Bullion Committee, and from its being known to several of my friends that I had taken a part in the discussion which preceded the Report, I have been pressed, by more than one of them, for some explanation of my opinions respecting the state of our currency and circulation, and of the grounds on which those opinions are founded.—Gratified to find their attention awakened to all the importance of the subject, and with my own feelings fully alive to it, I committed to paper the substance of my opinions, in part before, and the remainder very soon after, the publication of the Report.

Proportionate to the general interest excited by that Report, has been the clamour raised against it. That clamour, and the strange doctrines which are set up in opposition to the principles and conclusions of the Committee, have induced some of those who had originally read what I had written with the partiality of friends, to express a wish that I would publish it.

If this wish had not been fortified by other considerations, I should not, by yielding to it, have exposed myself to the imputation of that vanity, to which such indiscreet compliance is generally, and perhaps often justly, ascribed. But when so many pens are employed to propagate what appear to me most false and dangerous theories upon the subject of our currency; when several of those who have taken upon themselves to controvert the Report, have gone out of their way to misrepresent the conduct, and to cast obloquy on the characters and motives of those who concurred in it; and above all, when the many evil consequences of an erroneous, or even an unsettled state of the public mind upon a question of such vast importance, are considered; I trust that I shall be justified in submitting, what was originally prepared for an indulgent and limited circle only, to the examination and judgment of a more extended and impartial tribunal.

With deference then I venture to offer to the public an exposition of the course of reasoning which led my mind to the conclusion which I have formed upon a question in which the public has so deep an interest.

Any man, I think, who has read the pamphlet of Sir JOHN SINCLAIR, or the speech of Mr. RANDLE JACKSON to the Proprietors of Bank Stock, (as reported in the newspapers,) must admit that I have not unfairly described the attacks which have been made upon the Report of the Bullion Committee.

Both these productions appeared long after the following observations were written. To enter into any examination of their contents is not compatible with the object and limits of these introductory remarks; nor indeed, if it were, should I be tempted to such an examination, notwithstanding the circular invitation with which the Right Honourable Baronet is said to have accompanied the distribution of his pamphlet.

When among other theories equally extraordinary,—(whimsically dignified with the name of *axioms* in the work itself)—this author, before he is well clear of his preface, lays it down as a leading principle, "that the abundance of "circulation is the great source of opulence and strength;" and emphatically styles it "*the mine of national prosperity*;"—when he defines *Money* to be "a well regulated paper cur-"rency with a certain proportion of coin"—I should be at a loss how to deal with such *axioms*. They appear to belong to that class of propositions which have been sometimes characterized by rhetoricians as being "neither true nor "false;" and as they are (to me at least) wholly unintelligible, they must of course be unanswerable.

There is, however, one charge against the Committee, much dwelt upon both in the speech and in the pamphlet to which I have referred, with which I must detain my readers for a few moments. It is that of having made a Report directly contrary to, and altogether inconsistent with, the evidence.—This assertion has surprised me: and I have looked in vain for any proofs in support of it.

The Committee endeavoured, in the first instance, to collect and place upon their records certain *facts;* such, for instance, as the continued high price of gold bullion, and the great depression of the foreign exchanges.—To any *explanations* that were offered by the witnesses, of the causes which had produced this state of things, they listened with the most patient attention: and have given them a place in the Appendix, in the words of the parties examined. But when these explanations appeared to the Committee to be either unfounded or insufficient; to be contradicted by the experience of former times, or by the actual state of facts; to be inconsistent with each other, or with the admissions of the witnesses themselves; could it be the duty of the Committee to adopt them as their creed? Was it not rather their duty to state, in what respect, in what degree, and in what instances these explanations appeared to them unfounded or insufficient; and to point out the circumstances by which they were contradicted, and the inconsistencies which they involved?

It was indeed for the House of Commons to consider whether they would appoint such a Committee at all, or refer such a subject to such a mode of examination: and if it was foreseen that the promulgation of an opinion, such as that which the Committee have formed, would be attended with public mischief, (which I however am very far from thinking) it might, in that case, be matter of regret that the House should have consented to its appointment. But, even in that case, nothing can be more unjust than to impute as blame to the members of the Committee, acting under the orders of the House, the due discharge of a duty which the House had thought proper to impose upon them.

In the execution of this duty it became necessary to ascertain the principles by which the Directors of the Bank of England had been governed in the issues of their paper since the restriction.

This information could not be obtained from them in their corporate capacity: it could only be collected from those who were at the head of the Direction.

This forms by far the most important part of the evidence: because the supply of our circulation being now without control in the hands of the Directors, it was essential to ascertain by what rules and principles they were guided in the exercise of this extensive discretion. Before this enquiry, these rules and principles were, I believe, unknown to the public: they were certainly unknown to me. The Committee have stated them in the words of the Governor and Deputy Governor of the Bank; and have assigned reasons for thinking that they do not afford a check constantly and sufficiently operative against an over-issue, and consequent depreciation of Bank paper.—Is this what is called making a Report directly contrary to the evidence?

Mr. JACKSON, indeed, is of opinion that the Committee ought to have surrendered their judgment altogether to the authority of those witnesses who asserted, that Bank Notes are "*not* depreciated;" and who stated as the grounds of that assertion, that "in *their* extensive and various transactions, no difference exists between Bank Notes and coin."—As Mr. JACKSON is, unfortunately, not the only person to whom this inference appears to be conclusive, it may be regretted, as an omission, that the Report of the Committee did not more particularly guard against it. There is perhaps no part of the question which is capable of being settled with greater ease and certainty. The experience of our own, as well as of all other countries, has placed beyond the reach of controversy the proposition, that if *one part* of the *currency* of a country (provided such currency be made either directly or virtually a *legal tender*, according to its *denomination*,) be depreciated, *the whole* of that *currency*, whether paper or coin, must be *equally* depreciated. This proposition, I trust, the reader will find satisfactorily made out in the following pages.

.Whilst I am aware that I must despair of convincing persons so entirely at variance with the first principles of political economy, there is another, and I hope a larger class, to whose understandings the following observations must appear superficial and unnecessary. They certainly contain nothing which is new; or which can be striking or interesting to any readers of that class. A discussion which goes back to the first principles of our money system, and in which, at the risk of a wearying repetition, the same proposition is illustrated in several different modes, must appear superfluous to persons who are already well acquainted with those principles; and whose own ingenuity would supply them with illustrations more apt than any that I have been able to furnish.

But I am convinced, as well from the experience which I derived from the enquiries carried on in the Bullion Committee, as from every thing that has since come under my observation, that a great proportion of the public, including (even in the limited circle of my own acquaintance) many men of excellent understandings, have either overlooked the elements of the whole question; or, more probably, have never turned their minds to the course of enquiry, which, if properly pursued, must have prevented some of the misconceptions now afloat on this subject. To the want of this knowledge, to the want of time, or opportunity, or inclination to attain it, much of the error which prevails in some quarters, and of the doubts, uncertainty, and apprehension which exist in many others, is, in my opinion, to be ascribed.

In the present state of the question, surely, no man who takes any interest in public affairs, more especially if he have any legislative duty to discharge, will hesitate to acquire that knowledge; and to overcome any disinclination that he may feel from the natural dryness, or supposed intricacy of the question. The necessary information is to be easily obtained, by resorting to the history of our currency in former periods, and to those authors, in our own language, who are looked up to as of the highest authority in political economy. To which I may add that, since the agitation of the question in Parliament, several excellent publications on the subject have made their appearance.

Of most of these publications, however, including even the very able pamphlet of Mr. BLAKE,* I cannot help observing, that they appear to me, both to suppose a degree of elementary information in their readers, which all do not possess; and to take for granted, on the part of their opponents in the argument, a concession of principles, which have indeed, been long since established as fundamental truths; but which have been again called in question on the present occasion. To revert, therefore, to first principles, and to endeavour to prove again what has been already so often proved, may, as I presume to think, be a useful, though humble, help in the discussion which now agitates the public opinion of the country.

They who think with me, that it is by the establishment of sound, and the detection of false principles, upon points of general interest and leading importance in political economy, that the greatest benefits are secured to nations, or the greatest calamities averted from them, will not find fault with the mode in which I have ventured to treat the subject. They will even pardon the repetitions, which I have found unavoidable, when they consider that, in a question of a complicated nature, but admitting (as I conceive) of strict proof, one mode of arriving at the truth is more easily apprehended by some minds, and another by others; and that, in contentions, where interest and prejudice take a part, it is not enough to establish a proposition; it is also necessary to expose the fallacy of the reasoning by which it is attempted to be controverted.

Having once made up my mind to submit these remarks

* "Observations on the principles which regulate the Course of "Exchange, and on the present depreciated State of our Currency." By W. BLAKE, Esq. This pamphlet contains the most complete exposition of the whole doctrine of exchange that I have met with in any language.

to the public, I could not think of withholding my name. I am anxious to meet, upon a fair and equal footing, those persons who have publicly attacked the Report of the Committee. I wish to draw from them, either an admission of the *principles* which I state ;—or a clear and explicit exposition of their own. If they admit the principles stated by me, it is for them to reconcile their own deductions to those principles, so admitted; and to disprove mine. If the difference between us be as to *principles,* let them lay fairly before the public those, on which their theory is built; and shew the practical consequences, to which their own principles would, in their own opinion, lead.

I may add, that none of the considerations which sometimes disincline men in public life from this mode of declaring their sentiments, apply in the present instance. The question is already necessarily before the public. The parliamentary discussion of it is unavoidably at some distance. It is plain that the opinion of the public will not remain so long altogether suspended: and besides it is a subject upon which many persons would rather collect their ideas and form their decision in the leisure of the closet, than in the warmth of debate.

I have yet another reason for avowing my opinions as openly and as early as possible. If I know my own mind, those opinions have been formed as coolly and dispassionately, as they could have been upon any point of abstract science: and I should have felt it as impossible to avoid coming to the conclusion to which I have been led upon this subject, as to refuse my assent to the demonstration of any problem in mathematics. I say this the rather, because I see (and I see with deep regret) an attempt made to create political divisions on this subject: and to array particular parties against principles which, surely, are not to be classed among the articles of any political creed, or to be considered as connected with the separate interests of any party:—principles which, if false, may be disproved by calm argument, without the aid of influence or combination; but which, if true, cannot be refuted by clamour, and could not be overpowered by numbers or authority, without material hazard to the interests of the country.

So far as I know, and as I believe, this attempt has not hitherto been successful. The speech of Mr. RANDLE JACKSON, though it imputes *party spirit* to others, is obviously dictated by nothing more than a *corporation spirit:* a distinction which, fortunately, is too plain to be misunderstood. As to SIR JOHN SINCLAIR, the only other avowed author of such imputations, it would be most unjust, both to him and to mankind, to suppose him the organ of any other sentiments than his own.

Fatal, indeed, would it be for the country, if those who are to decide upon this question,—(a question which, while it is, on the one hand, so abstract as not to allow to error the apology of passion, yet, on the other hand, affects, in its practical consequences, the interests and the comforts of every class of society,)—could be persuaded to regulate their conduct, upon this occasion, by any feelings of political partiality or hostility. I trust that such feelings will not be allowed to disturb and exasperate this discussion: and, as to myself, I am most anxious to declare and record my opinions, while these feelings have not yet made any progress; and while the course of party politics, (if, most unfortunately, party politics are at any period to mix themselves with the subject,) is yet unascertained.

I am aware that I have already detained the reader too long upon points which are, in some degree, of a personal nature; especially as there is one other, more entirely personal, perhaps, on which I must request his indulgence for a few sentences. In discussions of an amicable nature which have arisen with those for whom these observations were originally intended, I have been asked, (and the question may possibly be repeated in a less amicable manner,) "Why I did not give to the public an earlier warning on the subject,—why not, while I was myself in office, and before the evil had grown to its present height?"

My answer is, first—that it is one thing to trace effects, the existence of which is manifest, up to the causes which produced them: but that it would have been another, to foresee all the possible consequences of a new measure; especially when those consequences were liable to be produced, or to be varied, by circumstances of which one had no knowledge. To the perspicacity, which alone could have qualified me for such foresight I do not pretend; but nothing more than diligence and impartiality was required to qualify for the task of that enquiry and examination which, where the conclusion is as plain, as to my understanding it appears in the present instance, could not fail to lead to conviction.

I answer secondly, that neither I, nor any man with whom I ever had intercourse, official or private, upon the subject, at any time considered the restriction of Bank payments as any other than an expedient, originating in necessity; and determinable whenever that necessity should cease. Nor could I have imagined, till the examinations before the Committee produced the disclosure, that there existed any individual who viewed it as an improvement in our money system, or who could look with satisfaction to the possibility of its indefinite continuance.

I answer further, that those consequences of this measure which are developed in the Report of the Committee did not arise till a late period. Up to that period, the foreign exchanges were not unfavourable; and the market price of gold not materially above the Mint price:—two circumstances, of which I felt assured that the Bank Directors never lost sight in regulating their issues. During the suspension of cash payments, a permanent depression of those exchanges, or a rise in the price of gold, appeared to be pointed out to them, by the principles of their institution, and by the course of all former experience, as the obvious and best criterion of any tendency to excess in the amount of their paper. It was therefore natural to conclude, that, in regulating their issues, they constantly and carefully watched these indications of the value of their notes. Persons more conversant, than I could be, with the course of business at the Bank, and whose opinions might naturally be supposed to have great weight with some of the Directors, whilst they urged the importance of this criterion, appeared to entertain the same confidence with myself, that to all practical purposes, it was duly observed.* It was not, till the Committee were furnished with the evidence of the Governor and Deputy Governor of the Bank, that I found that, in regulating the amount of their issues, the Bank had no reference to this criterion.

Before that declaration was made, I own that my opinions upon the whole subject were much more undecided. When the great fall in the foreign exchanges first took place, I ascribed it, without hesitation, and perhaps without much reflection, altogether to the effect of the violent measures, political and commercial, adopted on the Continent; and to the suspension of our commercial intercourse with the United States. When that fall had continued for near a twelvemonth, doubts arose in my mind whether, the cause of its long continuance might not be, that the Bank, from too much indulgence to their customers at some particular moment, had somewhat improvidently extended their issues; and too much delayed restoring them to a proper level. But as I still took for granted that they had not lost sight of the criterion above mentioned, my doubts went no further.

Such was the state of my mind at the time when I retired from office. Every month which passed from that time, whilst our exchanges were growing worse, and the price of gold rising, (notwithstanding that our expedition to the Continent was terminated, and our pecuniary aid to Austria discontinued,) could not fail to increase those doubts.

Under these circumstances, and very soon after the opening of the last session, the subject was taken up in parliament. When the Committee was appointed, I gave to the Enquiry all the attention in my power. The general principles which I carried with me to that committee were the same

* See—An Enquiry into the Nature and Effects of the Paper Credit of Great Britain. By Henry Thornton, Esq. M.P.

which I now profess; but the information which has led me to a more specific and particular application of them was chiefly derived from what came out in the investigation. When I found that the principle of regulating the issues and ascertaining the value of their paper by a reference to some *fixed standard*, and even the existence of such a *fixed standard* were either altogether overlooked by the Bank, (they could scarcely be unknown to them) or utterly disregarded in their practice, — my astonishment was great indeed. From that moment I was more at a loss to explain to myself why the evil was not greater, than to account for its present extent.

I am not ashamed to add that my individual efforts would not have enabled me to follow in all its practical bearings a subject of such extent and intricacy, without a far more regular and careful attention than was compatible with the incessant occupation, and multiplied duties of such public situations as it has been my lot to fill:—and this is far from the only instance in which the studies and self-examination of retirement have shewn to me how great in almost every respect (assiduity perhaps excepted) were my own deficiencies in office.

I can, however, conscientiously declare that whatever humble means I may possess of discriminating between truth and error, between degrees of probability and strict proof, between conjecture and certainty: have been recently and anxiously employed in the re-examination of the opinion which I supported in the Committee.

Eartham, 23d October, 1810.

THE

QUESTION, &c.

THE various definitions of the word *money*, and the different acceptations in which that word is used in the ordinary transactions of life, have contributed to produce much of the doubt and uncertainty which prevail at this moment respecting the state of our currency.

Money, in the popular sense, is frequently considered as having no other value than one purely arbitrary and conventional. It is sometimes defined to be the *representative* of all other commodities; and sometimes the *common measure* of them. These definitions are both incomplete, as applied to *money;* because they are equally applicable to every description of *currency*, whether consisting of the precious metals, of paper, or of any other article.

It is of the essence of *money* to possess *intrinsic value.*

The quality of *representing* commodities does not necessarily imply intrinsic value; because that quality may be given either by confidence, or by authority. The quality of being *a common measure* does not necessarily imply intrinsic value, any more than the possession of a *foot rule* implies the power of acquiring whatever it enables us to measure. *Money*, or a given quantity of gold or silver, is not only the *common measure*, and *common representative* of all other commodities; but also the *common and universal equivalent.*

Paper currency has, obviously, no intrinsic value.

A *promissory note*, under whatever form, or from whatever source it may issue, *represents* value. It does so, in as

15

much as it is an undertaking to pay, in *money*, the sum for which it is issued.

The *money*, or coin of a country is so much of its capital. *Paper currency* is no part of the capital of a country. It is so much *circulating credit.*

Whoever buys, gives — whoever sells, receives such a *quantity* of pure gold or silver as is equivalent to the article bought or sold:— or if he gives or receives *paper* instead of *money*, he gives or receives that which is valuable only as it stipulates the payment of a given quantity of gold or silver. So long as this engagement is punctually fulfilled, paper will of course pass current with the coin with which it is thus constantly interchangeable. Both *money*, therefore, and *paper*, *promissory* of money, are *common measures* and *representatives* of the value of all commodities. But *money* alone is the *universal equivalent; paper currency* is the *representative* of that *money.*

Of *paper currency*, however, there are two sorts; the one resting upon *confidence*, the other upon *authority.*— Paper resting upon *confidence*, is what I have described as *circulating credit;* and consists in engagements for the payment, on demand, of any specific sums of *money:* which engagements, from a *general trust* in the issuers of such paper, they are enabled to substitute for *money* in the transactions of the community. Paper resting upon *authority*, is what, in common language, is called *paper money;* and consists in engagements issued and circulated under the sanction, and by the immediate intervention of the public power of the state.

Paper, such as alone used to be current in Great Britain before the restriction on the Bank, was strictly *circulating credit.*—The paper current in *Austria, Russia*, &c., is properly denominated *paper money.*

The division and subdivision of the precious metals into various shapes and sizes; the proportion of alloy mixed with them in the coins of different countries; the stamp affixed upon such coins, and the names by which they pass current, are things in their nature arbitrary;

and subject to such regulations as may be made by the sovereign power of each independent state. By any alteration in these particulars, the *price* of all other commodities, or, in other words, the amount or denomination of money in which their value is stated, may be altered; but these changes cannot affect the relation which the value of the bullion contained in the coin bears to that of such commodities.

Price, therefore, is the value of any given article, in the *currency,* by reference to which that article is measured; and must, of course, be varied by any variation in the *quantity* of gold or silver contained in such currency.

Supposing, for instance, the currency of a country to consist of gold, and that, without any variation in the relative proportion of this metal to that of other articles, the *denomination,* of the existing coin should be raised, or its *standard* lowered, in any given proportion, the prices of all commodities would rise in the same proportion; although the *real* value of every such commodity, measured by a reference to the quantity of gold in such coin, would remain the same.—If, on the other hand, the quantity of gold in such a country (considered for the moment abstractedly from its intercourse with other countries) should be increased in any given proportion, the quantity of other articles and the demand for them remaining the same, the value of any given commodity, measured in the coin of that country, would be increased, or, in other words, the relative value of gold to other commodities would be decreased in the same proportion; although the *denomination* and *standard* of the coin should remain unaltered: and although no addition should have been made to the actual amount of that coin.

It must be almost superfluous to observe that by *denomination* is meant the specific name under which a piece of metal of a given quantity is known in the state of coin; and that *standard* is the precise *quantity* (ascertained by *weight* and *fineness*) fixed by law for pieces of each denomination. Thus the *standard* fineness of our gold coin is eleven parts of pure gold and one of alloy; and the *denomination* of a piece weighing 5 dwts. $9\frac{39}{89}$ grs. is a guinea.

It follows from this, that the right and duty of coining, which, in every independent state, is one of the most important attributes and functions of sovereignty, consists in affixing to certain pieces of the precious metals a *stamp;* which becomes to the subjects of that state, and to all the world, a public voucher, that each piece, according to its denomination, is of the weight and fineness fixed by the law of that state. The public honour and integrity of the legislature are pledged to the fidelity and exactness of the voucher, which is thus issued in the name of the Sovereign.

There is not therefore, nor can there be, any difference whatever, between any given coin, and an uncoined piece of the same metal of equal weight and fineness, except that the quantity of the former is accurately ascertained and publicly proclaimed to all the world by the stamp which it bears.

To apply these general observations to the particular money of this country:

I assume, as admitted, that, in Great Britain, gold is the scale to which all prices are referred, and, since the 39th of the King, the *only* LEGAL TENDER, except for payments under 25*l.*

I likewise assume, as unquestionable, both in fact and in law,

1st. That a pound of gold, of our standard, is coined into 44 guineas and a half; and that any person may, at the King's Mint, procure any quantity of gold to be so coined, free of any expense whatever; the officers of the Mint being obliged to return, in coin, precisely the same quantity which may have been deposited with them, without making any charge for the conversion of it into money.

2dly. That, by law, these guineas which, when fresh from the Mint, weigh 5dwts. $9\frac{39}{89}$grs. each, cease to be a *legal tender* if, by wear or otherwise, they are reduced below

5 dwts. 8 grs., which is a diminution in their value of a small fraction more than *one* per cent.

Consequently, the law of England, before the year 1797, distinctly secured to every man, that he should not be compelled to take, in satisfaction of a legal debt, for every guinea of that debt, less than 5 dwts. 8 grs. of gold of standard fineness; and, as distinctly, that he should not be obliged to receive, as the *representative* of a guinea, or a guinea's worth, any article or thing which would not purchase or procure that quantity of gold.

Such was the state of our current coin before the year 1797.

The Bank of England, as every body knows, is a chartered Company of Merchants whose promissory notes, for more than a century, have constituted a very large proportion of the *circulatiug credit* of this country. From the institution of that Company up to the year 1797, there had been no interruption to the convertibility of their notes into *money;* nor any interference on the part of the State in any thing that concerned the issue or circulation of those notes. This Company were simply the Bankers of the State, and, by a condition of their charter, its Agent for the payment of the dividends due to the public creditor.

In 1797, in consequence of a demand upon the Bank for gold, continued for a time, and in a degree, altogether unusual, and arising from a combination of untoward circumstances and events, partly political, and partly commercial; the Directors of that institution felt themselves bound to state to the Government the unprecedented difficulties and embarrassments of their situation.

It is but justice to them to remark, that they did not resort to this measure, till they had tried, and found unavailing, all those means of checking the drain of cash, which had been effectual on former occasions. On these former occasions the Directors had uniformly found, that to lessen the amount of their issues of paper, was the sure mode of checking and ultimately stopping the demand for gold. It was natural for them, as practical men to follow their established course; but when they found that, instead of abating, the drain increased every day, in proportion as they contracted the amount of their paper, it was equally natural for them to mistrust their own experience.

In this state of affairs, the remedy which was applied to the difficulties of the Bank and of the Country, was an act for the temporary suspension of cash payments.

It is material to understand precisely the nature of the change which this act created in the state of our circulation; a change, of the magnitude of which no man was more sensible than the persons whose duty it was to propose it to Parliament.

This act did not repeal any of the former regulations to which I have adverted, and which are the foundation of our money system. Neither did it make Bank notes a *legal tender*.—It did not alter in any respect the existing state of the law, either as to the weight or the fineness of the gold coin; or the act of the 39th of the King. It merely suspended other provisions of law (having in themselves no reference to our circulation, or *money* system) by which, in default of payment, the person and goods of a debtor are made liable for his debt. This liability it suspended, in cases where a *tender* shall have been made to the creditor of the amount of his claim in notes of the Bank of England.

If it had been proposed, at once, to make Bank notes a *legal tender*, and, in direct terms, to enact that every man should, thenceforward, be obliged to receive them as equivalent to the gold coin of the realm, without reference to the quantity of gold bullion which might be procured by a Bank note of any given *denomination*;—such a proposition would have excited universal alarm, and would have forcibly drawn the attention of the legislature and the public to the real nature of our circulation, and to the possible consequences of such an innovation. But, certainly, nothing of the sort was in the contemplation of any man when the first suspension act was passed.—That it was then considered and proposed, as an expedient which would be but of short duration, the course of the proceedings in Parliament abundantly indicates.

Such being the original character of the measure, it is not extraordinary that, in that crisis, Parliament, without much hesitation, and without any suspicion of the ultimate possible consequences, should have afforded a temporary protection from arrest to a debtor, who should have made a tender of payment in Bank notes. But if, in the year 1797, it had been foreseen that this temporary expedient would be attempted to be converted into a system for an indefinite number of years; and that, under this system, in the year 1810, every creditor, public or private, subject or alien, to whom the law, as it then stood, and as it now stands, had secured the payment of a pound weight of standard gold for every 46*l.* 14*s.* 6*d.* of his just demand, would be obliged to accept, in full satisfaction, about 10¼ ounces, or not more than seventeen shillings in the pound; with a prospect of a still further reduction in every subsequent year:—it is impossible to conceive that the attention and feelings of Parliament would not have been alive to all the individual injustice, and ultimate public calamities, incident to such a state of things; and that they would not have provided for the termination of the restriction, before it should have wrought so much mischief, and laid the foundation of so much confusion in all the dealings and transactions of the community.

Whether the actual state of things be such as I have just described, is the question upon which the public attention is now fixed:—and to which, I conceive, there can be but one answer. If the reader shall go along with me in the following statement, that answer will appear to him as obvious as it does to me.

1st. A pound, or twelve ounces of gold, by the law of this country, is divided into 44 guineas and a half, or 46*l.* 14*s.* 6*d.*

2ndly. By this division, which is made at the public

expence, and without charge for coinage, nothing is added to the value of the gold; and nothing taken away from it.

3dly. A pound of gold, therefore, and 46*l.* 14*s.* 6*d.* being equivalent, being in fact the same thing under different names, any *circulating credit* which purports to represent 46*l.* 14*s.* 6*d.* ought, by the law of this country, to be exchangeable at will for a pound of gold.

4thly. No alteration has been made in this state of law except by the Act of 1797.

5thly. The professed and intended operation of the Act of 1797 was not to diminish the *quantity* of gold for which any specific amount of *circulating credit* ought to be exchangeable, but merely to suspend, for a time, the option of the exchange.

6thly. But the sum of 46*l.* 14*s.* 6*d.* in our present paper, will procure in exchange for gold, only 10¼ ounces of that metal:—A pound of gold is now exchangeable for 56*l.* in *paper currency.* Any commodity, therefore, which is equivalent to a pound of gold, is also equivalent to 56*l.* in paper.

It follows that the difference between 56*l.*, and 46*l.* 14*s.* 6*d.* or between 12 and 10¼ ounces of gold, arises from the *depreciation* of the paper; and is the measure of that depreciation, as well with respect to gold, the *universal equivalent,* as to every other commodity.

Those who differ from me in opinion must be prepared to deny some one of these facts, from which, if not disproved, the conclusion necessarily follows. They must either shew, that I have mis-stated the *permanent* laws of the realm which regulate our coinage, and determine our *legal tender;* or they must shew, that gold is not the basis of our money—that its value is not measured by its quantity—that the value of that quantity is varied by its conversion into coin. But these are propositions which no man who has ever looked at the subject will attempt to maintain.

Otherwise they must shew that the intention of the *temporary* law of 1797 was different from that which I have ascribed to it: and that it was intended, by that law, either to lower our standard, to alter our *legal tender*, or to leave us without any standard at all.—But even if they should be able to shew, that the intention of this *temporary law* was to make any one of these alterations, still, by the establishment of their proposition, they will not invalidate but confirm the conclusion which I have stated. They will only have established, by their own arguments, the fact of the depreciation, and will no otherwise have varied the question arising out of it, than by making it appear, that such depreciation of our currency was not the unforeseen consequence, but the premeditated result of an act of the Legislature.

Although these appear to be the only imaginable grounds on which any exception can be offered to my statement, they are such as will not be taken by any man who does justice to the character of the Legislature, or has any recollection of the circumstances under which it passed the Act of 1797.

It would be monstrous to imagine that it could ever be in the contemplation and intention of either House of Parliament, that Bank notes, at their present, or at any less value, to which they might possibly be reduced, should be a *legal tender*. To entertain such an opinion would be to impute to Parliament a design to practise a deception, and to encourage a fraud. What would have been the consistency, what the integrity of a Legislature, which, leaving unrepealed and unmodified the regulations which take away the character of a *legal tender* from every guinea weighing less than 5 dwts. 8 grs. would give it to a Bank note, purporting to be a security for the same denomination, but the real value of which is, at this moment, 4 dwts. 14 grs., or, in other words, about three shillings less than the lightest guinea which is allowed to pass in payment?

If such be the effect of the Act of 1797;—let us see, by a comparison of that effect with the whole purport and tendency of all the antecedent laws, which regulate and govern our currency, what is the present legal state of that currency; and what the situation of the subjects of this realm, under the whole system as it now stands.

By law, a guinea which weighs less than 5 dwts. 8 grs. is no longer a guinea.—It is deprived of its quality of coin. It can no longer be tendered as *money*. But it may be sold for what it will fetch in the market as *bullion*, for the purpose of being melted down.

By law, it is an offence punishable with severe penalties to melt a guinea weighing more than 5 dwts. 8 grs.; or to reduce it, by clipping, filing, or any other process, below that weight.

By law, a guinea of that weight cannot be exchanged for more than the sum of 21*s.* which sum in *paper currency* is worth at present 4 dwts. 14 grs. of gold.—To sell, or to buy guineas at a higher rate than 21*s.* each in Bank paper, is an offence highly punishable.

For this last offence a man has recently been tried and convicted.

If the guineas purchased by him had been light guineas, viz. guineas weighing upon an average 5 dwts. 7½* grs. each, he might have bought and sold them without incurring any penalty.

The state of the law, therefore, is this.—The possessor of a *heavy* guinea, which is intrinsically worth about 24*s.* 6*d.* in Bank paper, who should exchange it for more than 21*s.* of that paper, would be liable to fine and imprisonment.—The more fortunate possessor of a *light* guinea is entitled by law to exchange it for what it will fetch, which would be about 24*s.* 3*d.*

A *light* guinea, therefore, cried down, no longer current, no longer a *legal tender*, is, at the present moment, more valuable than a guinea of *full weight*, in the proportion of 24*s.* 3*d.* to 21*s.*

The *light* guinea, by melting, is converted into 5 dwts. 7½ grs. of bullion.

The heavy guinea being, by law, incapable of being

* From the evidence of Mr. Merle, in the Appendix to the Report of the Bullion Committee, it appears that this is the average weight of light guineas.

converted into bullion, or of being reduced, by a diminution of *quantity*, into the more valuable shape of a *light* guinea, is equivalent to 4 dwts. 14 grs. of gold.—The difference of value in favour of the light guinea is 17½ grains of gold.

This is the present state of our currency; and the operation of the laws by which it is regulated.

Is it possible to conceive that this is the state of things, which the Legislature, in passing the Act of 1797, had it in contemplation to produce? Is it one, which, having been produced unintentionally, does not require such an alteration as would bring back the currency of the country to an agreement with its ancient legal standard?

For my own part, I confess that, if absolutely driven to the necessity of deciding between the alternative, of suffering the present state of things to continue, or of resorting at once to the stale and wretched expedient of either raising the denomination, or lowering the standard of our currency, in any fixed and limited proportion, I should not hesitate to prefer the latter. This expedient, I admit, though not unfrequently practised, in former and less enlightened periods of the history of this and other nations, is now universally and justly reprobated and condemned, as too disgraceful in its principle, and too ruinous in its policy, to be resorted to, even by governments the most arbitrary in their internal administration, and the most destitute of more substantial resources. Yet, let me ask any of those who would have been startled at such a proposal, what would be the real difference between a state of law, which, either leaving the guinea at its present weight and fineness, should raise its denomination to 24*s.* 6*d.*; or, leaving it at its present denomination, should lower its standard to 4 dwts. 14 grs.—and a state of law, which obliges every man to receive the latter *quantity* of gold as 21*s.*, or to give 24*s.* 6*d.* for the former?

One difference, indeed, would be this: that, the injury once done, the fraud once committed, the extent of the evil would be known and ascertained. Prices at home, and abroad, once accommodated to the change in the value of our currency, all uncertainty, and consequent speculation upon a further derangement, would cease. Creditors, annuitants, and all who possess incomes, fixed in their amount by a contract of any description, would be able to measure the extent of their loss. All future leases, and bargains for time, would be made with a reference to this definite alteration in the common measure of all exchangeable commodities. Salaries and wages of every description would be more speedily and more proportionably compensated for the change.—The existing evil, on the contrary, of which the present measure may be reckoned at about 15 per cent., is indefinite, uncertain, and fluctuating, though progressive in its growth. It has, consequently, a greater tendency to derange and unsettle all the transactions of society, and to depress the labouring classes, and all who derive their incomes from salary or wages of any description. It increases, at the same time, the foreign expenditure of Government, in proportion to the fall of the exchange; and its domestic expenses, in proportion to the increased price of all commodities at home. It adds, in the same proportion, to the amount of our annual loans and taxes. A saving, it is true, accrues to the State from paying the wages of valour, talent, industry, and labour, in a depreciated currency, and from the reduction which is thus made (really though not nominally) in the value of the dividend paid to the public creditor. But it is equally true that these unfair and unintended savings to the State are more than counterbalanced by its increased expenditure:—whilst this increased expenditure, and the increased taxation necessarily consequent upon it, doubly aggravate the evil on those classes of the community at whose expense these savings are made, by taking from each a greater proportion of their already depreciated income, for the payment of all the other charges of the State.

The propositions which I have stated appear to me so clear and conclusive that I am almost ashamed of saying anything more on this part of the question. But the doubt and confusion which prevail in the minds of many sensible persons, and the sophistry to which they have been induced to listen, from the want of clear and precise ideas on this subject, are quite extraordinary. There are those who reason as if they had persuaded themselves, and who endeavour to persuade others, that *Bank paper* is the *real* and *fixed measure* of all commodities; and that *gold* is only one of the articles, of which, in common with others, the value is to be ascertained by a reference to this *invariable standard* and *universal equivalent*, Bank paper. So widely extended is the error in this respect, that, however much in contradiction with some of their own principles, it pervades, more or less, nearly the whole of the evidence of the respectable merchants who were examined before the Bullion Committee.—For instance, in the examination of Mr. CHAMBERS, (p. 102), a gentleman who deservedly enjoys the reputation of great intelligence and extensive information in the commercial world, we find the following evidence.

"At the Mint price of *standard* gold in this country, how much gold does a Bank-of-England note for one pound represent?—5 dwts. 3 gr."

"At the present market-price of 4*l.* 12*s.* per ounce, how much gold do you get for a Bank note of one pound?—4 dwts. 8 gr."

"Do you consider a Bank-of-England note for one pound, under these present circumstances, as exchangeable in gold for what it represents of that metal?—*I do not conceive gold to be a fairer standard for Bank-of-England notes than indigo or broad cloth.*"

Question repeated—"*If it represents twenty shillings of that metal at the coinage-price, it is not.*"

In these answers this leading doctrine is manfully and ingenuously asserted and maintained; and all who stand up for the undepreciated value of Bank paper, however disguised their language, must ultimately come to the same issue.

Mr. CHAMBERS plainly avows, that "*He does not conceive gold to be a fairer standard for Bank-of-England notes than indigo or broad cloth*"—and that "*a one pound note does* NOT *represent twenty shillings of that metal at the coinage price.*"

These answers, to my understanding at least, completely give up the whole of the case.

If "*gold be not a fairer standard for Bank-of-England notes than indigo or broad cloth,*" I could wish to learn what *is* the really fair standard?

If "*a one-pound note does not represent twenty shillings of that metal at the coinage price,*" what *does* it really represent?

Need I recall to any man's recollection the obvious, and, as I till lately imagined, undisputed grounds on which the precious metals have, not in this country only, and by our system of laws, but in all civilized countries, and in all ages of the world, been received, by the common consent of mankind, as the fittest standard for measuring the value of all other commodities; and employed as the universal equivalent for effecting their exchange?—That the precious metals are less bulky in proportion to their value—that they are accurately, easily, and almost infinitely divisible—that they are less subject to decay — less likely to fluctuate in their supply,—less liable to be counterfeited or adulterated, —more homogeneous and uniform in quality, than either *indigo*, or *broad cloth*, or any other known commodity?

Gold in this country (as silver at Hamburgh) is really and exclusively the fixed measure of the rising and falling value of all other things in reference to each other. The article itself which forms this standing measure, never can rise or fall in value with reference to this measure — that is, with reference to *itself*. A pound weight of gold never can be worth a pound and a quarter of gold; and being divided, in this country, into 44 and $\frac{1}{2}$ pieces, called guineas, an ounce of this gold will always be worth $\frac{1}{12}$ of this sum, or 3*l.* 17*s.* 10½*d.* The truth of these propositions, which cannot, I conceive, be called in question, would not be affected by any imaginable increase or diminution in the quantity of gold in the country. By such an increase or diminution, indeed, the value of all other things, (the quantity of those other things and the demand for them continuing the same), would be increased or diminished in the same proportion, with reference to gold; but gold itself would still remain, just as much as before, the *fixed measure* of the rising and falling value of all other commodities, in reference to each other.

A Bank note is not a *commodity:* it is only an engagement for the payment of a certain specified quantity of *money.* It cannot vary its value in exchange for any commodity, except in reference to the general increase or diminution of the value of such commodity in gold, and in the precise proportion of that increase or diminution. Gold, therefore, is the test by which the value of Bank notes must be tried; and if a one-pound note, being an engagement to pay 5 dwts. 3 gr. of gold, is worth in the market only 4 dwts. 8 gr. as stated by Mr. CHAMBERS in his evidence, it is equally worth only 4 dwts. 8 gr. in exchange for any other commodity.

It follows from this;—that a general increase of prices in all the ordinary commodities of any country is not, in itself, an indication of the depreciation of its currency.—Such an effect may arise from other cause. It could not fail to be produced by an increase of the precious metals. But any considerable or durable increase of price in the precious metal which forms the standard of that currency cannot be ascribed to any thing but the depreciation of such currency; even if the price of all other commodities should be falling at the same time. This would happen in any country if, at the same period, when its currency is depreciated, in any given proportion, the supply of the precious metals were diminished, or the demand for them increased, in a greater proportion.

The currency of a country may be depreciated from two different causes.

1st. By the standard coin containing a less quantity of the precious metal which forms that standard, than it is *certified* by law to contain.

·2dly. By an excess in the amount of that currency.

A great depreciation, arising from the first cause, took place, in this country, in King WILLIAM's time, when the quantity of precious metal actually contained in our coin was upon an average, nearly 30 per cent. less than that coin was *certified* to contain. A smaller depreciation, arising from the same cause, was felt early in the present Reign, when the quantity of gold contained in our guineas was reduced by long wear, or otherwise, from 4 to 5 per cent. below the quantity they were *certified* to contain. To this evil, within these limits, it was then thought necessary to apply a remedy. That remedy was the general recoinage of our gold in 1773.

Since that period the first cause of depreciation has ceased to operate in this country.

The existing depreciation, therefore, must be occasioned by excess. Depreciation from excess, if the coin of a country be maintained at its standard, cannot take place to any amount, or continue for any length of time, unless the currency of such a country consists, partly of paper, and partly of the precious metals: except indeed in the extreme case of that currency consisting wholly of paper, without any reference to its value in coin.

If the circulation of any country were performed exclusively by gold, for instançe, and the supply of that metal in such a country were, from any imaginable cause, doubled, whilst the quantity of gold, and the demand for it should continue the same in all other parts of the world; the price of gold in such a country would be diminished. This diminution of the price of gold would appear in the proportionate rise of all commodities; but gold being so much cheaper in the country in which its quantity had been thus increased, it would be bought by other countries, and exported from that country, till its price was restored again to a level in the different parts of the world.

If the circulation of a country were supplied, partly by

gold and partly by paper, and the amount of that circulation were doubled by an augmentation of that paper, the effect upon prices at home would be the same as in the former case. But gold not becoming by this augmentation of currency more abundant, in such a country, than in other parts of the world,—as a *commodity*, its relative value to other commodities would remain unaltered;—as a *commodity* also, its price would rise in the same proportion as that of other commodities, although, in the state of *coin*, of which the *denomination* is fixed by law, it could only pass current according to that *denomination*.

When paper is thus augmented in any country, the exportation of the gold coin, therefore, will take place; not because gold, as a *commodity*, is become more abundant and less valuable with reference to other commodities in such a country; but, from the circumstance of its value as *currency* remaining the same, while its price in that currency is increased in common with the prices of all other commodities. So far as such exportation takes place, the diminution which it effects in the total amount of the currency, has a tendency to support the value of the remainder, just as much, and for the same reason, as if, in the case of the circulation consisting wholly of gold, first an augmentation, and then an exportation to the same amount, had taken place, according to the first supposition.

An excess of paper has, in the first instance, the same effect upon prices as an excess of the precious metals, to the same amount, would have, in any particular country. But it does not admit of the same relief: it cannot *right* itself by exportation.

The currency of a country, then, is depreciated,

1st, If its standard coin contains less of gold or silver than it is *certified* to contain. In that case, the paper, as *representing* that coin, is also depreciated, and precisely in the same degree as the coin:

2dly, If the paper is exchangeable for less of the coin than it *represents;* that coin containing the quantity of gold or silver *certified* by law. In that case, the coin, though undiminished in value, must, as part of the currency, partake of the depreciation of the whole.

Consequently, if the coin be itself, *as coin*, depreciated,— the paper which circulates with it cannot be otherwise than depreciated to the same degree. But if the coin be undepreciated as *coin*, and there be, notwithstanding, a depreciation of the general currency, the cause of that depreciation can only be in the paper: and that cause can be no other than the excess in which that paper is issued.

I shall now proceed to state some of the assertions, and to examine some of the arguments and explanations of those who maintain the sound and undepreciated state of our present currency.

The first and principal of these arguments and assertions is one which, if it could be established, would at once preclude all further discussion. It is this—" That there can be no " excess of Bank of England paper in circulation, so long as " it is issued only in the discount of bills of undoubted solidity, " founded in real mercantile transactions, and payable at " fixed and not distant dates (60 or 90 days at the utmost), " or upon loan to government for public securities." The limits of the latter description of advances are not quite so accurately defined, but the principal criterion seems to be " government not being able to dispose of such securities to " better advantage in the open market."*

* Vide examination of Mr. Pearse, the present Governor of the Bank, Bullion Report, Appendix.

It is now many years since I had occasion to look into the Treatise of the famous Mr. LAW;—and from not having it at hand, I have no opportunity of referring to it at this moment.—But I have a confident recollection that there exists a very strong resemblance between the principles on which his celebrated SCHEME was founded, and this leading doctrine of the Bank.—I mention this not invidiously, but by way of caution to those *practical* men, who see nothing in the Report of the Bullion Committee, but the production of *wild theorists*, and *speculative politicians*. I should be glad to know under what class of *theorists*, and in what order of *politicians*, they would have ranged any man, who, before the year 1797, should have ventured to recommend, as a safe system, the principles by which the Bank now professes to regulate its practice?

Now admitting, what the Bank itself however states to be impossible, that any extent of experience, or any degree of caution, can be sufficient to guard them against ever discounting bills which do not fully answer the above description—it must, I think, be matter of astonishment to any man whose attention has been at all turned to these subjects, that, in the new state in which the Bank of England has been placed since the suspension of cash payments, they could rely upon this mode of regulating their advances, as a perfect, steady, uniform and adequate check against any excess in the issues of their notes.

The confidence with which this doctrine was stated and maintained by the Governor and Deputy-Governor of the Bank, as well as by several eminent merchants, (not in the Bank direction,) before the Bullion Committee, is a strong proof, not only how much great corporate establishments are wedded to an existing system, and long established rules of action, however inapplicable to a new state of things; but how slow and reluctant, in such a state of things, individuals, otherwise of observing minds and excellent understandings, are, to call in question and examine the truth of early impressions adopted upon authority, and followed from usage. This tardiness and reluctance are naturally increased, when interest is manifestly on the side of the existing system.

The Directors of the Bank, governing themselves by the rule above-mentioned, had continued for a century to issue their notes, without those issues having ever led to an excess of paper circulation, at least of any continuance. But then, during the whole of that century, their paper was convertible into cash at the option of the holder. The security against excess was not in their rule, but in this corrective.

Their profits, as a Bank, depending on the amount of their issues, it was their interest, at all times, to make those issues as large as possible: in this, the public had a sufficient security that the supply of paper should not be less than the demand. But, on the other hand, it was the obvious and plain interest of the Bank to guard itself against direct and positive loss: and in this the public had another, and not less adequate, security, that those issues should not be carried to excess. The tendency and result of such excess, if continued, for any time, would infallibly have been the rise of the market price of gold above the Mint price; and the consequent return of such excess of paper to the Bank in demand for guineas. This demand would have imposed upon the Directors the necessity of purchasing and coining gold at a loss; until, by a diminution of their notes, they should have restored their value to a level with the standard of money.

By the conflicting action of these opposite interests, the currency was kept at its proper amount, and in its regular course. But one of these interests having ceased to operate, it is as vain to expect that the uncontrouled action of the other should continue to produce precisely the same effect, as it would be, in mechanics, to expect that a body impelled by two powers, acting in different directions, would continue in the same line of motion, if one of those powers were withdrawn.

The circumstance of the Bank confining its discounts to "bills of undoubted solidity, and founded in real mercantile transactions," has no connexion whatever with the question of sufficiency or excess in the amount of their notes in circulation. The "reality of the transaction," in which the bill originates, and the "solidity" of the holder, who, by the deposit of such a bill, obtains an advance of notes, are prudent considerations with the Bank, in their character of a mercantile company; but they evidently afford no security to the public, that bills, though uniting both these qualities, may not be discounted to excess.

The shortness of the date of any such bill, "60 or at most 90 days date," is another prudent banking precaution: and so long as the currency of this country continued in its sound and natural state, this regulation may, indeed, have been fairly considered as forming a part of the security of the public against any durable excess of paper. It gave the Bank a power, in the case of a drain of guineas, to diminish expeditiously the amount of their issues by contracting their discounts; to shorten the duration of the run upon them; and to restore the value of their paper without any large sacrifice of their gold.

Now, however, that they cannot be assailed with any such indication of excess—now, that they have every motive for enlarging their discounts, and no inconvenience to apprehend from such an enlargement, this regulation is only of consequence to themselves, as bankers, duly careful of their own interest, in selecting for discount the best and safest bills; but it is altogether without avail for protecting the public against the evils of a permanent excess in the circulation of their notes.

The present Governor of the Bank (for whom as a personal friend I have the most sincere respect) having, in his evidence before the Bullion Committee, stated that "*in his view of the restriction on cash payments, no positive inconvenience would be likely to result from its being made a permanent measure,*"* it may appear to him, perhaps, rather extraordinary, that I should recur to the aid of his arguments, and to the weight of his authority, in support and illustration of the proposition which I have now stated,

---

* In a subsequent examination this opinion was explained by Mr. Pearse, in the following manner.

"I have already stated that I am not aware of any positive inconvenience resulting from the present operation of the Restriction Bill, " or likely to result from its being rendered permanent, except as far as " regards an expectation on the part of the public that it will be " removed; but this circumstance is, in my opinion, essential, and " cannot be kept out of view in any consideration of the subject. " Whether it would be advisable to secure the public against a liability " to the recurrence of the inconveniences that led to the Restriction " Bill, by sacrificing their feelings on this point, and absolutely removing " all expectation of its being only a temporary measure, appears to " me to be entirely a political question, on which I do not conceive " myself qualified to give an opinion; but I may venture to observe, " that public credit and public opinion always go hand in hand, and " that the one is invariably influenced by the other."—Appendix, page 120.

It is therefore clear that, abstractedly of "this expectation on the " part of the public," the present Governor is of opinion, that "no " positive inconvenience would be likely to result from the restriction " being rendered permanent."

namely—that the security to the public against any excess in the circulation of Bank paper was the certainty of such excess being returned upon them for gold; and that this is the *only* check by which the amount of their issues can be permanently kept within its proper level.

In his evidence,* adverting to the possibility of an excessive issue of paper by the country banks, he says—

"*This excess (of country paper), in my opinion, would no*
"*sooner exist in any material degree, than it would be corrected*
"*by its own operation, for the holders of such paper would*
"*immediately return it to the issuers, when they* FOUND THAT,
"*in* CONSEQUENCE OF THE OVER ISSUE, *its value was reduced,*
"*or likely to be reduced below* PAR: *thus, though the balance*
"*might be slightly and transiently disturbed, no considerable or*
"*permanent over issue could possibly take place.*"

Now what is the state of a country bank? It will not be denied that it has the same interest, and the same tendency, as the Bank of England, to make its issues as large as possible. But then a country bank, from its being liable, at all times, to pay its notes in those of the Bank of England, at the option of the holder, is placed precisely in the same situation, by this check upon the amount of its issues, as the Bank of England itself was, by the necessity of paying in guineas, before the restriction. If, in any particular district of the kingdom, the circulation of which is supplied by country paper, an excess were to exist as compared with the circulation of the metropolis, which is exclusively supplied by Bank notes, the holders of such paper would immediately return it to the issuers, and would demand Bank of England paper, or, what is, for this purpose, the same thing in effect, bills upon London.

Whilst near 800 country banks, rivals of the Bank of England, and of each other, are exerting every endeavour to put forth their notes, what is it but the check created by this power in every holder of their paper to demand Bank notes, or bills upon London, that prevents any local or

* Report of the Bullion Committee, Appendix.

partial excess, and keeps the circulation of every district in the kingdom upon a PAR with that of the metropolis? Certainly not the description of securities on which the country banks make their advances: for, in this respect, they (at least many of them) are less prudent than the Bank of England, and do not confine themselves to "*good "bills of Exchange, founded on real mercantile transactions, "and payable at short and fixed dates.*" Yet it is admitted that they cannot make, or permanently maintain in circulation, any over-issues of their paper. On this point there is no difference of opinion in the evidence taken before the Bullion Committee.* Indeed it cannot be disputed, so long as the country paper is interchangeable at PAR with that of the Bank.

Again, what was it, before the restriction act, but the check created by the power in the holders of Bank paper to demand gold for it from the issuers, which prevented any material or durable excess of Bank paper? This check was constantly ready to be applied, if "*in consequence of an "over issue, the value of Bank notes was reduced or likely to "be reduced below* PAR," in reference to the price of bullion, either here, or in the other parts of Europe; the circulation of the Bank of England being, in this respect, to that of Europe, what the circulation of a country bank is now to that of the Bank of England.

Thus, as it is most correctly expressed in the words of the Governor of the Bank, "*though the balance might be "slightly and transiently disturbed, no considerable or perma- "nent over issue could possibly take place.*"

The circulation of country bank paper being, therefore, in exact proportion to that of the Bank of England, it

* After the conclusive evidence of the present Governor of the Bank, and of the other witnesses who were examined before the Bullion Committee on this subject, I have been rather surprised to find the proprietors of Bank stock at their late meeting (as far as the sense of that meeting can be collected from the language of their learned orator) disposed to contrast the sparing amount of their *own* notes with the profuse emission of paper by the *country banks*; and to charge the *latter* exclusively with any excess in the amount of our circulation.

follows, that, in whatever degree the issues of the latter shall be excessive, the former must partake of such excess; and, consequently, that no regulation, affecting or restraining country banks, could be of the smallest avail towards diminishing the total amount of the paper circulation of this country, so long as the Bank of England shall continue to act upon its present system. If, in any one district, or in all the districts, where country paper now circulates, one half of it were withdrawn or put down, its place would be supplied by some other paper. Otherwise, the proportion between the circulation of the metropolis and that of the districts so affected would be destroyed. The result, therefore, of any intervention of the legislature for this purpose, besides being highly objectionable as an interference with the rights of individuals and of private property, would be, only to add several millions more, and principally in small notes, to the amount of issues of the Bank of England; leaving the present evil exactly as it is:—a change which would open a wide door to forgery, and be attended with many other public disadvantages.

Whether security should be required from country bankers, before they are licensed to issue paper, is a subject which it would be foreign to my purpose to discuss. Such security, in a few instances perhaps, might improve the degree of credit which they might have a right to expect with the public. But this subject has nothing to do with the present question; which is simply,—whether there be an excess of paper now in circulation, and from what causes arising? and not—what may be the degree of confidence to which the issuers of any such paper may be respectively entitled? The depreciation occasioned by such an excess would be just the same, if every country bank were notoriously as solid and as rich as the Bank of England.*

* This is a part of the subject which it is material should be well understood; because many persons, witnessing the great multiplication of country banks within these two last years, are disposed, at first view, to think that in them is the root of the evil.—Let the parent stock be restored to its natural, healthy, and sound state, and the country will have nothing to apprehend from these ramifications of credit and

---

The explanations which have been offered by those who have endeavoured to shew that the high price of gold in England is not connected with any excess in the issue of Bank paper, are, 1st. That the immediate and operative cause is a great scarcity of gold, and a consequent demand for it, on the continent. And. 2dly, That speculation in the purchase of it in this country has been carried, and is still going on, to a very great extent, in consequence of the course of exchange with the continent having been for the last two years, and still continuing, so much against this country.

In these explanations everything is assumed. First, it is assumed that gold is very dear on the continent.—Dear, in exchange for what?—For the gold coin of the continent? Such an assertion would be ridiculous.—Dear, in exchange for any depreciated paper? This is very probable in several parts of the continent, but is surely not the criterion to which we shall be referred. Dear, in exchange for all other commodities? Is this a fact? Where is the evidence of it? Are cloth, corn, iron, or any other leading articles *twenty per cent.* cheaper on the continent, than they were, if paid for in gold? Certainly not. And if they were so on the continent, has not the drain lasted long enough to bring matters to a level, and produce the same effect in this country?—Has the price of commodities, in this country, fallen within these two years? Is not the contrary notoriously the fact?

---

circulation. No special interference with them would, in my opinion, be requisite or beneficial.

The Report of the Bullion Committee has been the subject of much artful misrepresentation; sometimes ascribing to the members of that Committee a *wish* to put an end to paper credit altogether; sometimes an *opinion* that it ought to be reduced to the same amount as in 1797. —Nothing like such a *wish*, or such an *opinion*, can be collected from the Report.--On the contrary, it speaks in the strongest terms of the advantages of an extensive circulating credit, and expressly states, that any increase in its numerical amount is, of itself, no proof whatever of its being in excess.

But it may be said, that we have Bank notes as a substitute for gold, and that it is by an abundant supply of them that prices at home are raised and improved. Be it so. In proportion as commodities are *dear* in Bank notes, Bank notes are *cheap* in respect to commodities. Gold, we are told, is scarce, and, therefore, must be *dear*, whether measured in those same commodities, or in any thing else. What is this argument, on the part of those who deny the depreciation of Bank notes, but to tell us, in the same breath,—that gold is *dear*,—that Bank notes are *cheap*—but that Bank notes are of the same value as gold?

Nothing appears to me to indicate that the value of gold, in reference to ordinary commodities, has increased in the general market of EUROPE.—The annual produce of the gold mines, it is true, appears not to have been so large, during the last half century, as at some former periods; but the supply does not seem to have suffered any diminution of late years.

The relative value of gold to silver may have been, in some trifling degree, increased. The quantity of silver lately imported from America, has been unusually large; while the demand from the East Indies and China has altogether ceased: nay, I am informed that a large supply of dollars was imported from the latter country, by the fleet recently arrived from *Canton*. Every presumption, therefore, is, that the value of silver continues progressively, though slowly, to decrease in Europe.

This alteration in the relative value of the two precious metals, may render it necessary, hereafter perhaps, to change the proportion which they now bear to each other in our Mint regulations.

In FRANCE, where the currency is chiefly silver, an alteration appears to have been recently made in the gold coin, to the effect of raising its proportion to that of silver, from 15⅕, to about 15½. According to Mr. GREFULHE'S evidence, this slight alteration appears, very nearly, to have put an end to the premium which before existed on the gold coin. In ENGLAND the present proportion of our Mint is about $15\frac{1}{5}$ to one. If, at any future period, it should be thought necessary to raise that proportion, the alteration would perhaps be best effected by lowering, in whatever degree it might be necessary, the standard price of silver, so as to leave that of gold, which is our currency and *legal tender*, always fixed and invariable.*

It is not, however, to a diminished produce from the mines, but to a greatly increased demand occasioned by the wants of the armies, or to the practice of hoarding, or to both, that the alleged high price of gold on the continent is imputed. The change in the proportion of gold to silver, by the recent alteration in France before stated, appears to have been rather less than 2 per cent. Now, for many years before this alteration, and consequently before the high price of gold in England, there was at *Paris* a premium or *agio* of about $1\frac{1}{2}$ per cent. in favour of gold. This *agio* is now stated to be reduced to $\frac{1}{4}$ at the utmost.—Consequently all the rise that can possibly be ascribed to the temporary causes to which the present demand for gold is attributed cannot exceed $\frac{3}{4}$ per cent.

It is true that, both at Hamburgh and Amsterdam, there appear to have been occasional fluctuations to a greater amount, and that, for certain short periods, a larger premium is said to have been given, sometimes for gold in bars, and sometimes for some particular coin; though very far within the limits of the difference between the Mint and

* It was once my intention, in the course of this discussion, to have made some observations on the state of our silver coin, and the many serious inconveniences which are brought upon the community, (particularly upon the lower classes) from its scarcity, as well as from its debasement; and also to have stated my ideas on the subject of a new silver coinage. But a very little reflection will satisfy every reader that, in the present state of things, and so long as we have no *fixed standard* of value for our currency, it would be absurd, and almost impracticable, to send into circulation any new coinage. The present evil, therefore, admits of no remedy; but will rather increase, so long as the depreciation of our currency is suffered to continue: when that shall cease, it will be time enough to consider what should be done in respect to our silver coin. The want of it is an evil, of no trifling moment in our money system, but secondary, as well in point of importance, as in order of time, to the question now under consideration.

market price in London. This must have been owing to some particular circumstance, having a temporary effect on those markets: otherwise the *agio* at Paris would soon have been affected in the same degree; which does not appear to have been the case.

But facts are not the only difficulty in the way of this explanation; it furnishes abundant argument to destroy itself. It will scarcely be contended by any one, that the commerce, the manufactures, or the internal prosperity of the continent, have so rapidly increased, of late years, as to require any great and rapid increase in the amount of its circulating medium. If, from any peculiar and temporary circumstances, a disposition exists to prefer gold to silver, as that medium, it cannot well be denied, that, in proportion as silver is discarded (especially whilst the supply from AMERICA is more than usually abundant, and the demand from ASIA stopped), *silver* at least ought to be particularly *cheap*, in exchange for undepreciated Bank notes, of the full standard value of the coin of this realm. Now is this the case?

Gold, we know, has risen so much above this newly established paper standard as to be worth 4*l.* 12*s.* per ounce in that paper. Has not the price of silver risen in nearly the same proportion? The present market price of silver of standard fineness is about 5*s.* 10½*d.* per ounce; which ounce, by the Mint regulation, is divided into 5*s.* 2*d.* only. If the relative value of gold to that of silver be somewhat increased, as there is reason to believe; if it should, in consequence, be thought expedient to vary the proportion of our Mint from 15⅕ to 15½, the depreciation of our paper, measured in silver, would then be very nearly, if not altogether, as great, as it now is, if measured in gold.

Let us now briefly inquire what aid the question of our foreign exchange can afford, in explanation of the difference between the standard of our coin, and the actual value of our currency.

Respecting the nature of exchange, and what is understood to be the *real* PAR between two countries, there is no point in dispute. The *real* PAR, it is admitted, on all sides, consists in the *equality of either of the precious metals measured in the respective currencies of the two countries.* So far, all the merchants who were called before the Bullion Committee concur with the statement of the Report. In substance, they are likewise all agreed with the Report, (however much the admission is at variance with some of their own arguments) that the *real* depression of the exchange can never exceed, for any length of time, the expense of transporting bullion from the debtor to the creditor country. Nothing can more strongly confirm the truth of this last position, than the evidence and calculations furnished to the Committee by Messrs. *Grefulhe* and *Goldsmid;* which prove that, at the period of the present year, when the *quoted* rates of exchange with the Continent were most unfavourable, the *real* fall did not materially, if at all, exceed this amount: consequently the difference between the loss on the *real* and the *nominal* rates of those exchanges was to be ascribed to some other cause.

Two very erroneous opinions on this subject are most generally received in the theory of the mercantile world.

1st. That, whenever the exchange is against any country, the natural and general course of balancing the account is by a payment in bullion.

2dly. That the balance of these payments in favour of any country is finally to be measured by what is called the *Balance of Trade;* or the excess of exports above imports.

These two positions lead to a third, which is the fashionable doctrine of the day; namely,

3dly. That the *Balance of Payments* may, for a time, be very much against a country, although the *Balance of Trade* is, at the same time, very much in its favour: that is, that a country, buying for ready money, and selling at long credits, may be exporting a great quantity of its bullion; although a much greater quantity is actually due to it, and will be forthcoming in the adjustment of its accounts, when these credits come to maturity.

Such is affirmed to be the present situation of this country, and the true explanation of the very depressed state of our foreign exchanges.

The first of these positions is so little conformable to truth, and to the real course of business between nations, that there is, perhaps, no one article of general consumption and demand, which forms the foundation of so few operations of trade between the different countries of Europe as bullion: and that the operations, which do take place, originate almost entirely in the fresh supplies which are yearly poured in from the mines of the New World; and are chiefly confined to the distribution of those supplies through the different parts of Europe. If this supply were to cease altogether, the dealings in gold and silver, as objects of foreign trade, would be very few, and those of short duration.

To establish and illustrate this view of the subject, let us suppose that, in consequence of purchases made by England on the Continent, greater than had been made by the Continent here, or in payment of any debt, service, or demand, bills upon England are offered for sale in the markets of the Continent; and that the supply of such bills exceeds the demand. Their price, like that of any other article, under similar circumstances, must fall; and the exchange, which we will suppose to have been before at PAR, will of course turn against England: but to this fall there are limits in the competition of the buyers. This competition commences as soon as those bills are offered at such a price as enables a buyer to use the credit which he obtains upon England by the purchase of such a bill, either as the means of paying for any goods for which he has already contracted; or of buying others, so as to afford him the prospect of a profitable employment for the capital engaged in the transaction. Much of the skill of a general merchant consists in these calculations; and his intelligence is aided by a comparison of *prices current;* as well as by the peculiar means of information which he may be able to procure from any other sources, respecting the state of supply and demand in the different markets of the world. Now, of all the articles of trade, bullion is the least likely to offer this temptation to the purchaser of a bill of exchange; because its price is more steady and uniform, and always nearer to a level (from which it never long departs,) than that of any other commodity, in the different markets of Europe. In proportion as these bills are bought at a greater difference below PAR, is any holder of them enabled to buy goods cheaper in England. For instance, if, for 100 ounces of gold at Hamburgh, of any given weight and fineness, he obtain an assignment for 105 ounces in London; it is clear that this is equal to a premium of five per cent, on the purchase of such goods. An unfavourable course of exchange consequently, operates as a bounty upon all exports, and as a tax upon all imports. This bounty and this tax necessarily excite a competition to export, and a diminished disposition to import; by the joint effect of which, in all ordinary cases, *without any transmission of bullion*, the *real* exchange is brought back to its PAR, and probably rises above it. In its turn, this rise is checked and counteracted by the operation of the same causes; and thus, like the mariner's compass, the exchange is in a state of frequent variation; but of variation confined within certain natural limits. If indeed a fall in the *real* exchange exceeds these limits, which are confined to *the actual expense of transmitting bullion from the debtor to the creditor country*, particular individuals will export bullion. They will be induced to do so by a profit much smaller than would tempt them to a speculation in any other merchandize, because such profit, however small, is in this case quick and certain. But, this exportation of bullion, in the ordinary transactions of trade, instead of being, as is supposed, the habitual mode of adjusting accounts between one country and another, is of rare occurrence, and, when it occurs, can never continue long, because the transmission of a comparatively small quantity of that metal which forms the standard and currency of a country, not only operates, like that of any other commodity, to diminish in so much the balance of debt to other countries; but likewise to force the exportation, and to diminish the importation of all other goods; and thus more rapidly to improve the exchange, than the export of any other commodity to the same amount. As the exchange improves, the exportation of bullion of course ceases.

The principle and its application are the same, whether we contemplate only one transaction, or embrace the aggregate result of all the different transactions in trade, and of all subsidies and government expenditure abroad, on the one hand, and payments to be made here, on the other, as well as all other causes and speculations influencing the bill market on both sides of the water.

The circumstances of the exchange between Ireland and Great Britain in the years 1803 and 1804, as stated in the very able Report of the Committee appointed by the House of Commons, in the latter of these years, "*to enquire into the state of Ireland, as to its circulating paper, its specie, and its current coin, and the exchange between that part of the United Kingdom and Great Britain,*" afford a striking illustration of the doctrine which I have endeavoured to explain, and of the fallacy of that theory, which refers all the variations of exchange to the *balance of payments* and the *balance of trade.*

The commercial intercourse between Great Britain and Ireland is exposed to no political interruption;—the trade between them in bullion is free;—the standard of both countries is the same;—the transfer of coin from one to the other is liable to no interruption or restraint;—the actual expense of transporting it was proved before that Committee not to exceed one *per cent.*;—it was then, as it is now admitted, that the fluctuations in the exchange between any two countries could not materially or for any length of time exceed this actual expense: and although the exchange had been for several months from 8 to 10 *per cent.* against Dublin;—although it was proved that what is called the *balance of trade* was in favour of Ireland;—although there was no reason to believe that there was any transmission of guineas from Ireland to Great Britain;—although the exchange between London and the north of Ireland, (Belfast), in which no paper currency existed, instead of being from 8 to 10 *per cent.* against, was, during the same months, about one *per cent.* in favour of Ireland;*—although this fact alone incontrovertibly proved that the *real* exchange was in favour of Ireland, and consequently that there could be no exportation of gold from it;—although it was a necessary consequence of this state of things, that the exchange between Dublin and Belfast was from 9 to 11 *per cent.* in favour of the latter; (just as in the last century, and from a similar cause, it had been from 1 to 6 *per cent.* in favour of London and Newcastle against Edinburgh;)—although it was impossible for the merchants and Bank Directors, examined before that Committee, to controvert these facts, or to reconcile them with their own doctrines and admissions;—still nearly all of them professed to be thoroughly convinced that *there could be no excess or depreciation of Bank paper* in Ireland. They persisted in ascribing the fall of the exchange altogether to the *balance of payments* and the *balance of trade;* and rejected all explanation which connected that fall with the depreciation of Irish paper.

Now, if under these circumstances Irish paper was not depreciated in 1804, with reference to the currency of other countries, it follows, that English paper was then, with reference to the same criterion, at from 8 to 10 per cent. *premium.* Does any man believe *this* to have been the case? If there be any man who does, he and he alone, has a right to maintain that our paper (having in some way or other, since got rid of that premium) is now at PAR.

Soon after the Report of 1804, the amount of issues of the Bank of Ireland being reduced, the exchange with Dublin was gradually improved; and the Directors of the circulation of that country have since kept the depreciation

---

* In the middle of February, 1804, for instance, the exchange of Dublin upon London was 17½—that of Belfast upon London 7¾.
Vide Appendix to the Report of 1804.

of their paper generally upon a level with that of English paper.

What the currency of Ireland was in 1804, as compared with that of Great Britain, the currency of the United Kingdom now is, with reference to that of Hambourg or Amsterdam. The arguments and preconceived theories of those who stood up for the undiminished value of the one, were the same as are now resorted to by those who deny the depreciation of the other.

If the reader should concur with me in the few observations, which I have ventured to submit to his judgment, he will now be able to form a tolerably just estimate of what is called the *Balance of Trade.*

If one country have a claim upon another, the holders of that claim have but two ways of using it; either they will leave the amount in the debtor country, as so much capital to be vested there at interest, or employed in such other manner as they may think proper;—or they will withdraw it. The latter is so much the more usual course, that, in the magnitude of the operations of this country at least, we may, except perhaps from very temporary circumstances, consider the former as having little or no influence on the exchange. Now, no claim can arise from one country upon another (except in the way of tribute or exaction) which is not founded in some *equivalent.*

An exchange of *equivalents* is the foundation of all *commerce,* from the simple barter of the untutored Indian, to the most complicated and extensive operations of the London merchant. No nation, therefore, can permanently export to a greater value than it imports, as far as exports and imports are created by a *commercial intercourse* with other nations. But a considerable part of our imports are not derived from *commerce.* From our colonies, a great proportion of them is in the nature of rent remitted in kind, to the owners of colonial estates who reside in England; to which are to be added, as farther exceptions, the produce of our fisheries;

and of any portion of our territorial revenue in India, or of the savings of public servants civil and military, in that quarter, sent home in goods. If these returns were abated from the sum total of our imports, the annual *Balance of Trade* in our favour, as stated to Parliament, would appear still more considerable. Yet, taken for any length of years, no part of this balance is created by our commerce. For every thing that we receive, through that channel, an *equivalent*, and no more, is returned. All that we send out, above the amount which is thus returned, is drawn from us by the remittance of the profits of foreign capital vested in this country, or is to be accounted for under the several heads of our foreign expenditure. A great balance of trade, therefore, instead of being the natural criterion of increasing wealth at home, is only a certain indication of a great expenditure abroad.—It is an indication of wealth, only in the same way as any other great expenditure, by proving the power and ability of the country to sustain it.

Whilst it is true, however, that the vaunted *Balance of Trade*, or the excess of our exports above our imports, is not, as it has been represented, and is generally believed, the *measure* and the *realization* of the profit derived to us from our foreign trade; but is, in fact, only capital sent out of the country for which no capital is returned to it; it is by no means to be inferred that this expenditure is without equivalent, though without commercial return: still less that it is not beneficial to the country, or that the sum so expended could be employed in any manner equally conducive to its interests. Nor is it to be inferred that the not incurring this expenditure abroad would be a clear saving, or, perhaps, any saving at all.

It must be obvious to every one, that the two great heads of this expenditure are our armies and fleets abroad; and subsidies to foreign states. Our soldiers, our sailors, the public servants of every description, so far as they are furnished abroad with whatever is necessary for themselves, or for the operations in which they are engaged, give, to those by whom they are supplied, assignments upon the produce of this country. These assignments, like any other bills of exchange, are converted into whatever articles the ultimate holders of them find it most to their advantage to export from this country. If this head of our foreign expenditure, therefore, were reduced by the recall of all our public servants, civil, naval, or military, now maintained abroad; still if the same number were to be maintained at home, the real saving to the country would not bear any considerable proportion to the reduction in our foreign expenditure. The *Balance of Trade* would be diminished in proportion to that reduction: but such diminution would obviously be no proof whatever of the declining prosperity of the country.

A subsidy to a foreign state may or may not be politically wise; but, in the view which is here in question, it must be considered as being paid for a service to be performed, which is held to be *equivalent* to the expense incurred. The withholding such a subsidy would, in many cases, be obviously the very reverse of economy; but it seems quite as obvious that, in whatever mode it be remitted, it must augment to that amount what is called the *Balance of Trade* in our favour.

It may, perhaps, be asked, if commerce is nothing more than an exchange of *equivalents*, and the *Balance of Trade*, taken for any length of time, only the measure of our foreign expenditure, in what way is a country enriched by trade? To those who may be disposed to ask this question I would, in the first place, reply by putting one or two others. What is the *internal* trade of any country, that is, the trade carried on between different districts of the same state within the limits of its territory, but an exchange of *equivalents?* Is this a trade by which the one gains and the other loses? by which *Yorkshire* is enriched at the expense of *Kent?* Then, if our internal trade be an exchange of *equivalents*, what is the distinction, in this respect, between it and foreign trade? What takes away this character from the latter?—and what, after all, is the latter?

To the question—how then are we enriched by trade?

the answer appears to me as obvious, as it is consistent with this doctrine.

The mind and faculties of man are constantly engaged in pursuit of his own happiness, and in multiplying the means of subsistence, comfort, and enjoyment. Trade, which effects the exchange of a part of the productions of the soil, industry, and talent of any one country, against those of the soil, industry, and talent of all other countries, is the great instrument of multiplying these means. By the aid of this exchange, not only those natural productions, which Providence has distributed in abundance in one portion of the globe, and refused to some other, are rendered common to all; but the soil of every country, and of every portion of every country, is left at liberty to be cultivated principally, or wholly, if necessary, in raising those productions for which it is best calculated and adapted; those which, by experience, it has been found to afford of the best quality, in the greatest abundance, and at the least expense of capital and labour. Labour or capital, employed in manufactures, is enabled to avail itself of local situations and natural advantages (for instance, a stream or a coal-mine), and to adapt itself, exclusively, to those pursuits, in which, from any peculiar disposition, dexterity, ingenuity, or fortuitous discovery, the people of any particular country, or any particular part of them, may excel. The advantage derived from the division of labour is well known. What is effected by the operation of that principle, for a single undertaking, is, by the aid of commerce, effected for the whole world. Commerce enables the population of each separate district to make the most of its peculiar advantages, whether derived from nature, or acquired by the application of industry, talent, and capital;—to make the most of them for its own consumption; leaving, at the same time, the greatest possible remainder to be given in exchange for any other commodities produced more easily, more abundantly, or of better quality, in other districts of the world. It is *thus* that a country is enriched by commerce.

Apply this, for example, to England. Much is required

for the subsistence, much for the comfort, much for the enjoyments and luxury, of the people of this country. Now, if we could not, or, by a mistaken policy, would not, procure salt meat from Ireland; a country, in which, we will assume, that, from its superior pasture, one acre will feed as many cattle as can be fed upon two in this country; it is obvious that, if we still wanted to consume the same quantity of meat, a larger portion of our soil must be allotted to pasture. —Consequently, we should have less of corn, hops, or some other article of our present growth.

In the same way, if we had resolved, that, instead of importing sugar, we would make it from beet-root, the sweet maple-tree, or any other vegetables, which could be raised in this climate; we should be obliged to allot a great portion of our soil to their growth: and, after all, we should have very little sugar; and we should have much less of other produce than we now have, together with an abundant supply of sugar. The same observation will apply to hemp, or to any other article principally imported from other countries.

Certain small states, which have been enriched by commerce, form no exception to the truth of these observations. —Favoured by natural advantages of situation; pursuing a more enlightened commercial policy than their neighbours; deriving commercial security from their own political weakness, and from the jealousy and wants of more powerful nations; they became, when trade was little understood and less esteemed, the carriers for all the other parts of the world. Great capitals were requisite for this purpose; and being thus concentrated in certain spots, they were gradually increased by thrifty management, till the owners were enabled, by successive accumulations, to employ part of their wealth in advances to the countries with which they traded, and thus to become partners in the produce of those nations. VENICE and AMSTERDAM, each in the days of its prosperity, may have been, what LONDON now is,—the *focus*, in which the greatest mass of capital is drawn together; the largest *emporium* of the goods and produce of all other countries; and the fountain-head of commercial credit.

The great profits, which centre in these capitals of the trading world, are the result of wealth gradually accumulated, or tempted from other quarters, by better prospects of advantage, and by confidence in a more assured state of property. It is this wealth which, in the first instance, creates the trade, and not the trade the wealth. But whatever may have been the profits and accumulation of wealth made by the mercantile community in any one of them, or the incidental advantage of such accumulation to the particular country; the benefits conferred on all individuals, and all countries, whose productions were exchanged by the intervention of *their* capital, industry, and talents, were reciprocal, and to each *equivalent.*

Every addition to the productions of a country, whether ultimately consumed at home or not, adds equally to its means of commercial exchange with other countries. To improve agriculture, therefore, is to extend commerce: and every new channel opened to the latter, affords additional encouragement to the former. It is thus that they both contribute to the wealth of a country; and that the improvement of that wealth is most effectually consulted by leaving to every part of the world to raise those productions for which its soil and climate are best adapted.—Yet, such is the barbarian ignorance, or detestable policy, which presides in the councils of France, and sways those of continental Europe, that we are boastingly told of whole districts in Italy and Provence, naturally fertile in other rich productions, being devoted to the raising, at vast expense, of a little very bad cotton. We hear of Princes in Germany devising wretched substitutes for coffee, or planting forests of sweet maple, and sinking great capitals in the erection of works for the manufacturing of sugar: and all this, at the same time that the natural productions of their agriculture, those best suited to their soil and climate, in exchange for which these articles might be procured in abundance, are rotting in the fields for want of a market.

If it were in the nature of violent passions and headstrong power to take lessons from experience, *Buonaparte* perhaps would begin to perceive, that the mercantile superiority, for which he envies and hates this country, grows, not so much out of commercial regulations, as out of a system of laws, which affords perfect protection to property, admits of no degrading distinctions in society, encourages industry, fosters genius, and excites emulation, and is supported by that moral, manly, and national character of our people, which is only another of the many advantages derived from that system; that the wealth, which is employed in commerce, is the result of long accumulation, uninterrupted by popular violence, or arbitrary exactions; that so long as these blessings are continued to us, on the one hand, and, as on the other, his warlike pursuits abroad, and capricious regulations at home, conspire to drive commerce from the Continent, the capitals engaged in trade will seek protection and employment in England; and that, whilst he is thus engaged in adding incalculably to the misery of Europe, by debarring it more and more from the benefits and enjoyments which commercial intercourse affords to mankind, the blow, aimed at this country is counteracted by the course which he pursues; and the national capital and resources of Great Britain are, upon the whole, perhaps, rather increased by the very system on which he has founded the vain hope of reducing us, either to submission, or to ruin.

These few observations would suggest many more on this interesting and important branch of political economy. But I am aware that I have already been guilty, in some degree, of a digression from my subject; to which, however, I have been tempted by a persuasion that there is no political question on which the prevalence of false principles is so general, as in what relates to the nature of commerce, and to the pretended *balance of trade;* and that there are few which have led to a greater number of practical mistakes, attended with consequences extensively prejudicial to the happiness of mankind.

In this country, our parliamentary proceedings, our public documents, and the works of several able and popular writers, have combined to propagate the impression that we are indebted for much of our riches to what is called the *balance of trade.* This impression, which has spread through Europe, has contributed, not a little, every where, to suggest the imposition of unnecessary restraints upon trade, and perhaps to render acceptable for a time, even to the nations who were suffering from it, the wild attempt to exclude British commerce from the continent. The jealousy, which our general prosperity creates, is enhanced by a notion that it is altogether the effect of our commerce. Whilst our merchants are individually reputed pre-eminent for good faith and fair dealing, the opinion entertained of us, as a nation, is, that we are little short of *sharpers* in trade; and that, whatever we gain by *it* is so much lost to those who deal with us.—For the countenance given to this opinion, prejudicial to every country, but not least so, to ourselves, we have, I think, more to answer than the most envious of our neighbours. Our true policy would surely be to profess, as the object and guide of our commercial system, that which every man, who has studied the subject, must know to be the true principle of commerce:—*the interchange of reciprocal and equivalent benefit.* We may rest assurred that it is not in the nature of commerce to enrich one party at the expense of the other. This is a purpose at which, if it were practicable, we ought not to aim; and which, if we aimed at it, we could not accomplish. Let us not then disclam a virtue, which we, perforce, must practise. The boast of wealth growing out of unequal advantages would be but a vulgar boast, even if it could, in the nature of things, rest on a real foundation.—Our legitimate pride should consist, not in the superiority of the means with which Providence has blessed us for the improvement and extension of our own commerce, but in the consciousness that those means cannot be employed for purposes purely selfish, and that we do not desire so to employ them. Our national character is to be exalted in the eyes of foreigners, not by a self complacent display of our own prosperity, but by shewing to surrounding nations that they have an interest in that prosperity, and that we prize it the more, not because we believe it to be exclusive, but because we know it to be communicable.

To come back, however, to the subject of foreign exchange. I have hitherto proceeded upon the supposition of the money of any two countries, between which an exchange is established, retaining their relative weight and fineness, according to the standard of their respective Mints, upon which the PAR between them was originally settled. If, in either country, the standard, or the denomination, be altered, whilst, in the other, they remain the same; of course, the *real* PAR will be altered in the same proportion, although this alteration will most probably be effected without any variation in the mode of stating the course of the exchange; just as a shilling is still called a shilling in Ireland, although its current value has long since been raised from 12*d.* to 13*d.* This gives rise to what, in the Report of the Bullion Committee, is called the *computed* PAR. Even without any change being made by law in the standard or denomination of the currency of either country, this PAR would seldom be found perfectly to accord with the real par; because the degree of wear might be different in the two currencies, or even in different portions of the same currency. It is only when both contain the full quantity required by the Mint regulations of the respective countries, or are equally diminished by wear, that the *computed* and the *real* PAR are, in fact, exactly the same. The *real* PAR will also vary where the standard of the one country is gold, and that of the other silver, with every fluctuation in the relative value of these two metals.

The regulation by which our gold coin, if reduced more than a small fraction above one per cent. ceases to be a *legal tender*, would prevent the foreign exchange from being affected to any greater degree, by the wear or clipping of our coin; even if the currencies of other countries were constantly of their full standard weight and fineness. It is owing to this regulation that the exchange became much steadier, and was more generally in our favour, after the re-coinage of our gold in 1773.

No alteration can be made in the standard, or denomination of the currency of any country, without the precise effect of it upon the value of such currency being immediately and generally known: and a corresponding alteration as immediately ensues in the rates of exchange with other countries, though the former mode of *computing* it may still be continued. In Ireland the *standard* is precisely the same as in England; but the denomination of the shilling being raised, in the former country, to *thirteen-pence*, the exchange is at the *real* PAR when it is stated to be $8\frac{1}{3}$ against Ireland: on the other hand, if the standard of our gold were lowered in England $\frac{1}{12}$, whilst it remained the same in Ireland, or if the denomination of our shilling were raised to thirteen-pence, or that of our guinea to 22*s*. 9*d*. the effect, in either case, would equally be to do away this *computed* difference against Ireland. It would be very easy to multiply examples of similar alterations in the currency of different countries, attended with a corresponding effect upon their respective exchanges.

Although our present situation is somewhat different from that which would arise from an alteration in the standard, or in the denomination of the coin, the effect on our foreign exchange is precisely the same.

Our gold coin is not materially deteriorated by clipping or wear; nor has its standard been lowered, or its denomination raised: but for coin we have substituted a paper currency; which, from being issued to excess, and from that cause only, no longer actually represents the quantity of gold which it purports to represent.

The following case will perhaps illustrate this part of the subject.

Suppose 12 ounces of gold, of standard fineness, to be converted at PARIS into French currency, and that, with the proceeds, is bought a bill of exchange upon LONDON for 56*l.* sterling. If, at the same moment, this last sum in English

57

currency (Bank notes,) would purchase exactly 12 ounces of standard gold in London, the *real* exchange of Paris upon London, it is admitted, would be at PAR.—If that sum would purchase 12 ounces and a half, the *real* exchange would be against London; if it would purchase 11 ounces and a half only, the *real* exchange would be in favour of London. Now, 12 ounces of gold being equal to 44 guineas and a half, or 46*l.* 14*s.* 6*d.* the difference between that sum and 56*l.* would, in the first supposition, be the measure of the depreciation of the latter sum in Bank paper. In the same manner, that depreciation may be calculated in the two other instances.

In the first case, the loss upon the exchange arises solely from the depreciation of the paper, and is exactly equal to it. In the second, the loss on the exchange is greater than the depreciation of the paper; in the third less: the difference, one way or the other, being half an ounce of gold, or 1*l.* 18*s.* 11¼*d.*

Whether, in point of fact, the *real* exchange with the Continent, be, at this moment, for or against this country, it may be difficult accurately to determine. If the difference, here, between the Mint and the Market price of gold, such as can be legally exported, be less than the loss on the *computed* exchange; the presumption is, that the *real* exchange is against us, in nearly the amount of that difference.

It being admitted, on all hands, that our currency has no value in a *foreign* country, except in proportion to the *quantity* of gold which it actually contains, or which can be procured for it by purchase in the market; I could wish that some of those who have made this admission, but who do not admit the depreciation of our paper, would explain, distinctly, what it is, other than that *quantity*, which determines the value of such currency amongst ourselves? Is it any thing in the coinage? Those who allow that 44 guineas and a half, new from the Mint, and 46*l.* 14*s.* 6*d.* in Bank notes, are *equal values*, and who cannot deny the fact that 56*l.* in notes, will not buy one grain more of gold than is contained in those 44½ guineas, will hardly contend that any thing is gained by the coinage. In truth, their position, as to the undimi-

58

nished value of our currency, can not be maintained at all, unless they can make out that two *unequal quantities* of the same article are *equal* to one another: and, if they can succeed in this, they may as well raise the guinea to the value of five guineas, and declare all our shillings crowns at once.

But, after all, the subject of *foreign* exchange is, of itself, of little interest or importance, compared with the question, to which it is incidental, of the diminished or undiminished value of our currency at *home*. It is, indeed, connected with the question of depreciation only as it is a symptom of that depreciation. Whether it be, as has been contended by me, and is, I think, satisfactorily made out, a symptom consequent upon the existence of the disease; or whether as others contend, it is the predisposing cause of it;—in either case, the disease equally exists, and equally demands a remedy. To talk of postponing the remedy until this symptom shall cease, is, in fact, to perpetuate the disease.

In King WILLIAM's time, the same disease (a depreciation of our currency) was accompanied, as it is *now*, with a corresponding depression of the foreign exchange. *Then* as *now*, there were not wanting those who wished to invert the relation which these two evils really bear to each other; who maintained that the high price of bullion, as measured in our currency, was produced by the unfavourable course of the foreign exchange; and who would fain have recommended to Parliament, rather to wait, in helpless expectation, for the disappearance of the evil over which they had no controul, than to apply themselves to the grievance which it was in their power to redress. But Parliament, at that time, felt, that, whatever might be the depression of the foreign exchange, it was their first duty to deal with the manifest evil in the state of our currency, from a conviction that it was, not only a question of policy, but strictly of good faith.

That it *is* a question of good faith, can any man doubt, when he considers that the *stamp* affixed to our coin is nothing more than a *guarantee* given by the sovereign that, in *weight* and *fineness*, the money of the country is in exact conformity to the *standard* fixed by law ?--when he considers that for the express purpose of making this *guarantee* completely effectual, the law which makes that money a *legal tender*, has at the same time, denounced the severest penalties against those who shall imitate or counterfeit such *stamp*; and takes away the character of *legal tender* from any portion of that money so *stamped*, if, from any accident or circumstance whatever, the *quantity* of gold certified by the *stamp*, is reduced in a greater proportion than about 1$\frac{1}{10}$ per cent.? —that the value of our money being thus accurately ascertained and determined, all pecuniary contracts and bargains have been made, and all engagements accepted, in the full confidence and assurance, that the public faith so firmly pledged, so strongly sanctioned, and so cautiously guarded, would never be violated or impaired?

Does it not follow from these premises, that any contrivance which, under the same *denomination* of money to which this *guarantee* applies, should compel any individual to accept, in payment of a legal debt, a smaller *quantity* of gold than is certified by the stamp to be contained in such *denomination*, would be a violation of the public faith; and a loss, to him as creditor, of whatever may be the difference between the *quantity* of gold to which he is entitled under the *guarantee* of the sovereign, and the *quantity* contained in the currency in which he is actually paid, or which can be procured for it at the time of such payment?

In truth there is but one security for the maintenance of the public faith of a country in this respect; and that is, *to preserve the* STANDARD *of its currency immutable and inviolable.* I have already shown that the intention of the Act of 1797 was not to introduce, or authorize any variation of our *standard*. Practically, for a series of years, it had no such effect. Within a late period such an effect has been produced. The *standard* of our currency has been virtually altered; and *that*, which no legislature would advisedly have consented to do, or could have done without violating the obligations of justice, has been unadvisedly and innocently done by the Corporation of the Bank. Not that the Bank were aware that they were exercising, any more than the legislature had it in contemplation to transfer to them, any such power. Yet, it is obvious that while in principle and in law our *standard* remains the same, in practice and in effect it is lost. If a foreigner had at any time enquired what was the standard of our currency ?—the answer at any period from the time of the TUDORS* downwards would have been, to refer him to the unvaried letter of the statute, as strictly executed in the regulations of our Mint. The answer to such a question must *now* be sought in the current price of bullion in the market, and in the discretion of the Bank.

Admitting these evils, however, it may yet be said, that the restriction is but a *temporary* measure, which once removed, every thing will return to its proper level. True:—but, if it be much longer continued, what confusion and derangement must, in the mean time, ensue in all the transactions of society? True:—but the very evils which this measure has created, and which it alone keeps alive, are assigned as the reasons for continuing it, so long as they exist. True, again, it is, that this is a *temporary* measure:†

---

* The last alteration in our standard was made in the 43d of ELIZ. when it was lowered between 3 and 4 per cent.

† I trust there is no doubt of this fact, but I am sorry to see that the Bank Proprietors (if their sentiments can be collected from the report of their proceedings at their last general meeting) entertained a different expectation.

An uninformed stranger, from reading the account of these proceedings, would be led to conclude, that the proposal of the Bullion Committee to allow the Bank two years to prepare for the resumption of cash payments, is a direct and gross infringement of their charter. It was condemned as a plan of *compulsion* and *injustice.* The Orator of the Bank, on that occasion, seemed to prefer even their dissolution, as a trading company, to this resumption of the functions for which they were originally instituted.—" Let Government" (he is reported to have said) " pay us the 18 millions they owe us, and we will make up the " remaining two millions by subscription among ourselves within an " hour, so as immediately to discharge all our notes."

In reply to this lofty language, I would observe ;—1st. that no one suspects the Bank of being insolvent, or of having made any advances without very good and ample security;—that no man has imputed the depreciation of their notes to any suspicion that their concerns as a Bank are not prosperous, and that their management for themselves is and, out of this very circumstance grow most important considerations for those whose high office it is to administer

---

not extremely prudent ;—2dly. that if the Bank Proprietors, as a body, should, after mature consideration, be disposed to petition Parliament for leave to surrender their charter, there would be no difficulty in finding other members of the community, who, upon a transfer to them of that charter, and the other advantages of the Bank, would be perfectly ready to make good any advances from the Bank to Government, and to take upon themselves the whole concern, without refusing to resume cash payments at the expiration of two years.—But I must add, that while on the one hand, I should be very sorry to witness such a transfer, on the other, I have not the smallest apprehension that the Bank Proprietors, when they shall come to weigh the arguments of their learned advocate, will put it in the power of any other body of men to acquire the advantages which they now derive—1st. from the exclusive privileges of their charter ;—2dly. from their being the agents of the state in all pecuniary matters ;—3rdly. from their being the Bank of deposit in which all the money arising from the receipt of the revenue, or issued for the expenditure of the state, is lodged.

With respect to the sum of 18 millions, which was said to be due by Government, it would have been well if, at the same time, that the aggregate was so ostentatiously announced, some of the heads of that debt had been stated. Such an explanation would have prevented many unfounded inferences, which, to the prejudice of Government, have been drawn from that statement in other quarters ;—as if sacrifices to such an amount had, since the restriction, and in consequence of the facilities which it afforded, been made by the Bank to the Government.—On the contrary, I believe, there never was a period of war in which Government were less, or so little, indebted upon floating securities to the Bank as at the moment of Mr. RANDLE JACKSON's assertion.

The first and largest *item* of which this sum of 18 millions is made up, is the advance *originally* made by the Bank of their capital stock amounting to 11,686,000*l.*—3 per cents; which advance has been carried on upon each successive renewal of their charter. This advance has no more connexion with the issues of the Bank than any other *three per cent. stock* which Mr. JACKSON, or any of the Proprietors may possess individually; or than the whole mass of the funded debt of the country. This stock, though ultimately liable for their engagements, is no part of the securities upon which their notes are issued · it is the *subscription* capital of the company, and the repayment of it is not due or *demandable* till the expiration of the present charter in 1833.

The next sum consists of two advances, of three millions each: the first lent in 1800, for six years without interest, as the price of the last renewal of their charter; and continued since the expiration of that period, at an interest of three per cent.:—the other advanced, without any interest, under an agreement with Government made in 1808. Both these advances are in consideration of the profits accruing to the Bank; from the deposit of the public balances in their hands. These deposits it is quite obvious, have no connection with the circulation of the Bank; and would be continued, to nearly the same amount, if that circulation were restored to its sound state. The average amount of these deposits exceeds *ten millions sterling.*

justice in equity, and to whose care and custody are committed the protection and preservation of property belonging to the most helpless classes of society.

No part of this advance of six millions is *demandable* until six months after the termination of the war.

The difference between the amount of interest paid to the Bank on this advance, and the amount of legal interest at 5 per cent. on that sum, is correctly stated by Mr. JACKSON at 210,100*l.*—per annum.

Thus are 17,686,000*l.* out of the 18,000,000*l.*—so confidently, but prematurely, called for by Mr. JACKSON, disposed of.

The small remainder of any debt from the Government to the Bank consists, either of the ordinary annual advance on the land and malt, the repayment of which is amply secured by those taxes;—their weekly produce being appropriated for that purpose, until the whole advance of each year principal and interest is repaid—or of any advances which the Bank may have voluntarily made, by the purchase of Exchequer Bills, for the repayment of which, with interest, they have the same security, and are upon the same footing, as any individual who may purchase such bills in the market.

With respect to the sum of 210,000*l.*, annually saved to the public upon the advance of the *six millions*, made, as I have stated, in consideration of a deposit in the Bank amounting, upon a permanent average, to more than *ten millions*;—I must be allowed to express my regret and surprise, that, at a general m eting of the Bank Proprietors, where the very Directors with whom the agreement for this advance had been so recently made on the part of the Bank, were probably present, (and surely the conditions and nature of such an agreement must be known to all the Directors) it should have been more than insinuated, without contradiction from any quarter, that this sacrifice of 210,000*l.*—per annum, is made by the Bank to Government, in consideration of the advantage which the Bank derives from the suspension of cash payments. —The words of Mr. JACKSON as stated in the report of his speech (Morning Chronicle, 21st September) are

" But when the Committee determined so earnestly to recommend " the resumption of cash payments, and a *compulsive* measure upon this " institution, it would have been but becoming in them to recommend, " as a preliminary step, the *repayment to the Bank of the* 18 *millions due* " *from the public, and also the restoration of the* 210,000*l. derived from* " *the Bank in consequence of the supposed advantages resulting from the* " *non-payment of cash.* This was a line of proceeding which at least " *common justice* should have urged the committee to propose."

Fortunately the correspondence on this subject between Government and the Bank in 1808 was laid before Parliament, and is published. By a reference to that correspondence every one may satisfy himself that this sum is the price paid by the Bank for the use of the public balances, and on no other account whatever: to which I may add, that it was the opinion of several persons in the House of Commons, and particularly of the leading members of the Committee of Finance, in consequence of whose report this bargain was made; that the advance obtained from the Bank was not adequate to the advantages which they derived from the agreement.

If the nature of our money be such as I have stated;—if the laws of England, by which its *standard* is *fixed*, *guarded*, and *guaranteed*, have been correctly described by me; (and upon these points, so well understood, and so long settled, there can be no difference of opinion)—if it be of the essence of those laws, that every legal bargain for money can only be satisfied by the payment of the stipulated *quantity;* I cannot help suggesting a doubt, whether the many important pecuniary interests committed to the care of our Courts of Equity may not be wrongfully deteriorated by the continuance of the present state of our currency?—Whether, for instance, an old lease, at the rent of 1000 guineas per annum, being virtually, though not in terms, a contract on the part of the lessee to pay in each year, at the very least, 266 oz. 13 dwts. 8 grs. of gold, (allowing each of these 1000 guineas to be of the lowest standard weight permitted by law) that contract can be equitably fulfilled by the payment of 220 ounces?—Whether even during the existence of this *temporary* restriction law;—which (be it always remembered) is to cease in six months after the termination of the war, and *must* be so construed and contemplated by every court, either of justice or equity,—1000 guineas, weighing any thing short of 266 ounces, would entitle the lessee to a discharge? By a *tender* of that which is equivalent only to 220 ounces, it is true, that he is now protected against the process of the court; but in *equity* is he entitled to a discharge? Will he be entitled to it, next year, if that which he may tender should be equi-

---

Be that as it may, I must decidedly protest against the assertion that Government has, at any time, demanded or received from the Bank any participation in the profits which accrue to them from the suspension of cash payments. Every administration, I am sure, since 1797, will join me in repelling this insinuation; and in maintaining, that, whatever measures Parliament may think proper to adopt, in consequence of the report of the Bullion Committee, their deliberations cannot be influenced or fettered by any direct agreement, or implied understanding, with respect to the continuance of the suspension. Nothing in fact has ever passed between Government and the Bank which can have the effect of preventing the Legislature from fixing the period for the resumption of cash payments, without reference to any other consideration than the interest and the safety of the country.

valent to 20 ounces only? Will he be entitled to it the day after the signature of a peace, although it is admitted and notorious that six months after that day, the law would compel him to pay 266 ounces?

I know not whether, by possibility, any man can have reflected upon this subject so little, or to so little purpose, as to object to the doubts which I have now suggested—that they proceed on the supposition that it belongs to the province of courts of Equity to take care that the value of money should never be altered. Nothing so absurd ever entered my imagination. The value of the precious metals relatively to other commodities, *cannot* be fixed. It is subject to be affected by the same circumstances of abundance, scarcity, supply or demand, as affect the value of all other articles. That it has greatly decreased within the period which has elapsed since the discovery of America is notorious– that it continues to decrease slowly and progressively, I am also disposed to believe. This is an inconvevience, but is not an injustice, to a creditor. All that he has any right to expect, all that his contract *stipulates*, and the law *guarantees*, is, that the *quantity* shall be the same: not that the value of that *quantity* shall continue invariably to bear a proportion relatively as favourable to that of other commodities. The reverse might have been the case: still he would have been entitled to the same *quantity*. True it is that the natural and progressive diminution of the value of money is peculiarly felt by that class of the community which depends for support upon fixed incomes; true it is that the unavoidable increase of taxation adds to this peculiar pressure. The more incumbent is it upon the Legislature not to aggravate this pressure by prolonging a system, which in its effects greatly outsteps the natural course of events; and not to augment the amount of the necessary deductions from income, by one which adds nothing to the revenue of the state.

One or two observations of those who maintain that there is nothing wrong in the present state of our currency remain to be noticed.

From the abettors of the present state of things, when they have been referred to the rapid rise in the price of all ordinary commodities as a *very strong indication* of the depreciation of our currency, I have often heard this answer,—"that this is sufficiently accounted for by the progressive diminution in the value of the precious metals; that is—by their *increasing abundance.* When the same persons, in consequence of this answer, have been referred to the high price of these precious metals themselves, if purchased in our currency, as a *more certain and unequivocal* proof of its depreciation, their answer has been "that this is the natural effect of the *scarcity* of these metals."

But, because gold that can be sworn off for exportation, is worth about 3*s.* per ounce more in our market, than gold, of the same fineness, which cannot be legally exported, an inference is drawn, that gold must be dearer abroad than in England, not only by this difference, but by all the expense of transporting it to the Continent; and that this circumstance accounts for its scarcity, and consequent high price here. This inference has already been so fully examined, and, I think, disposed of, in a former part of this Enquiry, that I shall, at present, content myself with offering what appears to me the real explanation of the fact with which it is here connected.

Since the Restriction Law, and the issuing of *one* and *two* pound notes, the quantity of gold coin in circulation has rapidly diminished; and within these last two years, guineas have almost entirely disappeared. For some years, prior to the autumn of 1808, the price of standard gold was pretty steady at 4*l.* per oz. and this was the buying price at the Bank. Towards the end of that year, the price rose very rapidly, and has since continued, with trifling fluctuations, at about 4*l.* 10*s.* per ounce; the Bank declining however to offer more than 4*l.*

It is within this last period, principally, that the difference in price between gold that could be sworn off for exportation, and that which was confined to the home market, has arisen.

Now, the demand for gold, like the demand for any other commodity, depends upon the consumption; and the price is regulated by the demand. The consumption in England, before the Restriction, was, either for the purposes of our manufactures, or for coin. The quantity used in the former was very inconsiderable, and probably still continues unaltered. The great demand was for the purpose of supplying and keeping up a certain amount of gold currency; and the great purchasers were the Bank. This demand has altogether ceased; and the purchases of the Bank, for these last two years, must have been suspended. The fact, I know, is not in evidence; but a comparison of prices sufficiently warrants the inference. Hence it appears, that the market of this country, for internal consumption, is fallen off almost to nothing, whilst the market of the Continent remains just as brisk as before. The necessary result is, that whatever gold there may be in England, or may come to England in the course of trade, and which can be legally exported, goes to the better market. It possesses a *privilege* which the law has taken away from other gold; and, under the present circumstances, this *privilege* makes it more valuable. There is nothing surprising in this, any more than there would be to find that a better price was given for *exportable* coffee, for instance, if that privilege were given only to a certain limited quantity, and the remainder of the stock in hand were confined to the comparatively small consumption of this country.

The only way to stop this exportation of gold is that the Bank should give the market price, and revive the use of it in circulation. If that price be 90*s*. per ounce, 90*s*. must be given: but, in proportion as the value of their notes in circulation shall be raised by the gradual withdrawing of the present excess, that price will diminish, until it shall be restored to the Mint price, and their notes consequently to PAR. On the other hand, if the excess of Bank paper shall continue progressively to increase, 90*s.* will soon cease to be a sufficient price for an ounce of gold: and either more must be given; or it will continue to be carried to other markets.

The difference between the market and the Mint price, it is true, will be just so much loss to the Bank upon all the gold which they may now buy, whenever they shall resume cash payments: but it is equally true, that this difference is, at this moment, just so much loss to the holders of their notes; and that the latter have no chance of that compensation which the Bank has so amply secured to itself, by the increased amount of its issues since the Restriction.

It is, therefore, because the use of gold has been superseded by the present state of our currency, whilst the over-issue of that currency has diminished its relative value; and because the Bank of England, not making a sufficient allowance for that diminished value, has ceased to offer the market price, that *exportable* gold is of more value than that which cannot legally be sent out of the country.

If the law which prohibits the melting of our gold coin, and its exportation, either as coin or in bars, could be much enforced, the difference of price would be greater than it now is: but every one knows how easily both these provisions are evaded; and how impossible it is to make them effectual. I have therefore no doubt that there has been sent to the Continent within these last two years, partly in bars, and partly in coin, a considerable quantity of gold not exportable by law; which would have remained in England, if the Bank Directors had raised their buying price in proportion as the value of their paper was depreciated.*

---

* Any bank of which the profits are proportionate to the amount of its issues, and which has nothing to consider, in making those issues, but the quality and character of the securities upon which its loans are advanced, must have a natural tendency to a continual increase of its paper. It appears to me, therefore, extremely probable, that, for some considerable time before the depreciation of our paper currency was materially marked by the high price of gold bullion, the amount of Bank issues was in excess. But the full effect of this excess was not so sensibly felt, because so long as our currency consisted of a mixture of

But the Bank, I may be told, could not buy guineas for more than 21*s.* each. Be it so: but it might have given 4*l.* 10*s.* for gold in bars: and, if this had been the Bank price, the guineas which have now gone abroad, either in bars, or in coin, (the latter to be melted abroad,) would have found their way, as bars, to the cellars of the Bank.

This is precisely what happened before the Restriction Law, whenever, from a temporary over-issue of paper, (to which the Bank, from the nature of its institution, must be ever prone,) the market price of gold was raised, for a short

---

gold and paper, the former would give way, and either be exported, or melted down—and by thus gradually making room for the augmentation of paper, the value of the latter would be, in a great degree, sustained. —But, when, by these successive additions to the amount of Bank of England and country paper, nearly the whole of the gold had been shoved out of circulation, whilst the same disposition and motives to increase the issues of paper still continued, the effect of any such further increase would be more rapidly and seriously felt in the diminished value of our remaining currency. By an unfortunate coincidence of circumstances, a disposition to apply for a great increase of discounts was excited in the mercantile world, much about the same time when the greatest part of our gold had already been driven away; and the facility with which these discounts were effected, must have contributed, in this state of things, to accelerate the depreciation of our currency.

I cannot help observing, on this occasion, that I have lately seen, with regret, that an issue of seven-shilling pieces (I hope to a very limited amount) has been made by the Bank. Such issues of coin can answer no good purpose, so long as the value of their paper is kept materially below PAR; for it is impossible that gold should continue in circulation, and the quantity of it remaining in the hands of the Bank is thus fruitlessly diminished.

The stamped dollars, though issued at five shillings each, which is somewhat more than their value at the present price of silver, will in like manner, (as indeed they do every day) though from a different reason, disappear. I say from a different reason, because it is true that for a one-pound note you may purchase more silver bullion than is contained in four stamped dollars. But each of these dollars, now worth about 4*s.* 9*d.*, is a substitute in circulation for five shillings of our silver coin, worth upon an average about 3*s.*—Any man, therefore, who exchanges five of these shillings for a dollar, gains about sixty *per cent.* —The profit on the purchase of silver bullion would be somewhat greater; but the dollar is preferred, because it is in the way of the shillings which would otherwise in a great degree soon cease to be current in circulation. This is no imaginary case, but a practice which, more or less, is going on every day.—So long as our silver currency shall be suffered to continue in its present state, the industry and ingenuity of individuals, however restrained by law, will not be wanting to keep up and supply its circulation. This debased currency will drive away any other which under the same denomination, possesses a much greater intrinsic value, just as our paper drives away the gold.

time, above the Mint price. Guineas, notwithstanding the law, were immediately melted, and the bars sold to the Bank at the advanced price: whilst other guineas were demanded from them, which were melted in their turn, if the difference of price lasted so long; giving to the melter a profit equal to that difference, and to the Bank a warning to reduce the amount of their paper.* Thus the gold coin did not go abroad, and though small quantities of it were occasionally melted down, no scarcity of coin was ever felt for any length of time.

Much less would it have gone abroad within these two last years if the demand and use for gold in this country had continued the same; or if the Bank price had at all corresponded to the market price: for it appears, by the evidence annexed to the report of the Bullion Committee, that, owing to political circumstances, the expense and risk of transporting gold to the Continent have been more than double what they were before the year 1797; and it must be obvious that any increased charge, in this respect, operates as a tax to discourage exportation.†

For these two last years, therefore, if the restriction law had not been in force, we should have had a greater security against our coin being exported, than at any former period: but, owing to that law, and to the consequent conduct of the Bank, a certain exportation has taken place, and will be continued, more or less, so long as the same circumstances shall continue, in spite of those laws, by which we in vain endeavour to restrain it. Those laws, indeed, it might be easily shewn, would be prejudicial to the public interest, if

---

* On this subject, the reader is referred to Mr. THORNTON's "*Essay on Paper Credit.*" *Ante* Page 215, &c.

† Owing to a great proportion of our guineas being locked up in the Bank, or hoarded by individuals, to the difficulty of collecting such as are still in circulation; to the expense, probably, of purchasing them at a premium, and the charge and risk of sending them abroad: the whole quantity of our gold exported has not, I conceive, been very large, and certainly not to such an amount as there would be any difficulty in replacing by purchases in the market here, or in the foreign markets which are open to us. I should very much doubt whether the quantity of gold which has been exported, by an evasion of the law, can exceed from two to three millions sterling.

they could be made effectual. Failing in their object, they are still highly objectionable, as holding out a strong temptation to perjury. On this ground alone, their repeal would be desirable. They are inconsistent with the true principles of commerce, and with the long established policy of the most enlightened commercial states of Europe;* —states, whose currency, amidst all the political calamities, and military exactions, to which they have been subject, for the last fifteen years, has suffered no debasement, nor ever made way for a system of paper currency, not convertible into specie at the option of the holder. Respecting these laws, all that I have further to observe, at present, is, that, however desirable it may be that the gold coin, which has been exported within these last two years, had been kept at home by a different system of policy; the eagerness for enforcing those laws, recently manifested by the very persons, who see, in the present system of our currency, nothing but sound wisdom and national advantage, appears peculiarly whimsical and absurd. Under this system, gold, a commodity of universal value, and of which we formerly possessed a great deal, ceases to be of use here, except to a very limited amount. Yet, in proportion as the system, which they applaud, becomes every day more complete, do they feel a perverse, but unavailing anxiety to keep at home so much dead and unproductive capital, instead of allowing it to be exchanged abroad for other commodities, for which there is a beneficial use and demand in this country.

So long as the present system is persevered in, there can be very little doubt but that the quantity of our gold coin will rather diminish, and that the small amount which still remains in circulation, if not hoarded, will be exported. Fortunately, there is quite as little doubt that, whenever, by the termination of this system, gold shall become again, *in fact*, what it is now *in law,—the foundation and standard of our currency*, it will again make its appearance; and that

* Such as Holland and Hamburgh. A similar policy prevails in the United States of America; whilst Spain and Portugal, who possess the mines from which the precious metals are drawn, have always endeavoured by the severest penalties, and always in vain, to prevent their being exported.

when we shall have a use for it, we shall be at no loss to procure a supply adequate to the demand.

Bullion is a commodity for which we must pay, as we do for any other which we want. But, for the same reason that, of all articles of trade, it is that which it is the most difficult for us to keep at home by any operation of law, now that it is not in demand; so would it be that which it would be impossible for the intervention of foreign powers to prevent us from importing, in proportion to the use and demand which we might have for it here. If a supply be necessary for our circulation, it must be procured, and may be procured, by an exchange of other commodities which we can spare, just in the same way as hemp, for instance, an article of which it is at least as much the interest of our enemies to intercept the supply. But, in as much as gold in the state of coin is so much capital engaged in an unproductive though necessary employment, it cannot be the wish of any man conversant with this subject, to proscribe the circulation of paper, or not to allow and even countenance it to the fullest extent; only taking care that all such circulation should be concurrent with the standard coin of the realm, and that such paper should be kept invariably at PAR, by being constantly exchangeable for that coin at the option of the holder.

It will be objected to me, perhaps, that, in this argument, I appear to have assumed that guineas were proscribed and excluded from circulation; whereas, they are still current at their standard price. This objection naturally brings me to the other main defence of those who stand up for the undiminished value of Bank notes: namely, "that commodities have but one price, whether paid for in "gold, or Bank paper; and, consequently, that the latter "cannot be depreciated."

This argument is altogether fallacious: whilst the fact on which it is founded affords the real explanation of the disappearance of our gold.—That our gold coin is not cried down and prohibited, is unquestionably true: and that the value of the gold contained in a guinea, in its state of coin, and when used as currency, is only $\frac{1}{20}$ more than that of a pound note, is not denied.—But then the question is this—Is Bank paper or gold our *standard?* If paper, then the value of a guinea ought to be measured by *it*; and the *denomination* of the guinea being fixed by law at only one shilling more than a pound note, its value can only be $\frac{1}{20}$ more than that of the note, be the latter worth what it may.—If gold, as I contend, and as I have been all along contending, then a one-pound note ought to be exchangable for $\frac{20}{21}$ parts of the *quantity* of gold contained in a guinea.—That it is not so exchangable is undisputed.—That, measured by this standard, Bank paper is depreciated, is undeniable: and it is only by making that paper a nominal standard, under the protection of law, that the value of coin exchanged for commodities, in the ordinary dealings of the community, becomes referable to this fictitious standard. The consequence is, that our coin is depreciated as *currency* to a level with the paper with which it circulates;—that twenty guineas, for instance, circulating upon this footing, lose as *currency* the value of all the gold which they contain above the quantity which might be purchased in the market by twenty-one Bank notes of one pound each.*

---

* The very able and elaborate essay of Mr. Thornton "On the Nature and Effects of Paper Credit," was published in 1802.

In this work, to which I have already had occasion to refer, the reader will find the true principles of political economy united with the practical, I might almost say hereditary, knowledge of a well informed merchant, and the extensive experience of a great London banker. In applying these principles to the actual state of our circulation in 1802, Mr. Thornton was led to the satisfactory conclusion, that, from the date of the restriction up to that period, our currency had not been materially depreciated;—perhaps not at all. This was the fair deduction from the facts to which his principles were then applied. From the application of the same principles to a different state of facts, such as were, at that time, matter of supposition only, the depreciation of our currency, it was shewn by Mr. Thornton, would be the necessary inference. The case which he then supposed, is now realized in all its parts. Every argument by which he proved in 1802 that our paper was not more than *sufficient*, equally proves its *excess* in 1810. But Mr. Thornton did not even stop here. In 1802, he appears almost to have fore-

No wonder then that guineas cannot be retained in circulation. By melting down, or by exportation, the gold they contain is restored to its intrinsic value, and relieved from the depreciation attached to it by law in its state of currency.

Laws, however severe, cannot alter the inherent and essential qualities, which determine the relations of value. They may, indeed, impose the same *denomination* upon values essentially different, but the difference will not be the less perceived; for no restraint upon human actions can permanently or effectually countervail the nature of things. When, therefore, the currency of a country consists, partly of gold of standard weight, and the remainder of a paper currency, in *fact* depreciated, but clothed by *law* with the character of a *legal tender*, the *denomination* fixed for such paper currency being the same as for the coin, the latter will have an irresistible tendency to escape from the depreciation in which it is by law retained, so long as it continues in the character of coin; and, either by melting or exportation, it will recover its intrinsic value.

This doctrine will, perhaps, be best illustrated by reference to a remarkable period of our history, and to the pro-

---

seen and anticipated some of the leading objections which would be set up against his conclusions in 1810:—this in particular;—that the deterioration of our gold coin to the level of the depreciation of our paper, would be confidently offered as a proof that the latter was not depreciated. His words are these:—"*Our coin itself, when paper is "depreciated, passes not for what the gold in it is worth, but at the paper "price, though this is not generally observed to be the case. It is the main-"tenance of our general exchanges, or, in other words, it is the agreement of "the Mint price with the bullion price of gold, which seems to be the true "proof that the circulating paper is not depreciated.*"

It is highly fortunate for the country at this moment, that the Bullion Committee had the benefit of Mr. THORNTON's most active assistance, and not less so, that the legislature possesses in him, not only a member unconnected with party, but one intimately acquainted with the whole business of banking, with all the details of commercial credit, and all the bearings of our money system.

The practical use of such knowledge in public life cannot be more forcibly illustrated than by stating, that the country is already indebted to Mr. THORNTON for the suggestions contained in the second report of the committee of Finance respecting the Bank. The consequence of those suggestions has been a saving to the public exceeding 250,000*l.* per annum.

ceedings of the English Parliament at a period to which, by common consent, Englishmen look back as a time when the theory of our government, in all its parts, was best understood, and the principles of justice and good faith, on which all free governments must rest, were most scrupulously practised:—a period illustrated by great names, both in the science and in the practice of politics, and which has this further recommendation to our attention, that it resembles our own times in one striking particular,—that of having been distinguished by a most anxious and energetic struggle for our independent existence, against the power and pretensions of France. I refer to the reign of King WILLIAM.

Towards the end of the 17th century, the current coin of this country had been reduced, by clipping and other practices, about 30 per cent. below the standard of the Mint. At that time, the pieces, new from the Mint, had no more value as *currency* than this debased coin: though no man, I apprehend, could now by any sophistry, however ingenious, convince, either himself or his neighbour, that the latter was really of the same value as the former. One consequence was, that the pieces of full weight disappeared as fast as they were issued, just as our guineas *now* disappear; another, that the exchange was permanently from 20 to 30 per cent. against this country, as it is *now* from 15 to 20; a third, that guineas (silver* being the then *legal tender*, and the silver coin that which was debased) rose to 30

* For an account of the circumstances which, in the course of the last century, gradually led to the substitution of gold for silver, as the sole *legal standard and tender*, I beg leave to refer the reader to the very clear and satisfactory treatise on our coin, contained in a letter from the late Earl of LIVERPOOL to the King. But this substitution, however produced, has taken place without any alteration in the *weight* or *fineness* of either of the precious metals in our respective coins, and, consequently, without creating any difference in their relative value to each other, as fixed by law, and the long established regulations of our Mint. It is obvious therefore, from this statement, as well as from the facts I have already mentioned, respecting the market price of silver, that the change in our *legal tender* has nothing to do with the depreciation of our paper; and that, under the like circumstances of excess in the amount of Bank issues, that depreciation would have been just the same, if no such change had occurred.

shillings each, as they have *now* risen to upwards of 24, measured in our new *legal tender* Bank paper: and a fourth, that silver which could be sworn off for exportation was, as *exportable* gold is now, at a premium.

But how little do nations profit by experience? The same fallacious explanations which are *now* given, were then offered to the public. The same delusive plans of relief were suggested—The *balance of trade* or the *balance of payments* was said to be against us. To this was attributed the unfavourable course of exchange: to the unfavourable course of exchange, the exportation and melting down of the *standard coin,* and the high price of bullion at home. The remedy proposed was, in the language of the day, "*to raise the value of our money,*" with a reference to the scarcity, and consequent high price of bullion: and the specific plan suggested was, to coin an ounce of silver into 6*s.* 3*d.* instead of 5*s.* 2*d.* These doctrines and this plan were supported by official characters of the greatest reputation and practical knowledge, and by persons of the most extensive experience in trade. Fortunately, the fallacy of them was detected and exposed, and the Government of that day was rescued from the adoption of a pretended remedy, which would have perpetuated the injustice, and aggravated the calamities for which it was confidently offered as a cure.*

The present state of our currency is, in its principle, and in its consequences, precisely the same as the case which I have now described. The effect is the same, whether the currency of any country being wholly metallic, consists in part of a coin, of full standard weight, and in part of a coin, which under the same *denomination,* should be materially deteriorated either in *weight* or *fineness*;—or in part of coin

* I would earnestly wish to recommend to my readers to look at the writings of Mr. Locke on this subject.—The arguments by which that great man was enabled to convince Lord Somers of the real nature of the evil, are worthy of their attention. The sanction of two such names, and of the Parliament of 1695, which had the wisdom and firmness to adopt their advice, in spite of all the interested misrepresentations of that period, will shew that the doctrines which I have attempted to establish cannot fairly be considered as either new or dangerous.

of the former description, and in part of a depreciated paper, discharging the functions of money in the same manner, with the same *denomination*, and under the same authority of law, as the light coin.

It being then, as I conceive, placed beyond all doubt that our paper currency is depreciated; that its depreciation is to be ascribed altogether to an excess* in the issue of that paper, and that without the restriction law no such excess could have existed, or at least have been permanently maintained; it follows, that the repeal of that temporary law is the obvious remedy for this evil. The precautions which it may be necessary to observe in removing that restriction, and the precise period when it ought to cease, are points upon which it would ill become me to anticipate the decision of Parliament.

I shall content myself with offering a few observations on the practicability of the measure, and with noticing such objections as have either occurred, or been suggested to me.

* It can scarcely be necessary to protest against any idea of the depreciation being, in any degree, to be ascribed to a want of confidence in the solidity of the Bank. A corporation originally possessed of a great capital, since increased by immense profits, which never makes an advance but upon the best securities, and which might call in the whole of those advances within three months, can never be exposed to any such suspicion.

Paper MONEY issued in the name of the state, in aid of its own Exchequer, and in compulsory payment of its expenses, such as has been resorted to in various parts of the world, is happily unknown to this country. Such paper is in the nature of a *forced loan*, which, in itself, implies a want of credit. From this circumstance alone, it falls below PAR; and its first depreciation is soon accelerated by the necessity of augmenting the issues in proportion to their diminished value. Thus an excess of paper co-operates with public mistrust, to augment its depreciation. Such was the fate of the paper issued by the American Congress in the war for their independence; more recently of the *assignats* in France: and such is now the state of the paper of the Banks of Vienna and Petersburgh. Whereas, the state of our currency, in regard to its diminished value, is no other than it would be if our present circulation, being retained to the same amount, were, by some sudden spell, all changed to gold, and, by another spell, not less surprising, such part of that gold, as, by its excess, created a proportionate diminution in its value here, with reference to its value in other countries, could not by exportation, or otherwise, find its way out of our separate circulation. It is excess not relievable by exportation.

In considering the great and general importance to the whole country of reverting as soon as possible to the former system of cash payments, it must be recollected that there are two parties more nearly and particularly concerned in the present discussion, namely—the Bank, and the commercial interest.

With respect to the former, it may perhaps be inconsiderately supposed, that, in case any specific, though remote, period should be fixed for the termination of the restriction, the interests of that corporation would lead the Directors, within the shortest possible time after the passing of a law for that purpose, to reduce the amount of their issues, until their notes should have been so raised in value, as to enable them to purchase Gold at a price not exceeding that of the Mint. Unquestionably it is in their power to effect such a diminution very rapidly. If the separate advantages of any part of the community could, in a matter of this importance, be held distinct from that interest which must be common to all, in guarding against any general pressure of public distress, those classes who suffer most by the depreciation, without deriving, even indirectly, any profit from it, and not the Bank, would be most benefited by their pursuing this line of conduct It is true, however, that, neither the great profits which the Proprietors of Bank stock have derived from the restriction, nor any circumstances by which they stand connected with the Government, or the trade of the country, would, of themselves, entitle the public to expect that the Directors should make any positive and considerable sacrifice of the interests of their constituents. But how far would this be the case, should they pursue a more moderate course? I assume that, in the event of a period for the opening being fixed, the Bank would find it necessary to buy gold. In order to purchase it they would be obliged to give the market price; and I admit that the difference between that price and that of the Mint would, ultimately, be so much loss to the Bank. But then, independently of the profits which they have made of late years by an enlarged circulation, unattended with any sacrifice for the purchase of gold; it is obvious, that, in whatever proportion above the Mint price their future purchases might be made, in the same proportion must their issues, bearing interest, be above the amount which ought to be in circulation, or which, in fact, they would be able to maintain in circulation, if the restriction did not exist. Suppose one million in gold to be bought at an average of *ten* per cent. above the Mint price, in the course of the first year after the Bank shall have received notice of a definite period for the resumption of cash payments:—if, during that year, the Bank should have in circulation, upon an average, two millions of paper, beyond the proportion, which, but for the restriction, it would have been able to issue, the immediate and accruing profit from the interest on the latter sum, would be exactly equal to the contingent loss upon the purchase of the gold, when cash payments should be resumed.

Without, therefore, exposing the Proprietors of Bank stock to any material loss, or probably to any loss at all, the Directors may effect a reduction in their issues, gradually and slowly, by apportioning that reduction over nearly the whole time which the law may assign to them to prepare for the opening. In the same manner they may, during the whole of that period, and without forcing the market, be adding to their stock of gold, of which the nominal price would continue to fall, in proportion as the amount of their notes was brought nearer to its proper level. This balance of profit, from excess of issues on the one side, and of loss upon their purchases of gold on the other, fluctuating, perhaps, in a trifling amount one way or the other, would of course cease altogether, so soon as the paper should be restored to the value it purports to represent.

The Bank, therefore, as a trading company, would have very little, or perhaps no inducement to make a sudden and violent reduction of its issues; such as might derange prices, and distress trade, or operate to the prejudice of the fair credit and legitimate dealings of the community. In all the other relations of life and public duty in which the Directors stand,—as merchants of the first eminence,—as men attached to the prosperity of their country, and studious to preserve that high estimation in which they are justly and universally held, they would find the most powerful motives for adopting a moderate and cautious line of conduct, in the reduction of their issues.

It will not escape the reader, that, in the view which I have taken of the mode in which the interests of the Bank would be affected by the necessity of purchasing gold under the present circumstances, the argument by which I have endeavoured to shew that it would be attended with no real sacrifice, is derived, not from a comparison with their present situation and advantages, but of what their situation and advantages would have been, from the circulation which they would now have been able to maintain, if no interruption had taken place in their cash payments. This, and not their present scale of profits, it must be obvious, is the fair comparison. These profits are increased, not only by an amount of issues carried beyond its proper limits; but by the Bank being relieved altogether from the necessity of purchasing gold in proportion to that circulation, or indeed of purchasing any gold at all.*

* Although the measure of the loss be different, in principle, and in degree, it is as much a diminution of profit to the Bank, to purchase gold at 3*l.* 17*s.* 10½*d.* as at 4*l.* 10*s.* or any other price. The notes issued for such purchases are the only part of their circulation from which they derive no profit. All their other issues are upon securities bearing interest. As a Bank, therefore, their policy, at all times, must be that the proportion of their notes issued for the former purpose should be as small, and for the latter as large as possible. Still better for them, if this buying of gold can be dispensed with altogether. This last advantage appears to be ensured to the Bank, so long as, by an excess of circulation, the market price of gold shall be higher than 4*l.* per ounce, which the Directors have fixed upon for their buying price. By every addition to their circulation, therefore, they not only secure to the Proprietors of Bank stock an augmentation of profit proportionate to the increase of that circulation; they also effectually guard against any drawback to that profit, by permanently maintaining the price of gold above 4*l.* per ounce. This course of proceeding is, at once, so ingenious and so simple, in its operation so effectual, and in its application so completely in the power of those who are exclusively benefited by it, so long as the restriction law shall continue, that it is not very surprising that the Proprietors of Bank stock should be disposed to resist any suggestion which touches that law; and to prefer the *sound discretion* of the Directors, unfettered by the control of cash payments.

Another difficulty may be started against the proposal for fixing a period, however distant, for the resumption of

---

Every one must be aware how very near this state of things, now openly avowed as a system, and almost claimed as a right, comes to a state of *paper* MONEY, according to the definition which has been given of *paper money*. It is paper rendered current by the authority, though not issued for the benefit of the State. It consists of loans advanced at interest: that interest being altogether for the benefit of the corporation of the Bank. I may be told, however, that there is no resemblance between Bank notes and *paper money*, because these notes circulate entirely upon *confidence*. To which I answer, that the law, which virtually makes Bank paper a *legal tender*, as much *forces* it into circulation in this country as *paper money* could be *forced* in any other country, by any law, which might, in the most direct terms, make the paper of such a country a *legal tender*. Whether the government first originate the paper money in payment of its own creditors, and *compel* all other persons to receive it from them; or whether it authorize a Bank to advance loans of such money for its own profit, and *compel* all other persons to receive it from those who obtain such advances, there is no difference as to the degree of *compulsion*. I may add, that in both cases, such paper will be received in the purchase of all commodities by a reference to the price of the precious metals in that paper; and consequently that the principle which determines the current value of Bank notes and of *paper money* respectively, is the same. *Confidence*, in the sense in which it is here used, is only the measure of that value.

I have thought it necessary to state thus much, because the assertion, "that a Bank note is never forced into circulation," is constantly put forward as an irrefragable proof that those notes cannot be depreciated. May I be allowed to ask, whether the Bank do not pay the public dividends, and whether, under the law for raising the Property Tax, they do not pay them at the rate of eighteen shillings for every twenty shillings stipulated for in the contract? What would be thought of the logic of any man who should tell the public creditor, that he is not compelled to take eighteen shillings in the pound, because he is at liberty to abstain from receiving his dividend at all?—But if he does receive his dividend, he is compelled to leave two shillings in the pound, or *ten* per cent. in the hands of the Bank, in trust for the use of the State.—He is equally compelled to receive the remaining eighteen shillings in Bank paper, subject, however, to the same option of not receiving them at all. A payment in such paper is, at this moment, a virtual deduction from his dividend of three shillings more, or of 15 per cent; just as much a real and a *forced* deduction, as if it were made directly from eighteen shillings of *standard* money, under all the powers and penalties of the Property Act. The public creditor, therefore, receives fifteen shillings in the pound of *standard sterling money* and no more. If the Bank of England were, to-morrow, to issue such an amount of notes as would reduce the *paper pound* in value to one shillingsworth of gold, every man would be *compelled*, just as much as he is *now*, when it is still worth seventeen shillings, to receive those paper pounds for twenty shillings each.

Preposterous as this extreme case may appear, there is no security, as the law now stands, against such an issue, except in the *discretion* of the Bank.

cash payments, namely—that the Directors of the Bank, notwithstanding any decision of Parliament, may increase the amount of their paper, or, at least, may not so reduce that amount, as to be prepared for the opening, when the time that may be fixed for it shall arrive: and that, by this expedient, they might compel Parliament to grant them a further term in the restriction.

That any provision which Parliament can make for terminating the restriction will be so far incomplete, that it will not necessarily carry along with it the means of enforcing its own object, is certainly true. This objection, however, to the specific period suggested by the Bullion Committee, would equally apply to any other proposal founded on the principle of assigning some fixed determination to the operation of the restriction law. But this difficulty, like that which would arise from an over-rapid diminution of Bank paper, rests on a supposition, possible certainly, but most improbable. They are both extreme cases.—Neither of them stated, nor contemplated, by those who concur in the principles and suggestions of the Report: though intimated in language too plain to be misunderstood, by those who profess themselves most anxious to prevent any change in the present system. As far as these insinuations affect the character of the Bank, they may do mischief, as coming from persons professing to be friendly to that institution. The conduct of the Directors, under whatever arrangement may be finally adopted by the wisdom of Parliament, will, I am confident, fully shew that all such insinuations are entirely unfounded.

With respect to the manner in which our trade may be affected by the resumption of cash payments, no argument has been offered to shew, and no statement, I am persuaded, can be produced to prove, that any serious difficulty or pressure is likely to arise, if the excess of our circulation shall be withdrawn in that gradual, cautious, and almost imperceptible manner, in which this change may be effected, in case two years shall be allowed for the purpose. This, beside, is a period within which every adventure now pending will probably be completed, and every credit now outstanding brought to maturity. Every merchant, consequently, will have ample notice, and full time to regulate his dealings, and to bring his affairs within such a compass, compared to his capital and state of credit, as he may think prudent and necessary. No one will be taken by surprise.—There will be no sudden fall in the price of goods;—no rapid fluctuations in the markets.—Our currency, I am sanguine enough to hope, may be brought back to its sound state, if not altogether without difficulty in some quarters; at least with much less difficulty than has been experienced, within these few last months, from the consequences of the speculation and over-trading, created and fostered by the excess of that currency.

Some persons, wholly unacquainted with the nature of commerce, or with any of the details or bearings of the subject, I am told, dismiss the Bullion Report with a short remark, "that it recommends what is impossible:—for that gold cannot be procured." To this, I think, I have already given a sufficient answer, unless the principles which regulate the purchase and sale of the precious metals are now become altogether different from those which have hitherto applied invariably to all commodities which can be the objects of barter. I may, however, further observe, that gold does not form the basis of the currency of any other country;—that the quantity of gold in Europe is not less now, and is probably greater, than it was at any former period; that the *price has not risen on the Continent*;—that it is to be purchased in the markets there; in the markets of Africa and America; in our own market. If, in these markets, the Bank will buy progressively, and, through proper agents, whatever gold bullion may be obtained without raising the price against itself, a very large quantity may be procured in two years, and, upon the whole, at a fair price. But then, in order to ascertain what is a *fair price* for *gold*, we must take its relative value* to *silver* such as it now exists.

* Supposing that value, as it appears by the evidence of Mr. Grefulke and others, to be on the continent 15½ to one: then 15½ ounces

It is no secret, that the Bank, soon after the Restriction, bought and imported a very considerable supply of gold. It has since issued very little. To these facts, I may add my confident opinion, (though this of course can be only matter of opinion) that it is, therefore, actually possessed of a large stock of gold. This stock, even without any addition, would, of course, be brought nearer to the proportion which it ought to bear to the amount of notes issued, as the latter is gradually diminished.

A great quantity of gold, which is now hoarded, would also make its appearance, if guineas were restored to their use and value as currency. In this respect, the country is in the same situation as it was in King WILLIAM'S time, when our metallic currency was so much depreciated. Before the determination to restore that currency to its standard, pieces of full weight were as scarce as guineas are *now;* but when that determination was taken and carried into effect, a great quantity of good money, which had been hoarded, was brought back into circulation.

In opposition to all these grounds of confidence, that the difficulty of resuming cash payments will not be so great as is generally imagined, it has been stated, that the increase of our commerce and of our revenue requires a vast increase of currency.

It might easily be shewn, indeed it is obvious, that in a country at once rich and free, in which, from these advantages, joined to the long enjoyment of public tranquillity, *credit,* either verbal or written, transferable or dormant, is extended to all the transactions of society, operations to a much greater amount may be carried on with a proportion of currency which would be altogether insufficient for the same operations in another country, not possessing these benefits,

---

of silver are equal to 3*l.* 17*s.* 10½d. or to an ounce of gold. In Bank paper 15¼ ounces of standard silver, at the present market price, which is about 5*s.* 10¼*d.* per ounce, cannot be purchased for less than 91 shillings.

or in which they might be less firmly established, or less amply enjoyed. In this country, where they are all united in the highest degree, the ingenuity of individuals, especially of our merchants and bankers, is constantly at work, to devise new means of substituting credit for the actual intervention of money, and to find fresh expedients, either to supply its place, or to economize the use of it, in their dealings with one another. If this were a proper occasion for such a detail, it might easily be shewn, that in this way, many improvements have been made, of late years, in the mode of carrying on the banking and commercial concerns of the metropolis, all tending to introduce a greater economy in the use of money. The quantity of currency, therefore, requisite for the purpose of exchanging and distributing the commodities of a country, is not to be measured by the extent of its wealth and commerce, compared with the wealth and commerce of other countries, or with its own, at former periods. Neither is that quantity to be measured by the public revenue. In proof of this assertion, as applicable to the present state of this country, it is not necessary to go into a minute statement of the course of proceeding at the Exchequer, although it is by such a detail that the proof would be most completely established. It is sufficient to state, that in the evening of each day, the whole receipt of the revenue, within that day, is carried to the Bank; and that from the Bank the whole amount of such receipt may be, and probably is, sent into circulation again on the following day, in the discount of commercial or Government securities. If the daily receipt of the Exchequer be, upon an average, increased from twenty to one hundred thousand pounds, it by no means follows that any thing like a proportionate increase, or indeed that any very considerable increase in the whole amount of the circulation would be requisite, in consequence of this increase in the revenue. Did any man, before the Restriction, ever dream of enquiring into the numerical amount of Bank issues, and of regulating and adjusting that amount by the quarterly account of the Consolidated fund, or by the annual return of our Imports and Exports? What is the link which connects the value of paper, regulated in its amount by some such numerical scale, with that of the precious metals? By what standard of value is that scale to be increased or diminished? Is that standard to be sought for in artificial checks and banking regulations—*bye*-laws of the Bank Corporation, made not for the object of restraining their loans, but for their own protection against the risk of insolvency in those to whom such loans are advanced?

But even if it were admitted that a much greater numerical account of money is necessary in consequence of the increased revenue and commerce of the country, it by no means follows that this augmentation would require to be made in the metallic part of our currency. Circulating credit, either in the shape of Bank notes, or in some other description of security, will always be preferred to coin in all the large operations of trade. For all considerable payments, paper possesses many obvious advantages over metallic currency. In other respects it is also more convenient. The actual holder of a note, convertible at will into cash, knows that the guineas which that note represents, and which it can always command, are not liable to be under weight, or to become so by wear in his possession; while every person who may receive that note in succession, equally knows that, without the trouble of weighing, or the risk of deception, it conveys the same title to him.

The Bullion Committee proposes that the small notes of the Bank of England should not be withdrawn till a certain period after the resumption of cash payments. If this precaution should be adopted, I have no doubt that many of those small notes will continue to circulate till the end of that period, from the preference, which, in many instances, will be given to them over gold.*

* The withdrawing of the small notes is a measure suggested by considerations of public expediency which ought to outweigh perhaps the economical advantages which the country derives from the use of them. It is not necessary at present to examine the question in this comparative view, although I own that I very much doubt whether

It has been suggested, as another objection, against terminating the Restriction law, that a state of circumstances might, by possibility, arise, in which it might be proper to re-enact that law.

I admit that it is possible, in the present extraordinary state of the world, that, in the course of events, a recurrence of similar circumstances, of general alarm, commercial pressure, and stagnation of individual credit, such as existed in 1797, may, at some future period, again compel the Government of this country to afford to the Bank a temporary protection against the demands which may be made upon it for gold. For it must be obvious, that no Bank, however cautious and prudent, can possibly exist, either with advantage to itself, or to the country, unless its circulation of Paper, upon an average, shall considerably exceed the amounts of its deposits, in cash or bullion, for meeting the possible demands that may be made upon it. The consequences of sudden public alarm cannot be measured. They baffle all ordinary calculation. Cash is then withdrawn, not because the circulation is excessive, but by the country Banks and the town Bankers, for the purpose of meeting possible demands upon them, and by the community at large, either directly from the Bank, or indirectly through the former channels, for the purpose of hoarding, from the dread of some imaginary or contingent danger. In such a crisis, every reduction in the amount of Bank paper, is so far from checking the drain, that it aggravates the general distress; because the gold which is taken out of the Bank, instead of being substituted in circulation for the notes withdrawn from it, is for the most part locked up, and thus, in proportion as the stagnant and straightened circulation wants life and aid, it becomes every day more embarrassed, whilst each new calamity produced by such a state of things, contributes to spread and increase the general apprehension. It is therefore manifest, that by a possible combination of circumstances, the Bank might be driven to part with its

country Banks ought not to be allowed to issue notes as low as two pounds.

last guinea, not only without having checked the drain, but with the certainty of increasing it, in proportion as the amount of their notes was diminished. At such a moment the preservation of the Bank from actual failure, though an important, is but a secondary consideration:—that of the country is the first. The possible cases, however, which may call for such an intervention of power, are not capable of being foreseen or defined by law. The necessity may not occur again: if it should, the application of the remedy must be left to those who may then be at the head of affairs, subject to their own responsibility, and to the judgment of Parliament. But I must observe, that in proportion as the knowledge to be derived from the experience of 1797, on the one hand, and of the two last years on the other, shall be more generally spread through the country, and as the principles of our money system and of circulating credit shall be better known and more generally understood, will the recurrence of such a crisis be rendered less probable, the danger of it more easily met and overcome, and the nature of the remedy, as well as the extent to which it may be used, more fully ascertained. It is a possible, temporary, and transient interruption of the ordinary course of our circulation, of which we are compelled to meet the risk, in order to insure to ourselves the habitual, permanent, and incalculable advantages of an extensive and secure circulating paper credit. This is the lesson we should learn from the use of the Restriction in 1797, on the one hand; and from the inconveniences to which the abuse of it has led on the other.

It has been objected, that the consequences derived from the arguments which prove the depreciation of our currency, if pushed to their full extent, would go to establish a title in persons, who suffer from being paid in that depreciated currency, to some compensation for the difference between the payment received, and the amount in standard money of their just and legal demands. According to the principles of strict justice, it may indeed be impossible to deny that this compensation is due to them. The injury which they now sustain, by being paid in Bank notes, is precisely of the same description as if they were compelled to receive in payment clipped and light coin. In the latter case, every man would agree that such coin ought to pass, not by *tale*, and according to its *denomination*, but by *weight* only. To the former, the same principle might apply. But no arguments are to be looked at with more suspicion than those, which, from the acknowledged impossibility of attaining to perfection, would infer, that it is absurd to attempt the nearest possible approximation to it. If a system be erroneous, the very consequences of its errors generally constitute the most powerful impediment to a correction of it.—But if that impediment were to be held conclusive, the result would be no other than this—that the errors of inadvertency, when they have prevailed for a certain time, are, upon a discovery of their nature, to be persevered in, from deliberation and choice. In the present instance, the result would be, that, a certain degree of injustice having been innocently done, and a certain degree of injury unavoidably suffered, the awakened consciousness of that injustice and that injury, should only lead to an advised confirmation of the system by which they have been produced. Any man who will give the slightest consideration to the subject, will see that it is not possible to redress the inconveniences which have been sustained; and to every man of sober understanding "*that it is impossible,*" is a sufficient answer. But the future is within our power. The legislature can prevent the continuance and augmentation of the evil; and it is, therefore, its bounden duty to do so.

I am not sure that some persons will not be found, who, however unable to deny that the depreciation of our paper is proved beyond all doubt, will still be disposed to maintain that the evil of such a state of things, great as it is, is more than compensated by some greater public advantages. It will be incumbent upon them to shew what those advantages are, that ought, in their judgment and in their morality, to outweigh the strongest claims of justice, and the plainest dictates of public honour; and distinctly to point out to what extent, and by what classes of the community, they are enjoyed. I purposely forbear again adverting to the various classes and descriptions of persons, subsisting upon fixed incomes, whom I have already shewn to be pre-eminently (though they are not exclusively) sufferers from the present state of things.

First, then, is it for the benefit of the landed interest that the present system should be continued? Surely this part of the community is too just to wish for profit to be obtained at the expense of others, even their nearest relations or friends; too enlightened to countenance a system which, progressive in its nature, would, if unchecked, ultimately lead to the subversion of all property.* One large class of landed proprietors indeed—those whose lands are actually under lease—being for the remainder of those leases within the description of persons of fixed income, suffer in the same manner as other persons which that class comprehends.—They even suffer more;—inasmuch as the reserved rent is generally subject to repairs and other outgoings, the expense of which is of course increased in proportion to the depreciation of the currency in which it is paid. In such a state of things, landlords will be naturally disinclined to grant new leases. Is this the way in which the cheapness of paper is to contribute to the improvement of their estates? So far from it that every landlord must be satisfied, by a moment's reflection, that the advancement of agriculture is best secured by holding out a fair inducement to the employment of capital in this most essential branch of national industry; and that it is, by the real improvement of the land, and not by a mere nominal increase in the annual rent, that he must measure the rise in

* If ever there was a proposition universally true, this has proved itself to be so in all countries in which *paper currency*, from any combination of circumstances, has been suffered to grow into a *paper* MONEY.

the value of his estate. If, by good husbandry, the produce of an estate be doubled, its real value will be proportionably increased; but, if the produce remain the same, and the increased rent, in Bank paper, be not exchangeable for a greater *quantity* of gold than the landlord was intitled to receive under the old rent, the real value of the estate will be any thing but augmented by such a rise in the rent.*

Secondly, is the commercial class really benefited by this state of things? It is impossible to deny that some, and, perhaps, many individuals, connected with trade, have derived advantage from the greatly increased facility which has prevailed, within these two or three last years, of obtaining credit upon the discount of commercial securities; and that a few, who have been fortunate, in watching their opportunities, and in boldly availing themselves of this facility, have made great and rapid profits by their speculations. But whether the mercantile body of this country, considered in the aggregate, has reaped any substantial advantage, or will ultimately derive any benefit, from the super-abundance of paper currency, is to me at least, a much more doubtful question. It is impossible for any observer of events accurately to discriminate between the adventures to which this excess has given rise, or, at least, a principal aid and support, and those which have their foundation in the mercantile capital and industry of the country, and would have been carried to the same, or, perhaps, to a greater extent, if the amount of discounts and circulation had been kept within those limits which are compatible with the sound state and undepreciated value of our currency. That some speculations which, it may be fairly presumed, belong to the former

* The price of land (either to rent or sell) like that of all other objects, is, of course, raised in proportion to the depreciation of our currency. But a great part of the increased value which landed property has acquired within these last ten years, is, I believe, fortunately for the prosperity of this country, of a more durable and substantial nature; and is fairly to be accounted for by the great improvements made in the science and practice of agriculture; by which the productions of our soil have been both ameliorated in quality and increased in quantity.

class, have turned out unfortunate; whilst others, which are still pending, are of precarious issue, is, I am afraid, an opinion but too well founded, and one to which, I apprehend, that recent and passing events have made many converts among those who have the best practical knowledge on these subjects.

The convulsions of the world have thrown a principal part of the trade of Europe and America into new channels. The first who explored those channels, and had the address to elude the difficulties and dangers which beset the approaches to them, were eminently successful. Their exports were inadequate to the demand abroad; their returns unequal to our wants at home. Great profits were the result. This result became generally known, and the temptation was irresistible. Not only the original adventurers, in most instances, re-embarked largely in the same pursuits; but hosts of new ones sprung up in every corner of the kingdom: every one, anticipating a gain like that of the first speculators, became of course, anxious to procure credit to the greatest possible amount—negotiable securities were multiplied in every shape—discount was sought for in every quarter—ingenuity was at work to multiply the means of obtaining and affording accommodation.* So long as the sales were

* It has been said, that any step which may be taken towards the resumption of cash payments, would immediately compel the Bank Directors to reduce, in a very great degree, the amount of their accommodation to the merchants; and some persons have gone so far as to insinuate that they would probably cease to discount altogether. The abettors of the present system have used this language with much success, as the means of creating an alarm in the mercantile world. To me there appears to be no necessity for making any sudden or violent diminution in their discounts; indeed there is no reason why they might not be continued to the same amount as at present. Every facility that could be required would, no doubt, be afforded by Parliament in this respect. The whole of the six millions, advanced in consideration of the deposits of public money, if necessary, might be repaid; and, instead of this advance, an annual sum might be paid by the Bank to the public equivalent to the saving on the interest of this loan. This repayment would afford to the Bank more than a sufficient latitude for gradually reducing their circulation without any diminution whatever of their commercial discounts.—But this is a narrow view of the question—The root of the evil is not in the discounts of the Bank.—Their power of giving an increased accommodation to the trade

brisk; so long as the demand, both for raw materials and manufactured goods, continued to increase, and prices to rise in the home market, every thing went on smoothly, as much to the satisfaction of the manufacturer and merchant, as of those to whom they were indebted for the discount of their bills. It was then that all these parties discovered to what a degree the suspension of cash payments afforded facility and security to the extension of this description of credit: but the currency, in which the discounts were effected, became depreciated in proportion to the rapid increase in its amount. If trade had continued in its ancient and accustomed course, and the spirit of rash adventure had not been excited by new prospects of extravagant gain, there is reason to believe that the expense of discount, aided by the strict adherence of the Bank to its long established regulations, and by the reluctance to engage in Country Banks, which had been created by the disasters of 1793 and 1797, might have afforded, for some time longer, (as they had for several years after the restriction was first imposed) a sufficient guard against any very material excess, or any great depreciation of our currency. But, on this occasion, the Directors of the Bank appeared to have considered the increased eagerness for dis-

---

of the country, and the extent to which it is now carried, depend more on the greatly increased amount of the balances deposited by Government in their hands, and which are lent out again upon good bills of exchange, than upon the enlarged amount of their circulation. The amount of these deposits is independent of the amount of the latter, and would not be affected by its reduction, whilst the effect of that reduction, in raising the value of their paper, would be precisely the same, whether it were brought about by a diminution of their loans to Government or to individuals; because it is to the aggregate excess of their issues, and not to the particular nature of the securities on which they are made, that the depreciation is to be ascribed.—That excess affords a facility to the abuse of credit, and gives birth to wild adventures in other quarters: those, I admit, will be checked by a diminution in the total amount of their currency; although it should be effected without any diminution in the scale of commercial discounts at the Bank of England. But have we not seen enough of the ultimate effects of this artificial facility, and these forced speculations? To those who still shut their eyes to the melancholy but instructive lessons which we have lately received in this respect, it would be useless to offer any other proofs of their dangerous tendency. They would remain unconvinced, even if all the follies of the South Sea adventure, or of the Mississippi scheme, were acted over again.

count as requiring some increased indulgence on their part; and, perhaps, whilst trade appeared so flourishing, it was not unnatural that they should consult their own fair interest as bankers in this respect.

The amount of their paper was, in consequence, considerably increased, although, by the great and simultaneous augmentation in the circulation of Country Banks, the use of Bank paper beyond the limits of the metropolis became every day more circumscribed. Under these circumstances, the rise in the price of goods, which, at first, was the effect of an increased demand, was soon considerably aided by the depreciation of the currency, as well as by the power which the facility of discount afforded to new speculators (calculating upon a still further rise) of keeping back their purchases from market. Thus the diminution in the value of our currency, brought on in a great measure by this *mercantile delusion,* has, in its turn, been one of the principal means by which the latter has been kept up and supported in the home market. Many a speculation, probably, within these two last years, for which the party takes to himself the credit of commercial acuteness and great foresight, was principally founded, however unconsciously to himself at the time, in the decreasing value of our currency.

In making use of the words *mercantile delusion,* as applicable to a considerable part of the trade, which has been created and fostered, within the two or three last years, by the circumstances which I have stated: I feel that it would be incumbent upon me to offer some more enlarged explanation of the subject, if, unfortunately, many recent occurrences did not, at once, establish the facts, and justify the terms I have applied to them. In the nature of things, such a speculation could not continue universally and uninterruptedly fortunate. The markets, at first scantily supplied, would soon be overstocked. Some of the adventurers, from being too late, others, from ignorance or misconduct, extravagance or misfortune, would fail. The chain was sure to give way in some of its links — great and numerous failures are the consequence—suspicion and alarm become general — securities, hitherto negociable, can no longer find discount — many of the discounters themselves are ruined, and all put upon their guard—the markets fall—goods are forced upon sale, when all are afraid to buy; and, whilst the fortunate *few* retire upon wealth rapidly accumulated, thousands are left to lament the ruin, which, deluded by the example of such rapid success on the one hand, and tempted by the facility of overtrading on the other, they have brought upon themselves.

I may therefore be allowed to doubt, whether a very great proportion of the more recent speculators to *South America*, as well as to *Malta, Heligoland,* and the *Baltic*, do not repent that they ever became acquainted with the tempting tale of a few early adventurers, or were so easily furnished with the means of engaging in similar risks, to an extent out of all proportion, either to the amount of their capitals, or to the demand from abroad; and whether, ultimately, the legitimate advantages of commerce, as well as the real interests of the trading and manufacturing classes, will not be injured, rather than advanced, by the consequences of the protracted suspension of cash payments.

This part of the subject reminds me that a few words are still necessary respecting what is called the "*balance of payments*" with foreign countries, to which I have adverted in a former part of these observations. I then left to the reader to judge for himself how far this fashionable doctrine affords a sufficient explanation of the long-continued depression of the foreign exchange, and of the high price of Bullion at home.

That a nation, like Great Britain, possessed of great commercial capital, should afford long credits to other countries, where capital is wanting, and where the rate of interest is consequently much higher, is certainly very natural; and it is an obvious advantage to us in trade. But these credits are given in succession, and some are daily coming to maturity, whilst others are created; so that, although the different parts of the world are constantly indebted to this country, the aggregate amount of those debts cannot, in the ordinary course of things, very materially vary.

But it is obvious, that if, from any peculiar circumstances, an unusual facility of discount exists at home, whilst abroad an advance in price, far exceeding the rate of interest here, is given for goods sold upon long credits, or a proportionate abatement made upon those bought by us for ready money, the balance of debt to this country may be somewhat increased, and the exchange thereby rendered unfavourable for a short time. This fall, if our currency were not depreciated, could not exceed the expense of transporting Bullion to the Continent, or continue, as it has done, for two years. Within that period too, it may be remarked, the longest of those credits must probably have come round, and consequently there would now be an end of the argument.

Besides, the increase of foreign debt, and whatever fall of the exchange it may, at one time, have occasioned, are to be ascribed to the abundance and cheapness of our paper; for, if the Bank, when it was liable to pay its notes in cash, had enlarged its issues, till the market price of Bullion, and consequently the course of exchange, were materially affected, these circumstances would have compelled them to make a diminution in the amount of their discounts. That diminution, by rendering money more scarce at home, would have prevented merchants from extending their credits abroad, and induced them, as far as possible, to accelerate the payment of those that were becoming due. The effect would have been to assist in improving the foreign exchange, till it was restored to its proper level, and, with it, the facility of discount at home to its ordinary course. This increased *balance of debt* (on which is founded the pretended "*balance of payments,*") is therefore only a further instance of the manner in which the harmony of the whole system is destroyed by the derangement of one of its parts, and an additional reason for restoring the value of our paper currency to the standard of our coin.

I will not add to the length of this discussion by examining more in detail the manner in which the interests of the mercantile and manufacturing part of the community are likely to be affected by the continued debasement of our currency. That they are not necessarily exposed to the same injury as is cast upon the other classes of the community I am ready to admit; but then let them recollect all the ties by which they are connected with those classes, and that the durable prosperity of the one cannot be built upon the distress of the other.

The business of a merchant is to buy cheap and sell dear. His general wish is to be able, for this purpose, to command as large a credit as possible. He must consequently, upon abstract principle, be favourable to any system which is likely to give facility to the discount of commercial securities. His interest, therefore, appears to be the same as that of the banker; whose profit increases with the extension of such discounts. His skill and his success depend upon his rapidly converting credit into goods, and, thereafter, re-selling those goods at advanced prices. Generally, therefore, a merchant is a large possessor, or *creditor* of produce, and a *debtor* for a considerable part of the sum with which it was purchased. If the currency, in which that debt is to be liquidated, be progressively decreasing in value, his profit, upon every transaction, will be augmented in proportion to the increased depreciation of the currency. But is this the fair profit of trade? Are these the gains to which the unsophisticated meaning of our laws, the clearest principles of justice on which they are founded, the sacred obligations of public faith, of which they are the pledge, and the rights and interests of the whole community are to be sacrificed? Is this the description of trade, or rather of gambling, which ought to find friends among the real merchants, or advocates in the Legislature of this country?

Besides, the continued success of such a trade depends upon the progressive increase of the depreciation of our currency. In the more probable case, of a fluctuating depreciation; liable to be increased or diminished by every change in the councils of the Bank; by any extensive or sudden failures of Country Banks, or by the doubts and suspicions to which all currency, if not referable to some established and certain criterion of value, must be obnoxious, it cannot, I think, be long before every *merchant* (if he be really worthy of that name) must wish for some *fixed standard*, by which he may ascertain the value of his commodities, may regulate his purchases and sales, and measure the extent of his engagements—before he must be convinced that paper, "*though never issued except in the discount of perfectly good bills, founded in real mercantile transactions*," may yet be carried to excess—that its real use and benefit (and they cannot be prized too highly) are not in what it adds to the currency of a country, but in what it saves of expense in providing it. That from the profit incident to the issues of such paper, the public derive a sufficient security that the wants of our circulation will be constantly supplied:—but that the full and safe enjoyment of this convenience, essentially depends on the assurance that such paper shall be strictly *circulating credit*;—that it shall retain its value in conformity to our own *standard*, and thereby, in reference to the currency of other countries;—and that nothing but its interchangeableness with cash, can now restore that assurance, or, at any time, permanently maintain it.

Lastly, is it the interest of the Government which calls for this system? This question can hardly be put without seeming to imply an admission which every man must be anxious to deny—that there can be an interest in the Government separate from that of the community. We are told, however, that the taxes could not be raised—that the loans for carrying on the war could not be negociated—and that the whole of our finance is a superstructure, built upon the basis of our present paper currency. These are assertions wholly unsupported by proof. Why could not the taxes be raised? How were they raised before the restriction? Would not the real wealth and capital of the country, as well as its population and industry, continue the same? and what are the taxes but a given proportion of the annual income, which the people of this country derive from their soil, their industry, and the employment of their capitals?

It is true that, the price of all articles being restored to their proper relative value, the taxes upon consumption would, in reality, bear a somewhat higher proportion to the prime cost of the commodities upon which they attach, than they do at present; but not higher than they did when they were first imposed. Besides, as this effect would be produced without any real augmentation of burthen, persons of a fixed income would be able to consume more, and those whose incomes have increased in proportion to the depreciation of money, would not (even should their incomes thenceforward be nominally diminished in the same proportion) be reduced to consume less than at present. The case of the assessed taxes, it must be admitted, would be somewhat different, some of them partaking of the nature of an *ad valorem* duty; but, upon the whole, there could be no very material or permanent diminution in their amount. The *ad valorem* taxes upon the transfer of property, such as the auction duty,* and the stamps upon conveyances, would

* This duty, in the year ended the 5th of April, 1808, produced 272,570*l.*, and in the year ended the 5th of April last, 363,434*l.*, being an augmention of *one-third:* although, certainly, in the last year, there was no pressure in the country to force property into the market. The auction duty is under the management of the excise; and it is not, perhaps, undeserving the attention of those who may wish to look at the difference in the first consequences of a depreciation in the currency of a country, upon the prices of labour and property respectively, that, whilst the produce of this tax has increased more than 30 per cent., most of the other taxes, in the same collection, being upon general consumption,—such as malt, British spirits, candles, soap, and glass, have within the same period, been rather decreasing; and others, such as beer, leather, salt, &c., have been very nearly stationary. The increased produce of taxes of this class must await an increase in the wages and salaries of labour and industry, proportionate to the decrease in the value of the Currency in which those wages are paid. To whatever degree that increase has already taken place, and in proportion as

certainly suffer a nominal diminution; but these branches of the revenue are not very considerable in their amount, and are the only portion of our *permanent* income which could be much affected. The property tax, being also an *ad valorem duty*, would be liable to some diminution, but as a great part of this tax is levied upon persons of fixed incomes, the falling off, in the first instance, would not be considerable, and would soon be made up by the growing wealth of the country.*

Why could not any loans, that may be necessary, be negociated? Is it not the amount of capital, compared with the demand for it, and not the amount of circulation, which regulates the rate of interest in a country? And what is it that supports the public credit of a country, except general confidence in the sufficiency of its resources, and a character for punctuality and good faith in its engagements? Are Bank notes not convertible into cash, the test of the solidity of our resources? Are payments made in a currency referable to no fixed standard of value, the essential criterion of punctuality and good faith?

It is true, that the abundance and cheapness of our paper have, in the first instance, a tendency to raise the price of the public securities, which enables the Government to borrow money on terms nominally better; but it is equally true that, from these same causes, the amount of the loans requisite for the public service is increased: and who does not see that the latter effect compensates the former? It does so, in the very year in which the loans are made. But if we consider its operation on posterity; if we consider that, in order to effect a small nominal saving *now*

---

it may become general (if the value and standard of our money shall remain unsettled), the nominal benefit of it will probably be felt in these branches of the public revenue. This appears to me a very strong proof that the effects of a depreciation of currency upon all the transactions, and upon all the comforts of life, are not merely imaginary.

* I have already observed in how many ways, and to what a degree our public expenditure is increased by the present state of our currency; and that the savings which form some set off to that increase, are neither honorable nor just, nor likely to be permanent.

in the rate per cent. at which our loans are borrowed, we engage to pay for all time to come an increased amount of interest:—That we contract to pay the more, because that contract is made in depreciated paper;—but that those payments are hereafter to be made in undepreciated money; —who does not see the improvidence of such a system? Who does not see that we purchase the show of what is at best a fallacious and temporary facility, at the expense of a more than necessary accumulation of real and permanent burthen? Can any one believe, that considerate men will much longer look to the public funds of the country as a safe and proper deposit for any permanent provision which they may be enabled to make for their families, if the principle on which the value of our currency now rests should either be countenanced and supported, upon system, as beneficial to the State, or defended and continued, as a necessary evil admitting of no remedy? This consideration alone forms a most important part of the subject, with a reference to the policy of the present system; and cannot be too seriously weighed by those who must ultimately decide upon the whole merits of this great question. In coming to this decision, let them also look to the character and honour of the nation, and to the impression which that decision will not fail to make in other countries. Foreigners will not be influenced, either by interest or prejudice, in forming their judgment respecting the value of our paper. If they see all the symptoms of a depreciated currency, such as they have witnessed in different parts of the continent, they will not doubt that our paper also is depreciated; and they would by degrees conclude (if all foundation for such a conclusion be not speedily done away) that the change in our money system, by which we have virtually made paper a *legal tender*, (however, in its origin the evil may have been unsuspected, or may still be palliated in its progress,) will ultimately produce the same disasters, which have marked the course and termination of similar attempts in other parts of the world. Respecting the language, or the predictions of our avowed enemy, on this subject, I am little solicitous; but from the dread and mistrust which prevail in every part of Europe, of any thing which, in principle, bears so near a resemblance to *paper* MONEY, I am convinced that the state of our currency, if not speedily rectified, will be a source of disquietude to all those whose hearts and wishes are really with us in this great contest. Nor must we allow ourselves to hope that our national character for strict integrity, and for a rigid adherence to good faith in all our engagements, would not suffer by the protracted duration of the present derangement in our currency. By a refined, and perhaps overstrained sense of our obligations in this respect, we have exempted that part of the interest of our public funds which belongs to foreigners from the property tax:—and shall we feel no scruples in paying that interest in a currency, of which the depreciation unavoidably exposes them to a much heavier deduction? How can we expect that our dealings and contracts will continue to be looked to with the same unbounded confidence, and to be held in the same high estimation, if *that* upon which they all turn, and by which their amount is measured, instead of being accurately ascertained and invariably fixed, is referable to no established standard of value whatever, and liable to fluctuations from causes over which the foreigner can have no controul? His apprehensions will soon outstep the reality of the evil, and his speculations on its future progress will contribute to aggravate its present pressure.

The occurrence of some general alarm, arising from preparations, or attempts which may be made by the enemy against this country, or possibly from some internal cause, should not be lost sight of in the consideration of this subject.

The difficulties incident to such a state of things, were confined in 1797 to a stagnation of sales, and to an interruption of credit in all the larger transactions of trade and of the community; but they were not felt in the exchange and distribution of commodities, in the common dealings by which the daily wants of society are supplied. But what would be the result of any general interruption of confidence in paper currency at the present moment, accompanied as it would necessarily be with an anxiety to part with that currency, and a refusal to accept it in payment for commodities on almost any terms?* In proportion as confidence would be suspended, would power be substituted to give circulation to our paper?—from the absolute necessity of the case, I apprehend that it would — and what power? Not indeed that of the state, as in despotic countries, but the power, probably, of every possessor of a small note, pressed by his own wants and by those of his family, against the possessor of the commodities by which those wants might be supplied.

But I have said enough, perhaps more than enough, both as to the certain and the possible consequences of the continuance of the evil. I feel that it is more than time to bring the subject to a close. Let it only be remembered, by those whose duty it is to consider this great question, that the existence of the evil cannot be disguised. It is too late to determine that we will not avow it, even to each other: —a policy, which, though it sometimes tricks itself in the garb of wisdom, is not a manly policy, nor one that, in the nature of things, can ever be long successful.

To recommend helpless acquiescence, or to attempt to palliate the mischief, is to hold out to all the world a discouraging picture of the real situation of this country. It is to represent, as our only support in the conflict, this system, which is, in fact, but the lengthened and distorted shadow of our real wealth; to represent the duration of that system, unsubstantial as it is, as forming the real measure of our resources.

Resources of a far different character this country possesses in abundance. They are to be found in the immense and increasing produce of its territory:—in the unwearied extension of its manufacturing industry:—in the elastic and

* Some idea may be formed of the distress which would result from such a state of things, by the sudden inconvenience which has lately been felt in some small districts of the kingdom in which the country Banks, by which their circulation was supplied, have failed.

expansive force of its legitimate commerce:—all mutually aiding and fostering each other:—all fed and put in motion by capital, the genuine growth of progressive accumulation —and not the factitious result of any artificial contrivance.

If, from the currency of a country thus circumstanced, the precious metals have altogether disappeared, it is idle to suppose, that such a disappearance can be the effect of natural causes:—it is absurd to exaggerate the process by which they are to be re-acquired into an effort, or a sacrifice;—or to suppose that any other process can be necessary, for that purpose, than that of restoring things to their natural course.

THE END.

INDEX.

C.

F.

G.

H.

M.

N.

Q.

R.

S.

T.

U.

V.

W.

Y.

For EU product safety concerns, contact us at Calle de José Abascal, 56–1°, 28003 Madrid, Spain or eugpsr@cambridge.org.

www.ingramcontent.com/pod-product-compliance
Lightning Source LLC
LaVergne TN
LVHW090253210926
848480LV00001B/8

* 9 7 8 1 1 0 8 0 8 3 7 4 4 *